BTEC national

2nd Edition

Children's Care ng & ment

Edited by Gill Squire

Studentship Book

Please do not damage this book which remains the property of The College. It must be returned to the Learning Resources Centre by the date below.

Issued to	Due for return
Lyazi Bear	June 2008
Danielle Bookman	June 09

www.harcourt.co.uk

✓ Free online support
✓ Useful weblinks
✓ 24 hour online ordering

01865 888118

Heinemann is an imprint of Harcourt Education Limited, a company incorporated in England and Wales, having its registered office: Halley Court, Jordan Hill, Oxford OX2 8EJ. Registered company number: 3099304

www.harcourt.co.uk

Text © Harcourt Education Ltd 2007

First published 2007

12 11 10 09 08 07
10 9 8 7 6 5 4 3 2 1

British Library Cataloguing in Publication Data is available from the British Library on request.

ISBN 978 0 435499 09 9

Edited by Stephanie Richards
Designed by Pentacor Big, High Wycombe, Bucks
Typeset by Tek-Art, Croydon, Surrey, UK
Original illustrations © Harcourt Education Limited 2007
Illustrated by Tek-Art, Surrey
Cover design by Pentacor Big, High Wycombe, Bucks
Picture research by Liz Savery
Cover photo/illustration © Photolibrary
Printed in the UK by Scotprint Haddington

Acknowledgements

Gill Squire would like to thank all the authors for their commitment and hard work on this book, and also the team at Heinemann, particularly Beth Howard and Kirsty Stroud, for their guidance and support throughout the production process. The authors and publisher would like to thank the following individuals and organisations for permission to reproduce photographs on the following pages:

Alamy/Sally and Richard Greenhill – 508; Alamy/Bob Johns – 376; Alamy/Brand X Pictures – Thinking points icon; Alamy/Bubbles Photolibrary – 177; Alamy/PBWPIX – 105; Alamy/Kari Marttilia – 303; Alamy/Ian Shaw – 297; Corbis – 344, 428; Corbis/ Philip James Corwen – 480–1; Corbis/Kevin Dodge – 108; Corbis/Reuters – 385; Corbis/Jennie Woodcock – 237; Corbis/Zefa – 118; Eyewire – 115; Fotolia – 66, 142–3, 210–1; Fotolia/Elnur Amikishiyev – 34–5; Fotolia/Jerome Berguez – 352; Fotolia/Peter Christensen – 2–3; Fotolia/Ieva Geneviche – 43; Fotlia/Hallgurd – 358; Fotolia/ Ade Hughes – 170–1; Fotolia/Kun Jiang – 292–3; Fotolia/Michael Kempf – 250–1; Fotolia/Pavel Losevsky – 4; Fotolia/Rob Marmion – 181; Fotolia/ Petr Nad – 13; Fotolia/Anita Patterson-Peppers – 71; Fotolia/Tom Perkins – 86–7, 102; Fotolia/Andrey Stratilatov – 20; Fotolia/Pascale Wowak – 427; Getty Images – 388; Getty Images/Photographers Choice – 514–5; Getty Images/Stone – 30; Harcourt Ltd/Jules Selmes – 99, 207, 244, 258, 451, 454, 467, 484, 486, 494, 498, 517, 519, 521, 522, 543, and icons for Theory into practice, End of unit assessment, Case study, Good practice checklist, Assessment activity; Harcourt Ltd/Tudor Photography – 104, 190, 308; Sarah Horne – 75; iStockPhoto/ Carmen Martinez Banios – 111; iStockPhoto/Kathy Hicks – 372–3; iStockPhoto/Sylwya Kucharska – 448–9; iStockPhoto/Kennith Ponder – 332–3; iStockPhoto/Jan Paul Schrage – 402–3; Rubberball Productions – Extension activity icon; Science Photo Library/Christine Hanscombe – 441

Every effort has been made to contact copyright holders of material reproduced in this book. Any omissions will be rectified in subsequent printings if notice is given to the publishers.

Contents

*The content of Unit 4 is also applicable to *Unit 38 Reflecting on practice in the children's care, learning and development sector*, which is available for the Award only.

About the authors and editor

Andy Boak

Currently Head of an adult education service, Andy previously managed health and social care provision in further education and taught on a wide range of courses at all levels, including the delivery of BTEC First and National qualifications, City and Guilds and Foundation degree, teaching assistants' courses and other childcare provision. With a background in research and special educational needs Andy has contributed to the development of other BTEC qualifications in health and social care and to earier editions of this and other texts.

Kath Bulman

Kath Bulman has many years' experience in the early years field, including health visiting, lecturing, work as an examiner and in developing qualifications. Kath now inspects education and training, including that for early years workers. Along with two grown-up children of her own and two stepchildren, Kath also has an army of nieces and nephews to add to her pool of observed examples for her books!

Joan Butcher

Joan has taught child development and child psychology for many years. During this time she established a pre-school for the local community which also provided work experience for her students. As an Ofsted Nursery Inspector she visited settings throughout the country. She has worked as a principal examiner for GNVQ and AVCE and is currently an external verifier for BTEC Introductory Level, First and National Diplomas. Joan has inspected examination centres in Europe and South Africa. In Uganda, she visited local nursery schools. In addition, she acts as a trainer for one of the awarding boards and has contributed to previous editions of this book.

Maureen Daly

Maureen has worked in early years settings for more than 20 years. For the last ten years she has worked in various colleges as a lecturer, curriculum leader and the Centre of Vocational Excellence co-ordinator. She is currently Head of School for care and early years at West Herts College in Watford. Maureen has contributed to several other books on early years, including *Understanding Theory in Practice*, *Management in Early Years Practice* and the BTEC National title *Protecting Children*.

Sue Griffin

Sue has been involved in the early years and childcare field for over 25 years. She worked for 18 years for NCMA – in latter years as National Training and Quality Assurance Manager, developing the first national qualification and quality assurance schemes for childminders.

She was a member of the Under Sevens Project team in 1989/90 which developed the first NVQs. She was involved in the playgroup movement in the 1980s and was national chair of PPA.

She is now semi-retired and works as a freelance consultant and writer for a wide range of organisations: National Children's Bureau, the Open University, Home-Start, CACHE, National Extension College, Practical Professional Childcare and NCMA. Sue is a magistrate and sits on the family panel for Cambridgeshire. She is also a member of the Early Education Advisory Group of the Sure Start Unit at the DfES and a trustee of the National Toy and Leisure Libraries Association. She enjoys being a granny.

Kelly Hill

Kelly Hill has been working within the early years and childcare sector for over 12 years. From nursery nurse to running her own successful early years training company. Whilst running the business, Kelly gained three business awards: New Business start-up of the year 2004, Young Entrepreneur of the Year 2004 and Business of the Year 2005.

Kelly has worked as an assessor, IV and EV for a number of awarding bodies, and as a freelance training consultant, advised many centres on the development of their awards, supporting them to gain scheme approval and developing Quality Assurance schemes.

Kelly has recently written the NVQ assessor's handbook for Children's Care, Learning and Development, published by Heinemann.

Sarah Horne

Having worked as a childminder and pre-school leader, Sarah progressed to employment as a lecturer in further education, tutoring on a wide variety of childcare courses. She has been an Ofsted Nursery Inspector and CACHE External Verifier. She is currently the Manager of the Childhood Studies Centre of Vocational Excellence (CoVE) at Blackburn College and works with a variety of regional and national initiatives developing work in the childcare sector. During the past few years she has contributed to a range of BTEC and NVQ texts and tutor resource packs.

Karen Hucker

Karen has worked in post-16 education for 20 years. She has taught food and nutrition in 11–16 schools and in post-16 establishments from Key Stage 3 to A-level. She has been an examiner for A-level home economics and Principal Examiner for food science and nutrition papers for the AVCE. Karen has also contributed to a number of books on food and nutrition.

Marjorie Snaith

Marjorie has a background of primary and special education and has taught in further education since 1992, involved mainly with the management and delivery of education and early years programmes.

She has contributed to the development of a range of courses in health, care, education and early years and has worked on programmes designed to raise literacy and numeracy levels for children and their parents/ carers. Additionally, she has been involved with the development of tutor resource packs for use in the delivery of social care and early years courses. She is currently an external verifier and examiner for BTEC NQF programmes in health and care and early years.

Gill Squire

Gill has a background in nursing and social sciences, and has taught in further education and sixth form colleges since 1992. She is currently an external verifier and examiner for BTEC NQF programmes in health and care and early years at levels 1–4 and is engaged in a range of projects relating to current BTEC courses. She has contributed to the development of a range of courses in health, social care and early years in relation to current National Occupational Standards for the UK, as well as working on courses designed to meet the requirements of training for international care workers.

Penny Tassoni

Penny is an education consultant, author and trainer. She specialises in the whole spectrum of early learning and play. Penny has written over 20 books, including the popular *Planning Play and the Early Years*, and is a regular contributor to *Practical Pre-School* and *Nursery World*.

Introduction

Working with children and their families is a rewarding and special career. Time spent with children is usually hard work, but exhilarating and varied. Not many careers offer people the opportunity to genuinely influence and shape young lives. The BTEC National in Children's Care, Learning and Development is a qualification that gives students many entry routes into the early years sector. It will provide you with a firm foundation for your future work.

This book contains information you will need to help you to complete the essential requirements to pass your BTEC National course. All the core units for the Award, Certificate and Diploma are included in the book, along with some of the more popular specialist units.

About the qualification

For the Certificate and Diploma there are 7 core units:

1. Positive Relationships for Children's Care, Learning and Development
2. Positive Environments for Children's Care, Learning and Development
3. Promoting Children's Development
4. Reflecting on and Developing Practice for Children aged 0-8 years
5. Protecting Children
6. Promoting Children's Rights
7. Children's Learning Activities and Play

For the Award there are 5 core units:

1. Positive Relationships for Children's Care, Learning and Development
2. Positive Environments for Children's Care, Learning and Development
3. Promoting Children's Development
5. Protecting Children
38. Reflecting on Practice in the Children's Care, Learning and Development Sector

This book covers all of the above units. If you are working towards the Award you will find that unit 4 in the book covers everything you need to know for unit 38.

This book also contains the following specialist units (for Certificate and Diploma):

8. Research Methodology for Children's Care, Learning and Development
9. Promoting Healthy Development and Living for Children and their Families
11. Diet and Nutrition for Children
14. Psychological Perspectives on Behaviour
17. Supporting Children's Numeracy Skills
18. Supporting Children's Literacy Skills
35. The Development and Care of Babies and Children under 3 years.

To achieve the Award you will need to successfully complete 360 hours of study (5 units); for the Certificate you will need to successfully complete 720 hours of study (normally 12 units of 60 hours); and for the Diploma 1080 hours of study (normally 18 units of 60 hours). It is worth noting that not all units are given a 60-hour weighting, as the units where more in-depth knowledge is required (such as Unit 3 Promoting Children's Development) is given 120-hour weighting, and some units may be as short as 30 hours. So, the number of units you will actually study for the Certificate and Diploma will vary according to the different specialist units your course includes.

Work placement is an important part of the Award, Certificate and Diploma courses, as it is the basis for applying and developing the skills and knowledge you have gained from your studies. It links with and is supported by Unit 4 Reflecting on and Developing Practice for Children aged 0–8 years (or unit 38 for the Award). Reflection is an essential skill that you will learn from the course and – when you are qualified – will use throughout your work with children to continue to improve and develop your practice in line with ongoing changes and developments in early years practice.

All the course units are linked to the National Occupational Standards for Children's Care, Learning and Development, which currently form the base for recognised courses in this vocational area.

Achieving the qualification

To achieve the Award, Certificate or Diploma qualification, you will need to successfully complete the required number of units of study. To pass each unit you must achieve all the Pass criteria. To achieve a Merit you must achieve all the Pass and Merit criteria for that unit. For a Distinction, you must achieve all the Pass, Merit and Distinction criteria for that unit. The type of assessments that you will do may vary considerably, from practical tasks to presentations and written assignments. You will get feedback from your tutor or teacher to show the criteria that you have met, with guidance for any further work you may need to do to achieve any criteria not yet achieved, or to show you how to achieve the higher level Merit and Distinction criteria where possible. You will be awarded a grade for each unit, and when all the units are completed you can use the conversion chart in the syllabus to calculate your overall grading, and the equivalent UCAS points.

About this book

Each chapter in the book is written to match the syllabus content of a unit and is organised into sections which relate to the learning outcomes of that unit. Throughout the book there are Assessment activities for you to do. These should help you to address the grading criteria given at the end of each unit of the syllabus.

It is essential that you address the criteria fully, and do what is asked, e.g. if a description is required, then you must describe, either in writing or possibly verbally, the activity or thing that is being addressed. If your description is verbal, then you, or the assessor (probably a tutor) must keep a record of what you say, to show that you actually did complete the criteria. A description is normally a Pass level criterion. To meet the higher level criteria, such as Merit, or Distinction, you will usually need to compare, analyse or evaluate the information. You will be guided by your tutor as to what is needed. It is important that you understand that to successfully address the higher level criteria, your work will not necessarily be much longer than that required for a Pass, but the content and depth will be greater and show that you have a more in-depth understanding.

The criteria in the grading grid at the end of each unit state what you need to do to achieve Pass, Merit and Distinction grades, using 'instruction words' such as:

- *Identify* – list, or briefly describe (in one or two sentences)
- *Describe* – write/report what you see, or know of a particular thing, e.g. 'Joe used blue, green and red paints in his picture. He drew 3 recognisable figures and said these were Mum, Dad and Joe.'
- *Explain* – describe something in detail, and say why, how and when, to show your understanding
- *Evaluate* – say how good something is, and consider (say and discuss) the weak points. Through your evaluation you will probably come to a conclusion
- *Justify* – give the underlying reasons for an action or situation
- *Compare* – use at least two examples, and explain the differences and similarities between them
- *Analyse* – identify strengths and weaknesses of a subject.

The book contains a number of features to facilitate learning and help you get the most out of your studies.

Key terms

Important concepts and terms are defined as they occur and are brought together in the Glossary at the back of the book.

Case studies

These contain scenarios with a 'real-world' feel to help you relate what you have learned to a practical situation. Case studies are followed by questions increasing in difficulty.

1.3

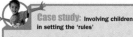

▲ Use puppets or dolls to talk about how other people feel

Perhaps the most effective way you can help children to learn these important life skills is by providing a positive role model in the way you relate to other people. Children learn so much by watching how adults behave, and they will copy the way you treat other people and how you speak to them.

Extension activity

During your work placements, monitor your own behaviour towards children (and adults) over a period of two days.

What does the way in which you speak to and behave towards others demonstrate to the children in the setting about how to relate to other people? What sort of role model do you provide for respecting the feelings and rights of others?

Frameworks for behaviour

Whatever setting you work in, there will be an established 'framework' for the behaviour of the children. This will set out what sort of behaviour will and will not be acceptable in the setting. It may be expressed as **rules**, **boundaries** or **expectations**.

Key terms

Rules describe what children may or may not do.
Boundaries indicate the limits to acceptable behaviour.
Expectations indicate to children how adults expect them to behave.

A framework like this is positive and helpful to children to make clear to them what the limits are for the way they behave. It can be very reassuring to them because they know what they may not do, how far they can go and how they are expected to behave.

The rules/boundaries/expectations are likely to be based on guiding children away from doing things which:

- are dangerous, hurtful or offensive to others (other children, adults)
- are a danger to the children themselves
- damage other people's belongings
- will make the child unwelcome or unacceptable to other people.

A framework for behaviour helps children to begin to understand that they must learn to control their own actions and behaviour – not only to protect the rights of other people but also for their own sakes and for their future happiness. Uncontrolled behaviour in older children, teenagers and adults becomes a serious problem for the family and, ultimately, for society.

Settings also have guidelines for applying sanctions when rules are broken, boundaries are crossed or behaviour falls short of expectations. It is essential that sanctions are applied fairly and consistently when children's behaviour is unacceptable within the setting's framework.

Theory into practice

Describe the frameworks set for children's behaviour, including the guidelines for sanctions, in each of the settings where you have work placements.

- What do the frameworks have in common?
- Where there are differences, why do you think this is so?

A crucial factor in being able to behave in ways which are acceptable to others around them is children's ability to cope with their strong emotions. A well thought-out framework for behaviour and guidelines on sanctions can help children move towards self-control as they:

- learn to deal with their strong emotions
- develop the ability to understand and respect the feelings and rights of other people
- start to accept rules and to apply them for themselves, without external pressure from adults.

You can play a role in helping children to accept rules and understand why they are necessary.

Case study: Involving children in setting the 'rules'

Beth is starting work in a new after-school club and holiday play scheme with children aged 6–10. The staff team have made a start on a set of expectations for children's behaviour, and now want to involve the children in agreeing what the framework should contain.

1 How can Beth and her colleagues approach this? What contributions can they invite from the children, and how?

2 What should they do if the rules the children come up with are very different from the ones they have already thought of?

Resolving conflicts

It is inevitable that the children you work with will at times have disagreements and be in conflict with one another. Very often, your best strategy is to hold back, observe what is going on and not intervene. You will find out that the children who have developed a sense of what is 'fair' and learned some emotional control will be able to resolve a conflict for themselves.

However, on other occasions, you may need to intervene – especially if one child is being hurt or verbally abused and is unable to respond on their own behalf. Children

may need your support to work through what is going on. You may be able to help them take partial control of the situation, which will help them in future to manage conflict for themselves.

Good practice checklist

You can help children resolve conflicts by:

- providing comfort to a child who is distressed by what is happening, perhaps who is the object of some unacceptable behaviour such as racist remarks
- acknowledging the feelings of that child
- asking each child to explain what is happening
- reminding a child whose behaviour has fallen short of the expectations of the setting that the way they have behaved is unacceptable, and explaining the hurt caused
- asking the children how the situation might be resolved, and giving them time to make suggestions
- praising the good suggestions they make and helping them put them into effect
- reminding the child who behaved unacceptably that that form of behaviour falls short of expectations – but making clear your continued affection for the child – 'I didn't like what you did, but I still like you.'

◄ Help children to resolve conflicts for themselves

Theory into practice

These provide an explanation of how a theory or concept is applied or can be seen in practice. They will give you a greater understanding of important concepts.

Good practice checklists

These are bulleted checklists of advice that will help you work towards good practice.

Assessment activities

These activities appear throughout, usually at the end of each learning outcome. They are tasks which map directly to one or more of the criteria related to that learning outcome.

Extension activities

These are stretching activities that build on knowledge gained in the unit. Doing these activities will help increase your understanding.

End of unit assessments

These are larger assignments appearing at the end of each unit, covering the assessment criteria in more depth. They are intended to help you achieve the best grade possible.

■ Websites

The websites used in this book were correct and up to date at the time of publication. It is essential for tutors to preview each website before using it in class so as to ensure that the URL is still accurate, relevant and appropriate. We suggest that tutors bookmark useful websites and consider enabling students to access them through the school/college intranet.

The book has been written by people with great knowledge and expertise, and is designed to help you to successfully complete your course and provide the basis for a rewarding career in early years work.

Gill Squire, Editor

Positive relationships for children's care, learning and development

Introduction

As a childcare practitioner, the relationships you form with children will be at the heart of your practice. The basis of any relationship is effective communication. You need to develop your skills in:

- building good relationships with children
- communicating with them in a variety of ways.

Your work will bring you into contact with many adults:

- the parents of the children you work with
- your colleagues in your setting
- other professionals working in other agencies and organisations.

You need to be able to communicate effectively with all these adults, and be able to build good professional relationships with them. You need to:

- show them respect
- express yourself clearly in ways that they understand
- be confident in your communications with them
- maintain confidentiality.

What you need to learn

- How to develop relationships with children
- How to communicate with children
- How to support children as they develop relationships
- How to communicate with adults

Thinking points

Working with children is a job that depends on having good communication skills. You must be effective in the way you communicate both with children and with adults.

During her day working in a small nursery, Leila came into contact with:

- the three children for whom she was key worker – a baby of 11 months and two toddlers of 16 and 20 months
- several of the older children in the nursery
- the parents of the children for whom she was key worker, one of whom had a hearing impairment, and another whose first language was Urdu
- two of the other workers in the nursery, one of whom was new to the profession
- her manager
- the caretaker
- the woman who cooked the children's meals
- the physiotherapist who came to advise her on exercises to do with one of the children for whom she was key worker
- the local authority adviser who was making a routine visit to the nursery.

What do you think would be the differences in the way she communicated with each of these people? Why was it important that she was able to communicate with them all effectively?

In your professional role it is essential that you focus on building strong relationships with the children you work with. Building relationships with others is never an easy or quick process. You will have to put thought into establishing and sustaining your relationships with children. The effort will be worthwhile because, if you form a good and positive relationship with a child, they will be more likely to:

- feel they can trust you
- be able to form relationships with others
- become confident and able to cope with the world
- respect your views and values, and respond to your guidance about how they behave.

Good practice checklist

You can build positive relationships with children by:

- giving them a warm welcome, smiling and making eye-contact
- finding out about what is important to them in their lives and what they like to do
- paying attention to what they are saying and showing that you are interested in their ideas and opinions
- talking about the things you like about them – for example, when they are kind and considerate or helpful
- showing respect for and interest in their parents and family
- being fun to be with – using lots of humour and laughter.

Building strong relationships ▶ is a key part of your role

The basis of a good relationship is showing an interest in the other person as an individual, and showing that you value and respect them. Each of us is an individual, different from all other individuals. We each have our own characteristics, strengths and weaknesses, and needs and wishes, which are not the same as anyone else's. Don't expect a child to behave in a particular way because you have known another child of that gender, age, ethnicity or family background who has behaved like that. **Stereotypes** can be a major barrier to seeing and treating each child as an individual. They are generalisations about people, assumptions that because a person is part of a particular group, they will be the same as others in that group. Such assumptions are usually inaccurate. There are as many differences within groups in our society as there are between them. Not all deaf people have the same needs as other deaf people; not all members of a religion adhere strictly to its dietary laws or rules about dress; not all children with Down's syndrome are docile and affectionate.

Key term

Stereotypes are generalisations about people, assumptions that because a person is part of a particular group, they will be the same as others in that group.

As you start to form relationships with children, you have to begin by:

- recognising that each child is an individual
- showing that you value each of them as a special, unique human being.

Theory into practice

Josie has a variety of ways of showing children how she sees them as individuals and values them for who and what they are. She says:

- I work hard at getting people's names right because our name is a key part of who we are. I never use another name just because I find it easier to pronounce. I check how to pronounce and spell a name I'm not familiar with, especially if it is from a language other than my own.
- I make life-size cut-outs of the children and ask them to decorate their own cut-out. I ask them to tell me things about themselves, and I write what they tell me on their cut-outs – things like 'Leah likes …', Jacob is good at …'.
- I talk with children about the characteristics that make each of us special and individual – our skin colour, our hair texture, our features – and I show that I admire theirs.
- I ask parents to contribute to our activities. When Parvinder's father came to show us how to put on a turban, Parvinder was bursting with pride!

Changing relationships

Babies and young children need to **bond** with the key adults in their lives, to have close and positive relationships with a limited circle of adults. Their relationships with these adults are the basis of their social development, enabling them to learn to have relationships with other adults and children. As they get to know an adult, they begin to trust that person to look after them and to understand and respond readily to their needs, both physical and emotional. These relationships are also essential to their healthy emotional development.

Key term

Bonding or **attachment** is the process through which young children form close relationships with a small number of well-known adults – their parents, their grandparents, their key worker in a nursery, their childminder or nanny.

Sustained close relationships give young children a feeling of security, and help them to cope with new experiences. They become confident that they can depend upon 'their adult' to be available and to help them understand their surroundings and the things that happen to them. Continuity in the availability of a known and trusted adult is essential – babies and young children whose main carer is constantly changing find it difficult to develop self-confidence; they remain fearful that there will not be a trustworthy adult at hand to 'rescue' them.

Good practice checklist

Building a close relationship with a baby or toddler depends very much on physical contact and touch. You should:

- handle the babies and under-3s you work with gently – cuddle and stroke them
- look into their eyes and smile at them
- show affection towards them
- observe them closely and get to know and understand the ways they are trying to communicate by learning what their different types of crying mean
- make the child the centre of your attention, and keep distractions from colleagues to a minimum
- not hurry through routine care tasks such as feeding and nappy changing, so you can enjoy one another's company.

Some settings have introduced policies which limit practitioners' physical contact with children. But babies and under-3s need affection, expressed by physical contact, to develop in a healthy emotional way. If the adults caring for these very young children do not have close physical contact with them, they will not be able to build a strong relationship with the children and that will deprive them of an essential element of a secure emotional environment.

Extension activity

Why do you think some settings have introduced policies which limit physical contact with children?

When other adults who are less familiar appear on the scene, and/or the familiar adults are not present, babies and under-3s can become anxious and even fearful. Both **stranger anxiety** and **separation anxiety** are common in babies and under-3s. You need to understand these normal, healthy stages of development and adjust your care to help children cope with their feelings.

Key terms

Stranger anxiety Towards the end of their first year, many babies develop an aversion to people they don't know. They cling to the familiar adults they trust and feel safe with.

Separation anxiety Many children aged 2 and under find it difficult to part from people and places they know and feel secure with.

If a baby or toddler is experiencing stranger and/or separation anxiety, they are likely to find it difficult to settle into a new childcare setting and form a relationship with a new carer during this time. You need to provide plenty of individual attention and reassurance, so they can gradually adjust to their new surroundings, and develop trust in you. As they get to know you, they will cease to see you as a stranger to be anxious about, and become more able to separate from their other, well-known carers. You can't form an instant relationship with a young child – it takes time and patience.

Stranger anxiety is a normal part of development ▲

As children grow and develop, their dependence on their key adults changes. As they become more confident, they may need less frequent physical contact, and be sustained by verbal support – praise and reassurance. They may appear to need you less, but your reliable presence and availability when needed will continue to be an important element in their confidence in becoming more independent.

There is more about attachment and separation anxiety in Unit 14, page 424.

Negotiating – choices and decisions

Part of developing a relationship is to be prepared for give and take. You should listen to:

- children's opinions and take them seriously
- what they say they want and, if it is possible, practical and realistic, find ways of responding positively to what they want.

Your relationships with children change as they grow and develop, and you should:

- make this sort of negotiation an increasing part of your relationship with them
- give them opportunities for taking control of more aspects of their lives.

Case study: Making choices

Sunita works in a nursery with babies and under-3s.

Miriam works in a pre-school with 3- and 4-year-olds.

Fiona works as a classroom assistant with children aged 6–8.

Pete works in a play scheme with children aged up to 16.

1 **What sort of choices and decisions could each practitioner offer to the children they work with, suitable to the stage of development of the children?**

2 **What guidance might they need to provide the children with?**

3 **What difficulties might they encounter in letting the children make choices and decisions?**

Adults tend to take over and run much of what happens in children's lives and it is important sometimes to stand back a little and be less controlling. You will have overall responsibility for their safety and well-being, but children need to practise making choices and decisions. If they don't have experiences which offer them the chance to practise the skill, they will become:

- over-dependent on others
- unable to take responsibilities for themselves
- frustrated or rebellious.

By involving children in making choices and decisions, you can help to build their self-esteem. This can start very young, though you might want to offer younger children limited choices which they can understand, such as deciding whether to read a story first or go for a walk first. You can offer older children wider choices but you are likely to have to continue to offer guidance to help them develop a realistic view of what is possible, and where there are limits so they can make sensible choices and decisions. You might offer them the chance to decide what to eat, but also provide guidance on healthy eating and help them learn about the cost of various sorts of foodstuffs.

Professional values of the sector

We have emphasised that young children need you to be ready to form close personal relationships with them. Children who are cared for by people who maintain physical and emotional distance cannot develop trust in their carers, and will not feel secure and valued. You must be prepared to commit yourself as a person to making relationships with children.

On the other hand, they are not and never will be *your* children – they are their parents' children. Your part in their life is temporary, whereas their parents remain central to the whole of their lives. So you have to be ready and able to put a lot of yourself into forming relationships with the children you work with, but equally ready and able to move on from those relationships. It will never be easy to say a final goodbye to a child you have worked with closely for a lengthy period, but it will be part of your professional career to cope with this. But you must never let the knowledge that you will eventually have to say goodbye hold you back from committing to a strong and positive relationship during your time with a child. This is what makes working with children such a demanding and challenging job, requiring personal maturity and a professional approach.

You will have to get used to saying goodbye ▼

The relationships you develop with children must always be within the professional values which are so important in work with children. These include:

- promoting the welfare and rights of children
- valuing children and listening to them
- promoting children's self-esteem
- working in ways which are anti-discriminatory and inclusive
- maintaining confidentiality.

Children's welfare and rights

The Children Act 1989 and the United Nations Convention on the Rights of the Child (UNCRC) require you always to put the welfare of each child at the top of your priorities in all your work. It is the child's right that their interests always take priority over the interests of their parents, your colleagues, you and your setting.

Children's rights are covered in detail in Unit 6.

Theory into practice

When Gina was on one of her work placements, she began to realise that some of the safety procedures in the setting were not carried out rigorously. The bolt on the outside gate was often left unfastened, and children were sometimes handed over to adults the staff did not know without the methods for using passwords being used. At first, she felt a reluctance to say anything about this – either to the nursery manager or to her tutor. She was afraid the manager would be offended and perhaps would refuse to allow her to remain on the placement – maybe the college might not be able to use that setting for placements in future. But she remembered her duty to put the welfare of the children first and discussed with her tutor the best way to bring these matters to the attention of the manager.

Children should be given the opportunity ▶ to explore their ideas and feelings

Valuing children and listening to them

We have seen how valuing each child as an individual lays the basis of forming relationships with them. Later in this unit we will look at how to listen actively to children. The UNCRC also sets out children's rights to express their views and have them taken into account, according to their age and maturity. As your relationship with a child develops, you will become aware of their views and preferences, and your responsibility is to take those views and preferences seriously and respond to them in the way you behave towards the child.

The Coram Family project 'Listening to Young Children' has developed the 'Mosaic approach' to help us to listen to what children tell us about their ideas and feelings, so we are more aware of their opinions and can take account of them. The approach uses various methods:

- observing pre-verbal children and children with limited speech
- 'child conferencing' – talking with children in a structured way, using a checklist of simple questions to 'interview' children, such as asking them what they like best about their setting
- cameras – giving children disposable cameras, showing them how to use them, asking them to take photos of things in the setting that they like and dislike, and discussing the photos with them
- tours – children taking an adult on a tour of the setting, explaining and commenting on each area.

These methods can be combined in various ways, helping children to express their ideas and feelings. You can find out more about this in *Listening to Young Children: the Mosaic approach* – see References and further reading, page 32.

Theory into practice

Maggie decided to use some of the Mosaic ideas in her childminding setting. She bought disposable cameras for the children aged 3, 4 and 6 that she cared for and asked them to take pictures of the things they enjoyed most in their time at her house – and the ones they didn't. When the photos were developed and printed, she was fascinated to find that the two younger ones took photos of the school gate and told her that they didn't like waiting for the big ones to come out – it was boring, Maggie was always talking to the mummies who were waiting too. But all the children took photos of corners of the garden where they could play hiding behind the bushes.

Maggie thought about what the children were telling her, and took their views seriously. She decided to be more careful to talk to the children while they were waiting and to think up some games like 'I can see something that's the colour …' to make the waiting time a little more interesting. She also decided not to cut back the bushes as much as she had intended.

Promoting children's self-esteem

A central part of children's emotional well-being depends on them developing **self-esteem**. Children with good self-image and self-esteem are more confident – they know what they are capable of and can achieve, and this makes them more resilient and able to deal with their lives. Children's self-esteem suffers when they are criticised, ignored, blamed, humiliated or belittled.

Key term

Self-esteem means having good feelings about ourselves and knowing that we are valued, lovable and loved.

Good practice checklist

If your relationship with children includes:

- listening to them
- showing that you respect their views and opinions
- giving them encouragement and praise for their efforts and achievements
- showing them affection
- letting them take responsibilities and make choices and decisions

you will build their self-esteem.

Valuing ourselves, and seeing ourselves as of value in other people's eyes, makes it possible for us to value others and to develop good relationships.

Extension activity

Think about your practice in your work placement over a period of days. Note down examples of when you helped to enhance children's self-esteem as part of your relationship with them. What did you do and say? What other actions could you have taken to boost their self-esteem? You can learn more about this in Unit 14.

Relationships that are anti-discriminatory and inclusive

It is essential that your relationships with children are **anti-discriminatory** and **inclusive**.

When people experience **discrimination**, they are treated as though they are inferior to other human beings, and of less worth and significance. It is prejudiced attitudes that lead to assumptions that, because someone's skin is not white, or they belong to a minority cultural group or religion, or they are disabled or female or homosexual, they are in some way less valuable and less worthy of respect. People who experience discrimination have fewer opportunities in life than other people. Openly expressed **prejudice** is a daily part of life for many black people in Britain, even for small children. Disabled people and gay people also frequently experience prejudice and discrimination.

Your relationships with the children you work with must always be underpinned by a determination to challenge and reject prejudice and discrimination, in order to ensure that all children have an equal chance to achieve and progress. This applies wherever you live and work. Many people who are in areas of the country where there are few people from minority ethnic groups often feel this aspect of practice is not relevant to them – but it is. Children in predominantly white areas will grow up to be adults in a multi-racial, multi-cultural society and will live and work with people of various racial origins and cultural backgrounds. They need to learn to respect other people's ways of life and to value individuals equally, not to see other people's ways of life as 'abnormal' or of less value than their own way of life.

We have already seen that you can also ensure your practice is anti-discriminatory and inclusive by avoiding stereotypical assumptions about the children you work with and ensuring you value and welcome each as a unique individual.

Another key element in your relationships with children which will enable you to be anti-discriminatory and inclusive is to treat each child 'with equal concern', making sure that they have the opportunities which will help them to get the most out of life. You should not treat children 'all the same', but respond to each as an individual. Sometimes this means you have to treat children differently from one another, adapting the way you work to the individual needs and characteristics of a child, making specific arrangements for them or taking a different approach.

Theory into practice

These practitioners treat children 'with equal concern', not all the same.

Rhian works with a 6-year-old boy with physical disabilities which mean that he finds it difficult to sit up unless his back is well supported. She makes sure that he has his foam shapes comfortably in position so he can sit up at the table to play board games with the other children. He needs that extra attention so he has the same opportunities as the others to join in and enjoy the games.

Morag works with children from African-Caribbean and Asian backgrounds as well as white children. She provides paints and felt-tip pens in a wide range of skin tones so all the children have an equal opportunity to paint and draw accurate pictures of themselves, their families and one another.

Sinead works with children from Chinese and South Asian origins. Her setting has been using an assessment schedule that referred to the ability to use a knife and fork in assessing a child's manipulative skills. She points out to her manager that this meant that the nursery is under-estimating the capabilities of some of the children who are very skilful at eating with chopsticks or with their fingers.

Emma ensures that the girls in her setting know that it's perfectly OK to climb and play football, and that the boys don't feel that they can't play in the home corner.

Giving all children opportunities

You can learn more about confidentiality in Unit 3.

Children learn values and attitudes by copying adults so, above all, you must show in the way you behave towards others that you value people equally, whatever their ethnic or cultural background, gender or disability.

You can learn more about discrimination and inclusion in Unit 6.

Maintaining confidentiality

As you get to know children well, building your relationships with them, you will acquire a lot of information about them and their families. Some of this information may be sensitive and must be treated in a confidential way.

Maintaining **confidentiality** means not sharing with other people, or passing on, personal information about the children and families you are working with, unless:

- parents have given permission for you to do so
- it is essential to do so in the interests of a child, for example where abuse is suspected.

Key term

Maintaining **confidentiality** means not sharing with other people, or passing on, personal information about the children and families you are working with.

Case study: Confidentiality

Ramini is a childminder and looks after a 2-year-old she has got to know well. She is concerned about the slow rate of development of the child and she would appreciate the advice of a health visitor about whether her concerns are justified.

Gill works with a 5-year-old boy in her classroom and has a good, trusting relationship with him. The child's mother has told the school that his father has just been sent to prison.

A 9-year-old child who Mark works with in the after-school club has told him she is being sexually abused by a member of her family at home.

1 **What should Ramini do before she approaches the child's health visitor?**

2 **Should Gill share this information with anyone else? If not, why not?**

3 **Should Mark promise the girl that he will not break her confidence – or should he pass on this information to someone else? If so, to whom?**

Assessment activity 1.1

Choose a child you have worked with in each of your work placements – choose children of different ages.

Describe how you built the relationship with each child.

Give examples of how you:

- offered them the chance to make decisions and choices
- treated each as an individual, 'with equal concern', showing that you valued them.

 P1

You must work at your skills in communicating with children because the way you communicate with them is important not only for their communication and language development, but also the development of your relationship with them.

The link between communication and relationships is two-way. Being able to communicate effectively is an essential element of having social relationships with other people. Experiencing social interactions helps to develop communication skills. Children are strongly motivated to make social contact with adults and other children, and to communicate with them. Although most children don't learn to talk until between their first and second birthdays, babies are able to communicate from birth, and eager for others to communicate with them.

Non-verbal communication

The ability to communicate is not only about spoken language (**verbal communication**) but also **non-verbal communication**, through **body language**.

Your body language consists of:

- your tone of voice (how loudly you speak, the softness or harshness of your voice, whether you end on an 'up' note, as in a question)
- your facial expressions (frowning, smiling)
- your stance (tense, relaxed, hands on hips)
- your gestures (pointing, arms crossed)
- the way you touch others.

Key terms

Verbal communication means using the spoken word.

Non-verbal communication occurs without words, for example, through body language or by signing.

Body language is how you communicate non-verbally, including tone of voice, facial expressions, stance, gestures, touch.

When someone speaks to us, we receive more information from body language than from the actual words spoken. It is said that only 10 per cent of what we communicate is in the form of the words we use, and the rest comes from non-verbal communication.

Much early communication from young children is through non-verbal communication. For example, babies have a range of different types of crying, differing in pitch, volume and persistence, and you need to tune in to these so you are able to respond appropriately. You will be able to recognise the difference between the half-hearted whimpering of a baby settling to sleep, the full-throated roar of a hungry baby and the heart-broken sobbing of a small child who has been separated from a known adult.

Young children, especially babies, also communicate through whole body movements such as:

- wriggling (to show that they don't want to be handled in a particular way or by a particular person)
- bouncing up and down (when they are enjoying playing)
- turning away (when they are distressed or bored).

'Listening' to young children is not just about hearing words. To be able to respond to their attempts at communicating to you, you must 'listen' to all forms of their communication, including non-verbal communication. You 'listen' to children not only with your hearing, but also by watching and touching them.

Similarly, children understand a great deal of what you are communicating long before they actually understand the words you are using. Your body language has a great effect on them – they are very sensitive to non-verbal communication. A stern look from you may mean much more to a 2-year-old who is doing something they know they should not than what you actually say to them. Young children pick up very readily on adults' physical tension and they can find this unsettling and bewildering.

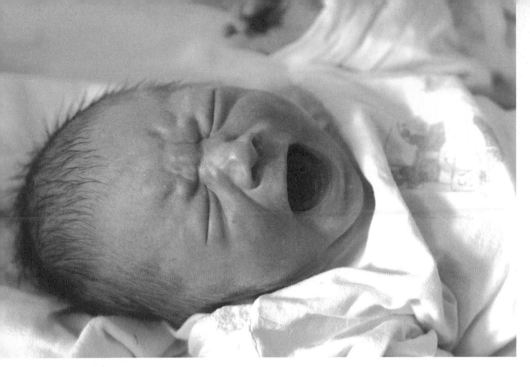

a child looks an adult directly in the eyes, whereas in other cultures it is considered evasive and impolite not to do so. There are also variations about attitudes to physical contact. In some cultural and social groups, body contact (especially between male and female) is limited to family members or certain situations (formal handshakes) only.

▲ Babies communicate through non-verbal communication

Verbal communication

We have already seen that when you talk to children, they do not just receive and understand the words you use to them; your tone of voice and body language are equally important. You will probably find that when you talk to babies you intuitively use what is called **motherese**. This is the way generations of mothers have talked to their babies and consists of:

- a higher pitch of voice and slower speech than when you talk to older children and adults
- simple vocabulary and sentence structure
- exaggerated intonation
- repetition.

Never feel embarrassed at talking in this way – it attracts babies to listen to you.

Good practice checklist

Think about how your non-verbal communication affects children:

- If you talk to them in calm and warm ways, you help them feel relaxed and comfortable.
- If you shout, you may frighten them.
- If you get down to their level and make eye-contact with them, they will know that you are talking to them specifically, listening to them and taking an interest in them.
- If you stroke them gently, you can soothe and reassure them.
- If you handle them roughly, you are likely to upset them.
- If you use positive body language like smiles and nodding, you will encourage them to communicate with you.
- If you are physically tense, you can make them feel anxious.

Key term

Motherese is how a mother talks to her baby; also known as infant-directed speech.

A significant aspect of body language is making eye-contact. However, you need to be aware how eye-contact is interpreted in different cultures. In some cultures, it is considered challenging or impolite if

Talking to and with children is not something that happens at planned and fixed times in the day. It is part of the natural everyday occurrences in your setting, accompanying all that you do with the children.

Get down to the child's level ▲

they know well who listens to them and responds to them.

An adult who is responsive is one who engages in conversation with children. They listen carefully to children, and use what they hear to communicate back to them. Unfortunately, observation and research has shown that pre-school children in a group setting may have as little as 3 minutes real conversation of this nature with an adult during a 2-hour session; most of what adults say to them takes the form of instructions ('time to put that away', 'put your coat on'). You must build your professional practice to ensure that you are a responsive practitioner who communicates frequently and regularly with the children you work with, and who listens carefully to them.

Good practice checklist

When you talk to and with children, make sure you:

- make eye-contact and make sure you have their attention
- get down to their level, and don't speak over their heads
- speak clearly
- use language that is appropriate to their level of development – keep your sentences short and simple and use words they can understand
- praise their accurate use of new language.

If a child makes a grammatical or pronunciation error, repeat the phrase back to them using the correct grammar and pronunciation.

But don't:

- ridicule their mistakes, their accent or use of dialect words
- constantly correct mistakes by telling them they are wrong or telling them that their accent is incorrect pronunciation
- try to get the child to 'perform' by asking 'What is this called …?'

Good practice checklist

Active listening to children involves:

- giving them your full attention
- not interrupting them
- giving them time to say what they want – this may involve you waiting silently for them to complete what they want to say
- picking up their non-verbal language as well as listening to the words they speak
- thinking about what they are saying to you
- repeating back to them what they have said, perhaps in a slightly different way, and expanding on what they have said.

Children will know when you are listening to them because you will respond in an appropriate way. A baby may cry, or a toddler may utter sentences using the few words in their vocabulary. They will know that an adult is listening when their needs are met – they are picked up and comforted, or given a drink. An older child will know that they have been listened to when their ideas are used to expand a play activity, or the adult responds to their anxieties by offering explanations and reassurance.

Listening to children

Listening is a key element in communication. As young children develop social and communication skills, the most important resource they can have is an adult

Ways of communicating with children

You communicate with children in a variety of ways. During your everyday routines with children, you will be:

- making task-oriented comments and questions
- giving instructions
- giving and receiving information
- **labelling**.

Key term

Labelling does not literally mean a written label, but

- using spoken words to give the names of objects and people
- supplying the vocabulary to enable the child to talk about the object or person.

Comments and questions linked to the tasks you do with children and instructions are inevitably part of your communication with children, but observation and research has shown that in some settings, these form too large a part of communication. When this happens, the children are not benefiting from all the other forms of communication and they are not able to express their own ideas and views.

The best forms of communication with children are:

- conversation, which consists of listening to and talking with others about any topic. A true conversation is always two-way – back and forth – and has a three-part structure:

  1 Person A makes an enquiry or a comment to Person B.

  2 B listens to A and responds – the response depends on, and arises from, what A has said.

  3 A listens to B and responds – the response depends on, and arises from, what B has said.

  If one person is doing all the talking, it is not a conversation!

- discussion, which is also a two-way exchange and centres on a specific topic, and enables children to explore ideas and gives you the chance to feed in new information.

It is very important to make time to have proper conversations and discussions with children, rather than just giving them instructions or 'talking at' them. Conversation gives children an interesting way to practise using language and explore ideas. Discussion is a good form of active learning, helping children to see things from different points of view and try out different ideas.

Good practice checklist

- When you give instructions, keep them simple and give one instruction at a time.
- Ask children for information as well as giving it to them.
- Do not bombard children with a string of questions so they feel they are being interrogated.
- Label everyday objects and parts of the body to children as a natural part of your running commentary on what is happening to and around the children, as a way of introducing them to new words, building on and extending their existing vocabulary.

Good practice checklist

When you are having conversations and discussions with children:

- listen to them carefully
- show interest in what they say
- respond accordingly
- give them time to think about what they want to say and finish what they're saying – don't prompt them when they need a little while to sort out what to say for themselves
- start conversations or discussions about everyday activities, routines and events – the weather, what activity to do after lunch, which way to walk to the library
- encourage children to feed their ideas, views and suggestions into discussion, and acknowledge the value of what they contribute.

What did you do at the party on Saturday Jasmin?

▲ Is this an example of an open question?

Open questions are a great aid to both conversations and discussions. They stimulate conversation and keep it going, and provoke discussion. They cannot be answered simply by a 'Yes', a 'No' or any other single word (such questions are 'closed' questions). Don't say 'Did you enjoy the party yesterday?' but do say 'What did you do at the party yesterday?'

Key term

Open questions cannot be answered by 'Yes', 'No' or any other single word (such questions are 'closed' questions).

As you converse and discuss, you will be:
- recalling – talking about what happened in the past
- expressing – talking about feelings and emotions.

Good communication with children through conversation and discussion contributes to various aspects of their development.
- Asking children about what they did yesterday or last week helps to develop their skills of memory.
- Providing them with an emotional vocabulary helps them to deal with their anxieties or fears and anger without becoming overwhelmed with strong emotions.
- Asking them what they think might happen 'if …' helps to extend their understanding of concepts and their ability to predict consequences.

Theory into practice

Jon decided to check his use of different forms of communication with children. He kept a small notebook by him and noted down examples of what he said to children over a couple of days. Later he looked through his notes and found that he had used a wide range of forms of communication:

- task-oriented comments: 'We're putting all the bricks back in their box.'
- task-oriented questions: 'Can you find the blue car to go in the garage?'
- instructions: 'Please go and wash your hands now.'
- asking questions: 'Which of these objects will float, and which will sink, I wonder?'
- answering questions: 'The new books we chose from the library yesterday are on the yellow shelf over there.'
- labelling: 'Here's your coat – let's put your arms in the sleeves.' and 'The leaves have fallen off the trees.'
- recalling: 'When Zainab came to the nursery yesterday she told us about her new baby brother.'
- expressing: 'Everyone is sad today because it's Mrs J's last day with us.' and 'You are very cross about that.'

He also noted a good conversation with Billy about a story they had enjoyed together, and a discussion with Taylor and Millie about how to build a bridge with some of the bricks.

Barriers to communication

You and the children you work with may have difficulties communicating with one another because:
- their communication development is impaired in some way
- you and they do not share a spoken language
- you do not understand them because:
  - you don't know them well enough
  - you are making assumptions about them.

Impairments to communication development

You are likely to work with children who experience hearing impairment to a greater or lesser extent, either temporarily or permanently. We know much sooner now than we did in the past if a baby has a hearing impairment because newborn babies' hearing can be tested, but a hearing impairment can develop later.

Many children suffer temporary hearing loss because of **glue ear**. Up to 70 per cent of children are likely to have a bout of glue ear before they reach their fourth birthday, but it is most common among:

- children who get lots of colds and ear infections
- children who live in homes where people smoke
- boys
- children who were bottle-fed rather than breast-fed.

Key term

Glue ear is a condition in which the middle ear fills up with a sticky fluid which muffles sound.

Glue ear usually clears up on its own, but some children are susceptible to recurring bouts, and a few need an operation to insert grommets. It can be very confusing for children who experience some periods when they can't hear properly, and other times when their hearing is fine and this can adversely affect the development of their communication skills.

You may encounter children whose development is on the autistic spectrum so they have difficulties forming social relationships. Their inability to relate to others impedes the development of their communication skills, and their poor communication skills hinder their ability to form social relationships.

About 5 per cent of children stammer for a time when they are learning to talk (four times as many boys as girls are affected). Stammering can have physical or emotional causes, but often there is no clear reason.

Shared language

You may work with children who are growing up in a home where their first language is different from the language spoken in their childcare setting or school. As they develop, they are likely to become bilingual which is a great asset in life. Even very young children quickly learn vocabulary in two languages, and are soon able to respond and apply them at home and in your setting. However, if you do not understand the home language of a child, you may have difficulty understanding their early attempts at speech, and you may not always respond appropriately to them.

Barriers to understanding

When you work with babies and older children who have little spoken language (or have a different spoken language from yours), you have to make sure that you arc open to non-verbal communications from them. To be able to understand the full range of a child's communications to you, you have to get to know them very well. A baby may be 'saying' that they want to be put down to sleep by starting to suck their thumb, rub their ear and pluck at their clothes. But an adult who does not know that baby would be unable to interpret that message, and the baby's needs would not be met.

Misunderstandings in communication can arise because of cultural differences. In some parts of South Asia, people use a sideways motion of the head which can mean both 'yes' and 'no' or neither 'yes' nor 'no', and this can be very confusing for European people who don't know how to interpret the gesture. You might assume that an African-Caribbean boy who refused to meet your eye when you were talking to him was being insolent or shifty. However, if you are aware that in some cultures making eye-contact is regarded as disrespectful, you would understand that he was in fact being polite.

Recognising and responding to communication difficulties

Your observations of children in a setting and attempts at communicating with them may lead you to suspect that a child is having difficulties in their communication development.

Theory into practice

Paulette and Jan are experienced practitioners who shared with some students their experiences of encountering children whose communication skills were not developing well. They described situations in which they had spotted that children were not developing as might have been expected.

Paulette described:

- a 6-month-old baby who didn't react to loud noises with a startled response and didn't turn towards the source of a sound
- a 3-year-old who persistently played on their own and didn't seek the company of others
- a child of nearly 3 who had scarcely any active vocabulary and the sounds or words they did make had little or inappropriate intonation.

Jan described:

- a 20-month-old toddler who didn't look up or respond to an adult or another child speaking to them
- a 2-year-old who was constantly puzzled or confused by the use of vocabulary for ordinary, everyday objects or actions
- a 4-year-old child who seemed to have difficulty in understanding other people's responses to them or recognising other people's feelings.

Difficulties in communication development can have wide-reaching effects on other aspects of development. A child who experiences barriers or difficulties in their communication development is likely to:

- find it difficult to form relationships and get left out of play with other children
- struggle to understand the basic concepts which underpin cognitive development
- encounter emotional and behavioural difficulties. A child who cannot hear or understand what is being said to them is likely to become bewildered and confused, and this may lead them to become angry or withdrawn. A child who cannot get across their feelings or what they want and need may resort to tantrums of frustration
- be delayed in learning to read and write.

You can do a great deal to help children who have communication difficulties. This may involve you in extending your skills so you can communicate in sign language or by using **Makaton**, a language system which uses signs and symbols and enables people who cannot speak or write to communicate. The signs are mostly black and white pictures which convey meaning more easily than words, which are more abstract. Children who experience communication difficulties may also need some specialist intervention.

Key term

Makaton is a language system which uses signs and symbols and enables people who cannot speak or write to communicate.

▲ Makaton symbols for everyday objects

Case study: How Shelley helps Daniel

Daniel is just over 2 years old and has had hearing problems for some time. He has recently been diagnosed as having glue ear.

Shelley is helping by:

- talking to Daniel clearly and loudly (not shouting!)
- getting down to his level and attracting his attention before she speaks to him, talking face to face
- cutting out background noise.

How can Shelley help further by talking to:
- **his parents?**
- **her colleagues?**
- **other professionals?**

Extension activity

What action would you have expected Paulette and Jan to have taken to get specialist help for the children when they spotted their communication difficulties? (See page 18.)

Assessment activity 1.2

Over a period of two weeks in your work placement, follow Jon's example of keeping a record of examples of the different ways you communicate with the children. **P2**

Alongside your examples, make notes of what you did well, when you knew you were communicating effectively with the children. Note how you knew this – how the children reacted and any feedback you received from adults in the setting.

Add some notes about the areas you are less successful in, and what you need to do to improve your practice.

You can learn more about this sort of reflective practice in Unit 4.

Case study: How Alex helps Raani

Raani is 20 months old and lives in a household where the first language is Urdu. She is beginning to say some words in Urdu at home, but remains bewildered by much of what is said to her at the nursery.

Alex is helping by:

- learning from Raani's mother some words of Urdu that are used for simple, everyday objects and using them when talking with Raani alongside the equivalent English words
- accompanying her actions with simple English, using lots of repetition
- learning some rhymes and songs in Urdu and including them in singing sessions with the other children
- giving Raani periods of individual attention and using body language to communicate with her.

How can Alex help further by contacting local agencies?

Human beings are social animals; we live in communities; to have a fulfilling life, children need to learn how to develop and sustain positive relationships with others. Fortunately, they are 'programmed' to want to interact with other people. Tiny babies gaze at human faces with interest and at a few weeks old start to smile which engages the attention and interest of adults and other children.

Developing relationships through play

As with so much of their learning, children learn the elements of how to develop relationships through play. They learn to:

- play and work co-operatively, sharing and taking turns
- have some understanding of how other people feel, and help to be considerate and care for others
- develop skills in dealing with disagreements and conflicts for themselves.

The way children play with one another changes and develops, from **solitary play** to **parallel play** to **co-operative play**.

- *Solitary play* Babies and under-2s mostly play alone. Babies are completely involved with what they themselves are doing and have no understanding of 'playing together' or 'sharing'. You may observe babies watching others and showing awareness of others, and there is evidence of communication between young babies, but they will not be truly playing together at this age.
- *Parallel play* By the age of 2 years, children may play side by side but are mostly engrossed in their own activities and do not interact very much. They may spend periods of time watching each other play, and they may even be chatting, but they still are not really playing together.
- *Co-operative play* As they move through 3 and 4 years, children begin to play with other children spontaneously. They work together to discuss, agree and implement ideas.

Key terms

Solitary play Babies and under-2s mostly play alone.

Parallel play By the age of 2 years, children may play side by side but do not interact very much.

Co-operative play By 3 and 4 years, children begin to play with other children.

▼ Developing relationships through co-operative play

You can help children move along the pathway from solitary to parallel to co-operative play by supporting their play – asking one child what the other is doing, encouraging children to share toys, showing them ways of playing together.

Case study: Supporting children's relationships through play

Jodie works in a small nursery, spending most of her time with the 2- and 3-year-olds. She notices that some of the children rarely play with others, and some have difficulty sharing play equipment and materials.

1 **How can she encourage children to play together and begin to develop relationships with one another?**

2 **How should she respond to those who do not want to join in and play with others, or will not share?**

3 **What clues can she pick up that indicate that children are moving on from one stage to another?**

Learning to understand others

By the age of 4 or 5, and especially when they start school, most children begin to form their own friendships with others of a similar age. During school years, friendships with other children come to play an increasingly important part in their lives. To be able to form friendships, children have to learn to feel **empathy**.

Key term

Empathy means understanding what it is like to be someone else.

Babies are fundamentally egocentric and have little empathy. They see themselves as the centre of the world and do not yet understand that there are other people who are separate from themselves and who have feelings like their own. But as children develop, they learn to empathise, and can begin to take other people's feelings and well-being into account. This will affect their own attitudes and actions, and they begin to make choices about how to behave. This is the foundation of ethical or moral development – what is sometimes referred to as 'knowing right from wrong' and what children talk about as 'being fair'. If children don't learn these skills, they will not be accepted and welcomed by other people, and that will lead to unhappiness and exclusion which are often the basis of various forms of anti-social behaviour, including bullying.

You can help even quite young children to begin to be considerate and caring towards others.

Theory into practice

Louise and Shamila work together in a children's centre. They discussed how they could help some of the 3- and 4-year-olds to begin to:

* know each other
* understand each other
* be considerate towards one another
* think about how other children feel.

Their ideas included:

* getting pairs of children to share information with one another about their favourite food, the pets and special toys they have at home, what they like to wear, special events in their lives such as the birth of a new sister or brother
* asking children to do things for one another such as handing out the apple slices or helping to clear up
* talking to children about they feel and helping them to learn the vocabulary of feelings – 'you look sad', 'you look very happy', 'you are so cross'
* using puppets and dolls to talk about thinking about how other people feel
* explaining children's reactions to one another – 'he is very tired today, so he wants to do something quiet and not join in that game'
* commenting positively on any acts of kindness or thoughtfulness they observed.

How do you think Hetty feels now?

Use puppets or dolls to talk about how other people feel

Perhaps the most effective way you can help children to learn these important life skills is by providing a positive role model in the way you relate to other people. Children learn so much by watching how adults behave, and they will copy the way you treat other people and how to speak to them.

Extension activity

During your work placements, monitor your own behaviour towards children (and adults) over a period of two days.

What does the way in which you speak to and behave towards others demonstrate to the children in the setting about how to relate to other people? What sort of role model do you provide for respecting the feelings and rights of others?

Frameworks for behaviour

Whatever setting you work in, there will be an established 'framework' for the behaviour of the children. This will set out what sort of behaviour will and will not be acceptable in the setting. It may be expressed as **rules**, **boundaries** or **expectations**.

Key terms

Rules describe what children may or may not do.

Boundaries indicate the limits to acceptable behaviour.

Expectations indicate to children how adults expect them to behave.

A framework like this is positive and helpful to children to make clear to them what the limits are for the way they behave. It can be very reassuring to them because they know what they may not do, how far they can go and how they are expected to behave.

The rules/boundaries/expectations are likely to be based on guiding children away from doing things which:

- are dangerous, hurtful or offensive to others (other children, adults)
- are a danger to the children themselves
- damage other people's belongings
- will make the child unwelcome or unacceptable to other people.

A framework for behaviour helps children to begin to understand that they must learn to control their own actions and behaviour – not only to protect the rights of other people but also for their own sakes and for their future happiness. Uncontrolled behaviour in older children, teenagers and adults becomes a serious problem for the family and, ultimately, for society.

Settings also have guidelines for applying sanctions when rules are broken, boundaries are crossed or behaviour falls short of expectations. It is essential that sanctions are applied fairly and consistently when children's behaviour is unacceptable within the setting's framework.

Theory into practice

Describe the frameworks set for children's behaviour, including the guidelines for sanctions, in each of the settings where you have work placements.

- What do the frameworks have in common?
- Where there are differences, why do you think this is so?

A crucial factor in being able to behave in ways which are acceptable to others around them is children's ability to cope with their strong emotions. A well thought-out framework for behaviour and guidelines on sanctions can help children move towards self-control as they:

- learn to deal with their strong emotions
- develop the ability to understand and respect the feelings and rights of other people
- start to accept rules and to apply them for themselves, without external pressure from adults.

You can play a role in helping children to accept rules and understand why they are necessary.

Case study: Involving children in setting the 'rules'

Beth is starting work in a new after-school club and holiday play scheme with children aged 6–10. The staff team have made a start on a set of expectations for children's behaviour, and now want to involve the children in agreeing what the framework should contain.

1 **How can Beth and her colleagues approach this? What contributions can they invite from the children, and how?**

2 **What should they do if the rules the children come up with are very different from the ones they have already thought of?**

Resolving conflicts

It is inevitable that the children you work with will at times have disagreements and be in conflict with one another. Very often, your best strategy is to hold back, observe what is going on and not intervene. You will find out that the children who have developed a sense of what is 'fair' and learned some emotional control will be able to resolve a conflict for themselves.

However, on other occasions, you may need to intervene – especially if one child is being hurt or verbally abused and is unable to respond on their own behalf. Children

may need your support to work through what is going on. You may be able to help them take partial control of the situation, which will help them in future to manage conflict for themselves.

Good practice checklist

You can help children resolve conflicts by:

- providing comfort to a child who is distressed by what is happening, perhaps who is the object of some unacceptable behaviour such as racist remarks
- acknowledging the feelings of that child
- asking each child to explain what is happening
- reminding a child whose behaviour has fallen short of the expectations of the setting that the way they have behaved is unacceptable, and explaining the hurt caused
- asking the children how the situation might be resolved, and giving them time to make suggestions
- praising the good suggestions they make and helping them put them into effect
- reminding the child who behaved unacceptably that that form of behaviour falls short of expectations – but making clear your continued affection for the child – 'I didn't like what you did, but I still like you.'

◄ **Help children to resolve conflicts for themselves**

Your aim should be to enable children to sort out their differences for themselves. This will be a valuable skill in their later lives, helping them to be confident, assertive and less likely to become victims of bullying.

Supporting other adults to relate positively to children

Besides working at the development of your own relationships with the children you work with, you can contribute to their relationships with other adults in the setting. You might play a role in helping a child to get to know and feel comfortable with an unfamiliar adult, for example when:

- a new colleague joins your team and has to get to know the children
- a child moves on within the setting – for example, from the baby room to the under-3s room – and they have a new key worker
- another professional comes to the setting to help provide specialist input, for example, a speech and language therapist.

Good practice checklist

To help a child become familiar with and begin to trust a new adult, you could:

- set aside some time when you can share as much information about the child as possible with the new adult, explaining all the child's individual ways of making their needs known, their likes and dislikes, etc.
- ensure that the new adult spends a little time with you and the child in their familiar surroundings engaged in familiar activities so the child begins to get to know the new adult
- show the child that you like and trust the new adult
- involve the child's parents too so the child can see that they also trust the new adult
- talk about the new adult in positive ways with the child, and encourage their parents to do the same.

Something to guard against when you work with other adults in a setting with children is not to let your attention drift on to the other adults and away from the children. When you get to know colleagues, you are likely to enjoy chatting to them and sharing information about personal as well as professional matters. However, it is important to confine this sort of conversation to breaks and out of work hours. When you are working with the children, they and your relationship with them must be the focus of your attention.

Case study: Keeping the focus on the children

Jess and Laura often spend time gossiping when they are supposed to be working with the children, so they don't observe the children closely and miss out on what the children are trying to communicate to them. They often try to draw Nina in to their conversations.

1 How can Nina avoid this?
2 What should she do to try to encourage Jess and Laura to concentrate more on their relationships with the children?

Sometimes you will find adults in your setting whose relationships with children do not seem positive. They may:

- make negative comments about the children in general, or about one particular child
- be very 'bossy' and controlling, always giving children instructions rather than engaging them in conversation
- show favouritism to some children and largely ignore others
- intervene too much in children's play and interfere in their disputes too early and too often
- show irritation towards the children, perhaps even shouting at them.

How you approach such a situation will depend on your role in the setting – whether you have management or leadership responsibilities and can take action to get these practitioners to address the shortcomings in their practice. Perhaps the most effective way you can encourage such colleagues to improve their relationships with children is by being a good role model; show by your practice how to develop and sustain positive relationships with children.

Extension activity

If you found yourself working with someone described in the list on the previous page, how would you try to help them change the way they related to children?

When children are distressed

Inevitably the children you work with will at times become distressed, and you will need to comfort them. Their distress may arise for a number of reasons, including:

- being hungry, thirsty, tired; becoming unwell; needing to have a nappy changed; being too hot or too cold
- the actions of other children such as having toys taken away, being hit by another child, being called names by another child
- feeling frustrated because they can't manage something for themselves, or they can't communicate their feelings
- having an accident such as a fall
- hearing other children cry
- being bored
- being separated from their parents or other familiar carers
- changes or new experiences they haven't encountered before.

Sometimes their distress will be obvious because they become upset and cry, but children can express distress in a variety of ways such as:

- losing their appetite
- becoming withdrawn and uncommunicative
- becoming angry and aggressive towards other children or towards adults.

If you have got to know a child well and observe them carefully, you will pick up such signals of distress and be able to respond appropriately.

When children become distressed, they need a sensitive adult with whom they have a close relationship to help them cope with distress. This enables them to become able to manage their feelings for themselves. In the past, some approaches to childcare included the 'let them cry' method. To pick up a crying baby was seen as 'spoiling' them. Current knowledge helps us to realise that it is bad for babies' emotional health if they are left to cry for lengthy periods because the baby who cries and cries feels abandoned, and that they can't trust adults to respond to their calls for help.

Good practice checklist

You might respond to children's distress by:

- cuddling them and stroking or gently rocking them to calm them down
- making sure they have their comfort object or 'cuddly'
- talking quietly and calmly
- sitting quietly with them, and perhaps beginning to sing
- distracting them by showing them a toy they particularly like or looking at a well-loved book together
- suggesting they play with water or play dough which can be soothing and relaxing, or giving them cushions to pummel or boxes to use as drums to help let off steam and relieve stress or tension
- reassuring them, and getting them to talk about what has upset them
- talking about feelings so they can learn the words to describe how they feel (angry, afraid) – for younger children, using pictures of different faces (sad, cross) – so that you can talk about which face looks like how they feel
- providing 'props' for make-believe play to help them act out what is upsetting them
- using books, stories and puppets to explore feelings that are strong and difficult to deal with.

Would you like to read your favourite book?

▲ Can you think of other ways to help overcome a child's distress?

seriously, that their anxieties or fears are important to you, and that you want to help put things right. You should also remember that a child who is often distressed may need protection from abuse, and it is your responsibility and duty to take action.

For more about child protection, see Unit 5. Distress is also discussed in Unit 14, page 433.

Assessment activity 1.3

As in the last assessment activity, over a period of two weeks in your work placement, keep a record of examples of the different ways you support children to develop relationships with one another. **P3**

Alongside your examples, make notes of what you did well, when you saw children developing relationships well with one another thanks to your actions. Note how you knew this – how the children behaved and any feedback you received from adults in the setting. **M2**

Add some notes about the areas you are less successful in, and what you need to do to improve your practice.

You can learn more about this sort of reflective practice in Unit 4.

It is important to respond to a child's distress because often the source of the distress can threaten their self-esteem. For example, if a child is being taunted or threatened, or called names, they can begin to lose the sense of being a valuable and loved person. They need you to show that you take the way they are feeling

1.4 How to communicate with adults

Working with children means that you have also to work with adults. There are three main groups of adults you will work with.

- *The children's parents* It is essential that you communicate closely with the parents of the children you work with, in the interests of consistency and continuity of their care and their learning opportunities. If you work in a community-based setting like a pre-school, some of the parents may

also be members of the management committee who will, in effect, be your employers.
- *Colleagues who also work in your setting* You must work as a member of the team and ensure that information is shared with others (you can learn more about this in Unit 4). Remember that your manager and support staff (such as admin, catering and cleaning workers) are also your colleagues.

- *Other professionals who work in a variety of other agencies and organisations* There is an increasing emphasis on multi-disciplinary working so that a range of professionals can contribute their expertise to promoting the overall welfare of the child. From time to time, your setting will be visited by inspectors and advisers.

You need to communicate effectively with adults in your work role because the children need you all to work together in the interests of their well-being. Children pick up very quickly on poor relationships and communication between the important adults in their lives, and will become unsettled and anxious if they sense tension and discord.

Much of what we have already looked at in communicating with children applies also to communicating with adults.

- Good communication is the basis of good relationships.
- Body language and other non-verbal communication is very powerful and often matters more than the words you use.
- Effective communication depends on active listening.

Being polite, courteous and respectful

Of course, as a professional, you should always communicate with other adults in a polite and courteous way. This means giving them your attention and showing that you are interested in them. Think how you feel if you approach a reception desk and the person behind it does not look up, but carries on with what they were doing before you arrived for some time before they acknowledge your presence. An adult coming into your setting should always receive a ready, smiling welcome from you.

Courtesy and respect also means addressing people as they wish to be addressed. This is especially important if you work with people from cultures you are not familiar with, since naming systems vary and a person's 'surname' is not always put last. Be wary about using people's forenames – some parents prefer to be called Mr X or Mrs Y. Always ask how you should address someone, make a note if you need to – and stick to what they see as respectful and courteous.

Good practice checklist

Think about the importance of your body language in showing respect and courtesy.

- *Your stance*
  - If you turn your body away from the person you're talking with, or cross your arms, you give the message that you don't want to listen to them.
  - If you sit or stand at a higher level, they could feel you are trying to dominate them.
- *Eye-contact* If you look directly at the person, and into their eyes, you will be more likely to give and receive messages accurately (but don't fix them in a glare, and remember that in some cultures, direct eye-contact is regarded as rude).
- *Facial expressions* Smiles and open gestures reinforce positive language and create a relaxed atmosphere, but looking bored or disapproving contradicts even the most positive language.
- *Touch* Great care is needed about touching or getting too close to other adults since there are wide variations in how people react to being touched or having someone coming into their 'personal space'. For many individuals it is unacceptable, perhaps for cultural reasons, or just uncomfortable. Think about how people from Mediterranean countries embrace and kiss even people they scarcely know, whilst northern European people stick to handshakes. Probably you should reserve touching or getting close to an adult for moments of great distress.

It is not necessary to get obsessive about 'political correctness', but you must remember that some words and expressions can be perceived as discriminatory or excluding. For example,

- Never ask someone for their Christian name – only Christians who have been christened have such names, and you could easily offend someone from a different religion or none.
- Do not refer to someone's child as 'an epileptic/asthmatic/diabetic' – this defines the child by their medical condition or disability, so say 'a child with epilepsy/asthma/diabetes'.

Listening

To be sure that you pick up other people's messages accurately and respond to them appropriately, you need to listen carefully to them. Remember what we said about listening to children, and apply it to listening to adults too. You need to listen actively to both their verbal and non-verbal communication. Their words may be saying one thing, but their body language may be giving an entirely different message, which may be a more accurate reflection of how they feel. If you show that you are listening carefully, people are more likely to feel confident in their relationship with you, and be more receptive to what you say to them.

▲ Crossed arms can give the message that you don't want to communicate

Good practice checklist

People will know you are listening to them when you:

- look at them, and nod and smile
- show you are interested in what they are saying, and concerned about them
- ask them questions which help them to continue with what they want to say
- wait until they pause before you ask questions
- leave pauses and silences in your conversation which give them time to think about what they want to say.

They will know you are not listening to them when you:

- keep looking round the room, not at them
- interrupt them and keep finishing off their sentences or jumping in with advice
- yawn or speak to someone else or answer the phone
- keep talking about yourself, capping everything they say about themselves with a 'better' story of your own
- keep looking at your watch and sitting on the edge of the chair (giving the message that you want to get away).

Responding to adults

Careful active listening will enable you to understand what others want and need, and put you in a position to respond to them. What you say in response to them helps them to keep communicating.

As we saw with children, a valuable technique in communicating with adults is to ask open questions, so you:

- gather information and explore ideas
- confirm and clarify what is being said.

Using prompts also helps to keep people talking and responding. For example, you can:

- reflect back what you observe and hear: 'You look worried', 'You sound disappointed'
- confirm that you understand what they're communicating: 'I was very interested in what you said about …'
- clarify and check that what you are understanding is accurate: 'I'm picking up that you feel …'
- summarise and focus on the main issues: 'From what you've said, the main problem is …'.

Be careful about using jargon and sets of initials. You might expect to share a lot of technical language with your colleagues, but parents may be bewildered by the terms you use. Even amongst colleagues, be alert to people who are newer to the profession or, in a multi-disciplinary team, may use terminology in a different way. Check that everyone has a shared understanding of a term. It will help if you restate a technical word in direct and easily understood language. Make sure your listeners understand the sets of initials you use.

Theory into practice

Ciara decided to monitor the way she spoke to parents, colleagues and other professionals over a period of three days, to spot areas of her communication skills she needed to work on. She caught herself:

- using the phrases 'motor development', 'first-hand experiences' and 'interpersonal skills' to some parents who looked at her blankly
- referring to the 'CIS', the 'EYFS' and 'CCLD NVQs' to the modern apprentice who had just joined the setting and who became very puzzled
- realising part way through a conversation with a speech and language therapist that they were using the terms 'inclusion' and 'integration' with different meanings, confusing themselves and one another.

It is important to pitch the vocabulary you use and your tone appropriately to the person you are talking to. Whilst you should avoid jargon, especially when talking to parents, and speak in direct ways, you have to be careful not to oversimplify. If you try to make everything very simple, you may miss out important information, and you run the risk of sounding patronising. There is a balance to be achieved. Many parents say they find professionals condescending at times, giving the impression that they feel superior because of their specialist knowledge. The professionals concerned may not have meant to give that impression, so it is important that you observe the person you are speaking to and pick up on clues that they are irritated or upset by the way you are speaking to them. The key is to acknowledge that parents are experts on their own child, just as you have expertise about children in general. This enables you to operate as partners, on an equal footing, each making a contribution.

It is essential that you express yourself clearly, so use language which is appropriate to the person you are talking to, and speak distinctly. If you have a regional accent or even use dialect phrases sometimes, you may need to modify the way you talk to make sure that everyone can understand your pronunciation and the phrases you use.

Communication difficulties

Just as you may encounter barriers in your communication with children, so you may sometimes find it difficult to communicate effectively with adults. There may be several reasons for this, and each will need a different approach to resolve the problem.

The most obvious barrier is lack of a shared language. If parents have a home language which is different from your own, you may need to rely on interpreters and this can bring difficulties. Professional interpreters will be impartial and simply pass on what the other person is saying, as accurately and completely as possible. However, if someone who is, for example, a family member or an official in a religious community acts as an interpreter, they may put their own 'spin' on what is being said. They may tell you what they would prefer the parent to be saying to you and include their own advice in what they tell the parent. Confidentiality issues may also arise. When you are speaking through an interpreter, pause frequently to allow the translation to take place.

As with children, the barrier may be related to disability, and you may need to use sign language or Makaton.

Good practice checklist

To help communicate with someone with a hearing impairment:

- find a quiet part of the setting to speak to one another
- make sure the person knows you are trying to communicate with them, gain their attention
- speak clearly and not too rapidly
- face towards the person you are speaking to and ensure there is light on your face so they can lip read
- use appropriate gestures to reinforce your spoken words
- take your time and check that what you are saying is being understood.

▲ Sign language can help to overcome communication barriers

Emotional stress is a significant barrier to communication. When we are upset, we find it difficult to express ourselves clearly and coherently, or to hear what others are saying to us. It is better to wait until someone has calmed down before trying to pass on important information, and understand that in the heat of the moment they may say things they don't really mean. You also need to understand that when people are overwhelmed by personal circumstances such as marital breakdown, serious illness or bereavement, they often build a shell around themselves which hinders them from expressing themselves or listening to others. They may also experience a low ebb of self-confidence, and you will need to make extra efforts to show that you seek and value their opinions and views.

Extension activity

Leo fell off the climbing frame this morning and gashed his leg on a protruding bracket. He has been taken to hospital to have stitches. Kelly phoned his mother at work and she has set out for the hospital. The other children are being kept away from the climbing frame until the manager can examine it.

Suddenly, Leo's father arrives, shouting angrily: 'You bunch of incompetent women. I'll sue you. You're not fit to be in charge of children.'

How should Kelly communicate to Leo's father what has happened and the actions that have been taken?

Remember that you can erect barriers to communication yourself. Some childcare professionals are always busy, busy, busy or have little patience with people who are not confronting life issues that they think they could resolve quite easily (leave an abusive partner, give up smoking, get a job). The barrier they erect means that parents can't get across what they think and feel because they sense that they are not being listened to or understood.

Communicating with someone is likely to become more difficult if you make assumptions about them rather than listening carefully to what they are actually communicating. If you rely on stereotyped views of people based on their cultural and social backgrounds, you are not focusing on them as an individual. For example, you might assume that a colleague who has had a university education grew up in a well-to-do family so they are out of touch with the reality facing many of the families you work with. In fact, they may have come from a low-income family and have a very clear understanding of living within limited resources in poor housing and dealing with uncertainty about future employment opportunities.

Conflict and disagreement

It is almost inevitable that at some time in your professional career, you will encounter a situation where you are in disagreement or even conflict with other adults. Sadly, things do go wrong at times between parents and settings; misunderstandings arise, and sometimes parents make complaints. In any work team, problems crop up.

Disagreement is not always negative – the expression of different points of view can be creative and help development. But conflict can cause:

- tension in relationships and anxiety and stress for individuals
- deterioration in the ability to work well so the quality of the services to children and families is disrupted.

It is important that serious disagreements are sorted out in a professional way as soon as possible so everyone is able to move on. The longer the situation is left, usually the worse it becomes.

Theory into practice

Josh worked in a nursery where there had been complaints from two parents about the way they were kept informed about what their children had been doing during the day. However, the staff responded to the complaints in a positive way, and retrieved the situation by:

- bringing the complaints and issues involved out into the open
- being determined to find a solution
- welcoming the parents' suggestions about finding new ways of working
- looking for solutions which everyone, or nearly everyone, could accept.

Jamila worked in a nursery school where resentment had built up between the teachers and the support workers about the failure to involve the classroom assistants in decisions which affected their daily work. Things just got worse when:

- the disagreements were not tackled head on but allowed to run on until they became intense and even personal
- confrontations developed to the point where someone had to back down or be the loser
- accusations were made, blame was apportioned, tempers were lost and the whole thing slid into gossip and backbiting.

If you are in a leadership role, you will have responsibilities for trying to avoid serious disagreements developing within your work team and dealing with conflict when it arises. However, every member of a team has a responsibility for contributing to avoiding

unnecessary disagreements and to resolving conflict. If you find yourself involved in a conflict, you must play your part in trying to deal with the situation.

Good practice checklist

If you are involved in conflict, you may find it useful to follow this approach.

Prepare yourself
- Write down what the problem looks like from your perspective and share it with someone you trust, asking them for their views on your situation.
- Think about various possible ways out of the situation, and the pros and cons for each.

Have your say
- Explain clearly and calmly to the people involved in the situation how you see it and say what effect it is having on you.
- Use simple, polite language and make sure your body language is open and non-threatening.
- Use 'I statements' to show that you are explaining things from your own point of view and not making assumptions about what other people think and feel.

Get the full picture
- Listen carefully when other people give their perspective, and show that you are listening – don't interrupt them.
- Ask open-ended questions to clarify any confusions or misunderstandings.
- Acknowledge the things you agree about and concentrate on where differences and difficulties lie.

Aim for a resolution
- Offer and consider several different options for the way forward.
- Be flexible and ready to reach a compromise.

Assessment activity 1.4

Think about the adults you have contact with during a work placement.

What sort of issues did you communicate with parents about? How did you communicate with them? Did you experience any communication barriers?

What was different about the way you communicated with your colleagues in the work setting compared with the way you communicated with parents?

What other professionals did you have contact with in your work placements? How did you feel about communicating with them?

End of unit assessment

Look back through your records of your work placements and use what you have recorded to help you answer these questions.

1 How does the way you communicate with the children help you to build relationships with them? Why are your skills of communicating with children important in the process of building relationships with them? **M1**

2 What are your strengths in communicating and building relationships with children? What areas of practice do you need to develop? **D1**

3 Why is it important that, as someone who works with children, you are able to communicate effectively with adults? **M3**

4 What are your strengths in communicating and building relationships with adults? What areas of practice do you need to develop? **D2**

References and further reading

Bruce, T. and Meggitt, C. (2006) *Child Care and Education*, 4th edition, Hodder & Stoughton

Clark, A. and Moss, P. (2001) *Listening to Young Children: the Mosaic approach*, National Children's Bureau

O'Hagan, M. and Smith, M. (1999) *Early Years Child Care and Education: key issues*, 2nd edition, Ballière Tindall

Tassoni, P., Bulman, K. and Beith, K. (2005) *Children's Care, Learning and Development*, Heinemann

Useful addresses and websites

The National Deaf Children's Society (NDCS), 15 Dufferin Street, London EC1Y 8UR; 020 7490 8656; Helpline 0808 800 8880; www.ndcs.org.uk

Royal National Institute for the Deaf (RNID), 19–23 Featherstone Street, London EC1Y 8SL; 020 7296 8000; www.rnid.org.uk

The British Stammering Association (BSA), 15 Old Ford Road, London E2 9PJ; 020 8983 1003; Helpline: 0845 603 2001; www.stammering.org

Makaton Vocabulary Development Project (MVDP), 31 Firwood Drive, Camberley, Surrey GU15 3QD; 01276 61390; www.makaton.org

Grading criteria	Assessment activity	Page number
To achieve a pass grade the evidence must show that the learner is able to:		
P1 use examples from placement to describe how relationships can be developed with children	1.1	11
P2 use examples from placement to describe how to communicate with children	1.2	19
P3 use examples from placement to describe how children can be supported in developing relationships	1.3	26
P4 use examples from placement to describe how to communicate with adults	1.4	31
To achieve a merit grade the evidence must show that, in addition to the pass criteria, the learner is able to:		
M1 explain why communication skills are important in developing relationships with children in placement settings	End of unit assessment	32
M2 use examples from placement to explain how children can be supported in developing relationships	1.3	26
M3 explain the importance of effective communication with adults in the children's care, learning and development sector	End of unit assessment	32
To achieve a distinction grade the evidence must show that, in addition to the pass and merit criteria, the learner is able to:		
D1 evaluate own communication skills in terms of developing relationships with children in placement settings	End of unit assessment	32
D2 evaluate own communication skills in terms of developing relationships with adults in placement settings	End of unit assessment	32

Positive environments for children's care, learning and development

Introduction

The care of babies and young children is central to all aspects of early years work. Keeping children healthy, safe and secure whilst in your care is your primary aim within any setting, and this unit will encourage you to think about how you can do this within your day-to-day practice.

Within this unit, you will investigate a wide range of relevant factors, which you need to consider to enable you to establish and maintain an environment where children are safe and well cared for. You will understand relevant current legislation relating to health and safety, and learn how to undertake risk assessments, investigating a range of procedures for hygiene control and the prevention of infection. In addition you will develop your knowledge and skills of supervising procedures for accidents, illnesses and a range of other emergencies. This unit also allows you to learn how to recognise symptoms of common childhood illnesses and investigate procedures for managing medications, and you are advised to complete a recognised first aid qualification so that you can respond appropriately in an emergency situation.

Throughout this unit, you will have an opportunity to learn how to care for babies and young children aged 0–8 and plan, implement and evaluate a range of care routines which are appropriate to the stages of development for individual children. Finally, you will develop the practical skills necessary to implement the full range of care routines effectively.

- How to provide a healthy, safe and secure environment for children
- How to supervise procedures for a range of emergency situations
- How to care for babies and children aged 0–8
- How to demonstrate the skills required to care for babies and children aged 0–8

Thinking points

If you asked a parent what was the most important thing they would consider when placing their child in a care environment, they will probably say that they want the child to be safe and happy. Safety is a basic human right, and this unit allows you to explore all the factors essential for keeping children safe and providing for their individual needs.

Imagine that your neighbour has been offered a full-time job and she has decided to find a nursery for 3-year-old Amy and 6-month-old Reuben. She is, however, very worried about leaving Amy in a strange place that she does not know. What will happen if there is an accident, or if Amy is ill? She isn't used to mixing with other children so she may get infections. How will staff know what Amy likes to eat, and will they make Reuben's bottle safely? What will they do when Reuben cries and who will look after the children when playing outside? There are so many things to worry about.

Your neighbour knows you are learning to look after children so she has asked you to make a list of all the things she should look for when she goes to visit different nurseries, to make sure that she chooses one where Amy and Reuben will be safe and secure and cared for effectively. What might you include on your list?

The safety and security of children is your main priority when working within childcare settings, and to do this, you need to consider and understand a range of factors:

- information
- legislation and guidelines
- risk assessment and procedures
- procedures for hygiene control.

Information

As an early years practitioner, you will be expected to follow the setting's **code of conduct**. You will have been given copies of (or access to) a variety of policies and procedures concerning the health, safety and security requirements of the setting. It is essential that you read and understand this information for your own safety and that of your colleagues and the children in your care.

Key term

A **code of conduct** contains the rules of your setting and practice you should demonstrate when working with the children in your care.

This information should be reviewed regularly by your line managers, and when alterations are made, details of changes must be passed on to you and your colleagues. Again, if you do not understand why changes have been put into place, you should discuss this with your line manager, to ensure your understanding of the practices of the setting. By ensuring that information is kept accurate and up to date, you are making sure that the health, safety and welfare of the children in your care is paramount.

The kinds of information that should be kept include:

- policies of the setting, for example the handling and disposal of body fluids and waste
- personal details of, and emergency contacts for, children

- details of staff of the setting
- statutory and regulatory arrangements covering health and safety
- evidence of drills and rehearsals of evacuation
- registers and daily records of attendance and adult–child ratios
- accident and incident record books
- medication records
- parental permission forms
- children's dietary requirements
- records of safety checks
- control of access procedures.

The Data Protection Act 1998

The Data Protection Act 1998 is legislation (a law) that is designed to prevent confidential information and personal information from being passed on without a person's consent. The Act originally applied only to information that was stored on computers, but it has been updated to include any information that is stored, either on paper or on computer databases. Under the Act, organisations that collect and store information must register with the Data Protection Commission. Anyone processing information must also comply with the eight enforceable principles of practice shown below. In terms of working with children and their families, this means that most information that is collected and held in an early years setting will be confidential. Passing on information to others would be in breach of the Act. This is one reason why consent has to be given by parents before you can contact other professionals such as speech and language therapists.

Information must be:

- processed for limited purposes
- adequate, relevant and not excessive
- accurate
- not kept longer than necessary
- processed in accordance with the data subject's rights
- secure

- not transferred to countries that do not have adequate protection
- fairly and lawfully processed.

Policies and procedures

Legislation requires settings to prepare **policies** and procedures that govern working practices and provide for quality and an agreed framework for action. The management is responsible for creating the policies and for checking that they are being followed, and the staff are responsible for implementing the policies.

As all staff and parents must be aware of these policies, you will often find them on a notice board, or in the setting's brochure. It is also important that new staff are informed of these policies and procedures during their induction.

Key term

Policies are documents to demonstrate how you should carry out your duties in certain situations, such as during an evacuation.

Maintenance of specified adult–child ratios

The National Care Standards for each country identify the adult–child ratios for registered settings to ensure the safety and well-being of the children in the group.

The National Standards in England require that the group size should never exceed 26 children. They also recommend that children should be in key worker groups. This means that each child has a named member of staff (key worker) who is responsible for their well-being and knows all the details of the child and the family. (It does not mean that they spend all the time with that member of staff.)

The minimum appropriate adult–child ratios in sessional care, full day care and out-of-school care are:

- 1:3 children aged 0–2 years
- 1:4 children aged 2 years
- 1:8 children aged 3–7 years.

Where a childminder is working alone in her own home, the ratios are as follows:

- no more than six children under the age of 8, including the childminder's own children under the age of 8
- of these six, no more than three children may be under 5 years of age
- of these three, normally no more than one child may be under 1.

It is essential that information regarding the ratios of children to staff are available. This may be through daily attendance registers or diaries. Accurate information should be collected daily regarding the times children arrived and were collected, and who their main carer was during their time in the setting.

Control of access, locks to doors, control of visitors and dealing with unwanted visitors

To ensure that the environment is secure, a setting will create procedures for managing access to the premises, with arrival and departure procedures for the children. This is particularly important where there are situations in individual families where one or other parent may have restricted access to the child. A setting will also want to provide some control over the people who are able to enter the building. All visitors will be expected to sign in when arriving at the setting.

The diagram which follows identifies some of the security measures taken to ensure:

- the safe arrival and departure of children
- that children are not able to leave the premises unsupervised
- that unwanted visitors are not able to enter the building.

Control of access – security

Locks/buzzers on doors
The locks on doors and gates will be placed so children cannot reach them. Buzzers will alert adults to opening doors.

Named personnel
Settings will ask parents to identify any adults who may collect their child. The child will not be allowed to leave the building with any other adult.

Panic buttons
Many settings now have panic buttons to enable staff to call for help if threatened.

Voice-activated or video access
Some settings may have voice or video identification systems. In large settings staff may have identification badges.

Care for all children
Settings will have a specific procedure to ensure that all children are cared for whilst other members of staff talk to parents.

Signing in
All settings will record the time children arrive and leave, many settings ask parents to sign their children in and out.

Transfer of responsibility
The policy will identify the point at which responsibility for the child transfers from the staff to the parent. This may be when the parent enters the building, or when the parent leaves the building.

A parent forgets to collect a child
Procedures will be in place to contact the parent or another adult.

Child collection policy

To ensure safety and security, settings will have a child collection policy which may include:

- a statement about the importance of collecting the child on time and the distress that not doing so may cause to the child
- a statement to suggest that regular episodes of non-collection might even be seen as neglect
- a statement that Social Services may be contacted if no one comes to collect the child
- procedures for a named emergency contact to be called if the named adult does not arrive
- procedures in place for when a different adult is to collect the child, which may include photographs, passwords and written instructions
- the point at which responsibility for the child transfers from the staff to the parent, which may be when the parent enters the building, or when the parent leaves the building
- a procedure that ensures that some adults can be free to talk to parents and still ensure there are enough staff to attend to the needs of other children.

Administration and recording of medication

There are two specific types of medication: those that are prescribed by a doctor, and those that can be bought over the counter. In early years settings, only medicines that have been prescribed by a doctor would normally be given.

People tend just to think of pills and syrups when talking about medicines, but medications can be administered in many different ways, including:

- pills
- nose, eye, or ear drops
- elixirs or syrups
- inhalers
- creams and ointments
- injections.

The National Standards provide specific guidelines regarding the administration of medications and all settings are expected to create a medications policy. The following aspects will be addressed within the policy:

- The parent must provide written permission.
- The medicine must be prescribed by a doctor.

- Written permission must include the name of the medicine, the dose, the time and instructions for administering the medicine.
- The medicine must be stored in the original container in a locked cupboard. If kept in the fridge, the fridge should ideally be locked.
- When administering medicine, another member of staff will act as a witness.
- The exact time and dose should be recorded and signed by both parties.
- A parent should also sign the record to verify the administration of the medication.
- If children attend different care settings, written information about the day's doses must be shared.
- For inhalers or injections, the practitioner should receive specific training from a health professional on how to administer the medication to that particular child.

Administration, recording and reporting procedures

Good practice checklist

Administering the medication
- Two members of staff check the label and the child.
- Shake the bottle.
- Measure the correct dose.
- To keep the label clean, ensure it faces upwards when pouring the dose.
- Sit the young child on the adult's knee.
- Talk to the child calmly.
- Have a drink ready to follow the medicine.
- Praise the child.

Never pour the dose into a drink, as the child may not finish the drink and you will not know how much they have taken. Both members of staff should then complete and sign the medication record.

Happy Days Nursery

Medication Record

Child's name _____
Date of birth _____
Parent/carer name _____
Emergency contact _____

Name of medication _____
Storage instructions _____
Dose _____
Instructions _____
Time to be given _____

I the parent of _____ give permission for the medication specified above to be administered by the staff at the stated time/s. I confirm that the medication was prescribed by the child's GP.

Signed _____ Date _____
Date _____ Time _____
Medication _____ Dose _____
Administered by _____
Witnessed by _____
Parent's signature _____

▲ An example of a medication record

Case study: Medication

Sarah has asthma and uses an inhaler. Today her mother brought her into the setting saying she had slight diarrhoea during the night and is feeling a little sick this morning. Her mother says she has an important meeting to go to today and cannot take the day off to keep her at home. She has given you a bottle of Calpol and asks you to give her a dose if she needs it. She has also given you some antibiotics prescribed by the doctor.

1 **What legislation provides guidelines for the administering of medication?**

2 **Explain in detail how you will respond to each of these situations.**

3 **Evaluate the role of legislation, policies and procedures in providing for health and safety.**

The legislation which underpins this procedure is to be found in the Control of Substances Hazardous to Health Regulations 2002 (COSHH), see below. The definition of 'substances hazardous to health' is given in Regulation 2 of these regulations and it covers all substances that are capable of causing disease or adverse health effects. It is therefore obvious that body fluids, blood, faeces, urine or vomit that may carry infections must be treated as hazardous substances.

Legislation and guidelines

Health and safety legislation

'Your health, safety and welfare are protected by law. Your employer has a duty to protect and keep you informed about health and safety. You have a responsibility to look after others.'

Source: Health & Safety Executive, 1999

Everyone working with young children must be aware of their legal obligations in relation to maintaining the safety of the children in their care.

■ The role of the Health & Safety Executive

The Health & Safety Executive (HSE) is the government agency which is responsible for health and safety. The HSE has responsibility for:

- inspecting places where people work
- investigating accidents and causes of ill health
- enforcing good standards by advising people how to comply with the law
- publishing guidance and advice
- providing an information service
- carrying out research.

■ Health and Safety at Work Act 1974

This is the most important piece of legislation relating to health and safety and includes the following:

- Employers must ensure, as far as is reasonably practicable, the health, safety and welfare of employees and those affected by their work. (This includes any person who may enter the premises, such as a caretaker, student or visitor.)
- Settings with five or more employees must have a written safety policy which must include specific procedures to cover emergencies such as accidents and events that require evacuation of the building (see page 58).
- Settings with five or more employees must carry out a risk assessment and show how risks are minimised (see page 45).
- Employers must provide for health and safety in relation to the provision, maintenance and use of premises and equipment.

Additional regulations, addressing specific areas of health and safety, have been added since the introduction of the Act.

■ Management of Health and Safety at Work Regulations 1999

These require employers to display official posters or provide leaflets for workers giving basic information on health and safety law. This is the reason that health and safety notices or leaflets will be on display in your workplace.

■ Control of Substances Hazardous to Health Regulations 2002 (COSHH)

These regulations require employers to control exposure to hazardous substances by ensuring they are kept separately in a marked, locked cupboard. It sets out eight steps that employers and employees should consider:

1 Assess the risk.
2 Decide what precautions are needed.
3 Prevent or **adequately control** exposure.
4 Ensure that control measures are used and maintained.
5 Monitor the exposure.
6 Carry out appropriate health surveillance.
7 Prepare plans and procedures to deal with accidents, incidents and emergencies.
8 Ensure employees are properly informed, trained and supervised.

Key term

Adequate control means to ensure that risks are sufficiently managed and organised to prevent injury.

■ Reporting Injuries, Diseases and Dangerous Occurrences Regulations 1995 (RIDDOR)

RIDDOR requires that all settings must provide an accident report book with separate sections for reporting accidents to children and adults (see page 56). All fatal and major injuries and dangerous occurrences not resulting in injury at work must be reported to the appropriate authority. Any injury that requires a member of staff to take more than three days off work must also be reported. The local Environmental Health or Social Services Department will advise on the reporting procedures.

■ Food Safety (General Food Hygiene) Regulations 1995

These state that settings which prepare or provide food for children must register with the Environmental Health Department of the local authority. They must ensure that people handling food have appropriate training such as the Basic Food Hygiene Certificate (see page 49).

■ Food Safety Act 1990

This Act affects everyone involved in the production, processing, storage, distribution or sale of food. It states that food must:

- be of the nature, substance or quality demanded
- not be falsely or misleadingly described
- not have been rendered injurious to health
- not be unfit
- not be so contaminated (whether by injurious matter or otherwise) that it would be unreasonable to expect it to be eaten.

The National Standards for Under Eights Day Care and Childminding

The four home countries each have a set of National Standards which identify a series of 'outcomes' that providers should aim to achieve. Each standard describes a particular quality outcome. Providers are currently being inspected against the *Every Child Matters* criteria.

Theory into practice

The National Standards are important legislation affecting early years settings and they underpin much of the work in this section of the unit.

- Find out which set of standards are appropriate for your setting, and consider how they apply to your practice.
- Compare the differences between the standards depending upon the setting, and consider why these differences are appropriate.

Risk assessment and procedures

Working with children means that there will always be an element of risk, running in the playground or climbing on apparatus, for example. Children should be encouraged to take safe risks as they explore their environment, and develop new skills. However, careful planning and thought will help to reduce the potential harm to any child.

Dangerous and non-secure areas

There are certain dangerous or non-secure areas within the setting where accidents are more likely to occur. The following tables identify some dangers and the actions taken to reduce the risks.

▼ Potential risks in the indoor environment

Area	The danger	Action taken to reduce risk
Toilet	Children locking themselves inside the cubicle Children slipping on wet floors Children falling while climbing Bacteria flourishing Burns from hot water Cleaning materials	Teach children about toilet safety High locks on cubicle doors Wet floors wiped immediately Child steps for high toilets Appropriate hygiene procedures Ensure thermostat controls temperature Cleaning materials in locked cupboard
Kitchen	Sharp knives and hot equipment	NO access to kitchen area
Floor	Children slipping on wet or polished floor Children tripping on carpet Rubbish left out by another user of the room	Non-slip floor covering Absorbent mat placed under water tray All carpets and mats fixed to floor with nails or tape Sweep and check floor before use each day
Stairs	Children falling	Ensure safety gates always closed Accompany children on the stairs ensuring they hold the hand rail Teach children safe use of the stairs
Windows	Children falling out	Safety glass installed Provide window locks and keep key out of reach of children Do not open window further than the child safety lock allows
Doors	Children 'escaping' Children trapping fingers	Locks on the doors, but keep the key in an accessible place Check the situation in relation to fire doors Supervise home time Provide slow closing mechanism and internal doors which are open during the session
Electrical sockets	Children poking objects into sockets	Socket covers for all sockets not in use

▼ Potential risks in the outdoor environment

Plants	Careful checks must be taken to avoid plants with poisonous leaves and berries.
Safe surfaces	Safe surfaces should be installed under climbing equipment. Areas where bikes are used must be flat and clear. Animal droppings must be cleared and disinfected. Surfaces must be checked for results of vandalism such as broken glass.
Access and fencing	Gates must be self-closing, at least 1.2 m high and locked. Fences must not have horizontal bars that children can climb. Fences and gates must be kept in good repair.
Dustbins and rubbish	Dustbins must be kept out of reach of children. If children are encouraged to pick up litter, they must wash their hands immediately afterwards.
Sun	Areas of shade should be provided. Sun screen and sun hats should be worn. Children should not be outside in the midday sun.

Where risks are identified, these must be shared with all staff within the setting to ensure that the safety of the child is paramount.

Security issues

When assessing the risks involved with security, the following issues may be considered:

- responsibility for keys
- responsibility for locking up
- systems for storing money and valuables
- setting alarms
- installation of CCTV
- security for the children (see pages 37–38)
- access to the premises
- arrival and departure procedures
- Criminal Records Bureau (CRB) clearance for all adults.

▲ Keeping safe in the sun

Dangerous substances and spillages

There are many substances in early years settings which may be hazardous. Spillages of any of these substances must be treated seriously and cleared up effectively using disposable gloves and appropriate cleaning cloths, which must in turn then be cleaned effectively or discarded (see the table below).

Policies and practice

In order to minimise risk, all settings will have policies and procedures in place to inform working practice. They are a legal requirement, which ensure quality practice. The management is responsible for creating the policies and for checking that they are being followed and all staff are responsible for implementing the policies.

▼ Dealing with hazardous substances

Substance	Hazard	Action to minimize the risk
Cleaning materials Washing-up liquid Toilet cleaners Bleaching agents	Poisoning Bleaching agents Unstable if mixed together Skin irritant	Store in a locked cupboard Ensure bottles are labelled Never transfer to another bottle Never mix different agents, e.g. toilet cleaners Wear protective gloves
Bodily waste Faeces Urine Vomit Blood	Transfer of infection	Wear disposable gloves and aprons Wash hands before and after dealing with incident Clean area after use Dispose of body waste and soiled nappies in separate container
Medicines	Poisoning	Keep medicines in a locked cupboard Follow 'administering medications policy'

Planning an outing

Outings are a regular feature of all early years settings. They may be a trip to the park, a walk to post a letter or full day outing to a wildlife centre or the seaside. Changing environments inevitably mean a new set of risks that need to be managed. Schools now follow national guidelines that were produced following a series of fatal accidents on trips, whilst pre-school settings have to increase staffing levels to comply with regulations.

Prior to any outing, you will be expected to undertake a risk assessment (as described below) to identify hazards such as the venue, traffic, weather, the activity. This list is by no means comprehensive.

In addition to undertaking a risk assessment you may consider the following checklist.

Good practice checklist

For all outings

- Ensure you have parental consent.
- Ensure children are adequately dressed.
- Take spare clothes, drinks, food and nappies and sun protection.
- Consider how to manage 'stranger danger' or children wandering off.
- Consider first aid/emergency arrangements.

For group-care outings

- Allow sufficient time to plan the outing.
- Find out whether you need insurance.
- Check what staffing ratios you need.
- Cost the trip carefully, allowing for hidden extras, for example driver's tip or parents who may not be able to contribute.
- Examine transport arrangements carefully, for example do coaches have seatbelts? Do volunteer drivers have the necessary experience and insurance?
- Ensure you have children's emergency contact details.
- Ensure that all staff and volunteers understand their role in the trip.
- Prepare and use registers to check that all children are present.

Case study: Staff induction

You work in a private day nursery. Your manager has asked you to prepare an induction session for new members of staff.

Consider what information is important to new members of staff and the best format to give them this information.

Theory into practice

Department of Health guidelines recommend the precautions for school visits to farms, which include:

- Wash and dry your hands thoroughly after touching an animal.
- Do not eat or drink anything at all while going round the farm, and only eat when well away from the animals, after thoroughly washing your hands.
- Do not put your face against an animal, and do not put your hands in your mouth after touching an animal.
- Do not touch animal droppings, but wash and dry your hands immediately if you do.
- Clean your shoes when you leave the farm, or when you get home, and then wash your hands thoroughly.

Look at your setting's outings policy. How does it safeguard the children whilst on farm visits?

Animals in the childcare setting

Scrupulous hygiene precautions are necessary in relation to any contact with animals. The following list describes some essential requirements:

- Wash hands before and after handling animals.
- Only introduce animals that are used to children.
- Always supervise children when with animals.
- Dispose of animal waste appropriately.
- Keep cages hygienic with a regular cleaning routine.

- Litter boxes should not be accessible to children.
- Keep all animal feeding utensils separately.
- Do not allow animals near children's food.
- Ensure that animals have regular checks with the vet and follow any vaccination requirements.
- Worm animals regularly.
- Check for fleas and treat appropriately.

Infection

Particular care needs to be taken to limit the spread of infection and efficient hygiene routines are essential (see page 48). Good ventilation can limit the build up of bacteria and viruses. It should always be possible to open windows to ensure a supply of fresh air to limit the spread of infection.

Lighting

- Lighting can affect mood – a sunny day can make people feel happier.
- Good lighting will avoid eye strain.
- Good use must be made of artificial and natural light.
- Flickering fluorescent light should be avoided – consider the use of daylight bulbs.

Heating

- Hot children are often irritable, cold children lethargic.
- The temperature should be kept at 18–21°C.
- The temperature must be monitored during the day.
- Heating systems must be maintained.
- Radiators must be protected.
- Carbon monoxide monitors should be provided.

Risk assessment

To ensure a healthy, safe and secure environment you must be able to identify potential hazards and take action to reduce the risk of accident or injury. Risk assessment is the process by which practitioners assess the level of risk posed to a child whilst using a particular piece of equipment or carrying out a particular activity.

Health and safety legislation

All settings are required, under health and safety regulations, to undertake risk assessments. While the responsibility for risk assessment ultimately lies with the management of the setting, the most efficient methods will include all members of staff.

Good practice checklist

Six steps for risk assessment

1 Identify the hazard. This may include identifying who is at risk (such as a member of staff using a cleaning product) or what specifically the risk is (e.g. bacteria flourishing in the toilet).

2 Wherever possible, remove the risk completely. If this is not possible, identify control measures to ensure the risk is minimised.

3 Identify who is responsible for taking action to minimise the risk.

4 Record the assessment. Ensure that the assessment is dated and signed.

5 Identify a timescale for the review of the risk assessment (this may be an annual inspection of the whole setting, or may be instigated if there is a change of staff or a new piece of equipment is purchased).

6 Monitor and document that the control measures are in fact in place and working effectively.

Settings will undertake risk assessments of the following:

- areas, such as indoor or outdoor environment (see page 42)
- activities, such as water play or outings
- times of day, such as meal times or arrival and departure times.

Examining the accident book may provide some evidence to identify specific risks and hazards.

Defective equipment

The table below identifies a range of examples of the equipment and resources within an early years setting that will be checked on a regular basis.

Equipment	Will be checked:
Electrical equipment	by qualified electrician
Outdoor play equipment	for rust and breakages
Games and puzzles	for broken or missing pieces
Books	for torn pages or scribbles
High chairs and prams	for cleanliness and safe harnesses
Play houses and climbing frames	for correct assembly and efficient hinges
Fire alarms, smoke detectors and carbon monoxide detectors	for low batteries

Physical environment

The National Standards address issues related to the physical environment. There should be an area where confidential information can be kept and where staff may talk to parents. Staff should have a room away from the children for their breaks and there should be separate toilet facilities for adults. There should be a kitchen which conforms to environmental health and food safety regulations.

The planning of the layout of the setting will have a direct effect on the children's experiences during the day. Their concentration, behaviour and sense of security will all be affected by the way in which the room has been prepared.

Positioning furniture and fixtures

- Furniture should be of an appropriate size for the children in the setting.
- Special consideration is required when premises are used for two different purposes or age groups, such as a nursery or school which is also used as an out-of-school club.

- Include some comfortable domestic furniture such as chairs or sofas, to create a comforting and homely environment.
- Provide a good variety of activities and make them available at all times.
- Provide some core work/play areas to ensure stability and continuity.
- There must be space to move between activities, to ensure no disruptions.
- Provide secure, stable storage at the child's height for self-selection of activities.
- Keep noisy activities away from areas near doors to ensure safety by the doors and a sense of calm for people entering the premises.
- Quiet areas where children can rest or read should be away from the noisy activities.
- Messy activities should be near a source of water for hand washing.
- Provide clear space for energetic play, or move the furniture for part of the session.
- Ensure that fire exits are unobstructed.
- Ensure good visibility throughout the room to aid supervision.

Adaptations for children with special needs

When working with children with identified needs, you will consult with parents or any professional who may be working with the child to ensure that you can adapt the environment to meet the child's needs. You may provide:

- ramps or wide doors for wheelchairs
- a quiet environment where background noise is reduced for a child with a hearing difficulty or autistic spectrum condition
- a safe area where a child with a visual impairment can move around by touching the furniture, or be introduced to tactile materials and resources
- opportunities to take an activity to the child, such as painting on a table rather than an easel.

Case study: Layout of the setting

Happy Days Nursery has been arranged according to the plan below.

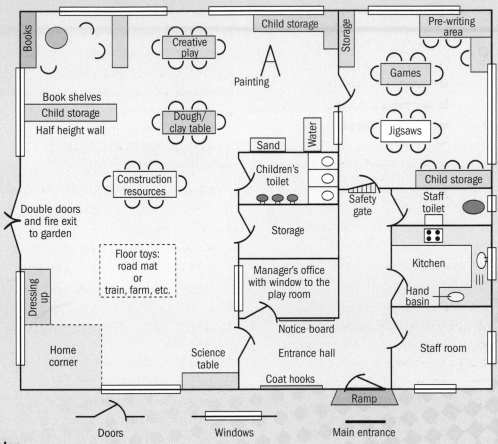

Examine the plan.

1 Evaluate the physical layout of the nursery using the information provided above as guidance.

2 Identify any potential health, safety or security hazards in the setting.

Supervision

It is important that there are quiet areas in the nursery where children can play in peace, but the staff must be able to observe and supervise effectively. The level of supervision will vary depending on the age of the child, the environment they are in and the activity they are undertaking. There are three distinct levels of supervision:

- *general supervision* – ensuring that you can see the children and are aware of what they are doing, for example being aware of what the children are doing whilst playing in the garden

- *close supervision* – being on hand while they undertake specific activities to help if required, for example sitting at the collage table to help with aprons or writing names on the paper

- *constant supervision* – interacting with the child during a risky activity, for example supporting children during a woodwork or baking activity.

Your responsibility is to ensure that children have the appropriate supervision at all times.

Procedures for hygiene control

Ensuring good hygiene practices within the setting will work towards reducing the amount of bacteria to a level which is no longer a threat to the children's health. How effective your procedures and practices are will depend on how they are applied and maintained. By ensuring that procedures are carried out effectively, thoroughly and correctly, you will minimise the risk of infection to the children in your care, other colleagues and yourself.

To ensure good standards of hygiene within the environment, settings should:

- address issues of hygiene within the health and safety policy
- include hygiene procedures in staff induction
- develop routines for cleaning the environment, equipment and toys
- provide appropriate hand-washing facilities
- use protective equipment as appropriate
- ensure safe storage of rubbish
- introduce appropriate food handling procedures
- promote personal hygiene routines
- introduce specific procedures when working with animals
- adopt appropriate measures for dealing with body fluids.

Personal hygiene and cleanliness

Babies' immune systems are not fully developed and they are vulnerable to infection. Adults must maintain high levels of personal hygiene to avoid bacteria transferring from their hands and clothing onto babies and children. Good hand washing is essential in preventing the spread of infection and reducing the risk of cross-contamination. It is best to use liquid soap from a dispenser rather than a solid bar, as liquid soap is less likely to become contaminated.

Good practice checklist

You should wash your hands:

- after going to the toilet
- before and after changing babies' nappies
- following any incident involving bodily waste
- before preparing food or bottles
- after touching animals and pets
- after undertaking domestic cleaning tasks.

Cleaning the environment

During the day a range of cleaning tasks will be completed by an early years professional, making sure the following are clean:

- toilets and nappy changing areas
- floors
- tables
- cooking utensils
- feeding equipment
- toys and equipment.

The most effective way to minimise the risk of spreading bacteria from one place to another is to use separate cloths and brushes, cleaning agents and rubber gloves for different tasks in the different areas. Toilet areas should be cleaned regularly using disposable cloths. Using disposable cloths is particularly effective, as they are thrown away with each use, and therefore cannot spread bacteria onto other surfaces. Nappy changing mats should be cleaned before and after each use, using a protective paper barrier between the mat and the baby's skin. Babies and young children who are crawling or playing on floors are at a higher risk of infection, and therefore you should also disinfect floors and surfaces regularly, wearing disposable gloves while doing so. Good hand washing and cleaning is essential when providing food for children. Cooking utensils, and eating surfaces should be spotlessly clean, and children should be encouraged to wash their hands thoroughly before handling or eating their food. Toys can carry bacteria from unwashed hands and from being put into children's mouths. Whilst it is not practical to wash each toy between use by individual children, it is important that toys are cleaned regularly and contaminated soft toys that cannot go in the washer should be discarded.

Food handling

All foods may be potentially hazardous if they are not handled correctly, therefore good hygiene in the kitchen is essential. Anyone who is involved in food preparation should undertake the Basic Food Hygiene Certificate.

It is essential that your setting considers:

- staff rotas, routines and areas of responsibility
- how food handling procedures will be reviewed and monitored
- how children will be monitored if they have access to the kitchen
- having a separate sterilisation area
- how food will be transported to various rooms within the setting.

This unit only provides simple basic guidelines as demonstrated in the diagram below. Detailed information can be found in Unit 11, page 392.

Dealing with body fluids and waste

While there is general concern about infections such as HIV (and small amounts of HIV have been found in body fluids like saliva, faeces and urine), there is no evidence to suggest that HIV can spread through these body fluids. However there is a risk that blood-borne viruses such as hepatitis B and hepatitis C and HIV may be spread by blood-to-blood contact.

A child may be HIV positive or have hepatitis without the carers knowing about it, so it is essential that all accidents or incidents that involve body fluids are managed by following the appropriate procedures.

Procedures for dealing with body fluids will include:

- Disposable gloves to be worn at all times.
- Where possible, hands should be washed before carrying out any first aid procedure involving broken skin.
- Hands to be washed after dealing with any spillages, even if gloves have been worn.
- Cover any skin abrasion with a waterproof plaster.

Storage
- Correct temperature: below 4°C for fridges, −18°C for freezers
- Stock rotation
- Raw food below fresh food in fridge
- All food covered
- Sandwiches should be prepared just prior to eating
- Dry ingredients in air tight containers

Preparation
- Hands washed before and after handling food
- Hands washed between handling raw and cooked food
- Disposable towels used
- Do not reheat food
- Food thoroughly cooked and cooled quickly if going to be stored

Food hygiene

Equipment
- Separate areas and equipment for cooked and uncooked food
- Separate chopping boards
- Can openers, slicers, food processors regularly cleaned and sterilised
- Cloths, tea towels, oven gloves boiled frequently
- Disposable towels used for hands and spills

Cleaning
- Surfaces to be cleaned regularly throughout the day
- Spills cleaned up promptly
- Food containers emptied and cleaned before refilling
- All signs of household pests reported immediately
- Waste disposal into sealed bins which are away from food area
- The bins must be cleaned regularly

Food handler
- No smoking
- Stay off work if any sign of diarrhoea or vomiting
- Complete food hygiene course

- Blood splashed onto the skin should be washed off with soap and water.
- Splashes of blood in the eyes or mouth to be washed out immediately with plenty of water.
- Spillages should be cleaned up as soon as possible using a solution of bleach diluted 1 part in 10 parts of water.
- Spillages should be wiped up with paper towels which are then disposed of as contaminated waste.
- Soiled clothing and linen should be rinsed in a cold wash and then washed in a hot wash, preferably at 90°C.
- Soiled items may be flushed down the toilet, burnt, or double bagged in plastic bags which have been properly secured and the waste collected for incineration.
- All gloves or aprons that have been worn must be disposed of with the affected items. Any carer who is concerned about the transfer of blood should seek medical advice from his or her doctor.

Reporting to the authorities

If there appears to be an outbreak of a particular condition, the setting must report the matter to staff at the Public Health Department. The Consultant on Communicable Disease Control will assess the situation. If the outbreak is food related, this must be reported immediately to the local authority's Environmental Health Department. It is essential that the information is accurately recorded and immediately reported to the authorities.

Reporting to parents

Some information must be shared with parents. This can be done through the daily exchange of information, through letters, or on an accident form. The following details may be shared with parents:
- any concern about the health of their own child
- specific information for all parents about a particular situation, for example a case of meningitis.
- an outbreak of head lice
- a child in the setting known to have developed Rubella
- accidents or incidents.

Whichever way you communicate with parents, it is essential that the information shared is recorded, accurate, and up to date.

Methods to minimise/prevent cross-infection

To appreciate the methods used to prevent cross-infection, you need to have an understanding of how infection is spread. The following table describes the different ways that infection is carried and identifies the precautions that are taken to minimise/prevent cross-infection. See also page 397.

▼ Minimising/preventing cross-infection

Micro-organisms enter the body via	Methods of prevention
Inhalation Breathed in through the nose and mouth	Ensure good ventilation
	Encourage hygiene practices, such as covering the mouth when coughing
	Use good hygiene procedures in relation to keeping the environment and resources clean
	Excluding children with communicable diseases
Ingestion Swallowed through the mouth	Use proper hand-washing procedures (see page 48)
	Practise good food preparation procedures (see page 49)
	Use good hygiene procedures in relation to keeping the environment and resources clean (see page 48)
	Use good hygiene procedures in relation to animals (see page 48)
	Exclude children with communicable diseases
	Safely dispose of waste products (see page 49)
Inoculation Penetrating the skin through cut or injection	Cover open wounds
	Safely dispose of waste products (see page 49)
	Use separate personal hygiene equipment
	Use rubber gloves

Extension activity

Using what you know about the stages of children's learning and development, identify a range of activities you could use with the following age groups to promote issues of hygiene:

- 0–3 years
- 3–5 years
- 5–8 years

Evaluate your activities making reference to the importance of personal hygiene, food hygiene and maintaining the environment. Consider additional learning outcomes the children from each age group may achieve through your activities, and how this might support them within the **curriculum**.

Key term

Curriculum A programme of study, set of courses or syllabus.

Confidentiality and reporting procedures

Every setting will have a confidentiality policy, and will have been required to register with the Data Protection Commission. The general rule is that information about a child or family should not be shared with any other person unless it is in the direct interests of the child, such as in the case of safeguarding children from harm. While in all general situations confidentiality must be maintained and personal or health details about any child or family must not be disclosed, there are some circumstances where sharing information is essential.

Case study: Reporting procedures

You are the manager of an out-of-school club.

- Jason has nits.
- Five of the children developed diarrhoea and vomiting last night.
- Farhan has German measles.
- Casey has a nasty weeping sore on her chin.
- Jamilla has eczema.

1 **Identify which of these situations you will share with:**
- **the parents of the child**
- **colleagues**
- **all parents**
- **the authorities.**

2 **Explain why you have decided to share this information.**

Assessment activity 2.1

1 Using the materials you were given during induction at your current workplace, identify the following policies and procedures:
- Health and hygiene
- Arrival and departures
- Child protection
- Behaviour management policy
- Smoking and drinking policy
- Fire procedure
- Medication procedure
- Illness, accident and emergency procedure.

Read through them, and ensure you fully understand them. Should you have any queries, consult your line manager.

2 Undertake a risk assessment of one particular area within your workplace to identify hazards.
- Identify potential hazards
- Describe procedures for dealing with them.

3 Explain how legislation, policies and practice support the provision of a healthy safe and secure environment.

Theory into practice

Simian, a nursery manager, is fully aware that accidents are the commonest cause of death in children over 1 year. These are some of the procedures which are carried out to keep the risks of accidents to a minimum:

- daily risk assessments
- regular fire drills
- safety film on all windows
- regular toy and equipment checks
- discarding broken toys
- non-slip mats
- supervised play, particularly around water
- safety gates.

What do you do in your daily work routine to keep children safe and free from potential accidents? See www.rospa.com for further information.

Procedures

First aid is the immediate assistance or treatment given to someone who has been injured or taken ill before the arrival of an ambulance, doctor or other appropriately qualified person. The aims of first aid are to:

- preserve life
- prevent deterioration of the condition
- promote recovery.

It is essential that any intervention should not harm the casualty and you should not take action just for the sake of doing something. For this reason, it is important that everyone who works with children should attend a relevant paediatric first aid course with a trained instructor which includes:

- dealing with emergencies
- resuscitation
- shock, choking and anaphylactic shocks.

A first aid qualification will need to be updated every three years.

The following information provides an outline of the procedures to be taken in an emergency, but is no substitute for attending an appropriate course. For further information look at: www.childcareapprovalscheme.co.uk.

Checking for signs and symptoms

It is important that you have a good procedure for responding to accidents and recognising the **signs** and **symptoms** of injury. In an accident situation, as a student, your first priority is to summon help from your supervisor, the identified first aider or the professional services.

Key term

A **sign** is anything that you perceive using your senses, for example something you smell, hear, see or feel.

A **symptom** is what the casualty tells you, for example 'I went a bit dizzy.'

A useful procedure for the assessment and diagnosis of injury is given below.

Prioritising treatment

Having completed the process of assessment, you need to be able to prioritise your treatment. It is important to remember the 3 Bs:

- *Breathing* Always assess the casualty's airway, breathing and circulation as the first priority and treat as appropriate.
- *Bleeding* Take the necessary action to stop bleeding.
- *Bones* If you suspect there may be injury to bone and supporting tissue, take the necessary action to support or immobilise the injury.

Assessment
Keep calm, don't panic.

Assess the situation
Ensure the area is safe. If a child has put their hand through a window and there is a lot of sharp glass, you may do yourself an injury. You may need to consider what to do with other children.

Assess the casualty
An initial assessment to ensure there is no life threatening condition. Check for consciousness, airway, breathing, signs of circulation and blood loss. If necessary start resuscitation.

Diagnosis
You reach a diagnosis by assessing the signs and symptoms.

Signs
Signs are evidence of a casualty's injuries that you can see, hear or feel. For example, burns, bleeding from orifices, swelling, unnatural shape, abnormal skin colour, noisy breathing, groaning, abnormal temperature.

Symptoms
Symptoms are sensations that a casualty can describe, for example, pain, loss of movement, weakness, tingling, dizziness, nausea.

▲ The procedure to follow in case of injury

Dealing with an unconscious casualty

An important aspect of first aid provision is the ability to deal with an unconscious person. These skills are best practised on a recognised first aid course. The following chart aims only to provide basic guidelines.

THE ABC OF RESUSCITATION

CHECK RESPONSE

Child 1–7

Talk calmly and shake very gently.

Baby (under 1)

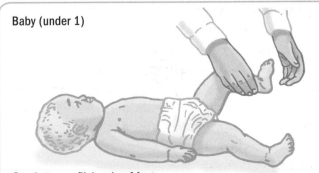

Gently tap or flick sole of foot.
DO NOT SHAKE A BABY.

CHECK AIRWAY

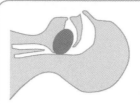

1 When unconscious the muscles relax and the tongue falls back.

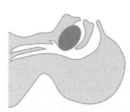

2 When the head is tilted and the chin lifted, the tongue will lift from the back of the throat.

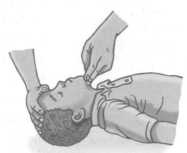

Open airway. Tilt head back slightly, one hand on forehead, two fingers under chin.

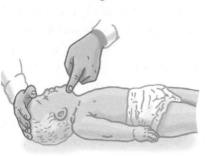

Open airway. Tilt head back very slightly, one hand on baby's head, one finger under chin.

CHECK BREATHING

Place cheek next to child's mouth. Listen for sounds of breathing and watch chest for movement. Listen for up to 10 seconds.

If breathing is not present, carefully remove any obvious obstructions from mouth. DO NOT poke down throat. Pinch child's nose, seal lips round mouth and breathe into the lungs until the chest rises. Give five breaths (known as rescue breaths), one every 3 seconds. Look for signs of recovery.

If still no recovery, begin chest compression.

CHEST COMPRESSION

Child 1–7
Place the heel of one hand in the centre of the chest. Press down one-third the depth of the chest 30 times at a rate of 100 per minute. Give two further breaths and continue at a rate of two breaths to 30 chest compressions until help arrives or the child begins to breathe unaided.

Baby (under 1)
Place the tips of two fingers in the centre of the chest. Press down one-third the depth of the chest 30 times at a rate of 100 per minute. Give two further breaths and continue at a rate of two breaths to 30 chest compressions until help arrives or the child begins to breathe unaided.

■ The recovery position

You will be able to practise the following technique on an approved paediatric first aid course.

1 Place two fingers under the child's chin and place your other hand on the forehead. Gently tilt the head back.

2 Straighten the limbs and place the arm nearest to you so it lies at right angles to the child's body. Check pockets for any bulky objects.

3 Bring the child's other arm across the chest and place the hand against the child's cheek with palm facing outwards. Holding that hand in position, use your other hand to pull up the child's far leg. Hold the leg just above the knee.

4 Gently pull the far leg towards you rolling the child forward until they are lying on their side. Use your knees to prevent the child rolling too far forwards. Keep your other hand holding the child's hand to their cheek.

5 Bend the upper leg so that it is at right angles to the body.

Throughout the procedure, ensure that the child's head remains well back and is supported on their hand to keep their airway open.

Treatment of minor and major injuries

Minor injuries

While it is fairly unlikely that you will have to deal with many major accidents, you will regularly be called upon to deal with minor injuries. Many minor injuries will respond to a cuddle and some adult attention, but however minor the incident you will always be expected to monitor the child's condition to identify any underlying problem. You may need to call for professional assistance even for what may appear to be a minor injury.

Major injuries

- Assess for danger.
- Give emergency first aid.
- Make it safe.
- Check the 3 Bs (page 52).
- Protect yourself.
- Keep calm and support others.
- Wear disposable gloves.
- Summon help.

The table below provides some basic information for use in an emergency until expert help arrives and highlights the actions you must *not* take. Remember, it is essential that any action of yours does not harm the individual or make the injury any worse.

▼ Basic emergency action

Emergency	Action	Do not!
Bleeding	Lay child down to reduce the possibility of shock Cover wound with pad or dressing Apply pressure for up to 15 minutes If there is a large foreign body in the wound, apply pressure on either side of wound Raise and support the injured part Bandage the wound	DO NOT remove glass or objects from a deep wound DO NOT apply a tourniquet, it can worsen the bleeding
Burns and scalds	Cool with sterilised water for at least 10 minutes Remove constricting clothing Cover with a clean cloth	DO NOT remove anything sticking to the burn DO NOT apply lotions or plasters
Choking	If obstruction visible, hook out with your finger Lean older child forward, or support baby's face down along forearm and give five brisk slaps between shoulder blades Stand behind child, place fist on lower breastbone, hold with other hand and press in sharply five times. For baby, use two fingers on lower breastbone	DO NOT risk pushing it further down DO NOT ever hold a baby or young child upside down and slap their back; you could break their neck
Convulsions	Cool the child by sponging with tepid water if they have a high temperature Clear the area and protect from injury by placing pillows or padding around the child Sponge with tepid water Put child in the recovery position once convulsions have ceased	DO NOT put anything in the child's mouth
Fractures	Keep the child still	DO NOT move the child until the injured part is immobilised
Head injury	Control any bleeding Monitor for consciousness, headache, drowsiness, vomiting or blood loss from nose, mouth or ears	If there has been a back or neck injury, DO NOT attempt to move the child DO NOT leave the child alone
Poisons	Check ABC (airway, breathing and circulation) Save sample of poison	DO NOT make the child vomit
Shock	Lay the child down, raise legs and keep warm Loosen tight clothing Treat any injury Monitor condition	DO NOT leave the child alone DO NOT give food or drink

In any of the incidents in the table you will have called for professional assistance. It may be tempting to put the child in a car to take them to the hospital, but some situations can deteriorate very quickly and you may need professional help and the ability to move through the traffic very quickly.

Accident procedures checklist

Accident procedures are specific to individual settings but will probably include the following points:

- A trained first aider must be on duty at all times.
- All adults should know who the first aider is.
- The person who witnesses the accident should inform a first aider.
- First aider will assess the situation and the injury and summon help if required.
- Another member of staff will comfort the other children involved in the incident.
- Remaining staff will maintain a normal play environment and move children to another area if necessary.
- If necessary, inform the parents or emergency contact if a parent cannot be found.
- In an emergency, dial 999 to call an ambulance. A member of staff may accompany the child to hospital if the parent has not arrived. (Ensure that the adult–child ratio in the setting is still appropriate.)

The Reporting of Injuries, Diseases and Dangerous Occurrences Regulations 1995 (RIDDOR) require settings to provide an accident report book. The member of staff attending to the injury is responsible for completing the accident report and ensuring that the parent signs the report.

Accident Report

Name _Farinda Patel_

Day/date _Tuesday 15 February, 2007_

Time _11.45 at home time_

Place _In the pre-school room_

Circumstances of accident _Farinda and another child were running to get their coats. They banged heads and Farinda fell to the ground_

Nature of incident _slight bump on the head_

Action taken _Cold water compress_

Person who dealt with injury _Zameera_

Witness _Caroline_

Parent's signature_____

▲ Injuries must be recorded in the setting's accident report book

Good practice checklist

If any of the following occur, you must call an ambulance:

- unconsciousness
- difficulty breathing
- severe bleeding
- serious burns.

You may also need to call for professional assistance for what may appear to be a minor injury. The table below provides details of some minor injuries and identifies some specific complications for which you should seek medical attention.

▼ Complications in minor injuries

Injury	Treatment	Monitor
Bump to head	Cold water compress	For drowsiness, vomiting, headache, bleeding from ears, nose or mouth
Nose bleed	Tip head forward and pinch nose below the bridge for up to 10 minutes	If it continues for more than 30 minutes, seek medical attention
Grazed skin	Rinse with clean water, do not rub embedded grit. Cover the wound while in the childcare setting to prevent infection and inhibit spread of leaking body fluids	For signs of infection, reddening of skin or discharge
Trapped fingers	Cold water compress	Check surface of skin for abnormal shape, or possible fracture

However, the final advice to any childcare practitioner is always that if at any time you are concerned about the welfare of the child you should refer the situation for professional assistance.

Signs and symptoms

There are many infectious childhood conditions. Some diseases can be very serious for particular groups of people, such as pregnant women and children with certain medical conditions which make them vulnerable to infections. Immunisation is available for some of the diseases, but not all families participate in immunisation programmes. The Department of Health provides

guidance on infection control in schools and nurseries and includes exclusion times. Many settings provide a policy for the exclusion of children who are ill, to limit the spread of infection.

The following table identifies the incubation and exclusion periods for some common childhood infections and lists some of the specific complications. (Exclusion details are taken from the Department of Health 'Guidance on Infection Control' poster.)

Children who are not well should not be at school or nursery even if they are not infectious, neither should children and adults with diarrhoea unless the diarrhoea is known to be of a non-infectious cause (for example, coeliac disease).

▼ Some common childhood infections

Infection	Incubation	Recommended period to be kept away from school (once the child is well)	Complications
Chicken pox	14–21 days	Five days from the onset of rash	Scarring or secondary infection from scratching. Can affect the pregnancy of a woman who is not immune
Diarrhoea and/or vomiting (with or without a specified diagnosis)		24 hours after the diarrhoea and vomiting have stopped	Dehydration
Impetigo	1–3 days	Until the lesions are crusted or healed. If lesions can be kept covered, exclusion may be shortened	Side effects are uncommon
Measles	7–15 days	Five days from the onset of the rash	Ear and eye infections, pneumonia and encephalitis
Meningitis	2–10 days	The Consultant in Communicable Diseases may be informed and will give advice. National Meningitis Trust help line (0845 6000 800) will also advise	Deafness, brain damage and death
Mumps	14–21 days	Five days after swelling appears	Meningitis (very rare). Infection of the testes in young men
Rubella (German Measles)	12–25 days	Five days from the onset of the rash	If contracted by women in first three months of pregnancy can cause serious defects in the unborn baby
Scabies	Until treated	Can return the day after treatment started	May trigger the onset of common conditions such as eczema
Whooping cough	7–10 days	Five days from commencing antibiotic treatment	Weight loss, dehydration, pneumonia

Theory into practice

A designated member of staff should be responsible for checking the contents of the first aid box, ensuring that contents are all still 'in date', and replenishing it as necessary.
Find out who is the designated first aider in your current workplace.

First aid

The Health and Safety (First Aid) Regulations 1981 require that all settings must provide a first aid box. The box should be green and marked with a white cross and should be waterproof and airtight. It must be kept in an accessible place, so that it can be easily found in the case of an emergency. Examples of what a first aid box may contain include:

- guidance leaflet
- 20 individually wrapped sterile adhesive dressings
- 2 sterile eye pads
- 4 individually wrapped triangular bandages
- 6 safety pins
- 6 medium-sized individually wrapped sterile wound dressings
- 2 large individually wrapped sterile wound dressings
- 1 pairs of disposable gloves (preferably latex free)
- alcohol-free cleansing wipes
- 1 pair blunt-ended scissors.

Theory into practice

It is essential that you carry out a first aid training course to ensure you feel confident and able to respond to emergency situations.

- Find out how many first aiders are within your setting, and how their competency is monitored.
- How do you feel you would cope in an emergency situation?
- What further training might you need to access and how might you go about this?
- If you need to, enrol on a first aid course. Your tutor can give you advice about where to go for this.

Emergency procedures

In any major incident, such as a fire, bomb or gas leak, you should call the emergency services. For major injuries, as described on page 55, you should always call for an ambulance.

The Health and Safety at Work Act 1974 requires that all settings provide procedures for use in the event of an emergency to ensure that everyone in the setting can respond quickly and effectively during any emergency incident.

▼ Types of emergency

Emergencies that require evacuation of the building	Other emergencies
Fire	Accident
Gas leak	Sudden illness
Flood	Intruder
Bomb scare	Missing child

The emergency process

It is not enough simply to plan the response to an emergency situation. The process must involve a cycle of specific procedures as shown in the diagram opposite.

Each setting will prepare procedures that meet the individual needs of its environment. In this section we examine some emergency situations following the process identified in the diagram.

■ Fire emergency checklist

All settings will prepare specific procedures that are relevant to their individual situations. However, a fire procedure will include the following guidelines:

- Display fire procedure notices prominently to inform people of the action to take in the event of a fire.
- Ensure all adults in the building are aware of the location and content of notices.
- Provide fire extinguishers and fire blankets in areas where they may be needed, such as the kitchen.
- Provide training in the use of extinguishers.
- Ensure all fire equipment is serviced once a year.
- Fire exits should be clearly signed, unobstructed and checked for ease of opening.

Prevention
Having an awareness of the causes of emergencies, and taking direct action to minimise these effects

↓

Procedures
Creating procedures that should be followed in the event of an emergency. Ensuring all adults are informed

↓

Rehearse
All procedures need to be practised regularly to ensure that all adults and children in the setting are aware of the actions they should take

↓

Record and review
Each practice will be recorded and reviewed immediately following the event, and an annual review will also be undertaken. This information will feed back into the process of PREVENTION

↓

Prevention
And the cycle is complete

▲ The cycle of specific procedures required to prepare for an emergency

- Evacuation routes should be planned with consideration for the different situations where a fire may occur.
- Fire practices must be carried out regularly at different times of day and using different evacuation routes.
- Fire practices must be recorded and evaluated.
- Registers must be completed as the children enter the building and must include arrival and departure time.
- Registers should include each child's emergency contact number and be held in an accessible place.
- Access must be maintained for emergency vehicles.

Even if you have fire-fighting equipment, the first priority is to evacuate the building. Do not fight a fire unless you know what you are doing.

Gas leak emergency checklist

- Raise the alarm. (Do not use an electrical alarm.)
- Turn the gas off at the mains.
- Open all doors and windows.
- Evacuate the building in a calm and orderly manner.
- Phone the Emergency Gas Number. (Keep the number by the phone.)

Flood or bomb scare

For all emergencies that require evacuation of the building such as bomb scares or floods, it is important to have a list of emergency numbers, and to have identified an alternative safe venue to take the children to.

Missing child

If a child goes missing whilst in the care of the setting, the missing child policy should be followed. This policy may involve the following:

- A thorough search of the area must be carried out immediately, taking care to search all areas that a child can access.
- If the child cannot be found, the emergency services must be called immediately and then the parent/carer must be informed.
- As soon as possible after the incident, an Incident Form must be completed and a copy retained by the setting.
- The events should also be recorded in the setting's Incident Book.
- An investigation should also take place to ascertain the reasons for the child becoming lost.

Rehearsing the fire procedure

In order to be able to respond effectively in any emergency situation, it is essential that everyone knows what to do and has had the opportunity to practise the procedure regularly.

Fire practices should be carried out at least once a term. Staff will ensure that they make provision for any children with special needs who may need additional help to leave the building quickly. It is important that even in domestic situations evacuation routes are planned and practised with the children.

If procedures are to be effective, all adults and children in the building need to be familiar with them.

It is the beginning of the new school year. The children joining the reception class are coming into school during the first two weeks. There are some new members of staff: the school secretary, the year 3 teacher, two teaching assistants, and two midday supervisors. The school runs a 'Parents as Educators' programme where parents volunteer to support work in the classroom. This programme is going to start at the beginning of week three. A small number of these parents have English as an additional language.

1 **How, and at what time, will you ensure that all adults and children are aware of the fire procedure?**

2 **How can you help parents who are not confident in their use of English?**

3 **What would be the result if some adults were not aware of their responsibilities?**

Reviewing and modifying the fire procedure

To ensure that fire practices are meaningful experiences, you will need to prepare criteria for evaluating their effectiveness. Suggestions could include:

- How long did it take?
- Was the appropriate exit used?
- Was the 'fire' in a different place from the previous practice?
- Was the alarm at a different time from the previous practice?
- Did all the adults know what to do?
- Did all the children know what to do?
- Did the children remain calm?
- Did someone remember the register?
- Was there a de-briefing discussion with the children after the fire practice?

- Provide a detailed log account of a fire practice you have participated in.
- Evaluate the effectiveness of your role during the fire practice and identify how you met the requirements of the policy in your setting.
- Identify the legislation which underpins the requirements of the fire procedure in your workplace.

You work in a two-storey private day nursery. There are three people working in the upstairs baby room with seven babies. During a fire practice last week Shabana and Dan were alone giving the babies their lunch. Natalie had just gone downstairs to collect some clean bibs when the fire alarm went off. It took Shabana and Dan 5 minutes to get all seven babies out of their high chairs and outside to the collection area. Natalie stayed downstairs to help one of the children who has special needs to get out quickly. Fortunately it was only a fire practice …

1 **What conclusions would you come to if you were to review this fire practice?**

2 **What difference does the time of day make to the fire practice procedures?**

3 **What difference does the age and ability of the children have to the fire practice procedure?**

Reviewing accident procedures

All accident procedures must be reviewed regularly and should involve an examination of the accident book. This will enable staff to identify any common features, such as the time of day or specific activities that regularly appear to cause accidents. This information can then be used to improve the accident prevention measures.

Assessment activity 2.2

You have taken a group of children to the local park. Suddenly a large dog appears and starts to chase Kerrie. She starts running looking backwards over her shoulder and crashes into Jack, and they both fall to the ground. The dog jumps on the children and bites Kerrie. Jack hit his head on the ground and is unconscious and breathing, and Kerrie has a deep bite on one leg and a dirty looking graze on her other leg. The other children are all screaming.

1 Describe what you will do in relation to the following:
   a) assessing the situation
   b) assessing the casualty
   c) diagnosing the injuries
   d) prioritising treatment
   e) providing treatment for both children
   f) recording the incident
   g) informing the parents.   **P3**

2 Undertake a recognised first aid qualification so that you are equipped to respond in emergency situations.   **P4**

Remember that in most situations you would call your supervisor, or the identified first aider, who will make any necessary decisions.

In this section you will develop the knowledge and understanding required to care for babies and young children and investigate the reasons why babies and young children need efficient care routines.

The early years services delivered in the UK are currently undergoing considerable change. The document *Every Child Matters: Change for Children* identifies five key outcomes for children and young people and describes the support needed from parents and carers to ensure these outcomes are achieved – these outcomes are described in the table below. The first three outcomes underpin all the work with children and these concepts run through the whole unit. (See also Unit 5 page 185.)

Key outcome	Support from parents and carers
Be healthy	Promote healthy choices
Stay safe	Provide safe homes and stability
Enjoy and achieve	Support learning
Make a positive contribution	Encourage community participation
Achieve economic well-being	Support career aspirations

Routines and care needs of babies and young children

Routines are important for both babies and young children. A good routine will not only meet their care and nutritional needs, but will also stimulate their development. The term 'educare' is now often used in this context, as child-rearing approaches in the past tended to focus more on meeting babies' and young children's physical and care needs whilst potentially overlooking the role of the adult in stimulating babies and toddlers. An efficient routine is not only valuable for the children but will ensure efficient working practice for the carer.

When working with babies, it is also important to understand the concepts embedded in the Birth to Three Matters framework. Some of the core principles relate directly to the work in this unit, as shown in the table below.

Principles within the Birth to Three Matters framework	Your working practice
Parents and families are central to the well-being of the child	You will consult with parents about all matters related to children's routines
Babies and young children are sociable beings, they are competent learners from birth	Your communication with babies and young children is an essential aspect of their care
Schedules and routines must flow with the child's needs	While establishing a routine the needs of the child must be your guiding factor
Children learn when they are given appropriate responsibility	As children grow and develop one of your primary goals will be to encourage their independence

Routines for children at different ages

The following table identifies core features of the **personal care routines** for babies and young children. You will notice how children gain more independence as they grow and develop. A detailed description of the reasons for individual care routines follows.

Age	Care routines
0–1 year	Babies, who spend considerable time asleep in the first few weeks of life, are totally dependent on the carer for all their needs. Routines will include feeding, sleeping, nappy changing, bathing and time for playful stimulation and interaction.
1–3 years	Young children begin the process of developing independence in feeding, toilet training, and helping to dress and care for their hair and teeth. While sleeping 10–12 hours a night, they will still need periods of sleep and rest during the day. They still rely on the carer to organise much of their personal care.

Age	Care routines
3–5 years	As children start accessing pre-school education, independence skills develop further. They can now feed and dress independently, need quiet periods rather than sleep times throughout the day, and are independent in personal care routines.
5–8 years	By the time they go to school, they are not only able to manage most of their physical needs but are also socially and emotionally more independent, able to relate to others and take more responsibility for their own behaviour.

Key term

Personal care routines Individual daily practices to care for personal hygiene, for example washing, cleaning teeth.

Care of skin, hair and teeth

■ Skin

Skin is the largest organ of the human body and has several key functions, which include forming a protective barrier to prevent germs from penetrating into our bodies. As babies are vulnerable to infections, it is vital that babies' skin is kept clean. Their skin is also sensitive and fragile which means that care must be taken in the selection of skin care products. Advice also changes over time with products such as barrier cream no longer being used systematically after a nappy change.

It is important to be aware of the different skin types and specific needs of all children. Black skin is often naturally dry and may need regular moisturising with creams and lotions. You will always ask parents for advice about the skin care for their child.

Children's skin needs to be protected from the sun's rays to prevent heat stroke and the occurrence of skin cancer in later life. Current medical opinion suggests that even on a cloudy or cool summer's day, the sun's rays can still be harmful to skin. Babies under the age of 12 months should not be exposed to the sun, and particular care needs to be taken between 11.00 a.m. and 3.00 p.m. when the sun is at its highest. Ensure that children wear light fitting garments, wide brimmed hats and high factor sun cream. Research into the effects of the sun on the skin is ongoing and adults caring for children will need to check for the latest available advice.

■ Hair

Care of the hair is important and often contributes to the development of children's self-esteem and self-image. Different types of hair require different care and you must ask parents for advice about the most appropriate care. Regular checking for the presence of head lice is essential.

Head lice

Head lice are parasites that live on the human scalp. They have become a common problem in many group-care settings, as children have more head to head contact. Children's hair should be checked each week for the following signs of an infestation:

- itchy scalp
- red bite marks
- lice – tiny wingless translucent insects in the hair roots, especially at the nape of neck
- eggs, known as nits – white or brown specks attached to hair.

Advice on treatment changes, although thoroughly combing with a nit comb is the traditional method. Other methods include the use of lotions containing pesticides and electric combs.

■ Tooth care

As well as for chewing food, teeth are important for the ability to speak clearly, so it is important that they are well looked after through good oral hygiene and regular visits to the dentist. The sticky layer of plaque that covers the teeth is home to the bacteria that usually live in the mouth. These bacteria are responsible for producing the acid that softens the enamel and causes tooth decay. Acid in fruit juice and fizzy drinks is also responsible for tooth decay so should be avoided where possible.

Bathing

The frequency with which babies and children are bathed is often a matter of parental choice. Topping and tailing refers to the process of cleaning the vital parts of a baby, for example their face and hands and nappy area, and is often an alternative to a full bath.

Nappy changing

In Western cultures, babies are put into nappies that require regular changing. There are three categories of nappies: disposables, traditional terry towelling (fabric), and more modern re-usable nappies. While the majority of parents currently choose disposable nappies, more and more parents are opting for environmentally friendly re-usable nappies.

Adults working with babies should check that stools and urine are normal for the age of the child. At first all babies produce meconium, which is sticky and greenish-black in colour. After a few days, the stools change according to whether the baby is being breast- or bottle-fed. Breast-fed babies have stools which are mustard in colour and fairly liquid. They should not smell unpleasant, whilst the stools of bottle-fed babies are browner, have some smell and are thicker in texture.

Once babies are weaned, their stools become firmer and have a stronger odour. The frequency with which babies pass stools can vary, although medical advice should be sought if no stools have been passed after a week or if the stools are watery, very pale or contain any signs of blood. Medical advice should also be sought if urine is not being frequently passed as this may indicate dehydration.

■ Nappy rash

While nappy rash affects many babies under 18 months, it is becoming less common as disposable nappies improve. The rash can cause severe discomfort to babies and therefore preventative steps are essential.

Ammonia dermatitis

Ammonia dermatitis is caused by the production of ammonia as bacteria from the baby's stools breaks down the urine. Ammonia is an irritant that burns the skin and thus causes nappy rash.

The table below describes the most common types of nappy rash. In all situations seek medical advice if the condition does not improve.

Care of skin, hair and teeth for children at different ages

The table opposite shows the principles of caring for children's skin, hair and teeth at different ages. Note how children need to be given more privacy and independence as they become older.

▼ Common types of nappy rash

Appearance	Cause	Treatment
Red rash forming around the genitals. Strong smell	Ammonia dermatitis	Increase frequency of nappy changes Wash and gently dry affected area thoroughly. Allow time after changes without a nappy to allow air flow
Spotty ulcerated rash covering the genitals and bottom	Ammonia dermatitis	Use steps above, but seek medical advice promptly
Pink and pimply rash forming around the anus and spreading to bottom and genitals	Thrush dermatitis	Seek medical advice – an anti-fungal cream is likely to be prescribed
Small blisters or pimples around the nappy area	Heat rash	Avoid using plastic pants if using terry towelling. Leave off nappy for as long as possible
Brownish-red scaly rash around genitals and anywhere where skin is greasy	Seborrhoeic dermatitis (similar to cradle cap)	Seek medical advice as an ointment may be prescribed

▼ Care of children's skin, hair and teeth

Age	Physical care
0–1 year	All aspect of physical care will be undertaken by the carer.
	Bathing Some babies become very distressed when their clothes are removed so bathing may not happen every day. As they get older babies can learn to splash and play and a daily bath becomes more common.
	Nappy changing Nappies should be changed after each feed and immediately following the passing of stools to avoid nappy rash.
	Hair care Babies' hair should be gently washed during the bathing process.
	Teeth It is important to start brushing teeth as soon as they begin to appear. The carer should clean the teeth twice a day with a small amount of baby toothpaste.
1–3 years	High levels of supervision are required at this age to prevent possible accidents.
	Bathing *Children should never be left alone in a bathroom or toilet.* Cleaning products must be removed from their reach. Children are likely to need a daily bath or shower. Water must be checked before children enter the bath and bath mats are advised to prevent children from slipping. Adults may need to make washing fun by turning it into a game as many toddlers intensely dislike having their faces, hands and hair washed. Children's skin needs to be dried carefully to prevent soreness.
	Hair care Hair will need to be combed or brushed regularly. Check with parents about preferred hair products and styles. Many toddlers dislike having their hair washed. Encourage toddlers to wet their hair themselves as they are playing in the shower or bath. Use mild hair products and make sure that a towel is handy to wipe away any water or soap from eyes.
	Teeth Milk teeth should be appearing. It is important that they are brushed twice a day by an adult as children of this age are likely to just suck the brush. To prevent tooth decay, sugary drinks and foods should be avoided and children should be seen by a dentist.
3–5 years	Children are taking more responsibility for their personal hygiene. Personal hygiene can be used as a basis for learning topics, for example 'Looking after our teeth'.
	Bathing Most parents will want their children to have a daily shower or bath. Children still need to be supervised at these times and the adult should take responsibility for running and checking the temperature of the water. They should encourage children to wash themselves, but do the final check to ensure that all areas of the body are clean, if necessary.
	Hair care Adults should encourage children to brush or comb their hair, but may need to give some assistance. Hair needs to be checked for head lice. Children should be encouraged to wash their own hair, but may need to be given assistance when rinsing.
	Tooth care Children can brush their own teeth, but adults should check and give a final brush. Avoid giving sugary foods and drinks to children. Six-monthly check-ups at a dentist are advised.
5–8 years	Children should be given increased privacy and the adult should be aiming just to remind and praise children about looking after their hair, skin and teeth. Some children become less enthusiastic and thorough about keeping themselves clean as they get older. Interesting bath products and toys can help if this is the case.

◄ Children should be encouraged to be independent when caring for their hair, skin and teeth

Theory into practice

Parents may have differing views on how best to care for their child's skin, hair and teeth. There are cultural and religious variations in the way physical care is provided. For example African-Caribbean children may be massaged after a bath and parents will know which skin care products suit their child best.

- Ask three parents of children at different ages what skin and hair care products they use.
- Use the internet to investigate products for black skin and hair.

Rest and sleep

The exact purpose of sleep is still being researched, but it is already known that the body requires sleep in order to maintain cells and also to process information and for the release of hormones required for growth. Lack of sleep can result in increased susceptibility to infection, a lack of concentration and challenging behaviour. Periods of rest are just as important as sleep, and there should be time each day when children can rest or be involved in some quiet and relaxing activity.

Play routines

Stimulation is essential for healthy development. As an early years practitioner, you will stimulate children's development through effective communication and by providing a range of age-appropriate play activities throughout the day (see Unit 7).

Planning implementing and evaluating routines

■ Planning a routine

Parents should always be involved in the planning of a routine as they may have particular preferences and knowledge of their own child that should be incorporated into any routine.

Good practice checklist

Consider these key factors when planning a routine:
- feeding and meal patterns
- bathing and skin requirements
- sleep and rest patterns
- opportunities to play and gain stimulation
- opportunities to interact and form an attachment to the carer.

■ Implementing a routine

Implementing a routine requires good planning, patience and good organisation. Most practitioners find that these skills develop with practice, especially as babies and children do not necessarily go along with any planned routine! They are also very aware of changes and react if they sense that their carers are not calm or are hurried. It is essential to be flexible enough to be able to respond to the child's needs and adapt the routine appropriately if required.

- Make sure that enough time has been allowed for feeding and various tasks such as nappy changing, bathing and feeding.
- Use any time when the baby is asleep purposefully, for example for making up feeds.
- Observe the baby and young child carefully for signs of tiredness or hunger.

■ Evaluating a routine

Routines are best evaluated by considering how the needs of the baby or young child have been met and how effective you have been in implementing the routine. The evaluation process could consider the following questions.

- Has the baby or young child:
  - showed signs of irritability or tiredness?
  - eaten a healthy diet and had enough to drink?
  - had plenty opportunity for communication and adult attention?
  - experienced a variety of stimulating activities?
  - had opportunity for fresh air and exercise?
  - had appropriate physical care?
- Have you:
  - managed your time effectively?
  - kept calm?
  - shared your time with different children?
  - kept to the schedule as planned?
  - been flexible enough to meet the needs of individual children?

Toilet training

The term 'toilet training' is in some ways misleading. It suggests that a child can be taught by an adult to use the toilet and this is no longer the approach taken today. It is now generally accepted that 'toilet training' needs to be a process which is child-led as it relies heavily on the child being physically and emotionally ready. This means that there is a wide variation in ages with some children moving out of nappies at 15 months whilst others are ready at around 3 years (see also page 76).

Physical activities

Physical activities should be included in all routines to promote development. Children at different ages have different needs and opportunities can be provided for the following:

- 0–6 months
  - time without a nappy to kick and play
  - baby gym
- 6–12 months
  - space to crawl
  - balls
  - objects to explore
- 1–3 years
  - time outside to run and climb
  - sit and rides
  - small slides
- 3–5 years
  - obstacle courses
  - climbing frames
  - music and dancing
- 5–8 years
  - races
  - ropes
  - bicycles
  - swimming
  - football.

Promotion of self-reliance and confidence

An independent child is a confident child who is able to develop a good self-image and self-esteem, both important aspects of development. The following table identifies care routines that can promote independence skills.

▼ Routines to promote independence

Age	Promoting independence
0–6 months	Can be encouraged to settle self to sleep
6–12 months	Begins finger feeding
12–18 months	Learns to use spoon Helps with dressing
18 months–3 years	More confident dressing skills Toilet training Learns to use spoon and fork
3–5 years	Learns to use knife and fork effectively Wash own hands and face but may initially need help with drying Learns to manage simple buttons and fastenings Can brush own teeth Learns to dress and undresses alone
5–8 years	Learns to tie shoelaces Can dress entirely independently

Feeding

Principles of nutritional requirements

In order to care for babies and children effectively, it is important to have some understanding of how the body uses food. To grow and develop, the body needs a diet that contains food with sufficient nutrients to meet its needs. You can find out more about this in Units 9 and 11.

Current nutritional practices

There are many concerns about the dietary habits of children and young people today.

- The National Diet and Nutrition Survey: Young people aged 4–18 years (2000) found that children eat less than half the recommended five portions of fruit and vegetables a day.
- The UK government's Scientific Advisory Committee on Nutrition (SCAN) recommends that children under 7 should consume no more than 2 g of salt a day. Most people do not realise the amount of salt

that is hidden in foods such as white bread, baked beans and tinned pasta.
- Children who do not drink enough fluids become dehydrated. This can have an effect on behaviour and learning ability.
- Research shows that children and young people eat too much sugar. More sugar comes from fizzy drinks than from any other type of food and drink.

Extension activity

Using the internet, prepare a short paper outlining some of the current issues in relation to the diets of children and young people, that you could share with parents to support them to promote healthy eating within the family. Some websites you can use: www.nutrition.org.uk; www.food.gov.uk, www.foodcomm.org.uk. Information about diet can also be found in Units 9 and 11.

Infant feeding

In the first four to six months of life, a baby relies solely on milk. There are two types of milk: breast milk and formula milk.

■ Breast-feeding

Human breast milk is considered to be the best type of milk for babies to receive as it changes to meet their nutritional needs. In the first two to three days, it is thick and yellowish in colour. This is called colostrum and contains antibodies to protect the baby from infection and high levels of protein to promote growth. Over the following days milk comes in and the quantity of colostrum reduces.

Most babies take the milk directly from their mother's breasts, although it can be expressed and used in bottles. Expressed milk is often given to premature babies who are not strong enough to suckle, and also to full-term babies to allow someone other than the mother to feed the baby.

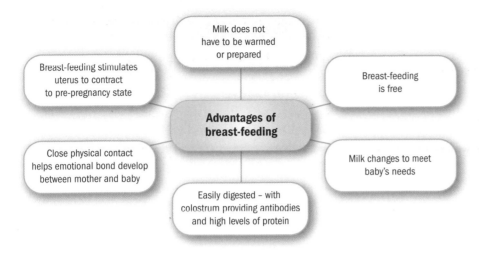

Milk does not have to be warmed or prepared

Breast-feeding stimulates uterus to contract to pre-pregnancy state

Breast-feeding is free

Advantages of breast-feeding

Close physical contact helps emotional bond develop between mother and baby

Milk changes to meet baby's needs

Easily digested – with colostrum providing antibodies and high levels of protein

For older babies and children (over one year of age), goat's milk may be used. However, goat's milk infant formulas and follow-on formulas have not been approved for use in Europe. Soya milk is used for babies who are allergic to cow's milk or whose parents have objections to using animal products. Formula milk is designed to reproduce the composition of breast milk as closely as possible, although it is not as easily digested. Formula feeds are available in powdered form to which water is added or in ready-mixed packs which although costly can be useful when travelling.

Whilst breast-feeding is strongly recommended, some mothers may bottle-feed. Common reasons include the wish to share the feeding with a partner, difficulties in establishing breast-feeding in the first few days or problems in coping with the night feeds. Mothers may also be advised to bottle-feed in cases where they have a medical condition which requires that they take medication or in cases where the baby has difficulty feeding or is not putting on sufficient weight.

Supporting breast-feeding

Breast-feeding is more likely to succeed when mothers have had information about it during the pregnancy and have been given help in the first few hours and days after the baby is born. Some mothers need help in getting their baby to 'latch on' to the nipple as this is a skill for both the mother and baby to learn. Once breast-feeding has been established, most mothers find it pain-free and very rewarding.

Key ways in which breast-feeding mothers can be supported

- Help the mother to rest and relax, for example changing nappies, helping with household tasks.
- Prepare nutritious meals – breast-feeding mothers need to eat well. Dieting when breast-feeding is not recommended.
- Offer drinks before and during feeds – breast-feeding mothers need sufficient fluid to manufacture milk.

■ Formula milk – bottle-feeding

There are two types of formula milk: cow's milk and soya milk. Cow's milk may be whey-dominant or casein-dominant. Whey-dominant milks are the most highly modified and are thought to be the closest to breast milk. Casein-dominant feeds have the same nutritional make-up as whey-dominant, however it is thought that casein takes longer to digest and is therefore more suitable for older babies.

Allergies to cow's milk affects between 2 and 7 per cent of babies under one year (Food Standards Agency). Therefore, formulas based on soya protein are available.

Frequency and amounts

You will follow the parents' advice about the frequency and amount of formula the baby will take. A new-born baby may need feeding every 2–3 hours progressing to 4-hourly as the baby grows. An approximate guide for each feed is as follows:

- new born: 30–60 ml
- 1 month: 90–120 ml
- 2–6 months: 120–180 ml
- 6 months: 180–220 ml.

It is most important to follow the needs of the baby who will soon let you know if he or she is still hungry.

Weaning babies

Weaning is the process by which babies learn to take foods other than milk. It is an important process because, after the age of 6 months, a baby's natural reserves of iron are running low and milk alone will not be sufficient to meet these or provide enough calories for the growing baby.

Key term

Weaning is the process of introducing solid foods to a child.

Weaning usually takes place between the ages of 4 and 6 months. It is currently recommended that babies should not be weaned earlier than 4 months because babies' digestive systems are not mature enough to cope with solid food.

Good practice checklist

Signs that a baby may need to be weaned
- Wakes in the night for feed after previously sleeping through
- Seems hungry after a feed
- Lacks energy and sleeps for longer periods

By 12 months most babies eat a wide range of foods and can feed themselves using their hands. Milk remains an important food in babies' diets during the weaning process, but as milk feeds decrease the baby needs to be offered drinks of cool boiled water or diluted fruit juice, as more water will be needed to aid digestion. More information about weaning can be found in Unit 35, pages 530–33.

■ Foods that should not be given to babies

Advice regarding the safety of foods can vary – always check the current advice. Some foods cannot be given to babies as they pose a health or safety risk.

- Salt should not be added to babies' food because the kidneys cannot process it.
- Sugar is not given to babies as it can cause tooth decay.
- Uncooked or partly uncooked eggs, such as soft boiled eggs, must not be served as they can contain salmonella, which causes food poisoning.
- Nuts can pose a choking hazard and also in some children provoke a serious allergic reaction.
- Liver is no longer recommended for children as it can contain high levels of toxins.

Communication with babies and children

As well as providing for care and nutritional needs, babies and young children also need to interact with their carers. Communication with babies helps them to 'bond' or form an attachment with their carer. Research on attachments (see page 104) has shown that a child who has formed an attachment with their primary carers will be emotionally secure. Interaction with others stimulates their language and aids overall development.

Extension activity

Using what you already know about developmental psychology, consider the impact of communication with a baby or child under 3 years of age on their all-round development. Which theories might you relate to effective early communication, and how can you develop strategies in your work place to ensure that this good practice takes place?

Touch and massage

Whilst hearing and vision are still developing in a young baby, they are able to process information by touching and being touched. Babies respond to being stroked, rubbed and held as this makes them feel secure. The use of massage in the everyday care of babies is increasing, although it is traditional in many cultures.

Crying

Babies are born with a range of reflexes (see page 99) including the crying reflex. Young babies rely on crying to signal their needs, although the amount of crying decreases as their communication skills develop. Primary carers are usually able to identify the needs of their baby through the type of crying, with breast-feeding mothers finding that some cries will stimulate the 'let down' milk reflex in their breasts.

Talking to babies and young children

The National Literacy Trust suggests that there is a growing realisation that the language and communication skills of young children are deteriorating. It would appear that there is less emphasis on talking to babies and young children. There are many reasons why this may be the case, which include:

- change in family work patterns
- lack of shared family time, for example meal times
- the predominance of television within the home
- lack of understanding about the importance of communicating with young children.

It is essential, therefore, for you to develop the skills of communication and use them effectively.

Stimulation

Babies and young children learn about their world by taking information in from their senses. This stimulates brain activity and creates pathways in the brain. Babies who have not been stimulated are likely to show signs of developmental delay. As children grow older, they need to be provided with a range of safe stimulating play experiences supported by a responsive adult who can interact effectively without controlling the play.

▲ A strong bond between carer and child is important for emotional security

Key term

Heuristic play is play in which children are allowed to discover for themselves. The adult provides a range of objects to explore but sits nearby and observes.

Good practice checklist

Examples of ways to stimulate babies include:
- talking and singing to them
- showing them books and pictures
- providing safe toys, such as baby gyms
- taking them for 'walks' and pointing out things
- placing the baby in front of a mirror
- mobiles and displays
- **heuristic play** and treasure baskets
- massage.

Case study: Communication development

Liam is 2½ and lives with his mother in a high-rise block of flats in a deprived area of town. His father is in prison and his mother has had depression since he was born. The health visitor has just arranged a place for him at the local children's centre as she is worried about his language development.

1 **Identify reasons why Liam has poor communication skills.**

2 **Explain the importance of communication with babies and young children.**

3 **Analyse the effect of poor communication on Liam's future development.**

4 **Create a list of advice you could give to Liam's mother.**

Babies and young children notice and respond to adults' tone of voice, gesture and facial expression as part of the process of learning language. Praise and encouragement helps children to feel secure and promotes self-esteem, confidence and independence.

Theory into practice

Observe three children receiving praise.
- Identify what they were being praised for.
- Describe how they were being praised.
- Analyse how that praise supported or extended the children's development.

Management of a distressed baby

Babies cry as a signal that their needs are not being met. These signals should never be ignored as they may mean that the baby is in pain or needs feeding. Babies who cry persistently must be referred for medical advice promptly, especially if they are normally easy to settle.

Some causes of crying

■ Colic: 0–3 months
- Acute pain in the lower abdomen causes the baby to draw up their knees and scream.
- It is common in babies under 3 months.
- It is often worse towards early evening.
- It may be linked to the immature digestive system or cow's milk intolerance.

■ Hunger
- Hungry babies may cry.
- They may suck their hands.
- If over 4 months, they may need to be weaned.

Good practice checklist

- Prepare feeds and meals in advance so that the baby does not have to wait long.
- Offer a sip of cool boiled water if feed is not immediately ready, to take the edge off hunger.

■ Tiredness
- Babies may fight to remain awake especially as they get older and more alert.
- They may cry intermittently.
- They may rub their head.

■ Loneliness
- The baby may feel lonely and want to be picked up.
- They can't entertain themselves so rely on adults for stimulation.

■ Pain and distress
Babies cry when they are in pain, which is why a baby should never be left to cry without being checked. Nappy rash and eczema can also cause babies distress and break their sleep patterns (see page 64).

■ Teething
- This is a common cause of crying in babies as they approach 5–6 months.
- Signs include hot, red cheeks, dribbling and restlessness.
- Babies often gain temporary relief by biting on teething rings.

■ Ear infections
- These are not uncommon in babies, especially after a cold.
- Signs include raised temperature, distressed cries and rubbing of ears.
- Medical attention needs to be sought promptly.

■ Separation anxiety
- Babies show separation anxiety from around 8–9 months, although it can occur earlier.
- Babies cry because they have formed a secure attachment to their primary carer and react if that person leaves (see Unit 1, page 6).

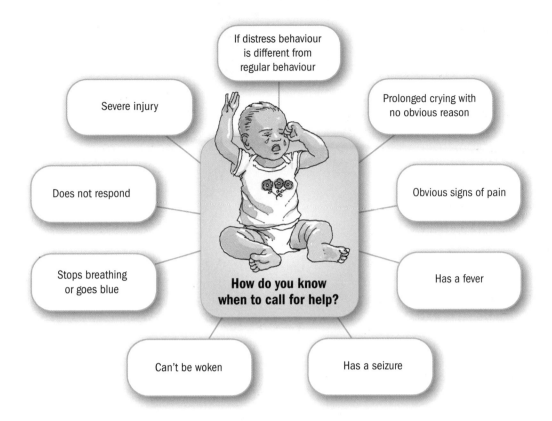

If distress behaviour is different from regular behaviour

Severe injury

Prolonged crying with no obvious reason

Does not respond

Obvious signs of pain

Stops breathing or goes blue

How do you know when to call for help?

Has a fever

Can't be woken

Has a seizure

Recognition of unusual conditions and reporting unusual conditions

There are many sources of support and advice for parents and carers. You might ask the health visitor, call the doctor, call NHS Direct or summon an ambulance. Your response will depend on the severity of the condition.

Clothing and footwear

Suitable clothing and footwear is primarily needed for warmth and protection of the skin. It has, however, also become important in our society as a way of projecting a self-image and it is not unusual for quite young children to have clothing preferences.

Although parents are largely responsible for buying and choosing their children's clothes, adults working in home settings may also have an input. Clothes and footwear should be suitable for the time of year and also for the type of play and activity that children are undertaking. Carefully choosing clothes for the activity prevents situations when children are told to 'try to keep clean' which effectively restricts their play.

Good practice checklist

- Clothes for toddlers and young children need to be easy to put on and take off.
- Garments should be easy to launder.
- Nightwear must conform with safety standards.
- Footwear, including socks and tights, should be checked for tightness.
- Garments should not restrict children's movements.

Care of clothing and footwear

For reasons of good hygiene and the child's self-image, it is important that babies and children should have clean clothes. It is important that clothes are washed in gentle and non-irritant detergent and you will need to ask the parents if they have any preferences. Children's feet need to be well supported and shoes should be the correct size and regularly be checked for wear. As children grow older, they can be encouraged to care for their own clothes, hang up coats, put clothes away or line up their shoes neatly.

Care of equipment and toys

An important aspect of providing care for babies and young children is the ability to maintain their equipment and toys effectively.

Good practice checklist

Care of equipment and toys

- Keep toys and equipment clean to prevent the spread of infection.
- Check for broken equipment to prevent accidents.
- Store toys and equipment safely to prevent accidents.
- Keep a stock list so new supplies can be ordered when required.
- Store toys and equipment in an organised way so items can be easily found.
- Encourage children to care for and value their resources.

Assessment activity 2.3

You are a nanny to 9-month-old Hollie. You have already introduced her to a range of mashed food and have just started finger foods. She wakes at 6.00 a.m., has a 45-minute nap soon after 9.00 a.m., and a 1¼ hour nap at 1.00 p.m. She goes to bed after her bath at 6.45 p.m. Her 3-year-old brother Jake goes to nursery from 9.00 until 11.30 a.m. and is in bed by 7.30 p.m. Six-year-old Julie goes to school.

1 Plan a routine which meets the care needs for rest, sleep, stimulation, fresh air and exercise for all three children.
2 Explain how the care needs change for all three children.
3 Evaluate the effectiveness of your plan in relation to providing care for the children.
4 Evaluate your own working practice.

2.4 How to demonstrate the skills required to care for babies and children aged 0–8

This section of the unit will support you as you develop the practical skills required to provide care for babies and young children.

Care routines

Bathing and care of the skin

The key to a successful bath time is to be well organised.

■ Items required
- Baby bath with warm water (38°C)
- Towel
- Non-slip mat (optional)
- Bath thermometer (optional)

- Clean nappy and other items
- Changing mat for nappy change.

Good practice checklist

- Do not leave babies in the bath or even near water without close adult supervision.
- Check carefully the temperature of the water.
- Make sure that room temperature is 20°C or slightly above.
- Remove any jewellery especially watches which can scratch the baby's skin.
- Be careful to bend from the knees to avoid back strain.

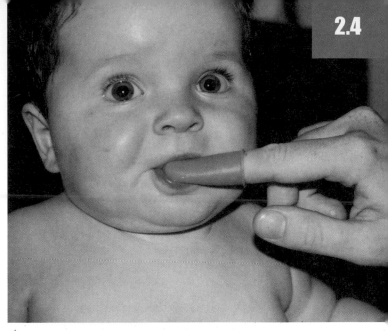

■ Bathing babies

It is important to be shown how to follow these procedures and to be supervised in doing so.

1 Prepare equipment and fill bath. Check the temperature by using a thermometer or dipping in your elbow. It should feel lukewarm.

2 Add bath product, if requested, to water.

3 Remove clothes from baby leaving on the nappy. Wrap in towel immediately.

4 Wash face using cotton wool. Wipe gently round the eyes from the inner corner outwards. Use separate piece of cotton wool for each eye. Using fresh piece of cotton wool, wipe face gently and clean behind the ears and under the chin.

5 Keeping the towel around the baby, tuck baby under arm supporting head, neck and shoulders. Baby must be securely held. Practise this position first with a doll if unsure.

6 Hold the baby's head over the bath and using the other hand, wet head to wash hair and scalp.

7 Dry baby's head.

8 Remove nappy and clean nappy area.

9 Hold the baby's arm that is furthest away from you and support the head with your wrist. Lower the baby into the bath.

10 Use your spare hand to wash the baby. Allow the baby time to kick and splash.

11 Lift the baby back onto towel. Do not allow the baby to become chilled.

12 Dry thoroughly, checking that folds of skin around the neck and groin are dry. Rub in moisturiser or massage oil if requested by parents.

13 Put on clean vest and then nappy. Check that baby is warm.

■ Bathing older babies

As babies become older, they can be bathed in an ordinary bath, although care has to be taken that they do not hurt themselves against taps and that they cannot turn on a hot tap. Water should always be kept shallow. Most older babies enjoy bath time and should be given time to play with the water.

▲ Using a finger brush

Hair and teeth care

The way in which babies' hair should be cared for depends largely on the type and quantity of hair and also on the family's cultural and religious wishes. Some babies have their hair shampooed and brushed, whilst others will need their hair oiling and plaiting.

When the milk teeth first come through, some parents use a finger brush to brush the teeth and gums before moving to a soft brush, as the babies get older.

Nappy changing

The key to a successful nappy change is good organisation and plenty of practice!

■ Items required for nappy changing

- Disposable gloves (usually provided in settings)
- Clean nappy
- Cotton wool or baby wipes
- Spare change of clothes if necessary
- Changing mat or towel in a safe place where baby is secure
- Nappy sack or access to bin.

■ Method for nappy changing

1 Wash hands and put on disposable gloves.

2 Remove clothes from lower part of the body.

3 Using a wet cloth or cotton wool remove stools from bottom, taking care to wipe from front to back. Use a new piece of cotton wool for each wipe.

4 Wipe girls from the vagina back towards the rectum to prevent the spread of infection.

5 Clean nappy area thoroughly, avoiding pulling back the foreskin on a boy.

6 Dry nappy area thoroughly.

7 Check that clothing is not soiled or damp.

8 If possible, allow time for baby to kick without nappy, especially if there is any indication of nappy rash.

9 Put on a barrier cream if requested by parents.

10 Place clean nappy on baby and dress.

11 Place baby in safe place and clean mat and dispose of soiled nappies.

12 Wash hands before handling baby.

Case study: Nappy changing

Jodie is in a hurry. She lays 8-month-old Farhan on the nappy changing shelf. There are no nappy bags left so she goes to the store cupboard to get a new roll. She comes back, removes his nappy. There are no stools, so she quickly puts on a new nappy and takes him for his dinner.

1 **Describe any mistakes Jodie has made.**

2 **Evaluate the potential outcomes of her behaviour.**

Disposable nappies are a popular choice due to their ease of use and 'disposability'. However, they do have a high environmental cost. The Women's Environmental Network (www.wen.org) has run the Real Nappy Project in an attempt to raise awareness of the problem of disposable nappies. By encouraging the use of washable nappies, they hope to reduce the waste and impact on the environment.

Toilet training

The key to successful toilet training is to make sure that children are relaxed and happy. Toilet training should only take place when children are showing that they are developmentally ready. Forcing children to sit on a potty often results in a child tensing up and so preventing the bladder from emptying. This in turn can lead to the child becoming distressed and associating the potty with the cause of their distress!

Toilet training cannot take place until:

- children can recognise the sensation of having a full bladder
- the bladder is developed enough to retain urine for long periods
- children can communicate their need to use a potty
- children are interested in and confident enough to stop using nappies.

Good practice checklist

Once a child shows signs of being ready to use a potty or toilet, adults should:

- make sure that clothes are easy to take off
- make sure that a potty is near the child
- avoid asking children if they need the potty as this creates potential pressure
- respond quickly when a child says that they need the potty
- react calmly to any accidents
- avoid putting undue stress on a child by bribing or rewarding a child for successfully 'performing' because if a child has an accident it can make them feel that they have failed
- teach the child to wash and dry their hands
- start to teach the child about hygiene issues.

Rest and sleep

As with all care routines, being prepared is the key to success.

■ Preparing to put a baby down to sleep

- Make sure they are not hungry.
- Change their nappy.
- Have a quiet time with gentle talking or a short story.
- Place them quietly in a darkened room.
- Check with parents if the baby likes to have a comforter.

Theory into practice

Latest figures show that 300 babies under the age of 1 year died suddenly and unexpectedly for no apparent reason in the UK in 2005 (FSID, November 2006). The number of deaths has recently been cut by following these steps with young babies:

- They should be placed on their backs and at the foot of their cots.
- Ensure that babies will not overheat. Room temperatures should be between 16°C and 21°C.
- Cot bumpers, pillows and duvets should not be used in cots.
- They should not be exposed to smoky environments or placed in rooms where adults have previously smoked.
- Mothers and fathers should cut smoking during pregnancy.
- Keep the baby's head uncovered.
- If the baby is unwell, seek medical attention.

Routines

It is essential that you consult with parents or carers to ensure that the home routine can match the care setting routine. Your primary aim is to meet each child's individual needs and adapt that routine as the child develops.

Theory into practice

Ask two children to brush their hands with paint.

- Give one child some hot water, soap and a towel to wash their hands.
- Give the other child some cold water and a towel to wash their hands with.
1. Which method of washing hands is the most effective?
2. Decide the age range that this experiment would be suitable for.
3. Consider the learning benefits for children.
4. Link this activity into the Foundation Stage or other early years curriculum.

Promotion of self-reliance and confidence

To help children develop independence, early years professionals will:

- have knowledge of the expected development milestones
- observe the child and talk to parents about the child's developing skills
- encourage the child's independence
- demonstrate and role model new skills
- assist the child in the early stages
- withdraw support as skills develop
- offer lots of praise and encouragement.

Good practice checklist

You can promote independence skills by:

- supporting children to tidy up
- encouraging children to wipe tables
- encouraging children to help prepare and serve food
- providing hooks for children to hang up their own clothes
- arranging resources so children can select them independently
- providing resources so children can clear up (spilt sand, etc.).

Feeding

Preparation of feeds

■ Sterilisation

It is important to learn how to sterilise feeding equipment. Sterilisation prevents babies from ingesting bacteria and is required until babies are at least 6 months old, although in group-care settings, this may continue until 12 months to prevent possible cross-infection.

Items that will need to be sterilised include bowls, beakers, spoons, bottles, teats, dummies and toys that are taken to the mouth, such as rattles.

Name	Method	Comments
Chemical or 'cold water' sterilising	Sterilising fluid or tablets are added to cold water. Items must be completely immersed and remain in solution till required. Check for air bubbles. Items must be rinsed in cool boiled water	Cheap Teats and rubber items need replacing frequently Solution must be made up accurately and needs changing every 24 hours
Boiling	All washed items are put in a saucepan with a lid. Items have to be completely immersed. Lid is placed on pan and water is boiled for at least 10 minutes although teats can be removed after 3 minutes. Items are left in the pan till required	Cheapest method Teats and rubber items need replacing often Saucepan kept just for sterilising
Steam steriliser	Steam circulates in the unit and items reach high temperatures	Expensive, but fast and efficient Manufacturer's instructions must be followed Care must be taken when opening the unit as steam can scald
Microwave units	Steam circulates in the unit and items reach high temperatures	Commercial units must be used for this method Follow instructions Allow items to cool Do not use metal items.

There are several ways of sterilising equipment. Many group-care settings use commercial sterilising units as, although expensive, they are fast and efficient. Whatever method is used, items have to be thoroughly cleaned first.

■ Preparation of a formula feed

Powdered formula feeds are significantly cheaper than the ready-mixed types. Bottles are usually made up in advance and stored in a fridge to save time and prevent babies from becoming distressed when they are hungry. It is important to find out from parents the type of powdered milk that should be used and also the weight of their baby, as this, not the age, determines the amount of feed required. Follow the stages in the following list.

- Check that bottles have already been sterilised.
- Boil kettle – allow to cool to avoid being scalded.

- Read manufacturer's instructions to find out about amounts of water and powder to be used.

- Wash hands.

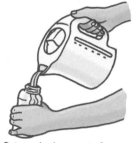

- Put required amount of water in sterilised bottle.

- Measure the exact amount of milk powder using scoop provided. Level off with a knife. The powder should not be pushed down as this wil increase the amount.

- Put powder into bottle.
- Screw on top and shake.

- Allow to cool if bottle is to be given straight away, otherwise store in fridge.

■ Bottle-feeding a baby

As well as feeding providing babies with nutrients, bottle-feeding also provides babies with emotional security. This means that whenever possible, babies should be fed by the same people.

1 Wash hands.
2 Warm bottle by standing in a jug of boiling water.
3 Check the flow and temperature of the milk by turning the bottle upside down and allowing it to drip onto your wrist.
4 Find a comfortable chair to sit in and have tissues or a towel to hand.
5 Gently touch the baby's lip with the teat.
6 When mouth opens, gently place teat inside.
7 Tilt the bottle to make sure that milk is covering the teat end of the bottle.
8 Allow the baby to take the milk at their own pace. Some babies can be slow feeders whilst others are quick.
9 Wind the baby after the feed. Sit them upright on your lap and gently rub their back or hold the baby upright slightly over your shoulder. Use a towel to protect your clothes. Babies sometimes bring up milk when they burp.
10 Offer bottle again after winding in case the baby is still hungry.
11 Throw away remaining milk.
12 Change the baby's nappy.

Good practice checklist

- Never leave a baby alone with a bottle.
- Do not heat bottles in microwaves as they can heat the milk unevenly.

Beginning the weaning process

Baby rice mixed with breast or formula milk is usually the first food that is offered to babies when beginning the weaning process as it is bland and is unlikely to provoke an allergic reaction. Some babies find it hard to feed from a spoon and choke or spit out food, and will need to be introduced to weaning slowly.

1 Choose a time when the baby is not tired or very hungry. Most people give the first spoon part way through a feed.
2 Place a bib on the baby and sit them on your knee.
3 Place a very small amount of food onto a sterilised teaspoon.
4 Gently rub the spoon against the baby's lips allowing them to suck it in.
5 Talk to the baby soothingly.
6 Follow the baby's lead – if the food is spat out, try again at the next feed, but if taken, encourage them to have another go.
7 Do not force the spoon into the mouth.
8 Be ready to take action if the baby chokes (see page 55).
9 Throw away any unused food.

Case study: Hygiene practices

Janine has just returned from shopping with 5-month-old baby Chelsea who is screaming. As she unpacks the shopping, Chelsea's dummy falls on the ground. Janine picks it up, wipes it on her sleeve, gives it a quick suck and pops it into Chelsea's mouth. She collects a bottle from the draining board, boils the kettle and using a teaspoon scoops some milk powder into the bottle. When the kettle boils she adds water to the bottle. Chelsea has started screaming again, so Janine tops the bottle up with cold water and gives it to Chelsea.

1 Identify all the mistakes Janine has made.
2 Explain the consequences of her actions.
3 Critically evaluate two sources of advice about hygiene procedures for feeding babies that have been designed for parents.

Communicating

Developing your communication skills is an essential aspect of your work with children.

Theory into practice

'Talk to your baby' is a campaign run by the National Literacy Trust (www.literacytrust.org.uk) to encourage parents to talk to their babies. Investigate current finding about the communication skills of babies and young children.

Holding and supporting

Young babies feel safe and confident when held firmly and securely. For the first few months it is important to support their head whenever you lift them. You may like to practise on a doll until you feel comfortable moving the baby around.

(a) Lift him carefully with your hands under his arms and your fingers supporting the back of his head.

(b) Turn him gently so that he lies cradled in your arms with his head resting in the crook of your elbow and his body resting on your forearm. Your other arm can then go under his bottom.

(c) Babies sometimes like to be held in the upright position with one hand under the bottom and the other supporting the back with the head turned to one side resting on your shoulder.

▲ **Picking up a baby**

Talking, eye-contact and interpersonal skills

Good practice checklist

When communicating with babies and young children:

- Do:
  - talk to babies while undertaking care routines, describing what you are doing
  - provide lots of eye-contact when talking and listening
  - provide a running commentary when undertaking domestic tasks or out shopping
  - allow 'turn taking' when babies start making noises
  - use facial expression to respond to communication and show that you are listening
  - reinforce communication with touch or gestures
  - as children get older, listen carefully to what they have to say
  - allow them time to respond
  - follow the child's lead in the conversation.
- Do not:
  - ask too many questions
  - use baby talk to toddlers
  - correct their pronunciation but simply repeat the word or sentence, for example 'Doddy done' could be repeated as 'Yes, daddy has gone'
  - jump into silences, the child may be thinking what to say.

Stimulation and play

To ensure you provide meaningful stimulation and play you will:

- make time for play
- provide a wide variety of different play experiences
- use good communication techniques
- follow the baby's lead
- notice when they are becoming tired or bored.

Extension activity

Using what you know about the Birth to Three Matters framework, and the developmental needs of babies and young children, prepare a plan for two days' activities which will encourage the developmental needs of the children in your care.

Praise

To promote good self-esteem, babies and young children need to receive lots of praise. There are many different ways to praise a child:

- shared praise, informal – telling mother in front of the child, 'He has been good today'
- shared praise, formal – showing good work in assembly
- verbal praise – saying 'Well done, that was excellent!'
- physical cues – hugs, clapping
- facial reinforcement – eye-contact, positive facial expressions.

Theory into practice

Think about how many times you have been praised in the past week.

- How did it make you feel?
- Can you think of three different types of praise you have received?
- Can you think of three times this week when you have praised someone else?
- What types of praise did you use?

Soothing a distressed baby

You learnt earlier (page 72) about some of the many reasons why babies cry. To soothe a distressed baby you should initially try to identify the cause of their distress and alleviate that.

Good practice checklist

Strategies for soothing a distressed baby include:
- distracting them
- picking them up and walking around with them
- rocking them gently in your arms
- making quiet, soothing noises
- rocking them in the pram
- giving a comforter if the parent wants
- placing them in a cot or bed and patting gently
- providing skin-to-skin contact.

Above all, be calm.

Clothing

Dressing and undressing

One of the key principles in dressing babies is to ensure that clothes are easy to put on and also easy to remove.

- Make sure that buttons on garments are sewn on securely.
- Avoid garments with ribbons as the baby may choke or be strangled.
- Dress babies in layers of clothes and check that they are not overheating.
- Do not put a baby down to sleep in a hat.
- Check homemade clothes carefully – babies tend to suck and handle their clothes.
- Make sure that garments are easy to put over a baby's head.
- Avoid garments that are difficult to wash.
- Make sure that any socks or garments with feet allow the baby to move their toes freely.

When dressing a baby, make sure that the room is warm before you remove their clothes.

Many babies do not like having clothes pulled over their head so it is sensible to choose clothes with wide or stretchy necks, or with fasteners or clothes that tie at the back. When putting on sleeves or tights, it is always easier if you roll up the garment before slipping the foot or hand through.

Clothes should be washed regularly. When working in a group setting, clothes that have been soiled should be double bagged and sent home with the parents. If working as a nanny, soiled clothes should be sluiced clean, and washed in a very hot wash using whatever detergent the parents normally use. Shoes should be cleaned regularly and checked for wear. It is particularly important that children wear appropriately fitting shoes as the feet can be damaged through ill-fitting shoes.

Care of equipment

The care of equipment and toys is extremely important, especially in group-care settings where there is a potential risk of cross-infection and potential for accidents.

- All toys and equipment should be age/stage appropriate for children.
- Weight bearing equipment, such as tricycles and climbing frames, should be regularly checked for signs of corrosion, metal fatigue and cracks.
- Equipment and toys that are damaged should be removed and discarded if necessary.

Cleaning feeding equipment

- Rinse as soon as possible following the feed.
- Wash in hot soapy water.
- Clean bottles with appropriate bottle and teat brushes.
- Turn teat inside out and squeeze water through the feeding hole.
- Rinse thoroughly under running water.
- Check for wear and tear.
- Equipment may be cleaned in a dishwasher.
- Sterilise, as described on page 78.

Bath and bedding

All equipment must be cleaned carefully on a regular basis. The bath will be cleaned after every use. The bedding does not need to be changed every day unless it becomes wet or soiled. The cot or bed will be wiped down occasionally using a spray cleaner. It is particularly important to keep the highchair clean as there are many corners where food debris can gather, harbouring bacteria.

Toys

- Toys that are frequently handled, such as Duplo bricks, should be wiped down regularly with a mild solution of disinfectant to destroy bacteria.
- Cuddly toys, dressing-up clothes and other fabric items should be regularly machine-washed.
- Manufacturers' instructions should be carefully followed when cleaning or using toys and equipment.
- The sand pit should be cleaned out regularly.
- Older children can be encouraged to help wash some toys in soapy water.

Storage

Resources and equipment must be stored safely. Items that children access themselves must be easy to reach. The shelves themselves must be securely fixed to the wall. Resources such as paint, glue and play dough should be checked regularly for freshness and disposed of appropriately. Where large items need to be stored, thought must be given to methods of transportation, as carrying heavy loads may cause injury to a member of staff. Staff should be taught safe handling techniques.

Equipment safety check

Cleaning — Date cleaned
- Sand tray
- Construction toys
- Dolls and dolls clothes
- Large mobile toys
- Baby toys
- Painting aprons

Maintenance — Date checked
- Climbing frames erected securely
- Jigsaws complete
- Farm complete
- Dolls house
- Train set complete
- All toys in correct labelled containers
- Containers in correct place on shelves
- Home corner equipment

Renewable materials — Date checked
- Paint
- Glue
- Play dough

Signed _____

▲ Sample safety checklist for undertaking regular assessment of toys and equipment

Case study: Health and safety

You work as a nanny in a family with two children: 9-month-old Zoe and 3-year-old Robert. On Monday when you arrive at work you notice some dog faeces just outside the gate. The latch on the gate must have broken over the weekend and it was impossible to shut the gate. Their mother has just finished giving the children their breakfast. 'I am so sorry, we slept in and I have not had not had time to clean up this morning,' she said. The highchair needs cleaning, and Zoe has got cereal all over her stuffed rabbit. Robert, who has only just come out of nappies at night, wet the bed so his bed needs changing. While their mother is talking, Robert has been scribbling on one of his books, and Zoe is sucking the ear of her stuffed rabbit.

1 **Describe the actions you will take as soon as their mother goes off to work.**

2 **Explain the importance of cleanliness and maintenance to the care of young children.**

Assessment activity 2.4

To demonstrate your developing skills, create two accounts about three of the following skills. One should be written at the beginning of a placement and the other near the end. Your log accounts will address children at different ages.

- Nappy changing
- Feeding
- Care of hair and skin
- Sleep and rest routines
- Promoting independence and confidence

Describe your practice, evaluate your performance and analyse how your practice meets the care needs of children. **P6**

End of unit assessment

Case study 1
A middle-aged man approaches you and a colleague whilst you are walking a group of children in the park. He asks personal details about a particular child, claiming to be a friend of the child's father.

Case study 2
You are in the wet play area of your nursery when a child slips on some spilt water. The child bangs his head and is knocked unconscious.

Case study 3
Your manager has asked you to prepare a light tea for the children in your care as the cook has gone home poorly with sickness and diarrhoea.

1 For each of the above case studies, think about and describe your response to the situation. **P2 P3**
   Identify and describe the legislation and policies which should be considered. **P1**

2 Design a PowerPoint presentation to 'teach' the rest of your class how to care for, and the skills required to care for, babies and children aged 0–8 years. **P5**

3 Explain how the legislation, policies and procedures you have identified establish and maintain a healthy, safe and secure environment for children. **M1**

4 Explain in detail your response to case study 2. **M2**

5 Present your PowerPoint presentation to your class explaining how to care for and develop the skills required for babies and children 0–8 years. **M3**

6 Evaluate how the legislation, policies and procedures you have identified establish and maintain a healthy, safe and secure environment for children. **D1**

7 Prepare a personal statement evaluating your own skills in caring for babies and children 0–8 years. **D2**

References and further reading

Bruce, T. (2004) *Cultivating Creativity in Babies, Toddlers and Young Children*, Hodder Arnold

Bruce, T. and Meggitt, C. (2002) *Childcare and Education*, 3rd edition, Hodder Arnold

Childs, C. (2001) *Food and Nutrition in the Early Years*, Hodder & Stoughton

Dare, A. and O'Donovan, M. (2000) *Good Practice in Child Safety*, Nelson Thornes

Dare, A. and O'Donovan, M. (2003) *A Practical Guide to Working with Babies*, Nelson Thornes

Dare, A. and O'Donovan, M. (2002) *A Practical Guide to Nutrition*, Nelson Thornes

Meggitt, C. (2001) *Baby and Child Health*, Heinemann

Meggitt, C. (2003) *Food Hygiene and Safety*, Heinemann

Meggitt, C., Stevens, J. and Bruce, T. (2000) *An Introduction to Child Care and Education*, Hodder & Stoughton

St Andrews Association, British Red Cross and St Johns Ambulance (2006) *First Aid Manual*, Dorling Kindersley

Sure Start (2002) *Birth to Three Matters: a framework to support children in their early years*, DfES

Sure Start (2003) *National Standards for Under Eights Day Care and Childminding Full Day Care*, DfES

Useful addresses and websites

British Red Cross – www.redcross.org.uk

Department of Health – www.doh.gov.uk

Food Safety (General Food Hygiene Regulations) – www.doh.gov.uk/busguide/hygrc.htm

Government health – www.wiredforhealth.gov.uk

Health and Safety Executive – www.hse.gov.uk

Infection control in schools and nurseries – www.phls.co.uk

National Literacy Trust – www.literacytrust.org.uk

National Standards and Guidance for National Standards – www.ofsted.gov.uk

Nutritional information – www.nutrition.org.uk

Royal Society for the Prevention of Accidents – www.rospa.com

St John Ambulance Association – www.sja.org.uk

The Hanen Centre – www.hanen.org

Grading criteria	Assessment activity	Page number
To achieve a pass grade the evidence must show that the learner is able to:		
P1 describe legislation and policies relating to the health, safety and security of children in a care setting	2.1 End of unit assessment	51 83
P2 describe procedures for risk assessment and hygiene control in a childcare setting	2.1 End of unit assessment	51 83
P3 describe procedures for dealing with accidents, injuries, illnesses and other emergencies	2.2 End of unit assessment	61 83
P4 undertake a recognised first aid qualification	2.2	61
P5 describe how to care for babies and children aged 0–8 years	2.3 End of unit assessment	74 83
P6 demonstrate the skills required to care for babies and children aged 0–8 years	2.4	83
To achieve a merit grade the evidence must show that, in addition to the pass criteria, the learner is able to:		
M1 explain how legislation, policies, and procedures for risk assessment and hygiene control establish and maintain a healthy, safe and secure environment for children	2.1 End of unit assessment	51 83
M2 explain how to ensure that procedures for dealing with accidents, injuries, illnesses and other emergencies are followed effectively	End of unit assessment	83
M3 explain how to care for and develop the skills required for babies and children aged 0–8 years	End of unit assessment	83
To achieve a distinction grade the evidence must show that, in addition to the pass and merit criteria, the learner is able to:		
D1 evaluate how legislation, policies and procedures in a childcare setting establish and maintain a healthy, safe and secure environment for children	End of unit assessment	83
D2 evaluate own skills in caring for babies and children aged 0–8 years	End of unit assessment	83

Promoting children's development

Introduction

This unit helps you to understand how to promote children's development from birth through to the teenage stage. In order to do this, you first need to understand children's expected development from 0–16 years of age and to consider the factors that affect growth and development.

Having acquired this basic knowledge, you can progress onto studying in detail how to promote development for different age groups within the sixteen-year period. This will include considering influences on development, such as the environment, communication, responding to physical needs, giving encouragement, as well as supporting learning.

You will then study how to observe children so that you can understand the stages of development and the needs of the child. Having learnt the methods involved in observing children and the importance of objectivity and ethics, you will undertake a longitudinal study of a baby or a young child.

Much of what you will learn when studying this unit will be invaluable when undertaking your longitudinal study. Some of the activities throughout the unit are of direct relevance to this study. They will help you prepare to work on this major project. By the time you have completed this unit, you should feel confident and be well equipped to undertake your own longitudinal study.

What you need to learn

- The expected patterns of development for children and young people aged 0–16 years
- How to promote development from 0–16 years
- The need for objectivity and ethics when observing children
- How to use observations
- How to undertake a longitudinal study of a baby or young child

Thinking points

The staff at a nursery are concerned that one of the babies appears to be making little developmental progress. The nursery manager discusses this with the parents and the child's health visitor. It is decided to ask the deputy manager to undertake a three-month longitudinal study.

The deputy manager has just returned to work after having five years off caring for her young children at home. She asks if she can attend a short training course to refresh her knowledge and understanding of children's expected patterns of development.

After completing the course, she starts to plan her work for the study carefully.

- What ethical protocols must she consider before, during and after undertaking the study?
- How can she be objective when undertaking the study?
- Which types of observation might she consider using during the study?
- What aspects of the baby's growth, development and activities might the deputy manager include in the longitudinal study?
- How might the completed study be used?
- Why is it important that the deputy manager feels confident that she understands the expected pattern of babies' development?
- How might the nursery promote the development of babies in their care?

Main principles of children's development

There are several aspects to human development. Development involves both the structure and the function of parts of the body. For instance, a baby during its first few months makes open vowel sounds, often called 'cooing'. The muscles of the mouth and tongue, which are important in producing clear speech, are still very slack. Later, when muscle tone and control improves, consonants can be formed.

- As the child grows, body actions become increasingly controlled and complex as **physical development** takes place. It includes changes in some of the sensory organs, such as the eyes.

- Children's thought processes become more organised and their understanding broadens as **cognitive development** progresses; this is sometimes called intellectual development. It involves an ability to develop ideas, or concepts, comprehend abstract ideas, to reason and to problem solve. It is closely linked to language development.

- Babies are born with some skills to enable them to interact with others, mainly parents and carers. However, the social skills and abilities of babies need greater refinement before they are competent in, and adaptive to, the social world around them. This is the process of **social development**.

- Feelings or emotions, both negative (for example, fear and anger) and positive (for example, happiness and pride), have to be both understood and controlled by children. This process is called **emotional development**. It involves the development of self-concept and self-esteem.

Key terms

Physical development is a gradual process by which children develop the use and control of muscles.

Cognitive development, sometimes called intellectual development, is a process by which thought processes develop so children are able to increase their knowledge and understanding of the world around them.

Social development involves children learning how to develop relationships and interactions with other people.

Emotional development is the process of a child developing an understanding of and controlling their own emotions and learning how to express and control emotions that they show to others.

All aspects of development are continually changing as children progress through life.

Holistic and interconnected development

The development of children is often studied as separate topics. However, each area of development influences the others and is interconnected.

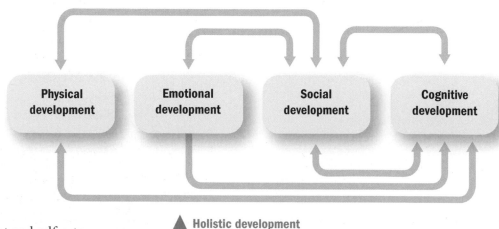

▲ Holistic development

Case study: Jay's play activities at nursery

Jay, who is 2 years old, attends a nursery. She enjoys trying to put on some of the dressing-up clothes and then role playing being a mummy pushing the pram. When trying to dress, Jay expresses great emotional pleasure by enthusiastically showing a nearby adult this achievement and using some words, which are not always correct, for the choice of clothes from the dressing-up box. Jay has had to develop cognitive skills in order to recognise that some words are used to describe clothes. In addition, developing physical skills of fine motor control and co-ordination facilitates dressing up, even if it is not quite accurate. Also, social development enables spontaneous role play. However, when another child wants to play with the pram, Jay resists any intervention. Due to a limited range of language and emotional skills to negotiate a sharing arrangement, Jay throws a tantrum using clumsy actions while trying to ward off the other child. This behaviour is due to the stage of physical, emotional, social and cognitive development that Jay has reached. Hence, the child's development should be seen as a whole or as **holistic development**.

Imagine you are working in Jay's nursery. Using examples from the case study, explain:

a) **how you might promote Jay's cognitive development**

b) **how you might promote Jay's social development**

c) **how progress in these areas might promote Jay's holistic development.**

Key term

Holistic development is defined in Birth to Three Matters as 'Seeing a child in the round, as a whole person, emotionally, socially, intellectually, physically, healthily, culturally and spiritually.'

The Department for Education and Skills (DfES) has produced a framework (called Birth to Three Matters) to support childcare providers and other professionals working with children aged from birth to 3 years. This framework emphasises that development should be viewed holistically and emphases the interrelationship between growing, learning, development and the environment in which children are cared for and educated. The four broad areas of development featured in the framework are shown in the table below.

Extension activity

In preparation for providing evidence for Unit 4, Reflecting on and Developing Practice for Children 0–8, undertake the following activity.

1 Before starting a work placement with children aged 0–3 years, familiarise yourself with the Birth to Three Matters framework.

2 Select three examples from the framework's suggested play activities which could promote children's holistic development.

3 Explain how these activities support specific areas of development and how they are interconnected.

▼ **Birth to Three Matters: areas of development**

Aspects	Components			
A Strong Child	Me. Myself and I	Being Acknowledged	Developing Self-Assurance	A Sense of Belonging
A Skilful Communicator	Being Together	Finding a voice	Listening and Responding	Making Meaning
A Competent Learner	Making Connections	Being Imaginative	Being Creative	Representing
A Healthy Child	Emotional Well-being	Growing and Developing	Keeping Safe	Healthy Choices

Source: Sure Start (2003)

Children develop at different rates for a variety of reasons. However, development does follow the same sequence. The upper part of the body, especially the brain and head, develops rapidly, while the lower part of the body follows more slowly. This is called head-to-toe or cephalo-caudal development. Also, development starts from the centre outwards. This is called inner to outer or proximodistal development. Hence, a baby can hold its head up before it can stand and can wave its arms around before it develops fine control over the use of its hands.

Theories of development

Nature–nurture debate

Every parent hopes for a healthy, beautiful baby who will thrive and reach the expected norms of development. The potential for growth and development is affected by inherited factors. This is called the interaction with nature. In addition, factors within our environment influence development. This is called the interaction of nurture.

There is much debate about how much and in what way either nature and/or nurture affects the process of development – known as the **nature–nurture debate**. Supporters of the nature side of the argument believe that intelligence is inborn, or innate, and the child's genes have determined their cognitive potential. Supporters of nurture believe that environmental factors, such as the child's stimulating experiences in the early years, have a strong influence on cognitive development. It is generally considered that both nature and nurture interact and influence the developmental process.

Key term

The **nature–nurture debate** is about whether children's development is influenced by nature (the effect of inherited factors) or nurture (environmental factors).

Conception to the end of the first year

Conception is a biological process but this does not diminish the sense of wonder we have at the creation of another human being.

Most conceptions occur as a result of sexual intercourse but, in a small number of cases, some embryos result from assisted conception techniques such as in vitro fertilisation (IVF). All conceptions require the presence of a gamete (sex-cell) from the male's sperm, and a gamete from the woman's ovum (egg-cell) in order to form the embryo.

The monthly menstrual cycle allows the release of the ovum. Good health, positive mental well-being and a balanced lifestyle provide favourable conditions for the efficient cyclic process. Factors such as poor diet, ill-health, stress (including both over-excitement and deep unhappiness) can influence the timing of the release of the ovum.

Changes occurring during the menstrual cycle ▼

| Day of cycle | 1 | 5 | 10 | 15 | 20 | 25 | 28 |

Follicle changes — follicle developing — ovulation — Corpus luteum developed — Corpus luteum degenerating

Changes in the lining of the uterus — menstrual flow — lining becoming thicker and more vascular

level of oestrogen

Changes in hormone levels

▼ **The menstrual cycle**

Day 1	The pituitary gland secretes a follicle-stimulating hormone. This causes between 10 and 50 follicles to form in the ovary. The developing follicles secrete oestrogen.
Day 5–14	Oestrogen causes the endometrium (the lining of the uterus) to develop and stimulate the cervix to produce a mucus to help the progress of the sperm into the uterus.
Days 11–17	Fertile phase when conception is more likely to take place.
Day 14	One follicle develops fully. When released from the ovary, it forms an ovum while the rest of the follicles degenerate. Sometimes, more than one follicle is released. This may result in a multiple pregnancy, for example twins. Luteinizing hormone is given off by the pituitary gland. This causes: • the ovum to be released • a small gland called the corpus luteum to form in the ovary after the ovum has been released, i.e. after ovulation. It secretes progesterone. The gland continues to form for the next ten days until the 26th day of the menstrual cycle.
Day 26	If fertilisation does not occur, the corpus luteum degenerates and the hormone progesterone is no longer produced. If fertilisation does occur the hormone progesterone will continue to be produced during pregnancy. Menstruation will stop and a softening of some of the muscles occurs, for example, in the uterus, intestine, bladder and blood vessels.

The pituitary gland in the base of the skull controls the menstrual cycle. This cycle usually lasts 28 days and during this time four different hormones are secreted. These are essential if conception is to take place.

The ovum is wafted towards the fallopian tubes through the oviduct. The minute hairs in the fallopian tube encourage the ovum to pass along the tube to the uterus. If a sperm cell, a gamete, swims along the fallopian tube and comes into contact with an ovum, it will pierce the jellylike coating around it and the sperm head will then go on to penetrate the ovum's nucleus. The two fuse together to form one cell, a *zygote*. Normally, the 23 chromosomes from the sperm join with the 23 chromosomes from the ovum to form a set of 46 which form 23 pairs. They are reproduced in every cell of the embryo.

The zygote initially divides into two and continues to divide rapidly with some cells forming the embryo and some the placenta. These cells, which look like a mulberry, are called the morulla and take four days to travel along the fallopian tube into the uterus. This is now called a blastocyst. It gets attached to the uterus wall by tiny projections called villi. When implanted in the soft wall, it connects into the bloodstream which allows it to absorb oxygen as well as essential nutrients and so it grows fast. When this stage is complete, usually between ten and fourteen days after conception, the developing baby is now known as an embryo.

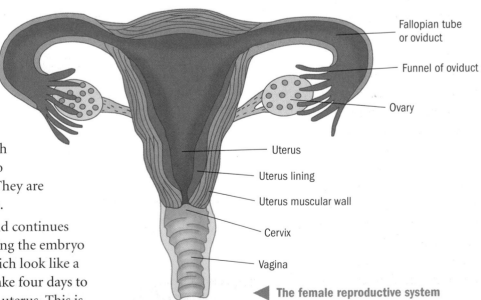

Fallopian tube or oviduct
Funnel of oviduct
Ovary
Uterus
Uterus lining
Uterus muscular wall
Cervix
Vagina

◄ **The female reproductive system**

▼ Development of embryo into a full-term foetus

Trimester (3 months)	Week no.	Stage of development
FIRST TRIMESTER, weeks 0–12	3	Embryonic stage • First missed period. • Foundation of the brain and nervous system is laid down. • Amnion sac is formed around the embryo which floats in a liquid, the amniotic fluid. • The placenta is formed which lies against the uterus wall and acts as the liver, lungs and kidneys for the embryo and the foetus. The placenta is connected to the embryo's circulatory system by the umbilical cord. Nutrients pass through to the embryo and digestive waste products and CO_2 pass from the baby to the mother.
	4	• Neural tube closes otherwise spina bifida occurs. • Length of embryo is about 6.4 mm.
	5	• Heart beat is detected and embryo is the size of a small seed.
	8	• Embryo has 10,000 cells and is about 2.5 cm long. • The formation of organs, eyes, ears and limb buds is at a rudimentary stage. • Embryo has developed the startle reflex.
	12	Foetal stage • All body parts are present, but still need refining. • The baby is now called a foetus. • It has developed the sucking reflex, can swallow, roll and somersault. • Organs are functioning. • Downy hair and fingernails are forming. • Foetus measures about 7.5 cm.
SECOND TRIMESTER, weeks 14–27	15	• Hears first sounds.
	16	• Genitals have formed. A female foetus has around 3,000,000 egg cells in her ovaries. • A greasy substance called vernix, covers the skin of the baby.
	20	• Weighs about 460 g. • The survival rate of babies born at this stage is very low.
	22	• Baby's body grows, bones harden. • Develops reflex to root and grasp. • Can dream and feel emotions.
	24	• Although the lungs are not yet fully developed, with intensive care, the foetus has some chance of survival. • The eyes open for the first time.
	27	• Weighs about 500 g and is approximately 33 cm long. • Is very active, e.g. twisting, somersaulting, kicking.
THIRD TRIMESTER, weeks 28–40	28–32	• Foetus grows rapidly to about 1800 g and is approximately 40 cm long. • It fills the space in the uterus and so rolls and turns less but can kick energetically. • The developing brain is able to process more information and respond more effectively, such as recognising the mother's voice. • Starts to develop a rhythm of sleeping and waking.
	33–36	• The foetus continues to grow and by week 35 is about 2800 g. It subsequently gains about 280 g per week. • The brain develops rapidly and the head grows more than the rest of the body to allow for this. • Fine hair covering the body starts to disappear. • The foetus can now swallow, urinate and make breathing movements. • A supply of glycogen forms in the liver which the baby draws on, together with its fat reserves, to provide energy during birth and immediately afterwards while feeding patterns are established. • The head will usually 'engage' in the pelvis for first pregnancies but during subsequent pregnancies it may not occur until labour.
	37–40	• The amniotic fluid reduces and the foetus grows to fill the space in the amniotic sac. • The foetus at 37 weeks weighs about 3 kg and is lying head down. • Birth may take place any time between weeks 38 and 42.

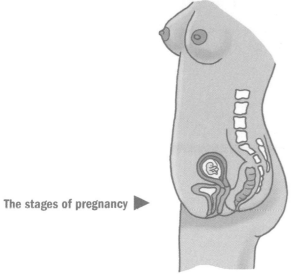
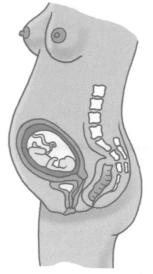
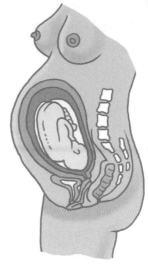
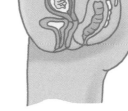

The stages of pregnancy ▶

Week 12 – first trimester   Week 26 – second trimester   Week 34 – third trimester

Factors influencing embryonic and foetal growth

Some factors can promote growth and the development of the embryo and resulting foetus and baby, while others can have a negative effect (see the table below).

▼ Factors affecting influencing embryonic and foetal growth

Factor	Effect
Age of mother	Under 15 and over 35 – increased risk of high blood pressure and pre-eclampsia. Under 15 – risk of under-weight baby. Over 35 – increased risk of diabetes, miscarriage, stillbirth and a baby with chromosomal abnormalities.
Diet	A well-balanced diet is essential. Nutritional supplements containing folic acid and a B vitamin help prevent neural tube defects and incidence of congenital abnormalities. Excessive amounts of vitamin A during first two months of pregnancy can cause birth defects.
Alcohol	Heavy drinkers or alcoholics usually have smaller babies, with smaller brains and with distinctive physical abnormalities or deformities. Affected babies display foetal alcohol syndrome. This can have long-term consequences including developmental delay, learning difficulties, impaired growth, affecting the functioning of the central nervous system.
Smoking	Nicotine constricts blood vessels reducing blood flow and nutrition to placenta. There is a risk of: • low birth weight • miscarriage • premature birth • still birth.
Medication	Some medications may cause congenital abnormalities, for example chemotherapy drugs.
Street drugs	Street or recreational drugs may cause congenital abnormalities, low birth weight, premature birth.
Infection	Some diseases attack the placenta, for example viruses such as HIV, and so reduce the nutrients passed to the foetus. Diseases with small molecules pass through the placenta and attack the foetus, for example rubella, syphilis, flu, chicken pox. Some diseases are present in the mucus of the birth canal and infect the baby during birth, for example herpes simplex.
Industrial hazards	Industrial hazards, such as exposure to solvents, oils, lead and pesticides, can have a radical effect on both embryonic and foetal growth.
Congenital abnormalities	Chromosomal abnormality – a defect in one of 46 chromosomes to be found in every body cell, for example Down's syndrome. Genetic abnormality – one of the genes found on the 46 chromosomes does not function properly, for example cystic fibrosis. Developmental abnormality during the embryonic stage, for example cleft lip, spina bifida. The reason for this is not fully understood. Genetic counselling and testing is offered when parents are concerned about congenital abnormalities.

When a baby is born, friends and relatives are usually very interested in who the baby looks like. We inherit genetic information from both parents. The millions of cells in our bodies arise from the division and subdivision of the single cell formed by the fusion of the ovum and the sperm.

Before a cell divides, its DNA is organised into paired formations called chromosomes. Human DNA forms 23 pairs of chromosomes. Each part of the pair is very similar but not identical. Units of DNA form a gene. Chromosomes are made up of hundreds of genes. Differences in details of our make-up are determined by our genes. For example, at a certain point on a chromosome, there is a gene determining the colour of the eyes. The mother may have a gene for brown eyes while the father has a gene for blue eyes. The brown gene is more dominant than the blue gene, which is recessive and, therefore, not so influential. Consequently, the child will have the mother's brown eyes. If both parents have blue eyes, the child would have blue eyes.

Genetic information affects other features of physical development, such as height and build. It determines the limits of each child's potential to develop and grow. Currently, much exciting scientific research is unravelling the mystery of our genes and it is hoped that soon scientists will understand much more about how we are formed and function.

■ Genetic disorders

Many human disorders are due to defective genes called mutants. Perhaps, the most common of these disorders is cystic fibrosis where the gene is recessive. The gene may have been passed down through many generations without difficulties. However, the medical condition may occur when both the mother and the father are carriers of this recessive gene.

Other disorders that are the result of inherited genes are sickle-cell anaemia and haemophilia (the latter is transmitted by a sex-linked gene and only occurs in males). Some diseases, such as Down's syndrome, arise due to a faulty allocation of whole chromosomes.

Early pregnancy tests such as amniocentesis and ultrasound scanning can reveal some of these genetic disorders prior to birth.

Birth

After the long wait during pregnancy, the mother has to work hard during the birth process to reach the moment of joy as she sees and then holds her baby.

During pregnancy the body secretes a number of hormones.

- Progesterone, relaxin and prostacyclin as well as nitric oxide are released, which inhibit the contractions in the uterus.
- Relaxin also helps to soften the connective tissue in the cervix and so prepare it for opening.
- Both baby and the mother produce oxytocin.
- The baby's brain signals via its pituitary gland to the adrenal glands to release cortisol. This stimulates the production of prostaglandins which are released when the baby has reached full-term. Prostaglandins trigger the uterus to contract. These are known as Braxton-Hicks contractions. These occur over the last weeks of the pregnancy.

Birth is a continuous process but is often described as progressing through three stages:

- *Stage 1* This is the longest part of the birth process, which lasts up to 12 hours

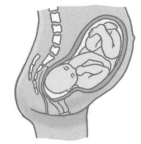

Before labour – head engaged in pelvis, cervix closed.

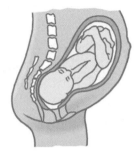

Stage 1 – cervix dilates gradually.

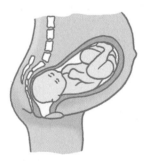

Cervix fully dilated.

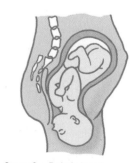

Stage 2 – Baby's head descends through cervix into birth canal, ready to be born.

 The stages of birth

or more. The cervix dilates (opens) gradually, from 0 cm to approximately 10 cm and flattens out. This is called effacement. At first, during the latent stage, the contractions are relatively spaced apart but later during the active stage contractions are more frequent and intense.

At the end of stage 1, called transition, the baby's head will be on the pelvic floor and contractions may be very close together, coming every 2 minutes. It is a very exhausting time.

- *Stage 2* This stage is shorter than stage 1 and may take anything between 20 minutes to 2 hours. The mother has a great urge to bear down and push resulting in the birth of the baby. The baby's head moves through the cervix, down the birth canal and then out of the mother's body.

Most babies are born head first, facing the back of the mother. Some babies are positioned before birth feet down on the pelvic floor in the breech position. Nearly all breech births are now delivered by caesarean section.

- *Stage 3* The placenta, also called the afterbirth, and any other material from the uterus is delivered. The uterus contracts with afterpains. If the contractions are not strong enough, the mother may be advised to put her baby to her breast as the baby's sucking will release the hormone oxytocin which stimulates the contractions.

Most babies are now able to breathe on their own and have a well-developed sucking reflex so are able to thrive. About 10 per cent of babies need extra support provided by the special care baby unit (SCBU) or the neonatal intensive care unit (NICU). Babies born before their full-term of 40 weeks, or who are small or very much below the normal birth weight, may need special or intensive care. A baby born before 35 weeks, which has a birth weight of less than 2.5 kg or has a condition that requires special care may need intensive care.

The midwife has a lead professional role preparing and managing the birth and also plays a part in providing a range of other services.

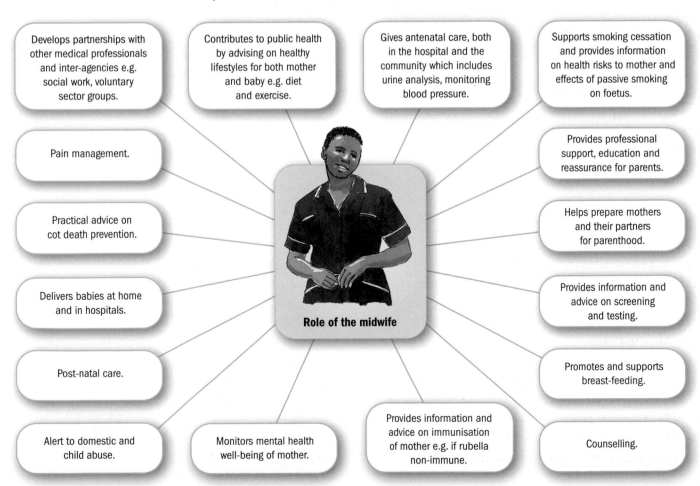

Develops partnerships with other medical professionals and inter-agencies e.g. social work, voluntary sector groups.

Contributes to public health by advising on healthy lifestyles for both mother and baby e.g. diet and exercise.

Gives antenatal care, both in the hospital and the community which includes urine analysis, monitoring blood pressure.

Supports smoking cessation and provides information on health risks to mother and effects of passive smoking on foetus.

Pain management.

Provides professional support, education and reassurance for parents.

Practical advice on cot death prevention.

Helps prepare mothers and their partners for parenthood.

Delivers babies at home and in hospitals.

Provides information and advice on screening and testing.

Role of the midwife

Post-natal care.

Promotes and supports breast-feeding.

Alert to domestic and child abuse.

Monitors mental health well-being of mother.

Provides information and advice on immunisation of mother e.g. if rubella non-immune.

Counselling.

Stages and sequences of development

We have already considered the debate surrounding the influence of nature and nurture in the development of babies and children, but there are other controversies surrounding the principles of development.

Developmental psychologists have differing views about the nature of the change in development. The issue of quantitative and qualitative change raises interesting questions.

- Is the development in children just an increase in the amount of the same progress (quantitative), such as increasing the number of the words they can use?
- Does the development involve different processes at different stages or ages (qualitative), such as when children string words together to form simple sentences?

Quantitative change is seen as a continuum and, therefore, stages are not viewed as being relevant. However, the qualitative approach to change accepts the idea that children at varying stages or ages have new approaches to problems and see the world around them differently and are concerned with different ideas. For instance, Piaget developed his theory of cognitive development based on a qualitative or stage approach.

Recently there has been much criticism of the qualitative or stage approach. For instance, John Flavell argues that children show sequences of development and these are found in a variety of areas, such as in the acquisition of language. They involve both qualitative and quantitative changes but the sequence for all children follows the same pattern. Progress can vary across different sequences, for example a child may proceed faster along the language sequence than along sequential change for moral development. While development does not correlate with age, it follows a similar pattern.

Children may reach **milestones** of development at different ages. For example, when children take their first step or speak their first word can vary greatly. Milestones are often used to measure development, such as when a child can sit without support. These milestones have to be used with care as the whole (or holistic) development of a child should be considered before drawing any conclusions. However, there is a generally accepted range of normal development.

Key term

Milestones are the ages at which the majority of children will reach certain significant stages of development, for example sitting up unsupported, walking.

Normal ranges of development

Generally, parents view their child as a unique individual but, nevertheless, are usually eager to compare their child with others. Health professionals use two approaches in assessing and trying to understand children's state of physical and mental health and developmental stages:

- The **nomothetic approach to assessment** involves comparing children's progress using

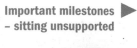

Important milestones – sitting unsupported

1 month – Held sitting, back a complete curve

6 months – Held sitting, back straight

9 months – Sitting unsupported

identified factors. These factors are expected to be the normal level of development according to age and other factors, such as racial origin. For instance, children from Thailand are generally smaller than those from Western European countries.

- The **idiographic approach to assessment** involves studying the child's individual progress, focusing on the unique aspects of the child's individual attitudes and behaviour that arise as a result of their own life experiences. It means that these attitudes and behaviours cannot be compared to the attitudes and behaviours of others and cannot be measured by a standard test.

Both nomothetic and idiographic approaches are sympathetic to the idea of change of personality, or to the behaviour that results from it, suggesting that this can occur as a result of support from professionals, such as a psychologist or child psychiatrist.

Key terms

The **nomothetic approach to assessment** involves comparing children's progress according to identified levels of development according to age and other factors such as racial origin.

The **idiographic approach to assessment** involves studying the child's own individual progress.

When a child is born, parents are given a Personal Child Health Record Book which contains charts on which the child's height, weight and head circumference are plotted.

Information is gained through monitoring growth:

- At birth the head circumference is measured to help detect any abnormality such as hydrocephalus. This is due to the accumulation of cerebro-fluid which can cause brain damage and is characterised by a large head. A small head, such as found in microcephaly, may arise from some abnormality of brain development in pregnancy, or may be a sign of impaired brain growth.
- Weight and length and height monitoring is also undertaken. These have to be interpreted with care. For instance, growth hormone deficiency may be linked with normal or even increased weight gain.

Temporary slow weight gain or loss may be due to minor illness or family disturbances. Parental build and height have to be considered. Hence, what is 'normal' for one baby may be a cause of concern for another.

Children's growth is usually plotted on centile charts. Nine centile charts were first published in 1993. These resulted from the study of and recording of the progress of thousands of children. They describe current growth very precisely. The horizontal axis, or bottom line, shows the age of the child in weeks up to 1 year. The vertical axis shows the types of development being measured and are given an age range. Blocks above the centile line show good development and those which appear below the centile line may indicate some developmental concern.

Centile charts are valuable since they allow a child's progress to be noted and comparisons made. Hence, a child can be compared with itself as well as with the average or 'normal' development. The charts can record all areas of development so a pattern of progress may be evident. Some areas may show advanced development while others may show slower development. These charts can alert early years workers to any progress which may give concern and is deviating from the normal pattern. Hence, this promotes the possibility of early intervention. Centile charts can be used up to the age of 20, but this rarely happens.

For further details of principles of growth and development see Unit 14, Psychological Perspectives on Behaviour.

Theory into practice

If the parent(s) of the baby or young child you are studying for your longitudinal study is willing to let you see the Personal Child Health Record Book, study it carefully.

- What evidence does it provide for the development of the baby since birth?
- How is the evidence recorded?
- Do any of the 'Factors affecting growth and development' listed in the Unit Content account for the pattern of development recorded?

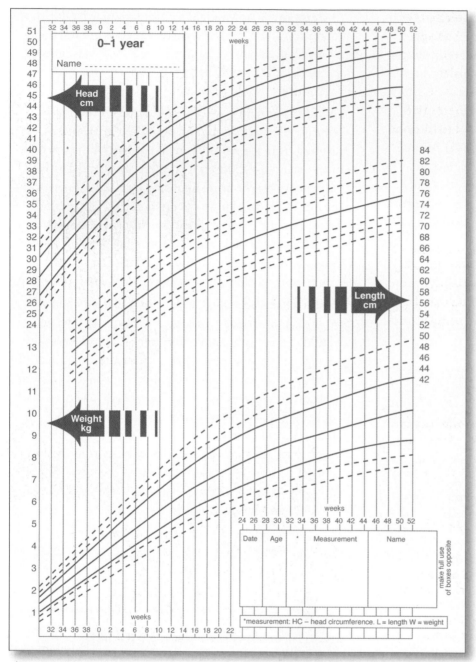

▲ Boys growth chart 0–1 year, from Boys Growth Charts (Birth–18 years), Child Growth Foundation, 1994

Physical development

This is the gradual process by which children develop the use and control of muscles, thus gaining a wider range of movements. Physical development includes:

- *changes in gross motor behaviour* – newborn babies display involuntary 'walking' movements arising from reflex actions. A 15-month-old child can increasingly voluntarily control their walking actions
- *fine motor development involving the movements of hands and fingers* – the early primitive squeeze grasp shown by some babies as young as 4 weeks develops into a very neat and co-ordinated grasp using the forefinger by 5 years
- *changes in some of the sensory organs, such as eyes* – the development of eye muscles enables most babies to see more clearly and over a larger area than at birth.

Why is physical development so important?

As a baby's physical development progresses, new skills are learnt. These enable the baby to become involved in more activities and to explore their immediate world and so promote their cognitive development. Further complex skills are learnt giving increasing control of activities. With success comes emotional development. The baby/child gains self-confidence through the control of their actions, thus promoting their self-esteem. With more mobility, children are able to play with others, thereby promoting their social development. The development of both gross and fine motor skills is important. Children become more independent and, for instance, start dressing themselves. Children can then proceed to acquiring more advanced skills which they need as they grow older for school, work and leisure.

Children progress at different rates but follow the same *sequence* of physical development. The age at which children develop physical skills, such as walking, depends on the maturation of their nervous system, strength of muscles, especially in their legs and back, and achieving balance. For most children physical development is a continuous process until maturity.

0–3 years

■ Reflexes

Newborn babies are born with certain reflexes. These are involuntary, automatic, physical responses, triggered by a stimulus and determined by impulses in nerves. Everybody has some reflexes, for example knees jerk when tapped, which you do not learn to do; they are inborn.

▼ Reflexes of new-born babies

Reflex	Stimulus	Response
Rooting	Stroking baby's cheek	Turns towards the side stroked as if seeking the nipple
Sucking	An object put into the mouth, e.g. nipple	Sucks rhythmically
Hand grasp (palmar grasp)	An object, e.g. finger put into hand	Grasps tightly into the palm of the hand
Startle (Moro) reflex	Baby is startled by bright light or loud noise	Arms and legs splay open, back arches and then arms and legs close as if to hang onto carer to avoid falling
Stepping/ walking reflex	Baby held upright with soles of feet on a flat surface or edge of table	Makes stepping/ walking movements

These reflexes enable babies to survive, for example seek for food and suck. Gradually the reflexes disappear and the baby develops voluntary actions, i.e. they learn and can choose to do the actions, such as making their own purposeful first steps unaided.

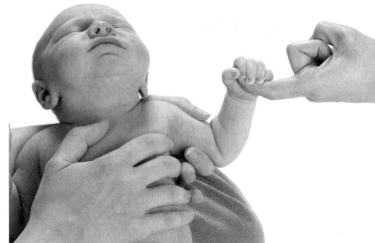

▲ Can you identify the two reflexes shown here?

■ Development of gross motor control in first year

These are large movements including:

- gross motor actions, which involve the use of the whole limb, for example when hopping
- locomotive skills, which are movements needed to travel, for example, crawling and walking.

They develop as described in the table overleaf.

▼ Development of gross motor control in the first year

1 month	3 months	6 months	9 months	12 months
Head droops if unsupported	Head held erect for a few seconds before falling forwards	Raises head to look at feet	Can lean forward to pick up toy	May stand upright alone for a few minutes
Pulled to sit, head lags	Pulled to sit, little head lag	Sits with support in pram	Can sit alone for 10-15 minutes	Sits confidently on floor for long periods
Lies with head on one side	Lies with head in midline	Lifts head from pillow to look at feet	Can turn body sideways to pick up toy	Can pull up to stand and sit down again
Large jerky movements of limbs	Movements smoother and continuous	Holds arms up to be lifted Can roll over	Moves on floor by rolling Tries to crawl When held, steps purposefully on alternate feet	Crawls Walks around furniture and may walk alone
Arms active	Kicks vigorously Finger play – brings hands together	In cot, lifts legs to 90° and grasps foot	Very active movements	Drops and throws toys purposefully

When these milestones of sitting, crawling and walking are achieved depends upon the development of neuro-muscular co-ordination and is also influenced by the inherited growth pattern from the parents. Other factors such as the weight of the child and fitness level can also affect progress. For instance, an overweight baby who has little exercise may take longer to be able to walk unaided. Children's pattern of walking changes as they become more confident.

Theory into practice

As part of your longitudinal study, study the child's progress either:
- towards being able to sit unsupported or
- towards walking independently.

Observe the child at the beginning of the study and three months later.

▼ Further development of gross motor movements, 12 months–3 years

Age	Pattern of development
12–15 months	Moves hesitantly and irregularly Poor balance, very unsteady, falls easily Body rigid, legs wide apart, arms outstretched to aid balance Arms and legs used to achieve balance by moving opposite each other
19–24 months	Body less rigid, feet only slightly apart, smooth pattern of walking Arms at side of body and not used for balance Stops and starts safely Runs carefully but cannot negotiate corners Walks upstairs with support, two feet to a stair, creeps downstairs backwards No attempt to move to catch a ball
2–3 years	Can throw a ball overhand Tries to catch large ball by extending arms Kicks balls enthusiastically Can ride a tricycle Walks alone upstairs using alternate feet

Development of fine motor skills

At the same time as a child's gross motor movements are developing, so too are their fine motor skills, as described in the table below. These involve wrists, hands and finger movements. It is important that these skills are fostered so children can develop good manual skills in adult life involving the use of tools and implements.

▼ Development of fine motor skills, 0–3 years

Age	Pattern of development
Birth	Reflexes give automatic tight hand grasp
4 weeks	Hands tightly clenched and will only open when touched Not yet able to control hands
3 months	Watches own hands Begins to clasp and unclasp hands together in finger play Presses palms together
5 months	Primitive squeeze grasp appears but movement of hands uncontrolled Finds it difficult to let go of object Enjoys practising dropping and throwing, e.g. toys, food
6 months	Uses whole hand to grasp objects which are held in palm of hand
9 months	Learns hand–eye co-ordination to pick up small objects – stretches out one hand leading to grasp of small objects when catching sight of them Handles objects enthusiastically – passing from one hand to another, turning over, etc. Early pincher grip – picks up small objects with finger and thumb
12 months	Picks up small objects, e.g. crumbs, with confident pincer grip – thumb and tip of index finger Uses both hands freely, but may show preference for one
15 months	Picks up small objects with precise pincher grip using either hand Releases objects from grip skilfully Manipulates cubes – builds tower of two cubes after being shown Grasps crayon with whole hand in palmar grip Imitates to and fro scribble after being shown (large, forceful movements)
18 months	Holds pencil in primitive tripod grasp Spontaneous to and fro scribble Builds tower of three cubes after being shown Turns pages of book
2 years	Picks up very small items, e.g. threads, accurately and releases with skill Builds tower of six cubes Holds pencil in preferred hand, well down shaft using thumb and two fingers
2½ years	Holds pencil in tripod position, using thumb, middle and index finger Can imitate circle, T and V
3 years	Builds tower of nine bricks Threads large wooden beads onto lace Enjoys painting with large brush Cuts with scissors

In order to develop motor control, children need to:
- practise to improve and master the skill
- concentrate on small parts of the overall skill, e.g. children learn to place two feet to a stair before developing the more complex skill of alternate feet action
- pay a lot of attention to the action; later they can do the action almost automatically
- have experience of a range of movement activities to develop their memory of motor actions enabling them to cope with more complex situations.

▼ Physical development – fine motor skills

Age	Pattern of development
4 years	Threads small beads Builds towers of ten bricks and makes bridges Holds pencil with good control in adult fashion Draws recognisable house
5 years	Threads large needle alone and sews real stitches Good control in writing and drawing using pencils and paint brushes Colours pictures neatly, staying within lines
By 8 years	Can build tall straight towers using bricks Drawings and pictures show increased recognisable detail Handwriting is even and may start to be joined Ties and unties laces

Extension activity

Observe two children of different ages and stages of motor development. Note their gross motor actions.

1 What locomotion differences between the two children do you notice?

2 In preparation for studying Unit 7, Learning Activities and Play, use the information above to identify at what age the following toys would be appropriate:
- baby bouncer
- rollerblades
- a trampette
- two-wheeled bicycle
- push-along wheeled toy.

3 How might their use benefit children's learning?

▼ Physical development – gross motor movements

Age	Pattern of development
4–5 years	Steady stride, arms used in walking action Can walk along a narrow line Runs lightly on toes Skips on alternate feet, can hop a short distance Moves rhythmically to music Skilfully climbs, slides and swings
6–7 years	Catches ball by holding hands in cup-shape, moves legs, outstretching hands to intercept ball, takes impact of catching by moving body Good balance both when moving and when static A smooth rhythmical action, arms and legs move in opposition to each other, feet close together Runs leaning forward slightly, arms swung backwards and forwards Co-ordinated jumping – can jump a distance Most children are seven times their birth weight
By 8 years	Precise gross motor movements, e.g. can walk alone along a line with arms outstretched for balance Expert rider of two-wheeled bicycle May develop skills in sport, e.g. swimming, rollerblading

A 4-year-old child's picture of the *Titanic*. Jim's picture shows that his fine motor skills are well advanced. He has good pencil control and his drawing is clear. He is starting to form recognisable letters ▶

The pace of physical development is slower but steady growth occurs. Children are notably physically competent. They can throw and catch accurately and can run fast. This is a very active period when they enjoy a range of sports which require different skills including a high degree of motor co-ordination and balance. Body proportions change. By the age of 12, the body's proportions are more like those of adults. For instance, an adult's head is only one seventh of the whole body whereas a 4-year-old's may be as much as one quarter of the total body size. The trunk becomes longer and thinner with the arms and legs being more extended. However, feet and hands grow more slowly which may account for some awkwardness at this stage. Boys are generally stronger than girls, while girls may be more graceful and precise in their movements. Fine motor co-ordination improves which is evident in children's handwriting and drawings.

There is an increasing number of girls who reach puberty by the end of this stage of development.

13–16 years

During these adolescent years, significant physical changes occur, if they have not already started in the earlier stage. Adolescence sees the end of childhood and the emergence of adulthood.

Body growth slows down just before puberty starts but physical changes occur during adolescence more rapidly than at any other stage of development, apart from during infancy.

The heart doubles in size and a growth spurt starts. Rapid skeletal growth occurs in both boys and girls. The timing of this may vary, with some young people showing significant growth during the earlier stage of 8–12 years while others may not see it until late into adolescence.

There is an increase in the levels of certain hormones, namely gonadotropins, gonadal steroids and adrenal androgens. At the same time, sexual organs mature with the enlargement of boys' genitals. The stimulation of gonads (ovaries and testes) by hormones from the pituitary gland prompts the onset of sexual maturity or fertility. The gonads begin to form ova or sperm and also secrete hormones which cause the adult sexual characteristics, such as female breasts and onset of menstruation in girls. In boys, the male voice changes and initially downy facial hair appears which later becomes more coarse. Hair appears on the chest and

under the arms. There is often a sudden increase in the grease glands of the skin, causing a potentially disfiguring skin complaint, acne.

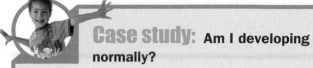

Case study: **Am I developing normally?**

This letter appeared in a teen magazine from a worried 13-year-old girl:

'My friend has grown much taller than me and has developed breasts. Hair has appeared under her arms and she also has pubic hair. She is very moody. Jane says this is because she is "full of hormones". Nothing has happened to me like this. Am I normal?'

1 How would you answer her query?
2 What other physical changes might have happened to her friend?
3 What physical changes might the boys in her class at school show at this stage?

Social and emotional development

Children's social and emotional development are closely linked. Social interactions are also linked with language development which facilitates communication with people. Research suggests that newborn babies have an inbuilt need to make relationships. They watch their carer's face, start to smile and make noises to attract their carers.

Emotional development

Attachment

John Bowlby thought both babies and mothers had a biological need to stay in close contact with one another. He suggested that an early, close emotional bond by the primary carer, usually the mother, with the baby and the baby with the mother was important for long-term development. This he called an attachment. He suggested that babies naturally want to keep close to their main carer. They engage in attention-seeking behaviour which promotes the adult's involvement with them. Behaviour such as clinging, crying and vocalising is focused on the main carer and is aimed at ensuring close contact with the carer. When this is achieved, the attachment behaviour, such as crying, diminishes. Babies play an active role in this and the attachment is reciprocated by the adult.

Bowlby also put forward the idea that babies have a predisposition to explore the world around them and to play. This involves the child in balancing the need for proximity to the carer and the natural desire to explore. When the child feels threatened, by such happenings as being in an unfamiliar situation or by separation from the carer, the child will initiate attention-seeking behaviour again, such as crying and clinging. This is intended to bring the carer in close contact with the child again.

Much research has been stimulated by Bowlby's theory of attachment. This has included research on the impact of early relationships with important carers on later cognitive and emotional development. However, it is generally acknowledged that the development of an attachment bond is not only important for infancy but it is also important throughout our lifespan.

Children and adults are:

'continually renegotiating the balance between being connected with others and being independent and autonomous as they encounter each new development phase.' (Cicchetti et al., 1990, p.3)

Early relationships have a strong impact on later development ▶

Rudolf Schaffer in *Mothering* (1977) puts forward the idea of the three stages of attachment in infancy:

- *Stage 1* The baby is attracted to other human beings in preference to other inanimate things in the immediate environment. By 6 weeks, babies smile more at human faces and voices than inanimate objects.
- *Stage 2* At about 3 months, the baby learns to distinguish between different human beings. The parent or carer is recognised as familiar and other unfamiliar humans as strangers. At this stage, the baby does not object to being handled by people other than its parents/carers.
- *Stage 3* At about 6–7 months, the baby forms a lasting, emotionally significant attachment to specific individuals and seeks their attention. The baby misses this significant person(s) and will fret for them if not present, even for a few minutes. The baby shows fear of strangers and becomes distressed and cries.

Schaffer stressed the importance of the attachment figure, for example the parent/carer, being responsive to the baby's behaviour and providing stimulation, such as talking and playing with the baby. He held the view that the need for stimulation was inborn. The baby then selects human stimulation and finally homes in on particular individuals to provide that stimulation. Schaffer and Emerson, as a result of a longitudinal study of babies, concluded that babies may become attached to people who do not carry out the normal caring roles, such as feeding and changing. Thus, the baby is capable of multiple attachments.

For further theories and studies related to attachment, see Unit 14, Psychological Perspectives on Behaviour.

Case study: When should my baby start at the college nursery?

A teenage friend has just had a baby and wants to return to her studies as soon as possible. She asks your advice about the best age for the baby to be placed in the college nursery.

Based on your study of attachment, at what stage might it be easier for a baby to cope with separation from the mother when being placed in a day nursery? Give reasons for your response.

Darwin claimed that basic emotions are innate in children, i.e. they are born with them. Research has supported this view that babies react with recognisable emotional expressions which mature as they get older and become more focused and differentiated. Infants are interested in and are responsive to the emotions shown by others. This recognition is the early stage of developing empathy. Babies learn appropriate emotional responses to happenings and people around them by observing other people's emotional reactions. They check their parents' facial expressions or body language before responding positively or negatively to a situation.

As children's language emerges, as well as their ability to pretend play, so they can explore imagining emotional events, and can question, think and comment on emotional situations. They can explore issues such as blame, responsibility and consequences. Social understanding is enhanced if children experience sensitive and emotionally relevant family relationships. Most children by the age of 6 can make judgements which take into account another person's wishes and beliefs. Children at this age are capable of masking their true feelings.

Between 8 and 12 years, children form strong relationships with others, mainly with their own sex.

Developing self-concept

One important aspect of emotional development is developing self-concept (the way we see ourselves). It is closely linked to self-esteem and revolves around the question: 'How do I feel about myself?' Self-concept relates to the child's view of their own personality and what they can do. It also involves the child's perception of how others view them and their abilities.

What am I like?

Developing self-concept ▲

This baby is starting to develop his self-image ▶

▼ Development of self-concept

Age	Pattern of development
0–3 months	• Babies' first important interactions are with family or carers. • They start to recognise their carer's face and voice and may stop being distressed if they hear, see, smell or feel their parent or carer. • These are the first steps to realising that they and their carer are separate beings.
3–6 months	• Babies start to develop their self-image so they will be able over the next months and years to discover the kind of person they are as well as what they can do. • Positive interactions between parent/carer and baby are important. The baby will learn to value themselves and their abilities and thus promote their self-confidence. A positive self-image enables children to feel they are valued and respected. A negative self-image makes the child feel worthless and results in lack of emotional stability during childhood and often into later life. • Babies are able to judge their self-worth by adults' and carers' responses to them.
6–12 months	• The opportunity to play increases. Encouragement to play and to interact will promote a positive self-image. • Through babies' awareness of emotions, they start to realise that others have emotional responses linked to their interactions. • Babies develop their understanding that they exist separately from others. They form a clear image that those around them are important.

Age	Pattern of development
1–2 years	• Children are now aware of themselves as persons in their own right. They show this sometimes in negative ways, displaying strong reaction to situations, i.e. throw a tantrum. Much obvious praise and encouragement is needed to foster children's positive self-image. Their relationships with others will depend on the development of their self-image. • By 18 months, children start to use language which reflects the development of their understanding of self. They use their own name and that of others. They vocally label things as 'mine' and can be very possessive. At times, they show an understanding of 'yours' and 'mine' but often prefer to have possession of both. • They have not yet developed effective co-operative playing skills but are starting to play alongside others, with mixed success. • They may start to form friendships with other children but their peers are not yet significantly influential on their developing self-image. • They are starting to look beyond themselves and understand how others feel, e.g. if someone gets hurt they can show sensitivity to their pain.
2–3 years	• Children continue to build up their self-image and self-concept. • Play, especially roleplay, is important in developing their understanding of self and others. • They like to imitate others, e.g. when speaking on the telephone. • Feelings of self-worth are enhanced through having special responsibilities and their identity recognised, e.g. hanging their coat on their named peg at nursery. • Increasing physical skills promotes their independence and self-reliance, e.g. being able to dress themselves. This has a positive influence on their self-image and self-concept.
4–5 years	• Children have usually by now developed a secure self-concept based on their own inner knowledge and understanding and on the views of others. Problems are likely to occur if children are unable to retain a stable view of themselves. • Acceptance by others, especially other children, is important to them. • They show sensitivity to the feelings of others. • They have internalised the social rules of their environment.
6–8 years	• They begin to compare themselves with others, e.g. 'I am better than Sian in Maths but she can run faster than me in games.' • They are more successful in controlling their emotions and having a private view of a situation but hiding their feelings. • Starting to progress from 'Who am I?' to 'What do I want to be?' • Friendship with others is very important to them.
8–12 years	• They are concerned about peer opinion which strongly motivates their behaviour. • They compare themselves with others but are more objective in their appraisal than previously. • Their developing sense of self helps them in setting their personal goals. • Relationships become more reciprocal. • Children acquire coping skills to enable them to adjust to stress.
13–16 years	• Self-esteem can be upset by body changes. • They have more open, flexible relationships to meet their increasingly complex needs. • They accept more readily the complexity of individuals, relationships and interactions. • Peer pressure is a very significant factor in emotional development. • Peer groups facilitate the forming of attitudes towards sexuality, sexual behaviour, moral judgements and values. They strongly influence self-esteem. • Many teenagers are sexually active. • Some teenagers use sexual experiences in a search for affection, rebellion or in alleviating boredom.

Good practice checklist

On work placement, support the emotional development of the 3–5 year-olds in a day nursery by:

• encouraging their sense of self-worth through giving them some responsibilities, for example to lay the tables for snack-time
• encouraging them to put on their own coats and hats for outdoor play
• participating fully, if invited, in their role-play
• addressing children using their correct name
• helping new children to be accepted within the group
• consistently following the nursery's social rules.

For theories of self-concept, see Unit 14, Psychological Perspectives on Behaviour.

Social development

What is personality? Helen Bee defines personality as:

'a broad range of individual characteristics, mostly having to do with the typical ways each of us interacts with the people and the world around us … and which tend to be persisting aspects of the individual.' (Bee, 1989)

Parents show a great deal of interest in their child's developing personality. Even babies only a few weeks old display distinct personalities.

Personality is thought to be a result of a combination of nature and nurture. In other words, it is influenced not only by what is inherited from parents, but also by our environment. The child's initial temperament affects the child's developing personality. Environmental factors then come into play.

Our experiences are very important in forming our personality. Some babies are very placid and easily soothed, whilst others seem to find it difficult to settle. The reaction of parents and carers to difficult children is thought to be crucial in reinforcing this type of temperament or helping not to emphasise it. Some studies, such as Olweus (1982) suggest that early aggression in children is a good predictor of later aggressive behaviour. On the other hand, sociability seems to be well established by the age of 2 years and is a good indicator of it continuing into later stages of development. Environment is very influential in reinforcing and encouraging aggressive and sociable behaviours.

One important aspect of social development is the development of children's moral or pro-social behaviour. The family, other significant adults and children have an important role to play in this. See the diagram below.

These theories ignore the fact that some people develop part of their moral sense through thinking carefully and logically about their actions.

Some psychologists believe that the rules of what is right and wrong are learnt through...

Conditioning
Classical conditioning may influence behaviour, e.g. the visit of a severe-looking great-aunt may cause a response of good behaviour. The child has come to associate the need for good behaviour with the sight of the disapproving old lady.

Role models
They may see members of their family as role models. For instance, an older sibling gets a reputation at school for behaving badly so the younger child feels the need to follow the family tradition by using the other child as a role model. Adults may reinforce this pattern of behaviour by their expectations based on their knowledge of the family.

Reinforcement
This good behaviour may be reinforced by a reward of a £5 note if the child's behaviour has been good during the visit.

Social learning
A child may learn behaviour from others who they view as significant to them. This may be parents or other children or perhaps an older brother or sister. For instance, they may develop anti-social behaviour which they have learnt within a dysfunctional family.

Imitation
A younger child imitates the older child's behaviour, e.g. a younger child may copy an older child's use of bad language.

By junior school stage, children are beginning to understand the distinction between conventional rules and moral rules. Conventional rules are set by the social or cultural group to which the child belongs, for example school uniform to be worn. Children begin to understand that these conventional rules are arbitrary and have only to be followed within the situation in which they are set. Hence, children do not have to wear school uniform at home. On the other hand, moral rules are seen as applying to all situations and are obligatory. These ensure that the rights for themselves and others are likely to be guaranteed.

For further information, see Unit 14, Psychological Perspectives on Behaviour.

Case study: Why this behaviour?

During a work placement in a pre-school, you notice that one child is very disruptive in the home corner. The toys are handled roughly. They and other children are often hit and subjected to verbal abuse. The child is constantly interrupting the circle time.

Using the approaches featured in the chart above, suggest how you might account for this behaviour.

Aggression

Freud believed that aggression comes from unconscious instinctive drives. He stressed the need to release this energy which would otherwise cause psychological disorders, such as depression. This act of release is called catharsis and may take the form of violent behaviour or more acceptable activities, such as sport.

There is some evidence to suggest that aggression may have a biological explanation. Connor's Danish study (1995) showed that if one of a pair of twins is a criminal, then the other twin is much more likely to have a criminal record than the average person. Brown et al. (1979) suggested that aggression is probably linked to high levels of certain hormones or chemicals. It is suggested that high levels of testosterone in males, women with pre-menstrual syndrome and increased levels of progesterone are linked to crime and negative behaviour.

Other theories stress that aggression may be reinforced and is, therefore, more likely to be repeated. For instance, parents may encourage boys to be tough and girls to be gentle. However, this is generally considered to be an oversimplified approach.

Patterson et al. (1991) studied families, some with aggressive children and some with children who were not a problem. Families were identified where the children were difficult to discipline. They seemed to have certain things in common, such as little affection shown, use of aggression to cope with tensions within family relationships, little use of approval and instead much use of physical punishment.

Factors in the home environment that can cause a child to be aggressive include:

- parental behaviour which provokes aggression, for example nagging
- harsh discipline
- lack of supervision, resulting in disruption of bonding
- poor housing, unemployment and marital strife which create tension in the home
- aggression displayed by other family members and seen as a norm.

An habitually aggressive child may become resistant to punishment, become harder to restrain, be rejected by their peers, fail at school.

For ways of managing unwanted behaviour see Unit 14, Psychological Perspectives in Behaviour.

▼ **Development of self-concept**

▼ Key stages in children's social development, 0–3 years

Age	Pattern of development
0–3 months	Smiles at 6 weeks Recognises people they know well When they hear, see, smell or feel their mother or carer reacts, e.g. may stop crying
3–6 months	Responds with pleasure to handling by carer and likes playful tickling, singing and other vocal playful sounds Friendly with strangers but starts to show shyness and some slight anxiety when carer out of sight
7 months	Reserved with strangers
9 months	Distinguishes strangers from known people Clings to adult and hides face when strangers are present Offers toy to adult
10 months	Needs little assistance to drink from cup Holds spoon but cannot yet use it him/herself Helps with dressing by holding out arms and feet Gives toys to carer on request Likes to be within sight or sound of carer Waves goodbye on request
15 months	Holds spoon but cannot prevent it turning over More co-operative with dressing Indicates when has wet or soiled nappy Unaware of dangers in the environment so needs constant supervision
18 months	Uses spoon successfully and drinks without too much spilling Takes off shoes and socks but rarely puts them on Knows where objects belong Will imitate simple everyday activities for short time such as reading book
2 years	Asks for food and drink Puts on hats and shoes Lets adult know of toilet needs Follows carer around and imitates domestic activities Takes part in simple role-play Defends own toys with determination Resents attention shown by carer to other children Plays alongside other children but not with them Unable to defer immediate wishes for satisfaction
2½ years	Continually asks questions Plays well with miniature toys, adding running dialogue
3 years	Eats using knife and fork Can pull up pants when going to toilet and is usually dry during the night Likes to help carer around the house Creative make-believe play Joins in playing with other children

▼ Key stages in children's social development, 4–16 years

Age	Pattern of development
4 years	Except for laces, back buttons and ties, can dress and undress More independent and very self-willed Needs the companionship of others but can be alternatively aggressive and co-operative but knows how to take turns and to share Likes dressing-up and dramatic make-believe play
5–7 years	More independent and sensible Understands need for order and tidiness but needs to be reminded Chooses own friends, is generally co-operative and appreciates need for rules and fair play and is developing an increasing sense of morality Displays a sense of humour Protective towards younger children and pets Comforts friends in distress
8–12 years	Strong gender segregation, favouring own gender and negatively stereotypes the other gender Different gender patterns of friendships. Boys' friendships are described as extensive and girls as intensive (Waldrop and Halverson, 1975); boys' friendships groups are usually larger, girls' friendships in pairs or smaller groups Reciprocal friendships formed and very important. Each partner names the other as a friend. Most spare time spent with friends Shows concern for others and very co-operative with friends
13–16 years	Adolescents focus great deal of attention on themselves and think everybody is looking at them. Some adolescents can develop a negative self-concept Peers are most important force in shaping adolescent sense of identity Intense conformity to values of peer group and behaviour Peer group used as support for transition from protected family life to independent adulthood, parental influences decrease Friendships are intimate with sharing of inner thoughts and feelings In early adolescence cliques form of usually 4–6 people of the same sex, with strong attachments to each other Gradually cliques combine into larger groups of both sexes, then break down into heterosexual cliques, followed by loose associations of couples (Dunphy, 1963) Heterosexual relationships explore physical sexuality and also personal intimacy

Cognitive and language development

Throughout our lives we develop ideas (or concepts) and are influenced by what we perceive about the world around us (our **perception**). Gradually our knowledge develops, together with an ability to reason, solve problems, comprehend abstract ideas and understand why people behave as they do. This is called cognitive development.

For further information on theories about how children learn and think, see Unit 14, Psychological Perspectives on Behaviour.

Key term

Perception is the process by which each of us gains direct awareness through our senses of the world around us (Sylva and Lunt, 1998).

Sensory development

Newborn babies take in, process and use a vast amount of information using their senses of sight, hearing, taste, smell and touch. This is called perception.

■ Hearing

From birth, babies seem to have an inborn preference for hearing the human voice. Condor and Sanders (1974) carried out some experiments on babies just a few hours old. Tapes of different sounds, including human speech, were played. After two days the babies started to move their arms and bodies in time with the human speech and showed little interest in the other sounds.

■ Vision

Babies' visual sensory system is not fully mature at birth. Vision is more blurred than in an adult and their eyes focus best at about 25 cm. Fantz (1961) carried out research with young babies who were shown different stimuli that were the approximate size and shape of an adult's head. Babies looked at the face-pattern more than any other pattern presented to them. Fantz concluded that babies have an inborn preference to respond to faces and an innate perceptual knowledge of the face. Other studies showed that babies have a preference for increasingly complex patterns and their capacity for differentiating patterns steadily develops.

■ Perception of depth and 3-D objects

Often babies roll and fall off chairs if unattended. They seem to have no sense of depth. Gibson and Walk (1960) tested babies' depth perception. They devised an experiment using a 'visual cliff' which consisted of a glass top covering a drop of several feet. Babies over 6 months refused to cross the 'cliff' which indicates that they are able to perceive depth.

■ Development of perceptual judgements

Vurpillot (1976) studied children between 3½ and 7½ years to discover how they use their perceptual skills. She showed them a series of drawings, all of which were slightly different. She asked them to spot the differences. Vurpillot found that:

- 3½-year-olds perceive anything missing in the picture and differences in form, e.g. round sun changes to crescent
- by 7½-years-old they perceive changes in sizes but not in location, for example the position of the house.

She concluded that younger children's perception is limited by their lack of capacity to gather, record and think about perceptual information, using only a few simple judgements. As children get older, they are able to make more visual comparisons and are more skilled at selecting from a range of information presented to them.

Case study: Using your knowledge of perception to good effect in a work placement

You are working in a family for one of your work placements. The mother, who is suffering from post-natal depression, has a 4-week-old baby, so you find yourself having to look after the baby most of the time. You have recently studied sensory perception and wish to apply your knowledge.

1 **Explain how you would hold the baby so you show your understanding of the baby's visual perception.**

2 **You wish to buy the baby a toy at the end of your placement. What might be your choice to stimulate the baby's sensory perception?**

▼ Theories of language development

Theorist	Type of theory	Main features
B.F. Skinner (1930s)	Nurturist: language is taught through imitation	Parents and carers reinforce and shape children's language
Noam Chomsky (1960s)	Nativist: language is innate – children are biologically programmed for language development	Children are born with all the things needed to produce language (called Language Acquisition Device) and are born with the potential to understand the structure of language (grammar)
Jean Piaget (1920s–1970s)	Interactionist input theory	Language results from children's cognitive development. As cognitive processes develop, so language develops. Language is influenced by the interaction with the environment. Children enrich the input and actively shape their perceptions through making it fit into pre-existing schemas, (patterns of understanding) or by generating new ones. They often use an expression which seems logical to them, but does not follow the more complex formal rules of grammar, e.g. a child says 'one mouse' but when another is present may speak of 'two mouses'

Theories of language development

The main theories of language development are outlined in the table above.

Sequence of language development

The following table shows the sequence of development which all children follow regardless of their ethnic origin. There can be considerable variation in the age at which children pass through the stages, depending on the environment and their speed of development.

Language development is fostered through independent reading ▶

▼ The sequence of language development, 0–2½ years

Age	Pattern of development
0–2 months	Cries to communicate need for attention Cooing – open vowel sounds like oooh, aah and uses gestures Shows skill of turn-taking in 'conversations'
3 months	Vocalises when on own and responds vocally to carer's interaction
6–10 months	Babbling – adds consonants and makes strings of sounds, e.g. dah, dah, dah Uses gestures as a form of communication
1–2 years	First words linked to familiar things, e.g. Daddy, car First one- or two-word sentences with gestures are called holophrases, e.g. child pointing to shoe with male figure, Daddy, meaning Daddy's shoe First sentences – from 2 years Telegraphic speech (short sentences – two or three words but only essential words, e.g. I play ball)
2½ years	50-word vocabulary Generalises speech, e.g. I goed instead of I went, 3 mouses

▼ The sequence of language development, 5–16 years

Age	Pattern of development
4–7 years	2500 word vocabulary Uses complex sentences and questions. Shows an interest in reading and writing. Can listen intently when interested Most children learn to speak well by the age of 5 or 6
8–12 years	By 8 years: Able to pronounce most sounds but may have difficulty with some consonants, e.g. v, s, l Speaks confidently and fluently Uses most plural and past tenses correctly Can express abstract ideas, such as emotions, through language Writes short pieces of writing independently Can read simple text accurately Can copy dialects Extends vocabulary, uses passive tense, pronouns By 12 years: Can write lengthy stories and can use a dictionary and become competent readers
13–16 years	Most adolescents use language competently to express complex, abstract ideas both orally and when writing Expert in reducing language to code when texting Often developing competence speaking a language other than their own native language

For further information on:

- language development, see Unit 14
- language development and supporting literacy skills, see Unit 18
- language development of babies and children under 3, see Unit 35.

Extension activity

1 When on work placement with pre-school children:
   - observe and record children at different stages of language development
   - identify the children's stage of language development.
2 Study the early learning goals for listening, speaking, reading and writing. By the end of the Foundation Stage what progress is it hoped a child will have made?

Factors affecting growth and development

Different factors may have both positive and negative effects on development as shown in the table below.

Factor	Positive effects on development	Negative effects on development
Social	Families with strong social networks provide opportunities for children to thrive socially and emotionally. Children gain confidence through mixing with others. This enhances language and cognitive experience.	Little experience of mixing with others in a variety of situations may affect social and emotional development. Restricted social experience and interaction means that there are inadequate opportunities for mental processes, such as those involving imagination and thought, to be fully stimulated. Thus, the potential for cognitive development is not fully realised.
Economic	Children living in favourable economic circumstances are more likely to have a healthy lifestyle. Their diet may include a wider range of foods, such as five servings of fruits and vegetables per day, thus enhancing their physical development. They may have more social opportunities, such as holidays and joining uniformed youth groups. They may have more fashionable, peer-acceptable clothes, thus promoting their self-confidence and feelings of social and emotional well-being. There may be less stress in the home thus increasing the likelihood of emotional stability. More affluent families may live in an area where schools enjoy a better learning environment. Active parent organisations often generously supplement core school resources. This supports and extends children's cognitive development. In addition, parents may be able to afford more out-of-school learning opportunities, such as music lessons, sports coaching and provide a wider range of toys and equipment including access to computers.	Children living in poverty are more likely to have a poorer quality of life. Poor housing, inadequate diet and higher rates of pollution affect physical development. There may be more stress, lower educational attainment and aspirations within communities with fewer resources. There may be higher rates of crime which may influence children's social and emotional development. However, affluence may have negative effects. For instance, diets of more expensive convenience and junk food, such as fizzy drinks and snacks rich in fats and sugar, contribute to childhood obesity. This may have a notable effect on health in adult life. Too easy access to resources and opportunities may present fewer challenges for these children, affecting their drive to develop and progress.
Cultural	Families where books and the expressive arts are valued stimulate children's creativity and widen their cognitive, social and emotional experiences. Some cultural groups value extended families. These enable children to have a good support network which may promote their development.	Some children in rural areas and areas of distinct ethnic groupings may have little experience of mixing with people from other cultures which can affect their social confidence and tolerance within culturally diverse situations later in life.
Gender differences	There is an increasing breakdown of traditional discriminatory attitudes to gender differences. All children are expected to have the same opportunities within the caring and educational services. These promote social, emotional and cognitive development for both girls and boys and so widen their future career aspirations.	Despite legislation to promote equality of opportunity, discrimination and stereotyping still exist. This can affect children's self-concept and their emotional and cognitive development. Some conditions, such as congenital deficiencies in colour vision, are more prevalent in one gender group. Boys are more prone to colour vision deficiencies.

Factor	Positive effects on development	Negative effects on development
Motivation	Children who grow up in a stimulating environment, experiencing interested, interactive parental support, are more likely to be well motivated to learn.	Children who have few stimulating resources and experience little interest by adults are less likely to be well motivated to learn and be aware of the world around them. They may start Key Stage 1 with a lower threshold of achievement. Some children have parents who are over-eager to motivate their children to succeed which may result in undue pressure/stress for the children. This may affect the children's mental and emotional well-being and have major repercussions later in life.
Health status	Children with health problems and special needs are, where possible, encouraged to attend mainstream schools and so avoid social isolation within special schools. This has a positive affect on healthy children who learn to value their peers with disabilities. Also, it promotes opportunities for children with special needs to maximise their development, especially socially and emotionally.	Frequent periods of ill-health and hospitalisation can have significant effects on children's development. Ill-health can slow down the rate of growth. Loss of time in school can restrict cognitive development. Little peer contact can delay social and emotional development.
Genetic inheritance	Some children's development is significantly affected by the genes they inherit from their parents (see page 94). Genetic counselling and careful monitoring during pregnancy results in the possibility of some genetic disorders being identified before birth.	
Adult expectations	Parents and carers who have achieved educational success are more likely to stimulate their children, be aware of their holistic developmental needs and actively seek and campaign for the best educational provision for their children. They are likely to have high expectations for their children's achievement.	Parents with little educational achievement may give educational progress a lower priority. They lack the skills and knowledge to enable them to access the best educational opportunities for their children.
Agencies working for and with young children	Families with favourable economic and social situations may need less support in order to thrive. The government has a positive strategy of supporting families and children through the Every Child Matters agenda. This initiative has the vision of all children living happy and healthy lives. It aims to achieve this through five outcomes: being healthy, staying safe, enjoyment and achievement, community participation and economic well-being. Through the Children Act 2004, a raft of measures are being put in place. Local authorities have a statutory duty to merge children's education and social services. Other measures include the appointment of a Children's Commissioner, better integrated planning, commissioning and delivery of children's services, Children's Trusts, the Children and Young People's Plan, as well as extended schools. Other measures include the National Service Framework for Children, Young People and Maternity Services, Ten Year Child Care Strategy, Children's Centres, free nursery education places for all 3- and 4-year-olds, Sure Start and workforce reform involving improving the skills and effectiveness of the workforce.	Neighbourhoods with high levels of deprivation, such as inner cities, often have less effective support services and have more problems attracting health, education and other support workers, such as teachers, doctors and dentists.

The role of play in supporting children's development

Professor Kathy Sylva is clear in her view of the value of play as 'one of the activities most significant to the (child's) development'. (Sylva and Lunt, 1998) Many other psychologists support Sylva's view:

- Erikson (1950) stressed the importance of children using play to help them deal with life experiences – the child tries to repeat, to master or to reduce their impact. Children try to organise their personal world in relation to the real world.

- Hutt and Bhavnani's (1972) research found that children who were assessed as being low in exploratory play when they were pre-schoolers tended to be low in curiosity and to experience problems in social adjustment five years later. Children judged to be active explorers were more likely to score high on tests of creativity and show evidence of being independent and curious.

- Connolly and Doyle (1984) found that the amount and complexity of fantasy play were linked to social competence.

Researchers stress the importance of the emotional atmosphere around children during play. This appears to be more important than a vast array of toys. For instance, parents can play an important role in enhancing their children's play experiences. Cohen (1993) suggests that parents can encourage imaginative play by accepting and respecting their children when playing with them. They give children confidence to explore the world around them and to try out new roles.

Research shows that play is vitally important in developing the children's ability to make good relationships. Children whose parents invite other children to come and play and have opportunities to play games involving co-operation are more popular among their peer group.

For more information about play, see Unit 7, Learning Activities and Play.

▲ Play is important in developing strong relationships

Assessment activity 3.1

1 Draw a timeline for the period of your development from 0–16 years of age. Divide your timeline into sections: 0–3 years, 4–7 years, 8–12 years and 13–16 years.

2 Describe the pattern of your development along the timeline.

3 Highlight and describe any factors which affected your development within the different sections of the timeline.

4 Describe any other factors listed in the Unit Content which you feel did not affect your development.

P1

Children have different developmental needs during their lifetime. However, there are some common features for all age groups.

- All children need to be provided with an environment which supports and allows their development to be promoted according to their developmental stage.
- They need to have both their physical and mental health needs met.
- Children need to feel valued and have their self-esteem appropriately promoted.
- Parents and carers need to provide encouragement for children.
- It is essential that adults communicate with babies, children and adolescents in order to promote satisfying relationships and also to encourage their language development.
- They also need to be aware of the child's stage of development, concerns, interests and so support their learning appropriately.
- Development needs to be promoted within an inclusive and anti-discriminatory environment.

Government initiatives, such as those promoted through the ten-year strategy for childcare, *Choice for Parents, the best start for children*, pledged to establish a single coherent development and learning framework for all young children from birth to 5 years of age. This was laid down in law by the Childcare Act (2006) and will be brought into force from September 2008 through the Early Years Foundation Stage (EYFS). It is planned to enable improved outcomes to be delivered for all children, across every area of learning and development. It is intended to assist in closing the gap between the achievement of disadvantaged children and those who are not disadvantaged.

The framework of the EYFS incorporates and develops the principles and practices laid down in *Birth to Three Matters*, the *Curriculum Guidance for the Foundation Stage* and the *National Standards for Under 8s Day Care and Childminding*. Hence, the EYFS covers both the requirements for learning and development and those for children's welfare from birth to 5 years.

Promoting development, 0–3 years

Environment

Both the home environment and out-of-home caring settings need to be safe, secure, encouraging and appropriate for the babies or children involved. High hygienic standards are essential for all, especially for babies who have limited immunity.

From birth, children need to feel secure and to be part of a stable, loving and consistent environment in order for their emotional well-being and mental health to be promoted. When cared for in an out-of the-home environment, children should have a key worker who is special to them and their family and so support their emotional well-being and help children to develop their independence through having someone on whom they can depend. This is especially important for babies or very young children. The key worker should get to know and understand the child and, in so doing, build up a warm, and at the same time, professional relationship, with both the child and the family. Interesting toys, equipment and activities should be provided to stimulate children to use their senses, interact, explore and so encourage cognitive development. Even newborn babies need to have stimulation, such as mobiles and music, to encourage their visual perception, listening skills and physical activity. Older children need a wider and ever-changing range of toys to handle which extends their rapid stages of development.

Out-of-home environments, such as children's centres and pre-schools, should be well-planned and organised to support children's learning and development. Ideally, children should have access to both high quality indoor and outdoor environments to promote their physical needs and to help their social development. Settings will need to work actively in partnership with parents and carers and respect them as the first educators of their children. When the environment is safe, comfortable, inclusive to all and provides good interaction with well-qualified adults, children are supported to become confident learners. Out-of-home environments should, where reasonable, be suitable for children with disabilities. Settings should show an awareness of, and respect for, the ethnic, cultural and social diversity of society in general as well that of the children attending. They need to be welcoming environments for all children.

Care settings will need to conform to the Disability Discrimination Acts of 1995 and 2005. Other relevant legislation includes the Sex Discrimination Act 1975, Race Relations (Amendment) Act 2000 and the Special Educational Needs Code of Practice. In addition, building and health and safety standards should be observed. Out-of-home environments have to be open for inspection by Ofsted which will monitor the learning and welfare standards of the setting. Ofsted has the power to close any which do not meet the standards laid down in current legislation.

For further information see:

- Unit 2, Positive Environments for Children's Care, Learning and Development
- Unit 7, Learning Activities and Play.

Physical needs

The EYFS places great importance on settings meeting the physical needs of children so they are kept safe and healthy. Also, as part of the Foundation Stage, settings need to teach children how to be healthy and safe. Equipment and toys, both at home and elsewhere, need to meet recognised safety standards, and should be used and maintained with the children's safety a priority. Staff need to be competent in first aid and are required to have up-to-date appropriate first aid training and qualifications. Staff preparing food for children should be trained to meet current food hygiene standards.

Much evidence supports the benefit of breast-feeding (see Unit 35, The Development and Care of Babies and Children Under Three Years). Weaning of babies and feeding of older children needs careful consideration to avoid infant and childhood obesity and to ensure healthy growth. Children need to be made aware of what constitutes healthy eating so they can learn to make informed choices when selecting their meals.

Toilet training needs to be sensitively undertaken so children are not under duress and they learn to adopt a healthy attitude to their toilet needs.

Encouragement

From birth, children need to be encouraged to take an interest in their environment and to be involved in playful activities – with their carer, alongside other children and, as they develop socially and emotionally, with other children. Babies and children need opportunities to play alongside and, later, co-operatively with their peers. This promotes awareness of themselves and others.

Children should be provided with appropriate opportunities for independence, given choices and allowed individual preferences. They need to be provided with opportunities and encouragement to progress within all the areas of learning of the EYFS. This includes the development of physical skills and creative skills.

Some children have several important transitions to make during this stage, such as being cared for outside the home, starting pre-school and moving between settings. Sensitive support needs to be provided to enable children to cope with these changes. The EYFS to be implemented in 2008 stresses the need for the sharing of information, such as the Early Years Foundation Stage Profile, between settings and other professionals to facilitate smooth transitions for children.

An understanding of children's pattern of behaviour enables parents and carers to adopt a positive, consistent and supportive response which encourages good behaviour. Praise, both verbally and in a tangible form such as stickers and certificates, enables children to be aware of what is regarded as appropriate. This encourages children to adopt a suitable approach to their activities and so assists in the development of socially acceptable attitudes and patterns of behaviour. Parents and carers need to adopt a realistic 'can do' approach so children are encouraged to persevere, enjoy challenges and are keen to learn.

Support learning

The Early Years Foundation Stage provides a flexible framework to promote development and learning from birth to 5 years for all children. It has built into it the expectation that early years practitioners will use observational assessment methodically to plan for supporting individual children's progression at their different stages of development.

Parents and carers need to provide play activities which support learning through exploration and problem-solving. Sensory learning opportunities are very important for young babies to promote their development. Toys and activities which stimulate visual alertness and involve children in listening and moving to the rhythm of sounds are invaluable (see earlier comments and Units 2 and 7).

The use of everyday routines, especially for older children, can promote learning within a meaningful environment, for example counting how many people need plates at snack time. Children need the company of their peers in order to promote their social, emotional and language development. A child's world can be extended through early literacy activities. These might include the reading and acting out of stories and rhymes, enjoying singing songs and taking part in role play with others. Awareness of the appropriateness of written words can be promoted through the use of words and labelling things of importance to the child, such as the nursery coat pegs with each child's name.

Parents and carers need to be aware of how, within both a play and home environment, children's learning can be supported within a meaningful context. A close partnership between settings and parents can extend the essential support needed to encourage children to learn.

Why is it important for children to be 'reading' at an early age? ▶

Communication

It is vital that parents and carers use a variety of ways of communicating with children to promote their emotional well-being, social skills and cognitive processes, especially their language development. Non-verbal communication, such as eye-contact and posture, as well verbal communication such as speaking, listening, singing, rhymes and story reading should all be utilised.

The use of sounds and language should be enjoyable. Hence, it is important for carers/parents to respond to babies vocalising and engage in turn-taking so babies are encouraged to explore how to communicate. Speaking and listening to children should be an important part of children's daily activities both at home and in other environments.

Being read to and the very early stages of beginning to read are an essential part of children's language development. Babies need to be introduced to books at an early age so they learn that reading in the close contact of a carer and/or parent is enjoyable. This will, also, encourage their visual alertness and concentration as well as provide opportunities for language awareness. Reading should be an important feature of children's

lives as they grow older. This will introduce them to the use of language including a wider range of vocabulary. It will, also, develop their imagination, their enjoyment of stories and competence of handling books.

Opportunities need to be provided to mark-make within meaningful situations as well as being part of more structured activities. Role play involving mark-making activities, such as recording the request of customers in a café, encourages children's interest in writing. The use of language associated with numeracy is also important. Children can be encouraged to sing and act out songs and rhymes featuring numerical language as well as using this type of language during planned, routine and spontaneous activities. Hence, parents and carers need to develop their children's communication skills and competence by providing them with appropriate opportunities, encouragement and support. This will help them to build up their confidence to use their developing skills in a range of situations and for a range of purposes.

For further information, see:
- Unit 7, Learning Activities and Play
- Unit 18, Supporting Literacy Skills.

Theory into practice

When undertaking Unit 4, Reflecting on and Developing Practice for Children aged 0–8 years, you will need to prepare carefully for the placement working with 1–3-year-olds. Prepare a checklist of strategies you need to adopt in order to encourage children's communication skills.

Promoting development, 4–7 years

Environment

The home environment and outside caring settings need to be safe, secure, encouraging and child-friendly.

These out-of-home environments need to meet the legal requirements explained earlier and are inspected by statutory authorities, such as the Fire Service and Ofsted, to ensure that they are safe, secure and appropriate for the age of children attending. The environment should be inclusive, anti-discriminatory and enable all children to have their developmental needs met, including physical, social and cognitive needs. The environment should, also, promote emotional well-being. Parents, early years settings and schools need to liaise closely with other outside agencies to maximise the opportunities for children's development and welfare. For instance, they need to work closely with social workers and the primary care team.

To maximise the effectiveness of out-of-home caring and learning environments, there has to be a close partnership with families. Children at this stage may be cared for at first within the home or an early years setting and then later at primary school and, perhaps, through extended school facilities or at before- and after-school settings. By September 2006, one in eight schools were providing extended school facilities. Schools work with local providers, agencies and sometimes other schools to provide access to high-quality childcare from 8.00 a.m. to 6.00 p.m. all year round. Such facilities also provide study support, such as homework clubs, sport and music clubs. Extended schools provide community facilities including adult/family learning and ICT. The benefits have included improved pupil attendance, improved pupil self-confidence and motivation as well as attainment.

Whether children in this age range are within the home, an early years setting, school or extended school facility, the activities, materials and experiences offered to them should be age-appropriate and support their learning and development as well as being child-friendly. Appropriate activities and experiences should be provided to stimulate further development and achievement within the Early Years Foundation Stage and later within Key Stage 1.

Physical needs

Healthy eating patterns and lifestyles need to be established particularly at this stage when children are more independent and should have more choices. The Early Years Foundation Stage promotes healthy lifestyles through the areas of learning of Physical Development and Knowledge and Understanding of the World. At Key Stage 1 children learn about healthy eating and lifestyles through Personal, Social and Health Education. For instance, the programme aims to enable children to choose different foods, to learn about different physical activities to promote health and how to keep themselves safe. The Public Health White Paper *Choosing Health* (2004) sets out the government's intention that all schools should become healthy schools by 2009. The National Healthy Schools Programme is promoted by the Department for Education and Skills and the Department of Health. It aims to:

- 'support children and young people in developing healthy behaviours
- help raise pupil achievement
- help to reduce health inequalities
- help to promote social inclusion.'

Source: National Healthy Schools Programme

Encouragement

Children need to be provided with, and supported to engage in, challenging and problem-solving activities but, at the same time, be made aware of the importance of assessing risks. Hence, children should be given some independence.

A sensitive approach has to be adopted so children are not over- or under-protected. They need to be encouraged to develop close, consistent and reliable relationships with their peers and their family so promoting their self-esteem, their resilience and thus their social and emotional development. Children still need support to cope with changes, such as when starting primary school so they can become more resilient and confident.

The policies adopted by settings and responses by parents to children's behaviour need to be consistent, realistic and supportive to encourage moral development. Inclusiveness is important for all children, both for those with special needs and for other children to promote respect for a diverse range of needs. The needs of all children need to be met including those with disabilities or special educational needs.

Learning through play is especially important for the younger end of this age range. All children need to be encouraged to learn through exploration in order to develop their inquisitiveness. Children need to be encouraged to extend their physical abilities through developing their gross and fine motor skills. Children should be encouraged to continue to be creative.

Support learning

Children need stimulating play and learning activities to promote their further development. Encouragement is important to progress both their language and numeracy skills, as well as giving support for their emerging writing and interest in books and reading.

Children should be made aware through enjoyable activities and experiences of the importance of books and stories as sources of information and for imaginative experiences. There should be a ready supply of books for children to access easily. Story reading to the whole group needs to be a feature of both Early Years Foundation Stage and Key Stage 1. In addition, children need to be encouraged to explore and enjoy books themselves. When learning to read they will need to have adult support and their reading carefully monitored so they are able to progress at their own pace.

Stimulating and relevant activities can help to promote mathematical understanding and the appropriate use of mathematical language. Activities need to be relevant and practical.

Children's development should be carefully monitored. Settings for children within the Early Years Foundation Stage will need to record progress using the Early Years Foundation Stage Profile. Children aged 5–7 will have their progress recorded within Key Stage 1. Through monitoring, children's learning needs can be identified and supported appropriately.

For further information, see:

- Unit 7, Learning Activities and Play
- Unit 17, Supporting Numeracy Skills
- Unit 18, Supporting Literacy Skills.

Communication

Children at this stage have similar communication needs to younger children with the use of both verbal and non-verbal communication, such as eye-contact, all of which are important to promote their language development. Children need opportunities each day at home, in their early years settings or at school to talk, to learn, to listen and to take turns in communication activities. The use of songs and rhymes are still important in promoting language development at this stage.

Children who are speakers of other languages than the one prevailing in the school, for example Welsh in English schools and English in Welsh-speaking schools, will need additional support in order to communicate effectively. Similarly children with disabilities and/or special educational needs will require their needs to be assessed and individual learning plans to be implemented.

A consistent, realistic and supporting approach to behaviour needs to be clearly communicated to children in order to promote their moral understanding and to develop their social and emotional skills. The policies of early years settings and schools need to emphasise the importance of a realistic approach which is both consistent and supportive in order to assist improvement.

For further information, see Unit 18, Supporting Literacy Skills.

Promoting development, 8–12 years

Environment

Children still need a safe and secure physical and emotional environment as a foundation for their increasing independence. A range of different, challenging experiences and opportunities should be provided to enable them to explore the world around them. Adults need to stand back but be available and aware of what is happening in order to allow children to develop a realistic awareness of their own abilities and needs, especially when assessing risks and undertaking activities. However, children should not be allowed to experience undue risk – their safety is paramount.

Children need meaningful praise and encouragement to promote their holistic development. Adults should provide a listening ear when children need support. They also need an inclusive and anti-discriminatory environment to support their emotional well-being for their self-esteem and self-confidence to develop. The milestone of starting secondary school requires some sensitive support to enable them to face this transition and other changes with social and emotional confidence.

Children need praise and encouragement ▼

What a lovely boat Aaron, how did you make it?

Extension activity

When on a work placement with 4–7-year-olds, find out how the setting:

- addresses the issue of inclusion for the children and their families
- monitors children's development
- provides appropriate activities and experiences to stimulate further development and achievement.

Physical needs

Healthy eating patterns, lifestyles and exercise need to be encouraged and established so physical and mental health is maximised ready for facing the onset of puberty. Children will have a varying range of physical needs which should be recognised. For instance, many boys need to be physically active in order to be part of their social group while some girls may wish to adopt a gentler approach to the use of their leisure time in order to be part of their social group. Sensitivity to the needs of all children, including those with special needs and disabilities, will promote individual development.

Support learning

Children's interest in information-handling and written communication, as well as mathematical and scientific understanding, needs appropriate support so both their self-esteem and cognitive development are promoted. Creative activities need to be encouraged in order to develop their imagination as well as their creative skills. Creative activities can provide a therapeutic channel for children to express their emotions, both their concerns and more positive emotions. A range of exploratory experiences are important at this stage since some children may become more intensely interested in certain aspects of learning to the exclusion of exploring others. For instance, some children become fanatically absorbed in using computers or playing computer games to the exclusion of exploring physical activities.

Communication

Children need to be encouraged to use a wide range of communication strategies. They need to expand their vocabulary and competence in the use of language, especially in the use of abstract concepts within their discussions and written work. The enjoyment of, and participation in, reading should be further promoted at this stage.

Children whose first language is not that used in the school will need support in order to develop their communication skills in the language that is used at school. Their questions should be answered with sensitivity and honesty, encouraging further exploration but, at the same time, respecting their level of understanding. Adults need to be available to act in a supportive role when this is needed.

Awareness and consideration of such issues as drinking, smoking, drug-taking and sexuality should be encouraged. These topics will feature within Personal, Social and Health Education programmes at Key Stage 2.

Case study: Development plans for extended school facilities

A local junior school is having an extension built to enable it to offer extended school provision. This facility will be used mainly for before and after-school care for the many children whose parents work. The school governors have been asked to make a list of what they would like to see provided in the new building and in the grounds around it.

1 Carefully read the section above on promoting development for 8–12-year-olds.

2 What facilities could be provided in the new centre which will:
   a) enable children to be safe
   b) promote children's independence
   c) provide stimulating play?

3 Which resources could be provided to support children's social and emotional development?

Promoting development, 13–16 years

Environment

Young people need information and support to help them make career choices and to be aware of further education and training. The services provided through schools and other agencies can be enhanced by parental interest and encouragement. Often opportunities are provided by families for adolescents to develop career choices.

Adolescents' emotional and social development is further promoted through challenging activities. The need to assess risks should be emphasised as this is a period of rash decisions which can sometimes result in unfortunate consequences. Opportunities offered to young people should encourage inclusiveness and be anti-discriminatory to promote moral development and to prevent resentment leading to negative emotional development.

Although adolescents actively seek independence at this stage, they also need an encouraging, safe and emotionally secure environment that recognises their need for increasing independence as they approach adulthood. Young people benefit from the emotional support of meaningful praise, the recognition of their achievements and the encouragement of adults and their peers. This is a period of transitions, for example passing from childhood to puberty, from secondary school to sixth form or college or into employment.

Although adolescents may appear to be emotionally, socially and intellectually competent, they may still need and often seek support from adults they respect or who act as parents or carers. If such support is unavailable within the family or caring environment, young people may seek help and advice from others including their peers, school counsellors or voluntary groups, such as Childline or Samaritans. Sometimes, help and advice may be sought from unreliable sources which may cause further problems.

Physical needs

Young people need to be made aware of healthy lifestyles to promote their holistic development, especially in relation to smoking, illegal drug-taking, sexually transmitted diseases and unwanted pregnancies. Several curriculum areas may include coverage of these issues, such as Science and PSE. Schools participating in the National Healthy Schools programmes will provide opportunities for consideration of such issues at this stage.

Support learning

Adolescents need encouragement to make choices and to play a positive role in decision-making. Opportunities for adolescents to take on roles of responsibility, such as prefect or serving on a school council, encourage serious decision-making. Much information about a range of issues is provided but they need support to handle this effectively. Opportunities should be provided so they can discuss things which are of importance to them. Hence, their understanding, moral and cognitive and, often, their social and emotional development can be promoted. Creativity and creative solutions need further encouragement at this stage.

Communication

Young people should be encouraged to use a wide range of communication strategies. They will usually use both verbal and written language confidently. They need to communicate and negotiate sensitively through effective, sympathetic communication with younger children. Sometimes, senior pupils undertake the role as mentor to younger pupils. The views and values expressed by adolescents need to be heard and shown appropriate respect in order for their self-esteem to be promoted and for their emotional development.

Assessment activity 3.2

Your local primary care trust has asked you to produce a leaflet on improving parenting skills. The leaflet will be made available in local health clinics. Produce the leaflet which describes how to promote development across the 0–16 age group. **P2**

Having now studied children's development and considered how to promote it, you are ready to progress to observing children and young people. As an early years professional, you will need to know how to do this in order to assess children's stage of development and, therefore, their needs.

Objectivity v. subjectivity

It is important that you approach observations in a scientific manner. You should avoid being **subjective** by introducing your personal thoughts and emotions which might influence the results of your work. It is important to be **objective** so your work is free of pre-conceived ideas or your personal viewpoint. This means reporting what you have seen or found out and what can be verified by other people carrying out the same research. This is not easy to do since we all have our own ideas and views, but these should be put aside and only the facts recorded. For instance, stating how you feel about a child's fine motor actions, 'She's always clumsy', is subjective. However, to observe a child trying to thread small beads onto a string and recording how many she is able to put on the thread and how many are dropped will give you objective evidence.

Key terms

Being **objective** means looking at the facts, being free from bias or your own point of view.
Being **subjective** means looking at things from your own point of view, being influenced by pre-conceived ideas, not looking at the facts and being impartial.

Closely linked to objectivity is **validity**. This means that the information you are gathering and the method you are using are relevant to the study being undertaken. In other words, they measure what is supposed to be measured. For example, if you were to carry out a test to measure sociability and recorded how much a child talked to you, would you be measuring language competence rather than sociability? Would the results be valid?

Reliability is also important. Consistent methods need to be used which can be replicated (repeated) in order to produce reliable information. For example, if you are measuring children's fear of thunderstorms and observed children during a particularly violent storm would you be able to replicate the same conditions next time there was a storm, since storms vary in intensity? However, it would be possible to video a storm and show the same video to different groups of children so making your observations more reliable because the children have all seen or experienced the same storm.

Key terms

Validity means that the information gathered and the method used are relevant to the study being undertaken.
Reliability means that the method used to obtain any information can be repeated and is consistent.

Your work will need to be free of error, i.e. the method used and the results obtained need to be accurate. For example, if using a time-sampling method of observation, the times recorded should be accurate, perhaps using a stopwatch, and not approximate or guessed.

Effects of perception

How often have you read through a piece of work before handing it in for assessment and not noticed an obvious error because you have read what you expected to see and not what you had actually written? Sometimes our senses play tricks on us and we see or hear things which are not quite as they first seem. So we perceive them inaccurately.

We receive sensory clues from our environment which stimulate us to search through our knowledge and past experience. If this matches some relevant ideas we have about the thing that stimulated us, it will influence how we see or hear it. If it does not fully match our knowledge or past experience, we may have to adjust our view or perception of it. Several psychologists have studied this phenomena including Rubin who devised the Rubin vase.

▲ The Rubin vase – what do you see?

It is clear that we should be aware of the way we perceive things when we are observing children. It is important we do not jump to conclusions based on what we perceive but rather on what we have objectively explored.

Effects of attitudes

Allport states that:

'An attitude is a mental and neural state of readiness, organised through experience, exerting a directive or dynamic influence upon the individual's response to all objects and situations with which it is related.'

Our attitudes, values or beliefs may affect our approach to our research. Attitudes may be positive or negative.

We develop beliefs (personal opinions) and come to determine our own personal set of principles, or standards of behaviour, which we adopt as our personal guidelines and which influence our behaviour.

Our beliefs are developed through the knowledge and information we gain from the world around us. People develop different beliefs.

So it is obvious that our attitudes, values and beliefs can affect our views or our interpretation of the results of our research. For instance, if we believe that the holistic development of all children would be better promoted if the under 5s were cared for during the day by trained early years professionals rather than their own parents, this may influence any research we undertook to study the day-care provision for under 5s.

Bias

Bias, whether intentional or unintentional, may affect the reliability of our research. When formulating questions for a questionnaire or for use during an interview, it is important to be as objective as possible. Often statistics may be gathered for a particular interest group so the results may reflect this bias. Similarly, when you select your child for your longitudinal study, the choice may be influenced by bias. You may have the view that a particular child will enable you to produce the results you think you want to obtain.

Ethical protocols to be met

When undertaking your longitudinal study, you should remember that you are studying a child who is important and precious to their family. The baby or young child is also very vulnerable and has the right, as well as the family, to be protected from any unpleasant or inappropriate intrusion into his/her life. Thorough consultation should be undertaken with the family and any other people concerned. This should be supplemented by a full written explanation of the nature of your study and how it will be carried out. It is essential, therefore, that written, not just verbal, permission is granted by the parent(s) for you to undertake the study and that explicit authorisation is obtained for the resulting written study to be used for your assessment as part of this unit. The parent(s) and any carer involved have the right to refuse your request even though you may find this inconvenient. Also, they have the right to withdraw from your study at any time. Thorough negotiation and involvement with the consenting adults is important from the outset. Good ethical practice includes giving access to the results of your study to the parent(s) who gave permission for you to undertake it.

Participants have certain rights which should be observed and which are set down in legislation: the United Nations Declaration of Human Rights and the Rights of the Child, the European Directive on Data Protection (1995) and the Data Protection Act (1998). The European Federation of Professional Psychologists Associations has an ethical code which all its member associations are expected to meet. So, ethical protocols are important.

Remember you have the right to curtail your study if you feel you are being put at any risk.

Extension activity

Copy this good practice checklist and complete it. The first three have been done for you.

Good practice checklist to ensure ethical protocols are met when undertaking the longitudinal study

- Ensure thorough liaison takes place with the family before commencing the study.
- Provide a full, written explanation of the nature of the study.
- Gain written permission from the child's parents or guardian to undertake the study.
- _____
- _____
- _____

Confidentiality

During the course of your longitudinal study you may have access to confidential information. Ethical conduct includes respecting the confidentiality of any information, however it is obtained. Your participants should have complete anonymity. Real names and details which could identify your subjects should not be included. You should not disclose to anyone any confidential material.

You need to know, however, your responsibilities in case during the course of your study you gain information which appears to provide evidence of child abuse or other criminal activity. Your responsibility in these circumstances needs to be made clear in the explanatory notes provided and when permission is sought from the parent(s) or other people/agencies involved. You will need permission from parents to use any photographs of the child being studied. They should preferably not show faces nor enable any reader of your study to identify the subject. Photographs should only be used if they provide valuable information or emphasise some important aspect of the study. They will need to be explained or commented on.

Case study: The absent-minded researcher

Gilly is an early years student undertaking a longitudinal study on Hannah, aged 1 year. The parents gave Gilly a photograph of Hannah in case she needed it for her study.

Gilly thinks Hannah is a very beautiful child. As a surprise for the child's parents, she has sent, unknown to them, Hannah's photograph to the local paper and entered it in the Bonny Baby competition. She is convinced the child will win and is sure the parents will be delighted.

She has made detailed notes in her file of the child's name, family details and address. Unfortunately, she accidentally left her file on the bus and it is now lost.

Comment on Gilly's conduct in relation to the confidentiality of the family.

Rights

As explained earlier, your child and the family have certain rights which you should respect. For instance, they can refuse permission for you to undertake the study and can withdraw permission at any time. The child has the right for your study not to prevent any development or cause any form of distress.

Responsibility

You have a responsibility to be accurate both in your observations and in the statements made within the study. The observations undertaken and the information gained should be purposeful, relevant and valid. They should not merely be motivated by inquisitiveness. This would be abusing your position and could be regarded as unethical.

Assessment activity 3.3

In preparation for your longitudinal study, write part of the written information you will provide for the parent(s), carers and other agencies involved. Explain how you intend to adopt an objective and ethical approach to your study. **P3**

Purpose of observation

Observation is to become a principle underpinning the Early Years Foundation Stage which will come into operation in September 2008. It will be a crucial part of the planning process for individual children. Sensitive observations and assessments will form the basis for planning the teaching required to meet the child's needs. Early years staff will be expected to observe closely what children can do and use these observations as the basis of assessments and their planning of the next stages of children's development. The observational assessments will identify and record children's progress towards the learning goals of the Early Years Foundation Stage. These observations will be recorded in the Early Years Foundation Stage Profile which will provide the framework for observations and assessments to be undertaken. Observation will, therefore, be a legal requirement within the Foundation Stage.

As part of your work with young children, you may wish to undertake observations in order to evaluate the effectiveness of planned activities or the relocation of activities or equipment within the setting. You may wish to observe in order to reflect on your own practice. Similarly, a manager may observe colleagues as part of a training and development programme.

Observation is also an important tool used by other professionals working with children. Health professionals may observe a child for certain aspects of their health and well-being. For instance, a speech therapist may observe a child's pattern of speech in order to gain information about any speech deficiency and plan an appropriate programme of support for the child. Similarly, a health visitor may observe a child in order to record the child's physical development.

Planning your observation

Good practice checklist

When planning your observation:

- Obtain permission to observe the selected child or the group of children. See ethics (page 125).
- Decide on your aim.
- Decide what you want to observe, who you want to observe, where and when you will undertake the observation as well as how you will undertake the observation.
- Plan thoroughly the type of observation to be undertaken. For instance, if you are going to observe a child's co-ordination skills through an activity using scissors, you will have to plan an activity which involves the use of scissors and prepare the materials needed for the activity. For example, you might plan for the child to help make a hat for Halloween which requires different shapes to be cut and then pasted onto the hat.
- Prepare any documentation to be used for recording your observation.
- Check that the place where the observation is to take place is thoroughly prepared, for example the correct number of chairs around a table, newspaper available if glue is to be used.

Undertaking observations

If undertaking an observation where you are not participating (a non-participant observation), you should aim to be as unobtrusive as possible to avoid the children's reactions being affected by their awareness of your presence. Ideally, position yourself a little away from the activity but at the same time near enough so you can hear and see what is happening. Try to avoid, or minimise, any distractions such as your mobile phone ringing during the observation.

If undertaking an observation where you are participating (a **participant observation**), be aware of the level of language used and ensure that the vocabulary is familiar to the child. Check if the child uses English as an additional language and adjust the type of communication used in order for the activity to be accessible to the child.

When working with children, ensure that you are at the same level or height as the children so they feel like an equal partner in the activity.

Make notes discreetly using abbreviations. Write up these observations as soon as possible after the event.

Key term

Participant observation occurs when the observer becomes involved with the children, either by working alongside a child or by becoming part of the group of the children being observed.

Case study: Madelon undertaking one of her observations

Madelon is undertaking a written narrative observation of a child writing a letter to Father Christmas. The child is being helped by a nursery assistant who Madelon knows well. Madelon is wearing a bright red jumper which has pinned to it a flashing 'Happy Christmas' badge which plays jingle bells. She sits at the same table as the child and chats to the nursery assistant. At one stage Madelon's pencil breaks and she asks the child for the use of one of her pencils. Madelon's tutor arrives and watches her making this observation.

Imagine you are the tutor. What would your feedback be to Madelon about the way she undertook the observation?

Structuring observations

Observations should be well organised so that they provide valuable evidence. They may be used to provide evidence for other health professionals, perhaps as part of the Code of Practice for the Identification and Assessment of Special Educational Needs. The observation may be used to assist curriculum planning. The evaluations and recommendations of observations can be used when planning activities either for individual children or small groups to meet their individual needs. For example, the observation could be undertaken in a foster home where a child has been placed after being abused. This may help a child psychiatrist assess the **target child**'s emotional needs and enable a social worker to provide an appropriate care plan. The observation should have a structured recording system.

Key term

The **target child** is the child being observed.

Observational methods

There is a wide range of observational methods to choose from.

Longitudinal observation

These observations are undertaken over a period of time. One of the most famous studies was the *Seven-Up* TV series when children were observed every seven years from when they were 7 years old until middle age.

Cross-sectional study

This involves studying subjects from several different age groups at the same time. For instance, you may wish to study (but not for your longitudinal study) intensity of attachment across the four different age groups used in this unit. You would select one child aged 0–3, one aged 4–7 years, one aged 8–12 years and, finally, one aged 13–16 years.

This allows progress to be reviewed across a series of observations

This will help you time a repeat observation

Although there may be only one target child, it is useful to know how many other children were in the group as this may influence the targeted child's behaviour

Only use the first name or a fictitious name so that the record remains confidential

It is important to know the exact age in order to assess the progress or behaviour

Do not record the name of the venue but describe the general environment

This should set out the broad area of development to be investigated

These identify the specific abilities or area to be investigated, e.g. a child's ability to use scissors

This depends on the format of the observation e.g. whether it is a time sample

Summarises what you observed

This summarises the findings with what is expected for the age group. Use a recognised source of reference to make a comparison. The targeted child can, also, be compared with the other children in the group.

How to help the child make progress

Observation: 1

Date:

Time commenced:

Time completed:

Number of adults present 2

Number of children 4

Name of child

Age 3 years 6 months

Setting The observation took place around a craft table in a pre-school

Aim To study fine motor skills

Objectives

Record of observation

Conclusion

Evaluation The developmental milestones for fine motor skills state that a child of 3 years should be able to cut using scissors. (Mary Sheridan: From Birth to Five Years.) Hannah is 3 years and 6 months. She is not yet able to co-ordinate the use of her hands so she can hold the paper and at the same time cut using scissors.

Recommendations More activities which involve the use of scissors need to be provided. Staff support on a one-to-one basis should assist Hannah when engaged in these activities. Undertake a further observation of Hannah's cutting skills in 6 weeks' time.

▲ A typical observation format

Written narrative/ running record

This involves watching a child or group of children and noting down what you see. The record is written in the present tense and usually covers a short period of time. It is necessary to describe the scene but the main focus should be on the child or children being observed. See the example (right).

There is no or little preparation involved. You may have merely carefully placed certain items within the home corner that you know are popular with the children so you might be able to observe certain reactions. You can use this method in a variety of situations. However, you may find it is difficult to record all the evidence if the situation is moving very fast. When writing up your notes later, you may inaccurately record what has happened.

Checklist

This is the list of skills or other attributes, for example attachment to carer, which you will be observing when assessing or checking the child's stage of development. The checklist has to be prepared beforehand and what is to be observed has to be clearly identified.

Standard tick charts can be purchased or early years staff can make up their own (see the example). There are also several commercially produced tick charts. These may record children's progress through the stepping stones leading to the early learning goals. If recording major developmental progress, the checklist is often supported by other evidence, for example a child's folder may include examples of written work to support the tick indicating progress made in writing.

Tick lists are simple to use if carefully constructed. They are an easy method of recording and, therefore, assessing a child's development.

Observation: 1

Date: 12/11/2008

Time commenced: 9:30

Time completed: 9.40

Age: 4 years 1 month

Setting: Home corner which is organised as a doctor's surgery

Child A barges in and demands the nurse's uniform to wear. She snatches it from a younger child who runs out crying. She tries to put the uniform on and has difficulty fastening the Velcro tabs. She leaves the surgery to ask for help, then returns. The other children leave the home corner. She opens the doctor's case and drops all the contents except for the stethoscope. She walks over the other items without any concern. She has difficulty sorting out the stethoscope and first tries to put the wrong part in her ear. A doll is grabbed and the stethoscope is pushed into the doll's chest. After a few seconds she throws the doll to the ground and lies on the bed herself.

▲ An example of a written narrative record

▼ An example of a tick list

Activity	Joe	Liam	Amin	Anne	Graeme
Talks to friend	✔	✔	✔	✔	✔
Talks to adult one-to-one	✔	✔	✔	✔	✔
Talks to two adults together	✔	✔	✔	✔	
Talks to small group of friends	✔	✔		✔	✔
Talks to small teaching group	✔				

Graphs and charts

For information, see Unit 8, Research Methodology for Children's Care, Learning and Development, page 316.

Time sampling

This form of recording consists of a series of written records at equal intervals throughout a period of time. The reason for observing the child will determine the length of each observation and the length of time between each observation. For instance, you might want to record a child's level of concentration so you may record what the child is doing each minute, as shown below.

Time	Activity
10.00	Sat at playdough, picked up playdough and felt it with hands
10.01	Rolled dough into ball, broke it into pieces
10.02	Ran to book corner, chose book, opened it, dropped it
10.03	Opened another book, lay kicking bean bag, did not look at book
10.04	Now sat at construction kit rug, tries to put two pieces together, throws pieces when they don't fit
10.05	Dressing up as a policeman, marches around room making noise of policeman

▲ An example of time sampling

Often coding is used in this method to provide a more detailed and valuable account, as shown below.

You might observe a child again at a later stage of a session when other activities are available, thus recording concentration levels for a range of situations.

This method can provide valuable information about a child's interest in activities, social development, concentration levels and overall development. However, it is sometimes difficult to record quickly enough to capture all that is happening.

Event sampling

This involves observing and recording certain events as they occur, for example temper tantrums, aggressive behaviour. The event may be planned or spontaneous, such as a child's reaction to an unexpected snow storm. So you may not have the appropriate documentation available to record reactions.

Participant observation

Participant observations can be valuable as the observer can see and understand the child's actions more clearly and may be able to influence what a child does so evidence may be collected more quickly. However, it is difficult to record discreetly and not distract the child while doing so. Also, an inexperienced participant may influence a child's reactions. The child may be aware of your intense interest in what is happening and so their response may be affected. See page 127.

Target child: Ros	Sex: F		Age 4yrs 11 mths	Date 10/10/2007	
Time	Activity	Code	Language	Social
10.00	TC sits at construction table	TC		SP
10.01	TC watches CL playing. Tries to make eye contact	TC-CL	NVC	IP
10.02	CL asks TC for a piece. TC snatches	TC-CL	Shouts 'No'	IP
10.03	CL hits TC	TC-CL	Cries and shouts	IP
10.04	A parts TC + CL Explains about please and thank you	A TC CL	CL asks + please TC nods (Yes)	IP
10.05	Both sulk	TC-CL	None	PP

Code

TC	Targeted child	CL	Child involved with	PP	Parallel play	NVC	Non-verbal communication
A	Adult	IP	Interactive play	SP	Solitary play		

 ▲ An example of time sampling using coding

Groups

You may wish to use a **sociogram** if you are observing a child within a group. This can show the social relationship between different people within a group or the relationships of one member within a group. Children are usually asked who their friend is so it is not strictly an observational method. The results may be recorded as shown (right).

Name of child	Child 1	Child 2	Child 3
Joe	Jay	Anne	Graeme
Liam	Liam	Jay	Jay
Amin	Amin	Graeme	Liam
Anne	Jay	Liam	
Graeme	Graeme	Amin	Anne
Jay	Anne		

▲ A sociogram of children's preferred friends

Key term

A **sociogram** can show the relationships between different members of a group or the relationship of one member within a group.

You may find it useful to map a child's movements around a nursery and to note how long they stay in each place.

You will most certainly want to make notes or field notes when observing a child, especially during an impromptu activity such as a baby's greeting of a close relative. These jottings should be made discreetly and then written up in detail as soon as practically possible. It will help if you use abbreviations when making the notes. You may find it helpful to look at the abbreviations used when assessments are undertaken for the Foundation Stage Profile, for example:

- SD – social development
- ED – emotional development
- LCT – language for communication and thinking.

When undertaking your longitudinal study, you will need to plan how often you are going to observe the child and the types of observations you will carry out during the time you have available for the study.

You may wish to record the child, using either an audio or video tape. These can be very useful as you can replay the tapes and note in detail the actions of the child. The audio tape is very valuable when studying a child's language development. However, the child's reactions may be influenced by the presence of the recording equipment. For instance, a child may play-up to the camera so not behave naturally.

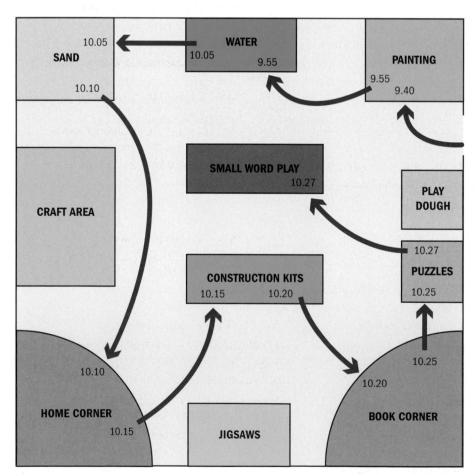

▲ A child's activities mapped during free choice time at pre-school

Comparison of methods

You will need to use a variety of methods when assessing a child's level of development and you will need to consider carefully the advantages and disadvantages of each method when planning the range of methods to be used. You need to think about the aim of your observation and then choose the most appropriate method for achieving that aim.

Repeat the activity using different scenarios, for example when testing a child's understanding of the number 3. Give the child different tasks involving the use of the same number. For instance, make three cakes using play dough, paint three mice or put out three plates in the home corner for the dolls' tea party. This will have the advantage of assessing the child's confidence of applying

▼ Comparison of observational methods

Observational method	Advantage	Disadvantage
Written narrative/ running record	Can occur spontaneously in response to a child or group of children's activities Can record significant details No pre-determined recording system needed Parents may find the information recorded helpful	Difficult to record/write down in longhand all the detail during the observation. Need to write quickly Child's reaction may be affected by presence of observer writing Not easy for observer to be inconspicuous
Target child	Allows detailed and informative observation of one child	Child may feel uncomfortable at being the focus of individual attention Target child may be absent when observation planned
Time sample	Gives a detailed, objective picture of children's activities, behaviour, developmental progress May highlight matters for concern	Takes time to do and to plan May be an intense observation for a limited period of time When recording, may miss some activities, especially if observer is inexperienced
Event sample	May give detailed information of a child's pattern of behaviour May highlight matters of concern May provide valuable information which can be easily understood by others	Child's reaction may trigger unusual behaviour if child feels they are being watched Need to concentrate hard on the event and children being observed
Checklist	Is easy and quick to undertake Has objective criteria, often linked to accepted developmental or behavioural norms Can be used with more than one subject to give a comparative result	Checklist needs preparing beforehand Observer must be professionally objective and familiar with checklist prior to completion
Graphs and charts	Allows data to be presented in an easy-to-understand format	May be time-consuming to construct Must enter data accurately to get reliable results
Longitudinal	Allows observer to see child's progress over a period of time	Child may be unavailable for the whole period of time, for example move areas
Cross-sectional	This allows comparison of results for different circumstances	May not have the right mix of subjects available to provide an appropriate cross-section
Structured recording system	Promotes the following of ethical guidelines Promotes objectivity in the observation Organises the evidence gathered into a logical format	Does not allow for spontaneity, for example recording of an unexpected happening

his/her knowledge. However, the child's attention may be distracted in one of the situations by the presence of others, so the results may not be truly reliable.

To help you compare different methods and to decide which method is most suitable for a particular observation situation, the table on page 133 highlights some of the main advantages and disadvantages of different methods. You may like to discuss these in a group and add to the table.

Limitations with methods

Many of the methods which can be used to observe children have limitations. For instance, the use of a video camera can be distracting for a child who may 'play' to the camera so an inappropriate record is made. When engaging in a participant observation it may not be possible to record all the information and your memory may not be reliable when writing it up afterwards. If you are unfamiliar with the documentation to be used, this can result in inaccuracies. It is important to remember before recording children that permission must be sought and given by parents or guardians.

Case study: Limitations of methods

Sian is on a six-week work placement in a pre-school for children aged 3–5 years. Her supervisor has asked her to work with a group of 3-year-olds. The children all come from the same centre for newly arrived refugees. While at the pre-school, Sian has asked permission to practise a range of observational methods. She intends to carry out:

- a longitudinal study
- a cross-sectional study
- a participant observation.

Sian likes playing with the children. Her supervisor has commented on her report form that Sian tends to control the children's play too much. She does not allow them enough opportunities to choose their play or show what they can do themselves.

What are the likely limitations for the methods that Sian wants to practise in this pre-school situation?

Limitations with recording

You may find that you are not able to write quickly enough when observing a child. When you lower your head to make a note, you may miss a vital piece of evidence. In your hurry to record information, the resulting scribble may later prove to be illegible when you are trying to write up your notes.

Interpretations

A single observation may highlight a problem, but important judgements should not be made on the basis of just one observation. This has to be followed up with subsequent observations in order to make an informed evaluation. For instance, children's awareness of the observation may inhibit their behaviour as they may feel shy. On the other hand, children may take the opportunity to play-act for the observer so the results will not be valid.

Judgements should, therefore, be based on sound evidence. The observer should avoid any personal or cultural bias. For instance, if the target child has an older sibling with behavioural problems, don't expect the target child to display the same problems. If a child comes from another culture, the parenting styles may be very different and this should be taken into consideration. In some cultures children are breast-fed beyond 1 year, so the child could have difficulty drinking out of a cup at this age.

When you are certain that you have carried out sufficient and varied observations and they all show a pattern of behaviour, this evidence can be used to plan appropriate provision or strategies. For instance, if all your evidence shows that the target child has difficulty sitting still for reasonable periods of time, such as circle time in pre-school, the staff can plan strategies to encourage an improvement.

Assessment

Good practice checklist

When using the evidence gathered through observations to assess a child, it is good practice to use one or more of the following strategies:

- Compare the results with commonly accepted milestones, for example using the tables of expected norms developed by Mary Sheridan.
- Relate the results to child development theorists, for example if studying attachment, to the work of Schaffer.
- Consider the child's achievement in relation to curriculum objectives, such as progress along the stepping stones leading towards early learning goals of the Foundation Stage.
- Use the assessment as the basis for planning future play/learning activities which will promote the child's learning or development.
- Use the assessment to plan provision to meet the child's needs, for example more one-to-one contact with an assigned key worker for a child who is very shy.

These strategies may assist you in identifying any developmental delay.

Your tutor may discuss your work with you during the course of your longitudinal study and give a **formative assessment** of its progress. This involves feedback to you in a way which enables you to improve the quality of your work. Formative assessment helps you to be aware of any gaps that exist in achieving the target of your learning, in this case a longitudinal study which meets all the assessment and grading criteria for the unit. It will guide you through the actions needed to achieve this goal. However, when you hand in your longitudinal study for final assessment and a grade is awarded for the unit, this is a **summative assessment**.

Key terms

Formative assessment involves a continual review by both you and the assessor during the draft process of producing your study.

Summative assessment is carried out at the end of your study in order to make final judgements.

Reporting

When reporting your findings, you should respect the confidentiality of your subject by not using the child's actual name or including any information which may cause the child to be identified, for example the actual address of the child which may be the place where the child was observed. The information gathered may put the child at risk, so strict confidentiality is very important.

The parent or carer must give the researcher permission to observe the child prior to the observations being undertaken. This is required under the Data Protection Act. Parents or carers must give informed consent. In other words they should be fully informed as to the nature of the observations and be allowed full access to your findings. The partnership with parents is important. Positive relationships with the parents can facilitate the sharing of information which can enrich your study. However, there may be occasions when it is inappropriate to share information gained through observations with one or more parent and it may put the child at risk, for instance, in suspected child abuse cases.

The early years setting may have strict guidelines for the sharing of observation records which you should follow. For instance, the setting may be reluctant for observations to be shared with others unassociated with the setting or who have no professional status, for example fellow students at college.

Your evidence may highlight particular difficulties which need further attention. Most observations will not present you with any concern. However, if your observations indicate that there are issues which you feel, in the interests of the child, you cannot ignore, it is your responsibility to act according to the policy of the setting. If the observations are being undertaken in a private home or on your school/college premises, it is important that you let your tutor know of your concerns. For instance, you may suspect that the child is being neglected or abused and this should not be ignored. It may be that your suspicions are unfounded, but you may have identified that the child is at risk and in need of protection. You will need to have available detailed, objective evidence which might have to be used within the legal system or be made available to the appropriate psychological service. Hence, it is important that your observations are thoroughly planned, objectively undertaken and reported. You should not share the information with anyone other than someone in authority, such as your tutor, who will regard the information as confidential.

Assessment activity 3.4

The local parent and toddler group has agreed to consider allowing some members of your student group to undertake a longitudinal study of their children. They do not fully understand the use of the observations which the students might undertake. They have asked for further information.

1 Prepare some handout notes for the session where you explain the use of observations. **P4**

2 In the handout notes, describe your own use of four observational techniques. **P5**

3.5 How to undertake a longitudinal study of a baby or young child

One way of noting a person's progressive development is to carry out a longitudinal study which involves research over a period of time. As part of the assessment for this unit, you will need to study a baby or young child for at least three months. It will enable you to study in depth various aspects of the child's development.

Baby or young child

You need to study a baby or a child between birth and 3 years of age.

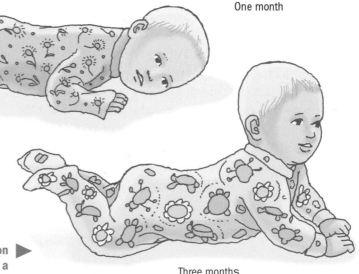

One month

Three months

Babies' prone position development over a three-month period ▶

Planning

It is very important that you give careful consideration to the choice of the baby or child to be studied. As you have to undertake the study over at least a three-month period, you will need to be confident that you will have access to the child for all this time. It is impractical to start studying a child who you know will be leaving the area in a few weeks' time as you may not be able to complete your study.

It is advisable to select a baby or child who has neither a known developmental delay nor an identified disability. When considering the choice of child, you need to try, if possible, to choose a baby or child who is at a rapid stage of development. For example, a child aged 6–12 months may progress from rolling over from front to back to moving over the floor by rolling, to attempting to crawl, to crawling on hands and knees and, finally, to bear-walking along the floor. You can observe the rapid change in the gross motor skills as part of the child's physical development.

You will need to plan a range of observations covering all aspects of development so you can see the holistic development of the child. This will influence the choice of the types of observations you make. For instance, the range might include time sampling in order to observe a child's level of concentration or a structured observation for fine motor skills observation. Ideally, one observation a week would give you a wide range of opportunities for your research and enable you to gather much valuable information. However, this might not be possible due to a number of factors. The family may go away on holiday or the child might be ill for one week or more. It is important to observe regularly. You will not get a true picture of your child's developmental progress if you carry out all your observations in the last month of the observation period.

Before starting your series of observations, you will need to gather some initial information from the parent or carer. For instance, it is helpful to know if the child was born full-term or prematurely. This could affect a baby's developmental progress.

Good practice checklist

Planning for selecting the child to be studied
Use the following checklist when deciding on the child to be studied.

		Yes	No
1	Is the child likely to be in the area in three months' time?		
2	Are you fairly certain that the child has no known disability or developmental delay?		
3	Will you be able to get regular access to the child?		
4	Is the baby/child you wish to study in a rapid period of development?		
5	Where will you observe the child?		
	a) If observing in the child's home, do you feel comfortable and safe visiting the home?		
	b) If outside the home, will the nursery or other venue give permission and the facilities for you to observe the child?		

If all the answers are Yes, then the child may be appropriate for you to select for your longitudinal study.

Ethical considerations

You should observe the ethical protocols already highlighted, including respecting confidentiality and appreciating the rights of the child and the family. Parents have the right to refuse permission for the child to be observed and can withdraw any permission previously granted at any stage of the observation process. You should be aware of the responsibility that observing a child places upon you. You should ensure that your work is accurate, so objective conclusions are reached as a result of your observations.

For more information, see Unit 8, Research Methodology for Children's Care, Learning and Development.

Range of observational techniques used

You will need to use a range of observational techniques. You may wish to be a participant in some of the activities and for some observations you may wish to be a non-participant. It might be helpful, for example if observing language development, to use an audio tape to record some evidence. It might be helpful to map a child's choice of play activities or toys or to undertake a time sample or event sample. All these techniques have advantages, but you should also consider their disadvantages for your situation. For instance, the audio tape recorder may prove to be too intrusive so the child is reluctant to speak freely.

Naturalistic observations may present some good opportunities for seeing the child behave in a relaxed, normal manner. This type of observation does not involve the child having to undertake a structured activity planned by the researcher. However, it will take patience waiting for the child to select any activity which you particularly want to observe. If you take advantage of a naturally occurring activity, you may not have any prepared recording sheets or paper, pen or video recorder available to record the event.

You will need to compare the value of different types of methods for achieving the range of observations you need.

Considerations of objectivity

The issues of bias, the effects of attitudes and perceptions, the importance of validity and reliability and the avoidance of error have all been considered earlier (pages 124–125). For your work to be credible, your study should pay attention to these issues.

Extension activity

Write a paragraph to explain how you intend to achieve objectivity when undertaking your observational study.

Carry out the observational study

The study will need to include relevant measurements, especially at the beginning and at the end of the study and perhaps during the study, if it is carried out over a long period of time. The parent(s) may be willing to report on birth weight and measurements as well as the results of developmental screening, such as that undertaken by the health visitor. They may be willing to give you access to the child's little red book, the child health record.

All areas of development should be observed. So you will need to plan observations of physical, social, emotional, cognitive, including language, development and consider how these contribute to the child's holistic development.

You will need to carry out secondary research to obtain information on measurements relevant to the age of the child studied, such as centile charts. You will need to research developmental needs based on the age and stage of development of the baby or child. You will have to be sensitive to the family's ability to provide for the baby/child and link your observations to both positive and negative factors affecting development. It will be necessary to obtain some case history of the child.

For further details of secondary research, see Unit 8, Research Methodology for Children's Care, Learning and Development.

Caring routines, feeding, play, toys and clothing should not only be described; you will also need to explain their relevance and whether they meet the developmental needs of your baby or child. It is essential to notice whether safety and security have been adequately considered. Safety and security are of first importance when you are undertaking the study. You should not put the baby, child or yourself at any risk of harm.

You should research suitable play activities for the age and stage of development of your baby or child. Play to promote all areas of development should be covered.

Use of observational study

Having undertaken the observations, you will need to interpret them – see Interpretations, page 134. When making assessments, refer to the earlier section on page 135. Your report should consider the implications of the study for planning to meet the needs of the child.

Assessment activity 3.5

One of the mothers at the parent and toddler group has agreed to allow you to undertake a longitudinal study of her 6-month old baby.

Describe how you will undertake this study. **P6**

End of unit assessment

The manager of Happy Days Nursery has been given the task of implementing a staff training and refresher programme. The nursery is planning to extend its provision by offering extended school facilities for both the local primary and secondary schools. You have been asked to help the manager to prepare for this project.

1 Prepare a PowerPoint presentation describing the expected patterns of development from 0 to 16 years. **P1**

2 Write the notes to go with the handout produced from the PowerPoint presentation. You will need to explain:
   a) the expected patterns of development from 0 to 3 years
   b) the factors affecting this development. **M1**

3 Produce posters describing the factors affecting children's development from 0 to 16 years. **P1**

4 Prepare to lead a group discussing how development can be promoted across the 0–16 years age range. Compile some notes to be given as a handout at the end of the session describing how development can be promoted across this age range. **P2**

5 The staff will be expected to do some further research themselves after the session and produce written evidence of this research. The task set will require an explanation of how development can be promoted across the 0–3 years age range. Imagine you are one of the staff and write your response to this task. **M2**

6 As a result of some recent high-profile cases, such as Victoria Climbie, where the abuse of children has gone unnoticed by a variety of agencies, the manager has decided to implement a regular programme of observations of children. In the training programme the staff are to consider how to undertake a variety of different types of observations.
   Produce a PowerPoint presentation to explain the importance of:
   a) objectivity
   b) the consideration of ethical issues when observing children. **P3**

7 The manager has asked you to lead a session explaining the use of observation of children. Prepare your notes for this session. **P4**

8 In order to assist staff doing observations, describe your own use of four observational techniques. **P5**

9 Show the staff how to interpret these observations, indicating how these can be used for assessing, recording and planning. **M3**

10 Having interpreted the observations, show the staff how to analyse them so they can be used to promote different aspects of development. **D1**

11 In preparation for this training programme, carry out your own longitudinal study of a baby. Prepare a leaflet for the staff. In the first section, describe your study. **P6**

12 In the next section of the leaflet, interpret your longitudinal study by assessing, recording and planning for the child studied. **M4**

13 For the final section of the leaflet, evaluate the observational techniques used. Also evaluate the longitudinal method undertaken. **D2**

References and further reading

Books

Barnes, P. (2002) *Personal, Social and Emotional Development of Children*, Blackwell

Bee, H. (1989) *The Developing Child*, Harper & Row

Bee, H. and Boyd, D. (2006) *The Developing Child*, 11th edition, Pearson International Ltd

Bowlby, J. (1965) *Child Care and the Growth of Love*, Pelican

Brown, G.L., Goodwin, F.L., Ballenger, J.C., Goyer, P.F. and Major, I.F. (1979) 'Aggression in humans correlates with cerebrospinal fluid amine metabolites'

Cohen, D. (1993) *The Development of Play*, 2nd edition, Routledge

Condor and Sanders (1995) *in* Davenport, G.C. *An Introduction to Child Development*, 2nd edition, Collins (page 235)

Connolly, J. A. and Doyle, A.B. (1984) 'Relations of social fantasy play to social competence in pre-schoolers', *Journal of Applied Developmental Psychology*, 20, pp797–806

Davenport, G.C. (1994) *An Introduction to Child Development*, Collins

DfES (2001) *National Standards for Under Eights Day Care and Childminding*, DfES

Dunphy, D.C. (1963) 'The social structure of urban adolescent peer groups', *Sociometry*, 26, pp230–246

Erikson, E.H. (1950) *Childhood and Society*, Norton

Fantz, R.L. (1961) 'The origin of form perception', *Scientific American*, 204 (5), pp66–72

Flanagan, C. (1996) *Applying Psychology to Early Child Development*, Hodder & Stoughton

Flavel, J. (1999) 'Cognitive Development: Children's Knowledge about the Mind', *Annual Review of Psychology*

Gibson, E.J. and Walk, P.D. (1960) 'The visual cliff', *Scientific American*, 202, pp64–71

Hobart, C. and Frankel, J. (2004) *A Practical Guide to Child Observation and Assessment*, 3rd edition, Nelson Thornes – very useful resource for the longitudinal study

Hucker, K. (2001) *Research Methods in Health, Care and Early Years*, Heinemann

Hutt and Bhavnani (1972) 'Predictions from Play', *Nature* 237, pp171–72

Olweus, D. (1982) 'Development of stable aggression reaction patterns in males', in Blanchard, R. and Blanchard, C. (eds) (1984) *Advances in the Study of Aggression*, Vol. 1, Academic Press

Patterson, G.R., Capaldi, D. and Bank, L. (1991) 'An early starter model for predicting delinquency', in Pepler, D.J. and Ruboin, K.H. (eds), *The Development and Treatment of Childhood Aggression*, Lawrence Erlbaum

Riddall-Leech, S. (2005) *How To Observe Children*, Heinemann – very useful for the longitudinal study

Schaffer, H.R. and Emerson, P.E. (1964) 'The development of social attachments in infancy', *Monographs of the Society for Research in Child Development*, 29 (3, Serial No. 94)

Schaffer, H.R. (1977) *Mothering*, Fontana/Open Books

Sheridan, M., Frost, M. and Sharma, A. (2005) *From Birth to Five Years: Child Development Progress*, Routledge

Sure Start (2003), *Birth to Three Matters: An Introduction to the Framework*, DfES

Sylva, K. and Lunt, A. (1998) *Child Development: A First Course*, Blackwell

Sylva, K.D., Roy, C. and Painter, M. (1980) *Childwatching at Playgroup and Nursery School*, Grant McIntyre

Tassoni, P., Beith, K., Eldridge, H. and Gough, A. (2000) *Diploma Child Care and Education*, Heinemann

Vurpillot, E. (1976) *The Visual World of the Child*, Allen & Unwin

Waldrop, M. F. and Halverson, C. F. (1975) 'Intensive and extensive peer behaviour: Longitudinal and cross-sectional analysis', *Child Development*, 46, pp19–26

Useful websites

Sure Start – www.surestart.gov.uk

National Children's Bureau – www.ncb.org.uk

Child Development Institute – www.childdevelopmentinfo.com

Children Webmag – www.childrenuk.co.uk

Grading criteria	Assessment activity	Page number
To achieve a pass grade the evidence must show that the learner is able to:		
P1 describe the expected pattern of development from 0–16 years and the factors affecting development	3.1 End of unit assessment	115 139
P2 describe how development can be promoted across the 0–16 years age range	3.2 End of unit assessment	123 139
P3 explain the importance of objectivity and the consideration of ethical issues when observing children	3.3 End of unit assessment	126 139
P4 explain the use of observation of children	3.4 End of unit assessment	136 139
P5 describe own use of four observational techniques to observe children	3.4 End of unit assessment	136 139
P6 describe own longitudinal study of a baby or young child	3.5 End of unit assessment	139 139
To achieve a merit grade the evidence must show that, in addition to the pass criteria, the learner is able to:		
M1 explain the expected patterns of development from 0–3 years and the factors affecting development	End of unit assessment	139
M2 explain how development can be promoted across the 0–3 years age range	End of unit assessment	139
M3 interpret observations to show how observation can be used for assessing, recording and planning	End of unit assessment	139
M4 interpret longitudinal study, assessing, recording and planning for the child	End of unit assessment	139
To achieve a distinction grade the evidence must show that, in addition to the pass and merit criteria, the learner is able to:		
D1 analyse observations to show how these can be used to promote different aspects of development	End of unit assessment	139
D2 evaluate the observational techniques used including the longitudinal method	End of unit assessment	139

Reflecting on and developing practice for children aged 0–8

Introduction

You are preparing to work in a very important profession which has profound and long-lasting effects on the lives of many children and great significance in the character of local communities and our wider society in future generations. Your work placements are a vital part of the BTEC course. They will enable you to have a taste of the reality of working with children, and to find out how a variety of settings offer services to children and families. From the beginning, what you do and how you do it will influence children so you need to understand how to work in professional ways.

At the heart of good practice in working with children is developing your observation skills. Observing children carefully and regularly will enable you to:

- reflect on your practice
- meet children's needs
- provide suitable opportunities for them to develop and learn.

A key element of working in a professional way in any career is to become a reflective practitioner, to be able to think about how you work and how you can develop and improve your practice. You must be prepared, throughout your career, to take responsibility for extending your knowledge and skills so you are able to go on contributing to high-quality services for children and families.

What you need to learn

- The roles and responsibilities involved in being a professional practitioner
- How to prepare for your work placements
- How to use your observations of children to enable you to promote their development and learning
- How to use your observations of children to meet their needs through routines
- How to reflect on your experiences and plan your personal development.

Thinking points

You are taking on a very important form of work. The future of our society depends on the early experiences and learning of young children who will be the citizens, parents, workers and leaders of tomorrow. When you complete your BTEC course and gain the qualification, you will be ready to move out into the world of work and get a job working with young children and their families. However, this will only be the beginning of your career. At all times, you must take a professional approach to your work, reflect on your practice and be responsible for your own continuing professional development (CPD) to meet the challenges of new developments in the sector.

Jo qualified and got her first job in a private day nursery. Within her first few months, she heard about government policy developments that would change the sort of settings in which there would be jobs in future, such as children's centres. She also heard that changes were proposed to the frameworks for children's learning in the early years.

How can Jo keep herself informed about changes and developments in working with children and families in the years ahead in her career? How will she know what is happening and what changes are on the horizon that will affect her?

Behaving professionally

The word 'professional' means different things to different people. It is essential that you develop a clear understanding of what it means in the context of working with children. Essentially, being a professional practitioner means behaving at all times in ways which:

- put the needs and well-being of children first
- contribute to the effectiveness of your work setting in providing a high-quality service to children and families
- are responsible, considerate, respectful and courteous towards other people
- provide a good and positive role model to children and colleagues
- promote the integrity of your profession.

Professional responsibility

It cannot be over-emphasised how important the work is in the career you are entering. The main influences on children come, of course, from their parents and family, but professionals who work with children in any role have an important influence on those children, some of them with long-term implications. The children you work with will be influenced by you and copy you.

Theory into practice

A group of BTEC students discussed what would represent good professional behaviour in the workplace, and what would not. They drew up these contrasting lists:

Professional behaviour	Unprofessional behaviour
Turning up for work on time	Persistently being late
Looking clean, neat and tidy	Wearing grubby or torn clothes; having dirty finger nails; hair hanging loose and untidy; poor personal hygiene; smelling strongly of cigarette smoke
Being dressed appropriately, in comfortable, practical clothes	Wearing high heels, revealing clothes or heavy or gaudy make-up
Being reliable in turning up for work	Taking odd days off ('duvet days') for no good reason; turning up the worse for wear after a good night out
Always being polite to children and families, colleagues and other professionals	Speaking abruptly, curtly or even rudely to others, or ignoring them
Being prepared to be flexible, to adapt to new situations and try out new working approaches	Complaining about and resisting change and developments in the work role
Focusing on the children and their well-being at all times	Gossiping with colleagues about personal matters during work hours
Taking responsibility for one's own safety	Taking risks such as climbing on a chair to reach a high shelf rather than fetching steps
Being pro-active about being well informed about the work and keeping up to date	Avoiding training sessions, never reading professional journals
Above all, being committed to the job, the setting and the children	Becoming uninterested in the job, setting and children – a 'couldn't care less' attitude

▲ Is this an example of professional behaviour?

You will be responsible for safeguarding them. You will affect their future chances of developing, learning and leading healthy lives. This is a great responsibility to take on and requires personal maturity. You must always keep that sense of the significance of your daily work at the front of your mind.

Guidelines for professional behaviour: codes of practice

In your chosen career, as in many professions, much of what constitutes professional standards of behaviour are unwritten and, although in Unit 1 we looked at some of the values of the profession, there is no single set of guidelines for all practitioners to follow. However, most settings have written policies and procedures which they require staff to comply with, and an increasing number have clearly set out aims or a 'mission statement'. If a setting is following a quality assurance programme, they will have a set of standards for the level of service which they are working towards. It is essential that you discover what these are for each of your work placements.

Case study: Sonali's sense of responsibility

Sonali thought back over her first year of working with children and drew up a list of situations and incidents when her sense of professional responsibility came home to her. Some of the examples she noted included:

- appreciating how much a child had progressed in being able to speak more distinctly after Sonali had done one-to-one sessions with him, following advice from a speech and language therapist
- overhearing a child telling another, 'I think you could be much kinder if you tried', using her own phrase and tone of voice
- passing on concerns to her manager about a child who was behaving in an inappropriately sexual way – later investigations by social services found the child was being abused.

1 Note down some examples of the professional responsibilities you find yourself taking on in your work placements.

2 What additional professional responsibilities do you expect to encounter when you are in employment?

Good practice checklist

In each of your work placements:

- note any aims of the setting, mission statement or quality standards you are told about or find printed in the setting's documents – if no one tells you about these, ask about them
- think carefully about the meaning of these aims, statements or standards – they are likely to be expressed in broad (perhaps even vague) terms, and you need to unpick what the intentions are that lie behind them
- use any opportunities that arise to discuss these aims, statements or standards with colleagues in the setting and find out how they interpret them
- gather together copies of the written policies and procedures that staff in each setting have to comply with
- check through these to see how they affect your daily work in the setting – what do they say you must do/must not do?
- during the course of each of your work placements, note down examples of how you comply with aims, mission statements, quality standards, policies and procedures.

If you follow this checklist for each work placement, you will be well placed to be able to compare how different settings set out expectations for practitioners' professional practice.

Policies and procedures are developed by settings not just to please inspectors but to ensure the smooth and safe running of a setting by:

- ensuring the safety, well-being and opportunities to learn for each child in the setting (for example, policies about equality of opportunity and anti-discrimination, procedures for referrals if it is suspected that a child is being harmed)
- protecting practitioners (for example, policies about recording an injury a child already has when they arrive at a setting)
- protecting the interests of the setting (for example, recording accidents in detail).

As a professional practitioner, you must adhere to the policies and procedures of the setting you are working in – for the sake of the children, your colleagues and yourself. This doesn't mean that you have to follow directives without thinking for yourself. No policy or procedure can cover all possible eventualities, and there will be times when you have to use your own initiative. If this happens, you will need to base your responses on the intentions of the policy or procedure and keep in your mind the key principle of the paramountcy of the welfare of the child.

Confidentiality

A very important part of professional conduct is maintaining confidentiality, and it is likely that your work placement settings will have policies about confidentiality.

As we saw in Unit 1 (page 11), maintaining confidentiality means not sharing with other people or passing on personal information about the children and families you are working with unless:

- parents have given their permission, for example, to talk to a health visitor about concerns about a child's development
- it is necessary to do so without parents' permission in the interests of the child, for example, in the case of suspected abuse.

You must always comply with the requirements of a confidentiality policy in any setting you work in. Not to do so would constitute unprofessional conduct.

Appropriate interpersonal skills

Your work will bring you into contact with a range of people:

- children
- their parents and other members of their families
- colleagues in your work setting
- other professionals.

The way you communicate with these people will be different from the ways you communicate with your own family and friends. Unit 1 (pages 12 and 26–32) covers communication in depth, and will help you to think about appropriate ways of communicating in your professional role, courteously and showing that you value and respect the person you are communicating with.

Working in a team

People who work with young children have contacts with colleagues and other professionals; they are part of a team working in the interests of the children and their families. The emphasis on working in wider **multi-disciplinary teams** is likely to increase in future, especially as children's centres develop and increase in number.

Key term

A **multi-disciplinary team** is one in which people from different professional backgrounds, training and qualifications work together to provide services for children and families.

Depending on their age, you may also see the children you work with as part of your team – and you should certainly see their parents that way, since they are your partners in achieving what is best for their children. In community-based provision such as pre-schools, parents are also part of the management committee so will certainly be members of the team.

The principles of teamworking

A team will be more effective if it is well led, but even a skilled team leader cannot make a team successful on their own – each person in the team must play their part. Teamwork is about working together and to do this effectively, as a member of a team, you should:

- be committed to working towards the shared goals of the team
- contribute actively and positively to the team
- respect and support other members of the team.

■ Working towards shared goals

People who work with children and families are usually very committed to their work, feeling that they can 'make a difference'. This makes them enthusiastic about what their setting is aiming to achieve, and motivates them to work with other members of the team. The team you join will be more effective if you understand clearly the overall purpose of the team, and take advantage of any opportunity to contribute to the development of the setting's goals. We have already looked at how a setting might have written aims or a mission statement.

Case study: Who's in Bushra's team?

Bushra works in a children's centre. She thought about the team she was part of, and drew a diagram to represent those colleagues who were part of her immediate work team, and those in her wider work team. It looked like this:

1 **What sorts of team have you observed and become part of in your work placements? Make a diagram like Bushra's.**

2 **What are the advantages of a multi-disciplinary team to:**
   a) **children and families?**
   b) **practitioners?**

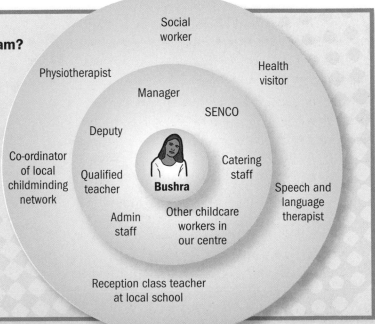

■ Contributing to the team

You cannot be an effective team player if you sit back and don't play your part.

Good practice checklist

To contribute actively and positively to a team of which you become a member, you will have to be prepared to:

- share your knowledge, ideas and information with the other members of the team
- contribute actively to discussion, planning and solving problems
- be open to new ideas and other people's suggestions
- take responsibility for aspects of work where you have the appropriate skills and knowledge
- hand over work to someone else in the team if their skills and knowledge are more appropriate than yours
- be reliable, completing work when and how you agreed to do it
- be prepared to be flexible and to adapt to changing circumstances
- maintain the confidentiality of what you hear in discussion and meetings, so others feel they can trust you with information about children and families.

■ Respect and support

Working in a team always requires a degree of give and take. To be a good member of your team, you must respect and support other team members.

Good practice checklist

When you work in a team, you should:

- listen to and respect the views of other team members
- offer support to other team members
- give other members of the team feedback
- thank others for their help and congratulate them on their successes
- don't gossip and criticise colleagues behind their backs.

In return, you can expect to:

- have your own ideas and opinions listened to and respected
- ask for support when you need it (don't pretend you can manage something when it's beyond your current skills)
- receive feedback on the way you work
- be thanked when you help others and have your own efforts acknowledged
- avoid being gossiped about and criticised.

▶ **Being an effective team member means taking part in discussions**

It isn't always easy to receive **feedback** from other people. We all tend to focus more on the negative things that are said about us and our performance, and we're not so good at remembering the complimentary things people say about us. A natural response to being told that you're not doing something well is to become defensive and to try to justify the way you have acted.

Good practice checklist

When you are offered feedback:

- listen carefully to what the other person is saying, and focus on their comments
- receive their positive comments graciously
- think about how you could use their constructive comments to change the way you work.

Extension activity

Your work placements will provide feedback on your performance and achievements. Look at the record of the feedback you have received. How do you feel about this feedback?

Don't let your personal feelings get in the way of working with others in a professional working relationship. There will always be individuals that you don't get on with – maybe they irritate you in some way, or you find their personality unappealing. You may have to make an effort to put this aside so that you can behave in a professional way which helps the team work well together.

If you are finding that a colleague is behaving towards you in a way which makes you uncomfortable in your work setting, or is undermining your role, don't let the situation simmer – it can only get worse. Always talk to your manager about what is happening. If your manager is the source of your difficulties, you may have to take it further up the structure of the organisation. Don't just complain in general terms. Describe specific instances of the behaviour that is causing you problems and explain why and how it is preventing you from working well.

Work roles and responsibilities

When you are offered employment in an organisation, you should have a proper job title and written job description. This should help you to be very clear about your work role, your place and responsibilities within your setting and how your role relates to the roles of others. Your job description should set out who provides you with management and support, and who (if anyone) you are responsible for managing and supporting. You should be careful not to stray into areas of work which lie outside your role and which are the responsibility of other people.

Theory into practice

Pete works in a large nursery, co-ordinating the after-school and holiday provision. His job description lists his responsibilities and duties as:

- taking overall responsibility for planning the environment, resources and day-to-day running of the after-school and holiday clubs
- liaising with parents
- recruiting and supporting the staff for the clubs
- managing the budget for the clubs.

He has been in the post for a while, and finds that he is now taking on activities which are outside his role, such as:

- applying for grants and fundraising

- speaking on behalf of the nursery to the local media.

He begins to realise that these are really the responsibility of the deputy manager, Rachel, and she is irritated by him encroaching on her work role. Think about Pete's position.

- What might the consequences be if nothing changes in this situation?
- What may happen if neither Pete nor Rachel do something pro-active?
- What could Pete and Rachel do to make it work better for everyone?

Assessment activity 4.1

Look through your collection of aims, mission statements, quality standards, policies and procedures from your various work placements.

1 Describe your own adherence to codes of practice for each placement setting. Use the Good practice checklist on page 148 as a reference. **P1**

2 Note the differences between the documents used in various settings. Why do you think there are these variations – is it to do with the nature of the setting (full-time/sessional, home-based/centre-based, maintained/voluntary/private/independent sector, etc.) or some other influence? **M1**

4.2 How to prepare for your work placements

Your work placements are a very significant part of your BTEC course; they are where you are able to put what you have learned in theory into practice in real-life situations. The reality of working with children and families is rather different from learning about it in the classroom and from books.

Your tutor will provide you with the necessary support to arrange work placements in four different settings.

The work placements you undertake will depend on what is available currently in your area, but they must provide you with experience of working with all four of the age ranges:

- 0–1 year
- 1–3 years
- 3–5 years
- 5–8 years.

Your work placements may be in a number of different settings:

- with a **childminder**
- in a **pre-school** (or playgroup)
- in a **private nursery**
- in a **nursery school** (or primary school).

Each of these settings offers you different experiences because of their differing locations, sectors and organisation as summarised in the table below.

A **children's centre** may offer experience similar to a private nursery and/or a nursery school. They are of varying sizes, offering a range of services to various age groups and managed in a variety of ways.

You may also have the opportunity to work in a setting for children with special educational needs or in a hospital setting.

Provision	Type	Age range	Number of children	Registration and inspection	Ownership/ management	Funding
Childminder	Home-based	Few months to teens	Up to six (of which only three under-5s)	Ofsted (England), CSIW (Wales)	Self-employed, has written contract with parents, runs independent business, sets own policies	Charge parents fees and a few receive state funding for 3- and 4-year-olds
Pre-school (or playgroup)	Community-based	2½ to 4 years	Usually up to 25	Ofsted (England), CSIW (Wales)	Many run by voluntary management committees largely composed of parents who employ the staff and work with them to develop policies	Receive state funding for 3- and 4-year-olds for several hours per week but also charge parents fees
Private day nursery	Centre-based	Few months to school age	Wide range from very small to very large	Ofsted (England), CSIW (Wales)	Private business, staff employed by owner who sets policies (working with staff)	Receive state funding for 3- and 4-year-olds for several hours per week but also charge parents fees
Nursery school or primary school	State maintained	3 to 8 years	Class sizes up to 30	Ofsted (England), Estyn (Wales)	Publicly owned, staff employed by governing body/local authority, governors work with head and other staff to develop policies	Funded by local authority, free to parents

You must prepare carefully before you start each work placement so you get the most out of your experiences, and also are able to produce the written evidence you need for your assessment for the BTEC qualification. This is all set out in the specification booklet, and you must read through carefully what is said in Unit 4.

Once you have chosen and arranged your work placements, you need to prepare to ensure that you assemble all the necessary evidence.

Making records of your work placements

To make the most of the learning opportunities of your placements, you need to reflect on what you learn and achieve during your time in the various settings, and to be able to do this, you need to keep a record of what you do and what happens while you are there in your Professional Practice logbook.

Talk to your tutor about how to make this record. You will need to build up a record of working:

- in a range of settings with different characteristics
- with children in a variety of age groups
- with disabled children as well as children whose development is following the usual pattern
- to provide a range of experiences and activities for children according to their stage of development and the nature of the setting

- with small and large teams of colleagues
- within the context of complying with different policies and procedures.

Your logbook should build into a valuable resource for you to reflect on your learning on the course and the development of your knowledge and skills as a professional practitioner.

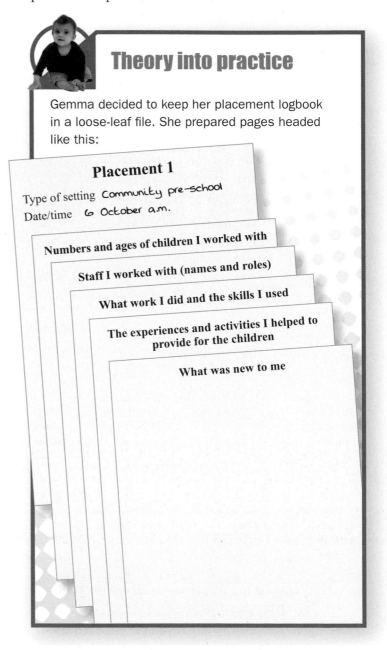

Theory into practice

Gemma decided to keep her placement logbook in a loose-leaf file. She prepared pages headed like this:

Placement 1

Type of setting Community pre-school
Date/time 6 October a.m.

Numbers and ages of children I worked with

Staff I worked with (names and roles)

What work I did and the skills I used

The experiences and activities I helped to provide for the children

What was new to me

This sort of diary record will provide a good overall picture of what you do in each placement setting, but you should supplement it with more in-depth records of particular aspects of your experiences.

Case study: Gemma's placements records

Besides her regular entries, Gemma made records of:

- her observations of individual children – she included what they were doing and saying, what they could do and what they could almost do (what they were ready to progress to next)
- her work with a disabled child
- the documents the setting showed her, such as policies and procedures, communications to parents, curriculum framework documents
- her attendance at team meetings.

For each, she noted the knowledge and skills she was using.

1 **From whom should Gemma have obtained permission to make these records?**

2 **What units of your BTEC qualification do you think these records would link to?**

Good practice checklist

When you are making records like this, make sure you:

- keep up your diary regularly – if you leave too long before you write it up after the session you spent in the setting, you will forget important details
- write legibly and set your records out clearly so you can share them with others – colleagues in the setting, your tutor and fellow learners
- pay attention to the quality of the content rather than getting caught up in spending time on beautiful presentation
- maintain confidentiality – be careful where you leave your records and who has the opportunity to look at them, and don't use the names of children or colleagues.

Assessment activity 4.2

Practise keeping records of your activities at your placements. Start a diary/logbook, and also prepare a more in-depth record of an observation of a child. (You learnt about observation in Unit 3 page 127.)

4.3 How to use your observations of children to enable you to promote their development and learning

Assessment for your BTEC qualification requires you to make records of observations of children and show how you use these observations. You will derive the greatest benefit from your work placements by making careful observations of children and using those observations to meet their needs and plan learning opportunities for them. Observation is the crucial element in the cycle of the **planned approach** to working with children.

The planned approach

The planned approach consists of the processes of:

- collecting information about a child, through observation and other ways such as talking to parents and other professionals
- assessment of the stage of development they have reached and identifying what interests them and what their needs are

- planning experiences, activities and routines to meet their current needs and help them progress
- implementation of your plans
- monitoring the child's progress and evaluating the success of your plans.

The processes in the planned approach make up a continuous cycle (see the diagram below):

- By reflecting on the information you collect, you can assess the stage of learning and development a child has reached and find out what interests them.
- These assessments point you towards the likely next steps in the child's learning and development and their current needs so you can plan experiences and activities for the child which will help them to progress and routines which suit them.

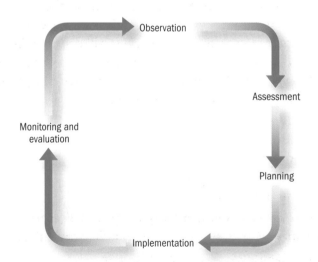

▲ **The planned approach**

- Further observations and other information are needed to monitor whether the child's development is progressing as you had hoped, and whether their

needs are being met, and to evaluate the success of the experiences/activities/routines you planned and provided.
- These observations take you back to the beginning of the cycle, ready to make the plans to continue to support the child's progress.

Observations

To be able to meet the needs of children and provide them with experiences and activities which will help them progress in their development, you must be a skilful observer. You learned about observations in Unit 3, page 127. Your work placements give you the opportunity to practise this all-important skill.

Observations are not an end in themselves – they are only of value if you use them to:

- assess a child's stage of development, their interests and their needs
- plan how to meet the child's needs and provide opportunities for them to develop and learn.

Remember, the aim of your observations is to collect information to help you identify the stage of development reached by the child. It should clarify for you what they can do, what they are already achieving. This assessment will in turn enable you to appreciate what the child can almost do, what they are ready to move on to next in their developmental progress.

Observation can also give you vital information about what interests a child has – what particularly fascinates or intrigues them at the moment, and that will be invaluable in helping you to plan experiences and activities to lead their learning forward. This may be just a broad interest an individual child has at the moment (tractors, bears or tall buildings) or their current 'schema' (putting things inside other things, investigating 'up' and 'down').

Over the four work placements, you must carry out observations of children in each of the age groups:

- 0–1 year
- 1–3 years
- 3–5 years
- 5–8 years

and also make sure you include observations of disabled children and children with special educational needs. You are required to carry out 20 observations across all your work placements. These must cover different aspects of children's development:

- physical
- social
- emotional
- cognitive (or intellectual)
- communication.

One observation is likely to provide you with more than one aspect of children's development.

Opportunities to carry out observations of children will need careful planning and the support of your tutor and work placement setting to ensure that you cover all the age ranges and disabled children/children with special educational needs, as well as all the aspects of development. You will need to keep careful records of which age groups and areas of development you have covered so you can make plans to fill any gaps left as you move from one work placement to another.

You must obtain written parental permission for your observations. For each one, you will need to select the type of observation technique and way of recording according to the age group of the child and the aspect of their development you want to observe and assess.

Theory into practice

Gemma's first observation and assessment of a child was of an 18-month-old baby, so she chose to use a descriptive narrative approach.

A subsequent observation was related to the pattern of behaviour of a 3-year-old, so she used event sampling and the ABC (antecedent, behaviour, consequence) recording technique. She recorded:

- the *antecedent* – what was going on immediately before the behaviour she was observing took place
- the *behaviour* being observed, together with a note of who else was present (adults and other children), how long the behaviour lasted, the time and place
- the *consequence* – what happened immediately after the behaviour she was observing.

She found this helped her to recognise the pattern of cause and effect and to work out whether there was a behaviour problem and, if so, what was prompting it.

Planning for learning

Once you have recorded your observations and made your assessments based on those observations, you are in a position to consider how to support the child to move on in their developmental progress. You will know what they are already achieving, be in a position to consider what they may be ready to move on to, and have some clues about what they will enjoy doing to help them learn. You will be ready to make plans for their learning and development, to contribute to the curriculum for children.

The curriculum provided for children in a setting consists of all the activities and experiences which enable them to learn and develop. Some of these activities and experiences will be planned, and some will be unplanned. Often, it is spontaneous learning opportunities, which have not been planned but arise out of events or changing circumstances, which provide the best learning. In England, the planned curriculum in your work placement settings is likely to be based on the Curriculum Guidance for the Foundation Stage and/or the Birth to Three Framework (combined into the Early Years Foundation Stage from 2008). You should make sure you become familiar with the relevant documents.

In each of your placement settings, you must plan and implement five experiences or activities for a child or a group of children which you consider will promote their development and learning. This means you have to make and implement 20 plans in all. Make sure that your plans cover all of the areas of development:

- physical
- social
- emotional
- cognitive (or intellectual)
- communication.

As with observation, an activity you plan is likely to contribute to more than one area of a child's learning.

Remember that young children learn from:

- play
- first-hand experiences
- talking

so your plans should offer opportunities for all of these.

Theory into practice

When Gemma began to think about making plans for the child she had observed and assessed, she considered the various play activities available in her work placement setting which might be relevant to the various aspects of the child's development. These included:

- drawing and painting
- dough or clay
- cutting and sticking
- water and sand
- role play, construction and problem-solving equipment
- books and tapes
- IT equipment
- singing and making music.

She realised she had a lot of scope to include these play activities in her plans. For example, she thought that cutting and sticking activities could help develop fine motor control.

Besides the usual play activities found in most settings, make sure you also include plenty of opportunities for first-hand experiences – experiences of the real world which enable children to explore, discover and learn through their senses. Don't just think in terms of limited little 'activities' for children – think in broader terms about the experiences of the world and life you want them to have. You could introduce children to the coldness of snow by bringing in a bowl of snow and putting on the table with some scoops – but for them to really experience snow, they need to put on coats, hats and wellingtons and go out into it. Singing 'Rain, rain, go away' while looking at rain through the window will not be as memorable or develop understanding of the wetness of rain as running around outdoors in the rain and singing as loudly as possible! Plan to give children exciting and vivid experiences, not dry 'activities' sitting around an 'interest' table.

And everything must be combined with lots of good talk between adults and children – making comments, asking questions, offering suggestions and giving encouragement.

Good practice checklist

- Base your plans around what you have found out about a child's interests. They will throw themselves into experiences and activities which relate to their current passion.
- As you develop your ideas for experiences and activities, discuss them with colleagues in the setting to be sure they feel comfortable and confident about what you plan.
- Make sure that your plans are realistic for the nature of the environment in the setting and the resources that are available in it. You can't expect to organise elaborate large-scale activities in the small domestic setting of childminding, and it may be more difficult to arrange to take a group of children out from a centre-based setting. Make all the necessary preparations – gather equipment and materials in sufficient quantities for the number of children involved.

▲ **Provide exciting and vivid learning experiences**

And the story does not finish with planning – or even with implementation. For every plan you make, your further observations will be needed to monitor the children's learning and to evaluate the success of your plans. Each time, take yourself round the cycle of the planned approach. You will then be able to see how you can improve your plans for experiences and activities for the future.

Using the planned approach of:

observation-assessment-planning-implementation-monitoring/evaluation

is not an easy skill to acquire and it is something you will go on working at throughout your career. Use your work placements to practise the approach and record what it is telling you.

Assessment activity 4.3

Begin practising the use of the planned approach.

1 Carry out and record an observation of a child. **P2**

2 Reflect on what this observation tells you about:
   • what the child can do – the stage of development they have reached and what they are ready for next
   • what interests this child. **M2**

3 Plan an experience or activity to help their progress. **P5**

4 Implement your plan.

5 Monitor the child's progress through further observation. **M4**

6 Evaluate how well your plan went and draw conclusions for future planning. **M4 D1 D2**

4.4 How to use your observations of children to meet their needs through routines

Some of the information you obtain from observation in a work placement will tell you how well children's needs are being met through the routines of the setting. These routines may be concerned with aspects of care such as:
- nappy changing or toileting
- rest and sleep
- washing (or even bathing) and dressing
- feeding and giving meals

or with aspects of health and safety such as:
- cleaning up
- preparing food in hygienic ways
- checking the safety of equipment or materials
- supervising children.

Make sure that during your placement in each setting, you observe and record four different routines – that will be 16 routines altogether across all your work placements. Include in your records:
- a brief description of what happened, what you see and hear, what was said by whom
- what your role is expected to be in the routine
- how the routine meets the needs of the child concerned
- any implications of the routine for the setting.

Theory into practice

Gemma's first placement was in a private day nursery. She spent part of her time in the baby room, and part with the 3–4-year-olds. She decided to observe and record routines for:

- bottle feeding and mealtimes
- nappy changing
- sleep and rest
- handover of children at the end of the day.

Her records included such content as:

- Babies are bottle-fed and their nappies changed according to a set routine, not when each one is hungry or uncomfortable. So there were some crying babies desperate for their next feed and I saw a few sore bottoms.
- The practitioner I observed just silently and briskly changed the baby's nappy. She didn't play with him or talk to him, and I thought that was a lost opportunity for getting to know him. When it was my turn, I took my time and smiled and chatted to the babies when I changed them.

- As I got to know baby J (10 months) well, I observed that as he began to get tired, he sucked his thumb for a few seconds at a time, but when he started rub behind his ear, he was really ready to be put in his cot and would drop off to sleep immediately. I was proud that my close observation of him led me to understand his individual needs so well and be able to meet them.
- The staff checked carefully that the person each child is handed over to is on the list on that child's file and if it was someone they didn't recognise, they asked for a signature. I think that protected each member of staff and the nursery from making a mistake.
- I was asked to help the children clear away at the end of the meal, letting them do as much of it as they could manage. I would just have gone ahead and done it for them, but I was surprised how confident and capable they were.

Assessment activity 4.4

Practise making records of your part in children's routines in your work placements. Include

- a brief description of what happened – what you see and hear, what was said by whom
- what your role is expected to be in the routine

- how the routine meets the needs of the child concerned
- any implications of the routine for the setting.

When you begin your career as a professional working with children and families, you must take responsibility for developing and improving your professional work practice, especially in response to changes. As you settle into your career, you will find that the context in which you work is constantly changing:

- You will take on new responsibilities or work roles.
- New ideas and practices will emerge in the sector, often based on new research findings.
- New legal requirements, frameworks and types of setting will come on the scene.

And, of course, the children you work with will be changing all the time as they grow and develop.

To be able to develop in your professional role, you will need to:

- understand your role and responsibilities as a professional practitioner
- reflect on your work practice
- examine how your values and attitudes underpin the way you work
- take advantage of any opportunities for increasing your professional knowledge and skills
- use what you learn to develop and improve your practice in meeting the needs of children and providing for learning experiences and activities them.

It is essential that you become a **reflective practitioner**. You cannot afford to feel that because you have a qualification, there is nothing left to learn. This is a challenging and constantly changing sector of work, and you must ensure that you continue to expand your knowledge, re-examine your values and attitudes and develop your skills.

Reflection or self-assessment is not something you do once; it's not taking a snapshot of yourself on one day or one week in your working life. The questioning approach needs to become part of your whole working life, a habit you get into, something you do regularly and throughout your professional life. It is worthwhile to put in the time and effort this requires because you will:

- get a clearer picture of what you actually do in your work role and whether you are really being effective
- feel more confident about how you work with children and families – you will feel more sure about the things you're getting right, and more able to take on new developments, new roles and other changes
- enjoy your work more and get on better with your colleagues and other professionals, and earn their respect
- be clearer about the things you are not so sure about or feel you need to learn more about
- reach higher standards in your work and provide a better service to children and families.

Monitoring and evaluating your work practice

Reflective practice is also not something someone else can do to you or for you – you have to take responsibility for your own professional development. The first step in this process is to review your own practice, first **monitoring** it and then **evaluating** it.

Key term

A **reflective practitioner** is someone who takes a questioning approach to their work, taking time to:

- think critically about what they do in their work, analysing how they do it and why they do it that way
- assess the effectiveness of what they are doing at work and how they can become more effective.

Key terms

Monitoring your work practice means taking a long hard look at the way you work, how you do it and what the results are, and why you work as you do.
Evaluating your performance means assessing the quality of your practice by asking yourself questions such as, 'Is what I do good enough? Does it lead to the best possible outcomes for children and families?'

To monitor and evaluate your own work successfully, you need to be honest with yourself. Admit to yourself what you really do and say at work, not what you would like to be doing and saying, or what you think you ought to be doing and saying. You will sometimes need to reflect on an area of your work which you are finding difficult or challenging. But remember also to reflect on areas of your work that usually go well – it's good for your self-esteem to celebrate your successes!

The records you keep of your work placements and the feedback you are given by colleagues in those settings will be the valuable raw material for this process of monitoring and evaluation.

Monitoring and evaluating your performance at work is not easy, so make sure you seek help and support from others. When you are in employment, your manager or supervisor should set aside time to discuss your work with you regularly. While you are studying, make full use of opportunities for discussion of your work placements with your tutor.

Identifying strengths and areas for development

As you develop your habit of monitoring and evaluating your work practice, you will become able to:

- value your own good practice (your strengths)
- identify any gaps in your knowledge and skills (your weaknesses or areas for development).

Many of us find it difficult to identify our strengths. We may have been brought up not to 'show off' about what we're good at, and feel it is conceited to talk about our strengths. It is really important, however, to know what our strengths are so we can build upon them.

'Weakness' is an uncomfortable word; most of us do not want to admit to weakness in any aspect of our life.

Theory into practice

Gemma used the diary and other records she had kept of her work placements to monitor and evaluate the effectiveness of her practice. She chose one aspect of her work practice to start monitoring and evaluating – supporting children to develop social relationships with other children. She read through her notes and picked out relevant aspects of her practice and added to her loose-leaf file by using this format:

Supporting children's social development: relationships with other children

This is what I have done:
I set up a play café so children could play together
I told P that he should share the bricks with R
I praised V when he helped C to pick up the books she had dropped
I tried to calm things down when T and J were fighting over the ride-on tractor

My practice has been successful in these ways:
Three children played together in a very co-operative way for over half-an-hour in the café, using their own ideas
V was much more confident later in the morning when it was his turn to hand out the slices of apple – he is usually too timid to take the plate round

Some examples of when things haven't gone so well:
P just refused and I couldn't find a way of persuading him
Both T and J got very upset – I obviously didn't go about it the right way

Perhaps it is more helpful in your professional life to think in terms of areas for development which arise from:

- gaps in your knowledge
- areas where you have had little direct experience.

Theory into practice

Gemma used her monitoring and evaluation of her practice to identify her strengths and areas for development, noting them like this:

Supporting children's social development: relationships with other children

My strengths

I have good ideas for play activities that encourage children to play co=operatively.

I am ready to praise children when they help others or are kind to one another.

My areas for development

I tend to 'tell' children to do things rather than showing them how.

I'm a bit too ready to leap in – I should let children work out their own problems and disagreements and only intervene when it's really necessary.

When you enter employment, your manager or supervisor should provide you with regular opportunities to think about your practice, providing you with feedback and support. This will help you to become a reflective practitioner.

Exploring your attitudes and values

An important part of monitoring your practice and identifying why you approach your work as you do is to think about how your attitudes and values affect your practice.

Your attitudes and values may come from:

- your personal philosophy on life which has developed from your religious beliefs or from values that reflect traditions linked to your cultural, social or family background. These might affect, for example, your attitudes about appropriate roles in families
- your experiences of your childhood – your memories of your personal life affect how you perceive other people
- what you are learning during your training – both on your course and in your work placement
- what you have read, especially research findings.

You may find it difficult to think critically about the effect of your personal experiences and memories on your beliefs and values. The attitudes that come from these sources are likely to be more subjective or negative than the attitudes you have developed through your training or from reading research findings. For example, you might hold the subjective view that all mothers should stay at home with their babies or you may have had negative experiences such as being bullied at school.

Extension activity

Think about some of your attitudes regarding what is 'correct' or 'proper' about how children should be brought up.

1 Where did you get these attitudes from? Perhaps from the way you were brought up yourself? (You might think that was the 'best' way or you might think the opposite!)

2 How do they affect the way you respond to the parents of the children you work with? Do you sometimes 'disapprove' of certain parents? How does that affect your relationship with them?

Tamsin has been thinking about how her experience of her own family life has affected her attitudes towards children and families.

She has a younger cousin, Mollie, who is disabled. Her aunts and her mother have always been very protective towards Mollie, and Tamsin remembers most of her childhood being told 'wait for Mollie', 'don't be so rough with her', 'you mustn't play that game because Mollie can't join in'.

The pre-school where she has had her recent work placement has three children with differing impairments, and Tamsin was surprised at the attitudes towards the disabled children there. They were not over-protected and the main approach seemed to be that all children should be helped to join in all activities. She was amazed at what the disabled children could do, given a bit of adult support and lots of encouragement. She now realises that she has had low expectations of what it is possible for disabled children to achieve, and that had prevented her offering them the full range of play and learning opportunities.

1. **What aspects of your personal or family life, including your cultural or traditional values, affect the way you approach working with children and families? Try to identify one or two attitudes to your work that are influenced in this way.**

2. **What positive effects do these attitudes have on your work?**

3. **Are there possible negative effects your attitudes might have? Discuss this with someone you feel could help you explore this in a professional way.**

4. **How can you guard against these potentially negative influences and make sure you work in a professional way in future?**

If some of your work practice is influenced by subjective emotions or negative experiences, you need to take a good look at whether this is preventing you from working effectively, so that you can do something about it. You will only be able to do this if you are honest with yourself. You will probably need the help of someone else to do this, and that has to be someone you can trust, have confidence in and respect as a fellow professional.

Methods of reflecting

The main route to becoming a reflective practitioner is to look carefully at the way you work, and why you work as you do (your underpinning attitudes and values). This involves you in asking yourself questions about your work:

- What did I do?
- Why did I do it like that?
- What do I do well (my strengths)?
- What do I need to improve (my weaknesses)?

Self-assessment and reflection can be a great help in everyday working life, enabling you to solve problems and giving you the confidence to tackle difficult situations. When you become aware that an aspect of your practice needs improvement or you are trying to resolve a problem, one approach is to look at things from a different perspective, to consider different ways of working and be ready to try them out. Ask yourself questions such as:

- What other ways of doing this do I know of?
- Are there alternative approaches I have heard of?
- What would happen if I did things differently?

Your answers may be based on what you are learning on your course and what you see being done in your work placements.

You may find different approaches to aspects of work with children and families in each of your work placements. These differences may be due to:

- the differing nature of the placements, for example, a childminder will have different relationships with parents from the sort of relationships you see between parents and staff in a large nursery. It is inevitable that a childminder, who has parents coming into their own home, will be more friendly in a personal way

- the ages of the children, for example, the attitude to the balance of risk and safety is likely to be very different in an open-access play scheme from that in a community pre-school
- the ethos or aims of the setting, for example, Montessori or Steiner establishments base their practice on specific theories of children's learning.

The variety of your work placements will give you the opportunity to compare and contrast various ways of working. Share what you learn at each work placement with your tutor and fellow learners. In discussion with them, identify the positive aspects of each approach. You will be able to draw on this analysis when you are seeking alternative ways of working for your own future professional development.

Theory into practice

- What different approaches have you seen in the various work placements you have spent time in?
- Why do you think there were these differences?
- Give some examples of how the different approaches might be useful in different situations.

To make this work, you need to have an open mind. You must be ready to consider methods of working that are quite different from the ways you have worked in the past, and be ready to take on changes which will mean you can be more effective in your work. In recent years, more and more long-established and experienced practitioners have opened themselves up to ideas from new ways of working such as:

- the High Scope approach
- the methods used in nurseries in Reggio Emilia in Italy
- the Thomas Coram techniques for listening to children.

Their readiness to learn these new ways of thinking and working have benefited the children and families they work with.

Extension activity

Use a search engine such as Google to browse the internet and find out more about High Scope, Reggio Emilia and listening to children the Thomas Coram way.

How to plan your professional development

Throughout your career, it will be your responsibility to plan how to develop and improve your practice (building on your strengths and tackling your weaknesses). You cannot take the view that you are ever 'fully trained' – there is always something new to learn which will make you better at your job. You need to learn how to plan for continuously changing and improving your practice.

Your professional development plans should consist of:

- setting yourself goals and targets
- deciding how you are going to move towards your goals and targets – what action you are going to take
- identifying the people who can help you
- deciding how you will monitor your progress.

Goals and targets

The first step in making a continuing professional development (CPD) plan is to decide what your goals or targets are.

'Goal' and 'target' have very similar meanings. A goal is what you want to achieve; a target is something you aim at. You can use either word to describe the results that you want from making and implementing your plan. Sometimes 'goal' is used for a long-term objective, and 'targets' used to mean the manageable steps (or 'milestones') towards your goal which you can achieve in the shorter term. Sometimes you will see the word 'objective' used, also with a similar meaning.

You will be led towards your goals and targets by looking at your strengths and areas for development.

- Your strengths will show you what you are already doing well and could build on and develop further.
- Your areas for development will show you what you need to change and improve.

Ask yourself, What am I trying to achieve? Where do I want to go next in developing my professional knowledge and skills?

Theory into practice

Gemma used the strengths and areas for development she had identified to help her set goals. She decided she wanted to:

- develop further
  - her ability to support children's co-operative play
  - her readiness to praise children
- tackle her tendencies to
  - direct and instruct children too much, rather than helping them to find things out for themselves and engaging in conversations with them
  - intervene too much too soon in what children were doing.

When you set yourself goals or targets, make sure that they are SMART, which stands for:

Specific

Measurable

Achievable

Realistic

Timed.

Good practice checklist

Be SMART:

- **S**pecific: be clear and precise about what it is you want to achieve; don't set vague or generalised goals.
- **M**easurable: decide how you will know when you have reached your target. What will your practice look like? What will be happening in your daily work?
- **A**chievable: will you be able to reach your goal in a reasonably short period of time (weeks rather than months)? Don't be hard on yourself and aim for huge changes all in one leap.
- **R**ealistic: set yourself targets that you can really do something about, which are possible in your work role and your setting.
- **T**imed: set yourself deadlines, dates for achieving your goals.

Theory into practice

Gemma defined her goals as:

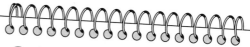

> By the end of my next placement, I want to receive feedback from others in the setting that I:
>
> - am skilled at supporting children's co-operative play, and at praising children for their efforts and achievements
> - support children's learning through conversations and asking them suitable questions
> - don't intervene inappropriately in children's play and disagreements.

Gemma's goals are SMART. It would not have been SMART to say, 'I want to be better at communicating with children.'

Deciding what action to take

When you have set your goals/targets, you have to plan what you need to do to achieve them. This might include:

- finding and using learning opportunities
- researching up-to-date information.

After you have completed your BTEC qualification and entered the world of employment, you will find that there will still be learning opportunities available to you such as:

- further formal courses leading to additional qualifications, either in a group face-to-face with a tutor, or as distance learning, or through a combination of the two (open or 'blended' learning)
- workshops, seminars, conferences
- 'on-the-job' learning, such as:
  - shadowing – working alongside and observing the practice of other practitioners, in your setting or elsewhere
  - coaching – a manager or other colleague encouraging you to develop new skills, demonstrating or modelling aspects of practice for you, and giving you constructive feedback on your efforts.

Theory into practice

Gemma felt that further study on her BTEC course, especially Unit 1, would help her achieve her goals, and she also discussed with her tutor how to seek support from the setting in her next work placement to allow her to observe the experienced practitioners there and benefit from their coaching.

Keeping up to date with new ideas and developments can provide you with insight to help you reach your goals.

Good practice checklist

There are different ways of keeping yourself up to date with the latest developments in your field:

- Magazines and journals like *Children Now, Nursery World, Who Minds?, Contact Under Five, Practical Pre-school* and *Practical Professional Childcare* contain articles and news which help you to keep abreast of new policies, emerging research findings, forthcoming conferences and other events, newly published books and government consultations.
- You can find out about books – both established texts and new publications – from reading lists provided for courses and resource lists in, for example, the Birth to Three Matters framework and by the library at the National Children's Bureau, and book reviews.
- Networking by taking an active part in local, regional and national networks of relevant organisations will be invaluable. You will meet a wider range of people working in your field, and find out about new developments and learning opportunities. The setting you work in may be a member of an organisation like the Pre-school Learning Alliance, or the National Day Nurseries Association; you may become a member of the National Childminding Association or the Professional Association of Nursery Nurses.
- Browsing on the internet by 'Googling' – enter key words which lead to relevant information and then select the most useful results – will help you to find out about current and recent research and government consultations and policy proposals. If you are not confident in using the internet, perhaps one of your early goals should be to acquire this skill.

When you look at the list of actions you have decided are necessary to reach your goals, you might feel it all looks a bit daunting. If it does, use the approach of 'eating the elephant'. The answer to the question 'How do you eat an elephant?' is 'One bite at a time'. Break down your planned actions into smaller steps, and tackle them a bite at a time rather than launching into the whole of it at once.

▲ **Using the internet is a valuable way of keeping up to date**

When you have listed your actions, put them into a logical time order – this needs to be done before that – so you know where to start.

Help from others

You are likely to need some support in putting your plan into action, and you need to think about this in advance and make it part of your plan. You may need to get the permission and/or co-operation of your manager or other members of your team. If you are asking your manager for coaching, or colleagues or other professionals for shadowing opportunities, you will need to discuss this with them well in advance. If you want to undertake a training course, or go to a conference, you will need to find out if it can be funded from your setting's training budget.

When you start putting your plan into operation, you are likely at first to feel enthusiasm and even excitement; you will enjoy doing new things. However, it is likely that after a while, you get a bit stuck because:

- you may find the additional work tiring
- you may encounter practical difficulties in your personal life such as illness (yours or someone else's)
- your confidence and initial enthusiasm may dip.

This is when you need to turn to other people for some support. Some people feel that to look for support from others is to admit to weakness and failure, but the opposite is true. We all need support when we are tackling challenges, and it is a sign of professionalism and personal strength to seek support.

You can turn to all kinds of people for practical, emotional or specialist professional support, such as:

- a colleague
- your manager
- a professional in another setting
- a tutor
- your partner or a member of your family
- a friend
- a helpline.

They may be able to offer you support such as:

- practical assistance in completing a task at work
- praise and encouragement to boost your confidence and morale
- crucial information you have not yet encountered
- a listening ear
- a chance to do something entirely different for a while
- a treat
- practical back-up such as giving you a lift or repairing your computer.

Monitoring your progress

You need to check regularly that you are putting your planned actions into effect and evaluate their success – looking at how close you are to achieving your goal. You could set yourself dates on which you are going to review your plan and the progress you have made.

Theory into practice

Leonie drew up her professional development plan using this format.

Leonie's goal is SMART, but if she had said 'I'll aim to be better at health and safety', it would *not* have been SMART.

My goal is that by the end of May, I will be able to carry out a risk assessment of a setting.

To achieve this goal, I am going to:
• complete the short course on risk assessment being offered by the local authority
• work with S in our nursery while she carries out next term's risk assessment.

The other people I will need to involve are:
• the manager of the nursery to get permission and funding for the course
• S – to get her agreement to my shadowing her
• C – to take over from me in the baby room when I'm working with S
• D – to fix the lights on my bike so it's safe for me to cycle home in the dark after the course.

I shall monitor my progress by
• making sure I've completed the course by the end of March
• after the work with S in April, reviewing my confidence to do risk assessment on my own.

Assessment activity 4.5

1 For each of your work placements, choose an aspect of your work to reflect on, as Gemma did (page 167).

  a) Monitor your practice: review the skills you used in your work placement related to that aspect of practice. **P6**

  b) Evaluate your practice: pick out examples of where you were effective, and those where things didn't go so well. Identify the strengths and areas for development of your practice. **D3**

2 Choose one of the areas of your practice that you identified as needing development. Draw up a plan
  • setting yourself goals
  • describing what you are going to do to build on your knowledge and skills
  • listing the people you will need to help you
  • setting out how you will monitor your progress. **M5**

End of unit assessment

Look through your placement diaries and other records such as observations.

1. Check that you have recorded what you did in each setting, and noted the feedback you received from colleagues there and your tutor.

2. Identify some examples of the knowledge and skills you used in each placement. **P6**

3. Choose one of the placements and select a specific example of your contribution to providing children with experiences and activities that support their learning. Describe what you did with the children in detail. **M4**

4. Compare how the policies and procedures of the various work placements affected the way you worked there. **M1**

5. Identify your strengths and areas for development revealed by your placement records. **D2 D3**

6. Which units of your BTEC course are relevant to each of your strengths and areas for development and can help you strengthen your professional practice for the future? **M5**

7. Now think about:
   a) How effective do you think your practice was in each of your placements? **D3**
   b) How do you plan to go on developing your practice? What will be your next steps? **P6 M5**
   c) What have been the benefits of reflecting on your practice? **P7**

References and further reading

Bruce, T. and Meggitt, C. (2006) *Child Care and Education*, Hodder Arnold

Hobart, C. and Frankel, J. (2004) *A Practical Guide to Child Observation and Assessment*, 3rd edition, Nelson Thornes

Grading criteria	Assessment activity	Page number
To achieve a pass grade the evidence must show that the learner is able to:		
P1 describe own adherence to codes of practice for each placement setting	4.1	150
P2 observe and identify the physical, social, emotional, cognitive and communication needs and skills of children in each age range and in four different settings	4.2 4.3	153 157
P3 observe and identify the individual needs of children with additional needs	4.2	153
P4 describe four different routines within each placement setting, including own role	4.4	158
P5 plan, consult on, prepare and implement five activities for a child/group of children to promote specific areas of development within each placement setting	4.3	157
P6 review own performance in each of the work placements and identify areas for further self-development	4.5 End of unit assessment	167 168
P7 describe the role of continuing professional development for workers in the Children's Care, Learning and Development sector	End of unit assessment	168
To achieve a merit grade the evidence must show that, in addition to the pass criteria, the learner is able to:		
M1 compare policies and practices at different placement settings	4.1 End of unit assessment	150 168
M2 interpret the observations undertaken in relation to children's skills and needs	4.3	157
M3 explain the importance of different care routines to the child/children, and the organisations/settings	4.4	158
M4 analyse each activity and suggest how each could be improved to increase the child's/children's learning and understanding	4.3 End of unit assessment	157 168
M5 produce a personal development plan and explain how it will potentially support own development	4.5 End of unit assessment	167 168
To achieve a distinction grade the evidence must show that, in addition to the pass and merit criteria, the learner is able to:		
D1 use the observations and interpretations to make recommendations for further action with respect to the skills and needs of the child/children concerned	4.3	157
D2 evaluate each activity in terms of its effectiveness in promoting children's development	4.3 End of unit assessment	157 168
D3 evaluate own effectiveness in each placement	4.5 End of unit assessment	167 168

Protecting children

Introduction

In the UK, in your town or city, and in your neighbourhood, there are children who are being physically, sexually and emotionally abused and neglected. There are adults who intentionally harm children or put them at risk from harm through neglect. The majority of families, however, care for their children appropriately and will not need intervention from professional services. This unit looks at how, by providing stimulating play and learning experiences for young children, early years practitioners are likely to become aware of children who give rise to concern because their behaviour and development are suffering. As an early years practitioner, you are in a prime position to alert others to possible abuse, support the child through any investigation that might take place and provide help for children who are known to have been abused. It is important, therefore, that you know about child abuse, why it may occur, how it may be recognised, its effects on young children and their families and what to do if they are concerned. It is also important to understand the importance of co-operating with other professionals using community support networks to assist in the protection of children.

What you need to learn

- How to recognise the indicators of potential child abuse
- How to work within the supporting legislation, regulation and codes of practice
- Good practice in responding to disclosure
- Strategies for supporting children, their families and other adults

Thinking points

There have been significant changes in the way we safeguard children and it is a responsibility that we all take very seriously as professionals. Over the last decade the services for children and their families have had to re-examine and evaluate ways in which the services could be made more effective and look closely at how professional judgements are to be made.

As an early years professional you may need to make some judgements about whether or not you have concerns about a child's safety. Imagine you have come across these scenarios in your setting:

- a 4-year-old child with fingertip bruising on his shoulder
- a 2-month-old baby who has severe nappy rash and appears to have not been bathed for the last two weeks
- a parent who looks tired and unwell, who has talked to you about her fears that she might 'do something she will regret' if she does not get some sleep soon
- a 16-year-old girl refuses to communicate and is depressed
- a young parent who asks you for advice on ways to get support in looking after her child as she has no extended family in the area
- an 8-year-old boy who has stolen food from other children's lunch boxes because he says he is always hungry.

Ask yourself these questions:

- Who do you think has responsibility for these children?
- What would be the most important thing for you to do first?
- What do you think you would need to consider first before making a professional judgement about whether or not there is cause for you to be concerned?
- What legislation and procedure will support the actions you might take?

Types of abuse

Abuse of children and young people is one of the most discussed issues of modern times. To recognise abuse, you need to first understand that life is potentially dangerous and that children and young people are vulnerable and sometimes need protection from adults and other children who may not treat them properly or who may cause them harm.

Child abuse is categorised into four main types:

- **physical abuse**: non-accidental injury; out of control punishment; shaken baby syndrome; deliberate harm; torture
- **sexual abuse**: incest; sex acts with children under the age of consent (16); sexual acts such as buggery/rape/oral sex; exposure; use of sexually explicit language; exposure to pornographic materials; photographing or videoing of children for sexual gratification; putting children under pressure to witness such acts
- **emotional abuse**: withdrawal of emotion and love; isolation; name-calling, ridiculing; threatening behaviour; humiliating the child; traumatising the child through one or more forms of abuse or torture
- **neglect**: when a child is neglected in a physical way, for example lack of food, not being kept clean and bathed or washed; clothes not washed – the extremes of all these examples.

There are also other particular types of abuse within these categories, such as bullying and domestic violence. These categories are nearly always linked to each other. For example:

- a child witnessing domestic violence (but not necessarily the victim of the violence) will suffer emotionally as a result
- a child who is raped (sexually abused) may also be physically harmed (physically abused) and suffer emotional trauma (emotional abuse)
- a young person who has been bullied could be injured (physical abuse), lose confidence and live in fear (emotional abuse).

Key terms

Child abuse is ill-treatment or harm inflicted on a child or young person, either deliberately or through neglect, which impairs or damages the child or young person's health, welfare or development.

Physical abuse may involve hitting, shaking, throwing, poisoning, scalding or burning, drowning, suffocating, biting, or otherwise causing physical harm to a child or young person; also referred to as non-accidental injury.

Emotional abuse is the persistent emotional ill-treatment of a child or young person which causes adverse effects on the child or young person's emotional well-being.

Sexual abuse involves forcing or coercing a child or young person to take part in sexual activities, whether or not the child is aware of what is happening.

Neglect is the persistent failure to meet the child or young person's basic needs.

Indicators of abuse

This section sets out to look at the *possible* indicators of abuse. When considering these indicators you should exercise caution as it could be tempting to see these as absolutes and there may be another perfectly reasonable explanation. The indicators are to be used as a guide. It is important that you always follow the guidelines and policies of the setting without jumping to conclusions or making assumptions.

When looking at the indicators of abuse we will categorise them just as the legislative framework does into four categories, but it is worth noting that when you are observing children many of the indicators will sit within all the categories, such as:

- lack of self-esteem
- loneliness and isolation
- over-anxiousness
- inappropriate behaviours
- overly aggressive or passive.

Physical abuse and injury

'Physical abuse may involve hitting, shaking, throwing, poisoning, burning or scalding, drowning, suffocating, or otherwise causing physical harm to a child.' (*Working Together to Safeguard Children*, 1999)

The table below shows characteristics that may be observed in a physically abused child.

▼ Indicators of physical abuse

Physical indicators	Behavioural indicators
Unexplained multiple bruises in unusual places (thighs, behind the knee, upper arm, back, neck, back of legs, etc. – see diagram of non-accidental injuries on page 174)	Unlikely or inconsistent explanations for injuries
	Withdrawn and overly compliant
Frequent bruises at different stages of healing	Aggressive
	Poor social skills
Bruises in the shape of objects, e.g. belts, rope, etc.	Low self-esteem
	Unusually fearful
Fingertip bruises	Hyper-alert to the environment (frozen watchfulness)
Unexplained/untreated burns and scalds	Reluctant to change clothing for swimming or PE
Unexplained/untreated fractures	Playing inappropriately with or without toys
Any bruising on a young baby who is not yet mobile	Inappropriately clinging to, or cowering from parent or carer
Cigarette burns	
Bite marks	
Internal injuries, which can cause pain, fever, vomiting, etc.	

It is important to remember that young children regularly develop bumps and bruises through falls and squabbles with siblings. You should also consider the age and stage of development of the child. For example, regular bumps on the head of a toddler who may fall or bang his head on furniture may be viewed differently from those of a 6-year-old who regularly appears with bumps or bruises on the head. When making a decision about a specific injury, you should also consider any explanation that has been given to you regarding the injury.

However, the physical signs of abuse are often different from those acquired through normal causes, as shown in the diagrams on page 174.

Parental attitude is important in assessing accidental and non-accidental injuries – when a child is suffering a severe and painful injury most parents would seek medical help. It is also important to remember that children of mixed race, of African or Asian heritage, may have dark pigmented areas at the tip of the spine, which at times extends into the buttocks. These spots are known as Mongolian Blue Spots. They are always of the same colour and do not go through changes of colour like bruises do.

Theory into practice

- A child has fallen over in the playground grazing both knees and his elbow.
- A child has bumped his head on the sharp corner of a cupboard.
- The child has pinch marks to his forearm.
- The child has bruising on his upper chest.

With a partner, discuss which of these injuries would be recorded on a body map.

Emotional abuse

'Emotional abuse is the persistent emotional ill treatment of a child such as to cause severe and adverse effects on the child's emotional development. It may involve conveying to children that they are worthless or unloved, inadequate, or valued only insofar as they meet the needs of another person ... Some level of emotional abuse is involved in all types of ill- treatment of a child, though it may occur alone.' (*Working Together to Safeguard Children*, 1999)

Emotional abuse is perhaps the most difficult and under-estimated form of abuse to detect because there are no physical indicators. There are also many other reasons why a child may be displaying these signs. Children may be unsettled by a change in the family function. There may be a new baby; a loss in the family or parents may have recently separated. There may be domestic violence in the home or an adult with mental health problems, putting the child under enormous stress. Older children and young people may be the

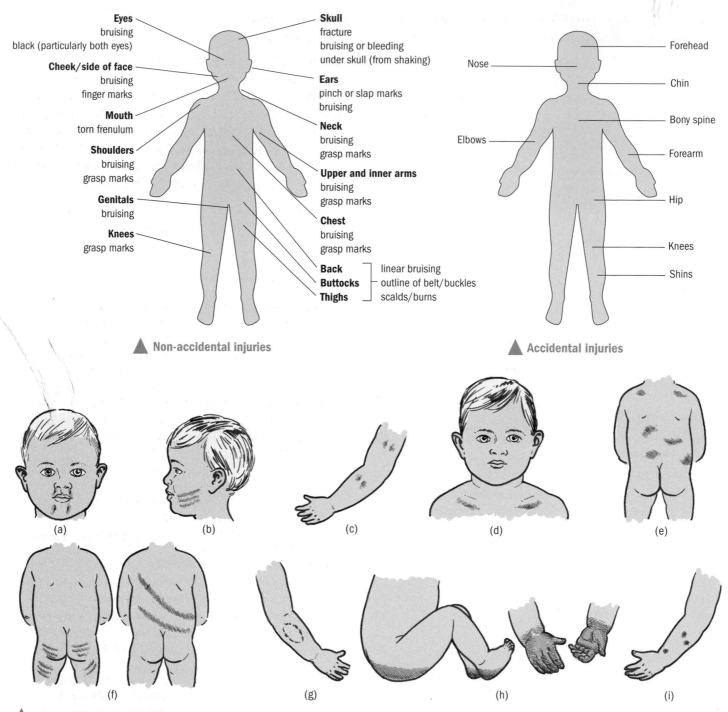

Non-accidental injuries

- **Eyes** — bruising, black (particularly both eyes)
- **Cheek/side of face** — bruising, finger marks
- **Mouth** — torn frenulum
- **Shoulders** — bruising, grasp marks
- **Genitals** — bruising
- **Knees** — grasp marks
- **Skull** — fracture, bruising or bleeding under skull (from shaking)
- **Ears** — pinch or slap marks, bruising
- **Neck** — bruising, grasp marks
- **Upper and inner arms** — bruising, grasp marks
- **Chest** — bruising, grasp marks
- **Back / Buttocks / Thighs** — linear bruising, outline of belt/buckles, scalds/burns

Accidental injuries

- Nose
- Forehead
- Chin
- Bony spine
- Elbows
- Forearm
- Hip
- Knees
- Shins

▲ Signs of physical abuse: (a) facial squeezing, (b) diffuse facial bruising, (c) pinch marks, (d) grip marks, (e) body bruising, (f) identifiable lesions, (g) bite marks, (h) burns or scalds, (i) cigarette burns

subject of domestic violence or forced to witness their parents being involved with drugs, sex or violence. Emotional abuse can include:

- parents or carers not giving love and attention
- constant shouting and screaming and insulting remarks

- continual criticism and threats
- humiliating punishments
- lack of approval – the child is never good enough, undermining their sense of self-worth.

Often parents are unaware that the way in which they are treating their children is abusive. Some emotional abuse can take place when families are under particular stress – bereavement; depression; separation. If this continues and becomes part of the normal day-to-day treatment of the child, this would constitute abuse.

It is important to have a good knowledge of child development and use regular observation as part of good practice to alert you to the subtle changes in a child's behaviour.

The table below shows characteristics which may be observed in an emotionally abused child.

▼ Indicators of emotional abuse

Behavioural indicators	
Attention-seeking	Fearful of parents/carers – reluctant to go home
Withdrawn and isolated	
Stealing or telling lies	Self-mutilation, e.g. head banging, hair pulling, picking at skin
Inability to have fun	
Low self-esteem	
Tantrums at an inappropriate age – over-reacting	Comfort-seeking behaviour, thumb sucking or rocking
	Over-anxious to please
Speech disorders	Poor concentration
Inability to play	Frequent toileting accidents in older children
Developmental delay	
Indiscriminately affectionate	

In the Birth to Three Matters framework (DfES, 2002) emotional well-being is recognised as an essential part of a child's right to be 'a healthy child'. It is important to be aware that parents are only human and may have moments of stress when they feel they cannot cope and consequently treat their children inappropriately. This may only be a temporary period of stress, but children need healthy dependent relationships in order to develop and express their feelings, and this kind of treatment, even in the short term, may have long-term effects.

Key term

Developmental delay is when a child or young person's development (physical, emotional, intellectual, language or social) is in some way delayed or regressing due to other factors, of which an abusive situation could be one.

Sexual abuse

'Sexual abuse involves forcing or coercing a child or young person to take part in sexual activities, whether or not the child is aware of what is happening. The activities may involve physical contact, including penetrative (e.g. rape or buggery) or non-penetrative acts. They may include non-contact activities, such as involving children in looking at, or in the production of, pornographic material or watching sexual activities, or encouraging children to behave in sexually inappropriate ways.' (*Working Together to Safeguard Children*, 1999)

The table below shows characteristics which may be observed in a sexually abused child.

▼ Indicators of sexual abuse

Physical indicators	Behavioural indicators
Pain, itching or discomfort in the genital area	Nightmares, night terrors and sleep disturbances
Difficulty when having a bowel movement, urinating or swallowing	Dramatic behavioural changes causing disruption of childcare activities
Recurring complaints such as frequent stomach aches and headaches	Clinging or compulsively seeking attention from both boys and girls
Eating disorders such as refusing to eat or eating constantly	Overly co-operative or aggressive
Torn, stained or bloody underwear	Destructive or anti-social behaviour
Bruising/bites to breasts, buttocks, lower abdomen, thighs, genital or anal areas	Apparent sadness almost all the time
Sexually transmitted diseases, promiscuity or pregnancy	Poor relationships with other children and lack of self-confidence
Semen on skin, clothes or in the vagina or anus	Frequent lying without apparent reason
	Self-destructive behaviour, e.g. biting oneself, pulling out hair, wrist-cutting, head banging
	Unusual distrust or fear of adults or specific adults
	May fear going home or being left alone
	Unusually secretive, 'special' relationship with an older person
	Unusual sexual knowledge and persistent, inappropriate sexual play for the child's age and stage of development

Neglect and 'failure to thrive'

'Neglect is the persistent failure to meet a child's basic physical and/or psychological needs, likely to result in the serious impairment of the child's health or development. It may involve a parent or carer failing to provide adequate food, shelter and clothing.' (*Working Together to Safeguard Children*, 1999)

The table below shows characteristics which may be observed in a child who is neglected.

▼ Indicators of neglect

Physical indicators	Behavioural indicators
Poor hygiene	Lack of interest, difficult to stimulate
Inadequate clothing, dirty, torn or inappropriate for weather conditions	Indiscriminately affectionate
Untreated medical problems	Persistently late to school or frequently misses school
Persistent nappy rash	Withdrawn
Poor nourishment	Low self-esteem
Emaciation	

Failure to thrive is when a baby does not meet its expected growth pattern, failing to put on weight. A baby would normally double its birth weight by 4 months old. There are many possible reasons for failure to thrive, one of which is that the parents/carer of the child are in some way limiting their diet and causing the failure to thrive. However, it can also be due to other conditions such as coeliac disease, liver disease or cystic fibrosis. If a baby fails to thrive it is vital that the situation is investigated thoroughly.

What is meant by 'significant harm' and 'cause for concern'?

When considering how to deal with possible child abuse, a decision will need to be made about whether the child or young person has suffered **significant harm** or whether there is a **cause for concern**. Flynn and Starns (2004, page 119) tell us that 'there is no absolute criteria for significant harm' and that each case is different. Child protection teams will make a decision by building a picture of the whole situation through a well-informed assessment. Harm can be caused by one serious event or by a series of events over time.

In the Children Act 1989 harm is defined as:

- ill-treatment (which includes sexual abuse and non-physical treatment such as emotional abuse), and
- the impairment of health or development (which means all areas of development and physical or mental health).

In practice you will need to consider the following elements suggested by Flynn and Starns:

- the family context
- the child's development within the context of family and wider world
- any special needs
- the nature of the harm
- the impact of the harm
- the adequacy of parental care.

It is important that you look at each child's circumstances to help identify whether the child is in need of protection (significant harm) or in need of support (a cause for concern). A professional and objective approach is vital and best practice must be pursued. It is also important that we ignore stereotypes and **pre-value judgements**, keeping an open mind, dealing with facts and reality and not jumping to conclusions based on assumption.

For further information on this important facet of child protection, refer to *Protecting Children: working together to keep children safe* by Heather Flynn and Barbara Starns (2004).

Key terms

A **cause for concern** is when there is need for support for the child and their family to ensure the needs of the child or young person are being met.

Significant harm The concept of significant harm is the criteria which helps professionals decide if there is need for intervention and/or support because there has been ill-treatment or impairment of health to the child or young person.

Pre-value judgement When a person makes a judgement about another person based on something they feel is the truth, for example that all poor people do not eat well.

Bullying

Although not in a category of its own, bullying is a form of emotional abuse and can cause long-term damage to a child. Abuse by older children can also be physical and sexual. In 1993 Jamie Bulger died at the hands of two 10-year-old boys, Jon Venables and Robert Thompson, in Liverpool. This highlighted the fact that children can also be the aggressors and abusers.

Children who are bullied at school or at home by older siblings often have low self-esteem and self-worth, they may begin to believe their attackers and feel worthless. Bullies may pick on the seemingly more vulnerable children, those less likely to fight back. They have often learnt this behaviour from their parents or older siblings, having been victims of violence themselves. Children who are the victims of bullying may go on to miss school in later years.

For older children, and young people too, bullying can take many forms – verbal, physical, racial or sexist. This can make the child's or young person's life miserable. You need to ensure that young people feel safe and supported in the setting and show that you feel this behaviour is unacceptable and that the adults are a source of trust and support.

▲ A child who is being bullied may have low self-esteem and become isolated

Good practice checklist

- Be a good role model for the children and young people in your care in your relationships with colleagues as well as children.
- Have clear procedures to deal with any incidents of bullying.
- Provide an anti-bullying policy.
- Discuss issues of concern with children and young people and make it clear that bullying will be taken seriously.
- Provide activities which enable children to discuss their feelings and anxieties.

Pre-disposing factors

In this section we will examine some of the factors that may lead to a child being abused. However, it is important for you to understand that children are *never* responsible for being abused. It is the adult or 'abuser' who is always responsible for the abuse taking place; the child is always the victim.

Key term

Pre-disposing factors are factors in the child's background or make-up which might make them more vulnerable or susceptible to abuse, for example if a child has parents who have themselves been abused.

Abuse within families

Contrary to popular belief, most child abuse and neglect takes place within the child's own home and family, by someone (usually a parent) that the child knows. Child abuse and neglect crosses all boundaries of culture, ethnic origin, religion and social status.

While no single factor can be seen to be responsible for causing an abusive situation, there are some factors which may make an abusive situation more likely.

Parents

Research into child abuse has shown that certain characteristics and experiences may predispose particular individuals to be more likely to abuse a child in their care than another individual. These include:

- parents who themselves have been abused
- parents who have experienced poor parenting themselves
- very young parents who may be unaware of the child's needs or are in fact still growing up themselves
- people who have unrealistic expectations of their child's behaviour
- parents who experience poverty, poor housing and social isolation
- parents who have a low self-esteem
- a history of alcohol or drug abuse
- parents with mental health issues
- an unwanted pregnancy and/or difficult birth.

None of these categories is applicable to all adults who may abuse or neglect their children, but they do need to be considered when addressing individual issues of child protection.

Children and young people

Some children are more vulnerable to abuse than others, for example:

- *a child with a disability*: a parent who has responsibility for significant physical care could become frustrated and resentful of the responsibility, taking it out on the child
- *an eldest child*: often the eldest child will be given more responsibility in a family under stress and this can lead to them being accountable and abused emotionally or physically as a result
- *looked after children*: children who are being looked after by the state may be cared for by an abusive person who is betraying their position of trust
- *a loner*: a child who does not have friends or social support may be preyed upon by paedophiles who exploit their vulnerability
- *a very young child who cries a lot or is difficult to feed*: parents who are tired or stressed can find it harder to keep calm and control their emotions
- *a child or young person who is unable to communicate*: the abuser will know that it will be more difficult for them to tell others. This applies to very young babies

and children but also to some children and young people for whom English is a second language.

Children with disabilities

All the indicators listed above apply to children with disabilities. However, the question still remains why children with disabilities are more vulnerable. *Working together to safeguard children* (DoH, 1999) also suggests that children with disabilities are at increased risk from abuse. Some reasons are:

- They receive less information on abuse and their rights, and may be less likely to understand it.
- They are often more dependent on physical care from different people.
- They may be less likely to tell what has happened due to communication barriers.
- They may be more likely to have low self-esteem and feel less in control.
- They may find it difficult to distinguish between good and bad touches.

Models of child abuse

In spite of the large number of theories put forward as to why child abuse occurs, there is no single theory which can be applied to all cases of abuse and neglect. Each situation is different and occurs for different reasons and cases therefore need to be viewed individually. The five main theories as to why child abuse and neglect occur are the:

- medical model
- sociological model
- psychological model
- feminist model
- contextual model.

Medical model

This theory addresses issues around the idea that the causes of child abuse were viewed as a disease. This came from the phrase coined by Kempe and Kempe (1962): the 'battered child syndrome'. This was later changed in 1976 to 'child abuse and neglect'. Kempe and Kempe applied Bowlby's thinking about attachment theory (see Unit 1) directly to child abuse and neglect. They concluded that many mothers (the main care-givers with whom the bond is made) who had abused their children had themselves suffered from poor attachment experiences in early childhood. Their response to this was to ensure that children in abusive situations were removed to places of safety and the parents were given 'treatment' to help with the bonding process.

Sociological model

This theory looks at changing patterns within society and believes that unemployment, poverty, poor housing and health deprivation are reasons for people abusing their children. Children need to live in healthy environments if they are to grow up healthy and well adjusted. Research has shown that there are links between rates of reported abuse and characteristics of social deprivation such as low income. Research also shows that many people who abuse children have very often been victims of abuse during their own childhood. These adults may go on to treat their children in the same way, as this was an integral part of their **socialisation**. This is referred to as the **cycle of abuse**. It is necessary, however, that practitioners do not make judgements about a family based on something the parent has told them about their background. Parents who have had poor parenting experiences may need extra support to enjoy being parents themselves and to get the very best from their relationships with their children.

Key terms

Socialisation is the process that happens during a child's early life – they are influenced by the people in environment around them.

The **cycle of abuse** refers to the situation when a parent who has suffered abuse as a child themselves then abuses their own child.

Psychological model

Family dysfunction theorists look at the dynamics within a family relationship. If this becomes poor or distorted, the family ceases to function as a unit. Dysfunction usually begins with the adult partners, who may then 'scapegoat', which means that all the family's problems become identified in one family member. Theorists argue that the scapegoat becomes necessary for the survival of the family unit.

Feminist model

This perspective addresses the imbalance of power between men and women within society and with particular reference to child sexual abuse and the abuse of adult male power.

Contextual model

Abuse can occur anywhere or at anytime but there is no particular type of family where abuse always occurs. Research has shown that there are four groups of factors which may lead to an increased increase:

- *unexceptional context*, when a family who would usually meet the needs of their children have particular stresses or problems which prevent them from being able to cope in their normal way
- *rigid context*, where parents are very strict and controlling and children appear to be fearful of making their parents angry. Parents are intolerant and focus on the negative, with high expectations of the child
- *deviant context*, where one or two of the parents abuse their power and are often mentally unwell themselves
- *chaotic context*, where discipline within the family is inconsistent and there is a lack of appropriate boundaries. Care of the children is often erratic and older children may be given adult responsibility.

Extension activity

Victoria Climbie was 8 years old when she died in February 2000. She had been tortured and died at the hands of an aunt, Marie Theresa Kouao, and her partner, Carl Manning. Find out about this case and, in a presentation to your group:

- Discuss the background of the case.
- Link the case to one or more of the theoretical models.
- Give reasons for your choice.

There are references at the end of this unit which may be useful.

Consequences and effects of child abuse and neglect

Studies have shown that child abuse has been a consistent factor in the backgrounds of criminals, substance abusers, prostitutes and runaways. Children who have experienced child abuse are likely to continue, or create, the cycle of abuse when they become adults. They assume that pain naturally accompanies intimacy. They are more likely turn to physical abuse, as well as substance abuse, in order to forget what has happened, or is happening, to them. Child abuse and neglect lower self-esteem and have a long-term damaging effect on the person's confidence, faith, relationships and future. Long-term effects of child abuse include fear, anxiety, depression, anger, hostility, inappropriate sexual behaviour, poor self-esteem, tendency towards substance abuse and difficulty with close relationships (Browne and Finkelhor, 1986).

While these effects are not always obvious, they are very important. Knowing this, there can be little doubt that children who are abused, as well as adults who were abused as children, need assistance to resolve the questions that the abuse experience has raised, even if that assistance does not come until years after the abuse.

In 2003 National Children's Homes (NCH) published *Working with Children*. This book provides an analysis of the latest government statistics on children and their families, looking at: children's services; health; population; education; children at risk; poverty and social exclusion. It stated that in 2003 the following numbers were recorded on the child protection register:

- 4,200 children under 1 year
- 7,600 children between 1 and 4 years
- 7,600 children between 5 and 9 years
- 7,000 children between 10 and 15 years.

At 31 March 2002, there were 25,700 children on child protection registers in England, a 4 per cent increase on the previous year. These were not all cases of abuse in the home. In 2002 a new 'mixed' category was introduced in recording these registrations because of the concerns about multiple risks. At 31 March 2002 the most commonly recorded risk category was neglect (39 per cent), followed by physical abuse (19 per cent), and then emotional abuse (17 per cent). (Figures from the *12th Annual Report of the Chief Inspector of Social Services 2002–2003*, Department of Health, 2003.)

There are also other areas of high risk and concern where children are being abused:

- child prostitution – this takes place in the UK today
- runaways
- drug use related incidents
- trafficked children
- domestic violence
- looked after children.

Extension activity

In small groups, research the following reports and other secondary sources. Produce a poster to inform the rest of the class about the areas of concern mentioned above.

- Trafficked children – Stop the Traffic (Unicef UK, 2003)
- Domestic violence – The Hidden Victims – children and domestic violence (NCH, 1994/Routes to Safety, Women's Aid Federation of England, 2002), www.avenueswomen.co.uk

Variation in family functioning

Family types

The family, in whatever form, is the unit that provides a home and care for dependent children. There are a variety of family types within our society:

- *Nuclear family* Parents and children live in an independent unit separately from other relatives. This may mean that the family is better off economically, but may also mean that if anything goes wrong between the parents, the family will experience considerable disruption.
- *Reconstituted family* Partners with children from previous relationships live together. This may provide a good level of support, but may also bring tensions for some individuals.

- *Extended family* Parents, children, grandparents, uncles and aunts live together in a supportive unit which has many advantages, but may limit the personal independence of some members.
- *Lone parent* A single parent, father or mother, living alone with a child. This may lead to financial hardship, or may induce feelings of isolation and lack of support.

Changing face of the family

While these definitions are fairly specific, it is important to be aware that there are many different combinations. The structure of the family has altered as a result of changes within the wider society. The increased incidence of divorce and remarriage, the development of a multi-cultural society and increased life expectancy has resulted in changes in family lifestyles and practices. Children may live in two households, moving from one to another at weekends or holidays; they may live with parents in a homosexual relationship, or grow up living with foster carers. Whilst family structures may vary in different cultures, it is very important not to generalise about any family situation.

More specifically, a change within any individual family structure, such as moving away from relatives, a grandparent dying or moving to a different country, can be quite disruptive for the family and the child. All families are different, have different practices and different values: there is no ideal model. What is important is that the children are fed, clothed and sheltered, are loved and have the opportunity to learn within a protective and caring environment.

Social disadvantage

There are many pressures on families, not least those caused by social or financial hardship. The cycle of poverty is difficult to escape and it places added pressures on the family. The following table identifies some of the factors which affect families.

All families are different ▶

▼ **Social factors which affect families**

Factor	Effect
Poor housing which may be overcrowded, damp and unheated with limited outside play space	Chest infections from living in damp conditions Lack of privacy or personal space Noise No safe outdoor play which may leave young children playing on the streets
Poor diet, cheap food with limited nutrients, high intake of fast foods, too much sugar and starch and too little fruit and vegetables	Illness and infections May affect growth Sets a pattern of poor eating habits which will last for life
Inadequate clothing	Discomfort in bad weather and may produce illness
Lack of stimulation and quality play resources, no holidays and limited travel	May affect intellectual development Makes times like Christmas additionally stressful
Low self-esteem	Feeling of worthlessness May cause depression May develop alcohol or drug dependency Leads to a feeling of being 'trapped'

Different concepts of discipline

All families have differing values and standards. These will have developed as a result of the personal experiences of the parents, who will bring their values and family practices from their own childhood. You will find that they have different ways in which they discipline their children as a result of these differences; what is acceptable behaviour in one family may be unacceptable in another. Some parents may feel that smacking their children is appropriate, for example. You need to take this into account as part of good practice. You may also need to support and advise a parent when their child's development is suffering as a result of their concept of discipline. You can do this primarily by being a good role model in the way you handle and work with their children. You will need to acknowledge their views and offer appropriate support and advice. The setting will also have a discipline policy that can be discussed with the parents.

Case study: Differing expectations of family life

This is an example of differing expectations of family life. You may find this strange, even unacceptable.

'When we were children we were expected to adhere to certain rules – we were not allowed to eat except at the table and were expected to sit together every evening for our meal. Table manners were very important in our house – if you did not follow certain etiquette my father would ask you to leave the table and you went without your dinner.'

In your group, come up with some similar examples of family life, as you remember them, and discuss whether or not you share the same experiences. Do you find some of these experiences unacceptable?

Assessment activity 5.1

List six possible indicators for each of the following:

a) a child age 3 who has been physically abused

b) a child age 6 years who has been sexually abused

c) a young person age 12 years who has been emotionally abused

d) a baby aged 9 months who has been neglected.

Make sure you include at least four **physical** and four **behavioural** indicators. **P1**

When you have compiled a list, write a short case study for each scenario in no more than 200 words.

5.2 How to work within the supporting legislation, regulation and codes of practice

The legal framework for protection of children

Before we look at the present framework, we need to understand something about how we came to this point. Prior to the implementation of the Children Acts of 1989 and 2004, there were many pieces of childcare legislation which were thought to be far too complex and incomplete for the needs of children, their families and the professionals working with them. As society's ideas and attitudes were changing (towards child abuse for example – more people were becoming aware of its existence and were no longer prepared to 'bury their heads in the sand'), it was evident that the existing legislation had to be updated. Another reason for this was the reports into the deaths of Jasmine Beckford (1985), Kimberley Carlile (1985), Tyra Henry (1985) and an inquiry into the handling of alleged child sexual abuse in Cleveland (1987).

The table below provides a summary of some of the major pieces of legislation affecting the protection of children and young people to date.

▼ Major legislation affecting the protection of children and young people

Legislation	Summary
Human Rights Act, 1998	This Act came into force on 2 October 2000 and details the basic rights of people in our society. The Act outlines rules to order and protect every person. Rules include the right to life, protection from slavery, the right to education and the right to marriage. These seem as though they go without saying, however, without the Human Rights Act we could live in a very different society. There are places around the world where freedom is restricted, people are used as cheap labour or are not allowed an education. The Human Rights Act is vital in keeping our society as fair and equal as possible and fortunately most of us have no idea what it would be like without such laws. We have the right to have an opinion – even that is not allowed in some societies.
United Nations Convention on the Rights of the Child, 1989	Children have rights and there is legislation to protect their rights. The League of Nations drafted the first Declaration of the Rights of the Child in 1924. The United Nations Convention on the Rights of the Child (CRC), containing 54 Articles addressing the rights of children, was ratified by the UK in 1991. Only the United States and Somalia have not ratified this declaration. The 54 Articles within the CRC address children's right to: • survival • development • protection • participation. The following articles are key in the protection of children: • Article 19: To protect children from all form of physical or mental violence while in the care of parents or others • Article 37a: No child shall be subjected to torture or other cruel inhuman or degrading treatment or punishment. The principles stated in the CRC underpin much of the current legislation of the UK designed to ensure that the views and the rights of the child are sought and upheld.
Special Educational Needs and Disability Act (SENDA), 2001	This Act is in two parts. Part 1 makes reforms to earlier legislation and gives rights to children with special educational needs to access mainstream education where they were formerly educated primarily in specialist schools for moderate and severe learning difficulties and specialist units. The Disability Discrimination Act of 1995 is extended in Part 2 of the Act which increases the civil rights of disabled children and adults in schools and further and higher education – giving them rights to equal access and the right to inclusion. The SEN Code of Practice 2001 was developed from this Act and this gives guidance to parents, schools and establishments receiving government funding. The guidance works on fundamental principles based on the social model of disability, so that their individual needs can be met. For more information on the Act or the Code of Practice, see page 239.
Children Act, 1989	This Act came into force on 14 October 1991. It is the most important reform of the law concerning children over the last century. It made the law simpler and easier to use. It brought together the legislation concerning the care and upbringing of children in both private law, which applies to children affected by a private dispute such as divorce proceedings, and public law, which covers children who are in need of help from a local authority. The five principles underpinning the act were as follows: • At all times, the welfare of the child must be the paramount consideration. • A new concept of parental responsibility. • The no order principle, whereby courts are instructed not to make statutory orders unless they are satisfied that the only way to safeguard the first principle (welfare of the child) is to make such an order. • The no delay principle, where children are involved in cases before the court, the court must set a timetable and ensure that the case is heard as quickly as possible. • The principles of corporate responsibility and partnership. These principles have remained valid in the 2004 Act.

Children Act, 2004	Built on the principles of the 1989 Act, and following the Children's Bill, the 2004 Act is part of a wider programme of change set out in the Green Paper Every Child Matters, see below. The Act amends sections 17, 20 and 47 of the former Children Act and includes a new framework of duties and accountabilities to develop high-quality services including: • closer joint working between various agencies involved with children • wishes of the children to be taken into account • greater sharing of information between professionals through databases • limits on the use of reasonable chastisement • a Children's Commissioner for England • better information-sharing between practitioners • Local Safeguarding Children Boards (LSCBs), of which there are 150, set up with statutory powers to replace Area Child Protection Committees in 2006 • groups to review unexpected child deaths in their area • improved local accountability (through a local Director of Children's Services and a lead council member for children's services) • a duty on local authorities to promote the educational achievement of looked after children.
Every Child Matters (Green Paper)	On 8 September 2003, the government launched the long-awaited Green Paper Every Child Matters (DfES, 2003). Improved information-sharing across agencies had been called for as result of the inquiry into the death of Victoria Climbie in 2000. Victoria's tragic death highlighted need for more effective communication and information-sharing. The Green Paper listed five key outcomes for children: • being healthy – enjoying a healthy lifestyle, good physical and mental health • staying safe – to be protected from neglect and harm • enjoying and achieving – to get the most out of life, to gain the skills needed for a productive adulthood • making a positive contribution – not to become engaged in anti-social behaviour but to make a positive contribution to the community and society • economic well-being – not to be held back by socio-economic difficulties. Chapter 2 of the Green Paper confirmed the government's commitment to: • ensure children are safe from bullying and homelessness • the Sure Start project • tackling child poverty • raising school standards • improving children's access to health services • more investment in the youth service. (See also Co-operating with Other Professionals, page 203.)
Protection of Children Act, 1999 (England and Wales) Protection and Supervision of Children Act, 2004 (Scotland) Protection of Children and Vulnerable Adults order, 2003 (Northern Ireland)	Created the PoCA list, a list of adults known to be unsuitable to work with children. All settings are required by law to consult this list via the Criminal Records Bureau. The Act also made it illegal to knowingly apply for a job if you have already been found unsuitable to work with children and/or vulnerable adults.
Data Protection Act 1998	This Act applies to the protection and security of all forms of data (information) – this includes written and spoken information, and information stored on film, video or tape recording or on computer. The Act safeguards people's rights when information about them is being collected as in a case of child protection or assessment of need. The Act covers: obtaining data, recording data, storing data, accessing data, using data, sharing data, disposing of data. There are two types of data used when you work with children and their families – person identifiable (things such as name and address, married status, number of children, etc.) and sensitive (more in-depth personal information). The good practice checklist opposite deals with handling sensitive data in line with the Act.

The UK government has published two useful guidance documents which clearly support legislation and set out ways in which legislation can be implemented. They are:

- *Working Together to Safeguard Children*, 1999. This acts as a guide for **inter-agency working** in childcare. It outlines the roles and responsibilities of the Area Child Protection Committees (ACPCs) or Children's Management Boards.
- *What To Do If You're Worried a Child is Being Abused*, 2003. This is an extremely useful document written for anyone coming into contact with children and young people. It gives clear guidelines about reporting your concerns and suspicions, and advice on respecting the rights of families and the need for confidentiality.

Key terms

The **local authority** is the local representation of government and law, which provides services to everyone in the local community.

Local Safeguarding Children's Boards (LSCBs) This system oversees inter-agency working in child protection in England, Wales and Northern Ireland; they replace Area Child Protection Committees (ACPS).

Inter-agency working is information sharing and shared decision-making between agencies to jointly and collaboratively meet the needs of families, children and young people.

Extension activity

Research the Children Act, 2004. With a partner, make a list of at least *four* ways in which it helps to meet the needs of children more effectively than the 1989 Act. You might want to use the current Children Act Report to aid your research. These can be found at www.dfes.gov.uk.

Good practice checklist

To ensure you meet the requirements of the Data Protection Act in your setting you must:

- collect all personal data with the parents'/carers' knowledge and consent – only collect as much as you need and be able to justify your reasons for the request
- record all data accurately – check all written information before retaining
- store data securely – only allow authorised people to access information and never store information on computer on shared drives
- use the data appropriately – for example, if you ask for a phone number, do not use it to give the number to someone organising an event at the setting
- sharing data – only share data on a need-to-know basis, such as a medical emergency
- safe disposal of data – permanently remove data from computers, shred or burn paper records. Do not dispose of inappropriately.

Who has parental responsibility?

All mothers automatically have parental responsibility for their children. In addition, the 2004 Act made changes to the 1989 Act which had said that all *married* fathers had parental responsibility and gave parental responsibility to all fathers who had been named on the child's birth certificate. This was a significant change. In the case of divorced or separated married parents, both parents, regardless of who the child lives with, retain parental responsibility.

Parental responsibility is very rarely lost except on adoption. Even where a care order is made, parental responsibility is retained, although the local authority may limit the extent to which that responsibility is exercised.

Parental responsibility covers both rights and duties. It includes the following rights:

- to give consent to medical treatment
- to determine the child's religion
- to choose the child's surname
- to apply discipline
- to give consent to marriage from the age of 16 to 18
- to give consent before their child can be adopted
- to appoint a guardian in the event of the death of the other parent.

It also includes the following duties:

- to look after children in a way which is not cruel or deliberately neglectful, and does not expose children to the risk of significant harm
- to provide maintenance
- to ensure that children of 5 and over receive full-time education.

Having looked at the legislation working for the protection of children, consider the case study below.

Framework for Assessment of Need 2000

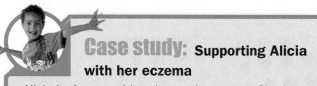

Case study: Supporting Alicia with her eczema

Alicia is 4 years old and attends nursery. She has lived in England with her mother for three years; they are refugees. Alicia and her mother have moved around the country a great deal and have never stayed anywhere longer than six months. Alicia's mother is being supported by a social worker from the local health authority, who takes Alicia to the hospital for regular appointments because she has severe eczema. Recently practitioners at the nursery are concerned because Alicia asks them if they can change her bandages and put her cream on. Her bandages are often dirty and smelly and she is continually scratching. When staff approach her mother, she does not appear to appreciate the importance of the situation. She says that the hospital social worker is dealing with that.

Which, if any, of the pieces of legislation could be put into effect here?

The *Framework for the Assessment of Children in Need and their Families* (The Stationery Office, 2000) is a common framework to be used by all professionals when an initial assessment establishes that there are child protection issues. In the majority of cases, **social services** will take the lead in carrying out the assessments. The framework lays out the roles and responsibilities of all the agencies involved, providing a common approach to assessment that everyone can understand when collecting information about the family. It also provides guidance on how education and day care services might contribute to an assessment.

The process for carrying out an assessment is:

1 Look at the **referral** to clarify if there is concern.

2 Gather information.

3 Look at all the facts and the feelings of the child and family involved.

4 Ask their opinions.

5 Gain an understanding of what is happening within the family.

6 Come to a conclusion about the needs of the family and the parenting capacity.

The framework is based on three domains and is called the assessment triangle:

- *the child's development needs* – their relationships, identity, emotional and behavioural development, health and education, social presentation
- *family and environmental needs* – income, employment, family history and functioning, wider family, community, housing
- *parenting capacity* – basic care, emotional warmth, stability, ensuring safety, guidance and boundaries, stimulation.

These three domains allow professionals to understand the world of the child and their family better in order to make an assessment. Each domain is split into dimensions – some of the dimensions of a child's developmental needs are health, education and identity.

For further information, Flynn and Starns (2004) have a whole chapter dedicated to the assessment framework and detail on initial and core assessment.

Health   Basic care
Education   Ensuring safety
Emotional and behavioural development   Emotional warmth
Identity   Stimulation

Child's developmental needs   Parenting capacity

Family and social relationships
Social presentation   Guidance and boundaries
Self-care skills   Stability

CHILD
Safeguarding and
promoting welfare

Family and environmental factors

Community resources
Family's social integration
Income
Employment
Housing
Wider family
Family history and functioning

▲ **The assessment triangle**

Key terms

The **Framework for Assessment of Need** is a common framework used by all professionals in an initial assessment to establish whether or not there are child protection issues; it provides a common approach that all professionals and agencies involved must use.

Social services are the services provided by the government to support those members of the community that are in need and often the most vulnerable.

Referral is when someone contacts social services or the authorities with concerns about a child or young person.

body in every local authority which has responsibility for producing a child protection procedure in line with *Working Together to Safeguard Children* (DoH, 1999). There should be a copy of the ACPC procedure in every setting for staff to refer to.

If you have concerns about a child or young person, you will need to report this concern using your setting's policy and the ACPC procedure. It is probable that the child and family you are concerned about will already be receiving support for their needs. The Children Act 1989 bestowed two main duties on local authorities in England and Wales to ensure that children are kept safe and well cared for. These duties are:

- to provide a service for children in need. Therefore, in some instances a 'child in need' meeting will be held to assess where the child's needs can be met. This might be in a number of ways: advice and support for the parent; respite accommodation for a child with special needs; better health care support; family centre intervention or a funded nursery placement (Section 17 of the Act)
- to investigate when a child may be in danger of, or be suffering, significant harm and therefore in need of protection (**Section 47 enquiry**). This will involve the police as there will be evidence that a criminal act may have taken place.

If you have concerns about a child or young person you must take action. The checklist below will answer some of the concerns you may have about reporting concerns.

Procedures

As a practitioner you are required firstly to follow the policies of the setting. Therefore it is vital that you know and understand your setting's policy. (There is an example of a child protection policy later in this unit.) You will also need to refer to the **child protection procedures** produced by the Area Child Protection Committee (ACPC). This is a multi-agency

Key term

The **child protection procedure** is part of the child protection service and starts at the point of referral; the child is the central focus.

A **Section 47 enquiry** is an investigation (legally supported by the Children Act 1989) where a child has been suffering significant harm.

Good practice checklist

- Raise concerns early with parents. If you can, give them the opportunity to seek advice themselves. You need not gain consent from the parent if you think the child is going to be further at risk by discussing the issues. Discussion with the parents could also put you at risk.
- Always keep good records of all concerns. These records must be clear and objective, stating the facts only. They are also highly confidential so they must be kept securely.
- If you are uncertain about the level of harm, seek advice and guidance from your line manager. Do not keep these concerns to yourself.
- Report to the designated child protection person in your setting.
- Remember at all times that the welfare of the child is paramount.
- The Children Act is clear in stating that there is a no delay principle –time is very important.
- Record all actions and referral.

All settings will have their own procedures for recording issues relating to child protection. Staff who are working directly with a family in relation to issues of concern maintain a contact sheet which provides details of all contact with the family.

While record-keeping is an important aspect of the care and education of all children, recording issues relating to child protection has particular importance. Any decisions that are made for a family may rely on the evidence gathered within the child's individual record. For this reason, it is important that all recording is:

- completed as soon after the incident as possible
- factual
- relevant
- detailed
- clearly written
- free from opinion.

The designated person may then seek advice from or report a case of child abuse to social services.

Not forming premature judgements

When reporting information relating to individual children, it is important to distinguish between directly observed evidence and evidence that someone else has told you. Second-hand stories may not actually be true, or they may have someone else's interpretation that is quite misleading. For example, the statement from a concerned neighbour that 'It's a terrible house, the children are screaming all night' may simply mean that there is a new baby in the house who cries all evening, or it may mean that children are being abused. As an early years practitioner, you need to be able to identify appropriate information that is directly observed, factual and relevant.

Theory into practice

During a staff meeting at the after-school club, the following information about Irfan (aged 13) is discussed. The staff say they are fed up with him, he is getting far too out of hand and destructive and is setting a poor example to the younger children. Irfan's neighbour has told one of the members of staff who lives in the next street that Irfan's father often hits the children. The incident book records show that Irfan has some bruises on his arms and neck which his mother said happened when he was playing rugby. His mother tells the manager that Irfan's elder brother, who has been attending hospital for some time, has leukaemia.

- Identify the relevant information in this passage.
- Which pieces of information would you record from the above case study?
- Do you think that Irfan is being abused? Give reasons for your answers.
- Share your decisions with a partner and compare answers.

After the referral

Once a referral has been made, the child protection team will consider the level of risk and then decide whether any further action is needed. They will then carry out an investigation. If necessary a child protection enquiry under section 47 of the Children Act will be instigated. Details of these procedures can be found in *What To Do if You're Worried a Child is Being Abused* (DoH, 2003).

If further action is taken, the assessment process will begin. The *Framework for Assessment of Children in Need and Their Families* underpins this process of assessing the needs of the child. A **case conference** will be held and information about the child will be shared so that decisions can be made to ensure the child's safety and well-being. Families are asked to attend the conference and occasionally the designated child protection co-ordinator from the setting, if it is felt necessary. It is at this point that records from the setting may be used to help create a holistic picture of the child's development and behaviour.

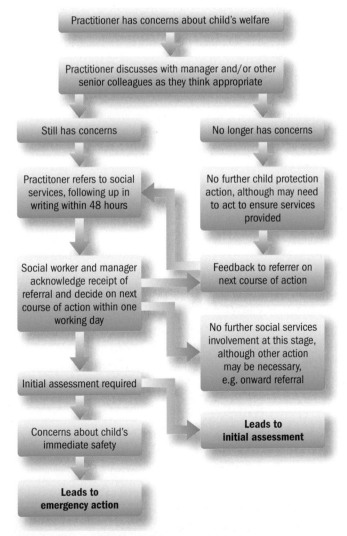

▲ Making a referral to social services

Key term

A **case conference** is a multi-disciplinary meeting to discuss a child or young person and their family.

Theory into practice

Using the document *What to do if You're Worried a Child is Being Abused* (DoH, 2003), investigate what happens after an initial referral of concern. Find out what is meant by:

- significant harm
- a core assessment
- the child protection plan.

Present your findings to the group.

You may also want to refer to the above *Framework for Assessment of Children in Need and their Families* (DoH, 2000: page 6).

Both documents can be found at The Stationery Office, or see Flynn and Starns (2004).

Confidentiality and storage of records

If you work in a team, it is usual to pass your concerns to the person who has the designated child protection role. Everyone in the setting should be aware of who this is in order to follow the setting's policy. The designated person will consider the concern and forward it to the authorities, police or social services. Local child protection teams will have someone on duty 24 hours a day. However, if you do not feel your line manager is taking your concerns seriously, you may need to report your concerns directly to the appropriate authority.

Records of all steps taken must be kept and these will need to be written in a factual and non-judgemental way – you must remain completely objective. All records will need to be dated and time recorded and members of staff involved will need to sign. Although you may not be directly involved in the procedures that follow reporting, there are occasions when your original reports are used as records in the initial investigation or later at child protection conferences.

All the records of such events must be stored securely where they cannot be accessed by anyone other than the designated child protection person and must be clearly marked as confidential. At this stage, it is worth remembering that these may only be concerns and that, should records of this nature be left around for anyone to read, people's lives and futures can be affected.

The role of the key worker

Following the introduction of the Early Years Curriculum, the concept of key workers is now firmly established within early years care and education settings. However, settings which provide for children's care have been operating key worker systems for many years.

The advantages of a key worker system are as follows:

- The key worker becomes a familiar figure for the child.
- The parent has one specific individual to communicate with.
- The key worker can build up a meaningful relationship with the family.

- The key worker can monitor and record progress and details of the child's care.
- Greater knowledge of the family situation will make the key worker more responsive to individual needs.
- When representing the family at meetings with other professionals, the close relationship and knowledge of the individual family is an asset.
- It provides consistency of care, which is of particular advantage for a child who is experiencing a traumatic period in their life.

Assessment activity 5.2

1 Write a brief summary (in no more than 200 words) outlining the legal framework relating to protecting to children. You must include references to at least three pieces of legislation. **P3**

2 Briefly describe the reporting procedures in a childcare setting. **P4**

3 Devise a detailed flow chart to explain the process of recognising and reporting child abuse. **M2**

5.3 Good practice in responding to disclosure

The principles of disclosure

There may come a time when a child tells you that they are being abused or have been abused. This is known as **disclosure**.

Key term

Disclosure is when a child tells you that they are being, or have been, abused.

In this section, we will be considering how to deal with and support a child who may disclose they have been

Often the child may feel it is their fault ▶

abused. It is important that you are aware of the policy of your setting should this arise. Some of the guidance may change in line with the most recent legislation, so you should ensure you are kept up to date. How a child is dealt with should this happen is crucial as you will have no advance warning and may be caught off-guard. On the rare occasion a child does directly disclose, you may be alone with the child. In these circumstances you are also vulnerable and must follow correct procedures.

You must also be aware of the boundaries of confidentiality. Although all practitioners and student workers are bound by confidentiality in all aspects of their work, disclosure or concern for a child is the only occasion when there may be a need to divulge information. This, of course, is to protect the child and ensure that their needs are paramount. If there are concerns or a disclosure, either direct or indirect, you are duty bound to report whatever information is needed in line with the policies of the setting.

There are two ways in which a child may disclose:

- *directly*, when a child talks to an adult or older child and explains that they have been abused in some way
- *indirectly*, when the professional is aware of possible abuse, through a variety of indicators or through a child's indirect attempts to disclose through art or other forms of expression.

Direct disclosure

Direct disclosure rarely happens in the majority of early years settings. However, in such a situation, you must ensure that you give the child your full attention. The child obviously feels they can trust you and you must not betray this trust. You may feel shocked by what the child tells you, but you must remain calm and not allow your own feelings to show, as this may affect what information the child then shares. Above all you must ensure that you show the child that you believe them and demonstrate unconditional acceptance of everything they say. It is vital that the child feels they are believed and that they can trust the adult not to question them and make them feel as if it is in any way their fault. The good practice checklist below summarises the main points when dealing with disclosure and responding to the child.

Good practice checklist

Support for children who disclose

- Do
  - Listen to the child calmly.
  - Tell the child they were right to tell you.
  - Believe them.
  - Tell the child that what has happened is not their fault or responsibility.
  - Acknowledge that they have been brave to tell you.
  - Reassure the child, telling them that their situation is not unique.
  - Be honest about your own position, who you will have to tell and why.
  - Keep the child fully informed about what you are doing and what is happening at every stage.
  - Give the child information about other confidential sources of help, for example Childline.

- Do not
  - Make promises that you cannot keep, such as keeping 'secrets'.
  - Ask the child lots of questions – investigation of the alleged abuse will be undertaken by a trained social worker.
  - Cast doubt on what the child tells you. It has taken a great deal of courage for them to tell you.
  - Say anything which may make the child feel responsible for the abuse, for example 'Why haven't you told anyone before?'
  - Communicate feelings of anger.
  - Ask leading questions, for example 'Was it your mummy that hurt you?'
  - Panic. When confronted with the reality of abuse there is often a feeling of needing to 'act immediately'. Action taken too hastily can be counter-productive.

Once the child has divulged this information, it is your responsibility to record what has been said as soon as you can after the event and report it to your supervisor/ line manager. When recording the event, it is important to give a factual account stating what the child said as clearly as you can remember. Do not make assumptions about the child's feelings or about the truth of what the child has told you. The good practice guidelines for observations and reporting should be followed. It is also important that you tell the child that they can come back and discuss it further if they wish.

Indirect disclosure

Indirect disclosure is when the child identifies abuse through their play and is more often the way a child demonstrates their pain about being abused. For example, they may demonstrate knowledge of abuse while playing in the home corner, using sexually explicit language or acting out an abusive situation. The child may make comments during a painting activity, or present paintings that reflect images or ideas that cause the practitioner concern. When and if this should happen, you should record the conversation or observation and present it to your line manager or designated child protection person in line with the setting's policy.

Theory into practice

One of the children in your nursery has been causing you concern. You have noticed that whenever she is playing alone in the role play area she appears to be 'playing out' acts of violence using the dolls. She also uses an aggressive tone and swears quite a lot. You are also concerned that during a cooking activity she becomes very frustrated with another child and shouts at the child: 'I will burn you in the oven.'

In a small group, discuss this scenario and decide:

- whether you should tell anyone your concerns and, if so, who
- how you would record these incidents in line with your setting's procedures and policy
- whether you should discuss it with the child's parents.

(Look at the Good practice checklist on reporting concerns (page 188) and use copies of your setting's policies.)

Why children do not disclose

You can understand children's reluctance to talk about their abuse if you consider the following:

- Very young children may not possess the language skills to tell you.
- The abusing adult may threaten the child physically or emotionally to keep the secret.

- Some children may think it is normal if they have never experienced anything else.
- Children may be afraid that adults will not believe them.
- Children may feel that it is their fault.
- Some children may emotionally separate home from the outside world accepting that both are different – they will isolate the traumatic feelings so that they can enjoy their time in the setting. This is of course far more difficult to identify.

Good practice checklist

If a child or young person does disclose to you or you have grave concerns that abuse is taking place, you should promptly follow the correct procedure of the setting.

Do not:

- investigate – it is never your role to investigate or make uninformed judgements
- examine the child – do not examine the child, for example asking to see further bruises. This is invasive and an abuse of the child's or young person's rights
- influence the child or young person – be very careful not to make comments or ask questions which may lead the child in a certain direction
- approach or accuse the perpetrator – you may endanger the child further or interfere with a pending investigation.

■ Dealing with your own feelings and emotions

It can be very distressing dealing with disclosure of abuse from a child or listening to details of an abusive situation, especially as you will know the child and family involved.

Some practitioners may find it particularly difficult if they have been abused in the past. In this situation, it is vital that you discuss your concerns with your line manager and ask for support. This distress may not occur initially as you will be concerned with the needs of the child and it often becomes a reality some time later. It may be possible to consider one of the following solutions:

- discuss with your GP and ask advice about local counselling services, some sessions should be available on the NHS

- talk to the social services contact as they have opportunities for supervision within their job role and they may be able to offer advice and guidance.

It is important that these concerns should not be neglected as you will need to remain professional when dealing with the child and family and cannot do so if you are upset and unable to remain objective.

Support for children who disclose and their families

It is essential that a child who has disclosed abuse is unconditionally accepted and never made to feel as if they are to blame. It is at this time that the child is most vulnerable and they will need help to feel secure.

Potential impact of disclosure on the child and the family

Disclosure may result in:

- services being provided to support the family and enable the child to remain at home
- the abusing parent being asked to leave the family home
- the child being removed to place of safety
- break up of the family structure.

If the abuser comes from outside the immediate family circle, such as an uncle or baby sitter, additional pressures relating to the wider community will be apparent.

Any of these situations will make the family feel very threatened. Parents may be angry because the setting has raised concerns. The initial shock may be hard to take in

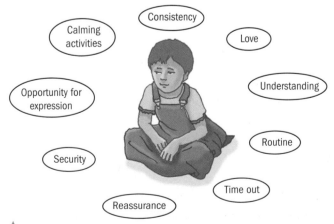

▲ The child needs to be surrounded with security in order to make them feel safe and accepted

and promote a feeling of disbelief. The shock is quickly followed by anger, which may be directed at the setting, the child or the partner.

There may often be feelings of guilt, as the non-abusing parent worries about their inability to protect their child and the abusing parent may be guilty about what they have done. The abusing parent, however, may feel that the complaint is unjustified, 'I was only disciplining the child.' There will also be a feeling of shame and embarrassment that the situation may become public. The child will also experience feelings of guilt and feel responsible for the family situation. This is particularly relevant if the abusing parent has issued threats about secrecy during the abuse.

Case study: Sahira's growing low self-esteem

Sahira is 4 years old and has been at the nursery for a year. When she began nursery, staff found her to be shy and a little withdrawn but, in the last few months, she has begun to take part more in activities and communicate more confidently with her key worker, Mita.

Her mother was managing her and her baby brother alone until about three months ago when a new partner moved in with them. Sahira's mother told staff about him and seemed very happy. Almost right away her new partner, Michael, began picking the children up from nursery and discussing their progress with staff, etc. Michael was very likeable and friendly and always made the staff laugh – sometimes joking about his new role as a 'father'.

After about six weeks Sahira became more withdrawn and participated less in activities. She didn't want to talk about home at all, even to Mita. When her mother dropped her off in the morning she begged her to come back and collect her. She had been overheard saying to her mother that she didn't want 'nasty Michael' to come and collect her. Sahira became more easily upset and when asked why she didn't want to join in activities, she would say: 'I can't do it ... I'm stupid ... I will make a mess.'

Discuss what action you would take as a team.

- **Would you talk to the mother?**
- **Would you ask Sahira questions?**
- **Would you have cause for concern?**
- **Which procedures would you consider?**
- **What would you do to monitor the situation?**

An allegation of abuse within a family will have a devastating effect. Parents may feel intimidated and embarrassed, or they may be hostile and angry. They will need support in the following ways:

- a clear focus on desired outcomes – this involves creating a specific action plan with specific outcomes and may be implemented with the support of other professionals
- supporting them to do what is best for the child and ensuring the child is the focus
- being responsive to parents' needs by showing some empathy for their difficulties
- opportunities to talk
- keeping them informed.

All human interactions involve communication, and many difficulties or conflicts may arise from failure to communicate effectively. Situations relating to abuse and the challenging of a parent's basic care of their child are very sensitive and as such require particularly sophisticated communication skills. For this reason, other professionals may undertake much of the direct work with children and families who are in abusive situations. However, it is important that you develop an understanding of essential communication skills. Much of this communication may be non-verbal, requiring careful observation to accurately interpret the messages being sent, especially emotions or feelings, for example through facial expression, gestures, body posture, lack of eye-contact or tone of voice.

Good communication first involves establishing and maintaining a good working relationship with the child and parent.

Recognising diversity

Here are some issues to consider with regard to child protection:

- Don't assume that a family from a particular background is more or less likely to abuse their children.
- Ensure that children and parents for whom English is an additional language use their preferred interpreter and access all the information they may need.
- Promote anti-discriminatory practice with the children. Challenge inappropriate behaviour.

It is important, when responding to disclosure of abuse, that you do not make assumptions about the family's situation based on their culture, racial background or gender. Very often we make assumptions based on what we *think* we know about a certain group in society or race of people. For example, we may assume that parents using physical punishment such as smacking are abusive, whereas many families consider this to be a fair discipline. We may assume that it is more natural for a man to be strict and less affectionate towards his children or we may decide he is a particularly 'good dad' if he spends time playing with his child.

In the case of Victoria Climbie, assumptions were made about Caribbean methods of discipline, suggesting that they were more authoritarian and some of these assumptions led to Victoria being ignored by the authorities. Whilst it is important to respect all parents and their styles of parenting, it is necessary to look deeper and think first before making an assumption. There may be times when a form of punishment considered reasonable by one culture is considered unreasonable in the UK and those parents may need support in recognising that. In such a case, it is important that the practitioner seeks advice from other professionals involved and actively challenges other team members who may make judgemental comments about the family.

Dealing with inconsistent care

As a key worker, you will work with many different families and you need to be aware of different cultures and social status within our society and ensure you are not judgemental in anyway. It is essential that the key worker is not critical of parenting styles, just because they do not view it as the 'norm'. For example, a child who is allowed to stay up in the evenings until the parents go to bed may be a concern in terms of how much sleep the child is getting, but it may be necessary to consider the additional adult attention the child may gain during this period. Families under stress may be able to take some advice about new strategies in coping with their children. However, when they are distracted by other problems or start to feel that the strategies are not having an immediate effect, they may give up and will need encouragement to persevere.

Stereotypes

You need to be very careful that you do not make assumptions based on stereotypes. Here are some examples:

- a drug user – poor and unemployed, always trying to get money from people, hanging around street corners
- an alcoholic – asleep during the day, out of control, always smelling of alcohol
- a child abuser – a man who hangs around school gates and watches the children in the playground.

Believing these stereotypes is not good practice and leads us to make assumptions about people. Good practice in the protection of children asks that we maintain a focus on the child and their family, which is not subject to bias or pre-value judgements.

Assessment activity 5.3

Compile a PowerPoint presentation for an audience of your peers, which describes the principles of responding to disclosure. Your presentation must include at least **five** slides with printed notes of the presentation attached (in no more than 50 words per slide). **P5**

5.4 Strategies for supporting children, their families and other adults

Safe practices in early years settings

Good practice within any early years setting involves working as part of a team, both within the setting and in respect of other professionals and local authority guidelines. This section enables you to explore specific issues of good practice related to protecting children.

What is a child protection policy?

All early years settings must have policies which outline procedures workers must follow in particular situations, for example on health and safety, and anti-bullying. They must also have a child protection policy in line with guidelines set down by the local authority, which contains information about what to do if you suspect that a child in your care is being abused or neglected. These policies should be written in a format that is easy to read for early years workers, volunteers and parents. It is important that they are reviewed regularly, and updated to keep abreast of any local and national changes in policy and law.

Standard 13 of the *National Standards for Under Eights Day Care and Childminding – Full Day Care* states:

'The registered person has a written statement based on the ACPC procedures clearly stating staff responsibilities with regard to reporting of suspected child abuse or neglect, including contact names and telephone numbers. It also includes procedures to be followed in the event of an allegation being made against a member of staff or volunteer.'

The Standards also state that there must be a designated member of staff who is responsible for liaison with child protection agencies in any child protection situation. The guidance to the National Standards provides the following advice about what to include in a child protection policy:

- the setting's commitment to the protection of children
- the responsibilities of all staff in child protection matters
- the steps to be taken when a concern is raised

- the name of the designated member of staff for child protection liaison and their role and responsibilities
- how and under what circumstances parents will be informed about concerns and any actions taken, and how confidentiality will be managed.

In relation to allegations made against a member of staff, the policy could include:

- the action to be taken with regard to the member of staff
- who should be informed
- how any investigation will be conducted and by whom
- how confidentiality will be managed.

Settings will also include statements about training opportunities, and the need to share the policy with all parents. An example of a child protection policy is shown opposite.

Guidelines for staff

As an essential part of good practice, all settings will have policies and procedures which are set down in line with local authority guidelines – we have already mentioned some of these in considering what to do if a child should disclose abuse or if staff at the setting

Happy Days Nursery

Child Protection Policy

Happy Days Nursery aims to provide an environment where children are safe from abuse and where any suspicion of abuse is promptly and appropriately responded to. In order to achieve this we will do the following:

- We will ensure that all staff have police clearance prior to the onset of employment.
- We will require at least one reference, which will always be followed up. Doubts regarding previous employment or gaps in employment will need to be clearly explained.
- We will require all appointments to be subject to a probationary period.
- We will ensure that all staff are trained in the identification of signs and symptoms of possible abuse.
- We will be vigilant when undertaking everyday routines, to allow for observation of the children.
- We will refer any suspicions to the manager, who will then take the decision as to whether further investigation is needed.
- We will ensure that all matters in relation to any child protection issue are treated according to the Confidentiality Policy of the setting.
- We will ensure that all parents are made aware of the Child Protection Policy when their children first enter the nursery.

- We will ensure that parents are informed of any changes noticed in the behaviour or appearance of their child.
- We will contact Social Services or the NSPCC, at the discretion of the manager.
- We will recognise the expertise of professional statutory and voluntary organisations and will endeavour to work closely with them, should the need arise.
- We will comply with the local ACPC procedures. The file is kept in the manager's office and can be examined at any time.
- Allegations of abuse against staff members/volunteers will be investigated immediately and relevant staff members will be suspended from their posts until investigations are complete. The manager will inform the Area Child Protection Team, who will undertake the necessary investigations. Persons found to be guilty of abuse of any nature will be referred to the appropriate agency. Support will be given to staff who may be the subject of wrongful allegations.

 An example of a child protection policy

▼ Promoting good practice

Promoting good practice	Examples of practical experiences
Appropriate physical care enables children to have respect for their bodies and to learn about the personal control they should have over their own bodies and what their personal boundaries are	Providing privacy during toileting Respecting privacy when dressing Encouraging independence in physical care routines such as bathing, feeding, toileting Promoting discreet behaviour such as not pulling your trousers down in public Drawing activities where the children can discuss: • who has the right to touch your body, for example doctors • what parts of the body should not be touched by others, i.e. areas covered by swimwear
Appropriate physical care enables children to learn about their bodies	Younger children learn body-part vocabulary Age-appropriate discussion about bodily functions
Appropriate physical care gives young children the opportunity for individual attention and appropriate affectionate touch which will enable them to recognise inappropriate touches	The cuddles a baby receives during nappy changing The physical touch during dressing activities The appropriate bed-time routine with bathing, story and cuddle
Appropriate physical care enables children to develop good self-image and self-esteem	Demonstrating respect during physical care activities, explaining to the child what you are doing, 'We are going to take your socks off now' rather than just pulling the socks off Positive comments during dressing activities can promote self-image
Appropriate physical care demonstrates how adults should behave towards children and young people	Appropriate support for toileting and bathing Privacy for older children

should have concerns about a child. All staff employed to work with children will have a 'police check' by the Criminal Records Bureau (CRB). This is a legal requirement for working with children. They will have also had an induction and regular staff training to ensure that they are up to date with current legal requirements and ways of working.

Affection

All children need physical demonstrations of affection. They need to experience appropriate touches during respectful contact. If they do not have experience of appropriate affection, they will not be able to judge what is inappropriate. Similarly a child who has limited experience of physical affection may be so desperate for affection that they accept inappropriate advances from adults. For this reason, it is important to role-model appropriate expressions of affection.

All children and families have different ways of demonstrating affection. It is wrong to demand expressions of affection such as sitting on your knee or being kissed if the child does not offer these spontaneously. Some children who crave affection may approach any new adult in the setting with overt physical attention. They may want to hold your hand, sit on your knee and always be physically close. For many new students in placement this message can be misunderstood and it is important that in this situation you do not promote unnecessary physical contact and maintain a professional approach to all children.

Visiting and access rights

In every setting, practitioners are responsible for the children in their care, this includes access to the children during the session times and what happens at the end of the session – 'going home time'. As part of the records kept on each child, there will be written clarification from the parent as to who is allowed to collect the child from the setting. A record of who is allowed to collect the child will be kept in the register. Should there be any changes to this, the setting will need to ensure that parents are aware of how to inform the staff of these changes. If a different adult should come to collect the child, members of staff would not be

allowed to let the child go with the adult unless a prior arrangement was made with the parent. This is when good communication is essential.

During the sessions the building needs to be secure. In some settings this can be in the form of an intercom or a reception area where visitors are met by a member of staff and not allowed to wander in to rooms occupied by the children. It is also necessary to ask all visitors to sign into the visitor's book, not only to protect the children but also for their own safety. Outside areas must also be secure, with gates locked permitting no access from outside but easy exit should there be a fire or emergency.

Case study: Sharing information with parents and carers

Read the following descriptions of children being welcomed into nursery:

- Zareena arrives at nursery with her grandmother, who does not speak English. Kate (her key worker) bends down to talk to Zareena and asks her if she has enjoyed the weekend. She takes her hand and walks in to the nursery, as she does so she turns and quickly says, 'Say goodbye to Grandma, Zareena.'
- Mark is a newly qualified practitioner. Whilst the children are arriving, he keeps busy trying not to make eye-contact with anyone. Kelly walks up behind him and says: 'My mummy wants you, Mark.' Mark replies, 'Can you ask her to talk to Marcia (the head of room) please, Kelly, I am a little bit busy now.'
- Brandon is not co-operating with his mother as she tries to change his shoes in the crowded hallway. She is looking a little anxious as some of the other mothers are staring. Louise (the practitioner) walks over to them and smiles at Brandon's mother. She says, 'Hello Brandon, how are you today? Have you told your mummy about the model you made yesterday? If you want, we can show it to mummy. Do you want to change your shoes and we can go through together?'

Identify areas of good and bad practice in communicating with each family. Give reasons for your choices.

When you are working with children and their families it is usual practice, indeed good practice, to involve parents and carers in all decision-making about the child, to have ongoing and open dialogue with them to support the developmental needs of the child and ensure that there is continuity between home and the setting. In doing so, you should ensure that you deal appropriately with confidential information about the family and the child.

However, sometimes it is necessary to breach confidentiality and share private information. Our duty to ensure confidentiality can only be overruled if the information reveals:

- a crime or intent to commit a crime
- an intention to harm themselves or another person
- that a person needs protecting from harm.

Parents have the right:

- to be informed if they are under investigation
- to have responsibility for their child
- for the child to continue to live in the family home.

However, these rights can be overruled if they endanger a child's welfare. It is, of course, in the best interests of the child to keep the parent informed and throughout any investigation they will be heard and treated with respect at all times. Although you will not be presuming guilt on the part of the parent you will always need to act on the best interests of the child and to advocate for that child or young person, even if this conflicts with the parent's rights being upheld.

Strategies with children and young people

The most important aspect of self-protection is the promotion of children's confidence and self-esteem. However, there are many other ways that you can empower children to protect themselves. Giving them information, promoting awareness and

encouraging coping skills can achieve this. You can teach children:

- the difference between good and bad touches
- to say 'No!' to adults that they know, as well as to strangers
- the difference between good and bad 'secrets'
- that their body belongs to them
- that they have a right to privacy
- older children will be listened to
- support older children to understand their rights
- ways of coping with bullying
- how to get help.

The table opposite identifies specific strategies that can be introduced to enable children to protect themselves. It is important to remember that children should not be made to feel totally responsible for their own protection, as in reality the adults who care for them are ultimately responsible.

Theory into practice

Make a game and plan an activity for children to develop body awareness.

- Provide a rationale for the activity.
- Identify some of the language or conversation you may promote.
- What will the children gain from taking part in the game?

Remember to ensure that your communication with children is age-appropriate. Your experience of working with children will be your guide.

- Use age-appropriate language.
- Check vocabulary and ensure that the child understands.
- Use pictures or drawings with younger children.
- Communicate at the child's pace; do not force the subject.
- Play therapists may use anatomically correct dolls to promote conversation.
- Do not lead the child.
- Employ effective listening.
- Work at the child's level; ensure good eye-contact.

▼ Strategies to enable children to protect themselves

Concept	Strategies
Good and bad touches Children should be able to identify good and bad touches. Touches that hurt, are rude or make them feel uncomfortable are not acceptable	Promote through appropriate daily physical care routines Support children who say 'No' to tickling games, hugs or kisses For older children, discussions such as 'I like hugs from ... I would not like a hug from ...'
To say 'No!' to adults they know as well as to strangers While it is important to promote the concept of 'stranger danger', more children are at risk from adults that they know well	Role play Books and videos, for example the NSPCC's *Emily and the Stranger* or Rolf Harris' *Say No video* Visits from a police officer Discussion about people you trust
Good and bad secrets You can provide opportunities for children to discuss good and bad secrets	Discussion about good and bad secrets. No one should ever ask children to keep a hug, touch or smack secret. 'Don't tell Mummy what we have bought for her birthday' = good secret 'Don't tell Mummy that I hit you' = bad secret
That their body belongs to them Children should be encouraged to know that their body belongs to them and that they have control over what happens to it	Young children can be helped by learning body vocabulary Songs such as 'Head, shoulders, knees and toes ...' Books such as *My First Body Book* (Early Learning Centre) Appropriate physical care routines Draw a picture of a body and discuss which parts of the body are the 'private' parts Body 'beetle game'
That they have the right to privacy Children have the right to their own privacy	Physical care routines
Getting help There are some situations where children can help themselves by getting help	Children should be taught their address and phone number in case they get lost Learning about which adults they can go to for help, for example the police, the person at the shop till, a lollipop lady, a mother with a pram or school teacher Visits from a police officer Shouting 'No!'

Empowering children to protect their rights

In protecting children we need to ensure that we **advocate** for them if they cannot speak for themselves. In supporting the child, we need to be aware of the rights of the parents so that we do not challenge their parental responsibilities.

Parents' *rights* were changed to *responsibilities* under the 1989 Children Act and the new concept of **parental responsibility** was added (see Key terms for a definition). This means that children are no longer seen as possessions of their parents, and that parents no longer have 'absolute rights' for their children. The parents never lose parental responsibility, unless the child is adopted or taken into care on a care order, and then parental responsibility is 'shared'.

Key terms

Advocate To be an advocate for a child or young person is to speak or act on their behalf to maintain their best interests if they are unable to do so themselves.

Parental responsibility In law, parents have both rights and responsibilities towards their children.

Children's rights have become increasingly central to legislation and have grown from the Children Act 1989 and the United Nations Convention on the Rights of the Child and more recently the Children Act of 2004. The table below shows some of the European and national rights of children.

▼ The rights of children

Children Act 2004	United Nations Convention on the Rights of the Child
To have their wishes and feelings taken into consideration	To non-discrimination
	To have their best interests as a primary consideration
To be brought up within their own families wherever possible	To an identity
	To express views and opinions
	To freedom of thought, conscience and religion
To decline medical treatment (Gillick v. West Norfolk Health Authority)	To protection from abuse and neglect
	To an adequate standard of living
	To an education
To adequate/ appropriate services	The Convention also details the rights of:
	• children when separated from parents
	• disabled children
	• children from minority ethnic communities

Theory into practice

Research the case of Gillick v. West Norfolk Health Authority, in which a parent took a health authority to court because they had prescribed her daughter (who was under 16) with the contraceptive pill.

- What were the outcomes of this case?
- What implication does this have on children and young people in respect of their rights?

Working with parents and families

Encouraging the development of parenting skills

The majority of parents, even those who abuse their children, do love them very much and want to do the best for them. It is important that you do not judge any parent and, despite any personal feelings you may have about their management of the child, you must treat them with professional respect. We are taught that to promote self-esteem we respond to a child who is behaving inappropriately by saying 'I do not like what you are doing, but I still love you.' In the same way, we can encourage a parent's self-esteem by acknowledging that as people and parents they are valued even though they may not be meeting all their child's needs. If you can initiate good relationships with the parents and work to promote their self-esteem, they will develop confidence in your ability to help and advise them.

Many people learn parenting skills within their own family but some parents, particularly young people and parents who have not experienced parenting themselves, may need help to develop these skills.

There are many ways of helping families to develop parenting skills. Working with parents is important because:

- parenting programmes can work in changing parents' behaviour and increasing their range of skills
- programmes can reduce the proportion of negative parenting
- parenting must be seen in the context of the relationship between the couple and other external stresses.

Parents and families involved in an abuse case will be involved in the assessment procedure identifying the needs of the child. Parents may attend case conference and will be involved in the identified plan of possible care and work with members of the core group to support the child.

The table below addresses some of the difficulties experienced by parents and identifies strategies to support them. Many of these activities will be introduced in all early years settings, but some will be used within settings where parents are required to bring their child under a child protection order.

▼ Difficulties faced by parents and strategies to support them

Skills	Difficulties faced by some parents	Strategies to support parents
Relating to children	Parents may not have experienced good parenting themselves and do not know how to relate to children In a stressful family situation, responding to children is a low priority, for example mental health, drug-related situations	Provide positive feedback whenever possible Encourage the parent to work beside you positively (role modelling) Help parents to develop listening skills Provide opportunities for parents to talk to children and share experiences with children Address any additional difficulties the parent may be experiencing such as accessing financial support
Informing parents about childcare and development	Parents may not see it as a priority to know about their child's development Parents may feel that the nursery is the expert and will deal with all such matters Parents may have literacy difficulties themselves and be reluctant that this should be 'found out', or have difficulty accessing information	Positively reinforce the value of shared care Exchange information on a daily basis Hold regular parents' meetings to discuss children's learning Arrange visits from the health visitor or dental hygienist Display signs and pictures around the setting describing development milestones related to individual activities Write reports about development in a jargon-free format which is accessible to parents
Developing practical caring skills	Parents may not have experienced the basic caring skills Parents may be isolated and have no support network and therefore no role models	Do not challenge the parent's method of working with their child. Suggest that there may also be some other ways of managing the situation. For example, rather than saying a diet of spaghetti hoops is not nourishing, suggest additional things that the child could eat Demonstrate practical skills such as nappy changing, bottle and hygiene routines. Involve the parent in cooking activities or meal times Identify or instigate support networks within the family and the community
Participating in play and learning	Parents may not have experienced play themselves Play may not be seen as a priority Learning may be viewed as the role of the nursery or school Financial difficulties may limit the provision of play materials or stimulating experiences	Provide opportunities for parents to share play experiences with children in the early years setting Provide workshop activities where parents can enjoy the play experience and make games or puppets to share with their child at home Use toy libraries Provide in-house 'stress free' courses
Adapting as children develop	For first children, parents may not know what to expect at different ages and stages, for example some parents will continue baby food long after the time the child should be on solid food Some parents have a need to be needed and are reluctant to allow their children to develop	Discussion about future developments, for example preparing for temper tantrums Verbal exchange on a daily basis preparing the way for additional development Linking the parent into family and community support networks Family workshop activities which enable the parent to meet other parents and observe the development of different children
Facilitating change	Accepting the need to change requires an individual to confront the fact that they may not have been doing well enough. This is very threatening	Parents need all the support they can to accept the need for change and to move forward positively. This relies on them receiving positive feedback and encouragement and the belief that they are valued as parents

Support for behaviour management

In the latest government guidance we are asked to work with both parents and other professionals to support families who are in need. This can be facilitated in all settings not just family centres.

A family may get stuck in a cycle where the child's inappropriate behaviour causes the parent to behave in an inappropriate manner. To ensure change, both children and parents may need help to modify their behaviour. There are many strategies for promoting positive behaviour. These can be reinforced through a variety of shared experiences, as shown in the table below.

▼ Strategies to encourage behaviour modification

Activity	Strategies to encourage behaviour modification
Women's group	The process is started by promoting the parents' self-esteem by providing the parents with some quality time where they can experience activities such as aromatherapy, make-up sessions, relaxation or stress management. It is an opportunity to have time for themselves and pamper themselves.
Fathers' group	Similar to above – fathers get the opportunity to meet with other parents and discuss their children and other topics. Many of these groups work within the community helping other parents and children and providing a good support network.
Family workshop	An opportunity for staff to work with the whole family, promoting positive behaviour such as encouraging parents to praise good behaviour, to give children lots of attention and encourage the child's self-control. There are opportunities for one-to-one support to help parents reduce the need to smack.
Outings such as shopping	This is a situation where children and parents often behave inappropriately. Staff can demonstrate effective behaviour management such as giving the child responsibility, or using distraction techniques and reinforcing appropriate behaviour.
Residential	An opportunity for children and parents to experience new and stimulating activities whilst staff introduce effective management techniques during normal family activities such as meal times and bed-time routines. Staff reinforce the importance of a consistent approach, of not nagging the child and of firmly reinforcing appropriate behaviour.
Home visit	Staff can visit at meal times to support what may be difficult situations, encouraging the family to sit at the table and to participate in conversation. Parents will be encouraged to set a good example and reward desirable behaviour. They can then encourage play experiences with new and exciting resources from the toy library.

Providing feedback to parents about their parenting

Factors to consider when providing feedback to parents are outlined in the diagram.

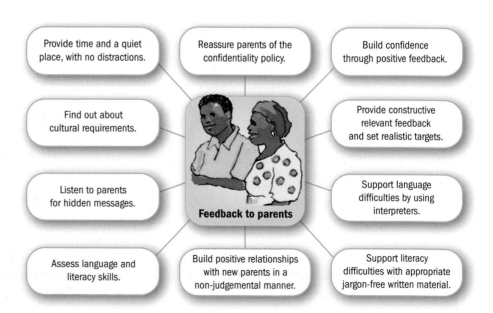

Provide time and a quiet place, with no distractions.

Reassure parents of the confidentiality policy.

Build confidence through positive feedback.

Find out about cultural requirements.

Provide constructive relevant feedback and set realistic targets.

Listen to parents for hidden messages.

Support language difficulties by using interpreters.

Feedback to parents

Assess language and literacy skills.

Build positive relationships with new parents in a non-judgemental manner.

Support literacy difficulties with appropriate jargon-free written material.

Whilst helping parents with their child's behaviour, it is important to take into account cultural and social factors. What might be viewed as unacceptable in one society may be viewed as the norm in another. We have already seen that standards of acceptable behaviour vary in different families (see page 182) and it may be difficult for children to conform to another expected standard within the early years setting. It is therefore very important to work with parents to achieve a consistent approach to managing behaviour. Communication barriers may also pose a problem when working with parents for whom English is an additional language – therefore a translator should be called upon. In the same way, for parents with a hearing impairment, a signer should be requested.

Sources of information and support

Co-operating with other professionals

Early years settings can provide key information to aid the assessment process and co-operate with other professionals. They can share information about:

- the child's development
- their relationships with their family members
- the child's health
- how the child interacts with other children and adults.

Everyday observation and monitoring of a child's progress will enable the setting to have a holistic view of the child. Other professionals, such as a health visitor or a social worker, may only see the child for short periods of time in a particular set of circumstances.

Early years settings can share information with other professionals to support the family and in some cases prevent an abusive situation occurring. This is what the Green Paper *Every Child Matters* called for by stating the need for:

- a common assessment framework (see the Framework for the Assessment of Children in Need and their Families, page 186)

- improved sharing of information between agencies
- a lead professional to be identified when children are involved with several agencies, i.e. health; social services; voluntary agencies.

It may not be necessary to allocate specialist services for the child if part of the protection plan can be supported in the early years setting where the child and their parents will have already formed good trusting relationships.

In all early years settings it is important to promote a collaborative approach to meeting the needs of a child. The early years setting can perform a role that supports a multi-disciplinary approach by:

- making other professionals welcome in the setting
- observing and monitoring children
- keeping good records
- recognising early indicators of abuse
- keeping staff up to date with training and legislation
- giving parents information about support services.

Theory into practice

You have a family at your setting who is causing concern – there are two children, one 2 years old and a baby of 9 months. The mother has expressed her anxiety about being able to cope as she has just been diagnosed with cancer and has no partner or family close by.

What would the early years setting do to:

- support and advise the mother?
- support the children?
- ensure the needs of the children were being met?

You will need to look at the possibility of involving other professionals. What might the setting put in place?

It is very important for all professionals working within this field and with cases of safeguarding children to respect confidentiality. When using a multi-agency approach, this needs to be handled carefully and information must only be shared with those who are directly involved with the case. It is also important that the information shared is only used to inform the professional in completing their part of the whole support package or care plan. They may not need to know or understand the finer details and background of the whole case.

Community support networks

The challenges faced by families who are involved in abusive situations are considerable and cannot always be addressed by one agency. A range of professionals with different skills and expertise will be able to work together to support the family.

Under the Children Act, social services has a duty to provide services for children and families in need. The law defines 'in need' in a very broad way. It covers:

- children who are not achieving a reasonable standard of health or development
- children whose health or development is likely to be damaged
- children with disabilities.

The services provided by social services may include:

- advice, guidance and counselling
- access to a family or children's centre
- occupational, social, cultural and leisure activities
- home help
- holiday provision
- day care provision for under-5s and specified activities after school and in the holidays for under-8s
- accommodation for children where the person caring for them has been prevented for any reason from providing accommodation or care, for example hospitalisation.

Voluntary and private organisations also offer services to families who are in need. The NSPCC is a voluntary organisation, which has the statutory power to remove children who are deemed to be at risk of significant harm from their homes. The NSPCC has been providing support to families in many communities for many years. Services vary widely, based on the needs of the local community.

Extension activity

Visit the NSPCC website and identify the role of the following organisations. Then visit the appropriate websites to identify additional facts about the organisations.

- The Children's Legal Centre
- Deafchild International
- National Association of Child Contact Centres
- Parentline Plus
- The Samaritans
- Women's Aid

Children and family centres

The responsibility for neighbourhood nurseries lies with the Early Years Development and Childcare Partnerships. They work with other services to provide a service for families in their area. Many of these services will be provided under one roof alongside:

- parent groups
- crèche facilities
- language groups
- baby massage
- mother and baby support groups
- fathers' groups.

Many of the families will have been referred by a social worker or health visitor.

Children's centres are very often centres of vocational excellence and provide care and education for children from 6 months to school age. Many offer 'wraparound care' to enable parents to work longer hours. Children attending such a centre will have access to a range of facilities as the centres work closely with other professionals, usually on the premises.

Extension activity

This activity will support work for assessment activity 5.4.

Working in a small group, research one of the following voluntary organisations:

- NSPCC
- Barnardos
- Kidscape
- NCH.

Prepare a presentation for the rest of your group. Address the following points, and present your findings:

- the history of the organisation
- the aims and objectives
- the main areas of work
- funding issues
- local contacts
- the role of the organisation in offering joint services with local authorities.

Discuss how you would disseminate this information to parents.

The range of professionals involved

The following list summarises the roles of some of the professionals who may support families to enable them to stay together and work to prevent problems.

- *Social workers* Many families will have regular contact with a social worker to support them. They are able to request services for the family.
- *Health visitors* Parents will have visits from their health visitor when the children are young. The health visitor may also pay regular visits to the early years setting on an informal basis to see if there are any concerns.
- *Drug and alcohol counsellors* These may be involved with parents or older siblings.
- *Educational psychologists* Support from an educational psychologist may be short term if there are behaviour or development problems or if a child has been abused.
- *Psychiatrists* These may be working with family members if there is a mental health issue or a child has been abused.
- *Family workers* These are very often attached to a family or children's centre. They may do some outreach work.
- *Play therapists* Play therapy has been found to be beneficial to children traumatised by abuse.
- *Child protection teams* These may only have contact in the initial stages of an investigation and assessment of a child. They may ask the setting for information to aid the assessment process.
- *Teachers* Schools can contact and refer for all sorts of concerns, including child protection concerns or individual needs.
- *General practitioners (GPs)* Very often GPs are the first port of call for many families. The GP will refer a child or family to the relevant services and will also be able to reassure and offer ongoing support to the family, having very often secured their trust.
- *Hospital staff* There are many ways in which families may become involved with hospital staff. This could initially be through the accident and emergency department. Vigilant staff will recognise a concern and offer support. The hospital will also have their own social workers who can be called in to help with things such as long-term illnesses, eczema and related problems.
- *Religious ministers* Many people will find talking to the minister of their own faith or religion an enormous comfort. Very often a religious minister can be involved with many of the family problems and challenges and will refer them to other services and professionals for support and help. A religious community can often be a source of strength for a family or child in need of support. They will feel they belong and are able to trust the advice given to them. Religious communities also offer a good role model for family life and stability in parenting.

Alternative forms of care

If, due to child abuse and neglect, a child has to be removed from the family home, they will be placed in foster care or in a children's home. Fostering, however, is seen as a good alternative to residential care in that it:

- can provide a family environment

- can be used for short- or long-term placements
- avoids children becoming institutionalised
- enables children who have been abused, and as a result possibly experiencing behavioural problems, the opportunity to experience family life.

If a child is fostered, temporarily, it may also be possible for them to remain at their normal setting and have continuity of care.

Voluntary organisations, such as Barnardos and the NCH, also provide this service. There has also been an increase in privately-run children's homes. These establishments consist of small family group homes, community homes and resource and reception centres.

Adoption is seen as another alternative to a child growing up in an abusive situation. This is governed by the Adoption Act 1976 and the Children Act 2004 and is a legal undertaking with all the responsibilities of caring for a natural child. As mentioned previously, with adoption, the birth parents lose parental responsibility, which is automatically given to the adoptive parents once the adoption certificate is processed.

Residential establishments for children are mainly provided by local authorities. However, respite care can also be advantageous for children who have been abused or neglected. Residential care is given to a child for a short period only, giving the parent and child the opportunity for some 'time out'.

Alleviating the effects of abuse

Once a child has disclosed that they have been abused, or you have observed indicators of abuse and referred to social services, your work with that child is just beginning. Below is a list of suggestions which may help with the after-effects of abuse:

- Consult other professionals for advice – this could be in the form of a specialist counselling service which supports children and their families through such events. Some of these services can be referred through the GP or, alternatively, advice and counselling can be given through voluntary agencies and support groups or charities such as NSPCC.

- Help the child to build trusting relationships – this could be achieved through a one-to-one relationship with a key worker.
- Remain consistent and allow times for rest and quiet periods.
- Always be willing to listen to the child should they wish to talk further about the abuse, but do not question the child.
- Meet the child's individual needs. Remember many children who have been abused display challenging behaviour and may need specialist help with this.
- Children may need support with language skills to express themselves.
- Provide appropriate play experiences to allow the child to explore feelings and promote self-image and self-esteem.

Case study: A parent seeks advice

Jamie is 3 years old. He has two older sisters, Sarah (age 9) and Emma (age 11). This week Jamie's mother has come into nursery very upset asking to speak to the manager. She explains to the manager that her partner (not the father of the children) has been arrested for sexually abusing a young girl. The police are not letting him return to the family home until further investigations take place.

1 Jamie's mother wants some advice. What do you tell her?
2 Should you report this to anyone? If so, to whom?
3 What strategies could you use to support Jamie at this time?
4 In what ways might Jamie be affected by this arrest?

■ Play experiences

The child may be referred to a play therapist whose role is to help children express trauma or emotions through play. You will also be able to offer a range of different play experiences, which will support all children's emotional and social development. The table opposite identifies some of these.

▼ Play experiences to support children's emotional and social development

Child's needs	Play activities
Expressing their feelings	Appropriate books dealing with issues such as bullying, or moving into foster care
	Dough, clay and malleable materials where children can give vent to powerful feelings
	Sand, water and messy play activities
	Happy/sad faces drawing activities to allow the children to give words to their feelings
	Self-portrait activities with sensitive non-questioning discussion
	Expressing feeling through music and dance
	Opportunities to explore feelings through role-play activities
	Controlled noise-making activities such as banging a drum, shouting out loud, etc.
	Puppets and doll play where children can describe feelings
Improving self-image	Body image activities such as self-portraits, use of mirrors, etc.
	Dressing up with mirrors and supportive discussion
	Books and stories such as Little Duck and the Bad Eye Glasses
	Circle time and discussion about objects from home
	Create 'A book about me'
	Invite parents from different cultural groups to the setting to share cooking or clothing experiences
Building self-esteem	Positive feedback during all interactions
	Dressing-up activities to develop independence skills
	Provide tasks and responsibilities, for example handing out biscuits, feeding the animals, and looking after younger children

▲ Creative play can give vent to powerful feelings

Theory into practice

- How do you think a child who has been abused might feel? Make a list of these possible feelings.
- Plan a list of one-to-one activities you might provide for the child and give reasons for your choice.

Assessment activity 5.4

1 Describe three activities you can use as strategies to support children who have been abused. **P6**

2 Describe three strategies you can use to support their families and other adults. **P6**

3 Write a guidance leaflet for families in need (two sides of A4), which explains the child protection strategies to support children, their families and other adults **M3**

4 Evaluate the strategies you have suggested (1,000 words). **D2**

End of unit assessment

1 Carry out some further research on four of the models of child abuse described on page 178.

2 Summarise your chosen four theoretical models of child abuse in no more than 100 words for each theory. **P2**

3 Write a short essay comparing your chosen four theoretical models, with at least two references for each theory. Include a chart demonstrating the practical advantages and disadvantages of each theory. **M1**

4 Evaluate how these models relate to practice. **D1**

References and further reading

Barker *et al.* (2004) *A Child Protection Handbook*, Routledge

Beckett, C. (2003) *Child Protection: an introduction*, Sage

Brown, A. and Finkelhor, D. (1986) 'Impact of child sexual abuse: a review of research', *Psychological Bulletin*, vol. 99, pp 66–77

Bruce, T. and Meggitt, C. (1999) *Childcare and Education,* 2nd edition, Hodder & Stoughton

Department of Health, *Framework for the Assessment of Children in Need and their Families* (2000), The Stationery Office

Department of Health (2003) *What To Do If You're Worried a Child is Being Abused*, The Stationery Office

Finkelhor, D. (1984) *Child Sexual Abuse: new theory and research*, Prentice Hall

Flynn, B. and Starns, B. (2004) *Child Protection: working together to keep children safe*, Heinemann

Full Day Care Guidance to the National Standards (2001), DfES

Herbert, M. (1996) *Working with Children and the Children Act*, BPS Books

Hobart, C. and Frankel, J. (1998) *Good Practice in Child Protection*, Nelson Thornes

Horton, C. (ed.) (2004) *Working with Children 2004–5: facts, figures, information*, Guardian Books in association with NCH

Kemp, C. *et al.* (1962) 'The battered child syndrome', *Journal of American Medical Association*, vol. 181, pp 17–24

Kempe, R. and Kempe, C. (1978) *Child Abuse*, Fontana

Lindon, J. (1998) *Child Protection and Early Years Work*, Hodder & Stoughton

National Standards for Under Eights Day Care and Childminding – Full Day Care (2001), DfES

Reder, P. *et al.* (1999), *Beyond Blame: child abuse tragedies revisited*, Routledge

Tassoni, P. (2003) *Supporting Special Needs*, Heinemann

Tassoni, P. and Bulman, K. (1999) *Early Years Care and Education NVQ 3*, Heinemann

Victoria Climbie Inquiry – Report of an Inquiry by Lord Lamming (January 2003)

Working Together to Safeguard Children (1999), The Stationery Office

Resources for children

Emily and the Stranger, NSPCC

Elliott, M. (1998) *Feeling Happy, Feeling Safe*, Hodder & Stoughton (colour picture book for ages 3–7)

Jody and the Biscuit Bully, NSPCC

Videos

Cosmo and Dibs Keep Safe, Kidscape and BBC (for children aged 3–6, teaching notes included)

Useful websites

Barnados – www.barnardos.org.uk

Bullying Online – www.bullying.co.uk

Childline – www.childline.org.uk

Children 1st – www.children1st.org.uk

Children's Legal Centre – www.childrenslegalcentre.com

Children's Society – www.the-childrens-society.org.uk

Criminal Records Bureau and the Data protection Team – www.disclosure.gov.uk

Daycare Trust – www.daycaretrust.org.uk

Deafchild International – www.deafchild.org

Department of Health publications – www.dh.gov.uk

Every Child Matters – www.dfes.gov.uk/everychildmatters

Gingerbread – www.gingerbread.org.uk

Kidscape – www.kidscape.org.uk

National Association of Child Contact Centres – www.nacc.org.uk

National Association for People Abused in Childhood (NAPAC) – www.napac.org.uk

National Children's Bureau – www.ncb.org.uk

NCH – www.nch.org.uk

NSPCC – http://www.nspcc.org.uk

Ofsted – www.ofsted.gov.uk

Parentline Plus – www.parentlineplus.org.uk

Planet One Parent – www.planetoneparent.com

Women's Aid – www.womensaid.org.uk

Save the Children (SCF) – www.savethechildren.org.uk

UNICEF – http://www.unicef.org.uk/tz/resources

Victoria Climbie – www.victoria-climbie-inquiry-org

Grading criteria	Assessment activity	Page number
To achieve a pass grade the evidence must show that the learner is able to:		
P1 describe four physical and four behavioural indicators of possible child abuse	5.1	182
P2 describe four theoretical models of child abuse	End of unit assessment	208
P3 outline the legal framework relating to the protection of children	5.2	190
P4 describe the reporting procedures in a child care setting	5.2	190
P5 describe the principles of responding to disclosure	5.3	195
P6 describe child protection strategies to support children, their families, and other adults	5.4	207
To achieve a merit grade the evidence must show that, in addition to the pass criteria, the learner is able to:		
M1 compare four theoretical models of child abuse	End of unit assessment	208
M2 explain reporting procedures in childcare settings	5.2	190
M3 explain child protection strategies to support children, their families, and other adults	5.4	207
To achieve a distinction grade the evidence must show that, in addition to the pass and merit criteria, the learner is able to:		
D1 evaluate four theoretical models of child abuse	End of unit assessment	208
D2 evaluate child protection strategies to support children, their families, and other adults	5.4	207

Promoting children's rights

Introduction

Britain is a diverse society with people from a wide range of cultures and backgrounds and with varying values and beliefs. Workers in any sector of childcare should recognise diversity as something to celebrate, but it is important to recognise that some members of society are disadvantaged in their access to the full benefits of our society, including education and healthcare as well social and economic provision.

Equality of opportunity, inclusion, and the rights of the individual are fundamental human rights, especially important for children and young people as they grow up.

This unit introduces learners to these fundamental concepts of diversity, equality, individual rights, and inclusion, especially in relation to the provision of services for children, and children's rights.

What you need to learn

- The meaning of diversity in today's society
- The importance of equality and recognising diversity and rights in services for children
- How services for children can recognise and promote equality, diversity and rights
- How to promote inclusion in your own practice

Thinking points

How do we develop our views and opinions about other people? Where does discrimination come from? Most people, if you ask them, would deny encouraging discrimination in their children, and yet discrimination is all too evident in society.

Imagine that you are working in an education setting and there is an unpleasant incident in the playground, with a small group of children bullying two others because of cultural and physical differences.

Your manager asks you to lead a project to improve understanding and promotion of diversity amongst the children. You start to think about why the children have developed these views and what the setting can do to improve them. What do you think you will need to consider? How can the setting start to improve attitudes?

So what is **diversity**? Isn't it just the same as equal opportunities? The short answer is: No! Diversity is at the heart of what makes everyone a unique individual. The human race is amazingly diverse. Look around any gathering of people – or just compare yourself to someone you sit next to on the bus to college. No two people are the same (even identical twins have some personality differences). You will see a whole range of differences from height, age, gender, skin and hair colour. Start talking to a few of the group and you will start to discover even more differences – including features that are not visible – experiences, education, family.

This section explores some of the crucial facts about these differences and later looks at how they can make a difference to lives.

There are many different factors that make up the diversity of an individual. Some of the important factors are race, culture, beliefs, values, age, health status, ability, place of origin, social class/stratification, economic status, family structure, sexuality, language, accents and codes of behaviour. It is very difficult to separate many of these aspects into individual points; many are very closely linked. For example, culture, language, beliefs and values may be very closely linked to a person's racial origin or place of origin. Economic status and accent is quite likely to be linked to their social class. Codes of behaviour, beliefs and values are closely tied to family structure, and age can be an important factor in beliefs and values, health, codes of behaviour.

Theory into practice

Look in the mirror and what do you see? What makes you *you*?

Look at the aspects of diversity above. How would you describe yourself in terms of race, culture, beliefs, values, age, health status, ability, place of origin, social class/stratification, economic status, family structure, sexuality, language, accents, codes of behaviour?

What do you think has influenced what?

Key term

Diversity recognises people's different characteristics, making sure they are considered so that they can get maximum benefit from their uniqueness. Treating people fairly means that their differences are recognised and are respected and acted upon as needed.

Diversity in British society

Race

The origin of the word 'race' is simply 'family'. In the nineteenth century it started to be used to describe the 'races of Man', defined as groups who were different to one another in terms of physical characteristics such as skin colour, hair type and body shape. However it is important to note that there are no traits, characteristics, or even one gene that is present in all members of one so-called race and absent in another. For example, all blood groups can be found in all the world's peoples (the percentage of Estonians and Papua New Guineans with A, B, and O blood are almost exactly identical).

As a word 'race' has no exact legal definition but the House of Lords defined an 'ethnic group' as a group that is seen as a distinct community because of certain characteristics that distinguish the group from the surrounding community. Two key characteristics are essential:

- a long shared history, of which the group is conscious as distinguishing it from other groups, and the memory of which it keeps alive
- a cultural tradition of its own, including family and social customs and manners, often but not necessarily associated with religious observance.

Other relevant characteristics may (but need not) include common geographical origin or ancestry, a common language (not necessarily peculiar to the group), a common literature, a common religion and the status of either a minority or a dominant group within a larger community.

Britain is a multi-cultural society. The percentage of the population in the UK who are from a minority ethnic background is 7.9 per cent, and around 50 per cent of this number were born in the UK (Office for National Statistics 2002).

According to the BBC's Born Abroad website (see page 248), in 2001, 4.3 million (7.53 per cent) of the total British population of 57.1 million were born outside Britain. This compares with 4.5 per cent in 1971, 5.14 per cent in 1981 and 5.75 per cent in 1991. The most common countries of birth were India (466,000), Pakistan (320,000), Germany (262,000) and the USA (155,000). Caribbean people accounted for 254,000 of the total.

Case study: Multi-culturalism is not new

In the 1700s, 20,000 of London's inhabitants were from ethnic minority groups.

The first documented instance of a black person in London was that of John Blanke, who was a trumpeter in the court of Henry VII in 1507. Fifty years later, black slaves were beginning to be brought from Africa, and this marked the beginnings of a continuous black presence in London. By the early eighteenth century, the number of black people in London had reached several thousand. Many had been brought to Britain as slave-servants of returning ex-colonial officials, traders, plantation owners and military personnel. However, the abolition of the British slave trade in 1807 effectively ended this first period of large-scale black immigration to London.

Source: Adapted from *Chronicle World: The shaping of Black London*

1 **What is the ethnic make up of the area you live in? How does it compare to the average for the UK?**

2 **Is the ethnic make up of the area you live in represented in your college and placement?**

Place of origin should not be confused with race. Many people who would describe themselves as belonging to a non-white ethnic or racial group were born in the UK. Place of origin or birth can be described as widely as the continent or the country or as locally as the county, town or even district. For example someone could describe their place of origin as Europe, the UK, England, Merseyside, Liverpool or Toxteth – and all would be correct.

The representation of different races is not equal across all aspects of society and is reflective of some of the issues affecting people of different races. Consider these facts:

- Around 10 per cent of children under 14 in the UK are from black and minority ethnic communities. The percentage in the north-east of England is much lower than in London.
- Over two-thirds of independently-owned local shops belong to people from minority ethnic groups.
- Almost 30 per cent of doctors and over 40 per cent of nurses in the NHS were born overseas.
- Twenty-one per cent of Asian people gain degrees, compared to only 16 per cent across the entire population of the UK.
- In 2002, there were only 12 black or Asian MPs in the UK. This figure should be between 55 and 60 to be a true reflection of the population.

Culture, beliefs and values

Culture can be part of race – as the definition of race suggests – but it is by no means tied with race. It has several senses.

- Culture is defined by the UN Covenant of 1966 on Economic, Social and Cultural Rights as education and participation in cultural life – the arts and sciences – books, theatre, dance, etc.
- Anthropologists (who study societies and cultures) define culture as the way of life of a particular group.
- Generalisations about the 'cultures' of all sorts of groups, large and small, are made not just by scientific observers but by anyone at all. People speak, for example, of an 'office culture' when describing the habits and conventions of those who work in offices. 'Consumer culture' and 'laddish culture' are common descriptions.

Key term

Culture is a set of attitudes, behaviour patterns and beliefs belonging to a group of people.

Culture can be seen as a set of attitudes, behaviour patterns and beliefs. There are indeed many different cultures in Britain, not least among the long-established population, where the differences may be defined by social class, region or dialect.

Age

Age has a great influence on how society and an individual view someone. The UK population profile is changing. Not too long ago, the population pyramid in the UK was a normal wide-based pyramid – with the majority of the population at the younger end. This has changed over the last 50 years to a bulging snake with the mass of population in middle to early old age.

The changing profile is slowly bringing about a change in attitudes towards older people in society. No longer seen as just a burden, the older population is now increasingly viewed as having power and influence – very different to 20 years or so ago, when the young were seen as the more important members of society.

The view of society as a whole on age can have a big influence on how people perceive themselves as well as the accessibility of goods and services.

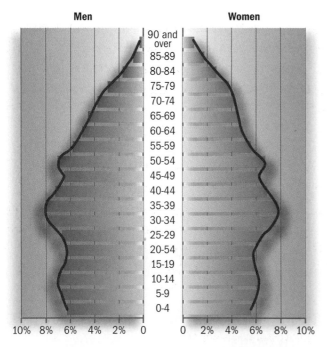

Men **Women**

90 and over
85-89
80-84
75-79
70-74
65-69
60-64
55-59
50-54
45-49
40-44
35-39
30-34
25-29
20-54
15-19
10-14
5-9
0-4

10% 8% 6% 4% 2% 0   0 2% 4% 6% 8% 10%

Source: Office for National Statistics

▲ **Population pyramid based on the results of the UK's 2001 census**

Health status

How healthy someone is can have a major influence on their life. Living with a chronic illness, that is one that continues for years, for example, arthritis or cystic fibrosis, can impose treatment regimes on daily life that can interfere with full participation in society. Health status can be closely linked with economic status as the cost of chronic ill-health can significantly affect earning power. The diversity of health status across any section of the population will be as diverse as any other individual characteristic.

Ability

Everyone has ability in some sphere. It is important to try to identify the particular ability that exists in individuals. The range of ability in any one skill will be diverse in a group of children or young people, for example the development of fine motor skills. When planning activities, it is essential to remember this and treat each child individually when deciding what level of skill or involvement in an activity is possible.

Family structure

The structure of families is almost as diverse as individuals. Sociologists divide family structures into a number of neat packages:

- *nuclear family* – parents and children living together in single unit
- *extended family* – parents and children living with or very near to grandparents, aunts or uncles
- *single-parent family* – one parent and children
- *reconstituted family* – two separate parents and children in a new relationship joined together.

This simple division hides a multitude of variations and it is important to remember that a family could potentially at different times fit into each different category! For example, a single-parent family could move into being a nuclear two-parent family. Subsequent separation could result in a single parent unit, but one that is part of an extended family network. A later new partnership could result in a reconstituted family. These family structures may or may not be legitimised through marriage.

▲ Family units can take many forms

Sexuality

The words 'gender' and 'sex' are often used interchangeably.

- Sex refers to 'some of the physiological differences which distinguish male from female'.
- Gender refers to the behavioural and societal differences between the sexes.

One of the variations on family structure can be due to sexuality. Same-sex couples may have children from previous relationships or by adoption, and may be nuclear, extended or reconstituted.

UK society has become much more relaxed about different expressions of sexuality, to the point that same-sex civil partnerships finally became law in 2005.

Sexuality can be expressed in a number of ways. Most people are familiar with heterosexuals, who form relationships with the opposite sex. Homosexuals, or gays, form relations with the same sex. Female homosexuals are commonly known as lesbians. Some people have no specific preference and are known as bisexuals.

Transsexuals are people who appear to be one sex, but have significantly characteristics of the opposite sex, in some cases requiring reassignment of gender to correctly place them in the right sex grouping.

Transvestites are different again and are usually men who enjoy dressing as women. They may be hetero-, homo- or bisexual in their sexual preferences.

There are a number of other sexual groupings of people, referring to their particular sexual interests, all of which add further to the pool of diversity. Some of these are illegal in UK society and can pose serious risk for children and young people, for example paedophilia.

Language and accents

The predominant language of the UK may be English, but it is important to remember that many other languages are spoken. Your own language may well be one other than English. Many people from an ethnic minority background speak two or more languages, for example many people with an Indian, Pakistani or Chinese cultural background speak three or more languages fluently.

Codes of behaviour

Most groups and subgroups in society have well-defined codes of behaviour. Not following these can result in exclusion from the group or society. Many of the codes of behaviour are clearly seen in our legal system. For example, it is illegal to:

- steal from others
- murder or harm others
- not take care of children and young people.

Society punishes people who do not follow these laws.

Many codes of behaviour do not have legal backing to enforce them, but nonetheless bring disapproval from others. Think about:

- queuing
- wearing appropriate clothing
- personal space.

Can you think of others?

Families with a history of offending

As we have just seen, some codes of behaviour have legal implications – if you are caught stealing. you will be punished by a fine, community service or even prison. Despite this, some families have a history of constantly breaking the law. Generations of a family can be traced with a history of convictions and imprisonment. The effect on children of a parent being in prison, along with the stigma, can be very damaging.

It is easy to condemn this cycle, but just stop and think for a minute. Is there a history of one type of behaviour in your family, perhaps playing a musical instrument or playing sport? You may see this as something that is a family tradition.

Theory into practice

Spend 15 minutes with a neighbour considering what the similarities and differences are between you.

1 Write down what you think are your unique points. Then swap thoughts and add more about each other.
2 Sort the lists into similarities and differences between the two of you.
3 How do the lists compare? Are there more differences than similarities?

Offending behaviour can be a family tradition. Much research has been carried out to try to identify why this particular tradition becomes embedded and what can be done about it. The next section (page 226) looks at the 'cycle of disadvantage' – see if you think that offending behaviour could be part of this.

Some causes of diversity are matters of fact and are unchangeable, for example where you were born, your age, culture and beliefs and values; others are potentially open to change, such as family structure, social class, health status. All can have a significant impact on your experiences in life.

Social class/stratification

There are few, if any, societies in the world that do not have some form of stratification and/or hierarchy. In some countries, class is based on religious groups. In the UK the stratification is based on social class.

Social class is a way of categorising the social status that different occupations have. In other words, some jobs are seen as high status or high class, while other jobs have less status. Your social class is concerned with the way other people think about your job – not just about the money you have.

Social class is a term that has been used to describe different groups of people for a very long time in Britain. Mostly, people are used to the terms 'upper class', 'middle class' and 'working class'. Upper-class people have more power, influence and status than middle-class people, but middle-class people have more power, influence and status than working-class people. Before the 1960s, class differences were open and obvious. People usually wore different clothes which showed the class they belonged to and they usually only mixed socially with members of their own class.

Historically, social class was often seen as being like a pyramid, the upper class at the top and depending on the work of the other classes.

Although it is common to think in terms of three classes, the official system for grading the jobs people do contains five classes. This system was officially designed for the Government Census in 1971 and is known as the Registrar-General's Social Class Index (see below).

Since the Registrar-General's classification system was developed, a number of variations have been developed

for different purposes. Market research agencies use a system first developed for the National Readership Survey, which divides the population into classes called A, B, C1, C2, D and E. These letters group people in a similar way to the Registrar-General's classification. Social Class I is known as A, Social Class II is known as B, Social Class III is known as C1, and so on. When companies want to send out advertisements to people through the post, they will often use postcode analysis of social class in an attempt to send product information to the right homes.

A new system to measure social class was introduced for the Census in 2001 and is known as the National Statistics Socio-Economic Classification. This system focuses on issues to do with job security and pensions as well as the skill levels needed to do a job. In general, the type of differences between occupations still show up in the new system. An outline of the new system is shown below.

▼ The Registrar-General's Social Class Index

Social class	Definition	Examples of occupations
I (1)	Professional occupations	Company secretary, doctor, judge, lawyer, university teacher, solicitor, scientist
II (2)	Intermediate occupations	Aircraft pilot, police or fire brigade officer, teacher, manager, farmer
III N (3N)	Skilled non-manual occupations	Cashier, clerical worker, estate agent, sales representative, secretary, typist
III M (3M)	Manual occupations	Bus driver, bricklayer, carpenter, electrician, hairdresser, baker, butcher
IV (4)	Partly skilled occupations	Agricultural worker, bar staff, hospital porter, street trader
V (5)	Unskilled occupations	Road sweeper, kitchen labourer, refuse collector, window cleaner, office cleaner

▼ National Statistics Socio-Economic Classification

Social class	Examples of occupations
1.1	Employers and managers in larger organisations, for example company directors.
1.2	Higher professionals, for example doctors, solicitors, teachers
2	Lower managerial and professional occupations, for example nurses, journalists
3	Intermediate occupations, for example clerks, secretaries
4	Small employers and own account workers, for example taxi drivers, painters and decorators
5	Lower supervisory, craft and related occupations, for example plumbers, train drivers
6	Semi-routine occupations, for example shop assistants, hairdressers
7	Routine occupations, for example cleaners, refuse collectors
8	Never worked and long-term unemployed

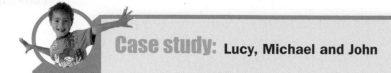

Lucy is 16, and her mother is a consultant in one of the London teaching hospitals. Her father works in the City of London as a financial analyst in one of the big commercial banks. She boards at a private residential school, which charges fees of £8,000 per term. In the holidays she stays with her parents either in their detached country house or with her aunt in London. Lucy is planning to study four A-levels and intends to go into medicine like her mother.

Michael is 16. His father is a teacher at a comprehensive school and his mother works part-time as a singing teacher. Michael attends a different school three miles away from the semi-detached home where he lives with his family. His father drops Michael at school each day on his way to work. Michael intends to stay on at school and take A-levels. He would like to get the qualifications to do engineering at university.

John is 16. His father is currently working as a technician at a car company, but the factory is threatened with closure and he may be made redundant. John walks or catches a bus to school each day from his home on a large housing estate in an urban area which is very congested with traffic. He is not sure how many GCSEs he will get and thinks he wants to leave school in the summer. John hopes he can get a job locally, hopefully with some training.

These three people are the same age – yet they have very different lifestyles. One boards at school, one travels by car to the best school in the area, and one walks to the local school. Their lives will be different in many other ways. Think of some of the differences they will experience in life.

Now think about their financial status. Lucy's family are wealthy. She mixes with people who are used to taking money for granted. If Lucy wants extra tuition to help with her studies, the money is there. If she needs a car, it will be bought for her. Lucy has already had many holidays in exotic resorts –she can expect to travel widely as expense isn't an issue. Lucy mixes with other people who have very high expectations of life. She is very clear about the possibilities for her future. Lucy works very hard, but she knows what she is working for. She would describe herself as middle class – but her father's occupation and family's status is social class I.

Michael lives a lifestyle that could be a bit like Lucy's. He can buy the latest clothing and CDs. He has a Saturday job that gives him a small income. Michael's parents can pay for little extras, but money is always an issue that has to be talked about. Michael mixes with people who don't know much about government or business, but they get advice on careers from the local school. Michael is interested in his future career and his parents put pressure on him to do well in exams, telling him that qualifications are very important. Michael's parents are middle class.

John's parents are working class. John goes to a school similar to Michael's, except that many of the students there don't believe that school is important. Most of John's friends say that school is boring and that what matters is getting out and earning money. Once you get some money you can be independent – you can do what you want. John hasn't got a job yet, but he is looking forward to getting the latest clothes, CDs, etc. when he can get one. John's parents often worry about money and are looking forward to John going out to work so that he can contribute to the household budget.

1   **What are the differences in lifestyle for these three people?**

2   **How do you think their views on education would be different?**

3   **What do you think might happen to each person in the future?**

Economic diversity

In 1998 the richest 10 per cent of the UK population had, on average, five times more to spend than people who had below average income, even after tax. Income varies widely between people, but one of the noticeable differences is between the regions of the UK, as shown in the diagram (right).

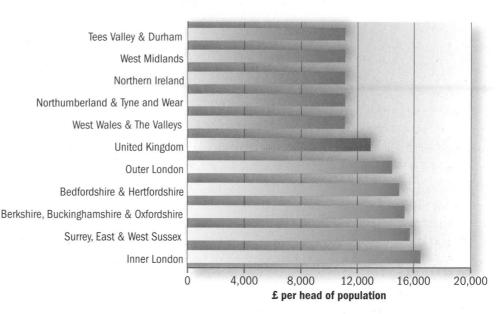

Source: Office for National Statistics

As you can see from the diagram, Inner London had the highest disposable household income (after tax) per head of population (£16,500) in 2004 – some 29 per cent above the UK average of £12,800. However in 2000 it was 36 per cent higher than the UK average. Tees Valley and Durham in the north-east had the lowest household income per head at £10,800. This was 16 per cent below the UK average in 2004.

Economic diversity is a feature of any community. Income and wealth are distributed on a variable scale in all societies. Even in the poorest communities around the world, someone will always possess more than their neighbour or friends, albeit on a very small scale.

Absolute and relative poverty

The definition of poverty used by governments to determine the level in the country can vary according to different factors. However, there are two fundamental definitions and it is the second one that has moveable goal posts for calculation purposes:

- **Absolute poverty** is a lack of income to provide all the basic requirements of living: food, housing, clothing, etc. This definition is universal and examples of absolute poverty are seen most often in developing countries after a natural disaster or when crops fail. Absolute poverty is rare in Britain as the state provides for basic needs.
- **Relative poverty** is having enough income for basics, but not for those items considered usual in the society you live in, for example not being able to afford a TV set, days out or for children to join in activities such as school outings. The level of relative poverty, as the name suggests, varies from society to society.

The **poverty line** is defined as the amount of money below which, after adjusting for size and composition of household and after housing costs, a family is categorised as being poor. In 2004/05, this was £186 per week for a lone parent and two children aged 5 and 11 and £268 per week for a couple with two children aged 5 and 11.

Key terms

Absolute poverty is a lack of income to provide all the basic requirements of living: food, housing, clothing, etc.

Relative poverty is having enough income for basics but not for those items considered usual in the society you live in, for example not being able to afford a TV set.

The **poverty line** is the amount of money below which, after adjusting for size and composition of household and after housing costs, a family is categorised as being poor.

What is important is the ability to be able to judge if more or less children in any place are in poverty from one year to the next. The Labour government, on gaining power in 1997, set great store by its promise to end child poverty by 2020.

There are different ways of measuring what it is to be poor. Some measures take housing costs into account, others do not. The picture of the number of children in poverty has varied since 1979. Child poverty grew rapidly in the 1980s, more slowly in the 1990s and has started to fall since 1998.

▼ **Number and percentage of children in poverty before housing costs**

Year	Millions	% of children
1996/97	3.2	25
1997/98	3.1	25
1998/99	3.1	24
1999/2000	3.0	23
2000/01	2.7	21
2001/02	2.6	21
2002/03	2.6	21
2003/04	2.6	21
2004/05	2.4	19

▼ **Percentage of children in poverty since 1979, after housing costs**

Year	% of children
1979	14
1987	25
1990/91	31
1992/93	33
1994/95	31
1996/97	33
1998/99	33
2000/01	30
2003/04	28
2004/05	27

Source: HBAI series

Extension activity

What do these two tables tell you about the complexity of comparing the progress of reducing child poverty?

In 2000/02, 30 per cent of children in Britain lived in households receiving less than 60 per cent of the median income after housing costs. Of children in single-parent households, the figure was 54 per cent.

Source: Department for Work and Pensions, 2003

Some 700,000 children (23 per cent of rural children) live in poverty in the countryside, representing 18 per cent of all poor children in the UK, and 45 per cent of single-parent households in rural areas live on low incomes.

Source: End Child Poverty, 2003

Inequality

The biggest single cause of inequality in the UK is poverty. There are a number of other reasons for inequality of access to services and provision, but most of them are related in one way or another to poverty. The following children are at great risk of living in a low-income household:

- children in single-parent households
- children in workless households
- children in large families
- children in families with one or more disabled persons
- children in families where the mother is aged under 25
- children in households headed by someone from an ethnic minority (especially of Pakistani or Bangladeshi origin)
- children in Inner London.

There are inequalities even amongst the poor population. Child poverty rates vary across the UK. The risk of poverty is around 28 per cent on average, but as high as 52 per cent in Inner London and as low as 21 per cent in the south-east. A child is less likely to be poor in Scotland (25 per cent) or Northern Ireland (23 per cent) than England (28 per cent).

Percentage distribution of income for children by having a disabled child in the family, after housing costs, including the self-employed

Family type	Quintiles by net equivalent disposable household income				
	Bottom	2nd	3rd	4th	Top
No disabled children	27	23	21	13	16
One or more disabled children	31	34	20	9	6

Source: Department for Work and Pensions, 2003

Extension activity

Look at the figures in the table above.

- What percentage of disabled children are living in the bottom two quintiles of income?
- Do you think these families will have more or fewer demands on their family income? Why?
- What effect do you think being in the bottom financial groups will have on the lifestyle of the families?

People who are poor may have enough money for food, for some clothes and for heating, but poverty means that there is little money for interesting purchases or exciting lifestyles. People who depend on benefits have limited life choices. Belonging to a sports club is not possible if you cannot afford the membership fees. Even jogging is difficult if you feel your neighbourhood is not safe to go out in. Children living in poverty may have limited life choices and limited life chances to develop their full social, emotional and intellectual potential.

Theory into practice

- How do you think the diets of people on average and low incomes generally compare?
- Do they tend to be more or less healthy?
- Compare the range of goods available in food shops and supermarkets in different areas – for example in a town centre supermarket compared with shops on a large run-down estate near a Sure Start centre. What are the differences in the range and quality of foodstuffs? How do prices compare? Are healthy food options available at a reasonable price in both cases?

Effects of poverty

Does it matter if one child is brought up in poorer conditions than another? Consider one baby born on a certain date into a comfortable, middle-class family whose parents are, say, an accountant and a doctor, and another child born on the same day into a working-class family, with one parent earning the minimum wage as a factory worker and the other parent working part-time as a cleaner. Sadly, the answer is that it matters very much. In the 1990s, an unskilled man aged 15–64 was three times more likely to die than a professional man. Males born between 1997 and 1999 to parents in the professional group can expect to live to the age of 78.5, which is seven years longer than males born to unskilled parents. For females the difference is 5.7 years.

Poverty has an impact on many aspects of our lives, including:

- our environment
- mortality rates
- housing
- education
- health
- cultural activities
- transport
- diet
- sport and interests.

The Health Divide carried out in 1988 was an important survey of the health of people in the UK. Some of its findings are shown in the table below.

	Social class 1	Social class 5
Infant mortality rates (death rate in the first year)	5 per 1,000 live births	11 per 1,000 live births
Childhood mortality rate (1–15 years) relative to 100	76	165
Men aged 20–64	62	170

Source: Whitehead, M. (1988) *The Health Divide*, London Pelican

At birth and during the first months of life the risk of death of a child in families in social class 5 is double that in class 1. In the first year this widens – for every death of a male infant from social class 1 there will be three among social class 5. Boys in social class 5 have a ten times greater chance of dying from fire, falls or drowning than those in class 1.

Certain minority ethnic groups have even greater differences. The infant mortality rates of children born to mothers born in Pakistan or the Caribbean are double those of mothers born in the UK. However, mothers born in Bangladesh have a higher risk of stillbirth but a slightly lower risk of the baby dying in the first year.

The Health Divide report is now regularly updated and used to recommend changes in our social and health system to improve the life chances of large groups of the population. Although some of the figures have improved, the gap between the richest and poorest members of society in health experience is widening.

A survey of 5–15-year-olds found mental health problems in 10 per cent. The risk factors included living in poor households, having unskilled parents and being in workless families (Office for National Statistics, 2000).

Compared with pupils who do not receive free school meals, those who do are more likely to smoke (14 per cent versus 10 per cent) and to take drugs (13 per cent versus 11 per cent). However, more children who do not receive free school meals report drinking alcohol (25 per cent versus 22 per cent) (Boreham and McManus, 2002).

■ Child poverty and education

Studies show that children from poor backgrounds do not perform as well at school. A variety of reasons have been given for this, including:

- their language (children from better-off homes are more likely to use language in a similar way to their teachers)
- lack of access to books and other resources at home
- lack of suitable places in which to do homework
- lack of access to educational visits and materials
- there is less parental encouragement, partly because the parents are less familiar with the education system.

Children from poor backgrounds lag significantly behind better-off children in educational development at 22 months. In 2000 in England and Wales three-quarters of pupils whose parents were in the highest professional group achieved five or more GCSEs at grades A–C, compared with only a third in the lowest group.

■ Child poverty and life chances

Poverty in childhood increases the likelihood of low income in adulthood. There is a strong link between children's earnings (as adults) and those of their parents. Only a third of boys whose fathers are in the bottom quarter of income make it into the top half when they grow up. Men whose fathers are unemployed are twice as likely to be unemployed for a year or more between 23 and 33 years of age (Department of Social Security, 1999).

■ Difficulties in accessing provision and services, and barriers to participation

Families who are poor often lack the means to search out services and facilities. For example, they are unlikely to have access to cars or the internet. Access to services may be further hampered by barriers of language and culture.

Better-quality early education delivers results for children. A child with pre-school experience has higher scores on pre-reading and number skills on entry to reception class compared with one without such experience. In turn, reception class attainment has an effect on attainment at Key Stage 1.

More and better childcare improves life chances and helps to tackle child poverty:

- Twenty-three per cent of non-working parents mention lack of access to affordable childcare as a reason for not working.
- Fifty-one per cent of non-working lone parents mention lack of suitable childcare as a barrier to work.

Research shows that low achievers from higher social backgrounds overtake high achievers from low social background by the age of 6–7 years unless intervention helps children from poorer backgrounds to realise their potential. Reaching children early through integrated services can help stop inequality blighting their chances and narrow the achievement gap.

Extension activity

The website of the Child Poverty Action Group (CPAG: www.cpag.org.uk) has a lot of information on research and campaigns relating to child poverty. Access this to study more detailed material on how poverty affects a child's life and future chances.

Hardship and meritocracy

We have looked at the effects of poverty in this unit, especially on a child's life chances. It is worth considering why some families live in hardship compared to others. The obvious factor is family income from employment or private means. But why do you think there are such differences in income between families?

Sociologists use the idea of 'meritocracy' – social inequality is assumed to be a more or less inevitable outcome of individual differences in intelligence or talent, given the 'need' in industrial societies to offer incentives to those of higher ability.

A meritocracy is by definition a society with in-built social inequality; all it promises is equal opportunity to compete for unequal power and rewards. In a meritocracy, the education system is not expected to eradicate privilege and disadvantage: it merely offers a sorting mechanism for recruiting people to subordinate or dominant positions.

It stands to reason, then, that if some jobs are seen as of less value than others, the rates of pay may well be lower. This can then result in hardship for some families, as a result of where they sit in the hierarchy of jobs.

Advantages of diversity

In twenty-first-century Britain, ethnic, cultural and religious diversity is a social fact. There are big differences, however, between the diversity of large towns and cities and the rural areas of Britain, and there is significant controversy about immigration.

Equal opportunities legislation focused people's minds on an image of treating everyone the same. Much was made of trying to homogenise people – to do away with their differences. Thankfully we have moved on from this approach to one where diversity is seen as something to celebrate.

Just think about the differences you identified in yourself and your friends. Diversity in musical tastes may well have led you to enjoy a different type of music, picked up from a friend. Food tastes are another example of how learning from others' views can change a person's tastes.

Britain is seen as an example of diversity across the world. A short walk down a main street of any city or large town in the UK will soon confirm this. The success of the British bid for the 2012 Olympics was in part due to this. The International Olympic Committee saw London as a place where anyone, whatever their background, could come and feel at home, could visit and know they would find a kindred spirit.

In the past 30 years the population of Britain has changed enormously. Many migrants who came to Britain after the Second World War from South Asia, the Caribbean and East Africa to help rebuild the country have remained here to raise their children and grandchildren. Their descendants were born here, have grown up here and, no matter which cricket team they may support, consider themselves to be British, English, Scottish or Welsh. Immigration patterns have changed greatly, with a high proportion of immigrants now coming from Europe, particularly the newer member states of the EU. In London alone, there are now 42 groups of over 10,000 people with recent foreign antecedents. There are also nearly a million people in Britain who have defined themselves as of mixed race.

Globalisation has meant that both labour and capital are increasingly mobile, leading to huge population shifts. Developments in technology and transport have made it possible for people to base their lives in two or more countries simultaneously (known as 'transnationalism'). All of these changes mean that what we used to call 'race relations' can no longer be understood using assumptions made 30 years ago.

The belief that all cultures are of equal value is publicly recognised as such, and that wider society should accommodate other cultures and beliefs without expecting any reciprocation.

Social harmony can only develop in a situation in which people share experiences and common ambitions whatever their cultural backgrounds – where people celebrate their diversity, but where difference does not have to mean division. Respect for individuals and acceptance of difference is an essential first step to achieving this.

Assessment activity 6.1

1 Describe the meaning of diversity in today's society. **P1**

2 Look around the areas you live and work in. Describe the diversity of the population in your area. How does it vary from another part of the UK?

3 Describe causes of economic diversity and potential effects on children, their families, and society. **P2**

4 Try to explain the reasons for the diversity in your area. How is financial diversity in evidence? Look at housing areas and shops. How do they vary? What do you think the different effects could be on children living in these different environments?

5 Describe the implications for children's settings of addressing issues of diversity. **M1**

6 Evaluate the value of diversity in today's society and its relevance for early years practice. **D1**

6.2 The importance of equality and recognising diversity and rights in services for children

Equity

Equity is defined in the dictionary as fairness, impartiality. **Tolerance** is an underlying part of equity, and means respecting difference and not expecting that everyone should be, act or behave as you think they should.

Care value base

The **care value base** was developed by the Care Sector Consortium in 1992 to improve clients' quality of life by setting standards and guiding professional practice in health and social care.

Considering the definition of equity above, it should not take long to realise that it is a fundamental principle for anyone working with children and young people and that if you work to the care value base you will be treating everyone fairly.

Key terms

Equity means fairness, impartiality.

Tolerance is an underlying part of equity. Tolerance means respecting difference and not expecting that everyone should be, act or behave as you think they should.

The **care value base** sets the standards and provides guidelines for professional practice in health and social care in order to improve clients' quality of life.

▲ The five basic tenets of good practice of the care value base

Principles and values of the sector

The principles and values set out in the Induction Standards of the Children's Workforce Development Council (CWDC) enshrine these basic principles and form the building blocks of all knowledge and practice in the sector. Read and remember – and above all practise!

Principles

- The welfare of the child and young person is paramount.
- Practitioners contribute to children's care, learning and development, and safeguarding and this is reflected in every aspect of practice and service provision.
- Practitioners work with parents and families who are partners in the care, learning and development and safeguarding of their children and are the child's first and most enduring carers and educators.

Values

- The needs, rights and views of the child are at the centre of all practice and provision.
- Individuality, difference and diversity are valued and celebrated.
- Equality of opportunity and anti-discriminatory practice are actively promoted.
- Children's health and well-being are actively promoted.
- Children's personal and physical safety is safeguarded, whilst allowing for risk and challenge as appropriate to the capabilities of the child.
- Self-esteem and resilience are recognised as essential to every child's development.
- Confidentiality and agreements about confidential information are respected as appropriate unless a child's protection and well-being are at stake.
- Professional knowledge, skills and values are shared appropriately in order to enrich the experience of children more widely.

Best practice requires a continuous search for improvement and self-awareness of how workers are perceived by others.

Source: Induction Standards, Children's Workforce Development Council, www.cwdcouncil.org.uk

Key term

Equality of opportunity means making sure that everyone, irrespective of their diversity (for example, age, gender, disability or race) has equal access to opportunities at work, through education and other services. There are a number of laws that help to make sure everyone does have equal opportunity.

Theory into practice

Think back to your most recent work experience.

- Give examples of how you have used the principles and values.
- Think about how you have seen qualified staff working to them. Have you seen examples of poor adherence to the principles and values?

If you have seen any what should you have done about it?

Cycle of disadvantage

In all societies, there are many people who do not have an equitable existence. All too many families live in a situation that is dominated by poverty, poor housing, poor education. Look back at the section on the effect of poverty. Do you remember how poor housing is often in areas with few shops and poor and expensive transport facilities? Families who are poor cannot afford the extras that enhance life, and children can be disadvantaged in terms of breaking out of the cycle of poverty.

Inequalities

Stereotyping, labelling and discrimination are all activities that result in the victim being marginalised and feeling disempowered.

Stereotyping

Life can be very complicated and sometimes people try to make it easier by seeing people in certain groups as being 'all the same'. One traditional stereotype is that people with red hair are bad tempered. A stereotype is a fixed way of thinking about a group of people. When people say 'All women are …' or 'All black people are …' or 'All gay people are …,' they will probably go on to describe a stereotype of these groups.

Skilled work with people of all ages starts from being interested in their individual differences. Stereotyping lumps people together as if they were all the same. Thinking in stereotypes usually stops a person from working well with people.

Labelling

Labelling of individuals and groups is the next step on the road to discrimination. With labelling, instead of having a set of fixed opinions about a group to which a person belongs (i.e. stereotyping), the person is summed up in just one word or term. Labels can be used to claim that a group of people are all the same. They may say that people are all only one thing, such as aggressive, emotional or very clever. When individuals are labelled, it is almost as if they stop being people – labels take away people's dignity and individuality.

Case study: Labelling

Some years ago there was a school for children with learning difficulties. When it came to mealtimes, the children had to sit down in order. The 'slow' children were allowed to start first because they took longer. Staff would label these children 'slows'. The 'slows' knew who they were and sat down when 'slows' were called for. Some children were not very skilled at holding their plates and so on, and they were labelled 'clumsies'. Children would describe themselves as 'slows' or 'clumsies'.

1 **What effect do you think describing themselves as a 'slow' or a 'clumsy' would have on children's development of self-esteem?**

2 **Think of an example of labelling a child that you have observed. How did it affect that child and what would have been a better way of working with the child?**

Prejudice and discrimination

The word 'prejudice' derives from the Latin for 'previous judgement' and means judging other people without the knowledge to judge properly. Moreover, new information is unlikely to undermine a prejudice. If people believe stereotypes about groups, they may go on to make judgements about individuals. For instance, an employer who believes that 'women don't really care about work, they only care about their family' may develop a prejudice that women are not suited for promotion to senior positions. Employers with such a prejudice might try to promote only men. Once people develop prejudices against groups of people they are likely to discriminate or treat them differently when in a position to make decisions.

■ The consequences of prejudice and discrimination

People who work with children have to make decisions about how to help others all the time. If you have prejudices or if you label or stereotype children or parents, you may discriminate against them in the way that you work. This is serious because:

- discrimination can damage people's self-esteem
- prejudice and discrimination can lead to verbal and physical abuse
- you may avoid or give a poor service to people you do not like.

Discrimination is not always obvious. It is often easy to make the same assumptions that everyone else does and this can come out in conversation. Children's and parents' rights can often be ignored as a result, and they can receive a worse service than others. When services or practitioners make assumptions about people, discrimination can easily follow. For example, the assumptions that everyone eats the same food or celebrates the same religious festivals results in people being excluded and discriminated against.

If, for example, an employer did not want to appoint a woman to a job, because she might leave to have children, the employer would be illegally discriminating against her. The discrimination would not be simply that the employer realised she was female. The discrimination would be that she was treated differently from a man who might want to start a family. A man in the same situation would be appointed while the woman would receive unequal treatment because the employer thinks she might leave the job or take maternity leave to have a baby.

Under the Race Relations Act 1976, racial discrimination arises when a person or group is treated less favourably than another in similar circumstances 'on racial grounds'. Racial grounds include colour, race, nationality (including citizenship), or ethnic or national origins. Discrimination might be on the grounds that a person is black (colour), Chinese (ethnic or national origins) or Pakistani (nationality), and it includes discrimination against white people (grounds of colour), or against Europeans of particular nationalities (for example, Germans).

It is important to find out about individuals and try to check that your own behaviour and the service you provide meet the needs of people. Where services do not provide equal quality to different groups of people, it is important to challenge discrimination, first by raising the issue with managers. There should be a policy in every setting that works with people to help prevent discrimination.

Good practice checklist

To work to the values and principles essential with children and young people, remember to
- see the individual – their diversity and difference
- look for features you like in every child
- work to inclusion for all children and their parents
- avoid seeing the world in terms of 'us and them'.

Theory into practice

What would you do in these situations?
- You are asked to line up the children ready for outdoor play with the girls in one line, the boys in another.
- Mrs Smith complains because her daughter has been playing with a little girl with cerebral palsy.
- A boy in the reception class uses abusive racist language.
- The owner of the nursery insists that all children wear shorts in nursery, although there are many children who are Muslim.

Vulnerable groups

Despite legislation and significant changes over the past 20 years, racism, sexism, disabalism and all other forms of discrimination do still exist. Many different people suffer as the result of inequalities and inequities. A significant proportion of children and families do not have equal access to facilities. There are a number of particularly vulnerable groups in society who are more at risk than others. Particular groups at risk include:

- children and families from black and/or ethnic minorities, including children from travelling families
- children and families which include a parent or child with disabilities
- children in care and young people leaving care
- families who are poor for whatever reason
- asylum seekers
- families who have a long history of unemployment
- children who have a parent who is an offender.

Human rights

It may be seen as stating the obvious that every single child, young person and adult should enjoy the same human rights as anyone else. The UN Convention on the Rights of the Child (discussed later in this unit) enshrines children's rights specifically as a follow-on from human rights legislation. For most children and their families, enjoying those rights is not a problem. For some, especially those from vulnerable groups, it can be very difficult.

The Children's Rights Director for England exists to protect the rights of children and young people. Children or young people who live in children's homes, family centres, foster care, boarding schools, residential special schools, or colleges of further education, or who are going through adoption, getting any sort of help from social services or who have just left care, should be aware of the Children's Rights Director. He/she is part of the Commission for Social Care Inspection (CSCI) and has an important role to ensure that children are being looked after properly in all of these places. The Children's Rights Director for England works with the people who visit and inspect settings and services used by children in care. He/she spends a lot of time listening to what children and young people have to say, and telling inspectors and the government what children think and want. The website is a good way for children in these circumstances to access the Director (www.rights4me.org.uk).

For some families the specifics of rights may not be so obvious, but they may have their rights denied in more subtle ways. Think about a child growing up in run-down housing, with a very young unskilled parent who is reliant on benefits. Accessing information on the best childcare provision in the area or indeed any provision may be difficult. As a result, finding a job or training to enable an improvement in finances is almost impossible. Exercising choice in health care or education, which is a right of all, is not even on the horizon for this family – their moral rights are being compromised.

Provision and services

The UK government has been keen to ensure that support is available for families with young children. The range of services available to support families and children has increased in recent years. But it is important to be sure that the various agencies work with the families to ensure choice and participation, rather than having support 'done' to them.

Choice is the key to success. For example, in the situation of a family with a child with special needs, an individual approach to decisions on integrated or specialist education is crucial, despite the prevailing educational policy.

Case study: Accessing services

Jill lives on the fourth floor of a block of flats with her 3-year-old twins. Her husband has a chronic health problem and cannot get out very much. The lifts in the flats are often not working and when they do they are dirty and smelly. It is a 30-minute walk to the local shops and community centre. The community centre has a Sure Start centre, which Jill would like to use so that she could perhaps work part-time, but she is too nervous to go. She worries that there will not be anyone she can talk to, and her husband is not happy at the thought of other people looking after their children.

1   What is stopping Jill going to the centre?

2   How could she be helped to access the services at the centre?

3   What could be done by the centre to reach out to families like Jill's?

Difficulties in accessing provision and services, and barriers to participation are discussed opposite.

Accessible and affordable childcare and early years services are critical for all children and key to reducing some of the serious social class differences. Parents cannot move out of poverty and into work or training without high-quality, affordable childcare to support them and their children.

Black and minority ethnic families tend to experience more barriers to access of childcare and early years services than white families and so do not take up places on offer. Do not forget that minority ethnic families also include 'new communities' of asylum seekers, refugees, travellers and gypsies – groups that have very different needs due to very differing circumstances. However, it is important not to stereotype all such communities as being unable to access childcare.

What are the barriers?

There are many complex barriers to the take-up of services and they vary according to ethnic community and, often, location. However, there are some common strands that were identified in research by Sure Start into four inclusion projects. (Sure Start is discussed below.) These related to the type of provision, its costs, a lack of sensitivity to language and culture, and a lack of information.

■ Type of provision available

- Families want flexible childcare that helps with the education and socialisation of their children.
- Some families need access to childcare only when they require it, for example, when a family member cannot offer support, or when work patterns demand it.
- Many families feel that most childcare settings cannot offer the level of flexibility or the type of programme that they require.
- Many minority ethnic families prefer community-based provision (for example, within local schools or community centres) but there is a perception that staff are not as well trained.
- Research shows that the take-up of places in the private and voluntary sector by black and minority ethnic families is much lower than the take-up of places in the maintained (mostly school) sector.

■ The cost of childcare

- The cost of childcare is seen as a problem for many families.
- The location of childcare settings outside their area can give the impression that they are only for the rich.
- There is a high level of take-up of free educational places for 3- and 4-year-olds by black and minority ethnic families.
- Families may not be aware of the Working Tax Credit to support childcare costs among black and minority ethnic communities.

■ Lack of sensitivity to language, culture and religion

- Many families feel that the childcare available is not sensitive to their language, culture or religious beliefs.
- Childcare staff are seen as having a lack of knowledge of, and sensitivity to, diverse cultures, especially in relation to food, language, dress and prayer.
- There is a lack of childcare staff from black and minority ethnic communities in many settings, which gives the impression that the setting is not reflective of their community and its cultures, or that it is tokenistic.
- Settings that do accommodate diversity in the language, dietary, religious and cultural requirements of their communities, and who recruit ethnic minority staff, are generally very popular.

■ Lack of information

- Some local childcare information services are not effective in getting the message into local communities.
- There can be a lack of knowledge about different types of provision, for example what childminders or private day nurseries can offer.

Theory into practice

Take a long, objective look at your placement or a local early years setting.

- Are the children and staff representative of your local community? If not, why not?
- What are the barriers to all the local community using your setting?
- What could be done to improve this?
- How could the provision start to work to improve access and remove barriers?

Overcoming barriers

The most important way to overcome barriers is to empower local communities to define their own ethnic description and to identify where, and from what, they feel excluded and included. Communication is essential to improve links between providers and communities. Successful methods used in Sure Start projects included:

- using recognised community workers who can communicate directly, in community languages, with enthusiasm, empathy and clarity
- developing 'child care champions' in the local community
- running information surgeries
- using community radio advertising
- using community press advertising
- being aware of the power of the spoken word (e.g. 'word of mouth' to relatives and friends)
- promoting 'childcare fairs' within community venues
- using more targeted mailing
- using local community and faith centres
- using high-profile and high-status venues for events to attract interest
- ensuring catering at events is culturally appropriate
- avoiding religious days and holidays for events
- use of interpreters
- literature in community languages
- face-to-face interaction in community and faith venues, at local festivals and community events
- developing promotional videos and audio CDs
- billboard advertising
- training 'information ambassadors' to work in black and minority ethnic communities
- targeting fathers and extended families with information
- outreach/home visits.

Other important points to consider for reducing barriers include:

- having culturally sensitive resources
- better on-site support and using local authority designated Equal Opportunities Co-ordinators (EOCs) and Equality Named Co-ordinators (ENCOs), where they are available
- more training in racial equality, and specifically 'race'/cultural awareness to improve awareness of the requirements of the Race Relations (Amendment) Act and good practice in working for equality.

Good practice checklist

Overcoming barriers
- Be aware of the particular barriers in your area.
- Explore the options that may help to remove these.
- Communicate with parents and children to try to understand issues affecting access for them.

Community resources, support and information, and the referral of children and families

■ Sure Start

Most communities have a range of services available to help children and families in need of support. The crucial all-encompassing service that uses the skills of health, education and social care services is Sure Start. As an early years worker you should be familiar with your local Sure Start provision, especially the information services.

Theory into practice

- What sources of information are there for parents and children in your area?
- How accessible is the information?
- Could it be improved? If so, how?

Sure Start is the cornerstone of the UK government's drive to eradicate child poverty. There is a range of different programmes aimed at widening access and improving children's chances. Sure Start programmes aim to:

- improve children's life opportunities by working with parents and parents-to-be in deprived areas
- provide better access to family support, advice on nurturing, health services and early learning
- identify babies and toddlers at risk of failure and help families to make sure that their children are ready to learn before they start school
- be responsive to local needs and preferences
- work closely with other local provision to offer a wider range of innovative services, including family learning.

By April 2003, 450 Sure Start programmes had been established. By October 2006, this had risen to 1,000, providing 800,000 children with the service. The target is for a total of 3,500 Sure Start Centres – one in each community.

Sure Start services include:

- early excellence centres, which offer high-quality practice as a one-stop-shop for integrated education and day care for young children, and services and opportunities for parents, carers, families and the wider community, both directly and in co-operation with other providers
- children's centres, which provide integrated healthcare and education based on previous good practice
- neighbourhood nurseries
- children's information services, which provide free information on Sure Start services for parents in every local authority
- ChildcareLink, which is a national helpline and website (www.childcarelink.gov.uk/)
- extended schools that offer a range of services for children, young people, their families and communities, including childcare, family and lifelong learning, parenting support, some health and social care services, and access to information technology, as well as sports and arts facilities.

The US Head Start programme was the inspiration for the Sure Start programme, because it proved that, at the age of 30, children from the programme who had had two years' early family help far outstripped those who had had no help. Every $1 spent on early years saved the state $7 later in crime, welfare, mental health and job prospects (Polly Toynbee in Horton, C. (2005) *Working with Children 2004–5*, Guardian Books).

■ Local authority social services departments

In a typical week in England in 2003:

- 384,000 children were in need (82 per cent of these were residing in families and the other 18 per cent, or 69,100, were being looked after)
- 224,000 (58 per cent) of children in need were in receipt of local authority social services

- abuse and neglect count as the single main reason for children receiving social service intervention (55 per cent of looked-after children and 26 per cent of others in need).

There are twice as many services for families of children under 5 than for families of children aged 5–10 years. Only 2 per cent of services are specifically aimed at minority ethnic groups, yet 8 per cent of the total population are from minority ethnic groups and the proportions of under-16s in this group are almost double those in the white population.

Theory into practice

Make a chart for your setting with the contact details of all the following services, and a summary of their services, either nationally or, if relevant, in your area for children and young people and their families:

- local social services
- Childline
- Children in Need
- local children's trust
- local Sure Start unit, including the programme manager
- local Connexions office if you work with young people
- local Area Child Protection Committee
- local contact for the National Society for the Prevention of Cruelty to Children (NSPCC)
- regional Commission for Racial Equality
- local Citizens Advice Bureau
- any local refugee support agencies
- local childcare information service
- any specialist support group for any individual needs of children you work with (for example, National Asthma Campaign, National Autistic Society, National Deaf Children's Society).

Identify any of these that you have had contact with. Finally, are you aware of any children or families that these services could help in any way?

■ Child development services

Children with multiple special needs often require specific, individual services, many of which are provided by community child development services organised by the National Health Service. The teams of specialists in these centres include:

- specialist health visitors
- physiotherapists
- speech therapists
- occupational therapists
- psychologists
- community consultant paediatricians
- social workers.

In addition, there are often a number of specialists for children with difficulties with their hearing or sight.

Theory into practice

- What services are available in your area for children with multiple special needs?
- Find out where your nearest child development service is and how referrals are made.

Assessment activity 6.2

1 Describe the importance of recognising equality, diversity and rights in providing children's services. **P3**

2 Spend some time researching the services in your area that are aimed at promoting equality and rights for children and their families. How effective do you think they have been?

6.3 How services for children can recognise and promote equality, diversity and rights

Formal policies on equality and rights

There is a raft of equal opportunities and diversity legislation relevant to children that we are all bound by. In addition, the UK is a signatory of the UN Convention on the Rights of the Child, which is an international treaty that sets out the human rights of children.

Race Relations (Amendment) Act 2000

This Act places a responsibility on public organisations to encourage racial and social harmony and requires schools and nurseries to:

- promote equality of opportunity
- promote good relations between persons of different racial groups
- eliminate unlawful racial discrimination
- prepare and publish a race equality policy
- monitor and assess the effect of their policies.

Special Educational Needs and Disability Act 2001 (SENDA)

Before SENDA, children and young people in education did not have the same protection from discrimination on the basis of **disability** as in their everyday lives. There is now a requirement to make reasonable adjustments to the educational **provision** where a child or young person may be disadvantaged without it. The implications of SENDA are discussed in the section on **special educational needs** below.

Key terms

Disability means a physical or mental impairment which has a substantial and long-term adverse effect on the child's ability to carry out normal day-to-day activities.

Provision can be a physical setting or a peripatetic service based in the community, or other service. Children with **special educational needs** learn differently from most children of the same age. They may need extra or different help.

National Standards for all early years settings

Ofsted monitors compliance with the National Standards for a range of early years settings. Many of the standards cover everyday practical issues relating to staffing, working with parents and behaviour, but two of them relate directly to **inclusion** and provide a strategic aim for addressing some individual needs:

- *Standard 9: Equal opportunities* The registered person and staff actively promote equality of opportunity and anti-discriminatory practice for all children.
- *Standard 10: Special needs (including special educational needs and disabilities.* The registered person is aware that some children may have special needs and is pro-active in ensuring that appropriate action can be taken when such a child is identified or admitted to the provision. Steps are taken to promote the welfare and development of the child within the setting in partnership with the parents and other relevant parties.

Key term

Inclusion is the process of identifying, understanding and breaking down barriers to participation and belonging, to make sure that everyone in an activity or setting is included.

Inclusion is recognising that we are all 'one' even though we are not the 'same'. Inclusion means children, young people and adults with disabilities and/or learning difficulties being included in mainstream society. Inclusive schools help the development of communities where all people are equally valued and have the same opportunities for participation. Think about what exclusion helps to promote – racism and sexism, for example – and you can see that inclusion is the exact opposite. True inclusion also involves making sure that all support systems are available to those who need them.

The key to making sure that your provision meets its responsibilities for promoting inclusion is simply to treat all children as individuals and assess and support their individual needs.

Recent changes in legislation now clearly support the needs of children with a disability even if they do not have special educational needs. A children's setting that considers all children as individuals, and seeks to welcome all children and parents, should not have difficulty in keeping to the law. It is useful though to think about the definitions of disability and special educational needs (SEN), and to know which legislation covers them.

Disability Discrimination Act 1995 (DDA) and the Education Act 1996

The DDA defines a disabled person as 'someone who has a physical or mental impairment which has a substantial and long-term adverse effect on his or her ability to carry out normal day-to-day activities'. This definition covers pupils with physical (including sensory), intellectual or mental impairments. The definition is broad and would include children with a learning disability, sensory impairment, severe dyslexia, diabetes or epilepsy, pupils who are incontinent, or who have AIDS, severe disfigurements or progressive conditions like muscular dystrophy.

The Education Act 1996 says that 'a child has special educational needs if he or she has a learning difficulty which calls for special educational provision to be made for him or her'. This is provided under the SEN framework, which can include a statement of special educational need.

Thus, a disability might give rise to a learning difficulty that calls for special educational provision to be made if it prevents or hinders the disabled child from accessing education. The SEN framework is there to identify and meet any additional educational needs of children. There is a duty under the DDA to make sure that disabled pupils are not discriminated against and so seek to promote equality of opportunity between disabled and non-disabled pupils.

Many, but not all, children who have SEN will also be defined as having a disability under the DDA. However, not all children who are defined as disabled under the DDA will have SEN. For example, those with severe asthma, arthritis or diabetes may not have SEN, but may have rights under the DDA.

National Standards for special needs and disabilities

The National Standards for early years provision laid down by the Department for Education and Skills and monitored by Ofsted include Standard 10, discussed above.

Special Educational Needs and Disability Act 2001

The Special Educational Needs and Disability Act 2001, supported by the 2002 Code of Practice, strengthened the right of children with disabilities to attend mainstream educational facilities. All education is covered by the Act: from nursery to higher education provided by local education authorities; education authority maintained schools and classes, and independent schools and grant-aided schools. Some private, voluntary and statutory providers of nursery education that are not constituted as schools are still covered by duties in Part 3 of the Act, which relates to access and 'reasonable adjustments'.

- It is unlawful for any school to discriminate against any disabled pupils and parents can lodge complaint to SEN and disability tribunals and via admissions and exclusions appeal panels. Ofsted inspect to check that schools, nurseries and so on are complying.

- The Act covers all education and associated services for pupils and prospective pupils. In essence, all aspects of school life are covered, including extra-curricular activities and school trips.

■ Less favourable treatment

If a setting treats a disabled child less favourably than another because of their disability without justification, they may be breaking the law.

Case study: Children with a disability

The parents of a boy with epilepsy want him to be admitted to a nursery school, but are told that the school cannot take him unless he stops having fits.

A girl who uses a wheelchair is on a trip with her school. The teachers arrange for the children to go on a walk over a very and rough and rocky path, but, having carried out a risk assessment, they decide that the disabled girl cannot go on the walk for health and safety reasons.

1 Do you think that either case is justified?

2 What do you think should happen next in each case?

Good practice checklist

- Do all senior members of the setting take their responsibilities under the DDA seriously?
- Are all other staff aware of their responsibilities?
- Has the setting reviewed its policies, procedures and practices to ensure that it does not discriminate against disabled children?
- Has the setting made 'reasonable adjustments'?
- Have staff had training on the new law and the broader issues of disability equality?
- Are there procedures in place to ensure that discrimination by staff will be identified and dealt with properly?
- Has the setting got an effective complaints procedure?

Anti-discriminatory practice means taking positive action to counter discrimination. This will involve identifying and challenging discrimination and being positive in your practice about differences between people.

Theory into practice

Have a look at the policies and procedures in your setting that relate to inclusion.

- How are legislation and standards referred to in them?
- How is it made clear that there are legal requirements to work in certain ways?
- What reference has been made in Ofsted inspection reports to National Standards 9 and 10?
- How could the policies and procedures be developed to make them easier to understand by staff?

Key term

Anti-discriminatory practice means taking positive action to counter discrimination.

Human rights legislation

Human Rights Act 1998

This Act mostly applies to adults, but by implication of their role as parents impacts on children as well. The Human Rights Act enshrines fundamental key rights that everyone should enjoy, namely:

- right to life
- prohibition of torture
- prohibition of slavery and forced labour
- right to liberty and security
- right to a fair trial

- no punishment without law
- right to respect for private and family life
- freedom of thought, conscience and religion
- freedom of expression
- freedom of assembly and association
- right to marry
- prohibition of discrimination
- prohibition of abuse of rights
- restrictions on political activity of aliens
- limitation on use of restrictions on rights
- protection of property
- right to education
- right to free elections
- abolition of the death penalty.

Theory into practice

- Which of the rights could affect a child or young person?
- How could some of the others affect them through their parents or carers?

UN Convention on the Rights of the Child

The United Nations Convention on the Rights of the Child was signed by all countries of the world (including the UK, but excluding the USA and Somalia) in December 1991. It is an international human rights treaty that applies to all children and young people under the age of 18 years. It gives children and young people a set of comprehensive rights, including: the right to express their views and have their views taken into account on all matters that affect them; the right to play, rest and leisure; and the right to be free from all forms of violence (see the table on page 236). Some groups of children and young people – for example those living away from home and young disabled people – have additional rights to make sure they are treated fairly and that their needs are met.

▼ Some key rights set out in the UN Convention on the Rights of the Child

Article	Essential feature of article
Article 3	• In all actions concerning children, whether undertaken by public or private social welfare institutions, the best interests of the child shall be a primary consideration. • The government must ensure the child such protection and care as are necessary for his or her well-being. • All services and facilities responsible for the care or protection of children shall conform with the requirements of safety, health, number and suitability of staff.
Article 6	Every child has the inherent right to life.
Article 7	A child has the right to a name, a nationality and, as far as possible, the right to know and be cared for by his or her parents.
Article 9	• Children shall not be separated from their parents against their will, except when such separation is necessary for the best interests of the child (for example, where there is abuse or neglect of the child by the parents). • A child who is separated from one or both parents must be able to maintain regular personal relations and direct contact with both parents, except if this is contrary to the child's best interests.
Article 12	Children who are capable of forming their own views have the right to express those views freely in all matters affecting them, and these views should be given due weight in accordance with the age and maturity of the child.
Article 13	A child has the right to freedom of expression; including freedom to seek, receive and impart information and ideas of all kinds, orally, in writing or in print, in the form of art, or through any other media of the child's choice.
Article 14	A child has the right to freedom of thought, conscience and religion.
Article 15	A child has the right to freedom of association and to freedom of peaceful assembly.
Article 18	Both parents have common and primary responsibilities for the upbringing and development of the child.
Article 19	Government must take all appropriate measures to protect a child from all forms of physical or mental violence, injury or abuse, neglect or negligent treatment, maltreatment or exploitation, including sexual abuse, while in the care of parent(s), legal guardian(s) or any other person who has the care of the child.
Article 23	• All mentally or physically disabled children should enjoy a full and decent life, in conditions which ensure dignity, promote self-reliance and facilitate the child's active participation in the community. • Disabled children have the right to special care with assistance appropriate to the child's condition and to the circumstances of the parents or others caring for the child.
Article 24	Children have the right to the highest attainable standard of health and facilities for the treatment of illness and rehabilitation of health.
Article 26	Every child has the right to benefit from social security, including social insurance.
Article 27	• Every child has the right to a standard of living adequate for the child's physical, mental, spiritual, moral and social development. • The parent(s) or others responsible for the child have the primary responsibility to provide, with government help if necessary, within their abilities and financial capacities, the conditions of living necessary for the child's development.
Article 28	All children have the right to free primary education and secondary and higher education should be available to all.
Article 32	Children must be protected from economic exploitation and from performing any work that is likely to be hazardous or to interfere with the child's education, or to be harmful to the child's health or physical, mental, spiritual, moral or social development.
Article 37	• No child shall be subjected to torture or other cruel, inhuman or degrading treatment or punishment. Neither capital punishment nor life imprisonment without possibility of release shall be imposed for offences committed by persons below 18 years of age; • No child shall be deprived of his or her liberty unlawfully.

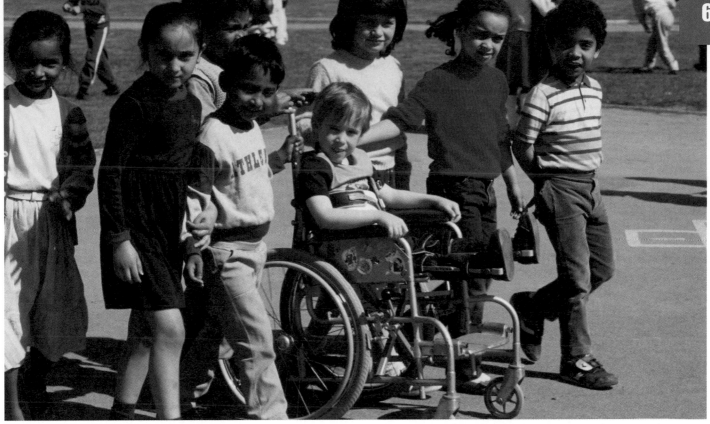

▲ The UN Convention on the Rights of the Child protects all children

Theory into practice

When you are working in your placement, find out how the rights of children are interpreted in everyday policies and procedures.

Extension activity

What is the relationship between human rights and children's rights legislation? Try to compare the differences and identify where the Human Rights Act has been translated into applying to children.

Overriding individual rights

Although legislation such as the Children Act 2004, Disability Discrimination Act 1995, Mental Health Act 1983 and the Human Rights Act is intended to protect the rights of everyone, there are occasions when those rights need to be discarded, usually on a temporary basis. Common law is intended to protect society or individuals and can override human rights.

Sometimes the rights of parents can conflict with the rights of a child, for example:

● for the safety of the child, when a parent's rights have to be outweighed by those of the child in the case of suspected abuse – this conflicts with the rights of the child article 9, the right to family life

● the use of power and force to make someone receive treatment if they have a mental illness

● statutory powers can be enforced, for example if a parent is not sending a child to school – the child's rights to education and the legal framework that requires children to attend school, are then used to make the parent send the child to school.

Working practices in children's services

Good practice in equality and diversity in children's services should involve active promotion of equality and individual rights, high-quality communication skills and well-developed partnerships with parents. One good way to test if this is happening is to monitor the quality and effectiveness of the provision in implementing inclusive and anti-discriminatory practice.

The regulations of the Race Relations (Amendment) Act 2000 require settings that are receiving funding to monitor participation by minority ethnic groups. The maintained early childhood sector has statutory obligations, but the obligations of the non-maintained sector, in which settings may be receiving direct or indirect funding, are not yet clear. The Department for Education and Skills does, however, require settings in the non-maintained sector to implement equality strategies and the effective collection, monitoring and analysis of ethnic data are seen as good practice.

The monitoring of the effectiveness of provision in children's settings is often not done well. Monitoring is important to check the effectiveness of your hard work as a setting to widen access. It is very difficult for authorities to get an accurate picture of minority ethnic participation in childcare services across all sectors, especially in the private and voluntary sectors.

Information that needs gathering includes:

- characteristics of the setting's catchment area – ethnic mix, age profile, social class, rural, urban mix and so on (such information is available from the Office for National Statistics at ward and postcode level)
- detailed statistics about the geographical spread of children who attend
- the ethnic status of children
- the number of children with registered disabilities
- the number of lone parents.

This type of information will help to focus on where action is needed to make the children attending the setting more representative of those in the locality. Once the base information has been gathered, regular checks can be made on the population of both staff and children to see if initiatives have worked. Information of this type can be very interesting. By starting to look for patterns in the way the setting is developing, and most importantly ask why this may be so, staff can start to improve services for the children who attend.

Remember that there are restrictions on collecting and keeping data about people. The basic tenet is that anyone can request to see information that is held about him or her.

Active promotion of equality and individual rights

Staff who work with children and young people and their families should have a commitment to equality and diversity embedded in them to the point that it becomes second nature. Pro-active attention should be automatic to ensure that *every* child or young person and their facility are treated as individuals and potential barriers to inclusion are identified and addressed. Achieving this requires close attention to staff recruitment and development as well as the right ethos of every organisation.

Ideally the staffing of every childcare and education setting should reflect the profile of the community it serves. This applies to all levels of staff, committees and volunteers.

Good staff training in equality and diversity involves challenging people's values and beliefs. Recognising your own prejudices and tendency to stereotype is crucial in order to work effectively with all children and their families. Working to identify and remove barriers to participation is also essential – as discussed in an earlier section.

Communication

One of the most important tools in promoting equality and access is the very simple one of communication. All too often families simply do not know about services available to them. Families who need information because they are not aware of services and support are often some of the more vulnerable groups, for whom finding information is not easy. This could be because of the very barriers that are preventing access to services, for example:

- communication
- transport
- money.

Good practice checklist

Throughout your professional career working with children you need to bear the following in mind

- Always share information with parents.
- Show that you value parents' role.
- Welcome their involvement in the setting.
- Make sure that you understand the diverse range of family patterns.
- Try to understand and meet different cultural expectations.

Theory into practice

- Put yourself in the role of a parent with a child with a learning disability living in your area. English is not your first language. How easy is it to find information out about:
  – the roles and use of advocates?
  – the availability of interpreters?
  – how to get leaflets translated into your first language?
- Now imagine you have recently moved to your area of the country. You have a teenage daughter without speech or sight. How easy would it be to have support for her using signing or Braille?

Partnerships with parents

Parents are usually far more important to a child than any professional carer may be. Parents are usually the primary socialisers of a child and have spent significantly more time with their child. They are usually a far more consistent and long standing part of a child's life. It is essential, therefore, that any relationship between a child professional and the parents should be positive.

The SEN (Special Educational Needs) Code of Practice 2001, which is used in England, outlines seven key principles when working with children. Many of these are based on partnership working with families. These principles are based on good practice and actually make totally good sense for working with the parents of any child:

- *Acknowledge and draw on parental knowledge and expertise in relation to their child.* This principle recognises that parents will usually be able to share some valuable advice, thoughts and strategies with practitioners.

- *Focus on the children's strengths as well as areas of additional need.* This principle is about remembering that children are 'whole people' and are not problems that need curing or sorting out. Think about the language you are using and also about how it might sound if it was said to you.

- *Recognise the personal and emotional investment of parents and be aware of their feelings.* Parents love their children unconditionally and see them as valuable. They may be very protective of their child and not be in full agreement about some aspects of plans for them.

- *Ensure that parents understand procedures, are aware of how to access support in preparing their contribution and are given documents to be discussed well before the meeting.* Meeting with parents and working through individual learning plans is an essential part of supporting children. This principle is about making parents feel at ease and ensuring that they can properly contribute to a meeting.

- *Respect the validity of differing perspectives and seek constructive ways of reconciling different viewpoints.* This principle is about understanding that parents are entitled to their own opinions about what is best for their child.

- *Respect the differing needs that parents themselves may have, such as a disability or communication and linguistic barriers.* Some parents may have particular needs that may prevent them from contributing. Inclusion means thinking about parents' needs and looking for ways of meeting them. This might mean translating documents, encouraging parents to bring along a friend or putting up a travel cot so that a baby can be brought along to a meeting.

- *Recognise the need for flexibility in the timing and structure of meetings.* This principle reminds you that parents may have jobs, difficulty with transport or other commitments. Partnership with parents means looking for times that everyone finds convenient, not just you!

Assessment activity 6.3

A new children's service providing day care to children under 5 and after school services is opening in a rural area of England. The service will be meeting the needs of a very diverse range of families – from relatively well-off families to families living in rural poverty. Many children are from families who have recently come to England from eastern European countries to work in the agricultural industries. Pay rates are very low and many of the families speak very little English.

1 What legislation will help to promote equality of opportunity, inclusion and rights in the new children's services? **P4**

2 How can the managers ensure that practices in this new service will promote equality of opportunity, inclusion and rights? **P5**

3 Explain how one policy from this new children's service meets the requirements of a piece of legislation. **M2**

4 Use examples from your experience to show how practices in children's services can promote equality of opportunity, inclusion and rights. **M3**

Personal awareness

Case study: Promoting inclusion

James, a student at college, was sent to see his tutor. He had been missing sessions in college, and his placement supervisor was also concerned with his attendance, although when he was there he was excellent with the children. His tutor noticed that James seemed to sit apart from the rest of the group, and was rarely in the canteen at lunchtimes with them. James was on the verge of leaving his course.

During the talk with his tutor it emerged that James was very unhappy as the rest of the group, in his words, 'viewed him as a freak', partly because he was the only male on the course, but also because he was well spoken. James had been to boarding school as his parents were in the army.

With James' agreement, his tutor decided to have a 'circle time' with the group and to encourage James to tell them how he was feeling. The session was very useful. Most of the rest of the group had not realised what they were doing, and one or two were able to express their thoughts about James, some voicing their surprise at a male early years worker, while others did not realise why his accent was so different from theirs. To his surprise, one or two others in the group also expressed that they felt excluded for various reasons.

James' tutor continued the work by exploring beliefs and prejudices and encouraging everyone to think about what their prejudices were and how to work with them. After several sessions there was a noticeable difference in the group's behaviours and, even better, professional journals for work experience were identifying clear links with improvements in practice at placement.

1 **What do you think had happened in this case before the discussions?**

2 **Has there been a time when you have felt excluded and identified as being different. How did it feel?**

The case study gives one example of how we can behave without thinking that we are showing bias in our beliefs.

There is a Native American saying about understanding others by walking in their shoes. That is a good basis for your dealings with anyone in any situation. Always consider how you might feel if you were on the receiving end of an interaction, and think about what you can learn from others.

Theory into practice

Everyone has beliefs and prejudices. Many of them will not be detrimental to other people, but some may well be. Always be alert in your dealings with others, especially children, to prevent your prejudices surfacing. Sometimes they may appear in the form of you not liking a child. It may be difficult to say why you do not, but just stop and think about it! Does he remind you of someone you didn't like at school? It may only be they have the same name, or colour of hair!

Challenge yourself to stop and think when there does not appear to be a rational reason for your feelings. Often you will identify some deep-set prejudice. And with most prejudices, recognising them is the first step to ridding yourself of them, or at least not letting them influence your professional behaviour.

As well as challenging your own behaviours, you have a duty to challenge oppressive and discriminatory behaviour in others – children as well as adults.

Theory into practice

Challenge others at all times:

- equally and inclusively
- as individuals
- with respect for their dignity, culture, backgrounds and values
- respecting confidentiality and the sharing of information according to the policy of the setting.

Inclusive practice

As you have seen, inclusion is basically about making sure that everyone is included in society and in all activities, regardless of their diversity. Disability history shows very graphically just how easy it is to exclude rather than include. Think about these two models of disability:

- The social model recognises that any problems of disability are created by society and its institutions. If someone is a wheelchair user, problems are caused not by the wheelchair but by the fact that some buildings do not have ramps and buses are difficult to access. The solutions to problems of disability are therefore in society's hands, and involve changing the attitudes of able-bodied people. The Disability Discrimination Act (DDA) is clearly a tool to help to improve the response of society in this manner. Inclusion is more easily achieved if the infrastructure of society is disability-friendly.

- The medical model views the disability as the problem. Disability is seen as a tragic, incurable fact that leaves the sufferer with little chance of a normal life. It focuses on the disability the person has, rather than his or her abilities. Under this model, people with severe disabilities are cared for in institutions and have little hope of independence. Until the 1980s, disabled children were seen as uneducable (which is totally at odds with the view today) as a result of a medical model approach. Society under the medical model is not disability-friendly as the infrastructure is developed only with able-bodied people in mind.

In your settings it is essential that you work from the perspective of the social model.

Is it the wheelchair that is the problem, or is it the steps?

Case study: Children with a disability

Lee, aged 7, was born prematurely after a pregnancy of 30 weeks. As a result of problems during his delivery, Lee has cerebral palsy. He uses a wheelchair to move around and a voice synthesiser to communicate. Although he cannot play sports, he loves watching football and enjoys playing games related to football. Lee and his friends spend a lot of time together playing games at weekends. School swimming sessions are his favourite. With the support of a personal assistant, Lee attends a mainstream primary school and is looking forward to moving to senior school with his friends.

Leila, aged 6, was also born with severe cerebral palsy and relies on her wheelchair to move around. Her parents were never encouraged to hope that Leila could attend a mainstream school. She attends

a special school with children who all live a long way from Leila. Her parents are not happy to let her visit the one friend she has nearby, as they worry she will not cope without them. Although Leila loves shopping, her parents do not take her very often as it is hard work, and they find it difficult to cope with people staring at her. They are thinking that Leila will eventually live in a residential unit with care assistants looking after her.

1 **Compare these two children. Why do you think they have different lifestyles?**

2 **Why do you think this has happened in each case?**

3 **How could you support Leila's parents to help them to encourage her to have a more normal lifestyle?**

Good practice checklist

To assess your setting, imagine you are a child who has some type of disability. Think about wheelchair users, children who move with difficulty, those with reduced vision or hearing, or any other type of disability you have seen or heard about. Ask yourself the following questions:

- Are all parts of the setting accessible?
- Can equipment be accessed by all children?
- Are there some areas of the setting that cannot be accessed by some children? How can this be addressed to avoid disadvantaging these children?
- Are any of the outings or activities that have been held in the past months restricted to any children? What could have been done to enable access for all?

Extension activity

1 Have a look at public buildings, shops, recreational areas and public transport and carry out your own disability access audit, i.e. how accessible is everything for people who need assistance with their mobility?

2 Now look at the same range of places and imagine you can understand little written English. How inclusive are these facilities for people for whom reading English is difficult?

It is important for practitioners to ensure that a child is not discriminated against in terms of the opportunity to reach his or her full potential. Look at these three examples:

- Yasmin has hearing difficulties and, as a result, her speech has been delayed. She experiences communication difficulties unless alternative methods of communication are considered. When her group at nursery has story time, the nursery nurse always makes sure that Yasmin sits at the front and that the story has a lot of visual appeal, to which end she uses puppets, pictures and miming.

- Ben has cerebral palsy, which means he has difficulty in controlling his movements without shaking. Playing in the home corner was difficult because it was a small area and he tended to knock things over. His teacher has resited the home corner so that it is in a bigger area and Ben can now play safely in it. His teacher has also realised that the new home corner is much better for Yasmin, who uses hearing aids. The new site is much nearer to the main classroom area and Yasmin can hear what is happening much more easily.

- Jason uses a lightweight wheelchair. He previously had difficulty getting into the playground as access to it was via two small steps. However, after the DDA came into force the school had a good-quality ramp installed and now Jason can get out into the playground easily and move very quickly around it. With the help of one of the staff, Jason's friends have invented a new form of football that allows him to use his arms instead of his feet.

There are many other ways to overcome barriers that face children and young people. It is essential to structure activities and opportunities for the entire group of children in your care, taking needs into account. All children can benefit when activities are adapted – for instance, making story time a wider experience, and learning new ways of playing traditional games.

Theory into practice

Sometimes special equipment may be needed to allow children with special needs to practise and develop all their skills.

- A child who has poor fine-motor skills and difficulty with fine hand–eye co-ordination may benefit from the use of thicker pencils and other tools.
- Children with delays in developing gross motor skills (large body movements such as walking or running), or sensory problems (vision, hearing, etc.) may enjoy large-scale toys such as ball pools and soft foam cushions.
- A child with a visual impairment may be able to read large-print books, and will enjoy listening to stories recorded on tape.

▲ Children with special needs may enjoy large-scale toys

Some centres are equipped with multi-sensory rooms that provide opportunities for children with a wide range of specific needs. These rooms feature a range of lights, sounds, smells and touch sensations that stimulate (or in some cases soothe) the senses.

Any activity, game or toy designed to develop an aspect of a child's skill should aim to allow the child to use the skills that already exist, and encourage them to extend them. For example, when a child reaches the stage of being able to turn the pages of a book, make sure they have books with thick pages, showing pictures of interesting objects.

Sometimes there is no need to adapt equipment, but instead you may need to change your methods of promoting an activity. A child who has difficulty sitting still for long will struggle to take part in a modelling activity lasting 15 minutes. You could, for example, sit with the child and keep up the encouragement, or ask to look at progress at frequent intervals, or you could give a child some responsibility for drawing all the children's efforts together, say for a display. This may help to prevent a child's behaviour becoming unacceptable.

In some cases there is simply a lack of resources for children who require support. For example recent research shows that blind and partially-sighted children throughout the UK are losing out on their education because they cannot always get hold of textbooks they can read. A report in 2006 showed that only 12 per cent of maths and 8 per cent of science GCSE textbooks in England are available in large print or Braille. Blind and partially-sighted pupils rely on teachers to photocopy and retype textbooks so that they can read them.

Implications of confidentiality

Confidentiality is essential in any care setting. Your placement will have a policy about confidentiality and the exchange of information. Sometimes information about a child may need to be shared with other professionals, for example health visitors, schools or the police or social services if a child's safety is at risk. This should be clear in the confidentiality statement.

Everyone's privacy is protected by a number of pieces of legislation, including:

- Data Protection Act 1984
- Access to Personal Files Act 1987
- Access to Medical Reports Act 1988.

As a student, your rule should always be, 'If in doubt, ask.' This applies to many aspects of your experience as a student, but especially in relation to confidentiality. When parents are in a school or nursery, they may confide personal information to staff. It is advisable to ask parents to talk to a member of the staff when you are a student, but if you are given confidential information by a parent you should make it clear you will have to pass it on.

Personal information about parents should not be the topic of gossip in the staff room and should never be repeated to other parents. In an early years setting you have to exchange information with other members of staff to help each other operate effectively. As life is busy in a nursery or school, this exchange of information may take place in the room with children. Ensure that parents

Case study: Abdul's story

Ten-year-old Abdul is registered blind. At school he doesn't get access to the same choice of books as sighted children. His mum says, 'It's not the fault of the teachers. It's the fact that many of the books he likes to read are not available in Braille or audio. I'd like the government to act now. If the situation doesn't improve, I'm worried that as he gets older, Abdul won't receive the books he needs.'

1 What effect do you think it will have on Abdul if he can't access the books he needs?
2 How could the school help with this?
3 Why do you think that the problem exists?

are not able to overhear such conversations or you will be guilty of breaching confidentiality.

Information that is divulged by parents is confidential to those who need to know, for example care staff caring for the child. You need to be aware of the pressures many parents are under in bringing up their children; these pressures can affect how they view the early years setting and indeed which they choose. Life events such as illness, moving house, divorce, death or redundancy can have a profound impact on parents and their children. Having to work very long hours to support yourself and your children may not be the choice of a single parent, but he or she needs support from you, not silent criticism because he or she leaves the children so late at the nursery.

Practitioners will often receive very personal information from parents. Some information has to be shared with others, even if the parent has indicated that he or she does not want the information to be passed on.

Most childcare settings hold a lot of personal information about their charges. It is important that everyone concerned is aware of the requirements of the Data Protection Act and the Freedom of Information Act. This allows people to view the information that is held on file about them or their children. Remember this when you are committing your thoughts to paper or computer; you must report facts and events objectively, factually and accurately. Parents should be made aware that they have rights under the legislation and be reassured that all files are kept in a secure environment.

Case study: Who should you tell?

- A parent confides that her new partner is hitting her children, who are already on the child protection list.
- You are given information by a grandparent that a child has developed asthma, but the parents have not mentioned anything.
- You are informed of changes in the child's circumstances that may affect his or her behaviour, for example a death in the family or a parent losing a job.

What should you do with the information disclosed in these scenarios?

Good practice checklist

- Ensure that parents know that confidentiality is respected when they are working in close partnership with carers.
- Everyone concerned must be aware of the rules of 'professional confidentiality', including which information must be shared with a line manager, such as issues relating to child protection.
- Let parents know that you may have to share some information with your line manager, before they start to talk about confidential issues.
- Never gossip about parents, children or other members of staff.
- Never discuss one parent with another parent.
- Do not make value judgements about a child or a family, but always respect a person's culture and identity.
- Remember to share information about a child's dietary needs, allergies, who collects the child and any concerns with the rest of the care team.

Respecting confidentiality and trust

In any area of care, you will hear and see a lot of confidential information about children and their parents. Remember that confidential information is not to be discussed with your friend on the bus or told to your family at home. It could be that the person sitting behind you on the bus is linked to the family concerned.

Sometimes, however, you have to share information with colleagues. As a student or a junior worker remember, 'If in doubt, shout!' but rather than shouting, have a quiet discussion with your supervisor. This is called 'professional confidentiality', sharing information for the good of the children in your care.

Theory into practice

- Ahmed, aged 7, tells you that he and his parents are going on holiday to Pakistan next summer, but that it has to be kept a secret in the meantime from his little brother, aged 4.
- Jane, aged 6, tells you that her uncle has been showing her his penis, but it is a secret and no one has to know.

Do you think you should keep both of these secrets to yourself or should you share either of them with a senior member of staff?

You do not need to share Ahmed's secret with anyone, but clearly Jane could be in need of protection, and it is your responsibility to share that secret. You should always tell a child that you cannot promise to keep everything they tell you a secret; if you do not say so, you may lose a child's trust.

Assessment activity 6.4

Whilst any setting you work in with children has an essential role in setting the environment to ensure inclusion and equality, it is down to you as an individual to make sure that you always promote inclusion personally.

1 Describe how you can work as an individual to promote inclusion. **P6**

2 Analyse the role of early years practitioners in ensuring the promotion of inclusive practice. **D2**

End of unit assessment

1 Consider the cartoon above. In the light of the material in this unit, why is this cartoon so opposite to the values and behaviours that we work to foster in children's settings?

2 With the cartoon in mind, work through the criteria for the unit, using them to demonstrate your understanding of the ways in which you and all children's settings should work to prevent the children you work with growing up with this as their idea of others.

References and further reading

Books

Boreham and McManus (2002) *Smoking, Drinking and Drug Use among Young People in England in 2002*, The Stationery Office

Casey, T. (2005) *Inclusive Play: practical strategies for working with children aged 3–8*, Paul Chapman

Cheminais, R. (2005) *Every Child Matters: a new role for SENCOs*, David Fulton

Thomas, E. (2003) *What About Me: an Equal Opportunities support pack*, HLB Associates

Clough, P. and Nutbrown, C. (2006) *Inclusion in the Early Years*, Sage

Davy, A. and Gallagher, J. (2006) *New Play Work: play and care for children 4–16*, Thompson Learning

Maloney, S. and Topping, K. (eds) (2005) *The Routledge Falmer Reader in Inclusive Education*, Routledge Falmer

Journals

Nursery World
Nursery Education
Practical Pre-School
Sure Start Magazine
Sociology Review

Useful websites

BBC – www.bbc.co.uk

Born Abroad: an immigration map of Britain – http://news.bbc.co.uk/1/shared/spl/hi/uk/05/born_abroad/html/overview.stm

Child Poverty Action Group (CPAG) – www.cpag.org.uk

Children's Rights Director – www.rights4me.org.uk

Children's Workforce Development Council (CWDC) – www.cwdcouncil.org.uk

Chronicle World: a history of black settlement in London – http://www.thechronicle.demon.co.uk/tomsite/capsule.htm

Commission for Racial Equality (CRE) – www.cre.gov.uk

Legalday – www.legalday.co.uk

The Equality Service – www.equality.leeds.ac.uk

Grading criteria	Assessment activity	Page number
To achieve a pass grade the evidence must show that the learner is able to:		
P1 describe the meaning of diversity in today's society	6.1 End of unit assessment	224 247
P2 explain causes of economic diversity and potential effects on children, their families and society	6.1 End of unit assessment	224 247
P3 explain the importance of recognising equality, diversity and rights in providing children's services	6.2 End of unit assessment	232 247
P4 identify how legislation promotes equality of opportunity, inclusion and rights in children's services	6.3 End of unit assessment	240 247
P5 describe how practices in children's services can promote equality of opportunity, inclusion and rights	6.3 End of unit assessment	240 247
P6 explain how the individual worker can promotion inclusion	6.4 End of unit assessment	247 247
To achieve a merit grade the evidence must show that, in addition to the pass criteria, the learner is able to:		
M1 describe the implications for children's settings of addressing issues of diversity	6.1 End of unit assessment	224 247
M2 explain how one policy from a children's setting meets the requirements of a piece of legislation	6.3 End of unit assessment	240 247
M3 use examples to explain how practices in children's services can promote equality of opportunity, inclusion and rights	6.3 End of unit assessment	240 247
To achieve a distinction grade the evidence must show that, in addition to the pass and merit criteria, the learner is able to:		
D1 analyse the value of diversity in today's society and its relevance for children's care, learning and development	6.1 End of unit assessment	224 247
D2 analyse the role of children's care, learning and development practitioners in ensuring the promotion of inclusive practice	6.4 End of unit assessment	247 247

Children's learning activities and play

Introduction

Play is essential to all children's development and acts as a natural learning medium. Through play children develop skills and language, and they learn about their immediate environment and those in it. This unit will help you to develop an understanding of the benefits of play and your role in maximising those potential benefits. You will develop an understanding of the major theories of how children play and learn. As you work through the unit you will gain confidence and understanding of how to plan, implement and evaluate activities for children and you will become more skilled at setting up play situations for children.

What you need to learn

- The major theories of how children develop and learn
- The role of play in the development of children
- The role of the adult in the provision and implementation of play and learning activities for children
- How to identify and promote learning opportunities for children aged 0–8 years
- How to plan, implement and evaluate learning activities for children aged 0–8 years
- How to set up play situations for children

Thinking points

Sunita works with young children in an early years care and education setting. She is involved in setting up activities and play situations for the children which promote a range of developmental areas. These activities include:

- physical development
- intellectual development
- communication
- emotional development
- social development
- explorative play
- imaginative play.

What do you think Sunita's role will be after these activities have been set up?

How might Sunita try to build the children's self-confidence and self-esteem?

Why do you think it is important for children to enjoy their time within the early years setting?

Development and learning

The importance of neuroscience and brain studies

Research into the development of the brain, especially in babies, has shown that they are very active in the early years and that the first three years of a child's life is an extremely important period. It has been shown that young children can learn new languages much better and with clearer understanding than at any other time in their lives. Studies concerning the brain have demonstrated that whilst the brain is capable of developing new circuits in later life it is much more active in laying down connections in the very young child.

The brain requires constant stimulation in order to function effectively and it is important that babies and young children have as wide a range of experiences and stimulating activities as possible. Children need exciting environments and activities; those who are deprived of stimulation in the early years will not develop as well as those who have rich and interesting environments with meaningful interactions with adults and peers.

Factors that may influence development and learning

There are a number of factors that influence development and learning in children and some of these are given in the table below, but note that the list is not exhaustive.

▼ Some influences on development and learning

Factor	Influences on development and learning
Settings	Childcare settings range from the home to more formal early years settings. One of the important factors is that the setting provides for the needs of the child and that the resources and environment stimulate and motivate the child to explore and experience new concepts. The role of the adult is particularly important as language is vital for the development of communication skills.
Timing	Children learn new skills and concepts when they are ready but the opportunities need to be present at the right time. Skills need to be built up over time, for example writing skills do not happen straightaway but build from the initial holding of a crayon, through mark-making to eventually being able to write recognisable words. Occasionally, children are encouraged to develop concepts before they are ready and this can lead to confusion and dislike of some areas of learning, for example maths. Regular and skilled observations enable practitioners to determine the age and stage of development and plan accordingly for the progression of skills and knowledge.
Support	All children need support and encouragement especially when endeavouring to develop new skills. Infants who are walking holding onto furniture and then stand alone are openly encouraged by the tone of voice, body language and smiles of the adults willing them to take the first unaided steps. The following praise and enthusiasm encourages the child to attempt this action again and so skills are developed and refined. Children who receive positive reinforcement in this way will be more confident and more willing to explore and take calculated risks with new activities. Children who have low self-esteem will be more reluctant and so it is important that children receive the appropriate support and encouragement at all times.

Genetics	The genetic make-up of children is set down at conception and there is a great deal of debate as to how this affects their ability to learn. This is covered in more detail under the nature–nurture debate. Under normal circumstances each person has 46 chromosomes – 23 from their mother and 23 from their father – and these determine eye/hair colour, blood group, etc. However, the genetic make-up of a child might also determine whether they are more prone to learning difficulties. Although genetics plays a major part in growth and development, there are also other factors to be taken into consideration such as lack of food and whether there are any ongoing health conditions.
Environment	Children need an environment which will enable and encourage them to develop in a healthy way. They need stimulating and motivating surroundings, which will promote enthusiasm and curiosity about events and activities. The environment should be safe and should have adults who will provide support and positive reinforcement and rich experiences tailored to the needs of the individual child. The home and its location as well as the early years setting will have an effect on the overall development of the child.
Health factors	The health of the child will have a profound effect on the individual's ability to learn and develop skills. Children in the UK are generally screened from birth for health and associated problems. Tests are carried out at birth and midwives and health visitors are vigilant for signs that a child is not developing as expected. Measurements such as height and weight are regularly monitored so that any problems can be dealt with sooner rather than later. The basic needs of the child must be met before the higher needs of learning and development can take place. Children need security, safety, warmth and nutrition before they can move on to higher skills.

Extension activity

1 In pairs, make a list of five environmental factors and five health factors that you feel could affect the development of the young child.
2 List the potential effects for the child.
3 List the potential effects for the family.

Major theories

Over the years theories have been developed about how children learn and what is important for that learning to take place. This section looks at some of the major theories and how they have influenced current practice.

The nature–nurture debate

This debate has been going on for many years and people hold strong feelings about it. The debate is about whether nature (genetics and inherited factors) or nurture (the environment and external influences) have the greatest effect on a child's development and ability to learn.

Genetic inheritance affects the colour of eyes/hair; it determines blood group, skin colour and influences many other factors. However, some theorists also consider that a child's level of intelligence is determined by genetic factors and that nurture cannot alter this level. They would acknowledge that nurture could affect how they might reach their potential level but would state that the child could only reach the predetermined level of learning laid down before birth.

Theorists who strongly feel that nurture is important believe that the environment and experiences of early childhood are vital to the overall development of the child and that each individual should have rich and stimulating surroundings in order to reach their full potential.

There are a great many people who hold the view that both nature and nurture have important parts to play in the child's development but acknowledge that nurture can affect the genetic factors. For example, if a child is from a family of tall people then the potential height might be genetically determined but health factors and dietary intake can affect whether or not that potential is achieved.

Transmission models of learning

John Locke (1632–1704) promoted the idea that a child is an empty vessel, which can be affected and shaped by adults. The transmission theories are concerned with the external influences on a child and do not take into account much of their genetic make-up.

Ivan Pavlov (1849–1936) carried out much research into the behaviour of animals, mainly dogs. When the dogs were fed, a bell was rung and at the introduction of the food the dogs would produce saliva as part of the digestion process. After a while it was noticed that the animals began salivating at the sound of the bell even if there was no food. He called this classical conditioning.

Burrhus Frederic Skinner (1904–1990) carried out further research into this field. He spent much time working with animals and he provided rewards, such as food, when they did as he desired. The food was positive reinforcement but he also used negative reinforcement, such as electric shocks, to deter the animals from carrying out unwanted behaviour.

This theory, known as operant conditioning, greatly influences how adults treat children on a daily basis (positive reinforcement such as praise is a powerful influence on children) and how professionals determine behaviour modification programmes. The emphasis is on positive reinforcement. Many children display attention-seeking behaviour which can be extremely disruptive, and part of the modification programme is to provide lots of positive reinforcement when the child displays desirable behaviour and not reinforcing undesirable behaviour.

Laissez-faire views

These views are based on the idea that children will learn naturally and in a set way, whether or not there is influence by adults or the environment. They link more closely with innate (inborn) structures, with little effect as a result of adult intervention.

Noam Chomsky believes that children have a structure in the brain, which enables them to develop language. This Language Acquisition Device (LAD), as he called it, means that children can apply the rules of grammar in their daily use of language. As spoken English is complicated, you will hear children applying certain rules which in practice are incorrect, as English has many exceptions to the rules of grammar, for example a child will say that they have 'bringed' you something (adding 'ed' to make the past tense or adding 's' to make plural as in 'mouses').

Constructivist view

This is based on the work of Jean Piaget (1896–1980) and has had a major influence on the work in the early years and education settings for many years. Piaget believed that we take in information and that our brains process it and as a result of this our behaviour changes. He believed that children pass through stages as they learn and, although the learning takes place at different rates, the order of the stages remains that same.

Piaget felt very strongly that children are active learners and he was one of the main exponents of discovery learning in early childhood. He also believed that children learn through a series of processes known as **assimilation, accommodation, adaptation** and **equilibrium**, and that they develop **schemas**, which are ideas or concepts linked to patterns of behaviour. Schemas include those linked to vertical and horizontal, enveloping, and rotational (see Unit 17, Supporting Numeracy).

Food arrives when the bell has rung.

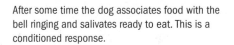

After some time the dog associates food with the bell ringing and salivates ready to eat. This is a conditioned response.

▲ **Classical conditioning (Pavlov)**

Key terms

A **schema** is a mental structure or concept which relates to a pattern of behaviour and can be used in a variety of situations.

In **assimilation**, new information is taken in which fits with the child's existing understanding.

During **accommodation**, information is modified and adapted to account for new experiences and knowledge.

Equilibrium is the balance of existing and new concepts as the child makes sense of its environment.

Adaptation is adapting thoughts and concepts through the process of assimilation and accommodation.

Theory into practice

When on your placement, watch the children at play.

- Do you notice any of them developing a schema as they go about their daily routines?
- Look for children who are working with activities and are concentrating on some of the following:
  - horizontal, for example laying objects or toys end to end or painting horizontal lines
  - transporting, for example moving objects from one place to another in a variety of ways
  - enclosing, for example placing toys and objects inside others
  - rotating, for example watching or playing with objects that turn, such as spinning tops, wheels.

Piaget's stages of development are given in the table below.

Stage	Description
Sensori-motor (birth to approx. 2 years)	The child initially has basic reflexes and gradually moves to learn through senses and movement. The infant will develop schema linked to grasping, shaking and hitting.
Pre-operational (2–7 years)	The child begins to develop symbolic play experiences. Language and literacy skills develop quickly during this period. The child is egocentric in that they mainly see things from their own point of view and have difficulty putting themselves into someone else's position.
Concrete operational (7–12 years)	The child is developing more structured and logical thought processes but still relates very much to concrete activities. Begins to understand abstract ideas towards the end of this period.
Formal operational (12+)	Abstract thinking is more noticeable during this stage and the child has a greater understanding of ethical issues and truth. They can develop hypotheses and make good attempts to test them. It is thought that some adults do not fully complete this stage of development.

Piaget also carried out numerous experiments to demonstrate children's understanding. Some of the most well-known experiments are those linked to the child's ability to **conserve**, particularly with mass, number and volume. For more about this, see Unit 17, page 454.

Key term

Conservation is the understanding that the number of objects (or the weight or volume) remains the same even when they are rearranged spatially.

Piaget demonstrated that children under 7 years cannot conserve number

Social-constructivist views

Jerome Bruner believed that a child is predisposed towards learning and that there are structures in place so that the child can follow a sequence of stages in their intellectual development. As a child has individual experiences, the cognitive schema provide meaning to these experiences. Children learn through doing, then imagining what they have been doing and then translating that into symbols of drawing, writing and numbers. Bruner believed that adults play an important role as they support children as they move through those different stages of development. Bruner's stages of development are:

- Enactive (0–1) – learning through doing – physical movements
- Iconic (1–7) – developing mental images
- Symbolic (7+) – using symbols such as language and other representational modes to transfer thoughts.

Lev Vygotsky felt that children's development is strongly supported by the adults. The level of development for an individual child became known as 'the zone of actual development' but Vygotsky felt that children were capable of higher levels with support and assistance from adults. The difference between these two levels was known as the 'zone of proximal development' and this has huge implications for the adult who would help extend the child's learning and reinforce it. Adult intervention is important so that the child can move from one zone to the next.

Advantages and disadvantages of each model

The advantages and disadvantages of the main theories are given in the table below.

▼ The advantages and disadvantages of each model

Model	Advantages	Disadvantages
Transmission	• Undesirable behaviour can be altered or modified • Children will learn through repeated behaviour patterns • Children will learn through direct experience	• No consideration given to children's stages of development • Adults take charge of learning process • Simplified view of children's learning • Children are less likely to take risks in play and exploration • Children not seen as active learners
Laissez-faire	• Children are directly involved in shaping the learning process • Development will progress regardless of adult intervention	• Children are programmed before birth as to their developmental level • Differences in rates of development linked to race or culture not recognised • Children are easily labelled if they do not fit in with recognised milestones • Children not seen as active learners
Constructivist	• Children are active learners • Children learn through discovery • Stages of development are clearly identified	Importance of social interaction is not recognised
Social constructivist	• Communication and adult involvement is recognised as important • Children are active learners • Parental involvement is encouraged • Stimulating environment produces observable positive results	Higher financial input required in terms of resources and staffing

Links to current research

Research on how the brains of babies develop and how children learn is going on all the time, for example:

- Chris Athey has carried out a great deal of work into children's development linked to schema.
- Janet Moyles has observed children at length to explain play as a learning spiral (see page 265).
- The work of Noam Chomsky concerning the Language Acquisition Device is ongoing.
- Many early excellence centres have based their programmes on the work of the social constructivist point of view and they are monitored on a regular basis as part of ongoing research.

The work of all the theorists is continually being challenged and developed as individuals seek knowledge about how the mind and thought processes in early childhood develop. Many children are observed and studied to substantiate or refute the theories. The results of such research have a direct effect on the way early years care and education settings are structured.

How children learn

First-hand experiences

Piaget firmly believed in discovery learning and that children should have first-hand experiences on which to build. Very young children, indulging in solitary play, are often engrossed in what they are doing as they investigate the properties of the objects they are playing with. Children need to experience as many things at first-hand as possible in order to build up their bank of learning. Allowing children to feel and experience things for themselves, within the bounds of safety, is far better than trying to learn by being told about them; for example we can tell children all about snow but they will never fully appreciate the wonder and the properties of snow until they experience it for themselves.

Through play

Play is vital to children. It is the main way by which they learn. Play that is self-initiated and free-flowing can produce deep and meaningful learning. It is through the various types of play that children can develop skills, gain knowledge and live out their hopes, fears and fantasies in a safe and secure environment. Language is developed and new vocabulary adopted as the children gain in confidence and enact plays, enjoy poetry and rhymes, and become lost in the world of storybooks.

Play can take on many forms and children will gradually move through the stages of play, as described on page 261, and eventually feel comfortable in co-operative play and solving problems with peers and adults.

Being active

Children are active learners. They learn best when they are actively involved with materials and people. Children usually have a great deal of energy and this can be beneficial for many learning experiences. They love to be running, skipping and climbing and in this way will develop gross motor skills. This in turn will promote spatial awareness, an understanding of speed, distance and height. The child's natural curiosity should be encouraged as they have a desire to find out for themselves. The role of the adult is always to ensure that the child is safe and that this curiosity does not endanger them in any way.

Using language

Children begin learning the basics of conversation at a very early age. When a baby is in the arms of an adult and there is eye contact and vocalisation, the baby quickly learns the concept of turn-taking during conversation.

Children need to engage in conversation with others and they will have opportunity to use language in many different ways during play situations. In fantasy and pretend play, the child will eagerly take on the role of another person and will use language appropriate to the role. Language and literacy development is promoted throughout the day in early years setting as children listen to stories, sing songs and rhymes, paint, draw and spend time mark-making and writing in various forms during role play, for example telephone messages,

▲ Engaging with stories is an important part of language development

making notes, recipes, menus, orders, etc. The adults that children come into contact with should extend the vocabulary used and reinforce good pronunciation and grammar incidentally and sensitively.

See Unit 18, Supporting Literacy.

Stimulation

The environment should be one that is stimulating and welcoming. It has been found that in some East European countries children in some orphanages have been kept in dingy rooms with no stimulation. These children have demonstrated developmental delay and have indulged in banging their heads against cot rails in order to have some external contact. Once people began talking to these children and introduced them to toys and other stimulating activities they improved dramatically and began to take an interest in their surroundings.

Working with others

Children enjoy the company of others and as they mature their play moves gradually from solitary play to co-operative play. They are able to discuss and try to solve problems as their play becomes more detailed and intricate.

Children's learning experiences do not occur in isolation. Use of language, being active and learning from first-hand experiences are all important and come together when play moves to deeper and more complex levels. Children need to interact with adults as well as peer groups and they will enjoy stories and discussions on a one-to-one as well as a group basis. As children work with others they will develop their social skills and will become more considerate as time progresses.

Doing meaningful activities

Children like challenging, meaningful activities and play. If they understand the rationale behind an activity it often helps increase their motivation. From a very young age, children will involve themselves in the daily activities in the home such as dusting, washing up and baking. They quickly learn that the activity has a goal and that positive reinforcement follows in terms of appreciation. Children will become engrossed in certain activities and will persevere for longer periods than their usual concentration span. Motivation and interest are vital aspects of this type of play.

Feeling secure

Children need to feel secure. This is one of the basic principles of childcare. If children are not safe and secure, they will not be able to move to the higher levels of activities. In order to allay their fears they will cling to an adult or familiar person and not venture to play or become involved in other activities.

A feeling of security is one of those things that is more evident when it is lacking than when it is present. In order to ensure that children feel secure, they need to be surrounded by people who are pleasant, helpful and who will make them feel valued and worthy. They will need to be praised and encouraged and should not feel criticised. Many early years care and education settings have a key worker system whereby the child has a nominated adult who will be their main contact at all times. This helps them to feel secure.

Once children feel safe and secure, they will feel that they can explore and experiment in a sheltered environment that will allow them to build their self-confidence and raise self-esteem.

Theory into practice

Children need to know that they are valued and have a sense of belonging. When on your placement observe the ways in which the children are made to feel that the setting is welcoming and belongs to them. For example:

- Do you see any posters that are brightly coloured and would appeal to children?
- Do the children have name cards or pictures?
- Is their work valued and displayed?

Make a note of other points.

Appropriate adult intervention

Adult intervention can enhance or ruin an activity. It takes time to develop the skills of sensitive and appropriate intervention. The child's safety is paramount and intervention on those grounds must never be compromised. However, there are many times when the situation can be enhanced and moved to a deeper level by your sensitive intervention. If a child is struggling to complete something or is experiencing difficulty then intervention might be appropriate. You should be careful not to take over the task but rather offer help which the child can refuse. Entering into the play situation takes skill and sensitivity and many practitioners have joined a tea-party in the role play area to find that they are virtually alone after a few minutes. When working with children during art and craft activities, it is important that you do not correct or neaten up the child's work unnecessarily as it indicates that what the child did was not to the required standard.

Influences of the major theories

On the organisation of the early years environment

The organisation of the early years environment is directly influenced by the theories mentioned earlier. It seems that the social constructivist point of view has

Case study: Will it do?

Joy is an early years worker in a private nursery and enjoys working with the children during art and craft sessions. She is currently working with children who are 3 and 4 years old, helping them to produce work for a wall frieze for the book area. They have decided on a spring theme and have produced flowers, kites, lambs and ducks. The children have painted pictures of themselves and other people, and are in the process of cutting them out ready to go on the frieze. Joy is watching the children and one little boy is cutting around his picture and is concentrating very hard. He leaves a few ragged edges, especially around the hands on his painting, but when he is finished he hands it to Joy who then picks up her scissors and trims the edges. The child looks at Joy as if his attempt was not good enough.

1 **How might Joy deal with this situation now?**

2 **How could she have avoided this situation?**

3 **What could she have done or said to the child?**

4 **Why is positive reinforcement and sensitivity important?**

been adopted by many settings as the way forward in providing opportunities for children. However, this has a cost involved and it is expensive in terms of resources and staffing ratios. As the child is seen as an active participant in the learning process, a stimulating and exciting environment is important and the social interaction with adults is an equally vital part of the process. Practitioners must also be trained appropriately so that they are aware of the different stages that children move through and that all activities and resources are age- and stage-appropriate. It is vital to have an in-depth understanding of child development and related activities in order to be an effective practitioner.

On resourcing

Appropriate resources are vital for the overall development of the child. This includes human resources as staffing ratios are important, not only for safety reasons but also so that the child can experience the stimulating interactions with adults during conversations, stories and rhymes.

Other resources include books, art and craft materials, table-top games and activities, large and small construction toys, sand, water and outdoor toys. The list is endless and all aspects of child development must be catered for as the child should have the opportunity to explore and experiment in a safe and stimulating environment. Simple science experiments should be made available as well as a range of role-play scenarios, which will encourage imaginative play.

It is important that the resources link with the areas of development – social, physical, intellectual, communication and emotional. Aesthetic awareness should not be neglected as children need to be allowed to experience a sense of wonder and awe. They should be exposed to a range of types of music, poetry and art so that they can develop a range of tastes and experiences.

On the role of the adult and their interaction with the child

When you consider the role of the adult, you need to think about what the various theories have to say on this subject. If you adopt the *laissez-faire* approach,

for example, then adult interaction will not be seen as important as if you consider the social-constructivist approach. The theories of Vygotsky and Bruner promote the sensitive involvement and intervention of the adult in order to help the child move to the next stage of development, in bridging the gap between the Zones of Actual and Proximal Development and providing 'scaffolding' to support the child's learning processes.

Most early years care and education settings regard adult interaction as an important part of the daily routine for young children. Well-trained practitioners are an asset to any setting as a good knowledge of child development is essential for the planning of appropriate activities. You should be able to use detailed child observations to advantage in planning for the future development of individual children.

Additionally, adults must ensure the safety of children at all times and check resources for any flaws or defects. The whole environment should be checked regularly and you should be ever vigilant for health and safety issues. You should be aware of parental wishes and ensure that dietary and religious requirements are met at all times, keeping in mind any allergies and fears/dislikes. It is an important and demanding but very rewarding role when working with young children.

Assessment activity 7.1

Look at the following grid in which the concepts and theorists are mixed up. Match the theorist to their concept. **P1**

Theorist	Concept of how children learn
Chomsky	The child is egocentric in that they mainly see things from their own point of view and have difficulty putting themselves into someone else's position.
Skinner	A social-constructivist who felt that children move through specific stages in their intellectual development and that adults play an important role as they support children as they move through those different stages of development.
Bruner	A child achieves 'the zone of actual development' but this theorist felt that children were capable of higher levels with support and assistance from adults.
Piaget	He believed that positive reinforcement as praise is a powerful influence on children.
Vygotsky	He believed that children have a structure in the brain, which enables children to develop language.

The nature of play

It is increasingly being recognised that play should be central in children's lives, both in and out of early years settings. This section looks at the stages of play and the types of play, as well as the benefits from different types of play.

Definitions of play

Play is not as easy to define as one might at first think, although the following characteristics as provided by Catherine Garvey (1991) are often agreed upon:

- Play is pleasurable, enjoyable. Even when not actually accompanied by signs of mirth, the player still positively values it.
- Play has no extrinsic goals. Its motivations are intrinsic and serve no other objectives.
- Play is spontaneous and voluntary. It is not obligatory but is freely chosen by the player.
- Play involves some active engagement on the part of the player.
- Play has certain systematic relations to what is not play.

Motivational value of play

One of the difficulties when providing play centres involves the role of the adults and the way in which adults might structure play opportunities for children. How can play be 'real play' if adults have chosen and planned it, bearing in mind that one of the key characteristics of play seems to be that it should be spontaneous and voluntary? This is a fair question and in reality what tends to happen is that adults are using play as a vehicle for learning. We know that children respond to playful experiences and that they are likely to be motivated to learn if play is used as a tool. Play is so fascinating and pleasurable that children are often able to persevere at a self-chosen activity, concentrate and repeat skills.

Cultural variations

It is important to be aware of any cultural variations when children are in an early years care and education setting. It is often easiest to gain knowledge directly from the parents as making assumptions can sometimes lead to difficulties. Parental wishes should always be taken seriously, and if they are in conflict with those of the setting, this should be explained, giving reasons. Often a compromise can be negotiated. Parents like to be involved and will be only too happy to explain their child's needs to you.

Stages of play and how they relate to developmental stages

The way in which children engage in play changes as they develop new skills and learn how to relate to others. Play begins early on in life. A young baby enjoys being played with and quickly learns how to smile and gain the attention of adults. By 8 months, most babies are starting to enjoy peek-a-boo and will even initiate this type of play by pulling something over their faces. The way in which children are gradually able to play together with children of their own age suggests that there are social stages to play. These were first recorded by Mildred Parten in 1932 and are still referred to today. Note that the age guide in the table below has to be considered as very approximate and that although most older children are capable of social activity, there will be times when they wish to play alone.

Age	Stage	Description
0–2 years	Solitary play	Babies and toddlers spend time playing 'in their own world'. Babies for example may spend time touching, feeling and talking to their toes.
2–4 years	Parallel play	Children are beginning to notice other children and may play alongside each other. They may also imitate each other's play. Gradually children then become more and more involved in each other's play.
4–7 years	Collaborative play (also known as co-operative play)	Children are able to play co-operatively together. They can decide how they want to play and make up rules for their play. They can also play complex games that require turn-taking.
7+ years	Competitive play	Some children from around 6 or 7 years onwards enjoy play that is collaborative and often structured, but also has a competitive dimension. Good examples of this are children playing board games, such as chess, as well as sports such as football and tennis.

The links between stages of development and play

The speed at which children's play becomes more social and sophisticated depends on their overall development and so you need to be able to observe children playing in order to assess their play needs.

The table below shows the stages of play and development that most children show, although it should only be used as a broad guide.

▼ The links between stages of development and stages of play

Age	Stage of development	Social stages of play	Features of play	Examples of resources/ equipment
0–6 months	During this period, babies gain some control over their limbs. They learn about communication by cooing and babbling.	*Solitary play* Babies enjoy playing with adults and older children, but also play and 'talk' by themselves.	Senses are used to gain pleasure and explore. Repetitive actions are used.	Baby gyms, rattles
6–12 months	Most babies become mobile in this time. They are learning to gain adult attention by smiling, babbling and, towards 12 months, pointing.	*Solitary play* Additionally, babies often show things to adults and initiate movements which will gain adult responses, for example dropping a toy on the floor.	Senses are still being used. Play is repetitive and exploratory.	Activity quilts, balls, books, pop-up toys
1–2 years	Toddlers are mobile and gaining gross and fine manipulative skills. They can feed themselves and can stack bricks and manage very simple puzzles. Language is just developing with first words emerging at 12–14 months. By 2 years many children are beginning to put two words together. Children are very reliant on adults and want to be close to them.	*Solitary play* Most activity is still likely to be solitary.	Trial and error learning. Repetitive movements and play. Toddlers 'talk' to toys. Imaginative play is developing.	Push and pull toys, dolls, trolleys

Age	Stage of development	Social stages of play	Features of play	Examples of resources/ equipment
2–3 years	Children's overall co-ordination is becoming developed, although strength is often lacking. Many new words are learnt. Sentences are short, for example three words and not always understood by others. Children often need adult to support their play and to help organise games.	*Parallel play* Children begin to notice other children playing and will happily play alongside.	Children enjoy imaginative play and imitate adult gestures, words and movements. They may take each other's toys and equipment. Sensory play is also enjoyed, for example water, sand. Play can be repetitive with children gaining mastery of their movements.	Dressing up clothes, props used in the home (for example tea sets, telephones), water, sand, paint and dough
3–4 years	Children are usually confident at this age. Most children are well co-ordinated and are able to snip/cut with scissors, run and partly dress themselves. They feel grown up as they are usually out of nappies. Language is usually understood by others and by 4 speech has become fairly fluent. Children require significant adult support.	*Parallel/co-operative play* The way in which children play is usually determined by their level of confidence and language skills.	Play is often imaginative play with children enjoying alongside or with others. Children also enjoy physical activities such as riding tricycles and climbing. Some play is beginning to be more planned, for example a child may tell an adult that they are making a house out of bricks.	Small world play (for example farm animals, train sets), dressing up clothes and home props, water, sand, paint and dough
4–6 years	Friendships are beginning to be formed. Single sex groups are not unusual. Language is usually fluent with only minor errors. Physically children are well co-ordinated. Children often require adult support and help.	*Co-operative play* Children are able to play together, share equipment and respond to each others' play.	Imaginative play remains important for some children, although other children are more interested in games involving physical skills such as football, riding bicycles or making things, for example construction toys.	Climbing frames, bicycles, drawing and painting, construction toys, creative materials
6+ years	Friendships are important to children. Children are starting to see others' points of view and can negotiate. Children are becoming increasingly independent.	*Co-operative play/ competitive play*	Children begin to have strong play preferences, for example some children enjoy making things, whilst others may enjoy physical games.	Very dependent on children's preferences – creative materials, board games, complex construction toys, footballs, climbing frames, hoops, dressing up clothes

Types of play activities and learning experiences

Play can be grouped into types, although remember that for children play is simply play! Categorising play into types helps you to plan effectively as each play type has particular developmental benefits. Categories of play can vary from setting to setting, but in this unit play has been grouped into the following types:

Free/spontaneous and structured/planned play

In order to implement the early years curriculum, children will need a variety of play experiences, both planned and spontaneous. Spontaneous play experiences are often those that the children find the most rewarding because they are often child-initiated and thus of interest to them. Sometimes spontaneous play arises out of planned activities, for example you may decide to encourage children to sort buttons, but a child may discover how to play tiddly-winks with the buttons. You can use this spontaneous play to further other learning by asking the child about the buttons, 'Which are the easiest to use?'

Structured play is sometimes the term used when adult involvement is an essential part of an activity, for example planting bulbs. In recent early years curricula documents, the terms 'adult-directed activity' or 'adult-initiated activity' are often used instead of 'structured play'. These terms reflect the growing view that if play is highly structured, it is unlikel`y to be in essence 'play' as play by its nature should emanate from the child.

There are many advantages of structured play or adult-directed activities. If sensitively led, they can support specific areas of a child's development or enable coverage of a particular area of the curriculum. An adult, for example, may put ice cubes in the water tray and ask a group of children to observe and play with the cubes to see if they float or sink. This activity would help children to notice the properties of ice and through the activity they may learn specific vocabulary.

Free-flow play

In contrast, free-flow play is play that is completely chosen by the child and relies on children's interests, hence the growing trend to call this type of play 'child-initiated' or 'child-led'. There are many advantages to this type of play as children are able to spend time following their own interests and set their own challenges. This type of play can provide deep learning experiences for the child.

Most settings aim to provide a mix of play opportunities, some of which would be considered as structured play and others as free play. The table below shows the advantages and disadvantages of structured and free play.

▼ The advantages and disadvantages of structured and free play

Free play or child-initiated play		Structured play or adult-initiated play	
Advantages	**Disadvantages**	**Advantages**	**Disadvantages**
• Children can set their own goals. • Children concentrate for longer periods when play is self-chosen. • Children are more likely to be creative. • Child-initiated activities are less pressured as the child is responsible. • Children learn how to choose. • Children can gain in confidence by being self-reliant. • Children can repeat activities until they feel they have mastered them.	• Children may not gain specific language or may choose not to engage in co-operative play. • Sometimes child-initiated play can be repetitive and not challenge the child. • Child-initiated play can be stereotypical. • Some children find it hard to cope with choice. • Children may not get a range of skills. • Children with learning difficulties may not receive sufficient adult input.	• Coverage of the curriculum is ensured. • Children can gain specific vocabulary and skills. • Areas of the curriculum such as mathematics need to be delivered sequentially in schools.	• Children's attention span is shorter during adult-directed activities. • Children may feel that they have failed if the adult's expectations are too high. • Activities may not be sufficiently challenging or creative.

Therapeutic play

Whilst play was once viewed as a waste of time, now we know that it benefits children's social and emotional development. Sensory activities such as sand, water and dough, as well as role play, are particularly seen as helpful. Being encouraged to play often helps children who have witnessed or been the subject of distressing events in their lives, including bereavement and abuse.

Combining types of play

As children do not see play in terms of 'types', they tend to combine play materials to support their ongoing play. The climbing frame may become the house, dough may be used to make cakes for the home corner or farm animals may need to go for a swim in the water tray! Insisting that play materials can only be used in a certain way or have to remain in certain places generally inhibits children's learning experiences and creativity. It is good practice therefore for settings to be as flexible as possible and, unless materials or equipment are likely to be damaged, to try to allow children to combine materials.

It is also possible to combine structured and free-flow play. As both child-initiated play and activities involving adults have advantages, there is a growing trend towards combining both ways of working with children. The Foundation Stage curriculum advocates play as a vehicle for learning but gives practitioners a vital role. To achieve this way of working, many settings now look for a combined approach, as illustrated by the case study below.

Moyles' play spiral

Janet Moyles (1989) put forward the idea that play is like an upward spiral that can lead to detailed meaningful play culminating in the mastery of skills and acquisition of knowledge. This spiral begins with free play, which may begin with a child exploring the properties of resources. The child may continue feeling and experimenting with the objects, for example clay, dough, construction toys, collage, and will become more and more familiar with them. Later the adult might initiate an activity involving the same materials, such as rolling out dough and cutting shapes. Over a number of days and weeks the child might initiate other play

Case study: All buttoned up

Anna, an early years practitioner, wants to encourage several 4-year-olds to practise their sorting skills as part of delivering the mathematical development area of learning within the Foundation Stage. She puts out a large tray of buttons on a table. Two children come and start playing and touching the buttons. Anna asks them to show her their favourite buttons. She gives each child a small box to put their favourite buttons in. As the children show her their favourite buttons, she comments on them, 'This one is shiny. This one has four holes.' She then asks the children if they could find her some black buttons with four holes. After three or four minutes, Anna leaves them to carry on playing.

The children make up their own sorting game using the small boxes that Anna has left.

Evaluate the effectiveness of this approach to learning by considering the following questions:

1 **How has the early years curriculum been implemented?**

2 **How are the children learning through play?**

3 **How is the practitioner able to meet individual children's needs and interests?**

4 **How did the practitioner's intervention extend the children's skills and language development?**

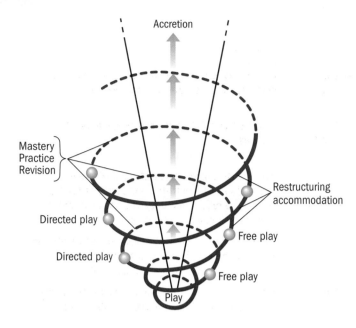

Moyles' spiral of learning

activities using the skills gained and these may be in different areas of the setting, for example the kitchen or role-play area. If the adult takes note of this pattern, they can direct play again towards the development of new skills to be practised and mastered and as this happens the child will wish to use these new skills in as many different ways as possible. As these skills build up the child is able to extend them and develop new ones.

Extension of play opportunities

You need to look at ways of extending children's learning whilst they are playing. This can take many forms and requires a flexible and thoughtful approach.

- *Providing further equipment* You may feel that a child may benefit from a more challenging jigsaw puzzle or could be given further choice of materials in order to make the play more enjoyable.
- *Asking questions* Sometimes you may ask questions to stimulate children's thinking and thus their learning about a situation, for example 'What would happen if you mixed the colours?' It is important that questioning is not carried out in the form of an interrogation and that the question is worth asking!

- *Playing alongside or with children* You can play alongside children as this may help children to gain ideas, for example you may start to make your own model and children may take some of the ideas and incorporate them into their own.

Imaginative play

This type of play is also referred to as 'pretend play' or 'role play'. It particularly stimulates children's language as at first they talk to themselves and later talk to each other. The language used often reflects the language that they have heard, with children sometimes using imaginative play to make sense of situations that they have encountered.

Theory into practice

- Make a list of different ideas for role-play situations, for example hospital, shop etc.
- Alongside each situation, make a list of the resources you might need.

Creative and expressive play

Creative play is a broad heading to encompass materials and play that encourage children to express themselves. It is important to differentiate between creative play and activities which are adult-led and result in children making things to a set formula. Creative play should allow children to be expressive and to bring to their play an interpretation of their own ideas, for example they may choose to paint but will not necessarily use the 'proper' colours. Another key feature of creative play is that it does not have to have a definite purpose or end product – only the purpose that the child ascribes it. For example, a 3-year-old may enjoy the texture of ribbons and laces and may choose to stick different pieces onto a piece of paper.

▼ Types of creative play

Type of creative play	Features	Resources
Collage	Children from as young as 2 years enjoy selecting and feeling different textures and finally sticking them.	Glue, selection of paper, fabrics, laces, ribbons, buttons, feathers, newspaper, magazines
Painting	Most children enjoy painting and printing with brushes, rollers, sponges and also with their hands.	Selection of paints, large brushes, rollers, fine brushes
Musical instruments	Children love to use musical instruments and can quickly learn to identify a beat or rhythm. Exploring the sounds of instruments helps children's auditory discrimination.	Homemade shakers and rattles, a selection of untuned percussion instruments such as tambours, drums and rattles; tuned percussion instruments such as xylophone, chime bars
Junk modelling	From a selection of paper, boxes and other materials, children enjoy creating 3D models.	Wide selection of interesting textures and materials which might include boxes, bubble wrap, corks, plastic lids, matchsticks, straws, tubing
Drawing and mark making	Early drawing and mark making forms part of the process of learning to write and communicate through symbols.	Selection of paper, type writer, crayons, charcoals, pastels, felt-tips, board markers, rubbers, etc.

Sensory play

Sensory play is sometimes referred to as 'play with natural materials'. It includes traditional nursery activities such as sand, water and malleable materials like dough. Sensory play has the capacity to hold some children's attention for long periods of time as the sensory nature of the materials seems to help them to focus. It is not unusual for quite sociable children to prefer to play in parallel with sensory activities, for example two 4-year-olds may stand side by side at a sand tray and, whilst looking occasionally across at each other, may not actually play together. Some examples are given in the table below.

▼ Types of sensory play

Types of sensory play	Features	Examples of resources – usually rotated to encourage children to play in a variety of ways
Sand	Sand can be provided in large walk-in pits, free standing trays or also in small trays on tables. Children tend to spend time scooping, digging and shaping sand, although the dampness of sand will affect the way they play.	Equipment for scooping and pouring (for example, spoons, spades, bottles, egg cups), toys with wheels (for example, trucks), animals (for example, dinosaurs, farm animals), objects for hiding (for example, shells, beads, 'treasure'), equipment for printing and making sand castles
Water	Water is usually provided in large trays. Children tend to enjoy changes in the water, for example bubbles, inclusion of ice cubes, coloured water.	Items for floating (for example, boats, corks, ducks), toys for washing doll's clothes, dolls, plastic animals, equipment for pouring and scooping (for example, beakers, bottles, tubes, funnels)
Dough, plasticine and clay	Dough is used for children to model with as well as to pound and cut. Dough is versatile, as there are many recipes which provide different textures.	Tools (for example, cutters, rollers, and scissors), moulds, plates and cake tins to encourage children to make items for their role play
Gloop	Gloop is cornflour combined with water. It forms a runny paste.	Trays and spoons, although many children simply use their hands

Social play

Through play, children learn how to relate to each other and learn how roles are developed in society. There are many beneficial aspects of play linked to the emotional and social development of the child. Play:

- provides opportunities for children to meet and interact with each other
- helps children to learn to co-operate and collaborate with each other
- provides pleasure, relaxation and enjoyment
- relieves stress and anxiety
- can help children to feel calm and soothed
- provides opportunities for children to feel in control and powerful
- helps children to feel good about themselves and to achieve goals that they have set themselves
- gives children opportunities to act out experiences and make sense of them.

Extension activity

Think of an activity that will encourage children to socialise and talk with each other. Describe the activity and list three learning outcomes.

Drama and role/fantasy play

Imaginative play encourages children's speech and language development. To develop children's overall language, many early years settings 'theme' the role-play area so that children begin to use new expressions and vocabulary. Themes tend to work well when children have had some actual experience so that they draw from it for their play.

Examples of themes that can be used in role-play areas include:

- school
- dentist
- train station
- post office
- hospital
- greengrocer's shop.

Locomotor skills

Locomotor skills encompass the use of gross motor skills and the development of skills used in crawling, walking and running. Children also develop the variations of these with skipping, hopping and jumping. Examples of the types of activities that promote development are:

- Children need to gain in confidence to use tricycles, scooters, bicycles – they need to develop good co-ordination skills. Protective headgear should be offered. This also helps children to learn about speed and distance.
- Obstacle courses promote gross and locomotive development. Hoops and play tunnels, as well as beams, can be used to encourage children to use a range of movements.
- Kicking helps with co-ordination and perceptual skills. Children enjoy kicking from an early age although they find it hard to play co-operatively with a football until they are older.
- There is a variety of 'running games' to help develop skills, co-ordination and spatial awareness, for example chase or 'What's the time Mr Wolf?'

Mastery play

Children will spend great amounts of time practising skills and activities. You may observe them carrying out the same thing over and over again, or you may notice that there is a theme to their play activities. They may paint horizontal lines in various colours, build tracks along the floor and place blocks end to end to make long lines. In cases like this, it is often the case that they are developing a horizontal schema. Similarly they may be mastering vertical schema and will build towers, etc. If children are motivated they will spend much time mastering skills and will use them in many activities in order to practise them.

Children become very skilled and gain confidence as they progress. Have you ever watched a child on a tricycle once they have mastered it? They can move very quickly and stop within centimetres of a wall. If you consider what is involved in that process, it is fairly complicated. The mastery of use of the tricycle and the understanding of speed and distance are all present in what at first appears to be a simple act.

Socio-dramatic play

Although the role-play area can be used to stimulate children's language, it should also be a place where children can go to dress up and take on any role that they wish. As children get older, they may wish to plan their play with others and this then becomes 'drama' or socio-dramatic play.

Children can also show self-expression when moving to music. They enjoy having space and music to move to. Props such as ribbons and scarves can be put out as some children enjoy moving and creating shapes with them.

Whilst concerts and plays organised by adults may be enjoyed by children, it is important to understand that generally they are not good vehicles for self-expression as they originate with the adult rather than with the child.

Symbolic play

Children indulge in symbolic play from an early age and it is characterised by children substituting one object for another, for example a cardboard box becomes the car; beads become food on the plate in the role-play area. This type of play is important as it assists with the understanding that one thing can represent another, as in the written word and the characters used in mathematics. Without the ability to recognise symbols we would have difficulty with many aspects of day-to-day living.

Play with objects

Children love to play with objects of various shapes and sizes and in

Studying mini-beasts ▶

doing so develop a number of concepts and skills. They are gradually absorbing information about the properties of each object. They will spend great amounts of time listening to the noises objects make and working out how they relate to each other or fit inside each other. This type of play helps children build up the skills and knowledge to develop other concepts, for example linked to science and mathematics.

Exploratory and technological/investigative play

Most children enjoy looking at things work, investigating and seeing what things can do. This area of play is about children acting almost as early scientists and mathematicians. They may go outdoors and look closely at things, want to dig and pour water into a hole or create a shelter. Indoors they might be interested in programmable toys, computers and technology. This is not a 'traditional' area of play, but one that reflects the growing interest in technology and also the realisation that children should also be spending time outdoors playing.

Examples of resources and activities for exploratory play include:

- magnifying glasses, bug boxes
- spades, trowels, buckets
- screwdrivers, tools
- programmable toys, computers
- gadgets.

The role of play

Play has an important role in the promotion of skills and learning in the main developmental areas:

- physical development, for example gross and fine motor skills
- language and literacy
- understanding of the world
- emotional and social development
- imagination and creativity.

Play also has a therapeutic aspect.

Physical development

There is increasing research to suggest that children's physical development is important in order to help their literacy. Physical skills also give children confidence and independence as, for example, they can put on their coats or complete a jigsaw. Physical skills can be divided into gross and locomotive motor skills (see Locomotor Skills on page 268) and fine motor skills, although some activities encompass both types of skill.

■ Fine motor skills

Children need to develop the muscles in their hands to allow them later to use tools such as scissors with accuracy and also in order to be able to write. Activities will include:

- using scissors, for example for collage
- threading activities such as beads, pasta and buttons
- jigsaws, small construction equipment such as Duplo, Stickle bricks, interlocking train sets
- junk modelling to encourage the use of tools such as staplers, scissors and rulers
- everyday routine activities such as pouring out drinks at snack time, stacking away toys, putting books onto shelves, folding away dressing up clothes
- dough, sand and water with tools and toys.

Language and literacy

A good starting point when considering speaking and listening activities is to revisit children's stages of language development including their ability to internalise thought and process information. This covered in more detail in Unit 18, Supporting Literacy Skills.

Child development theories suggest that children will find it hard to process information gained by the spoken word alone (i.e. listening) as they rely heavily on images to process information. In the same way, they find it hard to wait for their turn to speak because they cannot internalise their thoughts, which results in them needing to talk in order to think! It is therefore good practice for speaking and listening activities to be interactive and carried out with small groups of children.

Understanding of the world

Children need opportunity to develop an understanding of the world around them and will enjoy gaining information from books, stories and rhymes. Posters are useful in providing information from various sources, for example job roles, cultural artefacts, styles/types of housing. It is important that adults do not let the children develop stereotyped assumptions, for example all Native Americans live in wigwams, but use the endless opportunities to provide information about rich and varied lifestyles and experiences. Science and nature are important and children should have opportunity to care for or know about animals – but remember that some children have allergies to animal fur.

Emotional development

Role play often provides opportunity for children to explore their fantasies and fears. It may not remove the concern but opens it up to exploration and conversation. Activities might be used to help alleviate pent-up feelings of frustration and anger, for example using music and dance/movement or allowing the child to use hammering activities or pounding clay, etc. There are jigsaws available which display a person or teddy with different expressions on their face, such as anger, happiness, sadness, worry, and these can be used to initiate conversations as to what makes us happy or sad.

Social development

Children usually enjoy the company of other children and adults. Attending an early years care and education setting enables them to mix with other children in a structured environment. They also learn how to work together in a group and will develop skills and gain knowledge by observing others and then carrying out activities. Language development can be enhanced and vocabulary extended by listening to the conversations of others and by grammatical corrections being made in a sensitive manner. Children quickly learn what is acceptable behaviour and what is not and, providing the main attention is given to desirable behaviour, they can develop skills and manners that might not have been evident previously. Considering the feelings of others, having good manners and helping maintain a healthy environment are all life skills which will be beneficial as they grow and mature.

Imagination and creativity

Drawing, painting and making models are all ways of encouraging self-expression in children. The key to helping children show their creativity is to provide them with a good choice of materials rather than showing them what to make. Most settings provide a drawing and writing table as well as malleable materials and paint.

The therapeutic aspect of play

Anna Freud was one of the forerunners in the development of using the therapeutic aspects of play. She felt that play could be used in the diagnosis and the treatment of issues and conditions in young children. This type of play is often used today when working with disturbed children who have been harmed or damaged by life experiences. It has been found to be particularly beneficial for children who have been abused as they can deal with their experience in a safe and secure environment with individuals trained specifically to work in such situations.

Assessment activity 7.2

1 Provide a leaflet for parents at your placement in which you explain how play can provide for development in children.
2 Choose three types of activity, for example sand play, water play, creative activities, outdoor play, and explain in the leaflet how each is beneficial for holistic development. **P2**

You might like to illustrate your leaflet.

7.3 The role of the adult in the provision and implementation of play and learning activities for children

Role of the adult

The role of the adult is central to how well children are able to play and learn when activities are delivered using play as a medium.

Identify and promote learning opportunities

Whenever possible, it is beneficial to use the child's interests and likes and to develop them to promote and provide learning opportunities. For example, if a child

likes playing with cars, it is possible to incorporate them into many aspects of play. Sorting different types of vehicles, making patterns and 'roadways' in the sand, using different vehicle wheel patterns in art work, and developing themes of 'Road Safety' are just a few ideas when planning activities for the child.

Understand relevant curriculum requirements

In the UK, at the time of writing, there are several early years frameworks, which reflect the needs of the home countries and also the ages of the children. Each country within the UK has, or is developing, a framework for the under 3s as well as one for pre-school and school-age children. Settings in receipt of government funding need to show that they are implementing the curriculum in their country. In 2008 the framework in England will become the Early Years Foundation Stage and will take into account the care and education of children aged 0–5. School settings working with children aged 6 and above in the UK have to plan using the country's National Curriculum.

Using a balance of activities

As well as thinking about the activities, practitioners also have to think about the balance between structured, adult-directed play and play that is child-led or 'free'. It is essential that children do have sufficient time to explore and set their own challenges in the way they want and there has been some concern that time and opportunities for 'free play' have been crowded out.

Everyone has their favourite activities, but it is important to vary the approach so that the child has a good balance of activities throughout the day. Children should be encouraged to play outside and should be dressed appropriately. They should have opportunity to promote all aspects of development through a range of stimulating and exciting activities which will fire the imagination and encourage learning and the development and mastery of skills.

Implementing an integrated approach

Many settings choose to deliver part or the entire curriculum using themes. The idea behind themes is that play and learning activities are interlinked and that children benefit from cohesiveness. There are hundreds of popular themes including 'Myself', 'Growing' and 'Colours'. These can be used to incorporate all the areas of development and the range of curricular outcomes.

It is generally accepted that 'themes' are not really appropriate with babies and very young children, although many settings working with children over 3 years tend to have some type of theme.

Planning

The key to working well with children is often in the planning and preparation. This means that good organisational skills are required. Activities need to be age- and stage-related so that children can succeed and thus gain in self-confidence.

Preparing

It is important that all early years workers consider the materials and resources required for an activity. Part of the preparation process is to ensure that the right materials and equipment are available and that there are enough of them for the number of children involved.

Health and safety

One of the major aspects of the role of the adult is to ensure that children are safe from harm. All health and safety policies and procedures of the setting must be read, understood and adhered to by all members of staff including volunteers and those on placement or work experience.

Equipment and resources should be checked regularly for defects and removed if they are damaged. Risk assessments should be carried out prior to any activity being carried out and any risks minimised to an acceptable level. If they cannot be reduced significantly, the activity should not be implemented. There may need to be an increase in staffing for some activities so that the children can be monitored more easily.

Implementing

When implementing an activity, it is sometimes necessary to explain or show the children what to do. When playing games it might be useful to have a practice run. However, the creativity and ingenuity of children should not be stifled and the adult should always encourage them to think things through. It is important that language appropriate to the activity is used, and in this way the children will learn new words and reinforce others as they converse in a relaxed manner.

Providing encouragement

The work of B.F. Skinner demonstrated the importance of positive reinforcement and encouragement in building up confidence and raising self-esteem. Children need and demand attention and are keen to show adults what they have done. Encouragement and praise will promote and support further activity and the development of skills. The adult must show encouragement, not just with words but also using positive body language and enthusiasm in tone and facial expression. It is also important that adults praise children for what they are doing, rather than for what they are producing, for example 'You look like you are enjoying painting' rather than 'Well done, that's a lovely painting.'

▼ Enjoying creative activity

you look like you're enjoying painting, Caitlin.

Case study: Look what I've made

Amir is 3 years old and has spent a long time at the construction table making a model. He is very proud of what he has done and carries it over to Jamil (the early years worker) who is sitting at another table filling out some forms. Amir approaches Jamil from the side and says 'Look what I've made.' Jamil looks over her shoulder and glances at the model. 'Well, that's lovely, Amir – well done,' she says. She then continues to fill out the forms and Amir returns to the construction table.

1 **Did Jamil encourage Amir?**
2 **How might Jamil have improved her response?**
3 **How could she encourage Amir in other ways?**
4 **How might she extend the learning opportunity?**

Intervening as required

The adult must be able to intervene sensitively and appropriately and must never take over the activity from the child. Adult involvement can enhance or destroy a play situation and it is important to know when to join in and when to leave the children to play in a group. They will often indulge in role-play activities and will ask you to join them, and it will be beneficial if you can enter into the spirit of the play. You need not be inhibited as the children do not judge as adults might. Occasionally, you might see a child struggling to do something and it is good practice to ask if the child requires your help. Never step in and assume that they wish you to take over – they may need to persevere to master a skill.

Providing stimulation

The whole setting should provide a stimulating environment. Activities should be changed on a regular basis so that the children do not become complacent and bored. Using familiar themes and topics can encourage conversation and from these discussions activities can arise. Opportunity must be taken when unusual occurrences happen, for example if a fire engine stops outside the setting, or if the weather provides opportunity for new learning experiences, for example a snowy day, which enables the children to experience new activities and changes in the environment.

Building confidence and self-esteem

Many physical skills involve practice and early failure can discourage children from continuing. This means that activities need to be planned to ensure that whilst presenting some level of challenge, the child is likely to succeed. Children also need to gain in confidence before attempting some activities such as climbing or attempting to ride a bicycle. Adults therefore need to adopt a sensitive approach to encouraging children to attempt such activities and avoid pressuring children. Adults have to remember that children's ability to absorb the spoken word in the absence of pictures or gestures is limited. This is why many young children appear to find it hard to sit and listen. Listening activities need therefore to be kept focused and interactive, for example, 'Put your hand up when you hear a bell.' It is also very hard for young children to listen to each other – as young children do not have 'entertainment' skills. This means that activities relying on large groups are unlikely to meet the needs of all the children.

Activities that encourage self-expression help children gain confidence and build imagination, as well as developing language and fine manipulative skills.

Inclusion

All children should have opportunity to gain experiences from all the activities. However, some activities and/or equipment and resources may need to be altered or adapted to suit the individual needs of each child. It is your responsibility to ensure that no child is excluded from any activity and that the right resources are readily available. Here are some examples, but they are by no means exhaustive or restrictive:

- left-handed scissors
- access to activities for wheelchair users
- tactile collage for sight-impaired children
- paired activities for a child who is shy
- specialised equipment for children who have difficulty with manipulative skills and gripping.

Differentiation

Not all children work at the same level and at the same speed. You should provide activities that all children can work at and achieve. However, in order to provide challenges for others, you will need to provide or extend activities to stretch the learning in some children. For example, an activity may be designed to encourage children to sort by colour, but some children will be able to use two attributes and be able to sort by colour and shape.

Extension of activities

Extension activities may be developed from an initial activity. For example, the children may be making flowers, which might lead to discussions of the types of weather and may eventually lead to the idea of a frieze with flowers, kites, lambs and people. Alternatively it may lead to the design of a weather chart and topics on clothing.

Observing

It is an essential part of the role of the adult to observe children. This will enable you to ascertain the stage of development the child is at so you can plan for the future development of the individual. Observations usually relate to the individual child, but sometimes it is necessary to observe groups of children to see how they relate to each other. It may be beneficial to observe the use of an activity to see if it is fulfilling its intended role. It may need repositioning or changing altogether. It is also useful for new early years workers to observe more experienced staff to ascertain how they relate to children and implement activities. Observing children is covered in more detail in Unit 3, Promoting Children's Development.

Monitoring

Activities often need to be monitored to ensure that they are beneficial for the development of the child. When planning activities, a number of learning outcomes for the child may have been identified and it is good practice to check that these are being achieved. It may be that the activity needs to be altered or amended in some way or that the number of children at any one time needs to be changed.

Evaluating

The evaluation of the activity is of great importance. Have the learning outcomes set for the activity been achieved? Has the role of the adult been effective? The adult will have been involved in planning and preparing short-, medium- and long-term plans and will need to evaluate these to see what worked, what did not work and why, and how the plan might be altered for future use. All aspects of planning and implementation will need to be considered and recommendations made for the future.

Communicating with children and their families

An essential part of the adult's role is to work in partnership with children and their families. Good communication and interpersonal skills are vital for this and these skills are covered in more detail in Unit 1, Developing and Promoting Positive Relationships.

Communication starts even before the child enters the setting, with documented information being taken from the parents regarding emergency contacts and other essential information required before the child is left at the setting. Parents need to be kept informed at all times and especially in the celebration of achievements with activities and skills. Developing a meaningful professional relationship with parents is important, but it should not become overly friendly.

Individual learning programmes

Individual learning programmes are particularly suited to the needs of babies and young children, but are also used with older children. Many settings, particularly those working with babies and toddlers, produce outline plans that identify the needs of children and give strategies for meeting the needs. These types of plans can be known as individual learning programmes.

To design an individual learning plan, you need to find out what the individual child's needs are, by assessing their development and interests, and ensure that play opportunities will encourage their overall development.

There are several methods that can be used to assess children's development. Ideally, a range of methods

Case study: Keeping the right balance!

Janine works in a day nursery and has developed a very close relationship with the mother of one of the children. Sam, who is 3, gets on very well with Janine and Sam's mother has asked Janine to baby-sit for her while she has an evening out with the girls. Janine is only too happy to help out and as she is to be paid feels that she can use the extra money. This mutual arrangement works well for a while, but then Sam's mother starts to be late collecting him from the nursery, but she says that she knows it will be all right as Janine is there and Sam knows her well. Sam's mother also asked Janine to put in the money for a trip the children were going on as she said she was a bit short but would repay it later. Janine starts to feel uncomfortable about the situation.

1. **How might she have prevented this situation from developing?**
2. **How might she deal with Sam's mother to prevent the situation from deteriorating?**
3. **How might it affect her working relationship with Sam's mother?**
4. **How might it affect her relationship at work with the colleagues?**

should be used to gain a full picture of the child, although this in practice rarely happens as most settings find it hard to release one member of staff to carry out observations. It is also important to look at children in a range of situations, i.e. in group situations as well as when they are playing alone or with one other child.

Once you have completed some observations, it is important to develop an overall picture of the child's development. What strengths and interests has the child shown? Are there any areas where the child has specific developmental needs? It is also good practice for early years settings to involve parents in the process. Parents see their children in a different context and will be able to provide additional information. It is also important to find out what parents feel are the priorities for their child, for example a parent of a toddler may want to concentrate on feeding skills.

The actual layout and content of an individualised learning plan can vary, with some settings choosing to keep them quite brief. Most programmes contain a resumé of the child's developmental progress and some aims for the future. It is important that these aims are achievable otherwise the child may be put under pressure. Plans also have to be looked at when drawing up curriculum plans and overall plans for groups of children. Activities can then be added that reflect children's play interests, but also link to any developmental needs that they have. Babies and toddlers particularly benefit from this individual approach.

Case study: Matthew's individual learning plan

Matthew is 3 years old. His individual learning plan aims to promote his interaction with other children as, although he plays alongside other children, he rarely talks to them. A small group of children, which includes Matthew, is to play sound lotto. Matthew's key worker puts Matthew with a slightly older child to play the game together as this will encourage Matthew to work with another child. She encourages them both and Matthew begins to make eye contact with the other child.

1 **Why do you think it is important for Matthew to interact with other children?**

2 **Suggest two other activities that might encourage Matthew to interact with other children.**

3 **What do you think the adult's role is in the activities?**

4 **How might you record the progress made?**

Planning and preparation

In order for children to be able to express themselves, adults have to give them choices and a feeling of 'freedom'. Children will need to feel that there is no 'right' or 'wrong' way and that whatever they do will be free of judgement. Adults have therefore to learn to take a step back and support rather than direct children.

Environment

Children play and learn well when the environment not only meets their needs, but also excites their curiosity.

A good layout helps children to move around safely, but also allows them to get on with their play. Enough space needs to be provided for each type of play activity so that children do not become frustrated because other children 'walk' across their game or the table is not large enough for them to put out all the farm animals that they want. The environment also has to be safe for children. Good planning means allowing time before and during sessions to check that areas are clean, especially outdoor areas where vandals or animals may have created hazards.

It is also important that time is spent thinking about storage and accessibility. Messy cupboards and drawers where nothing can be found mean that neither children nor staff can find things. It also makes it harder for children to be given and take responsibility for tidying up and looking after their environment.

Resources

Planning and preparation are needed so that sufficient resources are put out and that they will actually grab children's attention and interest. The way that they are put out can also make a difference. Where children are spending several hours in a session, it will also be important to think about how the materials and equipment might be varied throughout the day – if children's interest wanes, there will then be something else for them to do that they will enjoy. In settings that share resources, planning is essential to avoid situations where two members of staff are both hoping to use the same resource with children.

Providing for children's play requires good organisation to ensure that there are sufficient materials, equipment and support to meet the needs of all children. This means that nearly all settings have some form of formal planning system in place, although the extent and type of plans can vary enormously.

Involving children

Children always play better and enjoy their learning more when they are involved and where their interests are reflected. Adults can make a difference to play and learning by observing children as they play and also talking to them about what they would like to do. It is good practice to make materials and equipment accessible for children to pick up and use when they want to.

Discussion with other adults

It is often a setting's policy to plan as a team. There are several types of planning and as this changes from setting to setting, it will be important to find out the type of planning that your setting uses. Good plans are based on correct assessment of children's stages of development and interests. It is important for everyone working with children during a session to know what is going on. This means that volunteers and parents, as well as staff, should have an idea of what is planned and the type of learning and play opportunities that are being created. Everyone also needs to know what their role is and also how best to work with individual children in the setting, some of whom may have an Individual Education Plan.

Health and safety

Health and safety is the responsibility of each individual within the setting and should not be taken lightly. Planning play opportunities should be done with safety in mind. However, this does not mean that safety becomes an excuse to prevent children from having fun or from doing things that will challenge them. Thought needs to be given as to the level of supervision that will be required during a session and during particular activities. Ideally a balance should be struck so that there might be some activities that children can do and enjoy without too much adult support, whilst others might need adults to supervise closely.

With babies and young children, safety is paramount especially when choosing equipment and materials. This is covered in more detail in Unit 2, Positive Environments for Children's Care, Learning and Development.

Good practice checklist

When setting up play activities for children, check for any safety issues:

- trailing wires
- wet floors
- damaged equipment
- spillages
- open doors
- sharp corners
- unsafe equipment, for example knives/sharp implements
- taps left on.

Remember to be ever vigilant.

Use of everyday routines to enhance learning

The routines that a child is involved in every day provide great learning opportunities. Health routines such as hand washing can lead to topics related to 'Myself' and other linked activities. Mealtimes and snack times can initiate further opportunities for creative activities, for example *The Hungry Caterpillar*.

Extension of play activities

During activities, sensitive practitioners will be looking for scope to extend children's language, skills or thinking. This requires an amount of skill and knowledge of child development as the practitioner has to consider the child's stage of development, their interest in the activity and ways of developing the child further. Opportunities to extend children's learning are sometimes built into the activity or they can be spontaneous. Good practitioners need to also look for ways of extending children's learning while they are playing. This can take many forms and requires a flexible and thoughtful approach.

Valuing children's ideas

Motivation is essential when working with children and if the children's own ideas are valued, used and adapted then motivation levels will be high. They usually spring from a desire to carry out certain roles and activities and adults should listen carefully to the wants and needs of the children in their care.

Understanding stages of development

You should have a clear understanding of the stages of development, as this will enable you to plan effectively for the needs of the individual child. Much research has been carried out as to what might be the expected stage of development for a child at any given age. It is good practice for practitioners to ascertain the stage of development an individual child is at and then plan for the next stage. It is also helpful to know if children are showing signs of delayed development so that appropriate strategies can be put in place.

Observation

The most effective way of finding out the stage of development of a child is to carry out a series of systematic and detailed observations, looking at each area of development. You will be trained in how to observe children and draw meaningful conclusions from your findings and plan for the future.

One observation will provide only a small amount of information and this may be limited as the child may not be well or may be upset, and therefore not behaving as they usually do. However, a series of observations over a period of time will enable you to build up a picture of the child's stage of development. When this is matched with the child's age, it is possible to make meaningful judgements.

Inclusion

It is the responsibility of the adult to ensure that all children are included in activities and play situations. During the planning stage, you should have considered the activity or situation and the equipment and materials required. Any specialised resources or adaptations should have been taken into account at this point so that all children have the opportunity to participate.

Monitoring strategies

Setting criteria for evaluations

One of the key ways of gaining information for use in later evaluations is through careful observation of children during the activity. Most students find it helpful to keep a pad of paper near them to make notes on:

- how engaged the children are in the activity
- whether the children appear to be interested and enthusiastic
- whether the children are easily distracted
- whether the children appear settled
- how confident the children seem
- whether their bodies are relaxed or tensed
- how easily the children are managing the activity
- whether any children appear frustrated or bored
- how much support is being given in order for children to manage the activity
- whether support is being given because the activity is too challenging
- whether the children are active or passive
- whether the children are using language during the activity
- what has interested the children during the activity – can this be used as a starting point for further activities?

Documentation

It is useful that all findings are recorded so that a profile of the individual child can be built up and their developmental needs identified. This record is confidential to staff and parents and the information should not be divulged to other sources without consent.

Discussion with colleagues

Although the child's record might include observations, examples of the child's work, activities and experiences the child favours and their levels of enjoyment, it should also include factual discussions between colleagues. These are useful in providing the overall picture of the child's development.

Evaluation

As a student, you will need to show that you can evaluate the effectiveness of your work as well as the activities. Student evaluations can also be used to provide evidence of your:

- knowledge of child development
- ability to assess accurately a child's stage of development
- understanding of the early years curricula
- awareness of your strengths and weaknesses
- ability to review and plan effectively.

There is no set format for producing student evaluations, although most contain:

- an overall introduction to the nature of the plan and the intended learning outcomes
- a brief review of how the plans were implemented
- an analysis of how the children responded and an evaluation of the effectiveness of the activity or activities
- an analysis of the effectiveness of your role and your planning
- detailed recommendations of how to extend the child's learning
- detailed recommendations of how to improve and consolidate your practice.

Child observation

Observations should also help us to reflect upon whether an activity is working well and is meeting children's developmental needs and interests. It is good practice to observe children and then use the information gained towards future planning. For example, a child who is fascinated by mixing red and yellow paint together should have future opportunities to explore the effect of mixing other colour combinations.

Observations skills form the basis of how to plan for children under 3 years and this is reflected in the Birth To Three Matters framework in England and the equivalent framework in Scotland. This will also be a major aspect of the Early Years Foundation Stage, which will incorporate the Birth to Three Matters framework and the Foundation Stage Curriculum and will be implemented in 2008.

Theory into practice

Carry out the following structured observation. Observe two children of different ages playing with the same piece of equipment, for example give a football to a child of 12 months and then later to a child of 4 years.

- Analyse the differences in the way in which the children have played.
- Evaluate the extent to which their play links to their stages of development.
- Consider ways in which their play links to theories of child development.

Monitoring of participation and learning

When the children are involved in an activity, you should note whether the children are actively involved or not. Some children will begin by observing what others are doing and not join in immediately. It may appear that they need to observe in order to gain the confidence to participate and it is useful for future activities if you are aware of this. Other children will be keen to be involved immediately and prefer to have a 'hands on' approach. Adults working with children need to be aware of the different types of learning styles in children.

Monitoring and evaluation of children's enjoyment

When children are highly motivated, they will spend time and concentration when working through an activity. They may well be very keen to talk about what they are doing and enter into detailed explanations about the processes. Enjoyment should not be confused or always linked with laughter as children can be very serious when involved with something they enjoy doing.

Reactions and responses

Sensitive observation and conversation will provide you with information about activities and play situations. Broaching ideas of future planning will evoke reactions and responses from the children and the adult should be able to form an opinion as to whether this will be enthusiastically received or not.

Reflecting on own practice

It is also useful for you to reflect upon your own practice and develop a plan for future training or staff development needs.

To analyse the effectiveness of your practice, it can be useful to ask yourself the following questions:

- How well have I prepared for this activity?
- Is this activity meeting the needs of all the children?
- Are the learning outcomes planned being gained by the children?

- What other learning is taking place?
- How much control do the children have over their learning?
- Am I encouraging children to be spontaneous and to develop their own thinking?

Assessment activity 7.3

In your placement, ask if you can observe a member of staff. Consider the different tasks that they are involved in, for example, planning for and setting up activities, interacting with the children and parents, etc. You should relate it to all aspects of providing and implementing play and learning activities for children.

Note the importance of the adult's role in providing for children's learning experiences.

7.4 How to identify and promote learning opportunities for children aged 0–8 years

Supporting early learning

For adults to support early learning, it is necessary for them to understand national requirements and how that support might be structured.

Early education framework

It is essential that you are familiar with the early education framework in your home country. Currently the curriculum framework in England is in three parts; the Birth to Three Matters framework; the Foundation Stage with the Early Learning Goals, and the National Curriculum.

Birth to Three Matters was established as an effective framework for children under 3 years of age. It is based on activities and experiences linked to the child's overall development and children are encouraged to learn through their senses. The framework provides a firm foundation for moving onto the Early Learning Goals in the Foundation Stage. However, the Early Years Foundation Stage will be implemented in 2008 and training events have been planned for at least 18 months prior to that. This will enable early years settings to make a smooth transition from other frameworks they have been working with. It will build on the existing Foundation Stage, Birth to Three Matters framework, and the National Standards for Under 8s Day Care and Childminding.

The National Curriculum in England was introduced following the Education Reform Act 1988 and has been used in all schools ever since. It is a set curriculum to ensure that standards are consistent across the country and is implemented in schools after children have reached their fifth birthday.

Cwricwlwm Cymreig is the Welsh equivalent of the National Curriculum and recognises the importance of the unique Welsh culture and heritage and includes the teaching of Welsh as a first or second language. The Northern Ireland Curriculum is structured in a similar way and has opportunity for the inclusion of Irish as one of the curriculum subjects in Irish-speaking schools, and again the unique culture and heritage of Ireland is encouraged at all times.

Learning aims and objectives

Careful planning should ensure that the activity will meet the required needs in the chosen area(s) of development. You need to consider the aim and objectives (learning outcomes) to be achieved by the child who will be involved in the activity.

- *Aim* The aim of the activity is what you intend to introduce the child to. It is an 'umbrella' statement that encompasses what is to be carried out during the activity. For example, 'to introduce the child to a simple science activity involving snow'. The aim sets the scene and limits the activity to a specific type of activity. However, the activity should be flexible enough to incorporate some change of direction if necessary.
- *Objectives* The detail of what is to be achieved is given in the objectives. The objectives are what the child will be able to achieve. In order to plan the objectives, it is quite useful to start with the words, 'By the end of the activity the child will (for example)
  - understand that heat causes snow to change
  - be aware that snow is cold
  - demonstrate that snow reduces in volume as it melts.'

The objectives break the activity down into small units, each of which is measurable. They might be measured by observation or by questioning, but it is always possible to ascertain if the objectives or learning outcomes have been achieved or met.

Theory into practice

- Devise a learning activity for a small group of 3-year-old children which will promote language development.
- Produce an aim for the activity and list three learning outcomes.
- Describe the activity.

You may be able to implement this activity in your placement but remember to seek the advice and permission of the staff involved.

Integrated approach

An integrated approach often provides a greater learning experience for the children. Very few activities are exclusively limited to one area of development, and activities and play situations which provide a wide range of learning experiences for children often hold their interest and motivation for longer periods of time.

Inclusion

In order for inclusion to work effectively, it is essential that barriers to learning are removed for all children. When we talk about inclusion, it is often referring to children with special or specific needs, but in essence it is much wider than that and relates to any barrier to any child that might hinder them from taking part and learning. This is covered in more detail in Unit 6, Promoting Children's Rights.

Anti-discriminatory practice

This is one of the fundamentals of early years care and education. However, discrimination comes from many different sources and young children may not realise what they are saying. Any discriminatory remarks or actions by adults or children must be tackled immediately otherwise the unspoken message is that this is not an important issue. It should always be tackled in as sensitive a way as possible and all participants need attention – those who made the discriminatory comment, those who are the recipients of it and those who witnessed it. This is covered in more detail in Unit 6, Promoting Children's Rights.

Planning activities to support early learning

Within any early years setting, it is important to plan so that all areas of learning are covered and a wide range of activities and play situations presented. Planning will be long-, medium- and short-term and will consider the curriculum to be covered as well as taking into account the needs of the individual child.

Long-term planning

The length of long-term plans varies widely. Some settings view a long-term plan as anything over six weeks, whilst in school settings it usually refers to a full academic year's work.

Common features of long-term plans include:

- an outline of how the curriculum is to be delivered
- a consideration of the themes that are to be used over the period.

Medium-term plans

Medium-term plans are in some settings called curriculum plans. The length of a medium-term plan depends on the long-term plan. In some schools a medium-term plan shows coverage for half a term, whilst in some pre-school settings it shows coverage for a fortnight or a month.

Common features of medium-term plans include:

- details of the types of activities to be offered
- how the activities link to the early years or National Curriculum
- the order in which the activities are to be carried out
- learning outcomes.

Short-term plans

Settings that plan for a month may also have short-term plans which show what is to happen each week or each session. Settings may refer to these type of plans as 'session planners' or 'weekly planners'.

Common features of short-term plans include:

- details of staffing and resources
- order of activities to be carried out
- details of how individual activities may be adapted or extended to suit particular children
- learning outcomes for activities
- which activities are to be assessed
- the role of the adult in supporting specific children.

Case study: Teddy joins in

Mike, an early years practitioner, has brought in a teddy bear. He tells a small group of children that teddy wants to see what happens in a nursery class. The children take turns at 'showing' teddy around and during the session he 'joins in'. Towards the end of the session, Mike asks pairs of children to use a telephone to tell 'teddy's mum' what he has been doing. To model the language to some of the younger children, Mike talks to 'teddy's mum' first. The children listen to Mike and then often repeat the same type of expressions and phrases when it is their turn. Mike planned this activity to encourage children to use description and also to recount events.

Using the current early years curriculum:

1 **Discuss how the above activity would link to the curriculum.**

2 **Explain the developmental benefits of these activities.**

3 **Produce a short-term plan with identified aims and objectives for this activity.**

Activity plans

These can be referred to as detailed activity plans or even in schools as lesson plans. Short-term plans are not used in every setting, but tend to be used by students to help them show that they can plan a single activity effectively.

Common features of an activity plan include:

- resources
- staffing
- specific learning outcomes
- how needs of individual children will be met
- the role of the adult.

Curriculum planning

A curriculum can be thought of as a programme of activities or learning outcomes. Some settings plan an overall curriculum, which may be based on areas of development or on areas of learning from the curriculum they are following. Other settings may produce a separate curriculum plan for each area of learning or subject, i.e. some schools have a curriculum plan for literacy, another one for mathematics, etc.

Individual needs

When planning for young children, it is important that the individual needs of the child are taken into account. All learning activities must be able to accommodate all children at whichever level they are working. If you have taken this into account, there will be aspects of differentiation incorporated into each activity.

Importance of observation

In order to find the correct stage of development of the child, you need to carry out a series of observations. It is only then that you can make an informed judgement as to the level of activity that will be most appropriate. If observations are not carried out then it will be difficult to plan effectively and any assessments will inevitably be flawed.

Use of different types of play

All types of play provide learning opportunities for children and all activities will include more than one type of play. For example, creative activities will also include physical activity and imagination; they may include more. Types of play are usually categorised as:

- imaginative
- creative
- sensory
- physical
- exploratory, technological/investigative.

Use of ICT

Many early years care and education settings use ICT to support learning. There are a great variety of programs that can be used for children of all ages. Children do not fear technology and use it as just another learning tool. Many areas of the Foundation Stage and National Curriculum can be met using ICT.

Involvement of others

Parental involvement is encouraged by many early years care and education settings and often parents and children have suggestions and the skills to introduce new ideas for the children. For example, parents may introduce activities/foods from different cultures. There are occasions when other professionals and agencies might be involved in providing learning opportunities for children. For example, visiting speakers might provide stories and activities about dental care.

Availability of resources

It is part of the role of the adult within the setting to ensure that the correct resources are available and that there are enough materials for any learning situation. Remember – the resources must be fit for purpose for all children and that will include any adaptations and specialised equipment.

Monitoring

In order to ensure that the children are receiving the support they require, the adults in the setting need to monitor the activities and ensure that the children are learning from the experience and that they are participating.

Learning

If the activity has been planned with aims and objectives, it will be possible for you to determine whether the desired learning outcomes have been met. This is usually achieved by observation and by discussion and conversation with the children involved.

Participation

Monitoring participation levels tends to be much easier as children will not spend time at an activity that does not grasp the imagination and stimulate learning. It may be that other activities are more popular on any given day and the activity may be a success another time.

Formative assessment

Formative assessment is ongoing assessment. Adults will monitor children's strengths and weaknesses and this often forms an informal part of an activity. Assistance may be provided so that the child can gain in confidence in developing new skills and plenty of opportunities are provided to enable the child to practise and master them.

Summative assessment

Summative assessment draws together all the information gathered about the child and is often used to compile a written report. It is the 'summing up' of a child's progress to date.

The assessment process

It is very hard for practitioners who are closely involved with children to be completely objective when observing and assessing them. This is known as observer bias. The danger of observer bias is that the observer tends to home in on behaviours or skills that confirm their current view of the child. One way of limiting observer bias is by setting clear aims for observations, for example noting down every time a child interacts with an adult in order to gain a picture of a child's interactions with adults.

When completing checklists or tick charts which require adults to ask children to do certain tasks, it is important to remember that children may not always 'perform' well if they think that they are being watched or tested. Many skilled practitioners therefore try to incorporate these type of assessments into planned play opportunities, for example putting out some buttons for children to play with and then asking them if they would like to count how many there are.

With babies and young children, it is also important to remember that the focus of their play and interests can change in a few days. A baby may suddenly 'discover' their feet or a toddler may spot a car that previously was not of interest to them.

Case study: Developing skills

Jo has planned a series of activities to improve cutting skills for 4-year-olds. She put out some scissors on the dough table and three children are happily snipping and cutting away. Jo sits with them and flattens a piece of dough. She draws a line on the dough and then cuts it along the line. One of the children looks at what she is doing. She then flattens another piece of dough and draws a line on it. She passes it to the child who smiles and then has a go. Jo notices how the child handles the scissors and how easily he is managing the scissor action. Jo also notes that the child is almost able to cut on the line.

1 **Discuss the advantages of this type of assessment.**

2 **Consider ways in which this assessment will help further planning of activities.**

3 **Think of an activity Jo might plan for the future.**

4 **List three learning outcomes for it.**

Links to planning

Once the child has been observed and assessed, this information can be used to inform the future planning of activities, which will help promote development for the individual child. Planning can only be effective when information gained from observation and assessment is used to structure activities, which will fulfil the child's developmental needs. For example, if a child cannot hold a pair of scissors, then providing a detailed cutting activity would be setting the child up to fail. This could have a detrimental effect on the child's self-confidence and self-esteem.

Evaluation

Most evaluation criteria involve checking whether children have gained the intended learning outcomes. This is difficult to measure unless some type of assessment is carried out either during or after the activity. A child may appear to have understood a concept or may have happily played with materials, but not necessarily have learnt anything new! By building in some assessment into the activity, practitioners can see what the child has understood and learnt. It is important that the assessment is not seen in any way as a test as this would undermine the child's confidence. Good assessment happens as part of the activity.

Assessment activity 7.4

From your placement experience, choose one of the following age ranges and describe how the early years setting implements the curriculum for those children:

- 0–3 years
- 3–5 years
- 5–8 years. **P4**

7.5 How to plan, implement and evaluate learning activities for children aged 0–8 years

Planning and preparation

The thought that is involved in an activity prior to it being implemented is time well spent. It will help ensure that the activity goes as well as can be expected and that details have been thought through. You must remember that even the most well-planned activity can go adrift due to unexpected circumstances, but you will find that time spent in planning and preparation will be beneficial in the long term.

Planning within a thematic and non-thematic framework

The activity may be free-standing and initiated by something the child or family has said, or it may be that the activity forms part of a theme or is within the topic planning of the setting. If there is a thematic framework within the setting, the planned activity must follow the topic closely and it may form part of a larger picture. For example, the children may be encouraged to make houses from the junk modelling box which will form part of a larger street model linked to 'Road safety' or 'Transport'.

Ensuring progression

The activity should be challenging enough for the children to ensure that they are able to progress, but not too demanding that they feel over-powered by the activity. Children need to be able to put into practice the skills they have already mastered and have opportunities to develop new ones.

Meeting children's developmental and specific individual needs

It is essential that you understand and are aware of the needs of the individual child and know their stage of development. Differentiation within activities is important, as children can easily be discouraged if tasks are too demanding or not demanding enough.

Planning and preparation of physical and human resources

When considering the activity, you need to run through it in your mind so that you can itemise all the physical and human resources required. If the activity has a higher than normal risk factor, for example a woodwork bench, then it may be necessary to have more staff present to reduce the risk of minor injury. The amount of other resources must be enough for the number of children involved. They need to be readily available so that you do not need to move away to collect materials in order to complete the activity.

Use of ICT

ICT is regularly used in early years care and education settings and you may be involved in planning an activity incorporating the use of ICT. You need to familiarise yourself with the software so that you are not disadvantaged in finding that the children are more familiar with it than you are.

Consulting with staff, children and families

It is always good practice to communicate at all times with staff, children and their families as information can be gained that will be of invaluable use. Other members of staff will be able to advise and support you in your planning and may have information concerning the needs of individual children. Families and the children themselves are, additionally, a good source of information and ideas and they will feel more involved in the life of the setting if there are good communication pathways.

Inclusion

When planning and preparing activities, it is essential that thought is given to the needs of all children and that the activity is adapted to suit those needs if necessary. Specialised equipment may be needed to ensure that all children are included and this can be as basic as making sure that there are appropriate scissors for children who are left-handed.

Differentiation

Within the planning process, play and learning experiences need to match children's needs. Experienced practitioners choose activities and resources that will allow the curriculum to be differentiated. For example,

one child may simply observe and play with ice cubes in the water, whilst another may be asked if they could find a way of keeping the ice cube from floating.

Role in formal learning

Many activities that help children to learn skills and concepts are now being planned using play as a tool. We have seen that children are responsive to play and so combining play with learning intentions can be extremely effective. The key to doing this successfully is to consider what children naturally enjoy doing and finding ways of building learning into them. The table below shows how activities can be planned that will promote children's learning whilst they are playing.

▼ Incorporating learning into play

Area of learning	Example of play activity
Literacy	**Reading** Children can learn to recognise their names by playing a treasure hunt game. Adults hide names outdoors and children see if they can find their own name. Children can then develop this into their own game – they may write notes to each other and hide them or want to hide each other's names.
Mathematics	**Subtraction** The sand tray has ten sand castles on it. Children roll a dice and take it in turns to squash down the sand castles. Children can develop this game by making their own sandcastles and choosing to knock them down.
Science	**Blowing bubbles** Children are given a range of bubble mixtures and shapes through which they blow bubbles. Adults might help them to notice that bubbles are always spherical. Children can develop this game by trying to blow the largest bubble.
ICT	**Using programmable toys** Adults show the children how a toy robot works and together they make a maze for the toy robot to travel along. Children can develop this by building their own maze and seeing if they can programme the robot to move through it.
Knowledge and understanding of the world	**Learning about immediate environment** Adults give children magnifying sheets. Children explore how to use them and make their own discoveries about what is outside.

Encompassing diversity

In the planning process, thought has to be given to what has been dubbed the 'hidden curriculum', i.e. the underlying messages that children will be learning besides the ones intended. Are the activities in any way discriminatory? Will the activities help children to take a positive view of the differences in others and around them? Are the activities reinforcing undesirable stereotypes? These key questions should be at the forefront of your mind when planning and evaluating programmes.

Note that the Early Years Foundation Stage curriculum reflects the growing sentiment that before children can learn about the cultures and beliefs of others, they should feel secure about their own background and values; so 'doing' major festivals that are not part of a child's life actually devalues and trivialises them as young children cannot conceive of things beyond their own world. This represents a major change in thinking as early years settings have previously been encouraged to celebrate a variety of religious festivals outside their immediate experience.

Implementation

Interpersonal skills

Adults working with children need to be friendly, approachable and send out these messages through their body language. Children often reflect how comfortable they are feeling through their behaviour and concentration. A good play activity can therefore be ruined if children do not feel at ease and are worried about 'being told off'.

Observational skills

We can learn enormously by simply watching children as they approach activities and whilst they are engaged in play. These observations should help us to decide whether we need to intervene or interact with children.

Good communication is essential when working with children. A good style to adopt is a 'chatting' style in which children are equal partners in the interaction. This allows them to talk freely rather than feel that they have to give a 'correct answer'. Questions need to be asked sensitively and ideally we should only ask a 'real' question rather than one that tests children's knowledge.

With younger children we need to provide a running commentary style of speech. This helps them learn new vocabulary in context and encourages them to tune in to speech patterns. Pointing out things and remarking on them is, for example, a way in which a young child can work out what the topic of conversation is, whilst also learning vocabulary that is linked to it. This style is also useful with children whose home language may be different to that of the setting and who are not yet fluent. (See also Unit 1 Develop and Promote Positive Relationships.)

Awareness of when to intervene

One of the great skills of working with children is to know when and how to intervene. It is useful to think about what children will gain from any intervention and whether the intervention will disrupt children's play. Sometimes children can solve their own disputes and squabbles whilst at other times they may need an adult. It can be useful to stand by and move closer rather than always directly intervening so that the situation can be monitored. When intervening with older children, it is worth seeing if they can suggest a solution to their difficulty. With babies and toddlers, distraction usually serves as a wonderful tool.

Involvement of children

It is now good practice for children to be involved not just in the play and learning, but also in other aspects such as tidying away and setting out. This is important as children gain many skills and it also helps their feelings of self-reliance and confidence. It is also important during an adult-directed activity to think about ways of encouraging children to take ownership even though the adult is central. This might mean asking children for their thoughts, giving them plenty of choices and looking for ways of making sure that they are active rather than passive. Plenty of props might be used at a small group story time or children go and collect all the things that they think that they would like to use to make a card.

Awareness of health and safety

Adults have to keep safety in mind, although it is important that this is not used as a reason to become controlling. During sessions, it is worth thinking about the noise level and the quality of the noise. Children should be talking, chatting, laughing and even singing, but shouts and shrieks might need a little further investigation. It is also essential that adults should discreetly think about the way equipment is being used to prevent accidents. It is good practice to keep a general overview of what is happening around you even when you are involved with a group of children.

Evaluation

Whilst play and learning activities are ongoing, we need to assess and evaluate their effectiveness. The focus should be on the children and considering how well the activities reflect children's needs.

Children need a good range of resources and activities in order for them to enjoy playing and learning. Reflecting on how well an activity has worked for individual and groups of children can help us to plan for the future. It is important to focus on the role of the adult during the activity as well as the responses of the children. This can help us to think about the contribution that we are making to children's enjoyment and learning.

- Did most children appear to be engaged and interested in the activity?

- Can you identify the ingredients that helped children to be interested? For example, the activity was sensory and children were active.
- Were children encouraged to take control and be active during the activity?
- How much input from you was needed?
- Why was this input needed?
- How did you encourage children to be active in their play and learning?
- What did the children learn from the activity?
- Was this learning planned or spontaneous?
- How could this learning be reinforced or built upon?
- What did individual children gain from the activity?
- What was your role in helping children to learn?
- What types of resources were used?
- Were there sufficient resources?
- Which resources attracted children's attention?
- What further resources could have been used?
- What were the limitations of this activity?
- How could these limitations be addressed?

Assessment activity 7.5

List three activities that children in each of the following age groups might be involved in within the setting and itemise the learning outcomes for the child for each:

- 0–3 years
- 3–5 years
- 5–8 years.

You should now be equipped to set up play situations for children and this section will help you carry these out in practical situations.

▲ An outside play area should be challenging and exciting

Good practice checklist

When thinking about setting up an indoor play situation, check that you:

- plan and design the play situation
- consider health and safety issues
- list potential learning outcomes
- include opportunity to develop literacy skills
- include opportunity to develop numeracy skills
- ensure there are appropriate resources
- ensure there are adequate resources
- make the play situation as stimulating as possible
- adapt or alter the play situation so that all children can participate.

Good practice checklist

When thinking about setting up an outdoor play situation, you should:

- carry out suggestions in the previous checklist
- check the area is clear of debris and other harmful matter
- ensure any equipment designed to encourage children to climb, etc. is on an impact-absorbent surface
- ensure children are appropriately dressed
- ensure adequate staffing and adult support
- make sure that the activity/play situation is challenging and exciting for the children, keeping in mind their age and stage of development.

Good practice checklist

When evaluating the play situation, consider the following:

- Did the children enjoy the play situation?
- Were the children suitably challenged?
- Were there enough resources?
- Would you change any part of the situation?
- Were the staff–child ratios balanced?
- Did the children wish to repeat the experience?
- Did the children achieve the intended learning outcomes?

Assessment activity 7.6

Identify a play situation for a child in the 0–3 age group and one for a child in the 5–8 age group. List the resources you might need and the potential learning outcomes and the value of these two situations for the children. **P6**

Once the play situation has been set up, and the children have had opportunity to access it and use it, you should then consider reviewing the situation.

End of unit assessment

You will need to demonstrate an understanding of this unit for your own development, but also you will need to be able to plan activities for children, which will help promote their overall learning and development.

1 You are working in the early years sector and have been asked to produce a display, on 'Play and learning situations in the early years setting', which will be useful for trainee early years workers and parents of the children in the setting. Remember to make the display bright and welcoming. You might like to illustrate your work.

   a) In your display, provide details of the major theories of learning. **P1**

   b) Add explanations of how children learn with reference to these theories. **M1**

   c) Look critically at the differences between them, giving examples from your experiences to support the theories or challenge them. **D1**

   d) As the parents and trainees might not be aware of how important play is in children's development, include a chart (or a number of different charts) in which you describe the value of play in the development of children under 8 years of age. **P2**

   e) Explain the value of play in your chart(s). **M2**

   f) Describe the role of the adult in providing and implementing play and learning activities for the children in the early years care and education setting. **P3**

   g) Analyse the role of the adult and consider the different aspects of involvement. **M3**

   h) Explain how early years settings provide learning opportunities for children in the following age ranges:
   • 0–3 years
   • 3–5 years
   • 5–8 years.
   You should provide some examples to give support to your work. **P4**

2 As an early years worker you will be involved in planning, preparing, implementing and evaluating a variety of learning activities and play situations for young children.

   a) Plan:
   • two learning activities in an early years setting **P5**
   • two different play situations in an early years setting. **P6**

   b) Implement the two learning activities. **P5**

   c) Explain the value of each of the two learning activities and the two play situations. **M4**

   d) Evaluate the two learning activities and the two play situations, making reference to the major theories of learning. **D2**

   Put this work in a separate folder and keep it safe as it may be useful at a later date.

References and further reading

Books

Daly, M., Byers, E. and Taylor, W. (2006) *Understanding Early Years Theory in Practice*, Heinemann

Garvey, C. (1991) *Play: the developing child*, Fontana

Macleod-Brudenell, I. (2004) *Advanced Early Years Care and Education*, Heinemann

Miller, L., Cable, C. and Devereux, J. (2005) *Developing Early Years Practice*, Fulton

Moyles, J. (1989) *Just Playing: role and status of play in early childhood education*, OU Press

Pugh, G. and Duffy, B. (2006) *Contemporary Issues in Early Years*, Sage

Tassoni, P. (2005) *Planning Play and the Early Years*, Heinemann

Useful website

Department of Education and Skills (DfES) – www.dfes.gov.uk

Grading criteria	Assessment activity	Page number
To achieve a pass grade the evidence must show that the learner is able to:		
P1 describe the ways in which children learn with reference to the major theories of learning	7.1 End of unit assessment	260 290
P2 describe the potential value of play in the development of children	7.2 End of unit assessment	271 290
P3 describe the role of the adult in all aspects of the provision and implementation of play and learning activities for children	7.3 End of unit assessment	280 290
P4 use examples to describe how early years settings provide learning opportunities for children from 0–3, 3–5 and 5–8 years of age	7.4 End of unit assessment	285 290
P5 plan and implement two learning activities in early years settings	7.5 End of unit assessment	288 290
P6 set up and review two different play situations	7.6 End of unit assessment	289 290
To achieve a merit grade the evidence must show that, in addition to the pass criteria, the learner is able to:		
M1 with reference to the major theories of learning, explain how children learn	End of unit assessment	290
M2 explain the potential value of play in the development of children	End of unit assessment	290
M3 analyse the role of the adult in children's learning	End of unit assessment	290
M4 explain the value of the two learning activities and the two play situations	End of unit assessment	290
To achieve a distinction grade the evidence must show that, in addition to the pass and merit criteria, the learner is able to:		
D1 evaluate the major theories of learning, using examples from work placement	End of unit assessment	290
D2 with reference to the major theories of learning, evaluate the two learning activities and the two play situations	End of unit assessment	290

Research methodology for children's care, learning and development

Introduction

Research forms an important part of work in children's care, learning and development and this unit underpins much of what you do in studying for the children's care, learning and development diploma. Whether you have to read books, magazines or journals, carry out observations, ask people about their experiences of bringing up children or study a child's development, you will be undertaking research in one form or another. So, regardless of what unit you may be studying, you will carry out research.

This unit introduces you to the basic theory of research in children's care, learning and development and more significantly takes you through the research process so that you can feel confident about conducting your own research. This will be especially important for those units where you may be expected to conduct research as part of the assessment and in particular for Unit 3, Promoting Children's Development.

By undertaking the end of unit assessment you will have the opportunity to complete a research project for yourself that addresses the majority of grading criteria for this unit. The assessment activities at the end of the first two sections allow you to address those grading criteria that may not be covered by a research project, whilst the assessment activity at the end of section three allows you to practise planning a project and undertaking associated secondary research.

What you need to learn

- The purpose and role of research in children's care, learning and development
- Research methods relevant to children's care, learning and development
- Identifying a suitable topic and producing a plan for a research proposal
- Conduct and present research information
- Evaluate the research
- Implications and ethical issues related to using research

Thinking points

What does the word research mean to you? You would be surprised about how much research is being undertaken by different organisations around the world and you may be even more surprised by the extent to which you are involved in the process.

- If you have ever been shopping in your local high street and been pounced upon by someone holding a clipboard who just wants a few minutes of your time then you will probably have been involved in market research to determine, for example, different people's shopping preferences.

- If you have ever completed a registration card after purchasing a new mobile phone or mp3 player that involved ticking a number of boxes to a variety of questions then you will also have been a participant in another type of market research.

- If you have a store reward card then the company operating the card will collect information on all your purchases and analyse the data to determine not only your shopping habits and preferences, but also those of others that can be used to promote particular goods or identify new markets in the future.

- If you have taken part in the National Census or even been interviewed about your views on some topic in the news then you will have been involved in social research.

- In science classes at school you will have carried out experimental investigations that are the basis of scientific research.

- You may have been involved with medical research as a result of being asked by your doctor to be involved in the trial of a new type of drug.

Can you think of any research with which you have been involved? Share this with other members of your group and between you identify the purpose of the research and the methods being used to gather the information. This will begin to prepare you for conducting your own research and enable you to see how the different elements of the research process fit together.

As you can see from the Thinking point, research is used in all sorts of different ways and for many different reasons, but its main purpose is as a tool to develop a better understanding of the world we live in.

Within children's care, learning and development research plays a crucial role. It can be used to:

- examine current issues
- extend knowledge and understanding of issues relating to children's care, learning and development
- identify needs
- evaluate services to highlight gaps in provision
- monitor progress
- inform and improve policy and practice.

Organisations such as universities and government bodies undertake research programmes in children's care, learning and development that can address one or more of the above.

The range of research is vast. It often reflects issues of political importance simply because a large amount of research is commissioned or funded by central government. Universities, private research companies, public services or voluntary groups conduct the research on behalf of the commissioning body or they may have their own source of funding that will enable them to carry out research independently.

Research is also a tool that childcare practitioners can use to support their work.

The result of any research, whether conducted by or on behalf of policy makers or practitioners, should be to ensure that children and young people receive the most effective care, education and support available.

Your ability to understand the research process and develop research skills by undertaking research projects during your course will prepare you for higher level study while also enabling you to operate more effectively as a childcare practitioner.

Research has a crucial role to play in supporting children's care, learning and development. It informs both policy and practice and whilst organisations such as universities and government bodies undertake a wide range of research programmes it is a tool that all childcare practitioners need to have a working knowledge or understanding of. By doing so, policy makers and practitioners can ensure that children and young people receive the most effective care, education and support available.

Theory into practice

In the passage below, the italicised notes in brackets identify the purpose and role of research in children's care, learning and development, as identified in the list above.

The purpose and role of research in children's care, learning and development can be illustrated by the range of research on literacy and numeracy in the UK relating to the introduction of the literacy and numeracy hours in primary schools (*examine current issue*). Research in this field initially highlighted the fact that the literacy and numeracy standards in the UK lagged behind those of other countries (*identified need*). Other research, not just in the UK, investigated different methods that could contribute to improving standards (*extended knowledge and understanding of issues relating to children's care, learning and development*). Research since the introduction of the literacy/numeracy hour has focused on the effectiveness of the literacy and numeracy hour, leading to modifications to the programme, but also to questions as to whether it is the best way of addressing standards (*monitor progress, inform and improve policy and practice*).

Assessment activity 8.1

This is an extract of summary information about the Effective Provision of Pre-School Education (EPPE), a major piece of research undertaken over the past few years. Its purpose and role was varied due to the breadth of the study. Read the summary and then answer the questions which follow.

The EPPE project was a national longitudinal study of young children's development (intellectual and social/behavioural) between the ages of 3 and 7 years. The project was set up to investigate the effects of the child's home background and pre-school education from the age of 1 to 7 years. The researchers collected a wide range of information on over 3,000 children, their parents, their home environments and the pre-school settings they attended using a range of methods (child assessments, interviews, case studies and observations). One hundred and forty-one pre-school settings drawn from local authority day nursery, integrated centres, playgroups, private day nurseries, maintained nursery schools and maintained nursery classes were investigated. Centres were selected from five regions that were chosen to cover a range of socio-economic and geographical areas including rural, metropolitan, shire county and inner-city. The regions were selected to include ethnically diverse and socio-economically disadvantaged communities. A sample of children who had no or minimal pre-school experience was recruited to the study at entry to school for comparison with the pre-school group.

The key findings of the EPPE programme were that:

- Pre-school experience, compared to none, enhances children's development.
- The longer a child spent within a pre-school setting, the better their intellectual development, level of independence, concentration and sociability at primary school.
- There was no advantage gained from attending a pre-school full time compared to part time.
- The quality of pre-school provision has a direct bearing on intellectual, social and behavioural development of children in school up to the end of Key Stage 1 and disadvantaged children can benefit significantly, though the development of children who experience multiple disadvantage can be affected up to the age of 7.
- Parental education and social class remain important predictors of intellectual and social development. However, what parents do with their children at home rather than the social class to which they belong is of more importance and children who undertook learning activities at home showed improved intellectual and social development at school.
- Parenting styles vary for girls and boys.

Identify the main purpose and role of this research using the following headings:
- examines current issues
- extends knowledge and understanding of issues relating to children's care, learning and development
- identifies needs
- evaluates services to highlight gaps in provision
- monitors progress
- informs and improves policy and practice.

Types of research

There are many different ways of undertaking research and all involve the use of what is termed **primary** and **secondary research**.

- Primary research is the gathering of information by the person or persons carrying out the research. Primary research provides up-to-date and hopefully relevant information about the topic being studied. You will use primary research to carry out your own studies, such as observing children in a nursery or classroom or carrying out a survey of parents or young people in schools.
- Secondary research is the use of information that others have collected. You will undertake secondary research to gather information for the completion of much of your coursework. The information you obtain may come from a variety of sources and will be based upon the published work of the original researcher or an interpretation of their work by someone else.

Secondary research is an essential part of primary research, as the researcher needs to be fully aware of what other people have studied in relation to their own work. It may be that one piece of research is based upon the work of someone else or that the same research is being carried out in a different context, i.e. in a different place or with different people.

The type of information obtained by primary or secondary research can be identified as either **quantitative** or **qualitative information**.

- Quantitative information describes information or data that is in the form of numbers, for example the number of children attending different forms of day care provision.
- Qualitative information is descriptive and in the form of the written or spoken word, for example mothers' experiences of childbirth.

Further distinctions can occur as a consequence of research in the early years field involving the study of people. These include **cross-sectional** and **longitudinal studies**.

- A cross-sectional study is based upon the investigation of people at a particular moment in time. Such research may form part of investigations into the differences or relationships that can occur between individuals or groups, for example finding out about the difference in ability to conserve (see 'The experimental method', Theory into practice, page 307).
- Longitudinal research studies individuals or groups over a period of time, in some cases many years, for example studying the development of a baby for the first six months of life.

The problem with longitudinal studies is the time required to complete them. Whilst the example given might be feasible for you to carry out, others may not, for example a lifetime study of the social and emotional development of twins. Note, however, that for part of Unit 3, Promoting Children's Development, you will need to undertake a longitudinal study of a child.

Key terms

Primary research is original research; the collection of information by the person or persons carrying out the research.

Secondary research is the use of information collected by others.

Quantitative information is gathered in the form of numbers.

Qualitative information is gathered in narrative (non-numeric) form, for example an interview.

A **cross-sectional study** produces information gathered about a group of people at one point in time.

A **longitudinal study** is the study of an individual or group of people over a period of time.

Secondary research

You will have seen from the previous section that secondary research is something you do as part of your studies whether or not you are doing any primary

▲ Research can be a communal and wide-ranging activity

research and you will do secondary research both before and during any research project. So secondary research is described first rather than the primary research.

■ Secondary sources

Secondary research involves finding out facts and figures on topics you may be studying that have been produced by others. Some thought needs to be given to possible sources of such information.

Books, newspapers, magazines, specialist publications

Books obtained from your school or college will probably be your main source of information initially, particularly if you have not had experience of using other sources. Whilst your tutors may direct you to some books and provide booklists, you will have to search out others for yourself. This can be quite a task if a library is well stocked. However, most libraries now possess computerised search facilities and these can be a great source of help in finding resources that cover the area of work you are studying. As well as the school/college library, your local library may have useful material and, depending upon where you live, it may be possible for you to access more specialist libraries, for example universities or local authority education centres which usually have libraries for teachers (access to such facilities may be restricted or involve paying a subscription).

Libraries often subscribe to, and keep back copies of, daily newspapers, magazines and more specialist publications produced for people working in specific industries/organisations. The types of publications you might find helpful include:

- *Nursery World* – a weekly publication for early years curriculum professionals
- *Nursing Times* – a weekly publication produced for nurses and other professionals in the health and caring services; often contains specialist articles relating to children
- *Times Educational Supplement* – published weekly covering newsworthy topics and developments in education
- *Social Trends* – published annually, this is an invaluable source of official statistics covering amongst others information on families, housing, health, education and work
- *Regional Trends* – similar to *Social Trends*, but contains information on a regional basis. Useful if you want data relevant to a particular area.

People

By talking to people who work in early years settings, your tutors, family and friends, you can get different views and ideas on subjects. Such views may reflect changing attitudes towards parenting and education and, as such, support or refute information obtained from books.

Organisations

There are voluntary and statutory organisations that you will have found out about by reading other parts of this book and through input from your tutors. They can be an invaluable source of help and information on specific topics.

Whilst the statutory services are available throughout the country, voluntary organisations may be concentrated in larger towns or cities. However, a good starting point to look for such organisations is your local newspaper or the library. Whilst many organisations offer support to sufferers and carers, they are usually more than happy to talk to students or provide information that helps to further their cause.

Computers and the internet

Computers can be used to obtain information from CD-ROMs, the internet or intranets. CD-ROMs are digitally recorded stores of information. Some are like electronic encyclopaedias, containing textual and visual information on a wide range of topics. Others are digital copies of the publications mentioned above that are updated annually. CD-ROMs are now the usual source of computer programs, many of which have an educational content.

The internet, as a worldwide information base, allows access to an enormous range of research information as full publications, reports, summaries or abstracts. Search engines such as Google, Yahoo, Ask and MSN, can be used to find information on subjects of interest or to look for current areas of research. However, you can waste a lot of time searching the internet and getting nowhere. You need to be quite specific in your search, but not so specific that the search engine comes up with nothing. Most search engines have help facilities to assist you in your quest. Note that to gain access to some research reports and papers of many research journals' sites you must register or pay a subscription fee.

To get you started here are some sites that contain abstracts, summaries or complete reports of research for which you do not have to register or subscribe:

- www.dfes.gov.uk/research – research page of the Department for Education and Skills website
- www.surestart.gov.uk – website for Sure Start
- www.ecrp.uiuc.edu/ – a bilingual internet journal on the development, care, and education of young children
- www.ltscotland.org.uk/earlyyears/Publications.asp – the early years page of the Learning and Teaching Scotland website that has easy to follow links through its publications page to summaries and full reports of early years research undertaken in the UK
- www.rand.org/research_areas/children/ – RAND is a non-profit research organisation providing access to research from around the world in a wide range of subjects via a range of links – not quite so easy to navigate, but allows you to look at research undertaken in other parts of the world
- www.statistics.org.uk – the official government site for statistics gathered about the UK.

Intranet sites are local versions of the internet used by organisations for exchange of information within that establishment. It is more than likely that the place where you are studying has its own intranet that may have pages devoted to your course and contain links to websites considered useful for your course. Increasingly colleges have virtual learning environments (VLEs) that offer integrated services and more sophisticated opportunities for learning than intranets. To access a college VLE, you generally have to be registered as a student at that institution and you will probably require a password. Organisations other than your own college that have intranets/VLEs may choose to allow you access via an internet website, but may limit use to specific parts of that site.

Other media

TV, national and local radio often reflect current attitudes and opinions about different issues. However, like newspapers, they may reflect the biased views of the publishers and in order to attract a maximum audience will latch onto subjects that are topical and emotive, for example sex offenders in the community, the link between the MMR (measles, mumps and rubella) vaccine and autism.

Museums

These are often disregarded but are potentially useful in terms of local history and the subsequent social changes in local communities. Such changes may reflect a wide range of issues relating to parenting and the development, education and experience of children in a community. Many museums operate interactive displays or operate as living museums to reflect social history, for example Beamish Museum in County Durham.

■ Using secondary research

Remember that information obtained from secondary sources is second-hand. As such, it may be biased towards the views of the person or organisation that has produced it. In addition the information may be out of date as the book or article may have been written some time after the original research was undertaken and you may be reading the material some years after publication. You should always treat such information with caution and have evidence from different sources to support your work and provide a balanced picture.

You should ensure that secondary information you use is appropriately acknowledged, otherwise you may be accused of plagiarism, which could have serious implications for your studies (see Authenticity (plagiarism and summarising information) on page 326).

Primary research

While secondary research can provide the background and basis for many of your studies, you will also need to be familiar with the process of primary research and the different primary research methods used. Whatever the nature of the research being undertaken, researchers make use of different methods to help them answer the questions they have posed. These include:

- surveys/questionnaires
- observations
- interviews
- case studies
- experiments.

Each method is considered in detail on pages 300–309.

You might find by reading specialist books on research that these methods are presented in different ways and that there are others. Each method has its own advantages and disadvantages and will consequently be used by researchers in different circumstances.

Research is regarded as a cyclical process that involves the following general approach:

1 Identify a topic to research (research commissioned by a government body or other organisation generally dictates the subject matter being researched), see section 8.3.

2 Produce a research question or hypothesis (this may again be dictated by the commissioning body and can be based upon the research programmes aims), see page 306 and section 8.3.

3 Select research and sampling methods (designing) and consider any ethical issues involved in conducting the research (see pages 324–25).

4 Collect the information (see section 8.4).

5 Present the information (see section 8.4).

6 Analyse the information (see section 8.4).

7 Evaluate and discuss the research and its implications (see section 8.5).

Discussion and evaluation of the research can lead to further or continuing investigations to complete the cycle.

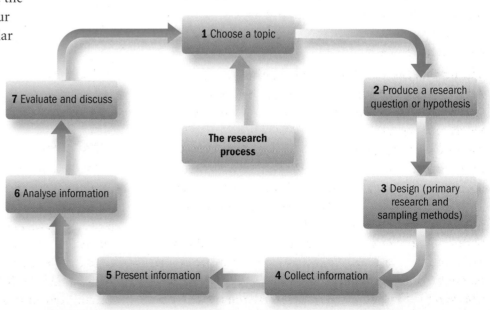

Primary research methods

Surveys

Survey research is based upon asking questions. This can be in the form of a questionnaire or an intensive one-to-one, in-depth interview.

■ Questionnaires

Questionnaires are usually a pen-and-paper exercise that people complete. The completion of a questionnaire can be carried out through a mail drop or group activity or as a one-to-one structured interview.

Advantages of questionnaires

- They are relatively inexpensive to administer, apart from the cost of photocopying and postage stamps.
- They can be sent to a large number of people.
- Respondents may fill them out at their own convenience.

Disadvantages of questionnaires

- Response rates from mail surveys are often very low.
- Postal surveys are not the best way of asking for detailed information.

The disadvantage of response rate can be overcome by carrying out the survey face-to-face, for example in your local high street. This also allows for the opportunity to question the respondent to clarify any questions or to gain a more insightful response. If you decide to use this method, it is important for personal safety that you conduct the activity in a small group and that you have some form of identification.

Alternatively, a group-administered questionnaire is an effective way of getting people to respond. It guarantees a high response rate and can draw on people who are readily available, such as in college, a school or workplace. However, it may limit the total number of people surveyed and can create a biased sample (see Use and misuse of statistics, page 322). Respondents are handed the questionnaire and can be asked to complete it immediately or you can offer to collect it the following week or whenever convenient.

How you administer the questionnaire is relatively easy compared to producing it. You might think it is easy to run off a few questions about, for example, the views of parents on raising children and keeping pets. You will find that it takes time, thought and practice to ensure that the questions you ask give you the answers you are seeking. You will also find that you need to undertake a trial to find out if it works (see section 8.3, page 311).

The types of question you can ask vary and include the following.

Closed and open questions

Closed questions lead to a yes or no answer, whereas open questions prompt the respondent to say something more. 'Are you married?' is a closed question; 'What are your views on marriage?' is an open question. Closed questions give information that can be easily quantified whilst open questions allow the respondent to express their own views. The difficulty with open questions is that respondents may have slightly different views, making the presentation of such information more difficult.

Information gathering questions

These usually ask for some numerical data, for example:
- How many children do you have?
- What is your age?
- In what year were you born?

The last is regarded as a more sensitive way of asking someone their age than the second.

Category questions

These offer a number of possibilities only one of which the respondent can fit into, for example:

Are you:	Male ❑	Married ❑
	Female ❑	Single ❑

Tick which age group you fit into:

15–25 ❑

26–35 ❑

36–45 ❑

46–55 ❑

56+ ❑

The use of categories such as age groups is another way of obtaining information that may be regarded as sensitive. It can also be useful to allocate people to age ranges if you want to see if there is any difference in response to your questionnaire between age groups, for example attitudes or changes to parenting between younger and older age groups.

Ranking questions

These are used to place answers in order and are useful for obtaining information on views or attitudes, for example:

> **Number the following emotional and social needs of children in order of importance:**
>
> Security ☐
> Discipline ☐
> Love ☐
> Encouragement ☐
> Responsible behaviour ☐

> **In order of importance, number your preferred method of pain relief during childbirth:**
>
> Gas ☐
> Pethidine ☐
> Epidural ☐
> Breathing and relaxation techniques ☐

Scale questions

These can also be used to obtain information about attitudes and beliefs, but must be used with care, for example:

> **Tick the box that best describes how you feel about the following statements:**
>
> **Children should be smacked if they:**

	Strongly agree	Agree	Disagree	Strongly disagree
hit or bite another child	☐	☐	☐	☐
wet themselves when being toilet trained	☐	☐	☐	☐
have a temper tantrum	☐	☐	☐	☐
play with their genitals	☐	☐	☐	☐

The scale question is quite controversial and may not be appropriate within a college-based project. However, it helps to illustrate how controversial topics may be investigated without having to ask someone directly about the subject, i.e. whether they smack their children.

A less controversial subject for using a scale question might be:

> **Tick the box that best describes your views on:**

	Strongly agree	Agree	Neither agree nor disagree	Disagree	Strongly disagree
Breast-feeding	☐	☐	☐	☐	☐
Fluoridation of water	☐	☐	☐	☐	☐
Homework for infant school children	☐	☐	☐	☐	☐

In this example, note how an extra column has been added to include the neutral response of 'neither agree nor disagree'. Whilst this allows people to express a neutral view, it can result in people avoiding the subject.

In addition to the style of questions used, you also need to consider the construction and presentation of your questionnaire. Follow the good practice below.

Good practice checklist

Creating a questionnaire

- Keep your questions as simple as possible. Two or three simple questions may be easier to answer than one difficult one.
- Do not ask too many questions. If there are too many, people will get fed up.
- Make sure your questions are unambiguous, for example 'Should a child be disciplined for being naughty?' This question begs the response, 'What form of discipline are you referring to and how do you define naughty?'
- Do not ask leading questions that imply a particular response, for example 'Do you think that it is better to breast-feed rather than bottle-feed a new baby?' The response may well be: 'Yes', but the respondent may be thinking 'Yes, but I'd rather bottle-feed.'
- Avoid grouping together questions that have a negative or sensitive context or, if you are seeking a more personal view, place them towards the end of the questionnaire, for example asking people's views on abortion, child abuse or drugs.

- Do not ask too many open questions as they can take time to answer and are difficult to analyse. Again, these are best placed towards the end of the questionnaire and can be a useful way of getting a response to more contentious subjects.
- Type or print your questionnaire in a format that is clear and legible.
- Set the questionnaire out so that simple closed questions which only require yes/no or one-word answers come first, followed by ranking and scale-type questions and finish with open questions to allow subjects to express their opinions more fully.
- Ensure that you include an explanation of who you are, where you are from and the purpose of the questionnaire. Also provide clear instructions and a statement to assure respondents that the questionnaire is confidential (see Good practice checklist – A code of ethics, page 325).

Theory into practice

The following questionnaire was put together by a group of childcare students to find out about mothers' views on breast-feeding and bottle-feeding. Read through the survey then see if you can answer the questions that follow.

1 Please indicate which age group you fit into.

   a Under 20   b 20–30   c 30–40   d 40+

2 How many children do you have and what are their age and gender?

3 Did you breast-feed or bottle-feed?

4 If you breast-fed, please state how long you breast-fed each child for?

5 If you did not breast-feed any of your children, please identify which type of infant formula milk you used

   SMA ☐   Cow & Gate ☐   Milupa ☐   Farley's ☐   Other ☐

6 Number each statement in order of importance.

   a Breast milk contains all the nutrients a baby needs.   ☐

   b Bottle-feeding is more convenient.   ☐

   c Breast-feeding is time-consuming.   ☐

   d Breast-fed babies are less prone to infections.   ☐

   e You know how much your baby has had when bottle feeding.   ☐

7 Tick the box that best describes how you feel about each statement.

	Strongly agree	Agree	Disagree	Strongly disagree
You should follow the advice of health professionals in deciding whether to breast- or bottle-feed.				
You should make up you own mind on whether to breast- or bottle-feed based on the experiences of friends and family.				

- Identify which questions are of the category, rank or scale type.
- How could you improve the presentation of questions 2, 3 and 4 and make it easier for you to summarise the results?
- Suggest what is wrong with questions 3, 4 and 6.
- Why is question 5 unnecessary?

■ Interviews

As you read through this section you will see that interviews, particularly at their simplest level, are no more than extended survey questionnaires. However, interviews are a far more personal form of research and can provide more detailed information particularly on sensitive subjects. They are usually carried out on a one-to-one basis. Whilst interviews are generally easier for the respondent, especially if what is sought is opinions or impressions, they are not necessarily easier for you. Interviews can be very time-consuming and they require good communication skills to complete effectively.

Interviews can be:

- *structured* – based upon a set of questions requiring specific answers, not very different from a questionnaire
- *open-ended* – little, if any, format and may take the form of a discussion
- *semi-structured* – a bit of both. If you use this form of research, semi-structured interviews are probably the most appropriate procedure to follow.

You are most likely to use interviews to find out about people's feelings, attitudes and experiences of, for example, childbirth, raising children, caring for a sick child, managing children's behaviour or the education of children. As a result, you will tend to choose one or more people to interview from those you know, have had contact with or have been put in touch with by your tutor or workplace supervisor.

▲ Conducting an interview

Once you have introduced yourself to the person to be interviewed, use the Good practice checklist below as a guide to help you complete the process.

Good practice checklist

Interviewing

- Give a brief explanation of the purpose of your interview and make arrangements as to the date, time and place of the interview. This will help prepare both the interviewee and yourself for the event.
- Make preparations for recording the interview. You can choose to use a tape recorder or take notes, both of which have their advantages and disadvantages as shown in the table below:

Tape recording	Note taking
Able to concentrate on interviewee, what he or she has to say and the questions to be asked	Need to give attention to both interviewee and note taking
Can make respondents anxious and not able to talk about sensitive issues	Can be distracting
Provides a complete account of what has been said, but can take a long time to transcribe and analyse	Allows a summary of what has been said to be noted and the main features identified, so analysis is easier. Important facts or remarks may be missed

Whichever method is used, ensure you have the agreement of the interviewee and, if note taking, have a spare pen or pencil and devise a system for abbreviating certain responses such as 'Q:' for your question, 'A:' for the respondent's answer, 'DK' for don't know, etc.

- In conducting the interview you need to take into account the beginning, middle and end. The beginning includes making appropriate opening remarks that put the interviewee at ease and doesn't ask too much of them. This can be achieved by explaining who you are, where you are from and re-emphasising what the research is for. The main thing here is not to be long-winded. Also provide reassurance that the interview will remain confidential. This can also include asking simple questions that only require one-word or short answers, such as 'How many children do you have?', 'What age and gender are they?' These simple questions can be memorised enabling you to give attention to the interviewee so helping to establish a trusting, honest, and non-threatening relationship that can lead into a more open-ended discussion about the main issues.

- If you are interviewing more than one person for your research, you must ensure that the questions asked are exactly the same, as altering them in any way can change their whole meaning and, as a result, the response you get.

- Ask all the questions in the order arranged prior to the interview so that nothing is missed out either by you or the interviewee. Do not finish people's sentences for them because it might not have been what they were going to say.

- If the beginning of the interview has gone well, it should lead naturally into the middle part of the interview where you hope to elicit a more open or detailed response for which you may find the following techniques helpful:
  - *Silence* One of the most effective ways to encourage someone to say more is to do nothing at all, just pause and wait. It works because people are generally uncomfortable with pauses or silence and it suggests that you are waiting, listening for what they will say next.
  - *Encouraging remarks* Something as simple as 'Uh-huh' or 'OK' after the respondent completes a thought can encourage the respondent directly.
  - *Elaboration* Asking a question such as 'Is there anything else you would like to add?' can result in the respondent providing more information.
  - *Ask for clarification* Asking the interviewee to talk in more detail about something said earlier can allow the discussion to explore new areas. This type of question also shows that you have been

listening, which can encourage the interviewee.

- *Reflecting* By repeating back part of what the respondent has said, you say something without really saying anything new. For instance, if the respondent just described a traumatic experience they had in childhood, you might say, 'What I'm hearing you say is that you found that experience very traumatic.' Then you should pause. The respondent is likely to say something like, 'Well, yes, and it affected the rest of my family as well. In fact, my younger sister ...', and so on.

- When the interview ends conclude by thanking the respondent and offering them the opportunity to read your completed work or at least a summary of it.
- Do give the respondent time to ask any further questions about you, your course or your research before you leave.
- You may have observations about the interview that you were not able to write down while you were with the respondent. As such you should immediately go over your notes and include any other comments and observations making sure you distinguish these from the notes made during the interview.

Case study: Interviewing: what not to do!

Suzanne chose to do a project on childbirth and decided to interview her friend, Danielle about her experience of childbirth as she was due to have her first baby.

The project was scheduled for submission four weeks after the birth of the baby. Suzanne thought this would give her plenty of time to complete the assignment. However, she hadn't bargained for Danielle's baby not being born until two weeks after her due date and that Danielle didn't come home from the hospital for five days as the baby was slightly jaundiced. Suzanne visited Danielle in the hospital and planned to arrange the interview for when she got home, but in the excitement of seeing the new baby and Danielle wanting to know about what was going on, Suzanne forgot. Fortunately, Suzanne managed to see Danielle in hospital again before she went home and this time organised the interview so that it gave her a few days to write up the assignment.

When Suzanne went round to Danielle's, she was about to feed the baby. Suzanne hadn't prepared any questions as she thought that as she knew Danielle so well it wouldn't matter, so they just chatted about her experiences. Suzanne realised it might have been a good idea to bring a notepad and pen. Suzanne asked Danielle if she had a pen and paper, but at that moment the midwife arrived. The midwife asked

Danielle about the birth and how she was getting on whilst Suzanne held the baby. When the midwife left, the baby was ready for a feed. No sooner had she finished feeding the baby when the door bell rang and another of Danielle's friends had come round to see her and the baby. Suzanne realised she had to go as she'd arranged to go into college to see her tutor about her progress with the project.

In a bit of a panic, Suzanne didn't know whether to go into college, but in the end took the plunge and found that, by talking through what she had discussed with Danielle and overheard what she had said to the midwife, it was obvious that she had gathered an awful lot of information. Suzanne's tutor suggested she spent the rest of the day getting her thoughts down on paper, checking any facts with Danielle the next day and that she would still have time to complete her report in time for the deadline.

Suzanne didn't mention to her tutor that she had previously arranged to go to the cinema with her boyfriend so was left having to decide what to do. As you can guess, Suzanne went to the cinema and ended up writing the assignment the night before the hand-in date, by which time she had forgotten a lot of what she knew and consequently failed the assignment.

What should Suzanne have done to ensure the project was successful?

Theory into practice

Interviews require good communication skills and take practice. If you are unsure about conducting an interview, try this activity to practise.

In groups of three, take turns in being an observer, interviewer or interviewee. Choose a topic which each of you feels able to talk about. Jot down some questions that will require closed and open answers. Use the good practice checklist above to help conduct the interview, with the observer making notes on both the verbal and non-verbal responses of the interviewee to the interviewer. The interviewer should remember to explain the purpose of the interview, ask some simple questions initially before moving on to more open questions.

If you found this easy, try repeating the exercise with a controversial or sensitive topic such as abortion, embryo research or cancer.

The experimental method

The experimental method is a standard scientific procedure whereby the researcher, possibly after some preliminary work:

- proposes a research hypothesis by which they hope to explain the initial findings
- designs an experiment or series of experiments to test the hypothesis.

■ The hypothesis

The hypothesis can be in the form of a very precise question, statement or prediction. The hypothesis suggests that there is a relationship or difference between two or more factors or **variables,** for example babies born to mothers who smoke during pregnancy are more likely to have a lower birth weight. The number of cigarettes smoked per day and the weight of the new-born baby are the two main variables being investigated.

Key term

A **variable** is a factor that changes or can be changed.

A relationship, often referred to as a correlation or association between variables, results from changes in one variable being *related* to changes in another, for example consumption of alcohol during pregnancy is associated (or correlated) with an increase in the incidence of babies born with foetal alcohol syndrome.

A difference between variables can be regarded as changes in one variable causing an *effect* in another variable, for example girls learn quicker than boys, often referred to as a cause and effect relationship.

The hypothesis can also be written in one of two formats:

- The experimental hypothesis predicts the outcome of an experiment, for example girls learn quicker than boys.
- The null hypothesis does not predict an outcome, i.e. it states that there is no effect or relationship between variables, for example there is no difference between the rate at which girls and boys learn.

■ The experiment to test the hypothesis

The next step is to design an experiment that will prove or disprove the hypothesis. The idea is to look at how one variable alters in response to changes in the other. With the cause–effect type of experiment, the researcher deliberately alters the variable known as the independent variable (IV) that is thought to be causing the effect and measures changes in the other dependent variable (DV).

The problem with this approach, particularly when applied to research on humans, is that there may be many other factors that could influence the results. These are called confounding or extraneous variables, for example:

- In the case of maternal smoking and birth weight, the age of the mother, the number of cigarettes smoked, the pattern of smoking before and during pregnancy, alcohol consumption, nutritional status and socio-economic status are extraneous variables.

- In the differences in learning between girls and boys, age, levels of intelligence, social class and income of parents are just a few of the confounding variables to be taken into account.

Consequently, the effect of such variables has to be eradicated or minimalised. This can be achieved by attempting to control as many of the factors as possible by ensuring the subjects are of the same or similar age, the same gender, etc. Alternatively, the experiment can be designed in such a way as to minimise the effects of such variables. This can be achieved using one of two approaches:

- *Repeated measures design* This type of study is carried out by working with one group of subjects so that each subject experiences both experimental conditions. For example, in an experiment looking at the effect of providing water during classes on children's attention span, each child experiences both conditions, i.e. having no water or water at different times.
- *Independent subjects design* In this case, each experimental condition is experienced by two different groups of subjects. For example, in the effects of water on attention span, two groups of children would be chosen, one of which has water available and the other does not.

Theory into practice

The aim of the following experiment is to study Piaget's theory of conservation (see Unit 17, page 454). It is presented as a step-by-step guide to provide an example of how you could use the experimental method to investigate a subject of your choice. It shows how the experimental and null hypotheses are presented and the need to design a suitable test based on Piaget's theories of cognitive development and conservation.

Step 1: Initial research into problem
Secondary research based on background reading shows you that up to the age of about 6 or 7 years, children are unable to conserve amounts or quantities and so you decide to look into the conservation of mass.

Step 2: The hypothesis
You produce an experimental hypothesis stating that children under 6 years cannot conserve mass compared to children over the age of 7. A comparable null hypothesis would state that there will be no difference in the ability of children under the age of 6 compared to children over 7 to conserve mass.

Step 3: Designing the experiment
- You now need to design an experiment to test your hypothesis. This involves selecting the children

to take part in your study and designing a way of testing the hypothesis.

- Selecting the children involves taking a sample (see Sampling methodology, page 309) of under-6s and another group of over-7s. In selecting the children you also hope to manage or control some of the extraneous variables that could affect the outcome.
- The design of the experiment is quite easy since you could use play dough moulded into two balls of the same size with each child asked if there is the same amount of play dough in each ball. Those children who answer correctly can proceed to the next part of the test which involves rolling one of the balls into a different shape so that the child can see, and the child again asked if each ball contains the same amount of dough. This would be repeated for every child and the results noted.

This experiment could be extended or redesigned to study the conservation of capacity (volume), length or number and could form part of a project in your placement having gained the appropriate permission (see *Good practice checklist – A code of ethics*, page 325).

Is this an example of structured or unstructured observation?

Observations

This section provides an overview of observation as a research method. Observation is dealt with in more detail in Unit 3, Promoting Children's Development.

Observation can be defined as the recording of facts or data through close examination of situations or events. There are two principal types of observation, participant and non-participant.

- In participant observation, you, as the observer, become involved in the activities you intend to observe.
- In non-participant, or passive, observation, you observe as an outsider and do not become involved.

In all likelihood, you will probably find yourself undertaking observations through placement activities that incorporate aspects of both types of observation. A good example would be during play activities where you might be assisting younger children whilst observing the interaction between individuals.

Observations can also be regarded as either structured (formal) or unstructured (informal).

- Structured observations are based upon predetermined criteria that will measure the duration, frequency, type or consequences of events.
- At the extreme, unstructured observation involves the researcher having some vague notion of what they wish to study, but through the observation process gathers information that provides a focus for developing a research question or hypothesis (the opposite of what has been suggested so far). The advantage of this approach is there are no pre-conceived notions or expectations about what the outcome of the research will be as such a large amount of information is gathered, which over time can begin to show patterns that can lead to broad generalisations. Herein lies the problem with this type of research – you need time both to carry out the research and to analyse the information.

The advantages of the observation method are that it is adaptable to many situations, can reveal unexpected relationships, draws on data not available using other methods, and can be used in conjunction with the experimental method. For example, the observation of behaviour before and after the introduction of a behaviour modification programme to assess its success or otherwise.

Case studies

The case study is not a method in itself, but an approach to research that is based upon the observation of an individual, organisation or culture. Case studies take into account historical evidence and are used to study the consequences of past and present events on the subject being studied. They can provide a unique insight into an individual or organisation but can be intrusive, therefore care must be exercised in carrying them out to ensure you have informed consent and to maintain confidentiality (see Ethical issues, page 324).

The gathering of information for a case study should initially focus on gathering historical information to prepare what is called a case history. This will usually be based upon interviews with the parents, teachers or other people associated with the child being studied, followed by observations of the child in different settings depending upon their age, for example home, playgroup or school, outdoors, in social groups.

Case studies also form part of a social worker's kit in relation to child abuse and whilst it would be inappropriate for you to be taking such an approach, you will find case studies very useful for finding out about the effects of disabling conditions such as Down's syndrome, cystic fibrosis or autism, for example, on a child's physical, emotional and social development. More in-depth studies may also consider the effects on the family or carers and the implications for health, education and social services.

Case studies are particularly useful for early years research being undertaken by students as they allow the opportunity to study something in depth over a relatively short space of time. They are also valuable for studying individual children as they enable a picture of the child to be revealed from which conclusions about their patterns of behaviour, their learning, their socialisation skills, etc., can be drawn and used to assist their development.

Sampling methodology

As well as choosing the primary research methods, some thought has to be given to the subjects who will be involved with the research. You need to consider some form of subject selection process since it won't be possible to include everyone. This selection process is known as sampling.

A **sample** is regarded as being representative of the group or population of people from which it is taken. Researchers hope to be able to draw conclusions about the population as a result of their work on the sample.

Taking the example of Piaget's experiment on conservation discussed in the experimental method (page 307), the purpose of the experiment is to see if there is any difference in the ability to conserve between children under 6 and children over 7 years old. Obviously, it would be impossible to carry out the study on all children, so the way forward is to observe a small number of children that can be regarded as representative of children under 6 and children over 7 years old. This group (or groups) of children will become your sample and the group from which they are selected is the **population**. For your work to be truly representative of the whole population, the sample selected must be **random**. This means that everyone in the population has an equal chance of being chosen to take part in your study.

Key terms

A **sample** is a subgroup of a population selected to represent the entire population, for example a selection of pupils from a year group within a school or group of schools.

A **population** is a group of people or objects that share particular characteristics, for example a year group in a school or group of schools that have similar characteristics.

A **random sample** is a subgroup of a population selected to represent the entire population in which the people in the population have an equal chance of being chosen to be in the subgroup.

Not all forms of sampling are random and the method chosen to select your sample will for the most part be dependent on the nature of the study, how easy it is to gain access to the people you hope to do research on and how much time you have. See the table below.

Type of sample	What it is	How to do it
Random sampling	Subjects are selected at random from a list created by yourself or someone else, for example class register, telephone directory or electoral register.	Everyone in a list is allocated a number and then a random number generator is used to select a sample of appropriate size. A random number generator is like the machine that spews out the Lotto numbers every week. Most calculators have a random number generator button that will perform this task for you.
Systematic sampling	From a list, every nth case is selected, i.e. every fifth or tenth person.	If you wanted to choose five children from a class of 25, everyone is allocated a number from 1 to 25, then the fifth, tenth, fifteenth, twentieth and twenty-fifth child is selected.
Stratified sampling	Stratified sampling involves taking a random or systematic sample from groups within a population.	If you want to find out if there is any difference in educational attainment or learning ability between girls and boys, you take a random or systematic sample from within a group of girls and a another from within a group of boys.
Quota sampling	Quota sampling is more or less the same as stratified sampling, but relies on the groups coming from a conveniently available population.	In the stratified sampling example above, the school in which you are on placement would be a convenient population from which to take your sample of boys and girls.
Opportunity sampling	This is simply based on taking a sample of subjects from those readily available	The most common form of sampling whereby the sample is selected from people you are associated with, for example students at your college.
Voluntary and snowball sampling	Involves people volunteering to be part of the research sample and may lead to others becoming involved through word of mouth.	You simply ask people if they wish to take part.
Purposive sampling	The selection of typical or interesting cases. Particularly suited to case study research or the investigation of a specific problem, such as a congenital disease.	The difficult part of this is finding people who wish to take part in your research. Usually the people come from those you know, but can be identified through your placement.

Whilst quota and opportunity sampling are the most likely methods you will use, whichever method you employ there may be people chosen who either don't start/join in or don't finish/give up. Never pressurise people into taking part.

Case study: Choosing the right sampling method

Andrea and Mahesh are undertaking a survey into parental preferences and purchasing habits in choosing and buying babies' nappies. They decide that the best way to get a suitable sample of people would be to take an opportunity sample based on people buying nappies from a local supermarket. As part of their questionnaire is about whether there are any differences between the purchasing habits of males and females, their tutor suggests they try to obtain a sample size of at least 15 males and 15 females. At the supermarket they very quickly reach their target sample size for females, but discover that males buying nappies are few and far between!

How could Andreas and Mahesh address this problem?

Assessment activity 8.2

Read again the extract of summary information on Effective Provision of Pre-School Education on page 295 and identify the key elements of the research process based on the following headings:

- the purpose or aim of the research or of any identified research question or hypothesis
- the research and sampling methods used to conduct the research (research design)

- the type of information collected (qualitative or quantitative)
- how this information was presented
- what the research showed (analysis)
- what implications the research has for children's care, learning or development (evaluate and discuss).

P2

8.3 Identifying a suitable topic and producing a plan for a research proposal

Topic and hypothesis

For any project you undertake the first three statements in the research process cycle (see page 299) are all about planning. The more effort put into planning and organising your activities, particularly where the research is a project for which you have been allocated a term or longer to complete, the better the end result. Once you have planned the research you are then ready to collect the data, after which you need to sort it out ready for presentation and analysis.

The following takes you through these first steps in the research process. At the end of this unit a checklist takes you through the whole cycle to help you with the organisation and planning of any research or project you undertake (see page 328).

Knowing you have enough time

Find out how much time you have got. You may have been given a deadline that only allows you a few weeks or even days to complete the work. Alternatively, you may be looking at a whole year. Whichever, you will need to plan your time effectively to ensure the work is completed on time and is of the standard that you feel justifies the grade you are aiming for. Do not leave things to the last minute, particularly with a longer term project.

Identifying a topic to research

As far as any research you undertake is concerned, different ideas may arise as a result of:

- reading or hearing about something that you think would be interesting and enjoyable to find out more about
- your own thoughts or experiences
- the ideas of others.

Your tutor may be able to get you started on suggesting topics that previous students have investigated or you may be able to use observations or other activities expected of you in placement.

The following may assist in generating ideas for topics:

- Your tutor may be able to get you started on suggesting topics that previous students have investigated, or you and your fellow students could try a brainstorming session. This is a popular technique used by businesses and organisations to generate ideas. You need a flipchart and marker pens. Your tutor may have given you a broad idea to think about or leave things very open. As a class, or in smaller groups of four to seven, agree who will write down the ideas (they need to be written large so everyone can see). The group should then start to think about what they could research and any idea that is suggested should be written down no matter how silly it may seem. Sometimes it can be difficult to get started but ideas will soon flow easily. From the list, choose two or three topics that sound interesting. Either as a whole class or in groups, discuss the ideas to see if they are realistic (in the time allocated, with the resources available, considering relevant ethical or confidentiality issues, etc.) and what research methods could be used. Your tutor will help you with this process. This should result in a research idea that you can begin to consider in more detail.

• Another starting point is the course syllabus, which should be available through your tutor. The syllabus identifies the outcomes and assessment evidence requirements for the units you will be studying. By reading through these, it should be possible to identify a topic that could be based upon a research project. Indeed, your tutor may give some direction or set specific assignments to ensure you meet such outcomes and assessment criteria. A number of units, both core and optional, refer to research projects as possible means of assessment.

• Talking to other people can be invaluable for helping to generate ideas and may include any of the following:

  – *Family* By virtue of being your parents/guardians, your mother and father will have a wealth of knowledge about bringing up children and, apart from seeing how difficult a job it is, you may be able to gain information from them that you can focus on in your study. Other relations may also be of assistance, not only as parents themselves, but possibly as someone who works with or on behalf of children.

  – *Employers and workplace supervisors* If you work in a care organisation either voluntarily, through an organised placement, or as an employee you could ask for advice and may find that they would like you to carry out some research for them. As you will be expected to carry out observations on children through placements, these may become part of your research project.

Once you have identified a topic, undertake an information search to gather some background information that will help in focusing on your study in order to produce a research question or hypothesis.

The research question or hypothesis

Having selected the topic or list of topics that you would like to study, or are thinking about studying, you should now begin to refine your ideas, focusing on what you would specifically like to find out. This will lead to producing a research question or hypothesis.

• A research question simply states the question or questions you want your research to answer.

• As already explained, an hypothesis is a special type of

Brainstorming is a popular technique for generating ideas

research question that tends to be used in surveys or experiments. It proposes the existence of a relationship between variables or factors and tends to suggest how the relationship will be tested (The experimental method, page 306).

Students often find identifying a research question one of the more difficult parts of the whole process and consequently try to opt out of making a decision about this until later. This is an error that could lead you to be unclear about the focus of your study. Time needs to be given to what you hope to find out. This part of the research process will involve you in doing some secondary research, reading around the topic, looking at recent research and talking to others. In this way you will begin to find out more about the area you are going to study that can then lead to the selection of a specific topic.

Once you have determined your research question, you need to select the primary research and sampling methods appropriate to your study. With a short-term project choose just one or two research methods that will provide information quickly; a longer term study can involve a variety of methods and allow a more in-depth investigation to be carried out.

Identify what resources you will require to complete your study. Do you need specialist equipment? Where will you get such equipment? Will there be a charge and how long can you have it for?

Produce an action plan that identifies your research topic, research question or hypothesis, the research methods to be used, any resources required and an approximate time allocation for each section. Submit this to your tutor for approval.

Conduct a pilot study of any survey you have planned. You may be quite happy with a questionnaire you have produced, but when it comes to people answering the questions, problems can arise over the meaning of words or misinterpreting of questions. Consequently, it is advisable to practise using your questionnaire on a small number of people to see whether questions need modifying to make them clearer. This is called a pilot or trial study, the results of which may still be used if you have not had to make any changes.

Continue reading around the subject, making notes that provide background information and that support or refute your research question or hypothesis.

Good practice checklist

Whichever research method you use it will be necessary to carry out the following to ensure the research is undertaken in an effective and efficient manner:

- Check your tutor is happy with what you are going to research and how you are going to do it. Make sure they have vetted your questions for a questionnaire, interview or case study or the way you intend to conduct an experiment or observation. This should have been addressed as part of any action plan you produce.
- Obtain written permission from anyone who may have some responsibility for your research. Verbal permission is adequate for a simple survey.
- Organise when and where the research will be undertaken:
  - Is it at college, in a school, nursery or playgroup, your local high street or shopping centre, at your own house or that of a relation or friend?
  - Timing can be important. For instance, Mondays tend to be quieter in town centres, young children may be more tired in an afternoon if you are conducting an observation or experiment, parents may be in too much of a rush to get involved when they are dropping off or picking up children from playgroup, school or nursery.
- Organise and prepare any materials or resources required:
  - Photocopy adequate numbers of questionnaires, having a few for spares if any get spoilt.
  - Have you got/do you need paper, pens or flip charts for you or the participants to write on?
- If you are conducting the research in a group make sure:
  - everyone knows what they are doing
  - everyone follows the same procedures
  - everyone uses the same style of questioning.

The way a question is asked can alter its whole meaning.

Assessment activity 8.3

This activity has been designed to help you develop secondary research skills. You should know how to conduct an information search or literary review and be able to identify examples of research that will help you understand both the research process and the key elements of research methodology and thereby prepare you for undertaking your own research.

1 Either on your own or in a small group, choose a topic to investigate.

2 Produce a research plan that identifies:
   - what you are going to investigate
   - how you are going to carry out the investigation, i.e. the primary research methods, timescales, sampling methods.

3 Go to your local or college library and look for texts on the subject or chapters or articles in books or publications. Note down the titles, the authors, date and place of publication as you will need this as evidence of your secondary research (see Good practice checklist Producing a bibliography (avoiding plagiarism!) on page 326).

4 Now carry out a search on the internet. Try using different search engines to identify online information on your chosen subject. Check out some of the website addresses and if they seem to contain relevant information, note down or copy the titles of the research together with their author and website address. If you have not used the internet before, ask your tutor, school, college or local library to help. **P3**

8.4 Conduct and present research information

Data collection

Having determined what method or methods you will use and the sampling strategy you will employ, you need to start collecting your data/information.

Again it is important to plan your activities. It would not be wise to organise a survey questionnaire in your local high street when the weather forecast is for gales or heavy showers or to find you had forgotten your recording materials when carrying out an observation or interview.

Having got yourself organised, you can now begin to collect the information/data. Once completed, the information collected will need to be prepared for presentation. This will be dependent upon whether it is qualitative or quantitative.

As explained earlier, qualitative data is descriptive information and can therefore be regarded as information collected in the format of words, whilst quantitative data is based upon numerical information. You may find that your study produces both types of information.

Dealing with qualitative information

Qualitative information may be in the form of directly written words, such as may be transcribed from an interview, or written notes that summarise what occurred. Both forms may reflect some selectivity on the part of the person who provided the information or by the researcher in summarising the information. In effect this shows that some analysis has already taken place and further analysis involves additional selection and refinement of the data.

Good practice checklist

Handling qualitative information

Initially you should take time to organise or manage the data so that the analysis and refining process becomes easier. Whilst you can do this in many different ways, here are some suggestions to assist you with the process:

- Use different coloured highlighter pens to highlight words or passages that say the same thing, that support or refute your research question and support or refute theoretical arguments.
- Add notes or comments alongside highlighted words or phrases that can help you relate the information to the research question or theory. This can include adding references to articles or books on the subject.
- Use a coding system to process information that repeats itself or could be grouped, for example males and females, different ages.
- Use tables to categorise words or phrases in particular groups. Open questions from an interview or questionnaire may elicit a wide range of responses. However, it may be possible to identify words or phrases that mean the same thing, allowing them to be grouped together. You need to be clear about how you have done this in presenting the data to show that you have avoided being biased.
- Cross out information that is irrelevant.

Once you have processed the information as described in the good practice checklist above, you can begin to select and summarise those bits of data that support or refute your research. Whilst this might seem like doing the whole thing again, it allows you to present a coherent argument in favour of or against your research question. It also enables you to tie your research into the information you will have gained by means of secondary research.

Where the information can be categorised into groups as with words or phrases that occur frequently, then the information may be summarised as numerical values, for example 'five respondents to an open question on experiences of childbirth referred to the desire for giving birth naturally rather than with medical intervention, whilst four preferred to have medical assistance'. In such cases the information can then be regarded as quantitative.

Dealing with quantitative data

Quantitative data will be based upon direct measurements; categories that have been assigned a value (for example, the number of males, females, the number in specified age groups), percentages or averages. Percentages and averages can form part of the next step to summarise and refine your data in order to make it clearer. You may also have obtained data as a result of secondary research that you need to prepare for presentation. Numerical information can be termed discrete or continuous.

- Discrete data is usually based on whole numbers that fit into categories, for example the number of boys and girls in a class.
- Continuous data is any numerical value within a range and can be a fraction of a whole number, for example heights and weights.

Good practice checklist

Handling quantitative data

The purpose of data presentation, be it discrete or continuous, is to make it easier to digest. This is achieved in the following ways:

- Organise the data into tables. Tables allow information to be set out in a structured way and can show simple trends and differences between numbers where there is not too much information.
- Use graphs to summarise more complex information that is difficult to digest from a table.
- Prepare statistics to analyse data in order to establish the proof or otherwise of the research question or hypothesis.

Modern computer programs enable you to complete all the above by entering the data into a spreadsheet program. Such programs include Microsoft Excel, Lotus 1-2-3 and more specialised statistical packages such as MINITAB and SPSS (Statistical Package for Social Science).

The figure below shows some data entered into a spreadsheet that is easily formatted into a table. Graphs can then be produced and formatted to show off your results to best effect. The difficulty is in deciding which graph is the most appropriate. The whole purpose of a graph is to make large amounts of data or more complex data more easily interpreted than might be possible from a table. This does not mean all data should be displayed graphically. The following information on the different types of graph is designed to help you choose which type to use given the data you have collected.

Methods of presentation

Pie charts

Pie charts are used when you have a single value for each category or set of data collected. They show each set as a percentage of the whole. The table below shows the number of 3- and 4-year-olds in education in England, Scotland, Wales and Northern Ireland in 2003 together with the total.

Region of UK	Number of 3- and 4-year-olds in early years education (thousands)
England	1190.6
Wales	55.6
Scotland	100.7
Northern Ireland	32.9
Total	1379.8

Source of data: Department for Education and Skills; National Assembly for Wales; Scottish Executive; Northern Ireland Department of Education

It can be seen that each bit of data is a proportion of the total. To produce the pie chart each value in the table has to be converted into a percentage of the total. Each percentage has then to be converted to the number of degrees as part of the 360° that make up a circle prior to constructing the chart. The data in the table were converted into the pie chart below using a spreadsheet program that does away with the need for changing to percentages and degrees required for producing the chart by hand.

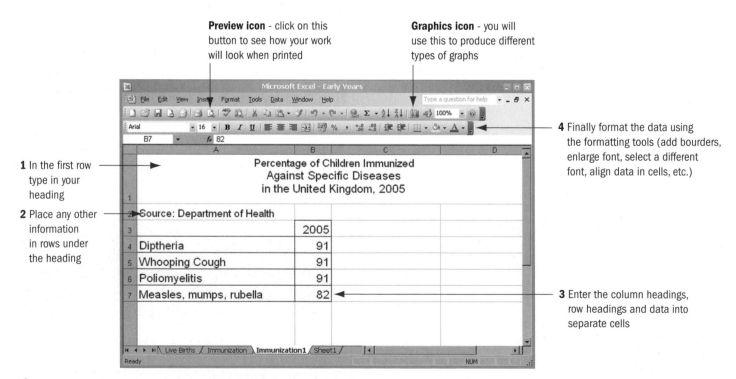

Preview icon - click on this button to see how your work will look when printed

Graphics icon - you will use this to produce different types of graphs

4 Finally format the data using the formatting tools (add bourders, enlarge font, select a different font, align data in cells, etc.)

1 In the first row type in your heading

2 Place any other information in rows under the heading

3 Enter the column headings, row headings and data into separate cells

Percentage of Children Immunized Against Specific Diseases in the United Kingdom, 2005

Source: Department of Health

	2005
Diptheria	91
Whooping Cough	91
Poliomyelitis	91
Measles, mumps, rubella	82

▲ Entering data into a spreadsheet (created in Microsoft Excel)

It is important to note that if we did not know the total number of children we couldn't work out the proportion of each and a pie chart could not be produced. For example, it would be impossible to produce a pie chart of different types of behavioural difficulty existing in a school because we are unlikely to know the total amount of behavioural problems exhibited. You should also avoid a pie chart where there are more than six sets of data as the information begins to look confused.

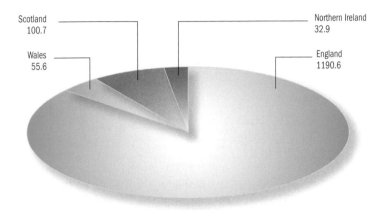

▲ Pie chart: numbers of 3- and 4-year-olds in early years education (thousands)

Bar charts

These can be used as an alternative to pie charts for displaying data as either percentages or whole numbers and can be used where there are too many categories to display in a pie chart.

In the table below, the types of day care are distinct from one another so the resulting bar chart below displays each group as a separate bar or line. It doesn't matter how wide the bars or gaps between the bars are.

▼ Numbers of children in early education, England, 2006

Provision	Numbers of children (thousands)
Private and voluntary	429.4
Independent schools	50.1
Maintained nursery and primary schools	657.7
Special schools	3.6

Source of data: Department for Education and Skills

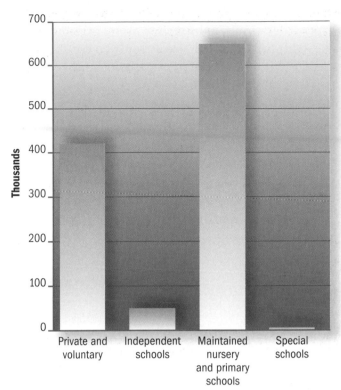

▲ Bar chart: numbers of children in early years education (England, 2006) by type of provision

Line graphs

When you have a considerable amount of data, especially when it is based on measurements taken over a period of time, the line graph is the best choice.

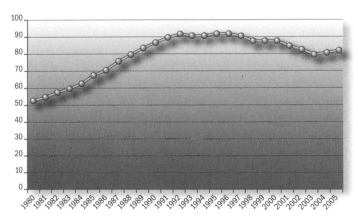

Source of data: World Health Organisation, 2006

▲ Line graph: percentage of children receiving measles vaccine in the UK from 1980–2005

This type of chart allows several lines displaying changes to several groups of data over a period of time to be displayed. This should only be done if it is necessary to compare different groups of data. As with the pie charts, avoid having too much data, i.e. too many lines.

Sometimes students aren't sure whether to join the data points with a line or a curve. A simple rule of thumb is that if the points for the graph when joined together look like a curve, then draw a curve. If the points form a line, connect the points to form a line. If points are scattered you can draw a line of best fit (see Scattergrams, below).

Frequency distributions (frequency histograms and frequency polygons)

These are rather more sophisticated graphs that are often confused with bar charts. They are used exclusively with continuous data. The data is grouped into what are termed class intervals, where the number or frequency of values falling into each class is found. In order to produce a frequency distribution, the raw data requires some manipulation prior to entering into a spreadsheet. This involves producing a tally chart (see below) and then entering the class intervals and frequency into a spreadsheet.

Live birth weights of babies born to a random sample of 128 women

Weights (g)	Tally	Frequency
1000–1499		0
1500–1999		0
2000–2499	‖	2
2500–2999	ﷺ ﷺ ‖‖‖	14
3000–3499	ﷺ ﷺ ﷺ ﷺ ﷺ ﷺ ﷺ ﷺ ﷺ ‖	47
3500–3999	ﷺ ﷺ ﷺ ﷺ ﷺ ﷺ ﷺ ﷺ ﷺ	45
4000+	ﷺ ﷺ ﷺ ﷺ	20

▲ Tally chart

Creating the chart is easier on some programs than others, but an IT tutor should be able to help you through any difficulties.

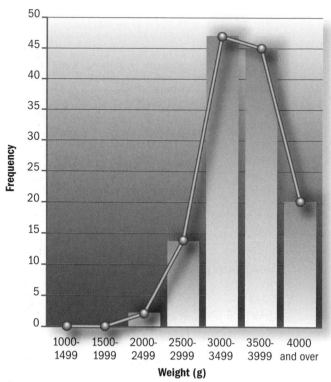

▲ Frequency distribution to show live birth weights of babies born to a random sample of 128 women

If you wish to compare frequency distributions of two or more sets of data, it is preferable to present the frequency distribution as a frequency polygon rather than a frequency histogram. A frequency polygon is simply a line joining the tops of each bar at their mid-points, though it is not necessary to do this when using a spreadsheet as you can simply follow the same instructions as for a line graph.

Scattergrams

Scattergrams are used specifically for displaying the results of correlational studies, i.e. data collected to compare one variable with another. It simply involves plotting the results of one variable against the other as a series of markers. The pattern created by the marks once the scattergram has been completed can indicate whether or not there is a relationship between the two variables. If it appears possible to draw a straight line through the markers then a relationship exists. In a spreadsheet, the computer can draw in the line. This trend line describes either a positive or negative correlation. If positive it shows that as one variable increases so does the other,

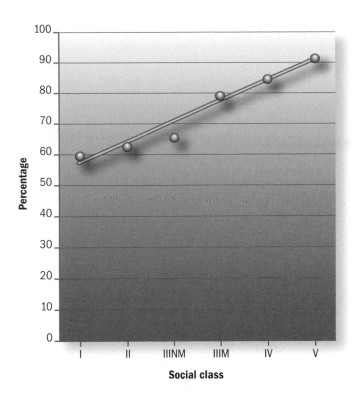

▲ Scattergram to show the relationship between the percentage of mothers who breast-feed and the social class of their partner

for example the higher the social class of the partner, the greater the incidence of breast-feeding (see above). If negative, as one variable increases the other decreases, for example the increase in media attention given to problems associated with vaccination correlates with a decrease in the number of children being vaccinated.

However, just because a correlation exists does not mean that a change in one variable results in a change in the other. For example, did you know that the amount of bananas imported into the UK after the Second World War correlated with an increase in the number of pregnant women! It is possible that the change in both variables is due to some other unrelated factor. Another example is the rise in asthma amongst children during the 1980s and 1990s. It has been found that this increase correlates well with the increasing use of diesel engine motor vehicles. Researchers proposed that this was due to the size of soot particles in vehicle exhausts polluting the air and irritating the lungs. However, there is also a correlation between the increase in rates of asthma and the use of double glazing in homes, central heating and fitted carpets, which encourage the increase in numbers of dust mites that also irritate the lungs. In more recent years, asthma rates amongst children have fallen, the reason for which is as yet unknown! Consequently, don't be tempted to draw a conclusion about a correlation unless it is backed up by the research of others, i.e. your secondary sources.

Mean, median, mode and standard deviation

Apart from graphs, numerical data can also be simplified and made more meaningful by determining the mode, median or mean. These terms describe different forms of averages known as measures of central tendency.

- The mode is the most frequently occurring number in a set.
- The median is simply the middle value in a set of results that have been arranged in ascending or descending order.
- The mean, as you are probably already aware, is calculated from adding up all the values and dividing by the number of values to give the 'average'.

The median is used where the data is discrete and is often used in conjunction with the range (the difference between the lowest and highest values in a set of data) to summarise the data. The range gives a measure of the spread of the data. Whilst this is satisfactory for many circumstances, the range will include extreme values and as a consequence may not be representative of the majority of the data, for example SATS results may include one or two very high or very low scores with the majority clustered around the median. As a result, it may be more appropriate to use the interquartile range covering the middle 50 per cent of the data.

The median and range, or interquartile range, are useful when working with discrete data, but where the data is continuous, the mean and another statistic, the standard deviation, tend to be of more value. This is because the standard deviation, whilst giving an idea of how much the data is spread either side of the mean also excludes extreme values and as a result is more representative of the majority of subjects in the sample. Whilst it is difficult to generalise, the larger the standard deviation, the greater the spread of the data about the mean.

The standard deviation is rather more difficult to calculate than the mean. However, scientific calculators that have statistical functions can determine the standard deviation at the same time as the mean. Alternatively, the standard deviation can be obtained from data entered into a spreadsheet.

The standard deviation and mean can be used to determine whether two sets of data, for example reading test results before and after an intensive reading programme, are *significantly different* from one another. Fortunately for you, the Children's Care, Learning and Development syllabus does not expect you to take your data analysis this far!

Triangulation

Your research may involve the use of a variety of methods, both qualitative and quantitative. It would not seem unreasonable to use the results of one to support or validate the results of another. This process is called triangulation. Researchers or research groups from different organisations who are studying similar subjects and applying similar research methods will use triangulation to compare the results and confirm the validity of their research (see Validity and reliability page 323).

Suppose, for example, you carried out a survey on a mother's experiences of childbirth. You may also have interviewed a small number to obtain more detailed information on these experiences. As such, the results of the interview would tend to confirm the accuracy of the survey results.

It is important to be aware that triangulation may not always confirm the accuracy of results from different methods or even of the same method used by different researchers.

Suppose you were investigating the behaviour of a class of children. You may have chosen to interview the children individually about classroom behaviour and then observed how they actually behaved in the class. The idea of triangulation is that the observation of classroom behaviour would back up the results of the interviews. As I am sure you realise, what children, or adults for that matter, say may not be what they do. Consequently, the interviews may suggest one thing and the observation something else. As such, triangulation would seem to invalidate your results rather than confirm them. The important thing is to recognise this and use triangulation as a way of evaluating your research. Equally, you could have identified that the different methods to be used in your research could produce conflicting results and as such modified the methods so that the results could support each other. In the example given you might ask the children in interview about the behaviour of others in their class rather than about their own behaviour that can be confirmed by the observation. Even here a child may not always say in interview something that is confirmed by observation!

8.5 Evaluate the research

This is perhaps the most skilled part of the research process and, as far as any research project you complete is concerned, tutors use what is produced in this part of a report to confirm decisions regarding the award of higher grades.

It is best to start the discussion with a review of the problem you chose to investigate together with the research question or hypothesis. This sets the scene and also helps to focus your mind on the purpose of the data collection and presentation.

You should then look at your results and summarise what they show. The idea is to highlight those features of your results that are important to your research question or hypothesis, i.e. whether the information supports or refutes the research question or hypothesis. Preparing your report for a presentation is a good way of summarising and picking out the most important features.

In the same way, you need to compare your findings with the information obtained through secondary research. Does this information support your study or contradict it? Differences between your work and those of others may reflect real differences due to the local nature of your research or it may highlight weaknesses in your study. Alternatively, the results may reflect something you hadn't thought of that could lead to the need for further research. In this case, you should attempt to suggest what that research could be.

If your results fail to support your research question or hypothesis, do not be tempted to manipulate them; instead draw on the information provided in the next two sections (Use and misuse of statistics and Validity and reliability) to evaluate the presentation of your data and the research and sampling methods used.

A further way of preparing your discussion is to talk to people who have had some involvement with your research and see if they agree with your conclusions, including your tutor. You could also sit down with someone else on the course and tell them what you have found out. If it makes sense to them then it should make sense on paper. You can do the same for them.

If your research was part of a group project, even better. Whilst you will probably be expected to submit individual reports, you can discuss your findings and help each other to draw relevant conclusions, evaluate and justify your approach to the topic.

If your research was based on interviews with just a few people or a case study, then it can be appropriate to discuss your findings with them. They may offer suggestions for development or identify things you have missed, and any discussion will help to keep them fully informed in line with the ethical requirements for informed consent.

Theory into practice

The following questions are based on the data presented in the section on Dealing with quantitative data (pages 315–20). By answering the questions and referring to the answers (pages 329–30, but see if you can do them on your own to start with), you will begin to see how to extract relevant information and draw appropriate conclusions that contribute to meeting different grading criteria.

1   With reference to the pie chart, what is the percentage of 3–4-year-olds in England, Scotland, Wales and Northern Ireland as a proportion of children in the UK?

2   With reference to the bar chart:
   a)   Which is the most widely available type of day care provision in England and Wales?
   b)   Why do you think there are fewer day care places for under 5-year-olds in out-of-school clubs?

3   Look at the line graph and suggest why there has been a decrease in measles-containing vaccine (MCV) vaccination rates from 1997 to 2003. (Refer to the 'Theory into practice', 'The publication of research and role of the media' on page 323 to help you with your answer.)

4   The trend in the uptake of the MCV vaccinations appears to be reversing since 2003. Why is this statement true and how can this change be explained?

5   With reference to the frequency distribution data on birth weights, which class interval would you expect the majority of babies to fall into?

6   With reference to the scattergram, a line of best fit has been added to show that there is a negative correlation between the proportion of mothers who breast-feed and partner's social class.
   a)   What does this tell you about the relationship between breast-feeding and social class?
   b)   Why do you think social class has a bearing on an activity such as breast-feeding?
   c)   What other aspects of child development could be influenced by the social class of the parent?

Use and misuse of statistics

Statistics provide a valuable tool for presenting and interpreting information so that the results of research are more readily understood. The use and misuse of statistics can arise as a result of problems with different aspects of the research process and not just the presentation and interpretation of the results. Such difficulties include the following:

- *Lack of clarity in the research question or hypothesis*, i.e. being unsure about what you want to find out. If you are unclear about the focus of your study, it can lead to selecting the wrong methods and consequently the production of data or information that is difficult to explain. It may also lead to a misreading of the results in trying to make them fit the hypothesis or research question. For example, you may have chosen to observe the behaviour of young children in a playgroup, but not clarified what sort of behaviour it is you are interested in. In all likelihood you will observe a wide range of behaviours and frequency of such behaviours that may produce too much information to organise and simplify with ease.
- *Use of inappropriate methods* The methods used must allow you to gather information that will support the research question or hypothesis. This means choosing methods that enable you to find out what you want to and that it is reproducible, i.e. Validity and reliability (see page 323).
- *Unrepresentative sampling* Remember that the purpose of sampling is to use people in your research who are representative of the whole population, which relies on obtaining a random sample of subjects. As discussed earlier, this is no easy task and there is often bias within a sample whatever the sampling method chosen. In particular, the most common sampling method used by students is the opportunity sample. As the people chosen are probably following some further education course like you, then the sample is biased towards students and misses out on all other people.
- *Inaccurate recording of information (sloppy techniques)* Failure to construct a questionnaire with

care or to undertake a trial can result in questions being misunderstood and answers being ambiguous. If you are administering a questionnaire as a group, failure for everyone to follow the same procedure can give misleading results. The results of an interview that you haven't prepared for in terms of questioning or recording may bear little resemblance to the actual interview itself and is more open to being biased towards your own views. A poorly prepared observation sheet or failure to conduct an experiment with care and precision will give inaccurate results.

- *Inappropriate presentation or misinterpretation of data* The following example shows how results can be presented in such a way as to change their meaning or to give misleading information. The bar chart below compares the attainment of children at Key Stage 1 in two schools, A and B. You can see that school A appears to be far more effective at

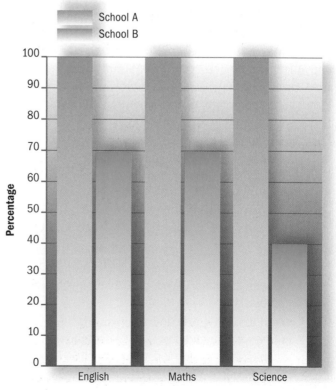

▲ Percentage of children at National Curriculum Level 2 (Key Stage 1) in two schools enabling the children to reach Level 2 of Key Stage 1 than school B. However, what you don't know is that school A is an independent school and school B has three times as many pupils as school A, and the children entering the schools come from different social backgrounds.

Good practice checklist

How to avoid misusing information

- Be clear about what you are trying to find out, i.e. ensure your research is focused.
- Be sure to use the most appropriate method or methods for your study.
- Try to ensure your sample is representative of the population in which you are interested.
- Do not try to use statistical methods in presenting your data to make it fit your research question when it doesn't, i.e. be honest. In using graphs make sure they are accurate.
- Do not misinterpret the data, i.e. don't say something is true when it blatantly isn't or say the results don't show anything when they do. Look carefully at, and use, all the results.
- Do not try to draw conclusions that do not exist. These can become discussion points for further research.

Validity and reliability

You have already met these terms in Unit 3 and earlier in this unit:

- Validity describes whether the results you obtain using a particular method tell you what you want to find out.
- Reliability is to do with the method being reproducible, i.e. if someone else repeated your work, would they get the same answers?

A method may be reliable but not necessarily valid. Whilst some methods are more reliable and others more valid, it is probably true that the level of reliability and validity is dependent upon how carefully the research has been undertaken. This surprisingly comes down to the conscientiousness of the researcher! One way of improving reliability and validity is to use more than one method in your study (see Triangulation, page 320) and you will find in reading many research reports that researchers draw on a range of methods.

Theory into practice

The publication of research and role of the media

The vast majority of published research is only read by those with an interest in the work, for example the commissioners of the research, other researchers and those who may be affected or influenced by the research findings. The media will report research findings if they regard it as being in the public interest. The effect of media interest can be profound, as for example in the case of the MMR vaccine and autism.

Look again at the line graph on page 317. It shows the change in vaccination rates against measles between 1980 and 2005. You will see that there was a steady increase in the percentage of children being vaccinated between 1980 to 1996 from 53 per cent to 92 per cent.

In 1998, research was published that suggested a link between the MMR (measles, mumps and rubella) vaccine and increasing rates of autism in the population. This was widely reported in the media, despite it being the only research at the time suggesting such a link. As a consequence, vaccination rates fell from a peak of 92 per cent and continued to fall to around 80 per cent in 2003 despite research evidence showing there was no risk to children's health and other researchers questioning the validity and reliability of the original work.

Research has continued to be published confirming that there is no link between MMR and autism. The media has reported the results of this research and the government, National Health Service, other public and voluntary groups have sought to persuade the public of the safety and benefits of vaccination. However, the subject continues to be shrouded in controversy, as there are many organisations that still support the findings of the original research and seek to influence the public in spite of research that suggests other factors may be involved in autism and its increase amongst children.

Ethical issues

Before undertaking any primary research that involves questioning, experimenting or observing people, it is important to consider the ethics of conducting the research and any issues of confidentiality that may be raised.

Ethics has been an issue in research ever since the Second World War when the Nazis were found to have submitted individuals to horrific experiments that resulted in death, disfigurement or psychological trauma. The Nuremberg trials that followed the war made researchers aware of the dangers of carrying out experiments on non-consenting subjects and it led to the development of a code of ethics for working with human subjects. Even so, there have been many cases of research carried out since the war that have subjected people to physical and/or psychological pain.

One famous experiment on obedience, carried out during the 1960s by Stanley Milgram, involved allowing participants to administer what they thought were electric shocks to other people they could communicate with but not see. Unknown to the participants, the subjects being 'electrocuted' were actors faking increasing discomfort as 'shocks' were applied. Participants were told that they had to continue applying shocks of increasing voltage even though the person being 'electrocuted' appeared to be in obvious pain. Whilst the experiment proved that people would follow 'orders' irrespective of the suffering they may cause, the justification for such deception of participants was regarded as immoral. Not only had Milgram deceived the participants, but he had attempted to alter their behaviour and used secret recordings to observe them.

Whilst such deception may be unethical, many drug trials rely on this to determine the effects of new drugs. Such trials, known as blind trials, involve two groups of volunteers, one of which receives the drug and the other a placebo (sugar pill). This experimental type of research works on the basis that any effect of the drug will only be seen in the group taking the drug as neither group knows whether they are taking the placebo or the drug under test. It has been found that some drugs have had as much effect on the placebo group as the test group!

Anyone participating in research is now covered by the United Nations Declaration of Human Rights, which is supported by European legislation enshrined in the EU Directive on Data Protection (1995) and in the UK by the Data Protection Act (1998).

Organisations conducting research implement a code of ethics to ensure these rights are protected. Such codes include the need for participants to give their informed consent. This is particularly important where research involving vulnerable groups, such as children, is concerned and should also take into account parental/guardian consent. This means that all involved are fully informed as to the nature and purpose of the research, what will happen, how and where it will take place. It also gives participants or their guardians the right to refuse or to withdraw at any time and ensures that the anonymity of participants is preserved. Many researchers also include the requirement to debrief those involved about the nature of the research and why any deception may have been necessary.

Even when codes of ethics are in place, cases of unethical research practice can still occur and organisations exist to investigate evidence of malpractice and take appropriate action taken where necessary. A recent example of this concerned researchers in a hospital who sought to study the effect of an exclusion diet on children with a food allergy. The research involved two groups of children being given a diet free of the allergen-causing food to determine any benefit. As part of the study, children thought to suffer from the allergy were given the food thought to trigger the allergic response. The researchers regarded the study as a trial and therefore did not seek approval from the hospital trust's ethics committee as would be expected. Subsequently an independent ethics committee that oversees research in the UK concluded that the study amounted to an experiment on children, that it could not be regarded as a trial and therefore required ethical approval. An investigation by the hospital trust where the research took place subsequently tightened its procedures for ethics committee approval.

Good practice checklist

A code of ethics

As far as any research you undertake is concerned you would be unwise to set about a project if it were to cause distress to the people involved as a result of the methods chosen, the sampling process or the reporting of the work. As such you should follow any policies and procedures which the organisation where you are studying has in place for students undertaking research. Such information should be available from your tutor. Alternatively, or in addition, the following code of practice can be followed to ensure your research meets basic ethical codes:

- Gain permission from appropriate authorities (employers, teachers, tutors) to conduct the research. This is important, as you may need their support if any problems occur. Generally, research at this level will be underwritten by your tutors or workplace supervisors due to your inexperience.
- Ask the subjects or, where children are concerned, their parents or guardians, if they wish to take part.
- As a consequence of the first two points, be in a position to explain your research.
- Be able to reassure participants or their parents/ guardians about the measures taken to maintain confidentiality.

Confidentiality

With regard to confidentiality, you must ensure the anonymity of all participants. This involves:

- changing names of subjects, particularly when using interview, observation, experimental and case study methods where the sample size might be small. False names, letters or numbers can be used instead, for example Fred, Miss X, subject 9
- avoiding descriptive language that could give away a person's identity as can occur in case studies, e.g. Mrs Y, the leader of the local Labour party, does give the game away a bit! You need to think whether such information is important to your study and if so, how else it can be worded, e.g. subject 8, a local politician
- taking care in conducting taped interviews when transposing the taped interview into a written format to avoid identifying the interviewee. It is important to recognise that the interviewee has the right to request that all or part of the tape is erased or destroyed at any time, and in any case the tapes should be erased once you have completed your work.

Another issue concerns what you may find out as part of your research. When gaining permission to conduct the research, you need to be clear about what you must do in the event of being told or finding out something of a confidential nature. If you find out or suspect that abuse has taken place, you need to know what your responsibilities are and to whom you should refer.

Case study: Ethical issues

From 1946 to 1956, nineteen boys with learning difficulties at the Fernald Waltham State Residential School, Massachusetts (USA) were fed radioactive iron and calcium in their breakfast cereal. The goal of the study was to gather information about nutrition and metabolism. The parents, who consented to the study, were not told about the radioactive substances.

1 This research provides an interesting topic for group discussion as it raises a number of issues that should be taken into account when planning any research project that involves vulnerable groups.

2 Alternatively, ask yourself the following questions about this research:

a) Is research dating back some 50 years relevant in modern society?

b) Would it have been more ethical for the research to be carried out on children without learning difficulties?

c) Should the research have been conducted if the parents had been fully informed?

d) If it were known that the radioactive iron and calcium were harmless would this have made any difference to whether the research was carried out?

These responsibilities should also form part of the information given to potential participants before the research is carried out.

Authenticity (plagiarism and summarising information)

When a piece of research is made available to the commissioners and/or public, it is expected that the person or persons undertaking such research have been honest and open about the research undertaken, information and data gathered and its presentation. The misuse of any secondary information used is generally a result of plagiarism, i.e. the direct copying of someone else's work, which is against copyright law. However, copyright does allow for other work to be used for research purposes as long as the original author is acknowledged.

The use of secondary information means that the researcher, and this includes anything you produce for assessment that uses other people's work, must produce a summary of the original. A direct quote can be made where the information contains specific facts or data relating to the study, but the information should be enclosed within inverted commas ('…'). Whether the information has been summarised or a direct quote used, a reference or acknowledgement to the author or producer of the information and its source must be included (see Producing a bibliography below).

With the advent of computers and the internet, plagiarism can be a problem where students cut and paste large chunks of material for inclusion in their work. It has been known for students to copy information from publications and not even take the trouble to remove the original author's name! Teachers and lecturers are becoming more adept at spotting such transgressions and students may be asked to do the whole assignment again. Colleges will also have policies in place that stipulate what should happen if a learner contravenes regulations relating to the copying of others' work.

Good practice checklist

Producing a bibliography (avoiding plagiarism!)
In producing your work you will hopefully have used a range of books, articles and other sources. Since you have summarised or extracted sections from such material for inclusion in your work, it is essential that you acknowledge the producers or providers of this information. Consequently, you need to produce a reference section, bibliography and/or acknowledgements section. Whilst these words can be used to mean the same thing they are used here as follows:

- A reference section is generally used for acknowledging information taken from the original author's work.
- A bibliography or further reading is used for information extracted from more general textbooks where the author(s) has drawn a wide range of material together from different sources.
- An acknowledgements section is to identify and thank those people who have given help or support or have contributed directly to your work by being a subject (remember not to identify anyone for whom confidentiality was promised).

You do not have to use this system and your tutors may prefer everything to be acknowledged within a bibliography only. However, whatever form you use, adopt a style or format for identifying information and material used.

One of the most commonly accepted formats for referencing is known as the Harvard system. Within the body of your report any book/periodical/newspaper report, etc. used must identify the author, the year of publication and the page number(s) referred to, for example:

'New and continuing research shows that the MMR or measles containing vaccine is not linked with the increased rate of autistic spectrum disorders (Szatmari, 2003, pp 173–174).'

If the author's surname is part of the sentence, then the date and page number(s) are sufficient, for example:

'Szatmari (2003, pp 173–174) suggested that new and continuing research shows that the MMR or measles containing vaccine is not linked with the increased rate of autistic spectrum disorders.'

If reference to a table or diagram is made, then the following is appropriate:

'In surveying the extent of extended schools provision in England, Clemens et al. (2005, p. 16, summary table)

showed the type of childcare or activities offered by primary and secondary schools.'

If you have copied or used part of a table or diagram from another source, this must also be acknowledged. This is normally done by identifying the author of the work and year of publication after the title of the table or diagram.

At the end of the assignment the information sources referred to are listed alphabetically by surname. The format depends on the type of resource referred to and is best shown by example as follows. For textbooks:

Meggitt, C. (2006) Child Development: An illustrated guide. 2nd edition. Oxford. Heinemann.

For articles from newspapers/periodicals/magazines:

Szatmarl, P. (2003) The cause of autism spectrum disorders. British Medical Journal, Vol. 326, pp 173–174.

Websites should be referenced in the same way as above with the author, year of publication, title and the website address, rather than the publisher (unless this is known). You should also include the date on which you accessed the site. Sometimes it may not be clear who the author is, in which case use the name of the organisation:

BBC News (2005) 'No link' between MMR and autism, http://news.bbc.co.uk/1/hi/health/4311613.stm. Accessed on 20/09/2005.

Seek advice from tutors with regards to other types of resource you may have referenced.

Some of this may appear rather confusing, but once you have got used to the idea, you will find that it helps in organising and presenting your work in a logical manner.

End of unit assessment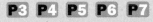

The purpose of this unit has been to prepare you for undertaking your own piece of research that will enable you to meet the majority of the pass grading criteria and to address the criteria for merit and distinction grades in Unit 8.

Careful selection of a project to research could also enable you to meet grading criteria for other units. The following ideas for research projects are offered as suggestions that could fit grading criteria for the units stated as well as those for Unit 8:

- Unit 3, Promoting Children's Development – Undertake a longitudinal study of a baby or young child
- Unit 7, Learning Activities and Play – An observational study of play
- Unit 9, Promoting Healthy Development and Living for Children and their Families or Unit 11, Diet and Nutrition for Children – A survey of nutrition in children
- Unit 14, Psychological Perspectives on Behaviour – Carry out an experimental investigation on Piaget's theory of conservation (see Theory into practice – An experiment to study Piaget's theory of conservation, page 307) or Observation of children's behaviour with the implementation of behavioural strategies.

If you choose to undertake a project that covers grading criteria for more than one unit, it is crucial to

ensure the grading criteria for both units are met.

To be considered for merit and distinction grades within Unit 8, you will need to address the relevant grading criteria (see the grid on page 331). Your ability to justify and review your research, analyse the results and discuss its implications are all features of effective research that can contribute to attaining higher grades. The following sections in Unit 8 of this book can assist you in addressing these criteria:

- Primary research methods, pages 300–09: This section, particularly the good practice checklists and theory into practice sections, can help you review the methods you used by comparing what you did with what is suggested as good practice.
- Discussing and evaluating your results, page 320, including the theory into practice – Analysing quantitative data on page 321: This section shows you how to analyse the results of your research and relate your findings to that of others
- Section 8.6 Implications and ethical issues related to using research, pages 322–27: This section provides information that can help you identify sources of bias or error in your results and consider the ethical implications of your study.

Good practice checklist

Your research project: a step-by-step guide

This checklist takes you through the whole research process as a step-by-step guide referencing back to appropriate sections if you need to check particular aspects of procedure.

1 Find out how much time you have got (see Planning your research, page 311).

2 Select a topic to research (see Planning your research, page 311).

3 Produce your research question or hypothesis (see Planning your research, page 312 and/or The experimental method, page 306).

4 Select the primary research and sampling methods appropriate to your study (see Planning your research, page 313 and refer to Primary research methods, pages 300–09). At this point it is also appropriate to take into account any ethical and confidentiality issues that may arise as a result of carrying out your project (refer to Ethical issues, page 324, the Good practice checklist – A code of ethics, page 325 and Confidentiality, page 325).

5 Identify what resources you will require to complete your study. Do you need specialist equipment? Where will you get such equipment? Will there be a charge and how long can you have it for?

6 Produce an action plan that identifies your research topic, research question or hypothesis, the research methods to be used, any ethical/confidentiality issues you have identified, any resources required and an approximate time allocation for each section. Submit this to your tutor for approval. The action plan can act as evidence of meeting specific grading criteria so make sure you have provided sufficient detail. This is also an opportunity for you or your tutor to consider any issues there could be with your study.

7 Conduct a pilot study of any survey you have planned (see Planning your research, page 313).

8 Continue reading around the subject, making notes that provide background information and that support or refute your research question or hypothesis (refer to Secondary research, page 296).

9 Draft an introduction and have it checked by your tutor. This is another opportunity to identify and address any issues that could arise with your chosen subject. Your introduction should provide the background to your study based on information you have gleaned from secondary research as well as your research question, the methods you are going to use and any ethical and confidentiality issues that need to be addressed.

10 Carry out the primary research (refer back to Primary research methods, particularly the good practice checklists or theory into practice sections on pages 302–07). Be prepared to answer questions that people may have about your research and, if they were actively involved, remember to thank them at the end.

11 Collate and present the results (refer to section 8.4 Conduct and present research information, pages 314–21).

12 Analyse, discuss and evaluate your research (see section 8.5 Evaluate the research pages 320–21).

13 Make recommendations for practitioners/users/policy makers.

14 The analysis, discussion, evaluation and recommendations can be presented after the results as a discussion section that will complete your assignment ready for submission.

15 Submit your assignment for assessment!

Finally, you may be asked to present the findings of your research to your peer group or others as part of the assessment process. You will not be alone in dreading this part of the project and may be unsure about what you should put into the presentation and what to leave out. A good way of tackling this is to produce a summary of your work. This is a paragraph or two of 100–200 words that states the:

- purpose of your research, the research question or hypothesis
- methods chosen
- most significant results that either support or refute your research
- conclusions drawn together with any implications and suggestions for further work.

The abstract can then be the basis for your presentation, which can be expanded on with references to:

- aspects of secondary research
- interesting parts of the data collection process (the interview that went wrong!)
- tables, diagrams and charts that display quantitative findings to good effect
- acknowledgements of the people who took part.

References and further reading

Bell, J. (2005) *Doing Your Research Project*, 4th edition, Buckingham: Open University Press

Blaxter, L., Hughes, C. and Tight, M. (2001) *How to Research*, 2nd edition, Buckingham: Open University Press

Hucker, K. (2001), *Research Methods in Health, Care and Early Years* (Professional Development Series), Oxford: Heinemann

MacNaughton, G. *et al.* (2001), *Doing Early Childhood Research: theory and practice*, Maidenhead: Open University Press

Meggitt, C. (2006) *Child Development: an illustrated guide*, 2nd edition, Oxford: Heinemann

Owen, D. and Davis, M. (1998) *Help With Your Project: a guide for students of health care,* 2nd edition, London: Singular Publishing

Peterson, R.A. (2000) *Constructing Effective Questionnaires*, London: Sage

Robert-Holmes, G. (2005) *Doing Your Early Years Research Project: a step by step guide*, London: Paul Chapman

Sylva, K. *et al.* (2004) *The Effective Provision of Pre-School Education (EPPE) Project*, Institute of Education, University of London

Szatmari, P. (2003) 'The cause of autism spectrum disorders', *British Medical Journal*, Vol. 326, pp 173–4

Answers

■ Theory into practice, page 302

- Category = question 1; rank = question 6; scale = question 7
- Combine all the questions together as a small table so respondents can tick a box or put relevant information into it.
- Question 3 does not allow respondents to say if they breast- and bottle-fed babies. Question 4 does not include bottle-fed babies. Question 6 contains a negative statement about breast-feeding and there is an imbalance between the number of statements for breast- and bottle-feeding.
- Why would you need to know about different types of infant formula when the survey is about breast- versus bottle-feeding?

■ Case study, page 310

Possible answers:

- Change the research question to exclude males.
- Visit more than one supermarket and try different times – the supermarket manager may have been able to tell Andrea and Mahesh the most likely times that men or at least couples shop for baby products.
- Change the research question to one that examines the differences between the shopping habits of men and women when buying baby products.

■ Theory into practice, page 321

1 This is a simple descriptive question that would be the minimum expected of a level 3 learner:

England	86.3%
Scotland	7.3%
Northern Ireland	2.4%
Wales	4.0%

2 These two questions are asking you to think a little bit more about the data. The first is still descriptive, but focuses on the largest value in the data set (it could equally have focused on the lowest value). The second is asking you to explain the reason why one piece of the data is different from the others and requires you to have some background knowledge or to have done background reading (secondary research). You should be able to do the same for any research you undertake.

   a) Playgroups

   b) Out-of-school provision is not offered by all schools.

3 This question is similar to 2b in that you are being asked to draw conclusions about the data from information presented and from secondary research information available in the case study. It can be answered fairly simply as: 'Parents are concerned about the apparent link between

the MMR vaccine and autism.'

If you wish to be considered for merit/distinction grades, you would need to answer the question more fully and refer to secondary research information as in the answer to the next question.

4   The answer to this question provides the opportunity to meet merit/distinction criteria since it is asking you to analyse the information and discuss its implications. You should begin to think about including references to background reading you have done that support or refute the information you have found out, as shown in this answer. It is reasonable to draw conclusions of your own based on qualitative as well as quantitative data you have gathered.

'New and continuing research shows that the MMR or measles-containing vaccine is not linked with the increased rate of autistic spectrum disorders (Szatmari, 2003 – *this is just one of many references on this subject and is presented here as an example*). The media have also reported on such research (BBC News, 2005) giving health practitioners evidence to present to parents that may persuade them to allow their children to be vaccinated.'

The last statement can be regarded as your own logical conclusion of what might have resulted from the new research and press coverage and can be regarded as a realistic and reasonable conclusion to draw. In some cases it may be possible to provide additional evidence that supports this statement including evidence from your own research. For example, if you had been investigating this subject you may have chosen to do a survey of parents asking them about their views on immunisation including a question on what influenced them to have their child vaccinated. From the responses obtained it may be possible to state that: a number of respondents to the question on what influenced parents to have their child vaccinated stated that their doctor/health visitor had assured them that research showed there was no link between the MMR vaccine and autism.

5   This is a pure data analysis question, but can lead into more in-depth discussion about the subject. The answer is 3000–3499 g as the greatest number of babies are born with birth weights in this class interval, but you could go on to say that almost as many are born with a birth weight between 3500 g and 3999 g. As such the majority of babies are born with birth weights between 3000 g and 3999 g. As a simple descriptive exercise this meets pass criteria and you would be expected to discuss the reasons for babies being born with higher or lower than average birth weight in order to gain merit grades.

6   Your answers to these questions can be influenced by your own attitudes and values and it can be easy to make assumptions. It is important, therefore, for you to be non-judgemental and to give answers based on factual evidence. This means you should back up your answer with reference to information obtained through secondary research.

a)   This question is asking more than it first appears. Whilst you could make the obvious statement that women from social class I breast-feed more than class II and class II more than class IIINM, you should really give an explanation of what social class is and what makes each social class group different in order to justify your answer. The social class definition used to produce the scattergram is based on a person's occupation (see the Registrar-General's social class index , Unit 6, page 217).

It may be appropriate to suggest that women whose partners work in professional and more skilled occupations will be more likely to breast-feed than women whose partners work in low or unskilled occupations.

b)   The answer to this question could become quite detailed as you can take the opportunity to discuss a whole range of reasons why women whose partners work in professional and higher skilled occupations are more likely to breast-feed. For instance you could explore the possibility that people from professional and higher skilled occupations have generally undertaken further and possibly higher education which may help them understand the benefits of breast-feeding.

c)   Other aspects of child development that could be affected by social class could be explored through an information search or literary review (see Assessment activity 8.1, page 295). A search on Ask.com for 'how does social class affect child development' produced over 18,000 results. You would only need to explore two or three of these sites to demonstrate that you had analysed the question.

Grading criteria	Assessment activity	Page number
To achieve a pass grade the evidence must show that the learner is able to:		
P1 explain the purpose and role of research for the children's care, learning and development sector	8.1	295
P2 describe the key elements of research methodologies	8.2	311
P3 identify and plan a research topic and carry out a literature search	8.3 End of unit assessment	314
P4 carry out the primary research and collect appropriate data	End of unit assessment	327
P5 present and report findings in a relevant format, identifying sources of bias or error	End of unit assessment	327
P6 discuss the findings of the research in relation to the original hypothesis	End of unit assessment	327
P7 outline any possible improvements to the research, referring to any relevant implications and ethical issues	End of unit assessment	327
To achieve a merit grade the evidence must show that, in addition to the pass criteria, the learner is able to:		
M1 justify the choice of topic and hypothesis	End of unit assessment	327
M2 review the research methods chosen in relation to the results obtained, any sources of bias or error and ethical considerations	End of unit assessment	327
M3 analyse the findings of the research in relation to the original hypothesis	End of unit assessment	327
M4 discuss the possible implications that the research results may have on current practice	End of unit assessment	327
To achieve a distinction grade the evidence must show that, in addition to the pass and merit criteria, the learner is able to:		
D1 discuss how the methodology of the research project could be altered to reduce bias and error	End of unit assessment	327
D2 analyse the purpose and role of research in the sector, drawing on the piece of research undertaken	End of unit assessment	327

Promoting healthy development and living for children and their families

Introduction

This unit enables you to develop your knowledge and understanding gained in Unit 3, Promoting Children's Development. You will study factors which affect the healthy development of children and also their families.

You will consider how healthy development involves gaining skills and competencies in order to maximise potential, thus extending life expectancy. In order to understand why this is more complex than it seems, you will research the factors which influence healthy development such as age, gender and abilities.

One of the key contributors to healthy development and living is diet. People's needs and the importance of criteria, such as government guidelines, are considered. A very important part of being able to promote a healthy diet is to understand the role different nutrients play in the body, which foods are good sources of these nutrients and what happens if we eat too little or too much of the foods containing them. Having studied nutrients, you will be ready to learn how to produce a balanced diet.

Finally, you will apply the knowledge of healthy diets and factors affecting healthy development and living to show how to maximise opportunities to promote health for all the family.

What you need to learn

- Factors which affect the health and physical development of children
- Nutritional needs
- How to maximise opportunities for promoting healthy living to children and their families

Thinking points

Parents are concerned that their children develop healthily, have a healthy lifestyle and progress to reach their full potential. In order to do this, parents need to understand about healthy living.

Nina manages a nursery in a very diverse area where children come from families who have a wide range of incomes, ethnic backgrounds and varied approaches to health. As an early years professional, she is in a unique position to promote both children's healthy development and to influence family lifestyles. Families who place their child in her care are eager to support the standards of the nursery by putting into practice some of these standards at home.

Nina takes every opportunity to promote healthy living and to understand what affects the healthy development of the children and families who use the nursery. She is sensitive to the different influences and situations which may affect the children reaching their potential. She is aware of the increasing concern about the nation's diet.

- How can Nina establish healthy attitudes towards eating through the meals provided in the nursery?
- How can she maximise the opportunities to raise health awareness among the children and so influence their families to prioritise healthy development and healthy living?

Healthy development and living

The majority of parents are very concerned that their children:

- develop healthily
- live a healthy lifestyle
- meet their full potential.

Meeting potential

Much research has enabled health professionals to monitor children's healthy development against accepted norms. Pioneering work, by such people as Mary Sheridan, has resulted in the charting of milestones to be expected for most children. Health professionals have a range of data, including centile charts, that they use to check that a child is showing healthy developmental progress. Much attention is paid by parents to physical development, such as when the child crawls or walks. However, a child's social, emotional and cognitive development are equally important as the child's development must be seen holistically (see Unit 3).

A programme of developmental checks takes place throughout childhood. The aim of the monitoring service is to enable each child to reach their individual potential. This reflects the UK government's policy, Every Child Matters. When a child's developmental progress gives cause for concern, there is a range of health professionals and services available to support the child's needs.

A healthy living pattern will support a child in achieving their full potential. Every child is different so the potential for one child may be very different for another. For instance, within a family you may have one child who has an exceptional musical talent and so will be able to play complex musical scores at a very early age but, perhaps, has poor sporting skills and, consequently, neither enjoys nor succeeds at ball games. However, his sister may have a highly developed ability to control a football but has no interest in playing a musical instrument and has no natural ability to achieve in this field.

Gaining skills and competence

A newborn baby is very dependent on others. He or she has to progress through an important period of transition from being highly dependent to being autonomous, especially in relation to their care and attitudes as well as their behaviour concerning their own health. In order to do this, they have to develop a wide range of skills and competencies. These include physical, social, emotional, cognitive and language skills and competences, as shown in the diagram (right).

For further information about growth and development, see Unit 3, Promoting Children's Development.

Ways of life to bring about good health

In order for a child to develop healthily, a pattern of living has to be established to promote health. The foundations for this pattern are laid down in the home and reinforced by health professionals, at school and by others. Healthy living involves children:

- being part of a loving, caring and stable relationship with others, especially adults
- having their basic physical needs met, such as a healthy diet, an opportunity to be physically active and a hygienic living environment which provides warmth, security and shelter
- being protected from disease, encouraged to develop good personal hygiene, having their health monitored, being cared for when ill and any appropriate health needs attended to
- having an opportunity to develop socially
- having their intellectual needs met through stimulation and through access to education
- being given the opportunity to maximise their potential for a full and rewarding life, taking into account their state of health and any disability.

As they grow older, children can learn more about healthy living through the wide range of information available to them, including internet websites. They can extend their skills, such as their competence to use the internet, reading

Language development
The ability to use and understand language extends children's worlds. They can learn more about their own bodies and healthy lifestyles, and are able to engage in a wider range of social and emotional experiences. Thus they become more autonomous in their own healthy development.

Emotional development
Secure relationships give children confident independence. They have to learn to manage their emotions in order to be accepted by social groups and society. A positive self-concept and self-esteem promotes stable mental health.

Social development
The child needs to build relationships, socialise successfully and understand the norms in their society. Social competence promotes the child's autonomy and healthy lifestyles.

Cognitive development
Problem-solving and developing their own ideas helps children to be able to deal with the complex issues that will confront them during their lives. As their cognitive development advances, they are able to promote their own physical and mental health.

Skills and competencies for healthy development

Physical development
The child needs to develop gross and fine motor skills in order to participate in activities exploring their immediate world. This promotes all the other areas of development and has benefits for mental health by promoting self-esteem.

ability, practical food preparation skills and physical skills to promote their health. The awareness of health is fundamental in promoting health. The understanding of causes of ill-health and how to improve health is essential in making decisions about healthy living.

As children mature they will need to accept responsibility for improving and/or maintaining their own health. They will need to adopt a pro-active partnership with health professionals. For example, before leaving for a gap year travelling around the world, they will need to have the correct range of vaccinations for the countries they intend to visit so they can, hopefully, remain healthy during their trip.

Life expectancy

Healthy living will also assist in extending life expectancy. For instance, in the nineteenth century many people had inadequate diets and very poor, unhygienic living environments. Infant mortality was high. Most families had a large number of children but did not expect all of them to reach maturity.

Infant mortality in the twenty-first century in the Western world is low and all parents expect their children to celebrate their eighteenth birthday and so reach adulthood.

The graph below shows that life expectancy has extended over recent years. Females continue to have a longer life expectancy than males. However, life expectancy for men has been rising faster than for women. Most notable is the gap between life expectancy and the number of years of poor health at the end of life.

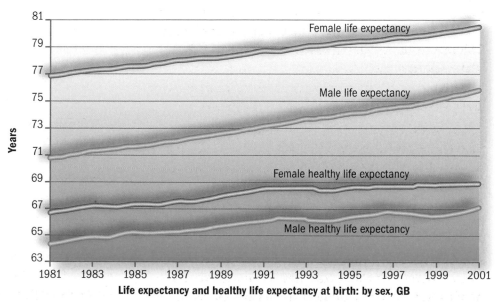

Life expectancy and healthy life expectancy at birth: by sex, GB

▲ Life expectancy

Source: National Statistics Online: www.statistiscs.gov.uk

Theory into practice

Study the graph on the previous page.

- What is the difference between life expectancy for males in 1981 and in 2001?
- What is the difference between life expectancy for females in 1981 and 2001?
- Discuss these changes in life expectancy with older members of your family and suggest how you might account for these differences.
- For how many years might a man expect to be in poor health at the end of his life?
- For how many years might a woman expect to be in poor health at the end of her life?

Key term

Good health Positive social and mental health and the absence of disease.

Factors which affect healthy living and development

Before we consider healthy living and development, we need to think about what is **good health**?

The World Health Organization describes good health as 'not merely the absence of disease; it is also a reflection of the social and mental well-being of people in a community' (Howard, 2002).

So in order to improve health, not only has disease to be reduced, but also there has to be a reduction of environmental social tensions and the incidence of mental ill-health.

Individual health and development needs

Age

■ Babies, young children and adolescents

It is estimated that between 2.4 and 3.4 million children are currently living in poverty in the UK. Where poverty exists, health and development are likely to be below the level for the rest of society.

The effects of poverty on children include:

- a reduced life expectancy at birth
- an increased risk of infant mortality
- a greater likelihood of living in temporary housing which may not have high standards, such as heating or cooking facilities
- poor physical, social and emotional development because the challenge to meet essential needs, such as warmth, getting enough food, etc. means that parents have less opportunity to support children in developing skills in emotional and social areas
- difficulty achieving or maintaining a satisfactory standard of personal hygiene so putting health at risk
- employment disadvantage as children living in poverty often leave school with the least qualifications, frequently because their parents may be struggling to provide for their family and so may not be able to encourage their children's academic progress
- a cycle of deprivation which results in the next generation subsequently living in poverty.

Some groups of children and young people have greater health and development risks. These include:

- looked-after children, such as children in care. Many of these children have a low rate of educational achievement which has implications for their future health and well-being – again, children whose social and emotional needs are not always able to be met will struggle to focus on academic or other developmental needs
- children in need of protection, previously known as children at risk, which includes children who have been abused which can affect their development especially physical, social and emotional
- children of travellers. They are often not involved in health screening and protection programmes because travelling families are not able to offer their children the opportunity for continuing attendance at a particular school, or within a healthcare programme.

The resulting lack of continuity is a contributory factor in determining the lifestyle that these children will be able to enjoy as adults.

- immigrant children, especially those of illegal immigrants. They often do not fully participate in health programmes due to social isolation and cultural factors
- teenage mothers, especially those living on their own. They have greater risks of health problems. Also, there are increased concerns for the development and the health of their babies
- those who are obese or are involved in substance abuse
- teenagers who drink heavily. There is an increasing number of under-age drinkers diagnosed with alcohol poisoning or 'behavioural disorders' due to excessive drinking
- young male teenagers, who are at greater risk of having accidents, especially risks related to car driving
- children whose genetic inheritance results in health conditions which may be disabling, such as cystic fibrosis
- children with disabilities, who are more at risk of bullying which effects their social and emotional development.

Chronic illness

Chronic illness among children affects not only their health, but also their development. Hospitalisation can cause social and emotional isolation and slows their cognitive development.

Role of infection

Infection, such as HIV, is a major health concern. In most childhood cases, HIV is acquired from affected mothers while the baby is still in the womb, or from breast milk. In the past, blood transfusions presented an HIV risk to children, but there are now improved practices within the transfusion services. Children are also at risk from HIV if they are living in situations where adults may be injecting illegal drugs, as the needles used for this are often dirty, thus putting children at risk if they accidentally handle the needles.

Infection can be acquired in other ways, such as through dirty home environments, through contact with others, for example the spread of meningitis among students living in halls of residence. The extensive UK vaccination programme has virtually eradicated some infections, such as diphtheria, from our communities. The effect on health of other forms of infection will depend on the type and nature of the infection. Some infections may have a temporary debilitating effect, such as the common cold, while others, such as meningitis, may result in serious illness or can even be fatal.

Role of immunisation

Immunisation helps to protect children from a range of diseases including diptheria, whooping cough, polio, measles, mumps, rubella and tetanus. The National Health Service organises a national immunisation programme. All children are invited to participate.

Substance abuse by family members

Substance abuse by members of their family may put children's health at risk. If pregnant mothers are involved in substance abuse, this will affect the health of their newborn child. Also, in home environments, where substance abuse is a significant feature of the lifestyle, children may be in need of protection as their welfare may be at risk. Children, especially older children, may start to adopt a similar lifestyle and so put their own health at risk.

Case study: A cycle of deprivation?

Leah, who is 15 years old, enjoys clubbing and drinking alcohol even though she is under age. She is living with her mother and three younger sisters in a bedsit, as they have been made homeless due to not paying the rent. Her mother smokes heavily and often there is little food in the house. Leah thinks she is pregnant as she had unprotected sex when she had too much to drink one night. She cannot remember who the boy was.

1 **What factors may have a significant effect on the developing baby's health and development?**

2 **What factors may have a significant effect on Leah's health and development?**

3 **Explain why this case may be an example of the 'cycle of deprivation'?**

■ Adults

Parents and families

Parents have to cope with their own changing physical, social, cognitive and emotional development as they move through the young adult stage to middle age and into older age.

Having a family can cause problems for some couples who are concerned about any problems arising from their genetic inheritance which they could pass onto their children. Certain rare diseases, such as cystic fibrosis, may be passed on through our genes. Genetic counselling, screening and tests during pregnancy may detect many abnormalities in the foetus before birth. Counselling can be offered to parents when problems are identified to discuss the options available to them which might involve the termination of the pregnancy.

In some families certain diseases appear to be prevalent. Members of such families may have an inherited predisposition for that particular medical condition, such as heart disease. Hence, people with a family history of heart disease need to make a special effort to keep fit, to control their weight and to live a generally healthy lifestyle. However, it may be that these family members have a similar lifestyle which leads to certain conditions.

Many family members may be obese, take little exercise and be heavy smokers and drinkers. All these factors make heart disease more likely.

Working parents may suffer from stress at work, such as adapting to the rapidly developing information technology age and the stress of learning new skills. For instance, 28 million working days were lost due to work-related ill-health in 2004–5.

Family pressures and other concerns, such as marital breakdown and balancing home and work commitments, can affect parental and adult health and well-being. These and other adverse family factors often cause children to have behavioural and emotional problems which further increases parental stress.

Many families living in poverty have one member of the family in work doing low-paid jobs. Hence, such situations give rise to frustration and social isolation which affect health.

It is estimated that over 8 million adults drink more than the recommended maximum units of alcohol per day which can affect the lives of both the parents and the children if emotional tensions arise and physical violence results.

Men, like women, have to adapt to the parent role ▶

Older people

Old age can be a period of enjoyment when older people are released from the pressures of work and raising a family and have the time to explore new activities. However, older people have many transitions to make in their development. As their physical strengthen lessens, mobility may be reduced and their senses are not so effective. They may tend to play a less active role within their family and social group, which affects them socially and emotionally. The death of friends, partners and contacts challenges them to adjust emotionally to their changing world. This affects their physical and mental health. In addition, some older people may suffer from cognitive deterioration, such as dementia.

Gender

- Women during pregnancy and immediately after birth, especially when breast-feeding, have specific health needs.
- During the menopause, women may have complex health needs including physical and emotional needs.
- Men, like women, have to adapt to the parental role and many other pressures as they face the transition to middle age which may affect their self-image and self-esteem.

Ethnic group

The ethnic grouping of the family may affect healthy development. Tensions may arise when one generation adapts differently to the ethnic climate of the environment. For instance, the second generation of immigrants often have a different viewpoint. Certain diseases, such as sickle-cell anaemia, are prevalent among some ethnic groups.

Abilities

Certain impaired abilities may affect children's health and development. For instance, poor hearing can affect cognitive and language ability. Low intellectual functioning, behavioural and emotional disabilities, poor physical health, and impaired physical potential can all restrict healthy development.

Theory into practice

A group of teenagers living in a deprived area are excluded from school for unacceptable behaviour. They are being educated in a special alternative education unit. As part of a citizenship course, they have been given the task of preparing a leaflet entitled: *Healthy Parents*.

- Write the section which explains the factors which may affect the health of their parents.
- Briefly describe the development which their parents undergo during early and mid-adulthood.
- Imagine you are one of the group. Write an action plan for when you become a parent to promote your healthy living in parenthood.

Environment

The environment in which we live includes our physical environment and our social environment. Both have significant influences on the state of our health.

- A clean physical environment helps to reduce the spread of disease. Dirty environments not only encourage the spread of disease but may have an effect on our mental and emotional well-being. Also, industry and traffic can affect health by causing accidents and the pollution of air, water and soil. Atmospheric pollution has given rise to an increase of asthma in children in the UK.
- In social environments, people may be marginalised because of factors such as gender, poverty, ethnicity, religion or other social groupings, including disability and gang allegiance. This may lead to a higher incidence of anxiety, depression and mental ill-health.

Location

Areas of deprivation show increased rates of ill-health. Twice as many men and women get lung cancer in deprived areas compared to affluent areas. Research has highlighted the so called 'north–south divide' in the UK. For instance, life expectancy in the north-east is two years lower than in the south.

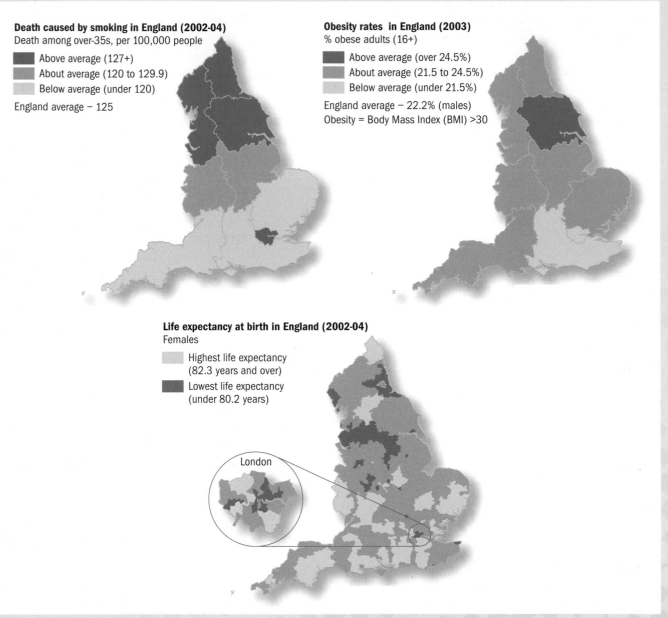

Death caused by smoking in England (2002-04)
Death among over-35s, per 100,000 people

- Above average (127+)
- About average (120 to 129.9)
- Below average (under 120)

England average – 125

Obesity rates in England (2003)
% obese adults (16+)

- Above average (over 24.5%)
- About average (21.5 to 24.5%)
- Below average (under 21.5%)

England average – 22.2% (males)
Obesity = Body Mass Index (BMI) >30

Life expectancy at birth in England (2002-04)
Females

- Highest life expectancy (82.3 years and over)
- Lowest life expectancy (under 80.2 years)

London

Source: Department of Health and Office for National Statistics

▲ **The north–south divide**

Study the maps above.

1 **Identify where you, or someone you know, live within the north or the south.**

2 **List the positive health factors to be found in this area.**

3 **List the adverse health factors to be found in this area.**

4 **Discuss these results with your group.**

5 **Suggest why these health factors are a feature of the local area.**

Extension activity

Look up your local community health profile on the internet at: www.communityhealthprofiles.gov.uk. This will give you more details of the health status of your area.

1 If you are asked to plan a health promotion activity in your work placement, which feature of this profile may be relevant in your choice of activity?

2 Briefly outline an activity which might be relevant in this situation.

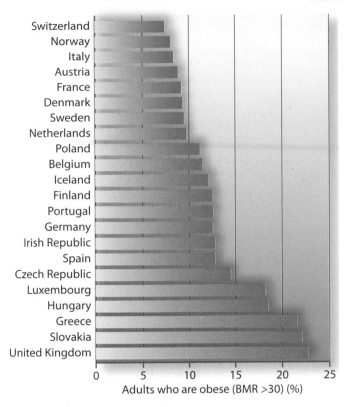

Source: *The Times*, 11 October 2006

▲ Adult obesity in EU countries, 2002–03

National guidelines on healthy eating and nutrition

Following nutritional guidelines promotes health and development, especially among children. The government advises us to:

- enjoy our food
- eat a variety of different foods
- eat the right amount to be a healthy weight and be active
- eat plenty of foods rich in starch and fibre (NSP), for example bread, cereals, rice, pasta, potatoes
- eat plenty of fruits and vegetables, i.e. five portions per day
- eat more fish – at least two portions a week including one of oily fish
- drink plenty of water
- cut down on saturated fat and sugar, for example butter and lard, cakes and biscuits, pastry
- not to have sugary drinks too often
- eat less salt – no more than 6 g per day for adults
- not to skip breakfast – this gives us energy and some vitamins and minerals at the start of the day.

Food and drink need to be selected carefully to meet nutritional needs and avoid obesity. The Food Standards Agency has warned that British people eat the worst food in Europe. Britain is regarded as the fattest nation in Europe. It has been estimated that bad diet kills 60,000 people each year in the UK. Levels of obesity have risen dramatically in the last 20 years. By 2010, a fifth of

all children and a third of all adults are likely to be obese. This will inevitably affect their health not only now but, also, in the future with death rates from heart disease, stroke and related illnesses rising even further and life expectancy falling.

A recent survey by the Food Standards Agency showed that half of all of Europe's ready-meals are consumed in the UK and that only half of UK households cook using fresh or raw ingredients every day.

Also of concern is the high intake of salt in our diets, with 75 per cent of our salt intake coming from processed food. The proportion of people in England eating five portions of fruit and vegetables a day is low. (*Health Profile of England*, DOH, 2006)

There is an increasing number of people who have special dietary requirements (see page 346), especially with the rise of the incidence of diabetes.

Healthy eating guidelines should be applied with caution to children. A low-fat/high-fibre diet would prevent a child obtaining the energy and

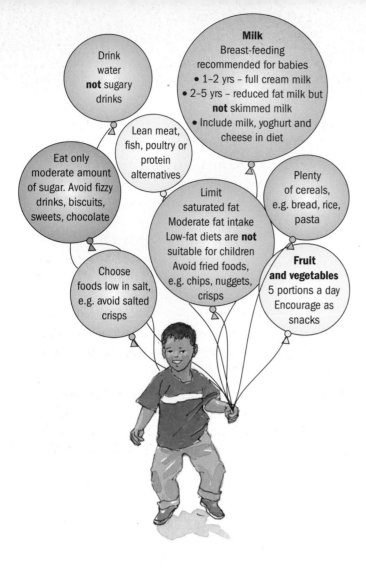

Milk
Breast-feeding recommended for babies
• 1–2 yrs – full cream milk
• 2–5 yrs – reduced fat milk but **not** skimmed milk
• Include milk, yoghurt and cheese in diet

Drink water **not** sugary drinks

Lean meat, fish, poultry or protein alternatives

Eat only moderate amount of sugar. Avoid fizzy drinks, biscuits, sweets, chocolate

Limit saturated fat
Moderate fat intake
Low-fat diets are **not** suitable for children
Avoid fried foods, e.g. chips, nuggets, crisps

Plenty of cereals, e.g. bread, rice, pasta

Choose foods low in salt, e.g. avoid salted crisps

Fruit and vegetables
5 portions a day
Encourage as snacks

▲ Appropriate and inappropriate foods for children

nutrients they need. However, a diet which is low in salt and sugar is advisable as it develops good eating habits and prevents a child getting used to sugary foods which can lead to tooth decay. The diagram above summarises appropriate and inappropriate foods for children.

For more about diet, see section 9.2 and Unit 11.

Key term

Nutrients are components in food which enable the food to produce energy, provide material for growth, repair of the body or reproduction, undertake vital chemical reactions to regulate the production of energy or the processes of growth and repair.

The importance of physical activity has long been recognised and it is one of the six curriculum areas of the Foundation Stage. Both indoor and outdoor activities are needed to promote the development of gross and fine motor skills as well as manipulative skills, balance and co-ordination. However, obesity among children and their inactive lifestyles are giving cause for concern. Children can spend too much time watching television and playing on computers. Some parents in urban areas are worried for their children's safety when they play outside. There is an increasing need for well-designed and maintained places to play. This is because there has been a decrease in the amount of public space and children's play areas over the last 25 years.

Physical activity programmes in schools and elsewhere prepare children to appreciate the need to rest after physical activity. Hence many nursery schools plan a restful activity such as quiet reading/looking at books after the physical activity session.

Assessment activity 9.1

Look back at the Case study: Regional differences in health on page 340.

1 Outline the factors which are affecting the health and physical development of children in your area.

2 What other factors may affect the health and physical development of children generally in the UK? **P1**

Needs

Different members of a family have different nutritional needs. Their needs will depend on such factors as their age, gender, level of exercise undertaken, their occupation, whether sedentary or active, body size (for example, heavy people use up more energy for maintenance), height and build, and their personal life stage or situation.

The body's **basal metabolic rate (BMR)** influences nutritional needs. BMR is higher in relation to body size in infants and growing children than in adults.

Key term

The **basal metabolic rate (BMR)** is the number of calories needed by the body when resting in order to breathe, for the heart to beat, for body temperature to be maintained and for other involuntary activities, including brain function to occur.

Nutritional needs according to gender

Until puberty, children need the same energy intake regardless of whether they are male or female. As they get older, into adolescence, boys need more energy intake than girls because they are physically larger and, therefore, their BMR is higher.

After the adolescent stage, the needs are proportional to the amount of lean tissue in the body. Therefore, women tend to have a lower BMR than men because they are usually lighter and because they have a lower proportion of muscle in their overall body weight. The BMR in older people is lower because there is less lean tissue.

Nutritional needs according to activity level

Active children who take part in a lot of energy-demanding activities such as sports like football, hockey or swimming, require high levels of energy. Some children are not very active and lead lifestyles which

would be classed as sedentary and therefore do not require as much energy.

- If you lead a sedentary life, perhaps work as a computer programmer and watch television most nights, you will need the calories for your BMR plus 30 per cent more.
- If you have a moderately active life, perhaps work as a sales assistant and go for a swim two nights a week, you will need the calories for your BMR plus 50 per cent.
- If you lead a very active life, perhaps you are a nurse, cycle to and from work as well as teaching aerobic dancing twice a week, you will need the calories for your BMR plus 80 per cent.

Regular exercise can burn up more calories than you consume if you eat very little. In this case, you would lose weight. However, different types of exercise use up different amounts of calories (see the examples in the table below).

▼ Examples of calories used in exercise

Activity	Calories used per minute
Average jogging	6.5
Dancing	4.5
Swimming	5.0
Walking moderately quickly	3.5

Together with an appropriate and adequate diet, exercise is essential for healthy living. The level of exercise undertaken may influence the energy intake needed in the diet. It will depend on whether the participant wants to maintain body weight or whether the exercise is aimed at losing weight.

Nutritional needs according to age

■ Babies

The nutritional needs of babies are generally met by either breast milk or formula milk. Babies get all their nutrients in the right amount from breast milk as well as immune protection. The baby requires more protein than an adult if considered per unit weight. Milk

▲ Active children require high levels of energy

heat over a large surface area relative to the size of the infant. Babies have a vital need for fluids due to the relatively small amount of water in their bodies. In hot weather or when ill they may need additional fluid to that obtained from milk. Milk generally provides an adequate supply of vitamins. However, human milk is low in vitamin D. The diets of breast-feeding mothers need to have an adequate supply of foods containing vitamin D or they need to take a vitamin D supplement.

In the second half of the first year, growth rate slows but the baby becomes more active as they learn to crawl and then walk at about the age of one year. As body size and activity increases so the energy needs are larger. A child at this stage has as much as four times the energy requirement as an adult when considered per unit of body weight.

▼ Nutritional needs of babies

Nutrients	Needs
Energy	Energy needs are determined primarily by body size and composition, physical activity and the rate of growth. As the child gets older, the energy requirements per unit of body weight decreases although total requirement for energy increases.
Protein	Protein in an infant's diet is used almost entirely to support growth. Two amino acids, histidine and taurine, are essential in the infant's diet for growth of body cells.
Fats	It is difficult to specify how much fat an infant needs. In breast milk, 50 per cent of the energy is provided by fat. Too much fat will remove some calcium and therefore reduce calcium absorption.
Carbohydrates	Carbohydrates supply about 40–50 per cent of energy in an infant's diet. The main carbohydrate in milk is lactose which is broken down into glucose and galactose during digestion.
Minerals	Babies need a wide range of minerals in their diet, in particular calcium and phosphorus for the development of skeleton.
Vitamins	Human and cow's milk provide all the required vitamins in reasonable amounts. Babies will also get vitamin D from sunlight which helps the absorption of calcium and phosphorus.

provides essential protein in the form of amino acids for growth. Adequate, but not excessive feeding, needs to be provided to allow the protein in the milk to be used for growth and not for energy requirements. Fats in breast milk supply 50 per cent of the energy needs. Carbohydrate, in the form of lactose, in breast milk supplies 40 per cent of the energy needs. Milk lacks iron and copper but these are already stored in the baby's liver before birth. Formula milk, which is milk without the immunity factor, can be used instead of breast milk.

Babies have a high BMR due to the large proportion of active lean tissue and the potential for loss of body

▲ **The challenge of weaning**

Weaning is the process of introducing new foods and so adapting the diet to include solid foods. Solid food should not be introduced before 4 months. It is needed because the milk diet cannot sustain some of the nutritional needs of the growing baby. These include the need for more energy, protein, iron, zinc and vitamins A and D. As the baby's stomach is small the foods given must have enough energy content to sustain the baby's needs. The diet should include a variety of foods so all nutritional needs are met. Foods rich in iron and vitamin C are needed to aid the absorption of iron. Milk is still important at this stage to provide protein, calcium and energy as well as some vitamins. It is recommended that breast or formula milk is provided up to the age of one year.

Weaning is discussed in detail in Unit 35, pages 530–33.

■ Young children 1–5 years

The baby experiences a change of diet to one that has 35 per cent fat and plenty of starch, non-starch polysaccharides (fibre) and 11 per cent extrinsic sugars which do not come from milk. These are sugars which are not contained in cells such as those contained within fruit cells. They are free sugars such as sucrose.

Foods should be nutrient-rich since the child's appetite is often small. A good supply of protein is needed for growth as well as food rich in a variety of vitamins and minerals. This is a period of activity so energy requirements are high in proportion to body size.

■ Schoolchildren

There is a steady pattern of growth up to adolescence which is reflected in a gradual need for an increase of nutrients in the diet. Children are very active so need plenty of energy, together with almost as much thiamin (Vitamin B1) as adults. Calcium is laid down for bone growth.

A healthy child should eat a balanced diet which contains all the nutrients they need in the right quantities. When ill, however, children often run high temperatures and have little appetite. Therefore their diet should contain a lot of liquid to quench thirst and prevent dehydration. Once they start to recover, they can be given small amounts of solid foods. Easily digested protein foods are particularly important as are those supplying calcium, iron and vitamins A, B complex and C.

■ Adolescents

Adolescents have higher nutritional needs than any other group. Well-balanced meals are preferable to high fat and sugar snacks. This is a period of growth and appetites are large. A good supply of protein is needed as well as calcium for strong bone formation. Thirty per cent of daily calories should be provided by fat or the diet will become too bulky. Vitamin C should be provided by eating at least five portions of fruit and vegetables. Adolescent girls need a good supply of iron or they may suffer from anaemia.

Adults

The nutritional needs of adults will be dependent upon lifestyle, for example whether someone has a sedentary or active job and lifestyle. Also, body size will influence the body's nutritional needs. Over-nutrition is a greater risk today for adults than under-nutrition. It is advisable for alcohol intake, especially among young adults, to follow government guidelines. Adults need to aim for healthy balanced diets which have:

- high amounts of starchy foods, especially those containing NSP (fibre)
- at least five portions of fruit and vegetables per day
- moderate amounts of protein foods and milk and dairy foods
- small quantities of foods with high concentrations of fat and sugar.

Adult women need a certain amount of body fat for normal fertility and a foetus is threatened if the mother is underweight. Various vitamins and minerals, including folic acid, aid a healthy pregnancy. A good supply of iron is needed to avoid anaemia and to provide the baby with sufficient iron to supply their needs for the first six months of life. Adequate supplies of calcium are needed, especially for women at risk of osteoporosis.

Older adults

The same basic guidelines for a healthy adult diet apply to older adults. However, it is important that nutrient dense foods are eaten since older people may have a lower food intake due to loss of appetite, sensory impairment (especially taste and smell) and, in some cases, a disregard for food due to depression or mental illness.

A good supply of animal protein is needed for body repair, as well as calcium and vitamin D to ensure healthy bones and to avoid decalcification. There is a loss of lean tissue which reduces the metabolic rate and, therefore, reduces the amount of energy required. Vitamins C and A are needed to combat infection and vitamin B group to assist healthy nerves. Iron is important as there is a tendency for anaemia.

Theory into practice

You are planning the meals for a nursery for children from 3 months to 5 years. In addition it has a before- and after-school provision for children aged 5–8 years.

- How might you provide for the babies in the baby room aged 3 months to 1 year?
- Suggest a suitable lunch for the children in the pre-school room aged 3–5 years.
- Suggest a suitable snack for the after-school children to be served when they arrive at 4.00 p.m.

Special dietary requirements

Some people require special diets due to an intolerance to certain foods, while other people require special diets due to medical conditions such as diabetes.

Food intolerances are usually due to a genetic predisposition to an allergic disease. Most food intolerances are caused by just a few foods, such as cow's milk in children, eggs, soya, wheat, peanuts, tree nuts and sesame seeds and lactose intolerance (lactose being a simple sugar found in milk). People who have these allergies need to consider their diet carefully and not only exclude these foods but also find alternative sources for the nutrients that the problem foods contain. For instance, if eggs cannot be eaten, increased protein and iron have to be obtained from other foods, such as red meat. Where diets have to be adapted for health reasons, advice can be obtained from community or hospital-based dieticians.

People may choose to adopt special diets for moral or religious reasons. For instance, vegetarians have conscientious, religious or aesthetic objections to using animal flesh as food. They may decide to follow a strict vegan diet where neither animal flesh nor animal products, such as eggs or butter, are eaten or they may decide to be lacto-vegetarians and not to eat animal flesh but to include dairy products.

Some religions exclude certain foods and follow certain dietary practices, as shown in the table below.

▼ Dietary practices of different religions

Religion	Excluded food	Other practices
Hinduism	Beef	Mostly vegetarian, fish rarely eaten and no alcohol. Period of fasting common
Judaism	Pork	Meat must be kosher. Meat and diary foods must not be eaten or prepared together
Islam	Pork	No shellfish or alcohol. Regular fasting including Ramadan for one month
Rastafarianism	Animal products, except milk	No canned or processed food, no added salt, no coffee or alcohol. Food must be organic
Sikhism	Beef	No alcohol

For more about special dietary requirements, see Unit 11, page 382 (religious practices), page 383 (vegetarian diets) and page 388 (food intolerances).

Government guidelines

The government has provided valuable guidelines to promote healthy eating, as discussed in section 9.1, page 341.

Hygienic preparation

It is important that food is prepared in a hygienic manner to minimise the bacterial content and ensure that food is healthy to eat.

See Unit 11, section 11.3, The principles of food safety, pages 392–98, for detailed information about the hygienic preparation of food.

Theory into practice

Write yourself some rules to follow when you are at your work placement and are asked to help to prepare and serve the children's mid-morning snack.

Encouraging independence

Some people proudly say, 'I can't even boil an egg!' However, it is important that we can feed ourselves adequately so we can be self-reliant and meet our own nutritional needs. Currently, half of all of Europe's ready-meals are consumed in the UK. Often these are expensive as well as being high in fat and sugar.

Interest in food can be promoted from an early age. Pre-school children love to cook and prepare their own snacks. If the food is well-balanced and healthy, this encourages healthy eating and food independence from an early age. Improved school meals have promoted interest in food and have prompted children to be more independent when making food choices.

The National Healthy Schools programme is intended to promote the health and well-being of pupils and staff. Initiatives are being introduced through this programme, and other initiatives, to enable pupils to have opportunities to learn about different types of food in relation to a balanced diet. Also, pupils will be able to prepare and cook meals which show awareness of the need to avoid food high in salt, sugar and fat and to use increased amounts of fruit and vegetables.

As people get older so they find shopping and preparing food more of a challenge. There are support services which enable older people to remain in their own homes and be adequately fed. For instance, there are many organisations which deliver ready-made meals directly to pensioners. The delivery person will help store the meals for them in their freezers. These meals only require microwaving. Luncheon clubs for older people make eating a more pleasurable, social experience and so encourage a greater interest in food.

Macro-nutrients

All food is made up of chemical substances called nutrients.

- **Macro-nutrients** occur in large quantities in the body. The macro-nutrients are carbohydrates, proteins and fats. These are usually measured in grams.
- **Micro-nutrients** occur in small quantities. These are vitamins and minerals and they are in smaller units such as micrograms (1/1,000,000 of a gram).

Key terms

Macro-nutrients are nutrients which occur in large quantities in the body: carbohydrates, proteins and fats.

Micro-nutrients are nutrients which occur in small quantities: vitamins and minerals.

Carbohydrates

There are three major groups of carbohydrates:

- simple carbohydrates – sugars
- complex carbohydrates:
  - starches
  - non-starch polysaccharides (NSPs).

■ Simple carbohydrates

Sugars are sometimes referred to as:

- simple sugars (or monosaccharides)
- double sugars (or disaccharides).

All carbohydrate foods digested in the body are converted to simple sugars which can circulate in the blood as blood sugar. The most common type is glucose, controlled by insulin from the pancreas and found naturally in ripe fruits and in some vegetables. Glucose passes into the bloodstream very quickly and is used in drinks for athletes as well as being a speedy source of energy for invalids. If there is not enough insulin to control the amount of blood sugar, diabetes occurs.

The other common sugars in food are:

- fructose, found naturally in fruits and vegetables, especially honey
- galactose, found as part of the lactose molecule in milk.

Monosaccharides can link together to form double sugars or disaccharides:

> 1 molecule of glucose + 1 molecule of fructose = sucrose (disaccharide or double sugar)

> 1 molecule of glucose + 1 molecule of galactose = lactose (disaccharide or double sugar)

- Sucrose is extracted from sugar beet or sugar cane. By-products of this process are molasses, golden syrup and brown sugar.
- Lactose is present in milk. Most lactose is provided by cows' milk and its products. Many products that contain milk powder or whey, such as milk chocolate, muesli or biscuits will have a lactose content.
- Maltose (malt sugar) is a disaccharide found mainly in sprouting grains such as barley and wheat. This occurs as their starch content is broken down into two glucose units. It is used in the manufacture of beer and may be found in some biscuits, breakfast cereals and malted drinks.

■ Complex carbohydrates

Complex carbohydrates (or polysaccharides) contain many monosaccharide units. Polysaccharides can be:

- 'available', i.e. they can be digested, such as starch
- 'unavailable', i.e. they cannot be digested by humans. They are sometimes called 'dietary fibre' but are more commonly termed non-starch polysaccharides (NSPs).

Starch

Starch is available from plants. Many plants store starch as their main food source, for example potatoes, cereal seeds (such as wheat) and pulses (for example lentils, chick peas). In this form it is indigestible so has to be cooked, usually in the presence of water. The starch grains swell and gelatinise so they are more easy to digest.

- Dextrin is formed from starch during cooking, for example when toasting bread or on the crusty outside of a loaf of bread. This is more easily digested than starch.

- Glycogen's composition is similar to starch but is made only by animals from glucose and not by plants. Small amounts are stored in the liver and muscles as an energy reserve.

Non-starch polysaccharides (NSP)

NSPs include cellulose, which forms the structure of plants, as well as complex non-cellulosic polysaccharides, such as pectins, found in fruit and useful for setting jam. It is generally recognised that a diet rich in NSPs is protective against common diseases such as coronary heart disease and diabetes. Foods rich in NSPs require more chewing and this slows down the process of eating and the passage through the digestive system which aids a more efficient excretion.

■ The function of carbohydrates in the body

- They provide energy. Between 50 and 60 per cent of the energy in the diet should come from carbohydrates. Energy can be measures in kilojoules (kJ) or kilocalories (kcal), commonly referred to as calories. Carbohydrates have an energy value of 4 kilocalories per gram.
- They help digestion and prevent constipation and bowel disease. NSPs cannot be digested by the digestive system but pass into the large intestine where they are fermented by bacteria. They provide bulk to the diet and aid the digestive process. They help the stools remain soft as they help increase the water content and move through the digestive system with ease. This bulk helps encourages peristalsis (the contraction and relaxation of the muscles of the digestive system).

Protein

No life can exist without protein. It is essential in our diet.

Proteins consist of 22 amino acids. They are rather like the number combinations of the Lottery. They can combine into millions of different arrangements along the chain of a protein. The sequence of their combination determines their properties and functions.

Most of the amino acids come from plants. Nitrogen from the soil and air combines with carbon and other substances to form amino acids which the plants then make into proteins. Our source of protein is from plant and animal foods, the animals having eaten plants which contain proteins.

When we eat proteins our bodies break them down into their separate amino acids. We then rebuild them and in some cases new amino acids are formed.

- We can make non-essential amino acids ourselves in our bodies.
- **Essential amino acids** cannot be made by our bodies and must be obtained from food in our diet. (This is why they are called 'essential'.) There are nine essential amino acids.

Foods which contain all the essential amino acids are known as high biological value (HBV) foods. Foods which are sources of protein but do not contain all the essential amino acids are known as low biological value (LBV).

It is very important that we eat plenty of protein foods. If we do not have an adequate amount of protein in our diets, our body's own proteins, which are part of our framework, are broken down to use for repair. At the same time, other functions which are reliant on protein, such as the production of hormones, fail. This can result in ill-health and, even, death.

Mixtures of vegetable proteins, such as baked beans on toast, and a mixture of animal and vegetable proteins, such as bread and cheese, are valuable in combining different amino acids.

Vegetarians need to have a varied intake of proteins in their diet. If they are lacto-vegetarians, they can replace meat and fish with additional milk, cheese and eggs but it will add bulk to the diet. Vegans, who eat no food of animal origin, will need to get their protein from plant sources only. They need to eat a wide variety of plant foods including those from cereals, peas, beans and nuts, in order to get enough protein in their diet.

Key term

Essential amino acids cannot be made by our bodies and can only be obtained from food.

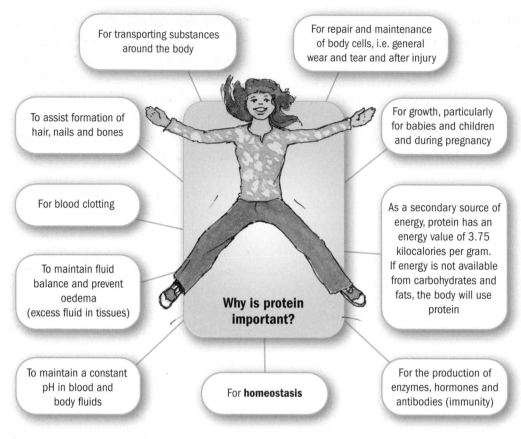

For transporting substances around the body

For repair and maintenance of body cells, i.e. general wear and tear and after injury

To assist formation of hair, nails and bones

For growth, particularly for babies and children and during pregnancy

For blood clotting

As a secondary source of energy, protein has an energy value of 3.75 kilocalories per gram. If energy is not available from carbohydrates and fats, the body will use protein

To maintain fluid balance and prevent oedema (excess fluid in tissues)

Why is protein important?

To maintain a constant pH in blood and body fluids

For **homeostasis**

For the production of enzymes, hormones and antibodies (immunity)

▲ Why protein is important for our bodies

■ Functions of protein in the body

Proteins have a wide range of functions in the body, as shown in the diagram above.

Key term

Homeostasis is the process of maintaining constant physical and chemical conditions within the body despite outside influences.

Fats

It is essential that we eat some fat in order for our bodies to work efficiently. Fats are made up of:

● glycerine
● fatty acids.

All living cells contain some fat in their structure and fatty acids are an essential part of cell walls and intracellular membranes.

Fats generally are needed as they are a concentrated source of energy, containing the highest amount of energy at 9 kilocalories per gram, but too much fat in the diet can contribute to obesity.

Fat can be:

● saturated – contain saturated fatty acids which are the main constituents of hard fats such as butter, lard
● unsaturated – liquid at room temperature, for example olive oil They are divided into:
  – monounsaturated fats
  – polyunsaturated fats.

The 'mono' and 'poly' refer to the chemical composition of the fat.

Essential fatty acids are fatty acids that cannot be synthesised in the body and must be supplied in the diet. Without them, retarded growth and skin conditions such as dermatitis occur. They are essential for our immune systems and for proper brain development.

These essential fatty acids are:

- linoleic acid, also known as an omega n6 fatty acid
- alpha-linolenic fatty acids, also known as an omega n3.

Visible fat is fat that can clearly be seen in the food, for example fat around meat, spreading fats such as butter.

Invisible fat is fat that is not so clearly evident, for example fat in egg yolk, in processed and manufactured foods.

Key term

Essential fatty acids are fatty acids which cannot be synthesised in the body and must be supplied in the diet.

■ The function of fats in the body

- They are the main source of energy for the body.
- They provide the body with warmth as they provide a layer of insulation just under the skin known as the adipose layer which helps reduce heat loss.
- They lubricate food and make it more palatable.
- They protect the vital organs such as the heart, kidneys and lungs from damage as they act as a shock absorber.
- They carry the fat-soluble vitamins A, D, E and K in the bloodstream – without fat, these vitamins cannot be carried in the body.
- They provide essential fatty acids which have a vital role in the formation of cell membranes and nerve tissues.

The table below summarises the sources of macro-nutrients in the diet and the effects of deficiency/excess.

▼ Macro-nutrients: sources in the diet and effects of deficiency/excess

Nutrient	Sources in the diet	Effects of deficiency/excess
Proteins	HBV proteins are from animal sources including meat, fish, eggs, milk and cheese. Soya is also classed as a HBV food as, although it does not naturally contain all the essential amino acids in the correct quantities, it is added during the manufacturing process. LBV proteins include peas, beans and lentils. If two LBV foods are eaten together, one may compensate for the deficiencies in the other, for example beans on toast. This is known as the complementary action of proteins.	Signs of deficiency include: • retarded growth • degeneration of the body cells as worn out cells are not replaced • organ malfunction due to hormone and enzyme deficiency • the body may be more susceptible to disease due to the lack of antibodies.
Fats	Sources of fat in the diet can be divided into four groups: • animal, for example fat on meat, lard, dripping • vegetable, for example olive oil, nut oils • marine, for example fish oils such as cod liver oil or oily fish such as herrings or mackerel • dairy, for example cream, milk, yoghurt. Animal sources are generally saturated fats and therefore should be eaten in moderation. Vegetable and fish sources are usually unsaturated.	Saturated fat contains more cholesterol and is linked with coronary heart disease and obesity. Excess cholesterol is carried in the blood stream by low density lipoproteins (LDLs) and can be laid down in the arteries causing the walls of the arteries to narrow. In some cases, the build up can be such that the artery blocks and prevents the blood flow. It is also possible for blood clots to get stuck in places where the arteries have narrowed, causing the same effect. Both can lead to thrombosis, a stroke or, if in the arteries around the heart, a heart attack.
Carbohydrates	Sugars are found in sugar itself and therefore in sweet foods. It is easily digested and can provide the body with an instant source of energy. Starch is found in cereals, potatoes and flour. As complex carbohydrates, they take longer to breakdown in the body and therefore provide a slow release of energy. NSPs are found in fruit, vegetables (especially beans), wholemeal bread, wholewheat pasta, breakfast cereals.	If carbohydrate is not available to provide energy for the body, the body will use protein for energy rather than growth and repair. Therefore, carbohydrates are known as 'protein sparers'. A lack of carbohydrate may lead to constipation or bowel disease.

Micro-nutrients

Vitamins and minerals are essential for the functioning of the body and our health, although they are only needed in small amounts.

Vitamins

Except for a few exceptions, the body cannot synthesise vitamins and therefore they must be in the diet. However, many vitamins can be synthesised in the laboratory and can be manufactured in bulk. The body cannot tell if a vitamin is synthetic or natural.

Vitamins are divided into two groups according to how they are dissolved and carried in the body:

- fat-soluble – A, D, E and K
- water-soluble – C and B complex.

■ Fat-soluble vitamins

These are found in the fat or oily parts of food, so are not found in foods that contain no fats or oils.

These vitamins are not excreted in the urine, as they are not water-soluble, so can accumulate in the body, especially in the liver and adipose tissue. Large amounts, especially of vitamins A and D, can be harmful. It is therefore important that excessive intakes are avoided. See the following table.

The sun is an important source of vitamin D

▼ Fat-soluble vitamins

Vitamin	Role in diet	Effects of deficiency	Dietary sources
A (Retinol) Retinol is found in foods of animal origin. Carotenes which have red and yellow pigments, found in fruits and vegetables, can be converted by the body into retinol.	Essential in the production of the pigment 'visual purple' needed to see in dim light. It is also needed for: healthy skin and keeping mucus membranes smooth and supple (for example, linings of eyes, vagina, etc.), normal growth of bones and teeth, health of reproductive system. It is thought that it may protect against certain disease processes leading to coronary heart disease and cancer. It assists immunity to infection.	• Causes 70 per cent of childhood blindness in the world. • Poor adaptation to dim light; in severe cases night blindness • Xerophthalmia or dry eye – failure to produce tears, eyes susceptible to infection, for example conjunctivitis • Blindness • Keratomalacia involves the cornea and can result in death • Children are more susceptible to respiratory infections and measles • Bones of skull thicken causing pressure on the brain • Mild anaemia, abnormalities of smell, taste and balance, roughened skin, nerve damage, inability to perspire, reduced resistance to respiratory diseases	*Animal sources* (as retinol): milk and milk products, butter, cheese, liver, kidneys, eggs, fish liver oils, oily fish, for example salmon, mackerel *Vegetable sources* (as carotene): carrots, dark green leafy vegetables, for example broccoli, red peppers, tomatoes, dried apricots, peaches, mango. Vitamin A is added to margarines (a legal requirement)
D	Maintains calcium and phosphorus concentrations for healthy bone formation. Known as the 'sunshine vitamin' because the body can make vitamin D itself through exposure of the skin to sunlight.	• Deficiency in children can cause rickets, with deformed bones too weak to support child's weight • In older people can cause bone softening (osteomalacia) • Asian migrants, premature babies and older people are particularly at risk of deficiency effects • Some evidence suggests deficiency of vitamin D increases risks of diabetes and some forms of cancer	Animal fats (butter), eggs, milk, meat, oily fish, liver, fish liver oils Foods fortified with vitamin D: margarine, infant foods, yoghurts, breakfast cereals Most people in the summer synthesise vitamin D through their skin
E	Essential in maintaining cell membranes, protection against effect of free radicals (unstable compounds that damage body cells), healthy reproductive system, nerves and muscles, protects against degenerative diseases, for example cardiovascular disease and cancer. It is suggested that it plays a role in healthy brain functioning.	• Premature infants may have low levels of vitamin E and may be at risk of anaemia • Oedema (excess fluid in tissues) • Neurological problems, for example loss of muscle co-ordination, impaired vision and speech • An inability to absorb fats	Most foods contain some vitamin E. Richest sources: vegetable oils, nuts and seeds, some cereal products, especially germs of cereals, egg yolk, animal fats, meat, green leafy vegetables
K	Aids clotting of blood	Rarely seen except in newborn babies. Blood fails to clot.	Some obtained through synthesis in the gastrointestinal tract. Green leafy vegetables (such as cabbage), peas, vegetable oils and margarines and foods containing them (for example, cakes), liver, cheese, cereals, fruits

■ Water-soluble vitamins

These are easily destroyed during food preparation involving heating, cooking in water and when exposed to light and air. Up to 75 per cent of vitamin C can be lost during cooking and can also be lost from cells of fruit and vegetables as they are cut and exposed to the air. Fruit and vegetables should be cut as close to the cooking time as possible, cook in as small amount of liquid as possible for the least amount of time and use the cooking liquid in gravy and sauces. Fresh foods eaten raw usually have a higher vitamin C content.

The body is only able to store limited amounts of water-soluble vitamins, with the exception of Vitamin B12. Excess amounts are excreted in the urine.

The vitamins in the B group (or complex) are numerous. The table below considers thiamine, riboflavin, niacin, vitamin B6, folic acid and vitamin B12, plus vitamin C.

▼ Water-soluble vitamins

Vitamin	Role in diet	Effects of deficiency	Dietary sources
Vitamin B1 (Thiamin)	Needed for the steady and continuous release of energy from carbohydrates Needed for growth and functioning of nervous system Maintains muscle tone Promotes a healthy appetite	Deficiency is rare. If foods are highly refined there may be an inadequate intake of thiamin. • Most vulnerable group are alcoholics, often at risk of a form of dementia. • In mild cases, tiredness, loss of appetite, feeling run down • In severe cases beri-beri • Retarded growth in children	Cereals, especially whole grain products. Thiamin contained in outer layers so is lost on milling. So white flour is fortified with thiamin. Many breakfast cereals are enriched with thiamin. Pulses, beans, seeds and nuts, brown rice, lean pork, liver, milk, eggs, fruit, vegetables
Vitamin B2 (Riboflavin)	Promotes growth and aids release of energy from food	• Inflammation of mouth, tongue, skin and eyes causing vision impairment • Check in growth of children • Anaemia may be a result of long-standing deficiency	Milk and milk products, meat, especially liver, eggs, fish, cereals if enriched with vitamin B2, dark green vegetables
Niacin (Nicotinic acid)	Promotes healthy growth and healthy skin, and release of energy from carbohydrates	Pellagra which includes dermatitis, diarrhoea and dementia	Can be converted in the body from the amino acid tryptophan, found in eggs and milk. Meat, especially liver, fish, peanuts, cereals, especially if fortified, milk and milk products, vegetables, especially potatoes
Vitamin B6 (Pyridoxine)	Assists in the digestion and the metabolism of proteins, fats and carbohydrates and glycogen, particularly in the muscles Essential for formation of haemoglobin (red blood cells)	Seldom seen. • Damage to nerves • Dermatitis • Longstanding deficiency – anaemia	Found in small quantities in all animal and plant tissues. Liver, chicken, fish, eggs, milk, wholegrain cereals, meat, including poultry, nuts (peanuts, walnuts), bananas, salmon, green vegetables and potatoes

Vitamin	Role in diet	Effects of deficiency	Dietary sources
Folic acid (Folate)	This is the generic name for a group of substances with related vitamin activity, including the synthetic form of vitamin folic acid. Needed for healthy cell formation, especially in the formation of red blood cells in bone marrow and lining of gastrointestinal tract. Intake is of particular importance at time of conception as it can reduce the risk of neural tube defect affecting the brain or spinal cord.	• Anaemia • Loss of appetite, nausea, diarrhoea or constipation • Inflammation of mouth and tongue Deficiency may occur in pregnancy.	Vegetables, (especially green leafy vegetables such as Brussels sprouts and broccoli, parsnips, beans), liver, fortified cereals, bread and whole wheat, oranges
Vitamin B12 (Cobalamin)	Numerous functions in the body. Essential for the functioning of the cells, from bone marrow to nerves, for healthy red blood cells. It helps to combat fatigue and anaemia.	Deficiencies take many years to develop. Most people have adequate reserves. If deficiency occurs cell division is affected and neurological damage can take place. • Anaemia	Animal foods – meat and fish, milk, eggs and cheese. Not found in vegetables, so vegans need to supplement their diet with specific vitamin supplement or vitamin B12-enriched products. Made from certain bacteria in small intestine.
C (Ascorbic acid)	Helps to develop and maintain healthy connective tissue. There is much evidence to suggest that a high intake of vitamin C is linked with a lower disease risk. It improves the absorption of iron by the body, aids healing of wounds and protects immune system.	• Bleeding from capillaries under the skin and from gums. There is delayed healing of wounds • Scurvy including weakness and fatigue, muscular and bone pains, oedema and depression. There may be roughness of the skin, anaemia and tendency for bone fractures. • Excessively high intakes of vitamin C can lead to diarrhoea in some people.	Fruit (especially oranges blackcurrants, strawberries), vegetables (green peppers, broccoli, cauliflower and Brussels sprouts), potatoes (particularly new potatoes but content declines with storage).

Extension activity

Imagine you are opening a new day nursery.

1 Design a checklist for the catering manager to use to record that the meals planned for the 3–5-year-olds contain vitamins A, B complex, C, D, E and K. This checklist record is to be displayed on the parents' notice board.

2 Identify the most common foods used in the nursery which provide these nutrients. Some foods may provide more than one vitamin.

3 As an example, plan one lunch meal and complete the chart yourself.

Minerals

There are 22 known minerals in the human body, most of which are thought to be essential. Minerals are seldom lost during cooking as they are generally resistant to heat, acid and air. In the table which follows, we consider the main minerals which play an important role in our bodies.

Mineral	Role in diet	Effects of deficiency	Dietary sources
Calcium	Calcium works hand in hand with phosphorus. Causes the hardening of the teeth and bones. Acts as a reserve supply for other needs, for example its role in body fluids. Essential in the contraction of muscles, including the heart muscle, for the functioning of nerves and some enzymes as well as the clotting of blood. Essential component of blood Essential in pregnancy as it is needed for the development of the foetus	• In children a deficiency can result in stunted growth and in rickets. • In adults it can result in osteomalacia (decalcified bones). • Women who have had repeated pregnancies and breast-feed are at risk of osteomalacia. • In older people, bone density decreases causing osteoporosis. The causes are not fully understood but it is preferable for young people under 30 to have plenty of dietary calcium and exercise to assist strong bone development. • High blood pressure	Milk and milk products, cereals and cereal products (but may not be easily absorbed from whole grains), small fish with bones (for example sardines), dried figs and nuts, parsley, watercress, black treacle Also from hard water
Phosphorus	Works in conjunction with calcium. It is the second most abundant mineral in the body. Excess is removed by the kidneys. Contributes to the formation of bones and teeth – it provides the strength Essential component of the blood Necessary for metabolism of energy from foods – component of certain enzymes and hormones	Deficiency is unknown	Phosphorus is present in most animal and vegetable foods. Phosphates are also added to a number of foods during manufacture.
Iron	Associated with the body's use of energy. Essential in the formation of haemoglobin molecules. Haemoglobin transports oxygen from the lungs to the tissues. Without iron the body cells, especially the brain cells, die due to lack of oxygen. Iron is used in enzymes. Iron is important during growth spurts and therefore is particularly needed during adolescence. An increased intake is needed during menstruation to cover the blood lost. Increased amounts are also needed during pregnancy and lactation.	• Iron-deficiency anaemia • Deficiency in the first two years can impair motor and mental development resulting in poor memory, low level of learning and attention span.	Offal (for example, liver), red meat, eggs, oily fish, cereals and cereal products, peas, beans and green vegetables, nuts, dried fruit, cocoa White bread is fortified with iron. The iron in animal sources is known as haeme or ferrous iron as it is the form of iron that is best absorbed by the body. Iron in vegetable sources of iron is known as non-haeme or ferric iron as it is not easily used by the body. The body has to convert the ferric iron to the ferrous state before it can use it. This occurs in the stomach during digestion. Both protein and vitamin C also have to be present for it to occur. Iron absorption can be inhibited by phytic acid which is found in wholegrain cereals. This acid binds with the iron and makes absorption difficult.

Mineral	Role in diet	Effects of deficiency	Dietary sources
Sodium	Body fluids contain sodium chloride (salt) particularly those outside cells such as blood. Sodium chloride is essential for homeostasis Sodium is vital for muscles and nerve activity	• Muscle cramps • Young babies cannot tolerate high sodium levels as their kidneys cannot excrete any excess, so no salt is added to weaning foods. Too much salt can be fatal. • High sodium levels can be linked to high blood pressure	Sodium occurs naturally in food in low amounts. However, processed food has significant amounts added to it.
Potassium	Potassium is found in the fluids of body cells. Regulates sodium–potassium balance in the body Stimulates kidney function and insulin secretion Helps to maintain acid–alkaline balance in the body Helps to convert glucose into glycogen Assists transmission of nerve impulses and contraction of muscles Stimulates mental processes by increasing the blood supply to the brain Higher intakes may counter the effects of sodium and assist in reducing blood pressure	Deficiency is unlikely to occur due to its presence in many foods. • Oedema • Hypertension • Irregular heart beat • Nervousness • Fatigue • Arthritis • Severe deficiency may cause heart failure	Citrus fruit, green leafy vegetables (for example, cabbage), bananas, potatoes, tomatoes, pineapple, dairy products, dried fruit and nuts, chocolate, treacle and meat
Iodine	Essential component of hormones manufactured by the thyroid gland in the neck, including thyroxine. These control the body's metabolic rate	• Lack of energy and obesity. • Goitre – a swelling of the thyroid gland in the neck	Good sources include seafood and seaweed. Iodine can be found in plant foods but the amount depends on the soil in which they are grown and therefore the amount is irregular.
Zinc	Essential for tissue growth Required for enzyme reactions including carbonic anhydrase which is the quick liberation of CO_2 from red blood cells in the lungs as part of respiration Involved in the development of the foetus during pregnancy	Symptoms of deficiency include: • taste impairment • poor immune response • skin problems • hair loss • check in growth or mental development • tiredness. Excess zinc is toxic.	Zinc is a trace element which is found in most foods particularly in association with protein. Good sources include: oysters, kidneys, green vegetables and wholegrain cereals. Less than half the amount of zinc consumed is absorbed and this can be reduced even more if wholegrain cereals are eaten. They are rich in fibre and phytic acid and these combine with the zinc and make it unavailable to the body.

▲ Dietary calcium can help to prevent osteoporosis in later life

Other nutritional needs

Fortified foods

Some foods have nutrients added to them to increase (or fortify) their dietary value. During the Second World War, when food was in short supply and rationed, the government ordered the fortifying of certain foods to protect the health of the nation. Food may be fortified with a variety of nutrients according to a country's nutritional needs or incidence of deficiency. In the UK today, there is no identified nutrient deficiency but the fortification of foods still continues.

Some foods are fortified by law, such as margarine, while others, such as breakfast cereals, are fortified voluntarily. A range of nutrients are added to food, including:

- vitamins A, C, D and a range of B vitamins
- minerals such as iron and calcium
- proteins.

Water

Water is essential for life. About 60 per cent of a young man's body weight is made up of water and approximately 50 per cent of a young woman's body weight. This is due to the average male body having more muscle than is found in female bodies. Muscle tissue holds more water than fat. Without water you will only be able to survive for about 10 days. If the weather is very hot and you are energetic, this time will be radically reduced to even 24 hours. However, if you run out of food, you can survive for several weeks.

Water is a solvent and dissolves other substances. It carries nutrients and other material, such as blood cells around the body.

We need to develop a habit of drinking water regularly. Most schools and colleges now have drinking water facilities. Natural water is preferable to sugary, commercial drinks in cans, bottles or cartons, since these

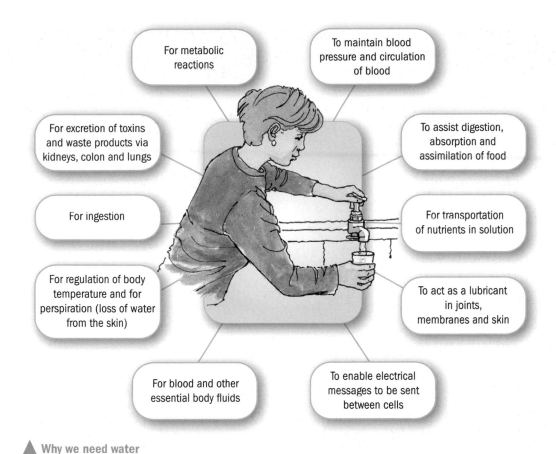

For metabolic reactions

To maintain blood pressure and circulation of blood

For excretion of toxins and waste products via kidneys, colon and lungs

To assist digestion, absorption and assimilation of food

For ingestion

For transportation of nutrients in solution

For regulation of body temperature and for perspiration (loss of water from the skin)

To act as a lubricant in joints, membranes and skin

For blood and other essential body fluids

To enable electrical messages to be sent between cells

▲ Why we need water

usually contain a lot of sugar. Other ways of obtaining water in the diet are through drinking:

- fruit juices, which will also provide some vitamin C
- milk, which also provides protein, calcium, riboflavin, vitamin A, vitamin B12 and potassium. It is advisable to drink milk with reduced fat, for example semi-skimmed. This is particularly important for anyone on a weight reduction programme
- tea and coffee, which provides some stimulants as well as nutritional content from any milk used.

Most adults with a sedentary lifestyle need to drink between 1.2 and 1.5 litres of water per day with a further 1 litre coming from food. However, people engaged in physical activity will need to manage their water intake to ensure they do not delay taking water until they are very thirsty. During the major marathon runs, there is always water on offer along the route for the athletes. In extreme conditions the sweat glands can give off as much as 10 litres per day. Babies can rapidly dehydrate, especially in hot weather or if ill with sickness and diarrhoea. Often older people dehydrate due to

overheating of their homes, depression and, therefore, lack of interest in looking after themselves and lack of mobility to make drinks for themselves.

Fibre

Another essential component of our diet is fibre, or non-starch polysaccharide (NSP). For further information, see page 349.

Concept of a balanced diet

Having learnt about the individual macro- and micro-nutrients, it is important to be able to use the information to provide what we call a 'balanced diet' – a diet in which the energy intake does not exceed the energy output. This means that we eat the correct quantity and proportion of nutrients to meet the body's requirements to work efficiently and to be healthy. Look again at the national guidelines on page 341.

An imbalance in the diet can lead to either weight loss or weight gain. An excess intake of energy and nutrients for any child will lead to obesity. Excess calories which are not burned up as energy are converted to fat by the body and laid down in the adipose tissue. Excess weight can put a strain on the body's organs and can also make individuals less mobile. Children who are overweight can be more prone to illness and have a higher risk of heart attacks, varicose veins and thrombosis later in life. Statistics show children who are overweight also have a higher percentage of accidents.

To get a balance of food, you need to eat a variety of foods from the groups in the table below. Choosing different foods from each group adds to the variety of nutrients eaten.

▼ Nutrients in the main food groups

Food group	Main nutrients provided
Bread, other cereals and potatoes (Other cereals: breakfast cereals, pasta, rice, oats, noodles, millet) Also included in the group are yams and plantains	Carbohydrate (starch) NSP (fibre) Some calcium and iron B complex vitamins
Fruit and vegetables	Vitamin C Vitamin A – carotenes Folates NSP Some carbohydrate – glucose, fructose and starch
Milk and dairy Milk, cheese, yoghurt and fromage frais	Calcium Protein Vitamin B12 Vitamins A and D
Meat, fish and alternatives Meat includes bacon and salami and meat products – sausages, beefburgers and pâté Alternatives are eggs, nuts, beans and pulses Aim to eat at least one portion of oily fish such as sardines and salmon each week	Iron Protein B complex vitamins, especially vitamin B12

Foods containing fat and foods and drinks containing sugar should be eaten sparingly. They are not essential to a healthy diet. However, they do add choice and palatability.

Theory into practice

As a nanny looking after a 3-year-old child, you have the responsibility of planning and providing well-balanced meals for the child. The parents leave early in the morning and do not return until after tea-time.

- Plan a suitable breakfast, lunch and tea for the child.
- Suggest healthy snacks for mid-morning and mid-afternoon.

For nutritional needs, see page 343 of this unit and for advice on planning a balanced meal, see Unit 11, page 374.

Dietary reference values

To give some guidance for the amounts of nutrients needed, some dietary reference values (DRVs) have been established. The actual amount needed for each individual varies according to height, weight, gender, physical activity undertaken and the climate. It is impossible to produce tables which match every person's circumstances. So experts have produced a set of recommended values which ensure that the needs of most healthy people are accommodated. They are, therefore, higher than the estimates of average requirements, except for energy and energy producing constituents. So if a person eats more of a nutrient than the recommended amount they will be getting more than is recommended. However, if it is calculated that a person is getting less than the recommended amount, they will not necessarily be deficient in the supply of that particular nutrient since the tables are set at a high level.

DRVs cover a range of intakes of the majority of nutrients. They can be used for working out the adequacy of diets for groups of people.

There are four values for nutrients:

- *Estimated Average Requirement (EAR)* which, as the name implies, is an estimate of the average need for food energy or a nutrient. This is the DRV for fats and carbohydrates.

For example, the EARs for energy for adolescents are:

Age range	Males		Females	
	Mj	Kcal	Mj	Kcal
11–14 years	9.27	2220	7.92	1845
15–18 years	11.51	2755	8.83	2110

Source: *Manual of Nutrition*, MAFF (1999)

- *Reference Nutrient Intake (RNI)*, which is the amount of the nutrient that is sufficient for almost everyone, even those with high needs. The RNI is also higher than most people need and it is most unlikely that anyone eating this amount will be found to be deficient in the nutrient being monitored. RNI is used for protein and for nine vitamins and 11 minerals.

- *Lower Reference Nutrient Intake (LRNI)*, which is the amount of a nutrient thought to be sufficient only for a small number of people with low nutrient needs. Most people will need to eat more than this. Anyone eating less than the LRNI will soon become deficient in that particular nutrient.

- *Safe Intakes* This is the recommended level for nutrients where there is no EAR, RNI or LRNI. The Department of Health has also safe intakes for riboflavin, niacin, vitamin B12, vitamin D, potassium, sodium and some other nutrients. The safe intake level is considered to be sufficient to meet needs.

Many of us are very interested in the amount and type of fat we are consuming. DRVs have now been set which indicate the levels for dietary fats and carbohydrates as well as NSPs (fibre). They are average values for the main population for good health. Fats are broken down into saturated and unsaturated fats as well as total fat intake. The DRV for saturated fatty acid has been set at a level to encourage reducing blood cholesterol levels for the nation.

Energy balance

Energy derived from fats and carbohydrate has to be carefully considered to avoid becoming overweight, which leads to obesity and resulting health problems.

Deficiencies

For deficiencies of vitamins and minerals, see pages 354–57. It is important to be aware of these so that problems can be remedied before they become too severe and life-threatening.

Malnutrition

For a healthy balance of foods, an individual needs to consume and absorb the appropriate amounts of energy and nutrients to meet their needs. **Malnutrition** occurs when the body receives the wrong amount or proportion of nutrients and energy. This can be too little or too much. Hence, the starving child from a economically developing country and the obese teenager from a developed Western country are both suffering from malnutrition.

The potential effects of an unbalanced diet, including malnutrition, are covered in detail in Unit 11, page 384.

Key term

Malnutrition is too much or too little food.

Assessment activity 9.2

You have been asked by the local children's centre to help them in a campaign to promote healthy eating.

Prepare a handout which describes the requirements of a balanced diet.

9.3 How to maximise opportunities for promoting healthy living to children and their families

Opportunities

During routines

Children benefit from the use of routines to promote learning of healthy lifestyles, such as the need to wash hands before eating. Nurseries build this routine activity into their daily plan, thus promoting healthy practices.

Some families may not have established routines which cause other family problems.

During activities

A variety of activities enable children and adults to learn about healthy living and health needs as well as how their bodies work. Children learn through curriculum activities. Programmes such as Food in Schools enhance the curriculum input through a range of activities and projects. These have been developed to complement and supplement existing healthier food initiatives in schools. Often these initiatives are developed through integrated activities within schools or other settings, such as nurseries. For instance, pre-school children may have a theme of 'Milk'. The children may learn about the value of drinking milk, take part in mathematical activities based on different numbers and the sizes of milk containers, and learn about dental health.

Adults' awareness of health living is raised through activities such as parentcraft classes, publicity, watching television programmes and, in deprived areas, through access to healthy living centres. These initiatives help adults to become aware of, and learn about, different health needs.

In today's society we have many facilities and opportunities for maximising health potential. Universal services are provided which are available for all, such as the health services provided by the primary care trusts and Child Benefit which increases the family's spending power. In addition, there are other facilities and opportunities. For instance, NHS drop-in centres and fitness centres support and promote the health of the local area. As living standards improve so the potential for maximising the health of the community increases.

Planned programmes

The government has certain targets, such as halving child poverty by 2010, improving health and reducing social exclusion. These targets are supported by programmes and initiatives, as shown in the diagram opposite. However, it has to be remembered that targets are not always realised.

In addition, there are targeted services for children with special needs or in special circumstances. These involve supporting children in adverse family situations. Children

Ten Year Strategy

Choice for Parents, the Best Start for Children, published in 2004

- Greater choice for parents to balance work and home life, enhanced parental leave, easy access to Sure Start
- Flexible childcare for all families who need it
- High-quality provision
- Affordable provision

Sure Start

- Government programme for all children.
- Aims to:
  - increase availability of childcare
  - improve health and emotional development for young children
  - support parents as parents and when they wish to work
  - help services develop in disadvantaged areas alongside financial help for parents to afford childcare
- Reaches over 800,000 children and has over 1,000 children's centres

Healthy Living Centres

- Set up in 1998
- Now 350 HLCs across the country in the most deprived areas
- Intended to reduce health inequalities by encouraging healthier lifestyles and actively involving the community

Recent government legislation and planned initiatives

Choosing Health (March 2005)

Identified public health priorities:

- Tackling health inequalities
- Reducing the number of people who smoke
- Reducing obesity and improving diet and nutrition
- Improving sexual health
- Improving mental health and well-being
- Encouraging sensible drinking and reducing harm caused by excessive drinking

Every Child Matters (ECM)

- Children's services are structured, commissioned and delivered through this approach
- Aims to improve quality of life and well-being for every child from birth to 19 years
- Key outcomes are for children to:
  - be healthy
  - stay safe
  - enjoy and achieve
  - make a positive contribution
  - achieve economic well-being
- Organisations to work together, e.g. education, social services, NHS, police and voluntary services
- First Children's Commissioner appointed in 2005

Childcare Act 2006

- First ever early years and childcare Act
- Takes forward some of the Ten Year Strategy initiatives
- Local authorities (LAs) required to
  - improve the ECM outcomes for all pre-school children
  - reduce inequalities in these outcomes
  - secure sufficient childcare for working parents
- Reforms and simplifies early years registration and inspection with a new integrated education and care quality framework and new Ofsted childcare register
- To be implemented by 2008

in need of protection, such as children who have been abused, will have social services involvement and care plans drawn up to meet their needs. Social services may support families through the deployment of outreach services, fostering and adoption, and other initiatives.

Voluntary support and lobbying programmes, such as the End Child Poverty group consisting of 53 children's charities, trade unions, faith groups and businesses, campaign to improve the well-being of children.

Case study: Planned programmes to promote healthy living

Jan, Liam and Jake have been absent from school for some weeks. The education welfare officer has contacted social services to report details of his recent visit. The children's mother has said that she has difficulty getting herself and the children up on time as she has no alarm clock and has not got the money to buy one. Also, the children refuse to go to school in old, dirty clothes and she has not enough clothes to wash and dry them so the children can have a change of clean clothes for school.

Social services visit the home. They find a disorganised house with piles of dirty washing and dirty dishes around the kitchen. Social services agree a care plan. This includes supplying the family with an alarm clock and providing an outreach worker who will help get the children ready for school and assist the mother to establish a routine with her washing and daily chores. There is also at home a 2-year-old child who looks under-nourished.

1 **Which of the government's programmes and legislation above might support the family?**

2 **How would they support the family?**

3 **How might the establishment of a routine by the outreach worker, helping the mother, provide an opportunity for the promotion of healthy living for the children and the family?**

During discussions

Discussions are an important way of providing opportunities for the promotion of healthy living. Children and parents need to discuss issues relating to healthy living, such as the dangers of substance abuse. Children need the chance to talk through issues at school which promote their health through such curriculum areas as Citizenship. Parents can use health services, such as their GP and NHS Direct, to discuss health issues of concern to them. For instance, if their child has a high temperature or severe pain, a parent can use these resources to discuss the problem.

Involving children

The importance of involving children in the promotion of their own healthy living is recognised. In 2005, a Children's Commissioner was appointed for England to enable children's views to be heard. The Commissioner pays particular attention to representing the views of the most vulnerable children and young people.

Involving families

Babies, children and young people need pro-active parenting. Loving, stable family relationships, together with appropriate care, promote children's growth and development. Healthy development is promoted by parental interest and encouragement, an understanding of their children's needs and the provision of resources, such as toys and activities. Parents need also to work in partnership with health and other professionals to maximise their children's potential. For instance, it is essential to attend health monitoring and immunisation programmes regularly and to respond promptly and responsibly to illness, accidents and other concerns.

Maternity and paternity leave, a minimum wage, increased support from the benefit system (for example, tax credits) have all supported and encouraged parents to play a positive role in their families. The government wants schools to be at the heart of the community, providing access to childcare from 8.00 a.m. to 6.00 p.m. all year, as well as providing a range of services. It is intended that schools will become linked to Sure Start children's centres. All schools are being encouraged to provide parental access to activities such as parenting skills programmes and child behaviour management courses. Some schools may offer activities such as healthy eating and nutrition courses and financial management. This is designed to help relieve the stress of parenting.

Parents benefit from support of other adults to cope with their changing physical, social, cognitive and emotional needs. For instance, working parents have to cope with stress of work, learning new skills, family pressures and other concerns, such as marital breakdown. Women need support through pregnancy and after the birth of their children, as well as during the menopause phase of their lives. Men, like women, have to adapt to the parental role and many other pressures as they face the transition to middle age. Support may come from the family or counselling services and voluntary groups, such as the Samaritans.

Many active grandparents value the opportunity to keep mentally agile as well as physically active in order to maximise the negative effects of development at this stage of life.

Inclusion

The government has actively encouraged social inclusion through many measures including those discussed above: the Ten Year Strategy, Sure Start, Every Child Matters and the Childcare Act 2006.

Health awareness

Health implications of different lifestyles

A 'lifestyle' can be described as a choice in personal behaviour. This includes choices made about such behaviours as the amount of exercise undertaken, the consumption of alcohol, substance abuse and high quantities of fatty and sugary foods consumed, addiction to smoking, pre-occupation with your health. The lifestyles adopted by people are influenced by three main factors:

- *biological factors*, which include a person's genetic inheritance and the way their body is or has functioned. Genetic factors, as explained earlier, may cause certain inherited diseases which are in themselves rare. A person's biological functioning may change as a result of past events which increase their likelihood of some health disorders in the future. For instance, it is thought that binge drinking when young may cause health problems such as liver disorders in later life

- *socio-economic factors*, such as income, nutrition, access to services and support, air pollution, living conditions and other factors

- *psycho-social factors*, which include ethnicity, religion, personal beliefs, educational achievement, relationships with others of importance to you, perceived stress levels, significant life events.

As we have seen earlier in this unit, lifestyles adopted have significant implications for health. Heavy smoking can shorten life expectancy and result in a less healthy life. Healthy eating and drinking and a sensible programme of regular exercise can prolong healthy life expectancy and the overall quality of life.

Short- and long-term effects of lifestyle choices

Lifestyle influences on health may have some short-term effects as well as long-term effects. For instance, a high energy intake may provide a satisfying feeling in the short-term and provide adequate energy for any activity undertaken as well as energy to keep you feeling warm. However, long-term over-consumption of food will result in surplus energy being produced by the food which, if not used up in the short-term, will be converted to body fat. This leads to the person becoming overweight and eventually obese, with the long-term health effects of increased risk of heart disease, anaemia and reduced mobility, as well as respiratory problems.

Case study: Lifestyle influences on health

Recent changes in school meals evoked protest from some mothers who objected to the more healthy school meals their children were expected to eat. Some took it upon themselves to pass chips and burgers through the school railings to their 'starving' children. However, as the news extracts below shows, not everyone agreed.

'Only 11 per cent of the public back their stance, while 86 per cent believe pupils should not be allowed out at break times to buy fast food and sweets from nearby shops, according to the survey conducted by pollsters Mori.'

Source: *The Observer*, 15 October 2006

1 **What might be the short-term implications for the children of their mothers' approach to healthy eating?**

2 **What might be the long-term implications for the children of the mothers' approach to healthy eating?**

3 **Explain why some of the factors listed above might have influenced the mothers' attitude to healthy eating?**

4 **Why might only 11 per cent of the public back the mothers' attitude?**

Case study: Chips or beans?

At primary school, Helen was given the nickname 'Beany'. At secondary school she continued to be friendly with some of her primary school peers but gained some new friends as well. Her primary school friends still called her 'Beany'. The new friends were mystified as to why she had this unusual nickname and asked why this was so. Helen recalled how when choosing her school meals, she always avoided chips as she thought that they were unhealthy and instead choose beans. Hence, her friends at primary school, who made fun of her reluctance to choose chips, nicknamed her 'Beany'.

1 **Was Helen's lifestyle approach to eating sensible?**

2 **In preparation for a placement in a primary school, plan an activity to make children aware of healthy eating.**

3 **How would this activity support the curriculum for the age group of children selected?**

Adults need increased awareness of the health implications of their lifestyles and both their short- and long-term effects. For instance, sexual lifestyle is an important aspect of adult life. Relationships with several partners, some of whom are relatively unknown to the consenting adult, may result in the short term in the uncomfortable symptoms of sexually transmitted diseases. However, the long-term effects may have very serious consequences, including sterility. For instance, if syphilis is contracted, the first stage or short-term effect is painless and may go unnoticed and untreated. If the second and third stages go untreated and the fourth stage or long-term effect kicks in, perhaps many years later, serious health problems may occur including paralysis and personality changes.

Healthy changes to lifestyle

Today we are made much more aware of the need to change our lifestyles in order to improve our health. Through health education our knowledge about health and the causes of illness is increased. For instance, every

Many people regard the British diet during the Second World War (1939–1945), when food was rationed, as being healthier than today. Then there were no problems of obesity which we see today and which in part is due to the easy access to foods contributing to an inappropriate diet.

Healthy living involves people accepting responsibility for improving and/or maintaining their health. It is important for people when trying to reach their health potential to adopt a pro-active partnership with the health professionals, such as ensuring their children have their full programme of immunisations. People also need to be adaptable to change, such as adapting the traditional British diet to meet healthy goals. Children need to be made aware of the health implications of their lifestyles.

- Enjoy safe, protected sex
- Balance work and family commitments
- Eat a range of foods for a balanced diet
- Eat 5 portions of fruit and vegetables per day
- Take part in appropriate vaccination programmes
- Cut down on salt in the diet
- **Healthy changes to lifestyle**
- Exercise regularly
- Eat less saturated fats and sugars
- Give up smoking
- Keep alcohol intake within the recommended limits/units
- Drink plenty of water
- Be a healthy weight

year a new health education campaign is launched to encourage us to not drink and drive, especially over the Christmas period.

Vigorous anti-smoking campaigns over many years have targeted heavy smokers. These have been complemented by an increase in the banning of smoking in public places, not only in England but in other European countries, such as Ireland. This has heightened the impact of the anti-smoking drives.

Much emphasis has been put on children's health and the importance of immunisation as a means of protecting children's health.

The public are eager to participate in opportunities to protect their health in later life. There is a ready response to invitations sent by the primary care trusts to have the flu vaccine and much interest is being shown in the development of a cervical cancer vaccine for 9–26-year-old females.

Facilitating change

Although we may be aware of what we should do to achieve a healthy lifestyle, we often do not achieve this. The author would be embarrassed to admit how many times she has set herself a weight reduction target but has failed to achieve it and, instead, has seen the scales registering a higher rather than a lower weight!

Health promotion campaigns are devised to help us achieve change. These are processes, activities or events that support and assist the improvement, protection or maintenance of people's health status. They aim to:

- improve the quality of life
- prolong life
- reduce the effects of ill-health, both physical and mental ill-health
- support the person directly involved (for example, the smoker) and those indirectly involved (for example, the victims of passive smoking).

Key term

Health promotion is a process, activity or event carried out with the aim of improving, protecting or maintaining people's health.

Theory into practice

- Identify a health promotion campaign.
- Is this a process, an activity or an event?
- Describe the health promotion campaign.
- Explain how it will fulfil the aims listed above for health promotion.

Health promotions may have an environmental intervention. For instance, a health promotion in an inner-city area to encourage under-5s to exercise may have an environmental intervention, which might involve fencing off a play area in a park specifically designated for the local Sure Start children's centre to prevent dog fouling. There may be local concern due to a child becoming blind in one eye as a result of playing locally and catching toxocariasis from dog fouling. The environmental intervention may involve legislation. In this case, the local authority may pass a local bye-law which imposes a fine on dog owners whose dogs foul the area. The intervention has not involved the under 5s but has involved the co-operation from others who do not directly benefit from the intervention.

Health promotions involve behavioural interventions which are concerned with the individual's actions. They aim to empower the individual by increasing their control, or feeling of control, over their lives including their physical, social and emotional well-being. This type of intervention includes:

- teaching skills, such as showing young children how to wash their hands thoroughly after going to the toilet
- raising awareness and knowledge about health hazards, such as the dangers of playing on the railways
- developing social skills, such as saying 'No' to unprotected sex
- cognitive behavioural techniques, such as how to relax after a stressful working day.

The success of health promotions requires the active co-operation of the individuals they are targeting. A key element of this approach is effective and persuasive communication with the target client group. The nature of this will vary according to the needs and circumstances of the group.

■ Approaches to health promotion

There are several different approaches to health promotion:

- *Medical approach* This involves measures being taken, often on a national scale, which are offered to the public generally. They are implemented by health professionals. For example, the flu vaccine is offered to all over 65-year-olds and those with certain at-risk medical conditions. The vaccines are usually administered by the GP or practice nurses.
- *Educational approach* Information is provided or appropriate skills taught to enable children or adults to make a choice for their actions. For example, health promotion programmes in pre-schools about not going with strangers uses this approach.
- *Behaviour change approach* This aims to bring about

changes in a person's behaviour changing the way they think. It is based on the key assumption that we are rational decision-makers. Campaigns with this approach rely heavily on factual information being provided about risks and health hazards through advertising campaigns and the use of the mass media. An example of this type of approach is the methods used in the annual Christmas drink-driving campaigns.

- *Self-empowerment approach* The aim is to empower individual people to make healthy choices. They have to consider their own values and beliefs and how certain factors affect the choices they make. It involves the individual being a participant in a variety of learning techniques, such as educational drama or assertiveness training. One example of this approach is a recent youth drama production which explored the dangers and consequences of joy-riding.
- *Collective action or community action approach* The purpose of this approach is to bring about an improvement in health by tackling local socio-economic and environmental causes of ill-health. It involves the close relationship between personal health and social, economic and environmental situations. People work as a group to bring about a change in their environment rather than a change within themselves.

For example, a local group of residents were outraged by the fouling of their grassed area in the centre of their estate. This facility is used by many young children as a place to play and is also enjoyed in the summer by many in the community for picnics and barbeques, as few houses in the vicinity have gardens. An illegal invasion by travellers resulted in human excretion and dog fouling as well as a large quantity of rotting rubbish being left behind after the travellers were evicted. The local residents called a heated meeting with their councillors and local authority officials and demanded that action be taken in the interests of health to prevent any future illegal trespassing. The local authority agreed to a councillor's suggestion that large boulders be placed around the area, thus preventing caravan access. In addition, the council undertook an extensive clear-up operation. This resulted in the grassed area being restored to its original state and being once again a valuable health facility for the community.

Assessment activity 9.3

You are on a work placement at a day nursery within a children's centre. There are many health problems within the area including obesity among young children and their families. The nursery has designated the last week of your placement to be called 'Let's Eat and be Healthy'.

You have been asked to contribute your ideas for how this opportunity for the promotion of healthy living may be maximised.

Prepare a presentation for the staff meeting where these ideas will be discussed. **P4**

End of unit assessment

Your tutor has been asked to send a student delegate to a conference being organised to improve the implementation of the Every Child Matters initiative. The conference has two principal aims:

- to highlight the contribution that different people can make to promoting healthy development and living for children and their families
- to develop stronger working partnerships between professionals.

You have been selected to attend the conference. Naturally, you are feeling a little nervous so you decide to research thoroughly the topics which appear on the conference programme.

1 In preparation for the conference, write some notes outlining factors that affect the health and physical development of children. **P1**

2 Prepare a handout for the conference explaining the factors that affect the health and physical development of children. **M1**

3 Produce a case study which evaluates the potential effects of two of the factors you have included in your handout that affect the health and physical development of children and their families. **D1**

4 One of the agenda items for the conference is: *How can different professionals contribute to promoting healthy eating for children and their families?* In preparation for the discussion on healthy eating, you decide to do some research on nutrition. Write notes:

a describing the types of macro-nutrients and micro-nutrients and their role in the diet. **P2**

b describing the requirements of a balanced diet. **P3**

c explaining the roles of the various components of a balanced diet including carbohydrates, proteins, fats, vitamins and minerals. **M2**

5 You have been asked to make a presentation at the conference to highlight the role early years professionals can play in promoting healthy living for children and their families.

a Use examples from your work placements to describe how opportunities for promoting the healthy living of children and their families can be maximised. **P4**

b Use two examples from your work placement to explain the role of the promotion of healthy living of children and their families. **M3**

c Using these two examples from your work placements, evaluate the promotion of healthy living to children and their families. **D2**

References and further reading

Barasi, M.E. (2003) *Human Nutrition: a health perspective*, Arnold

Davey, B. (ed.) (2001) *Birth to Old Age: health in transition*, Open University Press

Denby, N., Baic, S. and Rinzler, C.A. (2006) *Nutrition for Dummies*, John Wiley

Howard, G. (2002) *Healthy Villages: a guide to communities and community health workers*, World Health Organization

Marks, D.F., Murray, M., Sykes, C.M., Evans, B., Willig, C. and Woodall, C. (2005) *Health Psychology Theory: research and practice*, 2nd edition, Sage

Ministry of Agriculture, Fisheries and Food (1999) *Manual of Nutrition*, 10th edition, The Stationery Office

Wiseman, G. (2002) *Nutrition and Health*, Taylor & Francis

Software

EatMeter, British Nutrition Foundation, 2004

Interactive Food Facts (If2), British Nutrition Foundation, 2001

Useful websites

British Nutrition Foundation – www.nutrition.org.uk

British Nutrition Foundation, site for primary schools – www.foodafactoflife.org.uk

Central Liverpool Primary Healthcare Trust – www.tasteforhealth.com

Child Health Development Foundation – www.chdf.org

Community health profiles (DoH) – www.communityhealthprofiles.info

Every Child Matters – www.everychildmatters.gov.uk

Food in Schools (DoH/DfES) – www.foodinschools.org

Food Standards Agency – www.foodstandards.gov.uk

Food Standards Agency, Eat Well, Be Well – www.eatwell.gov.uk

ParentsCentre (DfES) – www.parentscente.gov.uk/family matters/childcare/extended schools

Sure Start – www.surestart.gov.uk

Wired for Health (DoH/DfES site for schools) – www.wiredforhealth.gov.uk

World Health Organization – www.who.int/

Grading criteria	Assessment activity	Page number
To achieve a pass grade the evidence must show that the learner is able to:		
P1 outline factors that affect the health and physical development of children	9.1 End of unit assessment	342 369
P2 describe the types of macro-nutrients and micro-nutrients and their roles in the diet	End of unit assessment	369
P3 describe the requirements of a balanced diet	9.2 End of unit assessment	362 369
P4 use examples from work placements to describe how opportunities for the promotion of healthy living to children and their families can be maximised	9.3 End of unit assessment	369 369
To achieve a merit grade the evidence must show that, in addition to the pass criteria, the learner is able to:		
M1 explain factors that affect the health and physical development of children	End of unit assessment	369
M2 explain the roles of the various components of a balanced diet	End of unit assessment	369
M3 use two examples from work placements to explain the role of the promotion of health living to children and their families	End of unit assessment	369
To achieve a distinction grade the evidence must show that, in addition to the pass and merit criteria, the learner is able to:		
D1 evaluate the potential effects of two factors that affect the health and physical development of children and their families	End of unit assessment	369
D2 use two examples from work placements to evaluate the promotion of healthy living to children and their families	End of unit assessment	369

Diet and nutrition for children

Introduction

This unit investigates the diet and nutritional needs of children in terms of what they should eat to be healthy, grow and develop, the effects of an unbalanced diet on health and issues relating to food safety.

The diet of children is very important in terms of healthy development. In this unit, you will learn about feeding children from birth to 12 years. You will learn how important the essential nutrients in the diet are to healthy growth and development. This introduction to the importance of good nutrition and diet for children will be invaluable to your understanding of how young children develop. Although you are studying children's care and education now, you may find yourself in another situation in the future where this information will become useful. Much of the information can be applied to all age groups.

The unit also covers diet-related disorders and explores the effects these can have on a young child's development.

Finally in this unit, you will investigate the importance of food safety and how poor food storage and preparation can so easily result in food poisoning. This knowledge can be transferred to other situations where vulnerable groups may be at risk from food poisoning.

What you need to learn

- The principles of infant feeding and diet of children
- The potential effects of an unbalanced diet on children's health
- The principles of food safety

Thinking points

Many different things influence what we eat and this is the same for children. Making good choices when eating is not always easy.

Think about your favourite foods. How many of these have been favourites since childhood? What did you eat in childhood that you don't eat now? What has changed and why?

Think about the children you know. What do they like to eat? Why do you think they like these foods? Are their favourite foods things that parents and carers would like them to eat?

Breast- or bottle-feeding and weaning

When babies are born, they are able to suck but not bite or chew. They are born with the sucking reflex and this means that their diet has to be a liquid one. The liquid designed by nature for its young is milk. Human babies are either breast-fed or bottle-fed with milk which has been modified to suit young babies. See Unit 2, pages 69–70 and Unit 35, pages 527–33, for information on feeding and weaning babies.

Diets of older babies and young children (aged 1–5)

By the age of 1 year, infants are able to feed themselves. By this stage the child will have up to eight teeth which help with the biting and tearing of food. Molar teeth for grinding of food develop later in the second year and the chewing ability becomes more fully developed.

Nutritional needs and nutrients in the diet

In order to understand the diets of young children, you need to have an understanding of the nutrients that are needed by all humans and which therefore have to be provided in the diet. Whatever the age, the nutrients needed are the same but the amounts in which they are needed may vary.

See Unit 9 for information on:

- nutritional needs, section 9.2, pages 343–47
- the main nutrients and their sources in food, section 9.2, pages 348–58.

Concept of a balanced diet

A balanced diet is one in which the energy intake does not exceed the energy output. This is discussed in detail in Unit 9, pages 359–62.

■ Planning a balanced diet

There are several ways in which you can plan a balanced diet for children.

One popular method is the nutrition pyramid (see below) which places the four main food groups at various positions on the pyramid in relation to the amount that should be consumed in the diet. Therefore, foods at the bottom of the pyramid should be consumed in larger quantities that those that appear at the top. In this case, fats and sugars, which contain few nutrients but have a high calorie content, are at the top to indicate they should be used sparingly in the diet, whereas starch foods such as bread and pasta are at the base of the pyramid to indicate they should be consumed most frequently in daily food choices.

Fats, oils & sweets group
Use sparingly

Milk, yogurt, & cheese group
2–3 servings

Meat, poultry, fish, dry beans, eggs, & nuts
2–3 servings

Vegetable group
3–5 servings

Fruit group
2–4 servings

Breads, Cereal, Rice, & Pasta group
6–11 servings

◀ The nutrition pyramid

The food plate ▶

Fruit and vegetables 30%

Bread, cereal or potatoes 30%

Milk and dairy foods 15%

Meat, fish or alternatives 15%

Fat and sugary foods 10%

Another popular method of meal planning is the food plate (see opposite). This aims to indicate the percentage of different food groups on any plate or meal.

Both these diet structures cover similar recommendations. They both avoid giving specific recommendations about portion sizes but give a guide on how a meal might be made up.

Developing a range of foods/food preferences

Children really begin to develop food preferences at this stage so it is important that they are encouraged to try as many different flavours and textures as possible.

Young children have a high requirement for energy in relation to their size. However, they are not able to eat large amounts of food at any one time. Whereas adults can cope with a bulkier diet, if this was applied to children, they would need to eat twice as much to meet their energy needs.

Therefore to meet their needs, children need to eat quite frequently and the foods need to be energy-rich. This means their diet will contain proportionally more high fat content and low fibre content foods compared to the diet of an adult. Children under 5 should not be given skimmed or semi-skimmed milk as they need the calories provided by whole milk.

Children also need more nutrients relative to their size. As they tend to eat a smaller selection of different foods, the range should be varied enough to provide a good mixture of nutrients in different amounts. Children should be encouraged to eat five portions of fruit and vegetables a day.

It is important to remember that children's appetites fluctuate as does their growth. Growth often happens in spurts and as long as the child is healthy and growth compares favourably overall, it is likely that all is well.

Some parents do not eat a variety of foods. Some families on low incomes or those who restrict their diet, such as vegans, may have a smaller range of foods and therefore children may not have a suitably balanced diet. In these cases, parents may need to offer children foods other than those in their own diets to make sure they have a balanced diet.

Ideally, children receive all the nutrients they need from their diet. However, vitamin and mineral supplements may be given to ensure this happens.

The pattern of regular meals is established in the first few years. It is important that children's eating patterns fit in with those of the family and that children become accustomed to eating regular meals with nutritious snacks in between. Children do need mid-meal snacks to ensure they meet their nutritional needs and energy requirements. Savoury snacks and non-sugary drinks are preferable. Encourage snacking on raw fruits and vegetables or cheese.

Extension activity

Make a list of 'good' and 'bad' snacks and drinks for children.

It is important that the diet of a child is not 'manipulated' too much. There is a great deal of confusion about what dietary trends should be applied to the diet of a young child. Healthy eating guidelines should be applied with caution (see section 9.1, page 341).

Parents may also decide to exclude certain foods from the diet as they believe they are linked to food allergies. In fact, the incidence of food-related allergies in children is very small and, therefore, self-diagnosis is not recommended.

Potential effects of food additives

In modern society, both parents often work and so look for ways to save time on food preparation. As a result, pre-prepared food (which contains food additives) now makes a significant contribution to people's diets. We also tend to go on just one shopping trip a week, rather than doing a daily shop as in the past, so we have to purchase foods which will last. Food manufacturers achieve this by using additives in conjunction with different food preservation methods to extend the shelf-life of their products.

Additives are also used to enhance the appearance of foods, for example by adding colourings and they are also used to provide flavour.

Food additives can have a negative effect on young children. They can contribute to allergies and hyperactivity. Therefore it is wise to try to reduce the amount of foods that contain artificial additives in the meals chosen for a young child.

More information on food additives and intolerance can be found on page 388.

Diets of older children (aged 5+)

The dietary needs of older children are similar to those of younger children except that the proportions of nutrients and energy intake needed increases.

School meals

Once children start school full time, they will generally be eating one meal away from home. Food provided at schools has been heavily criticised in recent years as being of poor quality and value. They have also been criticised for being unhealthy and providing a poor nutrient content. Many parents choose to provide their child with a packed lunch which is often filled with fatty foods such as crisps and chocolate biscuits.

▲ What should school meals provide?

Extension activity

1 What does the term 'school meals' bring to mind?
2 What should good school meals provide?

For many children, the school meal is the one hot meal of the day that they eat. In the past, the UK had nutritional guidelines for school meals, but these were abolished in 1980. Since then, school meals have been increasingly criticised for their poor quality and the fact that high-fat foods such as chips were being served several times a week. Older children were also more likely to eat off the premises. There have been increasing fears that this type of diet, if continued into young adulthood, would contribute to increases in cardio-vascular and diet-related diseases later in life.

Recent pressure has been placed on the UK government to improve the quality of school meals following media coverage of the poor quality. As a result the government set up the School Food Trust in 2005. This organisation has been given the task of transforming school food and food skills. To do this, it will be promoting the education and health of children and young people and improving the quality of food in schools.

This recognises the role schools have to play in helping children learn about food and healthy eating as well as developing practical cooking skills. If schools do not educate children in eating for health, poor eating habits may be reinforced. The changes will help reduce diet-related disorders. Childhood obesity is a major threat to long-term health. Statistics produced by the British Medical Association predict that by 2020 over one quarter of children will be obese. It is also suggested that as a result of this and other diet-related disorders, children will have a shorter life expectancy than their parents. Already, over 18 per cent of 2–15 year olds are obese.

By 2009, there will be new standards in place for school meals. These standards are far-reaching and cover all food sold in schools, including what is sold at the tuck shop and from vending machines. Many of the foods previously available in schools will no longer allowed as they are connected with the growing range of child

health issues, including diabetes, obesity, tooth decay and anaemia.

Why will the new standards make a difference?

It is believed that the new standards will make a difference because they will benefit children in a number of ways and this in time will have a positive effect on their health. Benefits will include:

- children eating balanced meals containing good sources of protein and starch, with plenty of vegetables, salad and fruit
- less access to unhealthy foods as unhealthy choices, such as foods high in fat, salt and sugar, are replaced by more nutritious options
- a positive impact on children's health; educating them in healthy eating and the effects on health of a poor diet should encourage them to eat more nutritious food
- an improved quality of school food nationwide
- better behaviour and concentration in the classroom.

Extension activity

Do you think that the proposed changes to food available in schools are a good idea? Do you think they will work?

What do the standards actually mean?

The standards require schools to ensure they follow the guidelines and these include:

- A variety of fruit and vegetables should be available in all school food outlets. This could include fresh, dried, frozen, tinned and juiced products. Not less than two portions of fruit and vegetables should be available per day per child.
- Manufactured meat products may only be included in the menu occasionally.
- Economy burgers are banned and so is certain offal.

- Oily fish should be available at least once every three weeks.
- Bread should be provided as an extra to the meal every day.
- Children must have easy access at all times to free, fresh drinking water.
- No sweetened soft drinks should be sold. The only drinks available should be water (still or sparkling), milk (skimmed or semi-skimmed), pure fruit juices, yoghurt or milk drinks (with less than 5 per cent added sugar), drinks made from combinations of these, low-calorie hot chocolate, tea and coffee.
- Milk should be either semi-skimmed or skimmed, not full fat.
- Confectionery must not be sold in schools or offered as part of a school lunch.
- Savoury snacks high in salt and fat, such as crisps, are no longer allowed. Only snacks such as nuts and seeds, without added salt or sugar, should be available.
- Salt should not be made available at lunch tables or at service counters. Condiments may only be provided in sachets to limit the amount used.
- Deep-fried foods (including those deep-fried in the manufacturing process) should not be served more than twice a week.
- Artificial sweeteners could be used only in yoghurt or milk drinks, or combinations based on yoghurt or milk.

To find out more about the new regulations for school dinners, visit www.schoolfoodtrust.org.uk.

Fast foods

As they get older, children socialise with their friends more and this may also lead to eating food away from the family home. Fast food outlets are very popular for children as they are relatively cheap so offer a social meeting place as well as a place to eat. Fast food is often high in saturated fat and many of the foods are fried which also increases the fat content. This can contribute to obesity. In recent years, the poor publicity about fast foods has led to many of the companies looking at ways to offer a healthier menu. Salads, fresh fruit, yoghurt and wholemeal rolls are just a few of the changes some of the popular fast food stores have introduced.

Theory into practice

Visit a fast food outlet and study the menu. How much of the menu would you say is healthy?

Diet during puberty

The nutritional requirements of adolescents reflect the period of rapid growth that occurs during puberty. In boys, the energy intake required increases from the ages of 13 to 16 and this parallels the growth spurt. In girls, peak energy requirements occur around the age of 12–13 years, the time when periods usually begin.

These extra energy needs can be met either by increasing the energy value of main meals or by increasing healthy snacks between meals. Many teenagers meet their nutritional needs by 'grazing', which means they tend to snack rather than eat three main meals a day.

Theory into practice

Make a list of healthy snacks a teenager could choose to eat. Explain why they are healthy.

Protein intake needs also increase during puberty to meet the increased growth rate. The need for iron increases progressively through adolescence. This is particularly important for girls as they will lose iron through menstruation.

A good intake of calcium is important at this time for skeletal development. All teenagers need at least 600 ml of milk per day plus 45 g of cheese or 125 ml of yoghurt to meet their daily requirements. Calcium can also be found in fish, fortified breakfast cereals and green leafy vegetables. Both calcium and exercise are important in the formation of strong, healthy bones and the prevention of osteoporosis later in life.

Many factors influence the diet of an adolescent:

- *Body image* Many adolescents want a good physique and sometimes eat an inadequate diet in order to achieve this. Adolescents are bombarded with images of thin, 'beautiful' young people in the media and many feel pressured to look like them. Obesity can be a problem for both sexes and young people should be encouraged to increase their physical activity rather than go on a diet.

- *Time management* Adolescents are often in a hurry and eating may well be at the bottom of their list of priorities. They may miss meals such as breakfast and this can make them feel lethargic and lack concentration. Missed meals are often replaced by snacks which are high in fat and sugar. A light breakfast such as cereal and fruit juice or a piece of fruit to eat on the run is better than no breakfast at all.

- *Financial limitations* Many adolescents are on a tight budget. Many have other priorities on which to spend their money, such as social life, and food will be a low priority. They therefore choose cheap food which is filling, such as chips or hamburgers. These are generally high in fat and salt, low in vitamins and minerals and do not contain much fibre. They are also high in calories. Adolescents may also be living independently and therefore the amount to spend on food could be limited.

- *Peer pressure* Adolescents may be pressurised by their friends to choose certain foods. It may not be seen as 'cool' to eat healthily and choose foods such as salads.

- *Limited knowledge of nutrition* Many adolescents have a limited knowledge of nutrition. Nutrition and cooking is no longer taught in schools as it used to be in the past so many young people have very limited skills in this area. This could mean that they rely heavily on pre-prepared foods which are not always nutrient-rich. They also will not know which foods they need to eat to obtain the nutrients they need.

Older children and teenagers can also be affected by additives in food. For detailed information about additives in food, see page 376.

Surveys have shown that many teenagers miss one meal a day and the most common one missed is breakfast. They tend to eat high fat and sugary foods such as chocolate and sweets on a daily basis. It is also believed that the majority of teenagers learn about nutrition through magazines, with school being a key source of information.

Theory into practice

Carry out a survey of your fellow students to find out about their eating habits. How well do your results reflect the comments above?

Presentation of food

There are many ways in which food can be made more attractive to children, particularly if they are fussy eaters. Some ideas include:

- making food into pictures such as faces, boats or castles
- cutting food, such as sandwiches, into interesting shapes
- involving children in the preparation of their food – this may encourage them to eat it
- thinking about colour – poached chicken with mashed potato and cauliflower is all white and will not look very attractive to children, whereas poached chicken with peas, carrots and potato wedges will be much more appealing

- giving children variety to encourage them to eat – always having the same foods will be boring and not encourage them if they are fussy eaters
- making sure food is moist and not too dry
- putting small portions on the plate – too much food will automatically put children off but they can always have more
- not forcing children to always finish everything on their plate – this can also put them off eating
- encouraging children to use cutlery – for young children, you may need to cut up the food for them and then encourage them firstly to use a spoon and later progress to a knife and fork.

Social aspects

Eating is a social occasion and children should be encouraged to enjoy meal times.

- Eating with the family at the table encourages children to develop good social habits which will mean that when they eat with others they will have established manners.

- Eating together also encourages conversation and communication in the family. This is an important part of eating.
- Food is also an important part of culture and many cultures celebrate using food and drink.

Theory into practice

Make a list of as many occasions as possible when food is used in celebrations in different cultures. Share your list with the rest of the group.

Personal preferences

Food choices

There are many reasons why people choose the food they eat. The following diagram summarises some of the

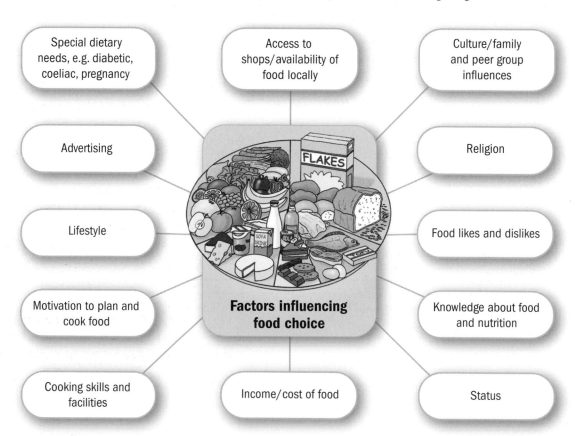

Special dietary needs, e.g. diabetic, coeliac, pregnancy

Access to shops/availability of food locally

Culture/family and peer group influences

Advertising

Religion

Lifestyle

Food likes and dislikes

Motivation to plan and cook food

Factors influencing food choice

Knowledge about food and nutrition

Cooking skills and facilities

Income/cost of food

Status

factors which influence food choice and therefore food intake.

For young children, the food they eat is influenced by:

- the food offered by their parents
- their own likes and dislikes
- advertising on children's TV
- peer group pressure.

For many children, their choice of food is limited by external factors. For example, a family with a low income may have their choice of food limited by cost and their own mobility – they may not be able to get to the large supermarkets for a greater choice of food due to lack of transport. Therefore they may have to shop in local corner shops where prices are higher and there is less choice. If the parents suffer from certain medical conditions, the child's diet may be affected by this. For example, if a parent has arthritis, this may make it difficult for them to prepare and cook fresh foods and the family may have to rely on convenience foods.

Food is also affected by regional variations. Different areas produce different products. For example, in the south-east of England, fruit farms are plentiful and fruit is readily available during the summer season. If you live near the coast, fresh fish is usually readily available in a way that it may not be in the Midlands.

The seasons also affect what food is available in the shops. Generally, food that is in season is cheaper as there is lots of it. However, preservation techniques and the improved transport systems mean that many foods are available all year round. However, this may come at a high price.

Culture and religion

Some individuals need or choose to have special diets as a result of lifestyle choices, cultural or religious issues, or health issues.

All religions of the world have their own beliefs, morals, ceremonies and celebrations. Many of these are linked to food either as food eaten at particular times or as restrictions on the diet. These can set a religion apart from others and give a sense of belonging to those who share the religion. A strict follower of religious laws is called orthodox. However, many people are relaxed about certain religious practices today. The table below outlines some dietary practices of religions.

Case study: Feeding a family

Fatima and Ahmed have three children aged 4, 8 and 15. They are concerned about their diets and do not feel they are as healthy as they need to be.

1 **What factors might affect what each of them eat? Are they the same?**

2 **What easy steps could Fatima and Ahmed take to improve the healthiness of each of their diets?**

3 **The 15-year-old, Janina, wants to become a vegan. How might this affect how the nutrients she needs are provided in the diet? (For information on vegan diets, see page 383.)**

Food restriction	Time of year/day	How food is prepared	Fasting practices
Judaism • Only eat animals with cloven feet and who chew the cud, for example beef, sheep, goats, deer • Do not eat pork • Only eat forequarters of the animal • Only eat fish with fins and scales • Do not eat shellfish • Do not eat foods containing meat and milk at the same meal • Do not eat blood	Do not prepare food on the Sabbath (Saturday).	Meat and poultry have to be killed in a particular way to drain the maximum amount of blood from the animal. The meat is then soaked in a salt water mixture and finally drained. This is called kosher. Separate utensils and cooking vessels must be used for meat and dairy products and fish.	There should be six hours between eating meat and dairy foods. If dairy products are eaten before meat, one hour must pass. Fasts occur in the Jewish calendar to represent sad events which have happened. All females over 12 years and 1 day and males over 13 years and 1 day must take part in fasting. Some fasting incorporates eating special foods which symbolise events in Jewish history.
Islam • Do not eat blood • Do not eat pork or pork-related products • Do not consume alcohol	Ramadam is a period of fasting where Muslims do not eat between sunrise and sunset. Therefore they eat light meals during the hours of darkness. Ramadam lasts for one month and occurs during the 9th lunar month. This varies from year to year. Strict Muslims also fast on Mondays and Thursdays and also between the 13th and 15th of each month.	Animals must be ritually slaughtered with a blow to the head. Certain words must be spoken whilst this happens. Meat slaughtered in this way is called halal meat.	Males are deemed to have reached the age of responsibility at 15, females at 12. All who have reached the age of responsibility must fast, except menstruating, pregnant and lactating women, sick or elderly people, those travelling long distances or those doing hard physical work. Must only eat with the right hand – left is considered unclean.
Hinduism • Do not kill or eat any animals • Usually lacto-vegetarians • Strict Hindus are vegan	Varies according to caste, family, age and gender	Ritual bathing and clean clothes are put on before food is prepared. Will not eat Western cheese	Hindu society is based on castes. Hindus from the upper castes cannot eat with the lower castes. Hindus from higher castes are more likely to be vegans.

Case study: Cultural diets

Mr Mohan Samarakeon is a strict Muslim. He is a widower and lives alone. He is 78 years old, slightly overweight and has high blood pressure which is controlled by tablets. He is not very active but enjoys sweet foods.

Identify the type of diet Mr Samarakeon could eat using the following headings:
- **Dietary restrictions**
- **Dietary requirements**
- **Foods to avoid due to health problems**
- **Foods to include in the diet and their nutrient content.**

Vegetarianism

A vegetarian is someone who chooses not to eat foods from animals and by-products of animals, such as cheese and eggs. Many people choose to be vegetarian and with careful food choices, all nutrients can be obtained from the diet. There are several different types of vegetarian:

- lacto vegetarians – eat milk and cheese, but not eggs, meat, poultry or fish
- lacto-ovo vegetarians – eat eggs, milk and cheese, but not meat, poultry or fish
- vegans – strict vegetarians who do not eat meat, fish, poultry, eggs, milk or cheese. Vegans also do not use any items which may contain animal products in them, such as make-up or soap, and do not wear leather.

Therefore, vegetarians cut out major sources of protein from their diets. Any diet in which one or more of the major food groups is omitted is not ideal. Each type of vegetarian diet has its own problems.

■ Lacto or lacto-ovo vegetarians

Few problems exist with this type of vegetarian diet as they still consume high biological value (HBV) proteins and therefore the essential **amino acids** – in the form of milk, cheese and, in the case of lacto-ovos, eggs. They can also obtain protein from peas, beans and lentils.

Soya or textured vegetable protein is a source of protein for this type of vegetarian. They can also eat Quorn, another source of vegetable protein.

However, lacto/lacto-ovo vegetarians need to watch the amount of saturated fat they consume as it is easy to eat large amounts through high consumption of dairy products.

Key Term

Amino acids The building blocks of protein.

■ Vegans

Vegans can find it difficult to obtain the correct amount of protein from their diets as they choose to omit all forms of animal protein. They rely on vegetable sources of protein and this can make the diet bulky and monotonous. They may also have low intakes of some of the vital micro-nutrients which are found in protein foods and dairy products, such as vitamins A, B1 and D and calcium, phosphorus and iron.

Theory into practice

Look at the tables of micro-nutrients in Unit 9, pages 348–51, and identify sources of vitamin A, B1 and D and iron, calcium and phosphorus that a vegan could eat.

To ensure they obtain enough protein, vegans should:

- eat a good supply of vegetable proteins which complement each other and therefore provide all the essential amino acids
- avoid too many foods which contain phytic acid, for example wholegrain cereals, as this will bind with any iron or calcium in the diet and make it unavailable to the body
- avoid too much bulk in the diet – vegetables are naturally more bulky and many absorb more water during cooking so increase their bulk; this can lead to constipation
- eat a broad range of fruit and vegetables as this will help cover the nutrient range needed.

Vegans cannot eat Quorn as egg white is used in its manufacture, which means it is not totally animal-free. They can eat soya protein and this is a good source of HBV protein for vegans as it contains all the essential amino acids at the correct levels, as they are added during manufacture.

The diet can provide less energy because it is bulky. There is also a risk of anaemia due to lack of iron, and the lack of calcium, phosphorus and vitamin D can affect the bone density. Children should not be vegans as the bulk of the diet means they do not consume enough energy to meet their growth needs.

Assessment activity 11.1

Jane and Aisha have both recently had babies. Jane has decided to breast-feed whilst Aisha has chosen to bottle-feed.

1 Describe the key principles of breast- and bottle-feeding. **P1**

2 Plan a bottle routine for a baby, explaining each step thoroughly. **M1**

11.2 The potential effects of an unbalanced diet on children's health

An excess intake of energy and nutrients will lead to obesity. Excess calories which are not burned up as energy are converted to fat by the body and laid down in the adipose tissue. Excess weight can put a strain on the body's organs and also can make individuals less mobile. They are more prone to illness and have a higher risk of heart attacks, varicose veins and thrombosis. Statistics show they also have a higher percentage of accidents.

Poor intake may lead to signs of deficiencies. There is likely to be a lack of energy and individuals may find themselves more prone to minor illnesses which take longer to clear up.

There are many different ways in which a child's health may be affected by diet.

Malnutrition

Malnutrition is long-term dietary imbalance. It occurs where the total intake of one or more nutrient is out of proportion to the needs of the body. It may lead to a deficiency disease due to a lack of a particular nutrient,

such as beriberi, a disease brought about by the lack of vitamin B1 (thiamine) – see page 387.

Under-nutrition

This occurs when the total intake of nutrients is less than that needed by the body. In most cases the total energy intake is inadequate and many essential nutrients are lacking. It can result in starvation.

Under-nutrition is rare in developed countries, but many children die from it in developing countries. Diseases linked to under-nutrition include:

- protein energy malnutrition (PEM) – a range of disorders which occur mainly in developing countries. It affects children under 5 years of age and is the result of too little energy and protein in the diet. Marasmus and kwashiorkor are the most common. Signs and symptoms include children with large stomachs and thin limbs
- zerophthalmia – a severe lack of vitamin A which leads to blindness.

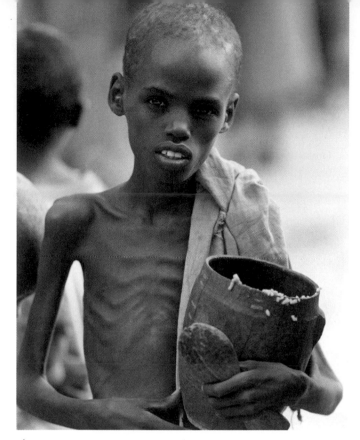

▲ **Under-nutrition is common in developing countries**

Over-nutrition

This is also a type of malnutrition, but it occurs when too much of a nutrient is eaten. One example is over-indulgence in food which leads to excess calorie intake and obesity.

Specific nutrient deficiencies

The lack of certain nutrients can lead to specific deficiencies.

Anaemia

Anaemia occurs due to a lack of iron in the diet or poor iron absorption because the diet is made up of a lot of non-haeme iron which the body finds difficult to absorb. Signs of anaemia include tiredness and lethargy. There may also be shortness of breath as the blood is unable to carry as much oxygen as it needs.

Anaemia can be common in Asian children due to their vegetarian diet.

Key term

Anaemia is a lack of iron in the diet or poor iron absorption.

Rickets

Rickets is a disease in children characterised by poor bone development. It occurs due to a lack of vitamin D, calcium and phosphorus in the diet. The bones become soft and the legs are unable to support the weight of a growing child. It results in physical deformity which includes bow legs and pigeon chest.

Tooth decay

Tooth decay is common in children. It may take two forms:

- *Dental caries* This affects the tooth itself and occurs where bacteria progressively attack the tooth causing pain and infection. It can result in the loss of the tooth.
- *Peridontal disease* This affects the gums or deeper tissue and leads to the gradual loss of bone which leads to loose teeth. This again will lead to eventual loss.

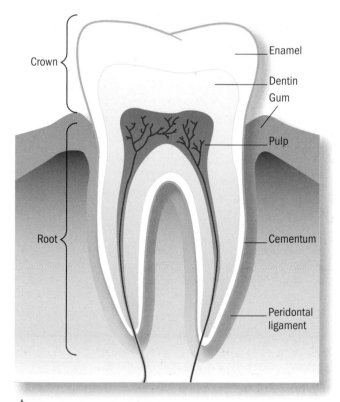

▲ **The structure of a tooth**

For tooth decay to occur, there are three contributing factors which must be present:

- *Agent* This is the bacteria. The bacteria which cause tooth decay are called streptococcus mutans. They produce acid in the mouth which attacks the teeth. The action of bacteria can be reduced by the presence of fluoride ions.
- *Host* This is the tooth. Teeth become susceptible to decay as soon as they are mineralised or formed. Tooth decay is irreversible damage and once teeth are damaged, they are more susceptible to attack. A reduction in the enamel on teeth, which can occur in malnourished children, will make the teeth more prone to attack. Other factors which contribute to this include lack of vitamin D and lack of fluoride in the diet.
- *Environment* This is the mouth, which is an ideal environment for tooth decay as it provides all the necessary raw materials. The bacteria are able to ferment sugar which is consumed in the diet and produce acid which attacks the teeth. The acid in turn dissolves tooth enamel. This occurs within minutes of eating sugar.

■ Foods that cause decay

Foods can be graded on a spectrum ranging from those which are most acidogenic, and therefore make most contribution to tooth decay, to those which are non-acidogenic (see the chart below).

Good practice checklist

Dietary changes which can reduce tooth decay

There are a number of small changes that can be made to reduce the risk of tooth decay. These include:

- Eat less sugary foods – tooth decay is less when sugar intake is rationed.
- Do not eat sugary food between meals – this reduces the exposure to sugar. There is evidence that sugar eaten within meals has less effect than sugar eaten between meals.
- Do not eat foods which provide prolonged delivery of sugar to the mouth, for example toffees, chewing gum with sugar.
- Chew sugar-free gum after a meal – this increases saliva in the mouth and neutralises the environment.
- Eat an apple or cheese after a meal as this will reduce the sugar in the mouth and so reduce decay.

Children should be encouraged to clean their teeth thoroughly at least twice a day using a toothpaste that contains fluoride. They should also visit the dentist regularly. Fluoride is added to tap water and this can help reduce tooth decay.

	Most acidogenic	Moderately acidogenic	Non acidogenic
Foods	Boiled sweets	Apples	Peanuts
	Toffees	Chocolate	Crisps
	High sugar foods, such as cakes and biscuits	Bananas	Cheese
			Eggs
			Dried apples
Nutrients/dietary factors	Sucrose	Galactose	Xylitol
	Fructose	Lactose	Mannitol
	Glucose	Starch	Sorbitol
	Maltose		(artificial sweetners)

Night blindness

Imagine you are lying in bed having just turned out the light. Initially the room is dark, but gradually you begin to see shapes of furniture and other things in the room. This is your night vision.

Night blindness is due to a lack of vitamin A in the diet. It occurs when the purple pigment in the eye is unable to adjust to dim light.

Beriberi

Beriberi is a nervous disease which is common in countries where rice is a staple food. Such diets can have a lack of vitamin B1 (thiamin). Beriberi attacks the nervous system causing paralysis and often death. It can also occur in chronic alcoholics.

Scurvy

Scurvy is due to a lack of vitamin C in the diet. It is rare in developed countries, although it may occur in those living on limited budgets as they are unable to buy foods rich in vitamin C.

Symptoms of scurvy include sore and bleeding gums, loose teeth, pain in the limbs and general tiredness.

Theory into practice

Make a list of the ways in which a parent on a limited budget can ensure their child gets a good intake of vitamin C.

Obesity

Obesity is a growing concern in the UK. To be clinically obese, an individual has to have a body mass index (BMI) of over 30; they are classed as overweight if their body mass index is between 25 and 30.

Theory into practice

BMI is a measure of body fat based on height and weight. You can work out your body mass index by dividing your weight in kg by your height in metres squared.
A BMI of:
under 20 = underweight
20–25 = normal
25–30 = overweight
30+ = obese

Obesity in children has tripled in the last 20 years. Currently around 10 per cent of 6-year-olds are obese and this rises to around 17 per cent of 15-year-olds. There are many reasons for this increase in obesity and both genetics and lifestyle play a part. Some reasons include:

- Children are less active than in the past and therefore burn fewer calories.
- High-calorie foods, such as those which contain high levels of sugar and fat, are more readily available. The increase in disposable income (income families have to spend on luxuries) has meant they can afford convenience foods which can be high in sugar and fat.
- Portion sizes have become larger – as we have become more affluent, we tend to eat more and this contributes to increased weight gain.
- Richer food often has more calories per mouthful.
- Sweet food is often given as a reward – this can help children to develop a sweet tooth.

What happens when a child becomes obese?

Fat cells are laid down in the first few years of life. If a child then eats more calories than they can burn, the excess will be laid down in the fat cells as adipose tissue. Fat cells increase in number to store excess fat and this can lead to an obese child having three times as many as a child who is not overweight. This is a change in body processes. These cells do not disappear if the child loses weight and therefore are fixed for the rest of their life. They will just swell or shrink according to the amount of fat that needs storing.

▲ Obesity in children has tripled in the last 20 years

Effects of being overweight

Being overweight can lead to health problems. Children can be short of breath and unable to take part in exercise. Being overweight also puts a strain on the heart and other internal organs. Other physical effects include damage to feet and the risk of long-term back and leg problems.

Overweight children are more at risk from type II diabetes (see page 390) as the pancreas cannot produce adequate insulin for their needs and size.

Being overweight can also lead to poor self-esteem. Children who are overweight often lack confidence and are sometimes bullied. They may find it difficult to take part in children's games and activities. They will have problems running, they walk more slowly than other children and have problems balancing. They may then turn to food for comfort and this in turn will lead to increased weight gain.

Food intolerance and allergies

There are three forms of **food intolerance**:

- *Food intolerance* This is a general term and includes all reproducible adverse reactions to food which are not psychologically-based. It includes reactions to additives, for example hyperactivity, natural components of food and inborn errors such as **coeliac disease** and diabetes mellitus. The body does not always produce antibodies in the case of food intolerance, but it reacts in the same way each time the particular food is eaten.

- *Food allergy* This is a form of intolerance which causes reproducible symptoms including abnormal immunological reactions to the food eaten. This means that the body produces antibodies when a particular food is eaten as it believes it is harmful. These antibodies can be detected in a blood test.

- *Food aversion* This includes foods which individuals choose to avoid for psychological reasons – there is no medical reason why they cannot be eaten. For example, some people cannot eat oysters because they do not like the texture or salty taste. This can make them feel physically sick.

Key term

Coeliac disease A condition where the body reacts to gluten, the protein which is found in wheat and some other cereals.

A **food intolerance** may be an adverse reaction, an allergy or an aversion to a particular food.

Theory into practice

Are there any foods which you choose to avoid because you do not like them?

Food intolerance

Food intolerance can affect many different parts of the body. Individuals suffering from food intolerance may not experience all the symptoms and each individual's symptoms will be different. The types of symptoms that food intolerance can cause are outlined in the diagram below.

■ Diabetes mellitus

Diabetes mellitus is a disorder caused by insufficient (or lack of) production of the hormone insulin by the pancreas. Insulin is responsible for the absorption of glucose into the cells for their energy needs and into the liver and fat cells for storage. A deficiency of insulin means that the levels of glucose in the blood become abnormally high, causing excessive urination and excessive thirst. The inability to store glucose results in weight loss, hunger and tiredness. Diabetes tends to run in families.

There are two main types of diabetes:

- *insulin-dependent diabetes mellitus (IDDM) – type I*
This is a more severe type of diabetes which usually appears in the under-35s and is often known as teenage onset as it most frequently appears in 10–16-year-olds. It develops rapidly and the pancreatic cells are completely destroyed, probably after a viral infection, and therefore

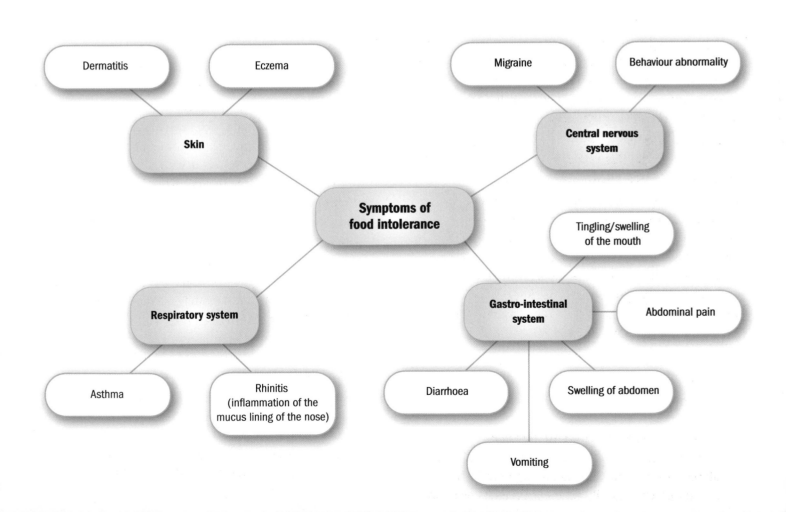

insulin production ceases immediately. The condition has to be controlled by hormone injections without which the sufferer would fall into a coma and die.

- *non-insulin-dependent diabetes mellitus (NIDDM) – type II* This type of diabetes is characterised by its gradual onset. It usually appears in the over-40s and is often so weak in the early stages that it is not obvious and only detected in medical check-ups. Insulin is still produced by the body, but not enough to meet needs. It is often linked to obesity and is the common form which older people suffer from. It is usually controlled by diet, weight loss and oral medication if needed. Injections are not required.

How to control diabetes

Diabetics should aim to keep the blood glucose levels as near to normal as possible through:

- maintenance of normal body weight for height
- regular physical exercise
- careful dietary management
- careful monitoring of blood glucose levels and insulin injections or oral medication if needed.

Dietary management

Doctors, dieticians and the British Diabetic Association all recommend a diet which follows the principles of healthy eating:

- high fibre/unrefined carbohydrates, i.e. starchy food such as wholegrain cereals, pulses, potatoes including the skin, brown rice, and most fruit and vegetables. Fifty per cent of energy should come from this. These carbohydrates are broken down and absorbed more slowly than others and therefore help to maintain the stability of the blood sugar
- low sugar intake – refined sugar is released into the blood stream very quickly and can cause a rise in blood sugar levels
- low fat content – to help manage weight
- low salt content.

It is important to ensure food is eaten regularly throughout the day as this helps to maintain the stability of the blood sugar levels.

- Too little insulin or too much carbohydrate for insulin levels means the blood sugar level rises too high – this is called hyperglycaemia. Insulin has to be injected.

- Too much insulin or too little carbohydrate means blood sugar levels are too low and this is called hypoglycaemia. Food or a sugary drink needs to be consumed. This may occur if a meal is missed or the diabetic takes part in physical exercise.

Food allergies

Allergies to food seem to be on the increase. This is partly because symptoms are recognised better. The most common types of allergy are milk, eggs, shellfish and peanut allergies.

Allergies are quite difficult for carers to deal with as they vary so much according to the individual. With acute food allergies, the first sign is usually a tingling in the mouth and a swelling of the lips. This may be followed by vomiting or diarrhoea if the food is swallowed. This is called an anaphylactic reaction.

An **anaphylactic reaction** is caused by the sudden release of chemical substances in the body, including histamine, from cells in the blood and tissues where they are stored. The release is triggered by the reaction between the allergic antibody (IgE) with the substance (allergen) causing the anaphylactic reaction. In the case of food allergy, the allergen could be any ingredient in the food.

This reaction is so sensitive that minute quantities of the allergen can cause a reaction. Therefore, even having peanut oil on a utensil which is then used to prepare another dish can cause a reaction. This is why you often see a warning on processed foods that the food is made on a production line where products containing nuts

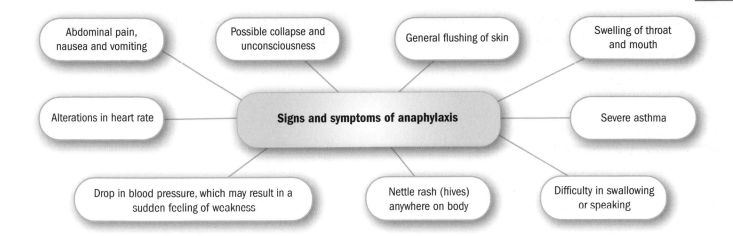

are also made – the manufacturer cannot guarantee that every trace of nut has been removed before they make the next product batch.

Anaphylactic shock is the most extreme allergic reaction. The whole body is affected, usually within minutes of exposure to the allergen, but sometimes the reaction is delayed and will occur hours after contact. This makes the cause more difficult to identify. Peanut allergy and nut allergy are frequently severe and for that reason have received widespread publicity. Other foods can also cause anaphylaxis, as can other triggers including insect stings, latex and drugs. On very rare occasions anaphylaxis may occur with no obvious trigger.

An individual would not necessarily experience all of the symptoms listed in the diagram above.

Key term

An **anaphylactic reaction** is an allergic reaction caused by the sudden release of chemical substances in the body in response to an allergen.

■ Treatment for anaphylactic shock

Any individual who suffers from anaphylactic shock will need adrenaline. Adrenaline injection kits are available on prescription for those believed to be at risk and these people generally carry kits with them. These are available in two strengths – adult and junior.

The injection must be given as soon as a serious reaction is suspected and an ambulance must be called. If there is no improvement in 5–10 minutes, a second injection must be given.

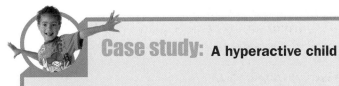

Case study: A hyperactive child

Matthew is 6 years old. His mother thinks he may suffer from hyperactivity. Hyperactivity is a reaction a child may have to a food or food constituent.

1 **What signs and symptoms might Matthew display if he is suffering from a food intolerance?**

2 **Name two foodstuffs that are commonly known to cause to hyperactivity.**

3 **Explain ways in which Matthew's mother could reduce the risk of hyperactivity through the choice and preparation of food.**

■ Milk intolerance

The most common reaction to milk is due to lactose intolerance which is the sugar found in milk. The body lacks or is unable to produce sufficient lactase, the enzyme necessary for the digestion of milk. As the milk sugar cannot be digested, it passes into the large intestine where it causes irritation and consequently pain and diarrhoea.

Sufferers from milk intolerance do not necessarily have to avoid all milk and dairy products as usually small amounts can be tolerated with little ill effect. Cheese has so little lactose that it does not produce the symptoms. Yoghurts also contain very little lactose as most has been converted to lactic acid during fermentation and this does not cause the same symptoms.

Sufferers may choose goat's or ewe's milk and cheese and these are low in lactose.

Extension activity

Plan one meal that is suitable for as many different special diets as possible. Explain why the meal meets the different needs.

Assessment activity 11.2

Eating a balanced diet is important for growth and development. A diet should include all the necessary nutrients for growth as well as being healthy.

1 Describe the potential effects of an unbalanced diet on babies and young children. **P4**

2 Produce a balanced menu for a 3-year-old for a week, justifying your choices. Make sure you think about nutritional content as well as presentation. Include variety. **M3**

3 Analyse the menu produced from the point of view of nutrients, balance and health of a child. **D1**

11.3 The principles of food safety

Safe practices

Food safety legislation

Food which has been prepared in unhygienic conditions can cause illness. Some illnesses can be life-threatening for vulnerable groups such as children. Therefore, anyone preparing food to sell for others to consume has to conform to certain food safety legislation. The principles and practices linked to good food hygiene are also important for food being prepared in the home to prevent food-related illnesses.

■ Food Safety Act 1990

This Act aims to protect consumers by:

- preventing illness from the consumption of food
- preventing them from being misled as to the nature of the food they are purchasing
- ensuring that all food produced for sale is safe to eat, of high quality and not misleadingly presented.

The Act covered four main areas:

- labelling
- additives and contaminants
- composition (or content)
- public health and hygiene.

Under the Act, it is illegal to sell food which has been contaminated or adulterated or is unfit for human consumption. It is also an offence to label or advertise food in a way that misleads the customer. The Act provides legal powers and penalties for companies and individuals who do not abide by it.

■ Food Safety (General Food Hygiene) Regulations 1995

These are regulations made under the Food Safety Act 1990. They apply to all types of food and food businesses, but do not cover domestic preparation in the home. They do cover non-commercial activities such as charity events.

The regulations set down standards that must be followed for food premises where food is being prepared. These standards include:

- *food premises* These must be kept clean and in good repair. There are regulations about design and layout; hand-washing facilities and toilets; hot and cold running water; ventilation; lighting and changing facilities

- *food rooms* There are specific requirements for rooms where food is being prepared which include the construction of ceilings, floors and windows and facilities for cleaning utensils and equipment as well as food

- *waste disposal* Poor disposal of waste can lead to food contamination. The regulations contain specific guidance about this

- *storage of food* The regulations outline how different types of foodstuff should be stored to reduce the risk of contamination

- *staff expectations* This covers ensuring staff follow good personal hygiene rules and are trained in these. It also makes it clear that staff should not work if they are ill.

Extension activity

The food safety regulations state that there must be changing facilities away from the food preparation areas where staff can change from their outdoor clothes. There must be toilet facilities which do not open onto the food preparation area and separate hand-washing facilities which are different from basins used for food preparation.
Why do you think these regulations exist?

■ Food Safety (Temperature Control) Regulations 1995

These regulations require that certain foods must be kept at temperatures that will prevent the growth of harmful bacteria or the formation of toxins. It is an offence to keep food at temperatures that would cause a health risk. Food should either be kept cold at below 8°C or hot at above 63°C.

Sometimes it is difficult to keep food at these temperatures, for example when on display or laid out for people to eat. In these situations, the food may be kept outside the designated temperatures for a short period of time, after which they must be discarded. For example:

- Chilled food can be kept unchilled for four hours, after which it must be thrown away.
- Hot food can be kept hot for up to two hours after which it must be discarded.
- Hot food should not be reheated more than once.

More information about the food safety acts and regulations can be found at www.food.gov.uk.

Hazard Analysis Critical Control Point (HACCP)

Hazard Analysis Critical Control Points (HACCP) is an approach to food safety that looks at the identification of Critical Control Points (CCPs) in food production and preparation processes. These are the points where there may be a higher risk of food contamination or food poisoning occurring. These points are then closely monitored in the production phase to ensure risk is reduced and food is safe for consumption.

Effects of unsafe practices

Food poisoning as a result of poor food hygiene is on the increase. Reasons for this include:

- increased incidence of eating out, where more food is prepared in a commercial setting and where hygiene faults can occur easily – one fault affects many
- mass catering, for example in schools, nursery settings and hospitals, where one fault can affect many
- greater use of convenience foods where temperature control is very important and is commonly misunderstood. This can also affect cook–chill food
- increased consumption of takeaways where food is kept at room serving temperature for long periods of time
- more cases are being reported as the public are more aware and there are also better laboratory techniques to identify causes.

Food may be poisonous or cause illness for several reasons:

- Some foods are naturally poisonous because they contain natural toxins, for example some mushrooms, red kidney beans (if not cooked correctly).
- Food may be contaminated with toxic chemicals, such as lead, copper, agricultural pesticides and herbicides, or chemicals such as disinfectants can contaminate food during growth, storage, preparation and or cooking.
- Food may be contaminated with pathogenic micro-organisms or toxic chemicals produced by micro-organisms. This is the most important type of food poisoning and is generally a result of poor food hygiene practices.

The main reasons for food poisoning are bad temperature control and/or incorrect storage. This often occurs because food is prepared too far in advance, cooled too slowly, stored incorrectly, for example at room temperature, not reheated sufficiently or incorrectly thawed.

Groups particularly at risk from food poisoning include vulnerable groups such as children, pregnant women, and those suffering from illness or convalescing. They are less able to cope with the symptoms of food poisoning.

▲ Would you like to eat food prepared in this kitchen?

Conditions in which bacteria multiply

Growth conditions need to be understood as preventing these conditions will help prevent the growth of harmful bacteria. To grow and reproduce, bacteria need:

- *a food source* Bacteria secrete enzymes to digest the main nutrients: sugar, proteins and fats in the food they are in. The simple products of this digestion are absorbed into the bacterial cell for metabolism
- *moisture* This is essential for all living organisms. Most foods are 55–98 per cent water and therefore readily supply the bacteria
- *temperature* The best temperature for bacterial growth is 37°C or room temperature. Rapid growth will occur at this temperature. Below 5°C bacteria growth slows or stops and above 100°C bacteria are killed
- *pH* Bacteria generally prefer a neutral pH in which to grow – most foods are neutral
- *time* Bacteria multiply by binary fission every 20 minutes – where 1 becomes 2, 2 becomes 4, 4 becomes 8, and so on. Therefore they have the capacity to rapidly reproduce given time
- *oxygen* Some bacteria are aerobic and therefore need oxygen in order to reproduce. Others are anaerobic and can reproduce without oxygen.

Most methods of food presentation aim to remove one of these growth conditions. For example, freezing reduces the temperature to a level where bacteria cannot multiply, canning heats food to a level where bacteria are killed, dehydration removes the moisture and pickling renders the pH too acidic for most bacteria to grow.

Common types of bacteria that cause food poisoning

There are many different types of food poisoning bacteria. The table below sets out some of the most common.

▼ Common types of bacteria that cause food poisoning

Bacteria	How food is contaminated	Affected foods	Symptoms	Onset	Duration	Special comments including groups most at risk
Salmonella	Found in the guts of humans, animals and insects; therefore their excreta are both a direct and indirect source of this bacteria. Poor hand-washing habits after using the toilet may be a cause of infection. Salmonella can also survive outside the body for long periods and therefore door handles, work surfaces and equipment can be contaminated. Meat and poultry may be infected at the slaughter house.	Meat, especially cooked meat and poultry, eggs, shellfish from polluted water, custards, cream and ice cream	Some fever, vomiting and diarrhoea	12–36 hours as the bacteria produces the poisonous substance in the cells and this is only released into the body when the cell dies.	1–7 days	This is the most common type of food poisoning and is responsible for two-thirds of cases. Salmonella can survive for up to three hours on unwashed hands. It is particularly dangerous for the very young and the elderly and can lead to death. It is easily destroyed by adequate cooking – food must reach a high enough temperature to kill the bacteria.

Staphylococcus aureus	Found in the human nose, throat and on the skin. Also found in whitlows, infected burns and wounds and in nasal secretions after a cold. Introduced to food directly from the hands or by droplet infection from coughs and sneezes or indirectly by licking spoons or from handkerchiefs.	Foods which are handled and then served without cooking, for example cream-filled cakes, precooked or processed meats and pies. Also meats that are precooked then reheated to serve as this allows the food handler to contaminate them after cooking.	Vomiting, diarrhoea, abdominal cramp (unpleasant but not serious)	1–6 hours (very rapid as the toxin is produced by the bacteria before it is eaten)	6–12 hours	Toxin is produced in the food before the food is eaten and therefore onset is quick but so is the course of the illness. Bacteria are easily destroyed by heat but the toxin can survive 20 minutes of boiling.
Clostridium perfringens	Found in soil and therefore infects fruit and vegetables. It can form spores and therefore can survive dry atmospheres – it is therefore often found in dust, on floors and on kitchen surfaces.	Meat, gravies, stews and large joints which are cooked and allowed to cool slowly	Diarrhoea and severe stomach pain	8–22 hours – because the bacteria produces the toxin when it reaches the intestines	12–24 hours	The spores are heat resistant and are not killed unless a temperature of over 100°C is reached. They germinate as meat and meat dishes start to cool.
Clostridium botulinum	Found in soil and decaying matter.	Bottled or canned foods particularly those which are not acidic. Vegetables, meat, fish and meat pastes where the processing temperature has not been high enough to kill the spores	Central nervous system is affected leading to paralysis and eventually death	13–36 hours	Prolonged illness which is sometimes fatal	Very rare disease. The bacteria produce a spore, which if it survives processing can reproduce without air and produces a very dangerous toxin.
Listeriosis	The bacteria can grow in low temperatures where other bacteria are usually dormant and it produces a toxin as it develops.	Found in pre-prepared salads, soft crusted cheeses, processed meats and pates, cook–chill foods and shellfish	Moderate flu-like symptoms – can cause miscarriage in pregnant women. Sometimes causes blood poisoning	5 days to 6 weeks	Various	Toxin damages the human cells involved in immunity and therefore abnormally weak people do not stand up well to an attack of this toxin. It is difficult to treat as it gets inside the cell which protects it from antibiotics.

Good practice checklist

Preventing food poisoning

There are a number of simple precautions which can be taken when preparing food which will help reduce the risk of food poisoning.

- *Food choice and storage*
  - Always choose fresh foods which look fresh.
  - Choose foods which are within sell-by dates.
  - Use a cool bag to transport cold foods from the supermarket to home/setting.
  - Do not allow frozen foods to thaw before needed for cooking.
  - Make sure the fridge is between 0° and 5°C and the freezer below −18°C.
  - Always store food which is labelled to be refrigerated in the refrigerator.
  - If food is to be served cold, always store in the refrigerator until it is needed.
  - To avoid cross-contamination, store cooked and raw food separately. Store cooked meat above raw meat to avoid blood dripping onto cooked meat.

- *Personal hygiene*
  - Cover sores and cuts with a waterproof dressing.
  - Wash your hands after going to the toilet and after blowing your nose.
  - Wash your hands in the hand basin and not in the sink.
  - Wear your hair tied back, no jewellery and no nail polish.
  - Wear clean protective clothing.
  - Wash your hands before preparing food and between handling different foods.
  - Do not touch your face, hair or nose when preparing food.

  - Do not cough or sneeze over food – if you are preparing food for others, do not do so if you are ill, especially if you have a stomach upset or diarrhoea.

- *Food preparation and cooking*
  - Clean work surfaces and utensils as you go using a clean cloth.
  - Eat foods by the use-by dates.
  - Keep animals away from food preparation areas.
  - To prevent cross-contamination, use separate utensils and chopping boards to prepare raw and cooked foods.
  - Thoroughly defrost food that needs defrosting before cooking.
  - Make sure cooked foods reach a temperature of over 63°C – they should be piping hot
  - Follow the instructions for pre-prepared foods and make sure reheated meals are piping hot.
  - Only reheat food once.
  - Check meat and poultry with a food thermometer to make sure the right temperature has been reached. Juices should run clear.
  - Keep hot foods hot and cold foods cold.
  - Do not keep food warm for long periods of time and particularly not between 5° and 63°C where bacteria multiply rapidly.
  - Cool foods as quickly as possible and within 1½ hours – cover and store in the fridge or freezer.

- *Reporting food poisoning* If you become ill after eating food bought from a shop or served in a café or restaurant, inform your local environmental health department so they can investigate the food hygiene standards of that food outlet.

Case study: Preventing food poisoning

Hamed Ali is a 6-year-old boy. His mother, Rashia, works full time and often relies on cook–chill meals during the week for quick and easy suppers. Rashia has been keeping the meals in the kitchen cupboard until they eat them.

1 Identify *four* conditions bacteria need to multiply.

2 What advice could you give Rashia to help her prevent food poisoning?

3 What effect might food poisoning have on Hamed?

4 Rashia still prepares some food from fresh produce at weekends. She particularly likes chicken and is therefore at risk from cross-contamination. What advice would you give Rashia about safe food handling?

Assessment activity 11.3

Food hygiene and safety are essential when producing food for anyone, but particularly young children who can be vulnerable to food poisoning.

1 Describe the principles of food safety and the potential effects of unsafe practice. **P5**

2 Explain the potential effects of unsafe food practices in a children's setting. **M4**

3 Evaluate the food safety practices in a children's setting of your choice. **D2**

End of unit assessment

Jane and Aisha's babies are now almost 4 months old. They would like some advice on weaning. This is Jane's first baby so she is unsure what to do. Aisha has a 3-year-old who is a fussy eater and wonders if weaning had anything to do with it.

1 Describe the process of weaning and feeding older babies and young children. **P2**

2 Explain the importance of the process of weaning. **M2**

3 Describe the main considerations in presenting food to young children. **P3**

References and further reading

Useful websites

Food Safety Acts – www.food.gov.uk

School Food Trust – www.schoolfoodtrust.org.uk

Grading criteria	Assessment activity	Page number
To achieve a pass grade the evidence must show that the learner is able to:		
P1 describe the key principles of breast- and bottle-feeding	11.1	384
P2 describe the process of weaning and the feeding of older babies and young children	End of unit assessment	398
P3 describe the main considerations in presenting food to young children	End of unit assessment	398
P4 describe the potential effects of an unbalanced diet on babies and children	11.2	392
P5 describe the principles of food safety and the potential effects of unsafe practice	11.3	398
To achieve a merit grade the evidence must show that, in addition to the pass criteria, the learner is able to:		
M1 plan a bottle-feeding routine for a baby, giving explanations for each step	11.1	384
M2 explain the importance of the process of weaning	End of unit assessment	398
M3 produce a balanced menu for a three-year-old child for a week, justifying the choices	11.2	392
M4 explain the potential effects of unsafe food practices in children's settings		398
To achieve a distinction grade the evidence must show that, in addition to the pass and merit criteria, the learner is able to:		
D1 analyse the menu produced, from the point of view of nutrients, balance and the health of the child	11.2	392
D2 evaluate the food safety practices in a children's setting	11.3	398

Psychological perspectives on behaviour

Introduction

When working with children and young people, you may find it useful to have a basic knowledge of child psychology as it helps you to work more effectively with children. Having an understanding of child psychology will support your day-to-day practice when carrying out observations on children, for example, or when considering why children behave the way they do. Using psychology can help you to manage children's behaviour and help children to settle in, as well as helping you to decide how best to present activities.

This unit will allow you to consider the psychological perspectives on children's behaviour and how you might implement strategies to promote positive behaviour within your setting. You will consider the effects of early relationships and look at the basic principles and theories relating to child psychology.

What you need to learn

- Theoretical perspectives of developmental psychology and the development of children's behaviour
- The formation of early relationships
- The factors affecting children's behaviour
- Approaches to challenging behaviour
- Techniques for monitoring the effectiveness of implementing behavioural strategies

Thinking points

You are working in a preschool nursery, supporting a new member of staff who has little practical experience. She asks you about how the children develop, and why some of the children, although at the same age, are very different in their abilities. She explains that she assumed all children learn the same things at the same age.

- How might you explain to the member of staff that children's development and learning is continual and that they do not necessarily jump from one stage to another?
- Do you think there are any areas of learning that are particularly stage-like?
- How might you demonstrate this to the member of staff?

The term 'behaviour' is used widely within psychology and it is worth noting that its use is not limited to appropriate or inappropriate actions that children might show. The term behaviour takes in all responses and actions that children might make. This section begins by considering some of the main issues in psychology before considering the ways in which children's behaviour develops.

Issues in developmental psychology

Why study children?

There are many different branches of psychology, but developmental psychology looks at the skills and thoughts that we have and considers how we might have acquired them. It studies how we grow and develop and includes areas such as how we learn, language and personality development. Having an understanding of how children learn will help us when planning activities, whilst knowing about the way children learn language will enable us to provide the best conditions for this.

The nature–nurture debate

Psychology as a separate subject has gradually evolved from biology. This means that many of the early theories were influenced by the idea that we inherit skills, abilities and behaviour. Work by behaviourists such as Skinner have since shown that our behaviour can also be shaped. The issue for many psychologists is to define how much of our skills, personalities, etc., are inherited (nature) and how much is influenced by our environment (nurture), as most psychologists accept that both influences are probably at work.

A practitioner who fundamentally believes that children's abilities and personalities are with them when they are born may take a non-interventionist approach, for example 'boys will be boys' or 'she's very shy'. A practitioner who believes that nurture has a bigger impact may take a different stance, believing that the children's progress and behaviour will be a reflection on their own abilities as an educator.

Continuity v. discontinuity

■ Is development continuous or does it occur in stages?

Some theories discussed in this unit are 'stage' theories, for example Freud's psychosexual stages of personality and Piaget's stages of cognitive development. Such theories are based on the idea that development passes through defined and separate stages and that each stage will have recognisable features; for example, in language development, children babble before they speak words, so babbling is seen as a stage in itself. Others feel that development is more gradual or a continuous process.

Nomothetic v. idiographic

This debate looks at whether we are all unique (the idiographic approach) or share essential characteristics but that we have some differences (the nomothetic approach). This debate is particularly relevant when we consider our personalities.

Theory into practice

Many early years practitioners may feel that children do not jump from stage to stage, but that development is often so gradual that it is hard to see, although over a few weeks they can see that children's development has progressed.

- In your work setting, ask staff what they think. Do they think that children's progress fits into stages or that development is continual? Ask if there are any areas of development which seem particularly stage-like.

Main theoretical perspectives

There are six main theoretical perspectives that keep occurring in developmental psychology. Whilst, originally, these were often seen as competing perspectives, increasingly today psychologists find that there are often overlaps between the different perspectives:

- biological perspectives
- social perspectives
- psychodynamic perspectives
- cognitive perspectives
- humanistic perspectives
- behaviourist perspectives.

Biological perspectives

Biology has a major influence on psychology. This is partly historic as the study of psychology grew out of the disciplines of philosophy and biology. Biological perspectives reflect the 'nature' element of the nature v. nurture debate. Areas such as aggression and the way in which we react instinctively in certain situations are sometimes linked to biological processes.

Social perspectives

Theories that have a social perspective look particularly at the influence of others on children's development. These perspectives link particularly to the 'nurture' element of the debate within psychology. Examples of social perspectives within psychology include the influence of parents on children's behaviour and the way in which social relationships affect us. Social perspectives also consider cross-cultural research, helping us to identify universal patterns and cultural variations that affect development, as well as the role of gender.

Psychodynamic perspectives

Psychodynamic perspectives consider the role of the subconscious on our actions. This area of psychology remains one that is quite controversial and is particularly associated with Freud.

Cognitive perspectives

Cognitive perspectives look at how children's actions are influenced by their thoughts and ability to process information. These perspectives also focus on the way in which thinking changes as children develop language and also mature.

Humanistic perspectives

Humanistic perspectives concentrate on the unique characteristics of human beings. It rejects the idea that children are influenced by their environment, but that, by exercising free choice and freedom of expression, they have a natural ability to make choices and decisions.

Behaviourist perspectives

Behaviourist perspectives consider the influences of the outer environment, rejecting the idea that children pass through stages, but that they are affected by the environment to which they are exposed.

The table below shows some of the key theorists that have influenced developmental psychology.

Name	Perspective	Key theory	Comments
Sigmund Freud	Psychodynamic	Psychosexual stages of development	Freud made a distinction between our conscious and unconscious minds.
Erik Erikson	Psychodynamic	Psychosocial stages of development	Erikson produced his theory based on Freud's work. He considered that our personalities carry on developing into adulthood.
John Bowlby	Biological	Maternal deprivation	Bowlby showed in his work that for healthy development, babies and young children need to form a bond with their parents or key carers.
Albert Bandura	Social/behaviourist	Social learning theory	Bandura showed that children can learn through imitating others.
Burrhus Frederic Skinner	Biological/behaviourist	Operant conditioning	Skinner suggested that behaviour can be manipulated through the use of reinforcements.
Ivan Pavlov	Biological	Classic conditioning	Pavlov through his works with dogs showed that humans can learn through association.
Jean Piaget	Cognitive	Stages of cognitive development	Piaget suggested that children's thinking passed through stages.
Lev Vygotsky	Social	Zone of Proximal Development	Vygotsky placed emphasis on the importance of adults to help children understand concepts.
Sandra Bem	Social	Bem Sex-Role Inventory	Bem created a measurement, which identifies masculine and feminine psychological traits.
Carl Rogers	Humanistic	Transpersonal psychology	Rogers suggested that all people have a need to be loved and respected, resulting in us becoming dependent upon them.
Abraham Maslow	Humanistic	Maslow's hierarchy of need	Maslow suggests that in order for us to feel fulfilled, we need to reach a state of self-fulfilment in which we may achieve our highest potential.

Acquisition of behaviour

When the term behaviour is used in ordinary conversation, we may think of actions of some kind – good or bad. Psychologists use the term in a different and broader way, i.e. the study of behaviour encompasses the way we learn, form attitudes and how we behave towards others.

Acquiring behaviour through learning

Behaviour and learning are linked. It is through behaviour that psychologists can see that learning has taken place. If we can understand how we learn, we could be more effective in our teaching and improve society. Psychologists in this area are interested in the process of *how* we learn rather than what we learn.

There are several theories that explain the learning process, broadly dividing into two strands: the behaviourist approach and **social learning theory.** There is also a third strand which centres around how children learn to think and develop thought processes (see pages 417–21).

The importance of learning theories in psychology

Learning theories are extremely important as they can be applied to many situations. This means that when studying other aspects of child development, such as language, behaviour management, etc., the same terms and theories will keep reappearing.

This approach suggests that learning is influenced by rewards, punishments and environmental factors. The term conditioning is often used by behaviourists – it means that we learn to act in a certain way because past experiences have taught us to do or not do something. We may know this as 'learning by association', for example not touching a flame because we were once burnt. There are two types of conditioning which are well documented: **classical conditioning** and **operant conditioning**.

Theory into practice

Classical conditioning can help us to understand how some children might develop seemingly irrational fears, for example suddenly being afraid of the dark, particular foods or animals. Consider this example: Mary was 5 years old and had gone to bed without being afraid of the dark. One night she was violently sick and her room was in darkness. Afterwards Mary cried if no light was left on at night.

Key terms

Social learning theory suggests we learn by imitating others.

Classical conditioning is a method of learning where a response can be triggered by a recognised cue.

Operant conditioning is a method of learning which is based on the type of consequence or reinforcement that follows our initial behaviour.

■ Classical conditioning

Ivan Pavlov was a physiologist who, whilst studying dogs, noticed that they always started to salivate before food was put down for them. He concluded that the dogs were anticipating the food and were salivating because they had learnt to associate the arrival of food with other things such as footsteps, buckets, etc. He devised an experiment where he fed dogs whilst a bell was sounded. Normally dogs do not salivate when hearing bells, but the dogs began to associate the bell with food and would salivate simply on hearing the bell.

Applying classical conditioning to humans

Pavlov's work was built on by Watson who showed that it was possible to use classical conditioning on humans. In a famous experiment he was able to make a baby of 11 months afraid of a white rat. The child had previously shown no fear of rats, but by pairing the rat with something that did frighten the child, the child was conditioned to be afraid of the rat.

■ Operant conditioning

The basis of the operant conditioning theory is that our learning is based on the type of consequence or reinforcement that follows our initial behaviour. B.F. Skinner (1904–90) is recognised as being a key figure in developing the behaviourist approach to learning theory and in particular for developing the theory of operant conditioning. His work was at first based on E.J. Thorndike's law of effect.

Thorndike's law of effect

The original concept of operant conditioning was first pioneered by E.J. Thorndike, although he did not use the term operant conditioning. Thorndike (1898) showed through experiments with cats that the results of behaviour would affect subsequent behaviour. This he called the 'law of effect'.

In his experiments, hungry cats were put into a 'puzzle box' which had a lever that allowed the cats to escape. The cats could see from inside the box a piece of fish which they were able to eat every time they escaped. At first the cats took about five minutes to escape and did so the first time purely through trial and error. Subsequently they were able to reduce the time that it took them to escape until they were able to escape in less than five seconds.

Thorndike suggested that the cats learnt to operate the lever because their behaviour had been rewarded or 'stamped in' by being able to escape and in particular by eating the fish.

Skinner

Skinner adopted and furthered Thorndike's work into the now accepted model of operant conditioning. Whilst Skinner accepted the work of Pavlov and Watson, he suggested, however that most humans and animals learn through exploring the environment and then drawing conclusions based on the consequences of their behaviour. This means that we tend to be active in the learning process, which is an important difference from classical conditioning.

Skinner divided the consequences of actions into three groups:

- *positive reinforcers*, which are likely to make us repeat behaviour where we get something we desire. For example, we may buy a new food product after having tried and liked a free sample. Skinner suggested that using positive reinforcement was the most effective way of encouraging new learning. Positive reinforcers for children include gaining adults' attention, praise, stickers, sweets and treats

- *negative reinforcers*, which are likely to make us repeat behaviour as well, but this is in order to stop something from happening to us. For example, we may continue to wear oven gloves to stop us from being burnt

- *punishers*, which are likely to stop us from repeating behaviour. For example, we may learn to stay away from an electric fence after receiving a shock.

- *Unexpected positive reinforcers* Skinner found during his experiments that it was often hard to predict what would act as a primary reinforcer and that it was sometimes only after the event that this became clear. An example of this is when children sometimes deliberately behave badly in order to attract their carer's attention. If they manage to attract the attention, they are more likely to show the behaviour again although they might be told off. Gaining the carer's attention in this case is the positive reinforcer even if they are being told off.

- *Primary and secondary reinforcers* There are some reinforcers that give us instant pleasure, satisfaction or meet a need. These are referred to as primary reinforcers. Chocolate is a primary reinforcer because most people find that once they put it into their mouths, they enjoy the taste. Secondary reinforcers are different because they in themselves do not give us satisfaction, but we learn that they symbolise getting primary reinforcement. A good example of secondary reinforcement in our daily lives is money. Coins and notes in themselves do not give us reward, but we learn that they can be used to buy something that will give us primary reinforcement, for example food. (The learning that is used when making the association with money and being able to get something is classical conditioning.)

Theory into practice

Operant conditioning is often used to encourage children to show wanted behaviour, although many parents and early years workers will think of it as offering a bribe! A child may be given a sticker if they have helped to tidy away. In this way, the child will be more likely to help in future as their behaviour has been positively reinforced.

Theory into practice

Young children do not understand the value of money because they have not made the association with money and pleasure. Toddlers, for example, are often more interested in the size, colour and shape of coins This means that offering money as a reward to young children is not very effective.

- *Frequency of reinforcement* Skinner looked at the effect that giving positive reinforcements at different intervals would have on behaviour. How long would behaviour be shown without a positive reward before extinction takes place? Interestingly, he found that unpredictable reinforcement works better than continual reinforcement. This would seem to work because it teaches the learner not to expect a reward or reinforcement every time. So they keep on showing the behaviour just in case a reinforcement is given. In everyday life, this is one of the reasons why gamblers find it so hard to stop playing. They know that they will not win every time, but carry on just in case they get lucky.

- *Delaying reinforcement* Delaying positive reinforcement, for example saying to a child that they can have a sticker at the end of the week, weakens the effect of the reinforcement. Immediate positive reinforcements are the most effective, partly because the behaviour is then more strongly linked to the reinforcement.

Social learning theory

This is another widely accepted learning theory. The key figure among social learning theorists is Albert Bandura (1925–). Social learning theorists accept the principles of conditioning, but suggest that learning by classical and operant conditioning alone would not explain other behaviours. Social learning theorists are particularly interested in looking at moral and social behaviour (see also Unit 7 and Unit 8).

■ Bandura's Bobo doll experiment

Bandura's famous experiment, often referred to as the Bobo doll experiment (1965), showed that children can learn behaviour by watching adults. Bandura showed a film to three groups of children. The film showed an adult in a room with a Bobo doll (a large inflatable doll). The three groups saw different versions:

- Group A saw the adult acting aggressively to the doll.
- Group B saw the adult being aggressive to the doll, but at the end of the film, the adult was rewarded with sweets and lemonade by another adult.
- Group C saw the adult being aggressive to the doll, but at the end a second adult appeared and told the adult off.

After the film, each group of children was shown in turn into a playroom that had a variety of toys including the Bobo doll. The reactions of the children were recorded. Group C were the least aggressive to the doll, but there was little difference between groups A and B. This suggested that they were less influenced by the reward that had been offered to the adult.

A follow-up to the experiment asked the children if they could demonstrate how the doll had been attacked and were rewarded for doing so. There was little difference between the three groups showing that they could all imitate the behaviour they had seen.

Theory into practice

Early years practitioners may agree that children learn through observational learning. A toddler may try to cross their legs in adult fashion after seeing an adult do so. If children do learn through observational learning, this has powerful implications for early years practitioners. We must act as good role models for children and be responsible when children are with us.

■ Reference group

It is thought that children's behaviour is also shaped by their reference group. In young children this is their families, but with older children, this extends to their peers. Reference groups provide children with models for behaviour and so can influence their behaviour. This can be particularly observed in adolescents who may develop their own fashion styles within a group.

■ Effects of parenting styles

As part of the social perspective on children's behaviour, some work has looked at the effects on parenting styles on children's behaviour. Parenting styles are usually grouped into four categories, as shown in the table below. It is important to realise that few parents consciously choose a style.

Style	Features	Outcome for child
Authoritarian	High levels of control and demands on child Low levels of warmth, negotiation and communication	Low self-esteem Lower achievement in school Subdued/aggressive tendencies
Permissive	Low level of control High levels of warmth and communication Indulgent	Slightly lower levels of achievement in school Less independent and mature May be aggressive, if aggressive behaviour is allowed at home
Authoritative	High level of control, but balanced by high levels of warmth and response to child	High levels of achievement Independent High levels of self-esteem
Uninvolved	Low levels of control Low levels of warmth and responsiveness	Low levels of achievement in school Low levels of self-esteem

Personality development

One of the greatest influences in psychology is Sigmund Freud. He is particularly famous for his psychosexual theory of development, often used to explain our unconscious thoughts and actions.

■ Freud's structure of personality

Freud suggested that there were three parts that made up our personality: the id, the ego and the superego. Not all of these parts are present at birth but develop with the child.

The id

This is the instinctive part of our personality, governed by the drives and needs of the body, such as hunger, pleasure. The id does not consider how meeting our desires and wants will affect others and so is often thought of as the selfish and passionate component. Freud suggested that babies only have the id when they were born – hence a baby will cry and cry until it is fed, regardless of how tired the carer is or whether there are other children that also need feeding. Getting the desire or need met is known as gratification.

The ego

The ego has a planning role. It works out how to meet the id's needs and desires in the best way. The ego develops from the id in the first few months – as babies might learn that by smiling in some situations, they are more likely to get their needs met, whilst in others it is

better to cry. In some situations the ego may sometimes make the id wait for its demands to be met. For example, a child may learn that if they snatch a cake from a tray, they may have it taken away from them, but by waiting to be offered it, they will eventually get it. The term deferred gratification is used when this happens.

The superego

The superego develops later in childhood and is that part of our personality that gives us our conscience. It tries to control the ego. It comprises two elements:

- the *conscience* will punish the ego if it misbehaves, i.e. does something that the superego considers wrong. This is the source of our guilt
- the *ego-ideal* will reward the ego if it shows good behaviour, i.e. pride, high self-esteem. This is the source of our pride and confidence.

■ Freud's psychosexual stages

Freud believed that our personalities are based mainly on biological needs or drives – the id factor! He felt that the main drives were sexual and aggressive ones and he shocked Victorian and Edwardian society by suggesting that the sexual drive was present in babies and children. The energy behind these drives, Freud called libido. He suggested that there were five stages through which we pass in childhood and on which our libido concentrated. The stages linked to physical development of the body. Freud felt that if we did not pass through these stages satisfactorily, part of our energy or libido would be stuck – or fixated. This would affect our behaviour and personality.

Oedipus complex

One of the theories that made Freud famous is the Oedipus complex. In the Greek tragedy, Oedipus falls in love with his mother and kills his father. Freud suggests that in the phallic stage, children fall in love with the opposite sex parent – hence the title of the theory. They then see the other parent as a rival. This is also a stage where children have become aware of the physical differences between men and women. Freud argued that the absence of a penis is thought by children to be as a result of castration. This leads boys to fear being castrated – 'castration anxiety'. Boys therefore have a decision to make, should they continue to love their mothers and risk being castrated by their fathers? Freud suggests that the conflict is resolved because boys decide to try to make a friend of their fathers by copying and admiring them.

For girls the situation is slightly different. Freud called this the female Oedipus (or Electra) complex. Girls will believe that they have already been castrated and develop 'penis envy'. Eventually realising that they cannot have a penis, they develop a desire for a baby and turn to their fathers. Freud is not so clear why girls then begin to develop closer ties with their mothers. He suggested that the ties are not as profound and that a girl tries to identify with the mother fearing that her mother will stop loving her.

Theory into practice

It is interesting that many children do have strong links with the opposite sex parent. We may hear the expression 'he's a mother's boy', for example, or hear a girl saying that one day she is going to marry her father. The phallic stage does correspond with children often showing very sex-stereotypical play. Freud would argue that this play helps the child to identify and copy the actions of the parent they fear. It is also interesting to note that boys do seem often to hold their penises at this age, particularly when they are anxious.

Erikson's theory of personality development

Erikson was influenced by Freud's work, but considered that the social environment, i.e. parenting and friendships, also affect personality. He accepted Freud's theory of the structure of personality being divided into three, but did not feel that Freud's work went far enough. He considered that our personalities were not fixed, and that we kept on changing during the course of our lives. His stages of personality development are life stages and are linked to social stages. He considered that at each stage, we face a dilemma or conflict and that, like Freud, the outcome of each stage would determine our personality.

Personality – a behaviourist approach

Do children learn some aspects of their personality from their parents through imitation and reinforcement? This would be the behaviourist and social learning approach to personality development. Many children share some characteristics of their parents. They can also develop similar attitudes to them. The difficulty with this approach is that it does not explain why children brought up in the same families can be so different.

Acquiring gender role

Gender concept and **sex-role concept** are an important part of self-concept and image. Our gender and the expectations of our gender become part of our self-image – of who we are. It is important not to confuse gender concept with sex-role concept. Sex-role concept is learnt alongside gender concept and means that children come to understand how as a boy or girl they are expected to act.

Key term

Gender concept is the understanding that gender is constant and permanent.
Sex-role concept is the understanding how, as a boy or girl, children are expected to act.

Gender identity

Children need to understand if they are a boy or a girl. By 9 or 10 months, babies are already starting to respond differently to male and female faces. By the age of 2 years, most children can correctly pick out a same sex picture (Thompson, 1975). Children seem to be using clues such as hair length and dress. Understanding gender identity is the first step in the gender concept process.

Gender constancy

Children also need to understand that regardless of the way people dress, act or cut their hair, they remain either male or female. This is called gender constancy. Understanding that some things remain the same, even if their appearances change, links to Piaget's theory of conservation (see also page 255) which suggests that this understanding marks a significant stage in children's cognitive development.

Sex-role concept

This is always an interesting area in the light of equal opportunities practice and policies. How do children learn the sex roles that are associated with gender? The table below outlines some of the stages of the development of gender concept and sex-role concept.

Age	Stage of development
9–12 months	Babies react differently to male and female faces
18–24 months	Toddlers start to show preferences for gender-stereotyped toys
By 2 years	Children can point to a picture of a same-sex child
2½–3 years	Children identify differences between genders by using clues such as hair length and style and dress
3–4 years	Children begin to associate tasks and objects with gender, i.e. some roles are determined through gender
5–6 years	Children have acquired the concept of gender stability. They know that gender is not dependent on type of clothes or hair cut

Sex-role behaviour

Researchers have found that sex-role behaviour is often shown earlier than we imagine. By 18–24 months, children start to show some preference amongst playthings, with boys choosing building blocks and cars, and girls choosing dolls and 'caring' toys (O' Brien, 1992). Even so, many children of this age are still not showing understanding of their own gender. Children as young as 3 years start to show a preference for their own sex playmates.

Children also seem to be quickly aware of stereotypical roles, for example tasks and occupations that are seen as men's or women's work are identified by children as young as 3 years.

■ How do children learn these stereotypes and sex-role behaviours?

There are three strands of thinking that relate to learning theories and theories of personality.

Social learning theory – Bandura

This theory suggests that children learn sex-role behaviour by the way in which they are played with and with what they see. Children will imitate their parents' and carers' roles and actions. There is some research to support this approach as parents seem to respond in different ways to boy and girls.

Cognitive development theories of gender

The idea behind one widely supported theory by Lawrence Kohlberg (1966) is that the child develops an understanding of what it is to be a boy or a girl – a schema – and behaves in such a way as to fit in with their understanding once they have understood that gender is permanent and they will always be a boy or girl. This would explain why some girls at around 3 years old refuse to wear trousers, because they know that they are a girl and believe that wearing trousers is what makes a boy a boy!

Gender schema theory

Another cognitive development theory put forward by Martin (1991) builds upon Kohlberg's theory. It suggests that children begin to develop an idea of what it is to be a boy or girl at around 2 or 3 years and show behaviour to match this. As they grow up, they learn more about gender roles and sex roles and adapt and develop their aggression without actual violence lead to the other party backing off and appeasing the aggressor. Through ritual aggression, animals avoid killing each other.

According to Lorenz, humans have inherited the 'warrior' instinct, but no longer ritualise aggression because they have developed weapons. Weapons where the aggressor no longer needs to make face-to-face contact with the other party has meant appeasement rituals such as cowering, begging for mercy, etc., are no longer so effective. Lorenz also suggested that aggression in animals and humans is spontaneous as if the aggression has built up inside and needs to show itself.

▲ Do girls learn about their gender by imitating their mothers?

ideas or schemas. It differs from Kohlberg's theory because the original schema is developed even though children have not shown an understanding that gender is permanent.

■ Aggression

In many early years settings guns are banned, but children may still go around waving a stick and pretend to be shooting each other. This begs the question whether aggression is instinctive or whether it is learnt – the nature versus nurture debate again.

The biological perspective (Lorenz) – nature

This considers whether aggression is an inborn instinct that has its roots in the survival of the species. This is an appealing theory – animals fight each other to protect their territory and females.

One famous psychologist, Konrad Lorenz, believed that the fighting instinct in animals has parallels with aggression in humans. He noted that fighting is often ritualised in animals – the triumphant male shows enough aggression just to make his point; shows of

Case study: Time to vent aggression

Little Boots Playgroup always structure time for physical play or activities that allow children to be 'legitimately aggressive', such as climbing, building with large blocks and running games. They believe that children need to 'vent their aggression', and activities such as these allow for this to happen at particular points during the day.

1 Is this the case in your setting?

2 What happens if the children are not able to go outside for vigorous play activity?

3 How might you instigate such activities, and support children to 'vent their aggression' in safe ways?

A theory known as the frustration–aggression hypothesis combines the instinctive nature of aggression with learning theory. It was put forward by Dollard *et al.* in 1939 although was later revised. The basis is that although there is an inborn aggressive instinct, it tends to be triggered when people are feeling frustrated. This linking of frustration with aggression may explain why some children have dolls or objects onto which they heap their anger! The later theory proposed by Miller (1941) suggested that although aggression can be triggered through frustration, other factors may prevent the aggression from being shown, i.e. realising that any aggression might be punished afterwards.

Aggressive cue-theory – nurture

This theory builds on the frustration aggression hypothesis, but looks carefully at why aggression is not automatically shown when people become frustrated. This theory suggests that although frustration causes anger, it might not necessarily cause aggression. Experiments carried out by Berkowitz (1966, 1967 and 1993) suggested that, in order for aggression to be shown, there needs to be some other triggers. Triggers used in experiments included weapons being available and participants seeing violent films. The aggressive cue theory would therefore explain why sometimes we can cope in some situations when we are angry, whereas in similar situations we might show some types of aggressive behaviour.

Aggression and biological factors

There is some support for believing that aggressive behaviour might be linked to biological factors such as hormones, drugs or alcohol. Chemicals produced by the brain may lead us to be more highly aroused and therefore more prone to show aggressive behaviour. A study in 1979 by Brown *et al.* looked at levels of serotonin. Low levels of serotonin are likely to produce high levels of arousal and therefore possibly aggressive behaviour. There have also been cases where women suffering from pre-menstrual tension have committed acts of aggression. These acts have been linked to the higher levels of progesterone produced prior to menstruation.

Social learning theory and aggression

The social learning theory approach suggests that our behaviour is shaped by what we have seen. Bandura's Bobo doll experiment (see page 409) seems to support this view. Children who had seen violent behaviour seemed more likely to show aggressive behaviour, whereas children who had seen how adults and other children control their anger were more likely to cope when they were angry. Although this theory is valuable, Bandura warns that not all children will be aggressive if they have seen an aggressive act.

Pro-social behaviour is the type that we tend to encourage in young children, e.g. comforting another child or sharing equipment. Psychologists have studied this behaviour to consider whether pro-social behaviour is instinctive or learnt.

At what age are children able to judge right from wrong? In the UK the age of legal responsibility is one of the lowest in Europe. The boys involved in the murder of Jamie Bulger faced criminal prosecution as our legal system felt that although they were 10 years old, they were at an age to know right from wrong. The Early Learning Goals for England suggest that by the end of the reception year 'most children will understand what is right and wrong, and why'.

■ Psychoanalytical – Freud and moral development

Freud suggested that moral development was also part of personality development. He suggested that moral behaviour is controlled by the superego (see page 410). He also suggested that children would be influenced by their parents through the process of identification during the phallic stage. Freud believed that children identify, that is to say, try to be the same as, their same-sex parents. This would mean that a boy who had an authoritarian father would be likely to show the same characteristics.

■ Piaget's theory of moral development – a cognitive approach

One of the most famous approaches to understanding

Children often worry about how an adult will react. Do they learn about right and wrong from these reactions?

Pre-moral (0–4 years)

Children learn about right and wrong through their own actions and consider the results of adults around them.

Moral realism (4–7 years)

Children's moral development is greatly influenced by the adults in their lives. Their judgements very much depend on what they think the adult's expectations would be.

Moral relativism (8–11 years)

Children are preoccupied with justice and following rules. This means that children have developed a concept of fairness. By 11+ years, children understand the concept of equity – that treating people in exactly the same way may not result in fairness. Children who do not understand their homework may need more of a teacher's time than those who do. The motives for people's actions are also considered by children.

▲ **Piaget's stages of moral development**

moral development is a cognitive, i.e. stage, model. This cognitive approach was put forward by Jean Piaget. Piaget used a clinical interview approach, asking children to explain how they were playing games and telling stories. He suggested that children's moral development was a three-stage process, as shown in the diagram above.

Theory into practice

If moral development follows a stage process, with children learning more as they develop, it would mean that an 'age' approach to children knowing right from wrong is not a helpful one. It also means that it is difficult to 'teach' children right from wrong.

• What do you think?

■ Kohlberg's theory of moral development – a cognitive approach

Lawrence Kohlberg's work on moral development is well known. He built on Piaget's description of moral development and suggested that, as with other cognitive areas, moral reasoning is linked to stages of development. He suggests that there are three levels of moral development that are subdivided into stages. The table on page 416 outlines the three levels and stages.

Pre-conventional level

This is divided into two stages. At this level, children are not being guided by their own moral reasoning, but following their parents or carers. They are doing this to either seek reward or to avoid punishment.

• *Stage 1: Punishment and obedience* The child finds out about what is wrong and right through seeing the consequences of their actions.

• *Stage 2: Individualism, instrumental purpose and exchange* The child is learning that some actions and behaviours are rewarded. The child is also learning to avoid behaviours that might mean punishment. By the end of this stage, the child is also beginning to enjoy helping people and has learnt the 'if I help you, you might be able to help me' approach.

Conventional level

The next level of moral development consists of an awareness of group behaviour and the idea that of what is and isn't acceptable in society.

• *Stage 3: Mutual interpersonal expectations, relationships and interpersonal conformity (often known as the 'good boy/nice girl' stage)* In this stage children come to believe that good behaviour pleases other people, such as friends, teachers and parents. Children are also becoming aware of the motive factor, i.e. 'he meant to help really'.

• *Stage 4: Social system and conscience (also referred to as law and order orientation)* This is a widening out stage – before children were wanting to show good and correct behaviour to please people they knew. In this stage, we become more aware of society's needs and interests and what is deemed by society to be right or wrong. People in this stage are keen to obey regulations and laws.

Age	Level	Stage	Explanation
6–13	Pre-conventional	1. Punishment and obedience	Children are not being guided by their own moral reasoning, but are following their parents or carers. They are doing this either to seek reward or to avoid punishment. They find out about what is wrong and right through seeing the consequences of their actions.
		2. Individualism, instrumental purposes and exchange	Children learn that some actions and behaviours are rewarded and they learn to avoid those that might mean punishment. By the end of this stage they are also beginning to enjoy helping people and have learnt the 'If I help you, you might help me' approach.
13–16	Conventional	3. Mutual interpersonal expectations, relationships and interpersonal conformity ('Good boy/nice girl')	Children come to believe that good behaviour pleases other people (e.g. friends, teachers and parents). They are also becoming aware of motive ('He meant to help really').
		4. Social system and conscience ('Law and order')	This is a widening-out stage. Previously, children were wanting to show good and correct behaviour to please people they knew. At this stage they are more aware of society's needs and interests and what is deemed by society to be right or wrong. They are keen to obey regulations and laws.
16–20+	Post-conventional/ principled	5. Social contract	At this stage rules and regulations are seen as useful tools to make sure that there is some protection and fairness in society. People working at this level are prepared to tolerate rules being broken, if they do not see that they are fair or just rules.
		6. Universal ethical principles	This last stage was in some ways an unclear one for Kohlberg and was difficult to test. People at this stage are extremely principled and not swayed by society. People in history who may have reached this level have been persecuted, as they are often seen as troublemakers.

Post-conventional or principled morality level

This level is very different to the others. At this level, people are not accepting the morality of the group or society unquestioningly. Demonstrators who break laws, for example animal rights' campaigners who illegally set animals free, would be demonstrating this level of morality.

- *Stage 5: Social contract* At this stage rules and regulations are seen as useful tools to make sure that there is some protection and fairness in society. People working at this level are prepared to tolerate rules being broken, if they do not see that they are fair or just rules.
- *Stage 6: Universal ethical principles* This last stage was in some ways an unclear one for Kohlberg and difficult to test. People working at this stage would

be extremely principled people who are not swayed by society and have inner principles which they have developed. People in history who may have reached this level were often killed or persecuted as they were often seen as troublemakers as they would be unwilling to compromise their position.

Testing moral reasoning

Kohlberg used hypothetical stories to test his theory (see Theory into practice opposite). His ideas have also been tested in many countries by John Snarey (1985) to see if his stage theory was relevant to other cultures. The result of his studies showed that the development of moral reasoning did fit the stage and level model, although in some societies, a norm of stage 2 reasoning was shown.

■ Behaviourist approaches

Behaviourist approaches to moral development would consider that children learn right from wrong through being reinforced. A child who is given praise because they helped another child would have this pro-social behaviour reinforced. Behaviourist approaches to moral development focus on rewards and also punishments, but the criticism of this approach towards moral development is that it will only give children a 'black and white' view of morality. This approach does not explain why adults sometimes act altruistically.

Cognitive development

Jean Piaget's stages of cognitive development are described in Unit 7, page 255.

Although Piaget's work is well known, there are two other approaches which are in some ways similar to Piaget's and have also influenced early years practice:

- Vygotsky's theory of cognitive development
- Bruner's developmental theory.

Vygotsky's theory of cognitive development

Vygotksy's work was not published in English until the early 1960s, even though his work was known in Russia in the 1920s and 1930s. He believed that children's social environment and experiences are very important. He considered that children were born to be sociable and that, by being with their parents and then with their friends, they acquired skills and concepts. Vygotsky saw children as 'apprentices', learning and gaining understanding through being with others. The term 'scaffolding' is often used alongside Vygotsky's ideas as the idea of the child being helped by adults around them to learn concepts is a strong feature of his work.

Vygotsky also suggested that maturation was an important element in children's development and that we need to extend children's learning so that they could use their emerging skills and concepts. He used the term 'zone of proximal development' to define this idea, although we might think of this as 'potential'.

Bruner's developmental theory

Jerome Bruner's work was influenced by Piaget but particularly by Vygotsky's work. Bruner's is not a stage theory as such but he suggests that children gradually acquire cognitive skills which he refers to as modes of thinking – see the table below.

Mode	Age (approx.)	Description and use
Enactive	0–1 years	Learning and thought take place because of physical movements
Iconic	1–7 years	Thoughts are developed as mental images
Symbolic	7+ years	Symbols including language are used in thinking

Information processing theories (IP) of cognitive development consider the actual processes used when information is presented to us. Information is constantly being gathered in the brain through our five senses – we may hear a sound in the street whilst also having the television on – some information we store and use whilst others we filter out and disregard. Information processing theories often use similar language to the terms used in computing as they suggest that the brain acts in similar ways! In much the same ways as computers, IP theorists suggest that tasks are broken down as part of the process involved in handling information. This breaking down into stages is often referred to as 'task analysis'.

■ Memory

Memory is an important component in our ability to process information. It was not until the 1950s that memory was really studied by psychologists and at present the most influential work carried out on memory has been by Atkinson and Shiffrin. They have proposed a 'multi-store' model which looks at the way information is coded and retrieved.

Theories about the way we store and retrieve information vary, but most psychologists agree that there is a process system to our memory – a simplified version of this process is shown below.

▲ The process of memory

Primary and secondary memory (short- and long-term memory)

Most psychologists also agree and have worked on the concept which William James (1890) suggested, i.e. that memory storage is divided into two – commonly called short- and long-term memory.

- Our short-term or (primary) memory is the one we use when we are holding in our minds a new telephone number a few seconds before dialling it. An hour later we might not remember the order of the digits.
- By contrast the long-term memory can hold information for a few minutes or for a lifetime! The long-term memory is seen as having unlimited capacity – this may come as a surprise if you are someone who has difficulty remembering things, but storage capacity is completely different to the process of retrieving information.

■ Encoding information

Children with **Attention Deficit Hyperactivity Disorder (ADHD)** may have difficulties when it comes to encoding or information processing. This is because their attention span may not always be sufficient for them to be able to take in the necessary information, although it is known that sensory materials can be a helpful tool to support their learning. Sensory materials such as sand seem to help children as they physically stimulate the hands and so increase arousal levels. This in turn can help children to focus their attention for longer and so helps them to take in information. It is also useful to remember that children with ADHD will benefit from being given information in a visual format as this can be easier for them to process.

Key term

Attention Deficit Hyperactivity Disorder (ADHD) is a disorder in which a child shows significant problems in focusing attention and hyperactivity.

In order to be able to retrieve information from either our long- or short-term memories, we have to encode it. If information is not encoded properly, it will be lost to us. Researchers are still looking at the way we encode information, but it would seem that our long-term memory uses three main methods: visual, semantic (signs, written and spoken language) and acoustic. In addition, we may also learn some of the following strategies that help us hold onto information that we do not want to forget:

- *Rehearsal* This involves repeating to ourselves what we want to remember, for example repeating a telephone number or practising actions to a song.
- *Clustering or chunking* This involves grouping pieces of information – rather than remembering a telephone number as 0-0-3-3-5-6-0-6-7-9-9-7, you would remember it in clusters or chunks 00-33-56-06-79-97. Children as young as 2 years can begin to chunk information.
- *Elaboration* This means finding connections between things that need to be remembered. If you find a person's name difficult to remember, you might think about one feature about that person to help you. Mnemonics such as Never Eat Shredded Wheat, to remember the points around a compass, are forms of elaboration.

Language development

Language, either spoken or written, plays an important part in most people's lives. Some psychologists, theologians and philosophers would suggest that our ability to use language to communicate and think separates us from the animal kingdom.

Understanding the structure of language

It is important to have some understanding of the structure of language. All languages have rules which are understood and used by both the speaker and listener. The rules are often usually referred to as grammar. By following the rules or grammar, speakers and listeners can understand each other. Linguists who study the structure of language use the term grammar to describe the 'package' of a language. This package is formed of three key elements: phonology, semantics and syntax.

■ Phonology

Languages have a sound system – phonology. When we hear someone speaking, we may recognise the language that they are using, even if we cannot speak it. This recognition may be based on listening to the sounds that are being used. The individual sounds that are used in a language are called phones – some languages use fewer phones than others, i.e. there are 40 phones used in

English. Individual sounds that are combined together are called phonemes.

■ Semantics

Languages are composed of words or units of meaning. When we learn a language, we also have to learn what these units are and how they can be changed. For example, if we add 'less' onto the end of some words, it changes their meaning.

■ Syntax

Finally, we have to learn the rules for using the words and how their place in a sentence can change their meaning. For example, 'The cat ate the mouse' has a different meaning to 'The mouse ate the cat' even though the same words have been used.

The sequence of language development

A good starting point when considering language development is to look at the pattern by which children learn to speak. It is interesting to note that babies and children, in whichever country they are born, all follow a similar pattern. The first year of a baby's life is spent trying to 'tune in' on the language that they are hearing and learning the skills of communication, i.e. making eye contact, responding to others' facial expressions and words. This first year is often known as the pre-linguistic phase and is now considered to be vital in children's overall language development.

The major stages in language development are shown in the table on page 420.

Theories of how children use language

The nature v. nurture debate appears once more when we look at the theories of how children learn language.

■ Skinner's operant conditioning theory – behaviourist perspective

This is a nurture theory, as Skinner suggests that we learn language mainly because when babies try to communicate their efforts are rewarded or reinforced in some way, for example a baby may get a smile from a parent if they gurgle. Skinner used this idea of

The stages of language development

Stage	Age	Features	Comments
Pre-linguistic stage			
Cooing	6 weeks	Cooing	Babies make cooing sounds to show pleasure. These early sounds are different to sounds made later on, mainly because the mouth is still developing.
Babbling (phonemic expansion)	6–9 months	Babies blend vowels and consonants together to make tuneful sounds, e.g. ba, ma, da.	Babbling has been described as learning the tune before the words. The baby seems to be practising its sounds. Babies increase the number of sounds or phonemes. This is sometimes called phonemic expansion. All babies, even deaf babies, produce a wide range of sounds during this period.
Babbling (phonemic contraction) Echolalia	9–10 months	Babies babble but the range of sounds is limited.	The range of sounds or phonemes that babies produce are used in the language that they are hearing. At this stage it would, in theory, be possible to distinguish between babies who are in different language environments. At 10 months babies are also understanding 17 or more words
Linguistic stage (CTD)			
First words	Around 12 months	Babies repeatedly use one or more sounds which have meaning for them.	The first words are often unclear and so gradually emerge. They are often one sound, but are used regularly in similar situations, e.g. 'ba' to mean drink and cuddle. Babbling still continues.
Holophrases	12–18 months	Toddlers start to use one word in a variety of ways.	Toddlers use holophrases to make their limited vocabulary more useful for them. One word is used in several situations, but the tone of voice and the context helps the adult understand what the toddler means. Most toddlers have 10–15 words by 18 months.
Two-word utterances telegraphic speech	18–24 months	Two words are put together to make a mini sentence	Toddlers begin to combine words to make sentences. They seem to have grasped which are the key words in a sentence – 'dada gone' or 'dada come'.
Language explosion	24–36 months	A large increase in children's vocabulary combined with increasing use of sentences.	This is a period in which children's language seems to evolve rapidly. Children learn words so rapidly that it becomes hard for parents to count them! At the same time the child uses more complicated structures in their speech. Plurals and negatives begin to be used, e.g. 'No dogs here!'
	3–4 years	Sentences become longer and vocabulary continues to increase.	Children are using language in a more complete way. Mistakes in grammar show that they are still absorbing the rules and sometimes misapplying them. Mistakes such as 'I wented' show that they have learnt that '-ed' makes a past tense. These type of mistakes are known as 'virtuous errors'.
Fluency	4–5 years	The basic skills of the language are mastered	Children have mastered the basic rules of grammar and are fluent, although will still be making some virtuous errors.

reinforcement to explain why babies stop making some sounds – he reasoned that when babies made sounds that parents did not recognise, they would not receive any attention, whilst sounds which were recognisable were noticed and reinforced. He called this process selective reinforcement. This approach would explain why children speak in similar ways to their parents, using the familiar phrases and intonation.

However, there have been criticisms of Skinner's theory. For example, the theory does not explain why all babies and children follow the same pattern of gaining language. If Skinner's theory was correct, you would expect to see that children's language would develop very differently depending on the amount and type of reinforcement that adults and others were giving. This is not the case, however, as most children seem to pass through the same stages. Also, the theory does not explain why children speak in different ways to adults around them, for example 'dada gone'. If children are learning by imitating what they are hearing and not having incorrect sounds or sentences reinforced, why do children say things such as 'wented' or 'swimmed'?

■ Noam Chomsky – nativist perspective

Chomsky's work on language is based on the idea that our ability to learn language is instinctive. This is a nature or nativist theory. His theory has been widely accepted as it is comprehensive and, unlike Skinner's ideas, explains why all babies' language development follows a pattern. He is famous for suggesting that humans have a Language Acquisition Device (LAD). This is not an actual physical part of the brain, but a structure within our brains that allows babies to absorb and understand the rules of the language they are being exposed to. The brain is able to analyse the language and work out the system that the language uses. This is a complex process, but explains why children can quickly understand and then use their language creatively and correctly without ever being formally taught or 'knowing' the rules.

Relationship between language and thought

There seems to be a strong link between language and thought, although there are different views of the relationship between them. Piaget differed in his views from Vygotsky and Bruner because he suggested that language was a tool that was used by us, whereas Vygotsky and Bruner suggest that language organises and drives the thought process.

■ Vygotsky – prelinguistic perspective

Vygotsky suggested that thought and language begin as two different activities – when a baby babbles they are not using babbling as a way of thinking. At around the age of 2 years, they merge and at this point the child uses language to help them think. Vygotsky also differentiated between two types of speech – inner speech which helps us to think and external speech which we use to

communicate with others. An example of inner speech would be when we say either aloud or inwardly, 'Then, I am going to ...' as a way of directing ourselves. Between the ages of 2 and 7 years, Vygotsky felt that children were not able to use them in distinct ways and therefore their speech was often a blend of the two, with young children often providing a running commentary of what they are doing. Vygotsky referred to this early speech and thought as egocentric.

■ Bruner

Bruner suggested that language is also linked to thought and that it was why children were able to develop a symbolic mode of thought. Previously children were using visual imagery to hold and use information in their learning, but language allowed them to use abstract, symbolic thoughts.

The development of self

Who are we? What are we like? These are fundamental questions for children, almost like being able to place oneself on a map. The development of **self-concept** is the process by which we gather information about ourselves. Self-concept is important because it is closely linked with **self-esteem**. It is useful to understand the difference between the terms used when talking about self-concept:

- *Self-concept* is our vision of our whole selves, which includes our self-esteem, our self-image and our ideal self.
- *Self-image or self-identity* is the way in which we define ourselves – who we are, where we live, our gender, etc.
- Our *ideal self* is our view of what we would like to be.

Key terms

Self-concept is our vision of our whole selves, including our self-esteem, our self-image and our ideal self.

Self-esteem is how we judge ourselves. This judgement either gives us high or low self-esteem, also referred to as self-confidence.

- *Self-esteem* is also referred to as self-confidence. Once we have developed a self-image and an ideal self, we then judge ourselves: how close are we to being the person we want to be? This judgement either gives us high or low self-esteem.

Developing self-image

Children gradually develop self-image. The first step for children is to be able to recognise themselves. A well-known test to see if children can recognise themselves is to put a touch of red lipstick on a baby's nose and then put the baby in front of the mirror. A child who is beginning to recognise themselves will touch their nose, rather than the nose in the reflection. Most babies are doing this by 18 months old.

Carl Rogers

Rogers described the development of self in principles rather than in stages, believing that conditional and unconditional regard was central to the development of self-concept. For example, he described how children raised in an environment of **unconditional regard**, i.e. praised and encouraged unconditionally, had the opportunity to realise their fullest potential. On the other hand, children being raised in an environment of conditional positive regard only feel valuable if they meet the set conditions. Rogers describes this as conditions of worth.

Key term

Unconditional regard is letting children know that they are valued just for being them, not always for what they can achieve.

Abraham Maslow

Maslow developed the hierarchy of needs which demonstrates how basic needs are inborn, and need to be satisfied in order to grow and develop. However, as a child moves up the hierarchy of need, the needs are less innate, and become more dependent upon the

▲ Maslow's hierarchy of needs

environment in which the child is raised. It is only when the lower order needs are satisfied that the higher order needs can influence personal development.

Robert Selman's levels of social role-taking

Role play or role-taking is seen as important by Selman, who concludes that children develop in their abilities to understand themselves and others – see the table opposite.

How self-esteem and self-image are linked

Once we have established what we think we are like (our perceptions of ourselves), we then consider whether we are happy with the result. Someone with a high self-esteem will be reasonably happy about their self-image, whereas someone with a low self-esteem may feel that they are not 'measuring up'. This means that self-esteem and self-image are linked. The process of how we come to make our judgements has been researched. There seems to be three main factors that affect this process which carries on through our lives.

- reaction of others to us
- comparison to others
- ideal self-image.

▼ Selman's levels of social role-taking

Stage	Age	Description
Stage 0 Egocentric role-taking	3–6 years	Children assume that everyone will be the same and feel the same as they do
Stage 1 Social-informational role-taking	6–8 years	Children see that others do not act or appear to have the same feelings, but do not understand the reasons behind this
Stage 2 Self-reflective role-taking	8–10 years	Children accept that others have different points of views to theirs, but find it hard to bring together the different perspectives
Stage 3 Mutual role-taking	10–12 years	Children can understand two points of view at the same time, and realise that other people can do the same
Stage 4 Social and conventional system role-taking	12–15 years	Adolescents are beginning to have a more detached view on how other people may be feeling and are able to understand behaviour in the light of this

Why does self-esteem matter?

Low self-esteem is linked to low achievement. Children who have low self-esteem will be less likely to put themselves in challenging and new situations. They have low expectations of what they can do and so do not meet their full potential. This means that early years practitioners must raise children's self-esteem through praise, showing genuine warmth and affection.

Albert Bandura

Bandura developed the theory of perceived self-efficacy, where a child's progress and development depends upon how they perceive their capability and performance. Their self-efficacy beliefs will impact upon the way they feel, think, behave and are motivated. Children with a strong sense of self-efficacy will be more likely to tackle difficult tasks and respond better to failure, whereas those that doubt their capabilities will be more likely to shy away from tasks they perceive as too difficult for them, and failure will reinforce this lack of self-efficacy.

Coppersmith's study of self esteem

Coppersmith (1967) carried out a large study in which hundreds of boys aged between 9 and 10 years underwent a series of tests to discover whether there was a link between achievement and self-esteem. Although the boys came from similar social backgrounds, he found that where the boys had high scores of self-esteem they were also achieving more highly. He found

that boys with lower self-esteem consistently under-estimated themselves.

Coppersmith then looked to see if there was a link between self-esteem and parenting. Using questionnaires and interviews, he found that children with high self-esteem had parents who had set firm boundaries but who had allowed them some freedom and security. Later, Coppersmith looked at the same children as adults. He found that men who had high self-esteem as children in the study had fared better in their education and careers.

Interpersonal theories

One of the ways in which we might develop a self-image is by considering the reactions of others to us. This is sometimes referred to as the 'looking glass effect'. This established theory was put forward by Cooley who suggested that in order for us to know what we are like, we need to see how others react to us. This theory is particularly important for adults to consider, as it means that we must be positive towards children so they are able to see themselves positively.

Symbolic interactionalism

A slightly different approach was taken by Mead (1934) who suggested that we developed self-image as a result of interacting with others and that role play was an important part of this process for children. Mead suggested that children's role play allowed them to understand different points of view. This would suggest that the home corner play is particularly valuable for young children.

Assessment activity 14.1

1 Produce an information sheet for other students on the theories of development.

   a) Outline each of the following theories: Piaget, Bruner, Maslow, Rogers, Bowlby and Vygotsky. **P1** **P2**

   b) Analyse the differences and similarities between these theories. **M1**

   c) Evaluate each theory's contribution to current early years practice using examples based on your placement experience. **D1**

2 Using at least three observations of one child in a setting, prepare a report about how the child is learning behaviour. The report should:

- analyse how the child's behaviour is being managed or reinforced in the setting
- explain ways in which the child is learning behaviours
- consider how the theories of how children learn behaviour link to practice. **M2**

14.2 The formation of early relationships

The study of children's early relationships and their importance in a child's overall development did not really start until the 1950s when John Bowlby published *Maternal Care and Mental Health*. The results of this and subsequent research has had noticeable and continuing effects on childcare practice. This means that adults working with babies and children need to have a good understanding of the stages in attachment, attachment theory and the effects of **separation**.

Key term

Separation The term used when a parent or main carer leaves the baby or toddler.

Theories of attachment

There are many key terms that are used in relation to the study of early relationships, three of which you will have come across earlier in this book:

- *Attachment* can be thought of as a unique emotional tie between a child and another person, usually an adult.
- *Socialisation* This is the process by which babies and young children gradually form a variety of relationships.
- *Separation anxiety* The effects on babies and toddlers when they leave their main carers.

Research has repeatedly shown that the quality of attachments will shape a child's ability to form other relationships later in life.

Stages of attachment

Attachment is often seen as a process, as outlined in the table opposite.

Key term

Multiple attachment Later theories of attachment proposed that babies were able to simultaneously make several strong attachments.

▼ The process of attachment

Age	Stage	Features
6 weeks–3 months		Babies begin to be attracted to human faces and voices First smiles begin at around six weeks
3 months–7/8 months	Indiscriminate attachments	Babies are learning to distinguish between faces, showing obvious pleasure when they recognise familiar faces. They are happy to be handled by strangers, preferring to be in human company rather than left alone – hence the term indiscriminate attachments
7/8 months	Specific attachments	At around 7 or 8 months, babies begin to miss key people in their lives and show signs of distress – for example, crying when they leave the room. Most babies also seem to have developed one particularly strong attachment – often to the mother. Babies also show a wariness of strangers even when in the presence of their 'key people'. This wariness may quickly develop into fear if the stranger makes some form of direct contact with the baby, for example, by touching them
From 8 months	Multiple attachments	After making specific attachments, babies then go on to form multiple attachments. This is an important part of their socialisation process

The quality of attachments

Some research has looked at the quality of babies' early attachments. It would seem that where babies and children are 'securely' attached they are able to explore and develop their independence. Babies and children whose attachment is less secure seem to show either indifference or clingy types of behaviour.

■ Ainsworth: the 'strange situation'

The quality of attachments was looked at by Ainsworth who is considered alongside Bowlby to be a key figure in this area of psychology.

Ainsworth and her colleagues (1978) created a scenario by which babies' reactions to being left with a stranger and then reunited with their mothers (and or fathers) were measured. This scenario is now widely used to study attachment behaviour.

The scenario is known as the 'strange situation' and is divided into eight parts with each part lasting about three minutes. During the experiment, the baby (a 1-year-old) has some time by itself as well as with a stranger:

1 Parent and baby enter room.

2 Parent remains inactive, baby is free to explore room.

3 Stranger joins parent and infant.

4 Parent leaves room.

5 Parent returns, settles baby and stranger leaves.

6 Baby is alone in the room.

7 Stranger returns and interacts with baby.

8 Parent returns again and stranger leaves.

Ainsworth and her colleagues were particularly interested in the reactions of the baby to the parent when they left or returned and the way in which the parent interacted with the baby. They categorised the behaviour into three types:

- *Type A – anxious-avoidant* Baby largely ignores parent and shows little signs of distress when parent leaves, continuing to play. Baby ignores or avoids parent on their return. Baby dislikes being alone, but can be comforted by stranger.

- *Type B – securely attached* Baby plays while parent is present, but shows visible distress when parent leaves and play is reduced. Baby is easily comforted on return of parent and carries on playing. Cries when alone because parent is not there, but can be partly comforted by stranger. Reactions towards stranger and parents are markedly different.

- *Type C – anxious-resistant* Baby is wary and explores less than other types. Very distressed when parent leaves and actively resists stranger's attempts to comfort. Wants immediate contact with parent on return but is ambivalent, showing frustration and anger alongside clinginess, for example wanting to be held but then immediately struggling to get down.

Why are some children more securely attached than others?

Ainsworth came to the conclusion that the quality of attachment depended on the parenting that the baby received. Where parents were able to sense and predict their babies' needs and frustrations, the babies showed type B behaviour. This meant that they were able to explore and play, knowing that their parent was a safe base.

What happens when babies and children are separated from their main attachments?

Most early years practitioners will notice that as children become older, they find it easier to separate from their parents. This is because they have formed other attachments to staff and, as they get older, to other children. They have also learnt that although their parent is absent, they will return. Babies and toddlers, however, find it difficult to cope with the absence of their main attachments and will show distress.

Bowlby noted that there seemed to be a pattern to the way children reacted if they were separated from their main attachments. This pattern is often referred to as separation anxiety. This is clearly seen in babies from around 7 months and seems to reach a peak at around 12–15 months. Older children will show separation anxiety if they are separated for long periods, for example if a parent dies or goes away for a period of time.

Bowlby's theory of attachment

The work of John Bowlby has greatly influenced social care policy, childcare practices and research into early relationships. Immediately after the Second World War, he was asked to investigate the effects on children's development of being brought up in orphanages or other institutions. In 1951 his findings showed that meeting children's physical needs alone was not sufficient – children were being psychologically damaged because of the absence of their mothers. The term 'maternal deprivation' was used to describe this effect. He reached this conclusion by looking at the life histories of children who had been referred to his clinic. He noticed an overwhelming trend – most of these children had suffered early separations from their mothers and families.

■ Main features of Bowlby's theory

- *Monotropy* Bowlby believed that babies need to form one main attachment and that this relationship would be special and of more importance to the child than any other. Bowlby suggested that in most cases this relationship would be formed with the mother, but that it could be formed with the father or another person.
- *Critical period* Bowlby was greatly influenced by ethnologists such as Lorenz and he believed that in the same way humans too would have a 'critical period'. He felt that babies needed to have developed their main attachment by the age of 1 year and that during a child's first four years, prolonged separation from this person would cause long-term psychological damage.
- *Children need 'parenting'* Bowlby showed through his findings that simply meeting a child's physical and care needs is not enough for healthy growth and development. Children need to have a main attachment in their early lives that gives them consistent support. His early papers suggested that the mother should play this role, although his position changed in later years.
- *Children show distress when separated from main attachment* Bowlby outlined a pattern of distress that babies and children show when separated from their carers. This is often referred to as separation anxiety. He also made links to show that when adults had been separated from their mothers in infancy, they would not form deep and lasting relationships. He called this effect 'maternal deprivation'.

Key terms

Monotropy In early theories of attachment, it was proposed that babies made only one key attachment.

Critical period A set period of time within which some theorists have speculated that an attachment must occur.

■ Criticism of Bowlby's work

There are many criticisms of Bowlby's theories and his work has been superseded by other research. When looking at the criticisms of his work, it is important to remember the political, economic and social climate of the time.

The role of the mother was over-emphasised

This has been a major criticism of Bowlby's early work. At the time he was writing, women were the traditional care-givers and economically after the war the government was keen for women to return to their traditional roles within the home. Bowlby's later work did emphasise that babies could form an attachment with someone other than the mother.

Attachments to more than one person were not explored

Bowlby placed a lot of emphasis on the importance of one single attachment. Subsequent research (Schaffer and Emerson, 1964) has shown that as children get older, they can develop equally strong attachments to other figures such as their fathers and siblings.

Quality of the substitute care was not taken into consideration

Bowlby did not take into consideration the effect of being in poor quality care. This means that it is hard to be absolutely sure that the psychological damage done to the children was only the result of maternal deprivation. Later studies have suggested that good quality care can help children to adjust to separation as children are able to substitute the main attachment to another person (Hodges and Tizard, 1989).

Maternal deprivation as a concept was too general

Michael Rutter criticises Bowlby's 'maternal deprivation' as being too general. Factors such as discord in the family, the nature of separation and the quality of attachments made would all affect outcome. This explains why some children are more adversely affected by their earlier experiences than others (see also Theory into practice about Koluchova, page 428).

▲ Children form strong relationships with both parents

Schaffer and Emerson's work on attachment

Until the 1950s, it was generally thought that babies and children automatically formed the strongest relationships with the people who fed them and met their physical needs. This is sometimes referred to as 'cupboard love'. Several pieces of research have shown that this is not necessarily true. One strong piece of research by Schaffer and Emerson (1964) showed that babies and children can form equally strong attachments to their fathers even when the father is not the main care-giver. Over a period of eighteen months, they visited babies at four-weekly intervals and found that most children by 18 months protested equally when they were separated from either the mother or the father. This piece of research showed that care-giving alone did not automatically mean that a child would form a main attachment.

Theory into practice

One of the major concerns most parents have when leaving babies with nannies or childminders is that the child will attach itself to the care-giver and not know who their parent is. Although in theory this is possible, it is unlikely providing the parents spend time responding to and interacting with the baby. This is the idea behind 'quality time' where the quality of the interaction and responsiveness of the parents is more important than the actual time spent with children.

Robertson and Robertson: short-term effects of deprivation

Robertson and Robertson carried out an investigation into the short-term effects of deprivation using children in hospital. As in the 1940s parents were not able to stay with their children in hospital, hospitalisation was a form of deprivation. Robertson and Robertson looked at how these children coped with the deprivation of their mother, and made distressing films of the children to illustrate their findings. Their investigation demonstrated that not only were the children extremely distressed whilst in hospital, but that they were also less attached than they were before going into the hospital. Robertson and Robertson worked with Bowlby to categorise the short-term effects of deprivation into three stages, which they called the PDD model, shown in the table below.

▼ Stages of separation anxiety: the PDD model

Stage	Features
Protest	Children may cry, struggle to escape, kick and show anger and distress.
Despair	Children show calmer behaviour, almost as though they have accepted the separation. They may be withdrawn and sad. Comfort behaviour, for example thumb sucking or rocking, may be shown.
Detachment	Children may appear to be over the separation and start to join in activities. The child is actually coping by trying to forget the relationship – hence the title 'detachment'. The effects of detachment may be longer lasting, as children may have learnt not to trust people they care for. They may ignore or reject the mother on her return.

There is a difference between the terms **deprivation** and **privation**. Deprivation means that a child has made a main attachment and then has been separated from the person. Privation means that the baby or child has never formed a main attachment. Fortunately, an increased awareness of child abuse and child protection has meant that cases of extreme privation in the UK are rare. There are, however, some famous case studies that have helped psychologists look at privation in children, for example the case of the Czech twins reported by Koluchova in 1972 (see right).

▲ Siblings can form strong attachments to each other

Theory into practice

In 1967, twin boys aged 7 years were found to be in a neglected state in Czechoslovakia. They had been cruelly treated and beaten by their stepmother and had often been locked in a cupboard together. They had little speech when they were rescued and after spending two years in a children's home were fostered. Follow-up reports in 1976 suggested that they had made significant progress in their speech and cognitive development and by 1984 they had completed an apprenticeship. They also seemed to be psychologically stable and had developed a good relationship with the foster parents.

This case seems to show that children can form main attachments to each other – almost as a survival mechanism. This and similar case studies also cast doubt on beliefs that poor early experiences will automatically create irreversible damage on children's social and cognitive development.

Key terms

Deprivation The term used when babies and toddlers are separated on a long-term basis from their main attachment.

Privation The term used when no attachment is made.

The role of fathers

Recent research has highlighted the importance of a father's role in children's social and emotional development. Fathers seem to offer a different type of contribution, which is nonetheless valued by babies and children.

Research also shows the following:

- Most children aged 7–30 months chose their father to be playmates in preference to their mother (Clarke-Stewart, 1978).
- Fathers hold their children in order to play with them, whereas most holding by mothers is linked to care-giving or restricting (Lamb, 1977).
- Fathers play in different ways with their children, giving children more vigorous physical play (Parke, 1981).
- Strong attachments to both parents rather than just one also seems to help children in unfamiliar situations (Main and Weston, 1981).

Theory into practice

Interestingly these pieces of research also coincide with a greater public awareness of the importance of fathers, although ironically, due to an increase in divorce and separation, a large proportion of children grow up in families without fathers. The understanding that men relate in different ways to children is also a reason why many early years settings are trying to employ male members of staff.

Development of attachment

It is important for you to be able to identify when babies and children have made attachments. This generally can be observed through looking at their behaviour. There are four broad indicators that babies and children might show:

- actively seeking to be near the other person
- crying or showing visible distress when that person leaves or, for babies, is no longer visible
- showing joy or relief when that person appears
- acute awareness of that person's presence, for example looking up at them from time to time, responding to their voices, following their movements.

There are some practical ways in which attachments can be helped to form. You need to focus on these particularly.

Feeding

The moment when babies feed is special as the baby is relaxed, secure and nestled into the adult. It is important that during this time, the adult focuses on the baby. It is good practice in childcare to ensure that the same person feeds the baby. This helps an attachment to be made. It is interesting to watch parents as they feed their babies. They may talk softly, stroke their baby's cheek or head and make eye-contact. These attachment behaviours need to be duplicated in childcare settings.

▲ **Children who have made an attachment show joy when that person appears**

Physical contact

Attachments are also reinforced through the handling of the baby. Cuddling, comforting and rocking are obvious ways in which parents and key workers respond to babies. Lack of physical contact can be damaging for babies and so it is now considered good practice for those working in childcare to spend time holding, rocking and responding physically to young children.

Time and care-giving

Whilst babies seem to recognise who their parents are, they still do need to spend sufficient time with them to build up an attachment. In the same way, babies and young children will feel more secure if they are regularly spending time in a childcare setting rather than sporadically.

Whilst research shows that simply responding to children's physical needs does not necessarily guarantee attachment, most strong relationships also have an element of care-giving. This might be passing a toy to a baby who is pointing towards it as well as other tasks such as bathing and washing.

Sensitivity and responsiveness

The way in which a parent or key worker responds and is sensitive to a child seems to be one of the strongest indicators of a strong attachment. Where there are strong attachments between babies and parents or key workers, the adults seem to be tuned in to what the babies want. This means that they can recognise the different types of cries easily and can interpret what the child wants and needs.

Individual differences

As with every aspect of early development, children will react to situations and the environment in different ways according to their upbringing. Children who are raised in cultures where many adults share the care of the child may develop less attachment to one particular care-giver, and central attachment may be less dominant. This may be observed when comparing a child from a large, close family who is used to lots of people around, and being cared for by grandparents or older siblings, and a child from a one-parent family without the support from others, and the child having a sole care-giver.

Historical theories of child rearing styles

Since the beginning of the twentieth century, texts on child rearing have been widely available. They are interesting to look at in terms of social history as they provide insights into the prevailing attitudes towards children at the time of their writing.

Truby King

One of the earliest influential experts was Truby King. Today, his method is much maligned. He suggested that babies should spend many hours outdoors, be toilet trained early on and that they should be fed on a schedule. From today's viewpoint, this seems harsh, but his focus was to prevent infant mortality. By cutting down contact and also putting the baby outdoors, the baby was less likely to pick up infections such as diphtheria. It is worth remembering that at this time there were no antibiotics or bottle milk if breast-feeding failed. Nappies were often not changed regularly as washing was not easy. Interestingly, Truby King was considered to be a hero of his time as his practices were credited with reducing the overall number of infant deaths.

Benjamin Spock

Benjamin Spock was influential in the UK in the 1950s and 1960s, although he began writing in America in the 1940s. His books were child-centred as he was influenced by the work of paediatricians, but more particularly psychoanalysts. He urged parents to move towards more flexible approaches to their children and stressed the importance of building relationships. He is known as being 'permissive', but in his later texts, he revised his position and aimed to give a more balanced view.

Penelope Leach

Penelope Leach has written many books, but one of the most influential was *Baby and Child* which appeared in 1977. Penelope Leach's approach is child-centred, arguing that by responding to babies' needs, parents will themselves feel happier.

Sheila Kitzinger

Sheila Kitzinger looks at child-rearing from both a child's and a woman's point of view. Interestingly her books are mostly about pregnancy, childbirth and breast-feeding. She draws upon other countries' and cultures' traditions to draw out what she believes is instinctive and natural in terms of childbirth and rearing.

Gina Ford

At the time of writing, Gina Ford's *Contented Little Baby* is causing much debate. She advocates that mothers have a definite routine and structure for their newborns. The book is a best-seller, but some experts have suggested that it is not child-centred and is a backward step in parenting terms.

Birth To Three Matters

The increase in the number of babies and toddlers being cared for in settings has prompted the arrival of frameworks of practice for professionals. The frameworks help practitioners to identify key aspects that will promote emotional as well as other areas of development. Good practice today centres on meeting the individual needs of babies and toddlers, observing them closely and thinking carefully about their attachment needs. See also pages 89, 463 and 524.

The role of the family

Throughout this book, you have looked at the impact the family has on the growth and development of children. Families should be a safe place, where children feel able to be themselves, learn from their environment and be nurtured. The complex nature of each family, and the diversity within it, will in itself contribute to the effect on each child.

It is essential that you show respect for the families and other people involved in children's care, and understand that they may not necessarily do things the way you feel is right. This does not mean they are wrong. The way a family brings up their children will depend on a number of factors, including:

- financial circumstances
- age of parents
- ethnicity
- culture
- social background.

Family support structures

Whilst working alongside children in any setting, you will come across a diverse range of family structures:

- *Nuclear family* The conventional nuclear family, with married parents and 2.4 children is rapidly disappearing. This type of family live independently from other relatives, and will live their day-to-day lives depending upon each other for support.
- *Reconstituted family* Made up of two adults who may have children together and children from previous relationships. This type of family is rapidly overtaking the nuclear family within society.
- *Extended family* Here aunts, uncles, grandparents and other family members live together as one unit.
- *Lone parent* This may be the mother or father of the child, living with the child without a partner.

It is unlikely that you will come across many families that fit perfectly into any of the above family types, but they will have a mix of the above within their lives. For example, a lone father may have the support of his parents and family, although they may not live together. The development of multi-culturalism within society may mean that siblings within reconstituted families have differing backgrounds and cultures, and therefore may be cared for differently within their family structure.

Within these varied family structures, the care of the child and methods of bringing up the child may differ, and it is essential that families have open and honest lines of communication, enabling them to agree on strategies and approaches. This is particularly important with the context of behaviour management.

Case study: Different parenting styles

Charlie, aged 10, lives with his mother and stays with his father, his new wife, and her two children at weekends. Charlie's mother believes in routine and strong discipline, and does not allow Charlie to go out alone with his friends. He has a strict daily homework and bedtime routine. His stepmother, however, does not share these views, and allows Charlie to go out with her children to the park, and allows the children to go to bed when they feel ready. Charlie is beginning to rebel against his mother's strict routines and develop negative behaviours.

1 **How do you feel this mix of child rearing is affecting Charlie?**

2 **How might these issues be resolved?**

Family-centred behavioural therapy

Supporting families who are experiencing difficulties with behaviour management may become part of your role. The latest governmental guidance requires practitioners to work together with families to support them in these times.

Behavioural therapy may be appropriate for families where they are experiencing difficulties, as it targets the whole family, not just the child or main carer, and as such, influences the lifestyle and choices of the family as a whole, which is beneficial to the child. Where families are no longer together, perhaps through a marriage breakdown, they may still come together for this behaviour therapy, meaning that the strategies will be used by whichever parent the child may be staying with.

Approaches to anti-social behaviour

There are a range of behaviours that are deemed as unacceptable within society, and it is part of your role to support children in understanding what is acceptable,

and that there are consequences for their actions. The types of anti-social behaviours you may come across might include:

- biting
- defiance
- violent outbursts
- bullying
- anger
- aggression
- manipulation
- attention-seeking.

How you deal with anti-social or unwanted behaviour will depend upon the behaviour, the situation and the child. For example, an 18-month-old child who hits another child who has taken their toy will be managed in a different way to a 7-year-old who does the same. When approaches are used, it is essential that you show disapproval of the behaviour not the child, by saying for example, 'It's not very kind to bite others because it hurts them', rather than 'You are a naughty girl for biting James'.

Good practice checklist

Dealing with anti-social behaviour

- Use eye-contact and facial expression to demonstrate your disapproval of the behaviour. A simple look will often be enough to demonstrate to a child that you do not want them to behave that way.
- Use a low voice, stating a determined 'No'.
- Explain the consequences of their actions in a developmentally appropriate way.
- Remove the toy or equipment.
- Give them time out to think about their behaviour.

It is important that the way the behaviour is managed reflects the age and the developmental level of the child, as well as the individual situation.

Conformity

Whilst children and families are unique in their characteristics, we all follow certain societal rules at some time, which allow us to **conform** and live happily. For example, adults go to work, children go to school, cars stop at traffic lights. Without these rules, society would break down. Children learn very quickly that certain behaviours will get them a certain response. For example, a child may learn that by sharing their book with another child, they will be praised, and therefore will build up interpersonal expectations, understanding what is expected of them.

Key term

Conformity is complying with social standards, attitudes and practices.

Approaches to distress

Children often become distressed for a variety of reasons, and will show you this distress in different ways, such as:

- crying
- clinging
- fear
- anxiety
- withdrawal
- anger and aggression.

It is important that each child's distress is dealt with sensitively and individually, in a manner that is appropriate to their developmental level. It is essential to communicate with the distressed child, and show support and understanding. The table below demonstrates some causes and signs of distress in children, offering possible responses.

Distress is also discussed in Unit 1, page 25.

▼ Some causes and signs of distress in children

Cause	Sign	Response
Pain	When children are experiencing pain, they will often show this by displaying comforting behaviour, thumb sucking, for example.	Children in pain without reason should be looked at by their GP. However, you may know that the child has a new tooth coming, or has just fallen over and hurt their knee. In these situations, you should comfort the child, explaining how they might help themselves to alleviate the pain, giving cuddles, and reassurance.
Grief (loss or death of a loved one)	This will also include a child who displays distress when a parent leaves them in your care. Children may cry, scream or become angry that they have been left by the parent.	Again, comforting the child and explaining where their parent has gone will help a grieving child. Where a pet or loved one has died, children will need time to talk about their feelings and be supported in understanding what has happened.
Communication breakdown	A child who does not feel understood can demonstrate aggressive behaviour or become withdrawn.	Give children plenty of time to communicate with you, supporting children with communication difficulties. Always check that you have understood them by repeating what they have said.
Frustration	Young children especially will become frustrated when they cannot explain their needs to their carer, or when tasks are too difficult for them to complete. Frustration may be demonstrated through aggressive behaviour or withdrawal. They may also have tantrums to demonstrate their feelings of frustration.	Use techniques such as baby signing to support your understanding of the child's needs, allowing plenty of time for them to communicate with you. Ensure that tasks set are developmentally appropriate, supporting children as they develop new skills, and praising them for having a go even if they do not complete the task.
Unfairness	If a child feels they have been treated unfairly, for example, another child has knocked down their tower, or they have been reprimanded for something that wasn't their fault, they may demonstrate this distress by acting aggressively or squabbling with the other child.	Listen to children before making judgements of what has occurred, and ensure that children are given the opportunity to communicate their feelings with you.
Negativity	Where a child has been bullied or has experienced negative responses from others, they may take this as a personal attack, feel threatened. Children who experience this may demonstrate withdrawal or aggressive behaviour.	Ensure that children understand the implications of bullying, and hurting others. Allow opportunities for children to voice their feelings in a controlled way, through circle time for example. Challenge negative responses given by parents and other carers.

Special needs

Children with special needs may require differing strategies to help them develop and form early relationships.

For example, children with autism have difficulties in communicating with others and are unable to share their feelings and thoughts. As a result, building effective relationships can be very difficult. Gifted children can also find difficulties in forming relationships as they experience frustration and low self-esteem, with a feeling of being different from others affecting how they form relationships.

By ensuring that your practice is inclusive, and that you strive to meet the individual needs of the children in your care, you can develop strategies to help children with special needs to form strong, lasting relationships with their families, friends and carers.

Assessment activity 14.2

Consider four different behavioural strategies which may be used with children in your setting. Decide how you might implement them and discuss this with your line manager. Implement the strategies in your work place, and evaluate the effectiveness of the strategy.

14.3 The factors affecting children's behaviour

Transitional stages

As children grow and develop, they will move through many stages which will inevitably affect their behaviour as they learn to cope and adapt. These stages are known as transitional stages. These transitions may be from home to nursery, nursery to school, or from one school year to the next. The transition may be moving home, or going to live with a different parent. Whatever the transition, you need to be aware of how these transitional stages may affect the behaviour of the child, and how you might support the child to move through the stage as smoothly as possible. The table opposite suggests some possible reactions to different transitions, and offers ideas on how you may support the child to cope with the changes.

Physical and health-related factors

A child may demonstrate different behaviours as a result of their physical health. For example, a child who is a wheelchair user may feel frustration and anger when he cannot do the things that his friends are able to do. This can cause tantrums, aggression, regression or attention-seeking behaviour.

Children who experience long periods of time away from school due to ill health may also find they have difficulties in maintaining friendships, resulting in low self-esteem and lack of confidence, all of which may affect the way the child behaves.

A young child who has to stay in hospital, for example, may not have developed the communication skills to explain how they feel, which can result in frustration and aggressive behaviour. They may kick out at a doctor who they fear may hurt them, or be anxious about a

▼ Dealing with transitions

Transitional stage	Possible affect on the child's behaviour	Possible practitioner response
Starting nursery	The child may feel vulnerable, and afraid, resulting in distress (see page 433).	Ensure that the child has a key worker responsible for settling the child in. Allow parents into the setting until the child feels relaxed. Allow the child and family to make several visits to the setting. Adapt routines around the individual child. Give comfort and reassurance to the child.
Changing school/ classes/teachers	As children grow in age, they are more able to understand and cope with change, but may still feel frightened and apprehensive of the changes ahead. They may demonstrate anger and frustration or become withdrawn. They may show extrovert behaviour in an attempt to become the class clown and therefore become liked by their peers.	Help children to work through their concerns together, perhaps by teaming children with others that they know, or putting an insecure child with a more confident 'buddy' may help the child to feel more settled.
Family breakdown	A child who experiences the break-up of a family may go through a grieving stage as a parent leaves. They may show anxiety and fear of what may happen through anger and aggression, or may become withdrawn. They may feel they have to take the place of the absent parent, and therefore strive to become more responsible and grown-up.	Giving a child the opportunity to discuss how they feel, and helping them to see that they are not the only one feeling like this may help. Assisting them to find alternative methods of venting their frustration, and explaining their hurt and concerns to their family may be helpful in a situation such as this.

procedure that they do not understand. If their parent cannot stay in the hospital with them, then feelings of grief, loneliness and anxiety may affect the behaviour displayed by the child.

As a child hits puberty, they will become aware of the growth changes within their bodies, and have feelings which they are unsure how to handle. They strive to become more independent, and as a result may become more argumentative and pushy with parents and carers. Girls in particular may develop low self-esteem as they question their individual development, and compare themselves with their peers.

▲ Children may feel frustration and anger when they cannot do the things that their friends are able to do

Socio-economic factors

The child's gender, background, culture, ethnicity, financial and housing situation and social class can all affect their behaviour as they grow and develop. A child who has spent their early years being cared for by a lone parent, without opportunities for social interaction with other children or adults, may find difficulties in sharing and co-operating when they begin school. Another example might be a child from a run-down estate, whose parents have little money, finding she feels a need to prove herself to her peers by acting in a particular way.

Family factors

On page 431 we looked at the diversity of family support structures, and how this can affect how early relationships are formed. These different family types will also affect how a child behaves, as a behaviour which is unacceptable for one family might be quite the norm for another. Changes within family structure may be a trigger to a change in behaviour for some children. For example, a divorce or separation may lead to a child becoming withdrawn or demonstrating regressive behaviour, or a child in foster care with many changes of family may become angry and aggressive. Obviously this is a generalisation, and each child will deal with changes within their family structure in their own unique way. The important point is to ensure that through open contact with parents and carers, you are aware of any changes taking place, and consider how this may affect the child. You can then discuss this with the child, and help them to manage their feelings in a more effective way.

Where a child comes from an extended family, other difficulties may present themselves. For example, if a child is cared for by grandparents during the day, whilst their parents are at work, their grandparents may have different expectations and rules from the parents. This will confuse the child, as they will not understand what their boundaries are. This may also cause stress on the extended relationships, which could cause further problems for the child.

Children with siblings may find they have problems as they feel they have to try to live up to the standards of older siblings or, on the other hand, feel second best to a new baby. At times like these, the older child may regress in an attempt to 'be looked after', or a younger child may demand attention by acting aggressively or withdrawing.

Acceptable behaviour, and the acceptable ways to manage it, will differ greatly between cultures, religions, ethnic groups and communities. Even the language that parents use to discipline their children will vary. Whatever the family circumstance, it is essential that the carers within the family work together, and agree common strategies that will be used. For example, a lone parent may be having difficulties with a child who is having temper tantrums, and discusses this with the nursery. They can then come up with a plan of action for each time the child demonstrates this behaviour, which will ensure the child is dealt with in the same way whether they are at home or at nursery. Parents should understand that they are role models for their children, and their children will model themselves on them, whether they portray positive or negative images. Within this context it is important to understand the **self-fulfilling prophecy**, whereby children will make attempts to live up to the expectations we impose on them.

Key term

A **self-fulfilling prophecy** is a prediction that, in being made, actually causes itself to become true.

As part of the **hidden curriculum** in schools, children can also learn behaviour through unintentional messages. Therefore, it is essential that when planning activities, you seek to understand the underlying messages a child may learn from the activities and consider this when carrying out curriculum planning. An example of this may be setting up a role-play area, with the intention of supporting a child who has begun to display negative behaviour towards a new sibling.

Key term

The **hidden curriculum** is the things that children learn at school that are not part of the formal curriculum.

The role-play area may contain dolls, and equipment for caring for dolls, and may help the child to communicate his feelings and thought through play. You may then be able to support the child to correct or alter his behaviour through this medium.

Theory into practice

In 1968, two researchers, Rosenthal and Jacobson, carried out a study on a class of children. They hypothesised that disadvantaged children make limited progress within school because that is what their teachers expect of them. They tested this by informing classroom teachers that a particular group of their class were more likely to make significant progress within their school year. These children had, in fact, been randomly chosen. When at the end of the year their progress was monitored, they found that those randomly chosen children had in fact made significantly better progress than their peers. They therefore concluded that there was correlation between the teachers' high expectations of the children and the children in turn living up to these expectations. This behaviour is known as the self-fulfilling prophecy.

Effects

As children grow and develop, they begin to visualise themselves, and develop self-concept (see page 421). This self-concept will become an important part of the way they view their capabilities and strengths, or self-esteem. With regard to behaviour, children need to have high expectations of themselves and believe they can behave in a positive way. A child who is regularly praised for their positive behaviour is more likely to continue behaving that way, as they have a firm belief in their ability to do so. Similarly a child who is constantly told that they are 'bad' or 'naughty' will develop low self-esteem, and feel that this negative behaviour is all they are capable of. It is therefore important to praise the positive behaviours that children show, and where possible ignore, or respond softly to, the negative

behaviours. Children will soon realise that they gain approval and praise from the positive behaviour.

Experiencing times of stress, or feeling unable to cope, can be devastating to a child, and you may find that the only way they feel they can communicate this feeling is through displaying negative behaviour. It is essential that where a child does this, regular observation of the trigger to the behaviour is made, to enable you to identify the times where the child displays these feelings. For example, a child who may be struggling with maths in school may become stressed at the thought of having to carry out the tasks. They may display avoidance techniques initially, going to the toilet, sharpening a pencil, etc. to avoid having to start the task. Once this is no longer available, they may display regression, have a sudden tummy ache or other behaviour to get them out of having to do the task. Regular observation of the child will enable you to pinpoint these areas of stress, and initiate coping strategies for the child.

Feeling socially excluded and marginalised can affect a child's ability to reach their full potential, leading them to feel frustrated and angry at the society or community in which they live. Feelings of disempowerment can lead to low self-esteem, and therefore to the behaviours discussed above.

Assessment activity 14.3

Design a leaflet for parents, detailing how nutrition, sleep and lifestyle may affect behaviour of a child, and give hints on how they develop positive routines to support their child's behaviour management. **P3**

Earlier in this unit, we looked at how we might approach anti-social behaviour, and the factors which might trigger unwanted behaviour in children. Here, we will look at how we might challenge behaviour using a variety of methods.

Approaches to behaviour

Using language

The language and tone of voice we use with children can be a clear indicator of how we feel, and demonstrate our approval or disapproval of their behaviour. For example, when we are praising a child, the pitch of our voice raises, and our facial expression and intonation demonstrates our approval. On the other hand, a disapproving look and a quiet low voice can show the child that you are not happy with their behaviour. As we have already discussed, it is essential to show disapproval of the behaviour, not the child.

Positive approaches to challenging behaviour

Challenging unwanted behaviour positively provides the child with clear guidance, role models, and examples of how to alter the behaviour. You may already be using some of these approaches within your setting;

- Always use positive reinforcement of desired behaviour; when a child is acting in a positive manner, tell them and ensure they understand what it was they did that you liked.
- Providing a reward when the positive behaviour is being demonstrated allows the child to connect positive behaviour with reward. This reward may be a sticker, a merit for their team, or some kind of reward chart, for example.

Negative approaches to behaviour

Children learn to associate behaviour with a response, and as such can learn that negative behaviour can be as useful as positive behaviour. If a negative behaviour is reinforced, the child will continue to exhibit the behaviour.

Think of a time when you have witnessed a child ask their parent for something, which is refused. The child will continue to ask in the hope that eventually their parent will give in. Should the parent give in, then they have reinforced the negative behaviour, giving the child the message that if they continue the negative behaviour for long enough, they will eventually be rewarded.

Children with additional needs

For some children, controlling their behaviour may be more difficult if they have additional needs which have to be catered for. A child with communication difficulties may find it difficult to express their needs or feelings, leaving them feeling undervalued and

▲ Lack of concentration may lead to low attainment, low self-esteem and poor self-image

frustrated, leading to aggression and displays of anger. To counteract this, you need to be aware of any communication difficulties, and try to develop and improve communication strategies with that child. Baby signing, Makaton or the use of picture cards may all be helpful in this situation.

Children with ADHD (attention deficit hyperactivity disorder) find difficulties with focusing their attention on particular tasks, especially those tasks which they find uninteresting. This lack of concentration may lead to low attainment as the child struggles to keep up with their peers, which may lead to the child having low self-esteem and poor self-image. It is important to provide these children with activities which will stimulate them and keep them aroused.

Good practice checklist

Support for children with ADHD

- Provide plenty of sensory activities to retain the child's interest.
- Develop and maintain routines and structure within the child's day.
- Avoid situations where the child is kept waiting.
- Provide activities which the child can leave and come back to when they are ready.
- Provide positive reinforcement, such as rewards or stickers, etc.
- Use visual props and cues.

You need to be aware of any additional need the child may have in order for them to address the need and provide strategies to deal with the behaviour displayed by the child. Where children feel their needs are not being met, or that they are being treated differently from their peers, they may become angry, aggressive and frustrated. It is essential that each child is treated individually, given equal opportunity and treated with respect.

Strategies

It is essential to have a range of strategies which may be used to challenge the behaviour of different children. Some of these strategies include:

- *Child empowerment* – teaching children how to have control over their own lives, allowing them to develop self-esteem, and confidence, and feel valued within society, enabling them to be proactive in their goals and outcomes
- *Assertive discipline* – helping children to understand that there are consequences for the behaviour, both negative and positive
- *Parent and child contracts* – an agreement between the parent and child which details acceptable and unacceptable behaviour from both sides and the consequences and rewards for their actions
- *Reward charts and incentives* – having visual targets, such as reaching the top of the tower, or collecting the most merit points for their team allows children to see how the behaviour is improving, and gives a positive incentive
- *Inclusion games* – children experiencing low confidence and self-worth may also find difficulties fitting in with their peers. Inclusion strategies such as selecting them to be responsible for the register or changing the reading books will help them to feel included within the group and empower them, thus supporting them with self-esteem and confidence development.

Specialised games and equipment

The use of specialised games and equipment can assist practitioners in supporting children with behavioural problems. As mentioned earlier, the use of tactile, sensory activities can help maintain the interest of a child with ADHD, therefore preventing unnecessary behaviour issues when the child's levels of arousal drop. Using visual games and activities for children with hearing impairments may also have the same effect. Board games which address personal issues around behaviour may provoke discussion and thought within a group of older children, encouraging them to consider how their behaviour affects others and work through alternative strategies which they may use.

Other more specific techniques such as **therapeutic communication** and **sensory integration therapy** can be useful for children with a range of needs which leave them feeling frustrated and misunderstood. **Cognitive behaviour therapies** may also be used depending upon the individual needs of the child.

Counselling models

A range of therapies and techniques may be used to support behavioural issues in children within counselling. Some of these may be:

- *colour/art therapy* – using art and creativity as a way of expressing emotion
- *persona dolls* – personality dolls used as a medium for exploring emotion, feelings, and other social issues
- *buddy schemes* – matching a child to a peer companion who will support the child socially within their environment.

Parent empowerment

Families may become stuck in a cycle where the child's poor behaviour triggers a poor response from the parent and so the behaviour continues. Providing opportunities for parents to learn new coping strategies will help break this cycle.

By supporting parents to develop their own self-esteem and confidence, you will be empowering them to believe in themselves as parents and educators. Some opportunities that settings may provide include:

▲ Persona dolls are used to explore feelings and social issues

- *family learning opportunities* – time for practitioners to work with the family as a whole, demonstrating and promoting positive behaviour techniques, and helping parents to see the value in family time for their children
- *single sex groups* – these might be fathers' groups or women's groups, which promote self-esteem to the group, providing time to discuss problems within the group and allowing others to offer suggestions or solutions. Opportunities to share common issues will help parents to feel they are not alone. The group may also offer relaxation time for parents to experience activities such as aromatherapy or vehicle maintenance
- *outings* – providing opportunities for families to experience new situations, and practitioners to offer advice and practical solutions to behaviour management within these situations. For example, a trip to a shopping centre may be particularly difficult for some parents. By going on the outing with the support of practitioners, parents can learn new strategies to cope with these situations.

Support roles and agencies

Where children are experiencing problems with behaviour, many professionals and support agencies are available to

▼ Some support agencies and professionals

Agency/professional	Roles and responsibilities
School nurse	Screening, health promotion within the classroom, initiating support for parents.
Health visitor	Work with parents when their children are young, offering support and guidance.
Educational psychologist	Support the identification of learning difficulties in children, working alongside families and professionals to draw up individual educational programmes.
Child and family services	Work with families and children to support them through difficulties, offering support and guidance.
Educational Social Work Service (ESWS)	This has the lead role in ensuring that legislation in relation to a child's school attendance and employment is being followed.
Social workers	Offer advice, counselling, support and protection to a wide range of people within the community, in hospitals, and other settings, supporting families under stress, older people, people with disabilities, people with mental health problems, homeless people, and children in need of care and protection.
Support teachers	Support children under the guidance of their teacher.
Counsellors	Provide opportunities for children and families to explore their problems from different perspectives.
Speech therapists	Work with children who have difficulties with communication, or with eating, drinking and swallowing. Work closely with families, carers and other professionals.
Holistic educational therapists	This is a pioneering new service which supports children with emotional and behavioural problems and their families. A range of complementary therapies are used to support children, which may include Hopi ear candles, aromatherapy, diet and nutrition and holistic counselling.

help families to overcome these problems. The table above lists some of the agencies or professionals which may be involved, and their roles and responsibilities.

Theory into practice

Find out about holistic education therapy and how it may be of use in your practice. The following website can give you further information: www.holisticeducationaltherapy.co.uk.

Complementary healthcare approaches

Alternative approaches to caring for children are becoming more popular, as families and practitioners strive to find alternative, non-invasive solutions to their problems. These may include:

- *Brain Gym* – an educational, movement-based programme which uses simple movements to integrate the whole brain, senses and body, preparing

the person with the physical skills they need to learn effectively (www.braingym.org.uk)

- *baby massage* – this can help to strengthen the bond between parent and child, as the parent becomes more confident in touching and holding their child, and the baby enjoys the feeling of being touched

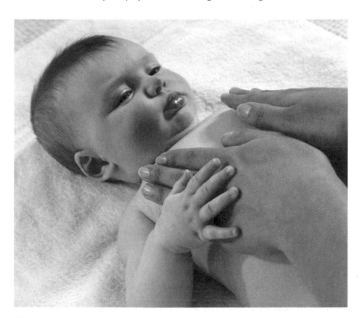

▲ Baby massage can help strengthen the bond between child and carer by the parent. As a relaxing approach, massage can soothe a child, and can also help the physical growth of babies, as they feel their joints and muscles moving and stretching.

■ The Behaviour Improvement Programme (BIP)

The BIP was set up in July 2002 as part of the government's Street Crime Initiative. Thirty-four local education authorities (LEAs) were selected for the programme on the basis of an indicator combining truancy and crime figures. In April 2003, the BIP was incorporated into the Excellence in Cities (EiC) initiative and rolled out to a further 27 EiC LEAs. This was followed by further expansion in 2004–5, when 26 Excellence Clusters were introduced to the BIP. Finally, a further 50 Excellence Clusters joined the programme in 2005–6. The programme came to an official end in the summer of 2006, but ex-BIP schools and authorities still receive funding through the School Development Grant (SDG) and most partnerships are sustaining the successful behaviour and attendance initiatives begun under BIP.

All participating LEAs and schools committed to achieving the following objectives:

'● **to improve standards of behaviour, and reduce the number of serious incidents**

● **to reduce truancy by agreeing 'stretching targets' for unauthorised absence**

● **to secure lower levels of exclusions than in comparable schools**

● **to ensure that there is a named key worker for every child at risk of truancy, exclusion or criminal behaviour**

● **to ensure the availability of full-time, supervised education for all pupils from day one of either permanent or temporary exclusion.'**

(www.dfes.gov.uk/behaviourimprovement)

■ Behaviour and Education Support Teams (BESTs)

These multi-agency teams work with children and young people aged from 5–18 years. It aims to carry out early intervention support and prevent emotional and behavioural problems. The team includes a variety of professionals, including social workers and police officers, bringing together a diverse range of experience and skills to provide individual support to families, depending upon their needs.

■ Every Child Matters policy

The Every Child Matters document details the UK government's policies on protecting the most vulnerable children within our society, and details how it will ensure that all children reach their full potential. The four main areas within this document are:

● Supporting parents and carers:
  – universal parenting services, for example family learning programmes
  – specialist parenting support, for example home visiting programmes

● Early intervention and protection:
  – improving information collection and sharing, for example common data standards on the recording of information
  – common assessment framework – this will draw on existing assessment tools
  – lead professional to take the lead on a child's case when the child is known to more than one agency
  – professionals encouraged to work in multi-disciplinary teams, and possibly be based in and around schools and children's centres

● Accountability and integration – locally, regionally and nationally:
  – proposed legislation to require the appointment of Directors of Children's Services – accountable for local authority education and children's social services and for overseeing services for children delegated to the local authority by other services
  – proposed legislation to create a lead council member for children

● children's trusts – most areas should have trusts by 2006. These will sit within the local authority and report to the Director of Children's Services
  – key services that should be within the trust are: education; children's social services; community and acute health services – including some tiers of child and adolescent mental health services

(CAMHS). They might include: youth offending teams(YOTs), and Connexions. The primary care trust (PCT) will be able to delegate functions into the children's trust, and pool funds with the local authority
– Local Safeguarding Children Board – these will replace Area Child Protection Committees
– an integrated inspection framework led by Ofsted
– appointment of a Children's Commissioner
- Workforce reform
  – workforce reform strategy to improve skill and effectiveness of the children's workforce
  – common occupational standards across children's practice
  – common core training for those who work solely with children and families and those with a wider role. For children's mental health, a coherent multi-agency strategy for mental health skill development is proposed within all children's agencies. The continuing and additional training needs of the CAMHS workforce, including all those agencies that make up the comprehensive CAMHS, will also be addressed and new career pathways will be developed
  – two new bodies are to be established: a Children's Workforce Unit based at the Department for Education and Skills (DfES) and a Sector Skills Council for Children and Young People's Services.

Look at the Every Child Matters website (www. everychildmatter.gov.uk) for further information on the Every Child Matters agenda.

Sure Start

Sure Start is a government programme which aims to achieve better outcomes for children, parents and communities by:

- increasing the availability of childcare for all children
- improving health and emotional development for young children
- supporting parents as parents and in their aspirations towards employment.

Sure Start plans to achieve its aims by:
- helping services development in disadvantaged areas alongside financial help for parents to afford childcare
- rolling out the principles driving the Sure Start approach to all services for children and parents.

For further information, look at the Sure Start website (www.surestart.gov.uk).

Confidentiality

Confidentiality is discussed in the following units:
- Unit 1, page 11
- Unit 2, page 51
- Unit 4, page 146
- Unit 5, page 198.

Assessment activity 14.4

Find out how support agencies are used within your setting to support the management of behaviour. Design a questionnaire to send out to support agencies, finding out how their job role supports the children you care for and evaluate your findings. **P5**

Observation

In Unit 3, you looked at the types of observational methods you might use in your setting to support children's learning and development. These observational techniques may also be used to monitor the effectiveness of the behavioural strategy being implemented.

Case study: Observing behaviour

James is 4 years of age and has been displaying negative behaviours such as biting and hitting other children. His mother informed you that his father has recently left, and although James still sees him regularly, he has taken it very badly. At home he has begun to wet the bed, and has regular temper tantrums. Together with both parents, you have drawn up a positive praise plan, in which all positive behaviour is reinforced with praise and negative behaviour ignored where possible, except for where another child is hurt.

How might you use observation techniques to monitor how effective the positive praise plan is?

The table below gives some ideas of how observational methods may be used to monitor the effectiveness of behavioural strategies.

Consultation

When evaluating the effectiveness of behaviour management strategies, it is essential that you consult others who are involved in the care of the child. This may include:

- parents
- carers
- teachers
- child
- support professionals.

An effective method of consultation is through questionnaires. Using set questions allows you to compare the answers given by different people, for example, does the teacher's response match with the response from the parent, and why? When devising the questionnaire, think carefully about the information you want, and the questions to ask. Decide whether the questions will be open or closed, and use them throughout.

Observation method	How it is used
Cross-sectional observations	Ideal for looking at how several children respond to situations, and how their responses differ or are similar. You may be implementing similar behavioural techniques with a small group of children, and use this method to see who is responding well and who is not.
Longitudinal observations	This may be the best observational technique for monitoring behaviour as it tracks one child over a period of time. While implementing a behaviour strategy, it will allow you to monitor its effectiveness over a set period.
Written narrative	Allows you to be descriptive about what you are observing, and therefore ideal as a starting point.
Structured recording systems	Allows you to focus your attention on the specific behaviour of the child that you are trying to target with a behaviour strategy.
Checklists	Easy to use, this type of observation allows you to tick off particular behavioural targets as you observe them.
Graphs and charts	Used to record information, this method enables you to track a certain behaviour, for example, the amount of times the child shows a particular behaviour within a timescale.
Time sample	Allows you the versatility to observe a child's behaviour at regular intervals, for example within five minute intervals.
Event sample	Possibly the most useful observation method for evaluating the effectiveness of behaviour management as it allows you to record how often a specific type of behaviour is shown.

Liaising with support professionals is vital for ensuring that behaviour management strategies are continually monitored and changed as necessary. External professionals may draw up behavioural profiles which will support the work with the child and can be shared with families to make the whole process more coherent.

Collecting data

Once you have decided on the methods and observation techniques you are going to use to monitor the effectiveness of behaviour strategies, you will want to collate the data into a reader-friendly format, enabling you to present your findings professionally.

Qualitative information

Qualitative information is presented in written form. You may have written down what someone has said during an interview, or made notes to summarise what has taken place. You will have thought about, and selected, the information required and, therefore, examined and evaluated the data. This selection process enables you to produce the factual information you require, producing qualitative information.

Quantitative information

This kind of information is based on direct measurements or categories that have a value – the number of times the child played with a particular toy over a set period, for example. This kind of information can be presented in tables or charts, demonstrating percentages or averages, and allows you to summarise your findings in a more methodical manner. You can use a computer to produce graphs, pie charts, bar charts, etc. to show the outcomes of the observations.

Diaries

Keeping diaries or logs of behavioural events can enable you to keep track of significant changes, and address what has happened in that day/week to trigger those changes. However, where a diary has been kept for a significant length of time, it may be wise to summarise its comments, and pinpoint particular events that are significant.

Behavioural incident logs

Incident logs may be effective in monitoring behaviour. Having a set format allows the user to ensure all the required information is detailed. It is essential that confidentiality is maintained and that these logs are stored appropriately.

Procedures for providing feedback

Giving feedback on the implementation of behavioural strategies to parents can demonstrate your commitment to their child's development, and help them to understand how the strategies have/have not worked. When providing feedback, always begin on a positive note. Feedback may be verbal or written, but it needs to be clear, concise and appropriate. You may feel it is best to ask the parent into the setting for a chat, or may arrange to visit them in their home. You may send a letter home with the child. It is important that when feedback is given, confidentiality is maintained, and that the feedback is factual.

All methods of monitoring the effectiveness of behaviour strategies have their limitations, and some will work for some children, but not others. It is important to remember that you should always take a holistic approach to monitoring behaviour, looking at the individual needs of the child and family.

Assessment activity 14.5

Prepare a presentation explaining how you might monitor the effectiveness of implemented behavioural strategies within your placement. Consider:

- the kinds of observational methods you might use, explaining their appropriateness
- others with whom you might consult
- how you might collate and interpret the data you have collected
- how you will use this information to support the behavioural development of the child. **P6**

End of unit assessment

1 Describe the major theoretical perspectives of developmental psychology relating to inappropriate behaviour that may be displayed by children in the following age ranges: 1–2, 3–5, 6–8. **P1**

2 Describe, with an example for each, how differences in the children's experiences of building relationships may have affected their behaviour. **P2**

3 Identify any other factors which may contribute to the children's inappropriate behaviour. **P3**

4 Outline strategies you might implement to support these children with behaviour management. **P4**

5 Identify the support agencies who might be able to offer support to these children. **P5**

6 Describe how you might evaluate the effectiveness of your suggested strategies. **P6**

7 Compare the major theoretical perspectives of developmental psychology relating to behaviour of the children you have identified. **M1**

8 Explain how practices that you have seen during your placement experiences have been influenced by these theories. **M2**

9 Explain the strategies you might implement to support children in the management of their behaviour. **M3**

10 Explain the methods you might use to evaluate the effectiveness of your strategies. **M4**

11 Analyse the contribution of the major developmental perspectives to early years practice in the context of behaviour management. **D1**

12 Evaluate the strategies you have suggested to support children with their behaviour management. **D2**

References and further reading

Books

Bee, H. (1999) *The Developing Child*, Longman

Bukato, D. and Daehler, M. (1997) *Child Development: a thematic approach*, 3rd edition, Houghton & Mifflin

Gross, R. (2001) *Psychology: the science of mind and behaviour,* 4th edition, Hodder & Stoughton

Gross, R., McIlveen, R., Coolican, H., Russell, J. and Clamp, A. (2000) *Psychology: a new introduction for A level*, 2nd edition, Hodder & Stoughton

Useful websites

Brain Gym – www.braingym.org.uk

Every Child Matters – www.everychildmatters.gov.uk

Holistic education therapy – www.holisticeducationaltherapy.co.uk

Sure Start – www.surestart.gov.uk

Young Minds (children's mental health charity) – www.youngminds.org.uk

Grading criteria	Assessment activity	Page number
To achieve a pass grade the evidence must show that the learner is able to:		
P1 describe the major theoretical perspectives of developmental psychology relating to behaviour	14.1 End of unit assessment	424 446
P2 describe the role of early relationships in the development of children's behaviour	14.1 End of unit assessment	424 446
P3 identify a range of significant factors that may affect children's behaviour	14.3 End of unit assessment	437 446
P4 outline four different behavioural management strategies	14.2 End of unit assessment	434 446
P5 identify a range of relevant support roles and agencies used in managing behaviour	14.4 End of unit assessment	443 446
P6 describe methods that could be used to evaluate the effectiveness of behavioural management strategies	14.5 End of unit assessment	445 446
To achieve a merit grade the evidence must show that, in addition to the pass criteria, the learner is able to:		
M1 compare the major theoretical perspectives of developmental psychology relating to behaviour	14.1 End of unit assessment	424 446
M2 use examples from work placement to explain how areas of early years practice are influenced by developmental theory	14.1 End of unit assessment	424 446
M3 explain four different behavioural management strategies	End of unit assessment	446
M4 explain the different methods used to evaluate the effectiveness of the behavioural management strategies	End of unit assessment	446
To achieve a distinction grade the evidence must show that, in addition to the pass and merit criteria, the learner is able to:		
D1 analyse the contribution of the major developmental perspectives to early years practice	14.1 End of unit assessment	424 446
D2 evaluate four different behavioural management strategies	14.2 End of unit assessment	434 446

Supporting children's numeracy skills

Introduction

Developing numeracy skills is an important life skill. There are so many occasions in everyday life when we use numeracy that we hardly think of it as being mathematics. Children need the opportunity to develop these skills in a supportive and secure environment and all individuals who come into contact with young children will have some influence on this.

In this unit you will have the opportunity to consider some of the theories relating to the development of numeracy skills. The role of the adult is particularly important in this area as you will need to be aware of the scope of your responsibility in planning, observing and assessing the development of children in your care.

As in all areas of childcare, it is important to be aware of the individual needs of the child and consider specific or special issues that may affect the child's ability to learn. In order to provide effectively for the child in the home or early years setting, you should be aware of current legislation and guidelines and how this has an impact on the early years curriculum. You will need to build up a range of activities designed to promote the development of skills related to numeracy, including shape, space and measures, as well as numbers. Involvement across the age range will provide you with the knowledge and skills required to support all children with the development of numeracy skills.

There will inevitably be some overlap with Unit 18, Supporting Literacy Skills and it is recommended that these two units are studied together.

What you need to learn

- The development of children's numeracy skills
- Current national initiatives and curriculum guidance relating to the development of numeracy skills
- How to develop a range of activities that can be used to support children's understanding and use of number
- How to develop a range of activities that can be used to support the development of children's understanding and use of shape, space and measures

Thinking points

Children in early years care and education settings regularly become involved in activities with strong mathematical connections. Early years workers will wish to promote the development of numeracy skills, which will be reinforced through play, structured and free-flow activities. They will need to develop a range of activities which can promote the understanding of mathematical concepts in the young child.

- How do you think mathematical concepts could be incorporated in the following activities?
  - Creative activities
  - Role play, for example shop, hospital clinic, post office
  - Construction toys
  - Outdoor play
  - Water play
  - Sand play
  - Cooking session
  - Story time
  - Singing and rhymes

- Why do you think it is important that children enjoy and have positive experiences of mathematics?

Relevant theories

How children develop an understanding of mathematical concepts

Each of the theorists mentioned in the table below have very positive and distinct views as to how mathematical thinking develops. Language development is also important as it has an impact on numeracy development (see Unit 18, Supporting Literacy Skills). You will be able to compare their views and form your own opinion about the process.

Key term

Numeracy skills are the skills required in order to be able to use numbers, shape, measures, time and space effectively.

▼ Theories on how mathematical thinking develops

Theorist	Theory
Bruner	Jerome Bruner believed that a child is predisposed towards learning and that there are structures in place so that the child can follow a sequence of cognitive processes. As a child has individual experiences, then the cognitive schema provides meaning to these experiences. Children learn through doing then imagining what they have been doing and then translating that into symbols of drawing, writing and numbers. Adults play an important role as they support children as they move through the different stages of development: • enactive (0–1) – learning through doing – physical movements • iconic (1–7) – developing mental images • symbolic (7+) – using symbols such as language and other representational modes to transfer thoughts.
Piaget	Jean Piaget's research led him to believe that we develop by taking in information, which is then processed by the brain and as a result of this our behaviour changes. He stated that there are stages of development that children move through. The ages are approximate but the sequence is the same for everyone. • sensori-motor (0–2) – using senses and reflexes • pre-operational (2–7) – using symbols and language • concrete operational (7–12) – developing more logical thought • formal operational (12+) – capable of abstract thought. He also developed the idea of schemas as ideas or concepts that children need to master in order to learn about relationships. In addition he carried out research into the ability to conserve mass, volume and number (see page 454).
Bruce	Tina Bruce suggested that as children play they strengthen and manage learning strategies and in this way they will develop concepts and ideas. She stated that children need to learn by direct experiences and that learning by observing others, either in reality or through television or videos/DVDs, they will not achieve the higher quality processes that will enable them to learn more effectively. Taking part enables children to socialise with others and they will gradually be involved in games with rules of varying degrees and they will also use language and activities such as drama, creative and music as tools to represent the thought processes.
Athey	Chris Athey further developed the concept of schema in the development of mathematical thought. These describe children's repeated behaviour patterns which children freely choose. It is through the development of schema that children develop as they explore and experiment. They form the foundations on which children build and develop more complex thought, especially about maths. The development of schema shows how the biological development of the brain is linked to the daily experiences of the child. Children become totally absorbed in the process and will spend a great deal of time carrying out related activities as they develop a particular schema, for example painting lines, building towers when developing a vertical schema. It is through the development of schema that children learn about the world around them and develop the skills required.

The development of schema

Piaget was one of the first theorists who felt that children formed specific schemas as concepts that must be established in the child's mind before they can develop an idea. However, the majority of theorists now accept that the development of schema is integral to the development of mathematical thought. Children will spend a great amount of time developing schemas. They may paint vertical lines in a variety of colours, build towers and stand objects on top of others when developing a vertical schema. Children who are developing an enclosing schema will place objects inside others and may even be seen doing this when eating, for example placing a piece of sausage on a fork and then covering it with mashed potato. They need to develop a whole range of schema to understand the world around them. These are some further examples:

- *transporting* – moving objects from one place to another in various ways, for example prams, trucks, trays and in bags
- *positioning* – placing objects in specific positions, for example playing under tables, asking for gravy in a specific place on the plate, walking in specific pathways
- *rotation* – enjoys playing with and watching things that turn and spin, for example spinning tops, wheels, enjoys being swung around.

▲ Developing schema?

Learning through play

Play is vital to the overall development of the child and is one of the main vehicles through which a child learns. Children always take an active part in play and it has a strong relationship with discovery learning. It is through play that children learn about all aspects of life and it is through play that they learn about:

- other people
- cause and effect
- objects (through exploration)
- time and space (through experimentation)
- making things
- solving problems
- mastering skills.

The adult or early years worker needs to provide a safe, secure and stimulating environment for the child with the resources to allow for play and development in all areas of learning.

Theory into practice

- Arrange to visit an early years setting and note all the mathematical processes in the play activities that the children are engaged in.
- Listen to the language they use and take note of mathematical language of comparison, number, measure and shape.

Sequences and stages

The table below provides approximate ages for mathematical development but it is important to remember that development in this area is very dependent on the opportunities a child has to hear mathematical language and practise the skills.

Correct use of mathematical words and knowing number names

Children will start to use mathematical words very soon after they begin to talk. It is all part of the development of mathematical concepts. Adults will often say 'How big?' and the child very quickly learns that this is rewarded by smiles of encouragement once they raise their arms. Gradually other ideas are introduced and reinforced, particularly at times of relaxation and when

▼ Ages and stages of mathematical development

Approximate age	Stage of development
Under 2 years	Children begin to become familiar with mathematical language, for example 'big', 'little', 'full', 'empty'. Some children will begin to count by rote – 1, 2, 3 but not much further.
2–3 years	Counting by rote to 5 with little understanding. Enjoys water and sand play and has an understanding of full and empty. Enjoys number rhymes.
3–4 years	Can often count by rote to 10. Some children developing an understanding of counting with meaning. Can sort by colour and size. Can match by colour, shape and size. Understands number names up to 10.
4–5 years	Sorting becomes more sophisticated and can sort by category. Enjoys simple number trails. Can bring correct number of items when requested. Can understand simple addition if language used is appropriate, for example related to objects rather than numbers. Starts to understand number shapes. More sophisticated addition – relating numbers and objects. Cannot conserve. Understanding of simple forms of measurement. Can place objects in order of size.
5–6 years	Spatial awareness is more developed. Starting to understand fractions, for example half, quarter. Greater understanding of numbers, volume, measurement.
6–7 years	Uses number lines effectively. Starting to understand time. Enjoys number puzzles.
7–8 years	More detailed and sophisticated use of number. Used of detailed measurement. Can conserve. Understands large numbers.

What stage of development is ▶ this child demonstrating?

the child has the full attention of the adult/carer. Meal times are valuable for this type of learning – 'one more spoonful'; 'all gone'; 'nearly empty' are all phrases used regularly and children quickly understand the concepts involved. Practising the number names in rhymes is one of the ways in which they can be reinforced in the child's mind and they are usually associated with finger play so that the number is also linked to the name. Games and stories that we enjoy with young children will also involve the number names.

Counting by rote

This involves counting without understanding, i.e. learning a sequence of words. They will later relate to objects but initially they do not. You might notice that some children when asked to count objects, will always end at five or ten no matter how many are there in reality. They have learned that number counting always tends to sound like 'one, two, three, four, five' even if there are only three objects. This will later progress into meaningful counting. However, songs and rhymes, for example 'Five fat sausages sizzling in the pan', 'Five current buns …', 'Five little ducks…', 'I have ten little fingers', all reinforce the pleasure of playing with number rhymes. Counting is reinforced throughout the day with the numerous activities that children become involved with.

Counting with meaning and one-to-one correspondence

This relates very closely to one-to-one correspondence when children realise that one number is linked to one object. Counting occurs in familiar stories, for example 'The Three Billy Goats Gruff', 'Goldilocks and the Three Bears'. In the latter, the number three is reinforced many times with the bowls, chairs and beds. There is also the song 'When Goldilocks went to the house of the bears', which can be used to reinforce learning from the story and this can be further enhanced if the children are encouraged to act out the story. This particular story also involves other mathematical concepts such as size, quantity, one-to-one correspondence and matching. Before a child learns to count, they need to be able to understand one-to-one correspondence. This is the

ability to match one object to another even though they might not look alike, for example realising that one cup goes with one saucer. Activities to practise and reinforce this concept include laying the table or preparing a painting activity so that each child has a brush, a paint pot, an apron and a piece of paper (one of each object for each child).

Addition and subtraction

Very young children can add and subtract but only if it is meaningful to them. They are unlikely to give the correct answer if asked, 'What does 2 + 1 make?' but when confronted with the problem, 'If you have two sweets and I give you another one, how many will you have?', very young children will often provide the correct answer.

Classifying

Children need to be able to classify or sort objects, initially by colour or shape, but will eventually be able to sort by category. Children often will automatically sort by colour and will place objects in sets, for example red plate, red saucer and red cup. They will also sort by shape, for example all the sheep in one field, cows in another and ducks by the pond. Sorting by category takes a little longer and is rather more complicated, for example asking a child to place all the objects that fly might prove to be more complex if the child has a group of objects which include helicopters, aeroplanes, birds, kites, sheep, horses, cars and lorries. Similarly a child may be asked to put all transport vehicles together.

Comparing

Children need opportunity to compare in various ways, for example light/dark, long/short, and there will be plenty of opportunity in the early years environment. Comparison of height of different children or of lines or towers made with building blocks will produce some interesting observations from the children. Similarly, comparisons of length of lines, tracks and pathways can also influence the development of other ways of measuring.

Ordering

Placing objects in order is an important part of mathematical development. Placing objects in order of size is one activity that children enjoy. The order of the day is another variation that children need to come to terms with. Children might be asked to place a series of pictures in order. One may have a child getting out of bed, another of the child getting into bed, eating breakfast and a fourth of the child going to school.

Volume, shape, measures, space and pattern

Children initially use everyday language to describe shapes and position. At first they are able to identify 2D shapes and later 3D shapes, giving them the correct name. They will develop skills of estimation and will make judgements as to whether a container is half-full or empty.

Recognising numerals

Children can recognise numerals, initially up to 9 and they will often attempt to copy these, sometimes reversing the shape. They will associate a numeral with the correct amount of items.

Symmetry

Children understand that some items are symmetrical and that there is a central line of symmetry. They will be able to fold paper patterns and design symmetrical shapes.

Conservation of number

Conservation of number is the understanding that the number of objects remains the same when they are rearranged spatially. Piaget carried out a number of experiments with children in order to demonstrate their ability or inability to conserve. Conservation in this context means that objects remain constant however they are arranged. He carried out experiments to demonstrate that children would not be able to conserve number, mass or volume until they have reached the concrete operational stage (around 7 years of age). Conservation of number is usually the first to develop but before a

child reaches that point they believe that objects may increase in number if they are arranged in a different pattern. The ability to develop an understanding of constancy comes as the child grows older. Piaget carried out a similar experiment to the one in the Theory into practice below. See if you achieve the same results.

Theory into practice

Try this experiment with a child approximately 4 or 5 years of age.

Put down two rows of counters, each containing five in number and each row a different colour. Talk to the child and ask which row had the most counters and the child will usually identify that each row has the same number.

Now, spread the counters in one of the rows so that they are spread out across more space. Do this in front of the child so that they can see that you have neither added nor taken away any of the counters. Ask the child which row has the most and the usually answer is that the longer of the two rows contains more.

▲ Conservation of number

Subitising

When Piaget carried out his experiments to demonstrate conservation of number, he related it to the ability to tell a number of items mainly by the pattern they made rather than by counting the separate items. This ability to instantly recognise the number in a group is known as subitising. If six items are placed in two rows of three, as in a domino pattern, then many people will be able to recognise the pattern even before counting the number of objects. It is easier to recognise five if placed in the domino pattern for five rather than in a straight line. This skill is developed over time but is often established to a certain degree by the time a child is five.

The role of the adult

Adults play an important role in the development of numeracy skills. Some of the first rhymes that we say to children convey numerical concepts, for example 'Round and round the garden, like a teddy bear, one step, two steps …'. Children love these types of rhymes and will develop a strong liking for early numeracy activities. Many adults will state that they do not like maths yet very young children have a good foundation and generally choose to play games linked to numeracy in preference for others. There is much speculation as to what happens between loving numbers and hating them. As early years workers and interested adults you can influence the understanding and development of numeracy skills in young children.

Extension activity

Make a resource that can be used with young children to extend their mathematical development. You could make a rhyme card or a recipe card, which has some counting or measuring related to it. When making cards of this type it is often a good idea to illustrate them so that they are interesting and the child will be able to count the objects in the picture, for example 2 eggs, 1 spoonful of sugar.

Using mathematical vocabulary

Using mathematical vocabulary is usually one of the things that occurs naturally. We talk about being 'big' or 'little', about containers being 'full' or 'empty'; we use positional vocabulary to describe objects, for example 'under', 'over', 'behind', 'in front of'. It is important that children are also encouraged in this way and that they become very familiar with mathematical language. It is generally part of everyday life and children should be encouraged to take part in a variety of activities and experiences and should be engaged in conversation. If this is the case, then mathematical vocabulary will be natural and part of everyday experiences.

Good practice checklist

When you are working with young children your role will cover many different aspects. Don't forget to consider them as you work with the children in your care:

- working with parents
- planning activities
- addressing specific needs
- observing and assessing
- using mathematical vocabulary
- reinforcing, praising and encouraging
- showing an awareness of cultural needs
- planning activities which build on previous experience and are child-centred
- inclusion
- confidentiality
- knowing how and when to intervene
- addressing diversity and cultural needs
- establishing an effective, confident and caring relationship with children.

Theory into practice

Watch a group of children at play and note the activities they initiate as part of their free-flow play. Take note of how many mathematical concepts are incorporated into their spontaneous activities and the level of enjoyment they get from these actions and words.

Observation and assessment

One of the main methods of assessing the development in young children is to observe them closely. This will enable you to assess the stage of development for that child and to plan effectively for future activities, which will aid consolidation and progression. It is mainly through observation, assessment and record-keeping that you can evaluate the provision and ensure that you are meeting the individual needs of the children. It is also necessary to check that you provide quality experiences, which extend learning.

As you have more contact with young children, you will become more aware of the importance of observation. This is covered in more detail in Unit 3, Promoting Children's Development.

Observing children and accurately recording your findings is essential. The conclusions you draw will be extremely valuable in your assessment of any individual child. Observing children effectively takes practice, but it is important to remember that a relaxed atmosphere will produce a more realistic observation than one where the children feel under scrutiny and may change their behaviour accordingly.

Reinforcement; praise and encouragement

B.F. Skinner was probably the best-known exponent for positive reinforcement and it should be recognised that praise and encouragement are very powerful, as children like to please others. In praising and encouraging a child, you are telling them that whatever they are doing is pleasing, good and gives pleasure to others and they will wish to repeat it. Some settings will use additional

methods of providing positive reinforcement, such as using stickers or star charts. However, it should always be remembered that these rewards should be attainable by every member of the class or group as it would be demotivating if a child did not receive a reward at all.

Theory into practice

Arrange to visit an early years setting (more than one if you can) and find out if they use any practical methods for encouraging children, for example stars on work or given to the child to take home. Make a list of the different types you come across and compare lists with your colleagues.

Working with parents

Parents are the child's first teachers and have much valuable information about the development of the individual child. It is important for you to build up a positive relationship with the child's parents so that each will be able to reinforce the work of the other.

Parents have a right to know about the structure of the setting and the curriculum planning and should be involved at all stages. Progress should be reported to them on a daily and regular basis and the child should be praised and encouraged when their parents are present so that they can develop their self-confidence and self-esteem.

The importance of planning activities which build on previous experience and are child-centred

Children need to build up skills and will need to use previous experience on which to do so. It is often said that 'success breeds success' and it is important that a child has confidence in what they are doing. If they are always presented with activities that they find difficult or that they are unable to complete, then their self-esteem will suffer as a consequence. This is not to say that activities should not be challenging but that they should be planned on an observed foundation. Many people have a great dislike of mathematics as adults because they have been confronted with new concepts before they have consolidated others and they have been 'moved on too fast'. In general, children love mathematical activities and we need to encourage that sense of achievement rather than lose it. Children will often initiate play activities and it is recognised that spontaneous play is vital to the holistic development of the child. Many of the self-initiated activities will include the development of mathematical concepts. These types of activities will always allow the child to continue with the mastery of actions and the development of skills. Children will reinforce and consolidate previous learning and children will freely choose play activities to strengthen and underpin knowledge.

Case study: Building for the future

Jasmine has been working in an early years setting for two years and is familiar with the development of activities for the children in her care. A small group of children are building the walls of a house using large plastic interlocking blocks. They are on the carpet area of the setting and are trying to join the oblong shape at the corners. However, there are too many blocks along one side for this to happen. They also want it to be large enough so that all three of them can sit inside and have a meal. They have already brought their chairs and a cardboard box as a table and one of the children has gathered cups, saucers, plates, etc. in readiness after the walls have been erected.

1 **How might Jasmine help?**

2 **What other resources might they need?**

3 **List the various mathematical concepts involved.**

4 **How might the activity be extended?**

Early years workers must be able to plan effectively for the needs of all children in their care, as shown in the table below.

Planning	Detail
Individual	It is important that you know about the individual needs of each child, including their actual stage of development. A child may be displaying signs of delayed development against the norms and it is essential that their needs be planned for, rather than a whole class or group approach. Individual planning is designed to address the specific needs of an individual child, for example a child may be having difficulty in gripping and picking up small objects and so the individual plan may include activities to strengthen muscles in the hand such as playing with clay or play dough.
Long-term	Long-term planning may be over a number of months with future targets set for the child. Details of the planning will include topics and strategies for each area of learning. The long-term planning might be in broad strokes with the detail more defined in the medium- and short-term planning. Long-term planning may be over a term or even a year when the plan and structure of the setting is set out. This must, in essence, be flexible enough to incorporate spontaneous activities and events.
Medium-term	Medium-term planning might be on a weekly or monthly basis, but will include detailed goals within the long-term planning. It is important that resources be available for all the activities planned and that they are set in a logical and structured way and cover all areas of learning. Medium-term planning will include goals set for children over a number of days and may include topical issues, for example festivals and related activities such as Christmas.
Short-term	Short-term planning may be on a daily basis and will have smaller goals to be achieved. You will have planned the small details and have decided on the resources, staffing and materials required. Achievements and progress will be recorded so that future planning can be based on realistic targets. Short-term planning will include achievable goals for the children, for example develop understanding of multi-cultural festivals, such as Diwali.

Topic: Myself	Monday	Tuesday	Wednesday	Thursday	Friday
Personal, social and emotional develpment	Parts of body Stranger danger	Emotions	Dental hygiene		
Communication, language and literacy	Stories, rhymes relating to parts of body				
Mathematical development	Sets				
Knowledge and understanding of the world	Stories of children in other countries				
Physical development	Movement and music				
Creative development	Our family	Frieze work			

▲ Example of a planning document

Awareness of diversity and cultural needs

All early years workers should be aware of the background of the children in their care and cater for cultural and religious specifics. In some cultures reading and writing does not follow the established pattern of reading in the UK. Remember, that letters are not always used and in some countries it is usual to use characters to convey messages rather than letters building up into words. Although this is important for developing literacy skills, this has an impact on the development of numeracy skills, as many mathematical problems are presented in writing, especially for the older child.

Establishing a positive relationship with children

Helping children develop numeracy skills is a very personal course of action and establishing a good relationship with children is vital in this process. It is through the building up of these relationships that the child's self-confidence and self-esteem will increase and so will their willingness to engage in conversation and interact with others. It is very difficult to think of activities that do not involve numeracy skills and children should be encouraged to feel at ease with mathematical problems and so build their self-confidence.

Knowing when and how to intervene

Knowing when to intervene in a children's activity takes sensitivity and experience. The child should be able to develop skills independently but occasionally adult assistance might be beneficial.

It is important not to take over the task but to ask if the child requires any assistance. You will need to observe the child and make a judgement as to whether your intervention is going to help the situation or hinder it.

Good practice checklist

When deciding how and when to assist a child, you should:

- observe the child and judge whether your intervention will help
- act in a sensitive manner that will not undermine their self-confidence
- ask if they would like you to help
- consider the form your assistance will take – a few verbal prompts may be all that is required to trigger their thought processes to move in a slightly different direction
- not take over the task!

Confidentiality

Confidentiality is one of the most important underlying basics for the early years worker. It is fundamental to the trust and respect that must be developed when building a positive relationship with parents and carers. Once confidentiality is broken, it is impossible to fully re-establish the relationship. Not only can a breach of confidentiality destroy carefully established relationships, it can also have far-reaching effects, which may even have legal implications for the setting and the staff involved. You will find more about confidentiality in Unit 6, Promoting Children's Rights.

Inclusion

It is vital that all children feel valued and are able to access the curriculum. Children will arrive at a setting with individual needs and abilities and the setting must cater for all. Activities must be presented so that they can be adapted to suit the needs of the individual child. It is part of your role to ensure that the needs of all children are met.

Addressing specific needs

The needs of each individual child must be met in the early years setting and, as the needs are specific to each child, it is important that you use individual learning programmes to meet those needs at all times. Some specific needs are mentioned below but these do not capture the vast range of needs that children present on a daily basis.

Specific needs

Meeting children's individual learning needs

It is essential that you meet the needs of all children and it must be recognised that certain conditions require additional resources including a higher adult–child ratio. There are a number of reasons why children will need an individual learning programme, including those shown in the diagram below.

It is important that the child receives the help and assistance required but equally important that they do not feel undermined or that their confidence or self-esteem is affected in a negative way. Adults must have the resources to provide the best for children and may require specialist input to meet the needs of children with specific needs.

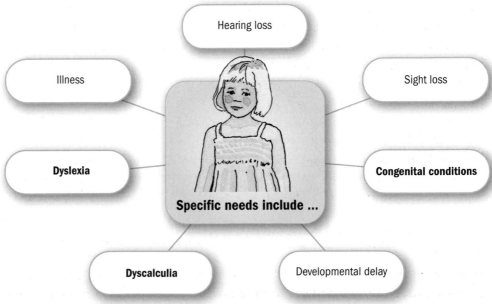

Hearing loss

Illness

Sight loss

Dyslexia

Congenital conditions

Specific needs include ...

Dyscalculia

Developmental delay

Key terms

Dyscalculia is a learning condition that affects the individual's ability to carry out calculations. This will also affect their general mathematical reasoning.

Dyslexia is difficulty with reading and writing despite the individual having normal development of cognitive skills and intelligence.

Congenital conditions are conditions that a child is born with; can include genetic conditions and those which occur during the pre-birth development of the child.

Dealing with difficulties in ways which do not undermine the child's confidence

Help is available to support children with any condition and you will be able to access specialist professionals in this area. It is vital that parents are involved at all times and that strategies are in place so that the child's confidence is not undermined. All adults involved with the child must demonstrate a sensitivity and awareness so that the child feels valued as an individual. Many early years settings have a **key worker** system where one member of staff is allocated to a child as their particular contact and link within the setting. The health visitor is often the first point of contact for many families when

▼ Meeting individual learning needs

Learning need	Detail
Developmental delay	Developmental delay might have a variety of different causes, for example illness, premature birth, separation, as well as congenital conditions. The situation may be permanent or temporary and will need to be addressed accordingly and on an individual basis.
Congenital conditions	There are a vast number of congenital conditions, which might result in learning difficulties and require specific help. Each condition will be individual to the child involved and require a personal or individual learning plan with short-, medium- and long-term goals to be achieved. In many instances, this will also involve guidance from other professionals, for example curriculum advisers and health visitors.
Illness	If a child has had a severe or lengthy illness, there may be delay in a number of areas of learning and this must be taken into consideration when preparing a programme of study. Many children 'catch up' quite quickly but may need more individual help for a while.
Hearing loss	This might be a permanent or temporary condition and you may be the first to realise that there is a degree of hearing loss. Children might only hear correctly if sitting close to the adult. They may be disruptive because they do not fully understand the situation. This must be diagnosed correctly and parents involved at all times. It may be that the child needs corrective treatment or to use an aid to help hearing. Adults should be aware of the situation and speak clearly when talking to the children. It is good practice to face children when talking to them but adults need to be careful to ensure they do not cover their mouth when speaking. This can affect development in many areas and particularly mathematics – if children find it difficult to hear the mathematical terminology, it will be more difficult to understand the concepts.
Sight loss	Sight loss or impairment can be in varying degrees and care should be taken to ensure the child has the best opportunity to see what is happening. Spectacles may be able to correct the situation to a certain degree, but there are screens for computers, which can enlarge the print, and large-print books. Bright illustrations and clear numbers can assist in this area. Many aspects of visual mathematics can be compromised and one-to-one assistance is often required to prevent further delay.
Dyscalculia	This is a learning condition that affects the ability to carry out calculations. It is also sometimes known as 'mathematical difficulty'. As it is thought to be related to difficulties in processing the visual image, it could be connected to dyslexia. Individuals with dyscalculia will often muddle up numbers and will appear to make very simple mistakes in their calculations.
Dyslexia	This is a difficulty with reading and writing despite the individual having normal development of cognitive skills and intelligence. Many children with dyslexia are capable, intelligent and articulate yet they are unable to read, write or spell at a developmental level appropriate for their age. As children with this condition have literacy problems in general, they will also have some difficulty with handwriting and this has a further impact on the development of numeracy skills. Again, children benefit from one-to-one help by specialist staff.

there is some indication that the child has difficulties with vision, hearing or developmental delay. Within an education setting, there is opportunity to contact curriculum advisers who can help staff provide a detailed learning plan for a specific child.

Key term

A **key worker** is a member of staff allocated to a child so that a strong relationship might develop. They will work alongside the child to get to know their likes, dislikes, interests and strengths.

When and how to access help

It is important that, as soon as any conditions are identified, the appropriate help is sought. There are a number of professionals that can assist when help is required for, example the GP, educational psychologist, health visitor. They will then be able to refer the family for further assessment and more specialist help, for example from a physiotherapist, speech therapist, etc. The earlier the intervention the better, so that the child and the family can access appropriate and relevant assistance.

Supporting children for whom English is an additional language

When English is not a child's first language, there are support mechanisms which can be put in place, and most early years settings have literature and welcome packs in a variety of languages. Books within the setting should celebrate the diversity of race and culture within the country and there should be books with stories in other languages. Multi-cultural images should be portrayed in posters and photographs, and labels should reflect different writing styles and languages. Numbers should also be written in different languages, alongside the numeral, to demonstrate the variety of words which might be used. There will also be interpreters who can provide support for the child and the family for as long as they require it. As the main thrust is for the child to understand the spoken and written word, it is usual for mathematical language and development to run alongside. Many rhymes and number songs have a repetitive pattern and often children feel more secure with this type of language.

Assessment activity 17.1

Produce a leaflet, for parents of children in an early years setting, explaining the development of mathematical skills in the early years. Give examples of activities that children might be involved in on a daily basis, drawing from your own experiences. Remember to make it interesting and lively. You might also like to illustrate your leaflet. **P2**

 Sources of support

Type of support	Support provided
Key worker	This is usually a member of staff in an early years setting who has particular responsibility for a small number of children. The key worker is the child's main worker in the setting and the child will develop a strong relationship with this person. The key worker is also the person within the setting that the parents/carers will share information with.
Curriculum adviser	This is usually an expert employed by the local authority who will advise staff on curriculum matters and how individual children with specific needs might access the curriculum within the early years setting.
Special Educational Needs Co-ordinator (SENCO)	The SENCO is the member of staff who is responsible for the identification of children with specific needs in the setting and also with the implementation of any recommendations from the statementing process or any other professionals.
Health visitor	The health visitor is one of the main supports that a parent has, especially prior to the child moving into an early years setting. If there are any concerns regarding health and delayed development then the health visitor can provide the contact for parents so that the appropriate assistance can be accessed.

Legislation

Relevant legislation relating to numeracy and literacy skills is summarised in the table below.

Legislation	Main points
Children Act 1989 and 2004	The Children Act 1989 was the legislative framework that set national standards for childcare services. It laid down quality standards by which all early years settings could be measured and it included that anyone running childcare services must plan activities, which would help children enjoy learning. The Children Act 1989 was later reviewed and after the Green Paper, Every Child Matters, the Children Act 2004 became the framework of legislation of services that are available to support children. This Act has five main outcomes. These were that every child had the right to: • be healthy • stay safe • enjoy and achieve • make a positive contribution • achieve economic well-being. In order to achieve the last three of these outcomes, the individual child needs to develop good language and literacy skills.
Warnock Report 1978	The Warnock Report was a report from a committee of enquiry into the education of children with special needs. The report estimated that up to 20 per cent of children would have special needs at some time during their school life. This report was directly responsible for the Education Act 1981 which had a profound effect on the way children with special needs were categorised and educated. The Act changed the whole ethos of special education and there was a greater move towards inclusion into mainstream education wherever practicable.
Code of Practice 2001	The Code of Practice is part of the framework of provision for children with Special Educational Needs. All education establishments used the SEN Toolkit, which provided a practical application of the principles of the Code of Practice.
Relevant curriculum framework	This depends upon the age of the child, with the curriculum being divided into three main areas: • Birth to Three Matters framework • Foundation Stage Curriculum • National Curriculum/Cwricwlwm Cymreig/Northern Ireland Curriculum. In addition, the National Numeracy Strategy and the National Literacy Strategy have formed an important part of daily life in mainstream education and these areas will be covered in more detail later in this unit (page 465) and in Unit 18, page 498. The new Early Years Foundation Stage (EYFS) is due to come into force in September 2008. The EYFS will provide a framework for care, learning and development for children in all early years settings from birth to 5 years. It will build on the existing Foundation Stage, Birth to Three Matters framework and the National Standards for Under-8s Day Care and Childminding. It is designed to be a flexible approach to care and learning and also to raise quality within the early years sector.

Two other reports which have had some impact on the development of numeracy are:

• the Cockcroft Report 1982, otherwise known as 'Mathematics Counts', which looked into the teaching of mathematics in schools

• the Rumbold Report 1990, 'Starting with Quality', which stressed the importance of good-quality early years education and recommended a curriculum, which included mathematics alongside other subject areas.

Curriculum guidance

The early years curriculum is generally considered in three broad age groups: under 3 years of age, 3–5 years of age and over 5 years of age.

Birth to Three Matters framework

Birth to Three Matters was established as an effective framework for children less than 3 years of age. It is based on activities and experiences linked to the child's overall development and children are encouraged to learn through their senses. Once a child is able, they will enjoy treasure baskets and take great pleasure from various types of tactile play experiences. They enjoy rhymes, stories and songs and, as they mature, they will learn through direct experiences and discovery learning. Many of these will involve the use of numbers and very young children take great joy in anticipating the next part of a rhyme or song and joining in with the finger play and counting activities. Parents and families are recognised as being central for the overall development of the child.

The framework is organised into four distinct areas:

- A strong child
- A skilful communicator
- A competent learner
- A healthy child.

▲ **Early learning**

The competent learner focuses on a number of different areas, such as:

- Making connections
- Being creative
- Being imaginative
- Representing.

These areas are invaluable for the development of numeracy skills, for example comparing, classifying categorising, making patterns, exploring, experimenting and discovering.

The framework provides a firm foundation for moving onto the Early Learning Goals. However, September 2008 will herald the implementation of the new Early Years Foundation Stage, which will replace a number of other frameworks, in order to provide a more structured and cohesive approach to care, development and learning for children in the birth to 5 years age group.

Curriculum guidance for the Foundation Stage, specifically the area of Mathematical Development

This is the curriculum for children aged 3–5 years. The Early Learning Goals are a series of targets that children work towards and they are linked to a series of Stepping Stones, which have been devised to assist early years workers in planning and preparation.

The Stepping Stones (non-statutory) and the Early Learning Goals (statutory) are used throughout the Foundation Stage and also help early years workers to assess children as they move through early years education. The Stepping Stones provide information concerning the knowledge and skills that children need in order to meet the Early Learning Goals. The Early Learning Goals are defined in six areas:

- Personal, social and emotional development
- Communication, language and literacy
- Mathematical development
- Knowledge and understanding of the world
- Physical development
- Creative development.

The third Early Learning Goal, 'Mathematical development', is divided into 'competences' linked to being able to count and recognise numerals up to 10; using mathematical language as a means to communicate and as a tool in thinking; developing the ability to describe position and use mathematical language in everyday contexts, for example big, little, more than, etc.

The final year of the Foundation Stage is what is often referred to as the Reception Year and it is expected that the majority of children will have achieved the targets set in the Early Learning Goals. Many children will have exceeded them and some children will not have reached all of them. The Foundation Stage Curriculum is closely linked to Key Stage 1 of the National Curriculum, which follows on in a logical sequence. The Foundation Stage has involvement with the Primary National Strategy and the renewed Mathematics Framework. This will be considered in greater detail later.

Extension activity

Research the Early Learning Goals for Mathematical Development and see how the Stepping Stones relate to that specific area. A useful website is www.dfes.gov.uk.

Early Years Foundation Stage

This will be implemented in 2008 and training events have been planned for at least 18 months prior to that. This will enable early years settings to make a smooth transition from other frameworks they have been working with. It will build on the existing Foundation Stage, Birth to Three Matters framework and the National Standards for Under-8s Day Care and Childminding. The approach is flexible and has been developed alongside the Rose Review so that the literacy and mathematics frameworks enhance the new developments.

National Curriculum/Cwricwlwm Cymreig/ Northern Ireland Curriculum

This is the curriculum for children over 5 years of age.

Cwricwlwm Cymreig is the Welsh equivalent of the National Curriculum and recognises the importance of the unique Welsh culture and heritage and includes the teaching of Welsh as a first or second language. A large proportion of the schools in Wales also use bilingual stationery when communicating with parents and carers and use English and Welsh when answering the telephone or when meeting people.

The Northern Ireland Curriculum is structured in a similar way and has the opportunity for the inclusion of Irish as one of the curriculum subjects in Irish-speaking schools, and again the unique culture and heritage of Ireland is encouraged at all times.

The National Curriculum in England was introduced following the Education Reform Act 1988 and has been used in all schools ever since. It is a set curriculum to ensure that standards are consistent across the country. Within certain guidelines schools are able to plan a flexible programme that meets the needs of the children locally. It consists of the following subject areas:

- English
- Mathematics
- Science
- Design and Technology
- Information and Communication Technology (ICT)
- History
- Geography
- Art and Design
- Music
- Physical Education.

Mathematics is sub-divided into areas covering the use of numbers, measuring, counting, calculating and shape and this has further been extended into, originally, the National Numeracy Strategy and, more recently, the Primary National Strategy, which covers the Primary Framework for Mathematics.

Theory into practice

Think of a general theme or topic, for example Myself or Toys, and list some activities around that subject that could promote numeracy skills in the 5–6-year-old child (Y1).

National Numeracy Strategy

The National Numeracy Strategy was first introduced in 1999 to raise the levels of numeracy in schools. Teachers and support staff were trained so that numeracy standards might be improved on a national level. The Numeracy Hour was devoted purely to the development of mathematical skills, sometimes on a small group or individual basis and sometimes with the children involved in whole-class work.

Theory into practice

Arrange to visit an early years department in a primary school and talk to staff about how numeracy skills are promoted in the classroom. Take note of sessions specifically designed to meet the Primary National Strategy.

■ Primary National Strategy (PNS)

In the spring of 2006 the Rose Review led by Jim Rose to look into the teaching of early reading became one of the main sources of evidence for the review and renewal of the Literacy and Numeracy Strategies. These became part of the new Primary National Strategy (PNS), which was made available in October 2006. The Rose Review drew on extensive research into the most successful teaching strategies and made recommendations based on its findings.

Under the PNS, children will continue to receive discrete teaching relating to mathematics. Greater emphasis is placed on group or whole-class work. It is anticipated that materials will be available from the Primary National Strategy to support this area of work.

The PNS suggests five key areas as laid down in the Primary National Strategy Bulletin. They are:

- Raising standards by encouraging flexibility in the teaching of mathematics
- Paying greater attention to structuring teaching and learning
- Raising expectations for all children
- More effective use of assessment
- Ensuring that children benefit from a broad and rich curriculum.

Extension activity

Carry out some research into the introduction of the Primary National Strategy and consider how it will positively affect early years education, and in particular numeracy. A useful website is www.dfesstandards.gov.uk.

There are three main differences between the renewed Mathematics Framework and the one introduced in 1999, as identified on the Department for Education and Skills website and the Primary Framework for literacy and mathematics:

- The new framework is an electronic version, which will enable users to access resources much more easily.
- There is a clearer structure with the curriculum laid out in seven strands.
  - Using and applying mathematics
  - Counting and understanding number
  - Knowing and using number facts
  - Calculating
  - Understanding shape
  - Measuring
  - Handling data.
- The objectives identified in the 1999 document have been 'slimmed down' to produce a more focused sense of what is important in the teaching of mathematics.

Learning through play

Play is the vehicle by which all young children find out and develop the skills and knowledge to extend experiences and move on to the next levels in learning. There are five main areas of development and early years workers, parents and carers need to ensure that all areas are catered for. The Rumbold Report (1990) 'Starting with Quality' stressed the importance of good quality early years education and recognised the importance of learning through a variety of play activities rather than the more formal learning of later years. Play is often a spontaneous activity that children engage in and it promotes development in all areas. Play has strong links to the curriculum guidance for the early years and is considered good practice in early years settings.

You will become skilled at providing for these areas of learning, but all areas of play will provide for mathematical development. Play and associated learning activities are covered in more detail in Unit 7, Learning Activities and Play, but it is important to ensure that children have ample opportunity to explore shape, space, capacity and other mathematical concepts. Children will take advantage of all the materials presented to them and will develop vital skills for the ongoing refinement of mathematical development.

Impact of legislation/guidance on practice

Legislation and curriculum guidance ensure that good practice is available for children at all times. The introduction of the Early Years Curriculum (incorporating Birth to Three Matters, the Foundation

Case study: Tea-time

John and his father are preparing tea for when his mother arrives home. They have discussed what they are going to prepare and have decided on ham and tomato sandwiches, meat pie followed by cake and scones. They will also make a pot of tea (John's father's job) and some juice. John opens the bread and says that they need two slices of bread for each sandwich. He counts it out by saying that there are 'two slices for mum, two for dad and two for me'. They proceed with the preparation of the food and then think about setting the table. John enjoys preparing meals and often cooks with both parents as he loves being in the kitchen. He also likes the washing up as he enjoys playing with the bubbles and cups in the warm water.

1 **Make a list of all the maths that might be involved in preparing the meal.**

2 **Make a list of all the maths that might be involved in laying the table.**

3 **Consider the mathematical skills involved in the washing up/water play.**

4 **How might you extend this activity?**

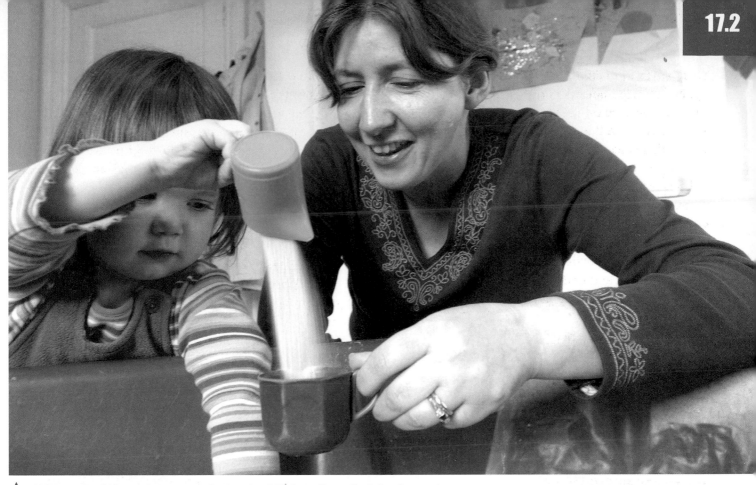

▲ Children should have the opportunity to extend their mathematical development

Stage and the National Curriculum) means that early years workers follow a flexible yet structured curriculum that will help raise standards in all areas of development, particularly mathematics. The detail of the curricula means that adults have a set of standards that the majority of children can achieve by the end of the curriculum stage. Training events are often arranged to provide for the development of staff and to ensure that standards are being maintained. Legislation and guidance on practice is continuously being looked at and revised. This is usually carried out by a group of people commissioned solely for that purpose and it is through their findings that legislation and guidance is amended and reviewed. As literacy and numeracy development has such an impact on the population as a whole, there are usually a number of resources available for early years practitioners especially on the Department of Education and Skills website or through the Standards Unit.

Theory into practice

Arrange to interview a teacher in a school and find out how current legislation impacts on their classroom practice.

Assessment activity 17.2

1 Produce a leaflet for a trainee early years worker, in which you explain how they could help children develop mathematical skills. **P3**

2 Link the work in the early years care and education setting to current legislation. Provide examples from your own experience to bring the leaflet to life. **P4**

Activities

There is a wide range of activities available to ensure that children have the opportunity to learn about numbers and mathematics. Each will have specific goals but many activities provide for overlapping aspects of numeracy. Some examples are provided below.

To ensure that children learn number names

Children need plenty of opportunity to hear the names of numbers and to be able to associate them with the correct number of items/objects. Children begin to hear about number names from a very early age with songs and rhymes that are said or sung to them. As they become older, the rhymes and songs become more sophisticated but a large majority still include numbers and they are also associated with finger play. Some songs and rhymes have the numbers in ascending order, for example '1, 2, 3, 4, 5 once I caught a fish alive …', and some will have them in descending order, for example 'Five little speckled frogs …'. There are many other opportunities through stories, creative work and incidental play for children to hear the number names and the associated number of objects.

One-to-one correspondence

Once children have developed the schema for dots and the horizontal and vertical, many will paint pictures which include grids with a dot in each 'square'. A great number of activities reinforce this concept, whether at home or in an early years setting. Some examples include:

- role play – sets, for example one cup, one saucer, one plate
- creative – one paint brush, one paint pot, one child, one apron

▲ Number rhymes

- cooking – one cake case, one space on a bun tray
- games – one counter, one space on game board.

Children might then develop activities in spontaneous play, for example role-play cinema when one person has one ticket. Once this concept has been mastered, children can start to identify number groups.

Theory into practice

Arrange to visit an early years setting and observe the children. Take note of occasions when they are developing the idea of one-to-one correspondence.

Matching and ordering activities

Early years workers can provide a range of activities, which involve matching and ordering.

- Matching activities include picture lotto games where the child is required to match the pictures and games where the shapes, colours or numbers are to be matched. You can make cards with a series of different shapes and the child might then thread the appropriately-shaped beads to match.
- Ordering activities include jigsaws which require the child to place the tallest at one end and the shortest at the other; placing numbers in the correct order; placing clothes for the dolls in order of size, lining up dolls in order. Children very quickly understand 1, 2, 3, but have more difficulty with the concept of first, second, third, etc.

Theory into practice

Draw around various shapes and objects on black paper then carefully cut them out. Let the children try to find the object and match it to the silhouette. (This is often a good way to ensure that tools are returned to the correct place, by matching them to their 'shadow'.)

Explore and record patterns

Children need plenty of opportunity to explore and create patterns and record them. Patterns are all around them and they may need encouragement to identify them. Creative activities provide an ideal opportunity for children to make repeated prints and develop their own patterns in shape and colour. They will be able to thread beads in a pre-determined pattern, for example follow a pattern from a card. Flooring and tiles provide patterns in the environment and children should be encouraged to take note of all the patterns that occur naturally, taking notice of the symmetry of leaves and flowers, considering the structure of webs. Children will often identify and point out patterns in everyday activities.

Theory into practice

Find some blocks of wood, approximately 6 cm × 6 cm. Glue a pattern onto the block using thick string. You might have a wavy line; three separate lines; a spiral; circle, etc. Once the glue has dried use the blocks to print with paint onto paper. Then you could make a display with the block and the pattern to find out if the children can match the two items.

Numerical problems

There are a variety of ways that we can encourage children to solve mathematical problems and a number of them are listed in the table on page 470. This list is not exhaustive and you will be able to think of many more.

Ways of encouraging children to solve mathematical problems

Activity	Detail
Counting games	Games using a simple die will enable the children to count the spaces or squares, for example snakes and ladders. It is good practice to vary the way the children identify the number of spaces to move, for example spots as on dominoes or numerals; activities where children count up to ten before looking for a hidden item.
Number puzzles	Jigsaws with number shapes are helpful with the identification of numerals. Puzzles where the number of items is associated with the numeral.
Nursery rhymes	There are many nursery rhymes and songs that include numbers, often in reverse order so that the child is encouraged to subtract as the rhyme progresses. There are rhymes when two items are subtracted and children need to concentrate when repeating it, for example 'Ten fat sausages sizzling in the pan, one went pop and the other went bang, eight fat sausages ...'.
Number lines	Children enjoy number lines and they can be very simple or more complex to suit the individual. They are often printed out on paper or card and the child is required to fill in the gaps. 1 2 ? 4 5 ? 7 OR 5 10 ? 20 25 ? 35
Maths trail	Children find maths trails very exciting and, if they are well designed, it is possible for the child to use an audiotape to follow the instructions. This will depend on the layout of the setting and the resources available. The maths trail follows a similar idea to an obstacle course in that there are a number of different activities which need to be carried out, but obviously with the maths trail each activity must be linked to mathematics in some way. The trail can be set using equipment and resources that are available in most early years settings, for example beanbags, hoops, tunnels, etc. and then a series of instructions can be prepared, for example 'Walk up the steps, one, two, three, then down the steps at the other side. Pick up the beanbags, first the red one, then the yellow and finally the blue. Carry them over the bridge to the hoops. Place the red beanbag in the large green hoop and the blue beanbag in the small yellow hoop ...'.

Extension activity

Individually or in pairs, devise and design a maths trail that you might be able to set out in your placement. It does not have to be too long or complicated, but should be interesting for the age group you are working with.

▲ Tallest to the left?

Materials, settings and environments

Importance of providing a wide variety of materials and resources for mathematical experiences

Children should have as wide a range of resources as possible and they should all be of good quality. As an early years worker, it is important that you always keep health and safety issues in mind. Most activities have some mathematical connotation and it is important that children should be able to take advantage of each opportunity and that the right equipment is available. The table opposite provides some examples, but it is not exhaustive and you will be able to add more of your own.

▼ Materials and resources for mathematical experiences

Play/activity	Materials and resources
Sand (wet and dry)	Containers of various sizes and shapes Sieves Balances Scoops Other items may be used depending on topic, for example cars
Water	Measuring containers and beakers of differing sizes and shapes Tubing Cups Water wheels Aprons – one per child (1:1 correspondence)
Role play	Plastic money Sets of items (for example, 1 cup, 1 saucer, 1 plate). Complete sets in different colours Clothes of different sizes to fit appropriate dolls Pans with matching lids – various sizes and shapes
Cooking	Different size bowls Different size spoons Measuring spoons Scales Aprons – one per child (1:1 correspondence)
Table activities	Jigsaws Matching games Construction toys Measuring activities for example growth of plants Symmetry – mirrors Woodwork bench
Creative	Collage – sorting Patterns – colour and shape Position Size, shape and colour
Outdoor	Patterns in nature Webs, leaves, etc. Patterns on and around buildings – fences, paving, windows, etc.

Enabling children to choose their own resources

It is important that children are encouraged to be as independent as possible so that they do not fall into a pattern of 'learned helplessness'. This might sometimes be observed when a child has been prevented from trying to do something themselves and loses interest. Occasionally you might see children standing waiting for an adult to put their coat on without any attempt to try for themselves. It takes time and patience to encourage children to develop such skills and it is often easier for the adult to take over. However, children will lose their will to try and so it is important to ensure that children have opportunity to make decisions and to explore and experiment within the bounds of safety. If resources are placed on low shelving, then the choice and responsibility will be up to the child. They will be able to make informed decisions and become more decisive as they mature and grow.

Good practice checklist

It is important that children are encouraged to be as independent as possible.

- Have resources that children can access easily.
- Encourage children to be independent in making choices with resources.
- Help children take responsibility for tidying away the resources.

How setting/environment may affect children's mathematical awareness

■ Displays

Children require the resources and the opportunities to develop mathematical awareness. The setting and the environment must be stimulating and conducive to children's learning. The setting should be bright, light and well ventilated so that the child feels relaxed and safe and will explore and experiment with the resources available. Most displays provide an opportunity to explore some mathematical concept and, depending on the age of the children, it is acceptable to incorporate mathematical ideas into display items, for example for 3–4-year-old children a springtime frieze could incorporate the song 'Five little ducks went swimming one day …' and might also include the written song, thus showing the numerals as well. Tabletop displays might include shapes and patterns, for example circles. The children could be encouraged to find shapes that might be added to the display.

Theory into practice

Arrange to visit two early years settings for different age groups. Take note of how the early years workers have made each setting a stimulating one and how the displays reflect the ethos of each establishment.

How to maintain interest, motivation and focus

Children will remain interested, motivated and focused if they are in a lively stimulating environment with activities that are fun as well as challenging. It is good practice to use observations to find out about the interests of a child and develop activities around them. If learning is fun and exciting, then children will wish to engage in more activities. Children are eager to learn and have a thirst for knowledge. However, if the environment is lacking in stimulating activities, the child will lose interest and focus.

How to use praise and constructive feedback to promote further learning

Children love to socialise and like to please those around them. You only have to watch a child at play and very soon they will wish to show their creation to someone else. Praise and encouragement is a powerful tool in the hands of the early years worker and children should be provided with positive encouraging feedback whenever possible. You must remember that praise and feedback is as much part of body language as the words spoken. If a child brings something to you and you look over your shoulder, glance at it and tell them that it is lovely, then turn back to what you were doing originally, then the message you have conveyed to the child is 'Go away, I'm busy'. The good early years worker will ensure that they face the child, maintain eye-contact and give them undivided attention, then provide the positive words and facial expression. It will make a great deal of difference and you will see it in the child's face.

Good practice checklist

When you are providing constructive feedback and praise to children, make sure that you:
- face the child
- give time
- maintain eye-contact
- show open body language
- smile
- be enthusiastic
- show that you are interested
- use positive language.

Remember, if you do not give the child your undivided attention, you are dismissing their efforts.

Case study: Farmyard fun

Jasmin and Peter are 4 years of age and have been working together for most of the morning in the early years setting. They are now engaged in play with the farmyard and have placed the toy animals in various places. They have the cattle in one field and most of the sheep in another, although one is by the pond with the ducks. One of the other children is passing by and begins to laugh at them and says how silly they are not to know that the sheep is not a duck. Jasmin starts to look upset as they have spent a lot of time sorting out the farmyard. Mark, the early years worker, is also nearby and overhears this.

1 **How might Mark relate to the children playing with the farmyard?**

2 **What might he say to the child who laughed at them?**

3 **How might he sensitively intervene?**

4 **How might he extend the play situation?**

Assessment activity 17.3

You have been asked by your supervisor to plan and implement some activities with children that will help develop number skills.

1 Plan one activity for children 3–5 years of age, and one activity for children 5–8 years of age. **P5**

2 State the aims and learning outcomes for the activities.

3 Implement and evaluate one of your chosen activities. **M3 D2**

17.4 How to develop a range of activities that can be used to support the development of children's understanding and use of shape, space and measures

Activities

To ensure children learn about shape, space, pattern and measure

Children require opportunity to explore and experiment with shapes, patterns, measures and space. It is the responsibility of the adult to ensure that resources are available so that children can play in a relaxed, safe and secure environment. In the table below you will find some of the resources that might be made available but you may be able to add to this, as it is not exhaustive in any way.

▼ Resources for learning about shape, space, pattern and measure

Resource	Mathematical relationship
Sand	Sand play provides opportunity for a wide range of mathematical activities depending on the other materials introduced to the play situation. Wet sand will allow children to make shapes and patterns by pressing objects into the sand or by pressing it into various shaped objects and tipping them out. Numbers and patterns can be drawn into the wet sand and it can be used almost as a marking board. Dry sand has totally different properties and will therefore allow children to work in a different way. Its properties mean that fine sand will flow like water and may be used in a similar way.
Water	Water play is therapeutic but additionally allows the child to develop skills and concepts in relation to mathematics. Different sizes of measuring containers are useful and it is also often helpful to colour the water so that measurements are easier to see. Any colouring agent used must be safe, so remember to check allergies and reactions to food colourings. Children will begin to use language related to capacity and measure, for example full, empty, and will move on to fractions in estimation, for example half full, etc.

Resource	Mathematical relationship
Cooking	This is an ideal activity to develop mathematical thinking and skills. Depending on the detail of the session, the children may well use: • counting – number of cake cases required; ingredients, number of spoonfuls, number of eggs • weighing – ingredients • measuring – spoons, cups • shape – cutters for scones, biscuits – cutting cakes, cutting sweets into squares or cutting sandwiches into varying shapes • volume – size of bowls to hold ingredients • pattern – decorating cakes • space – positioning biscuits on tray with space to expand as they cook.
Shaped objects	When children use objects of different shapes, it is important that you use the correct names and that any shapes drawn on card are accurately represented. Children will need access to the different shapes in both 2D and 3D and should have opportunities to find out their properties and how they fit together in reality. There are a number of games that children might play to help them recognise shapes and these are easily made in the early years settings.
Spatial awareness	Children best develop this concept by playing and carrying out activities outdoors. However, there are opportunities indoors through music, dance and drama. Outdoors, children will be free to run and jump, climb and skip. They are often unsure of their own relationship to the space available and it is common to hear children telling others to move back (even when they are obviously well out of the way) when they are going to jump or skip. As children become more aware of their self-image, they begin to develop a greater understanding of spatial awareness.

Extension activity

Make a game for a small group of children to help them develop an understanding of shapes.

For example, make four cards exactly the same with a picture made of different shapes (the same on each one) and then have different coloured pieces to match the different shapes within the picture. The game might be used on a very basic level, purely matching the shapes.

It might then be extended with the use of a colour die so that when the child rolls 'blue' they can place one of the blue shapes. It can then be further extended to a number die so that if 4 is rolled then they can have the coloured piece with the number 4 on the reverse. The basic shape might be a robot or a train.

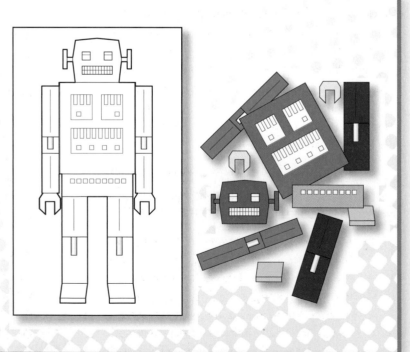

Recognising and naming 2D and 3D shapes in the environment

Children quickly become familiar with the shape and names of 2D shapes and this can be encouraged using songs such as:

'Draw a circle in the air, in the air.
Draw a circle in the air in the air.
Draw a circle in the air and leave it hanging there.
Draw a circle in the air in the air.'

However, they need opportunity to develop an understanding about 3D shapes and also need to know their names. It is good practice to try to develop links between the shapes as taught and their use and appearance in the environment, for example cones, pyramids, balls, bricks, etc. Helping children set up a display table with differently shaped objects, drawings, pictures and photographs will help reinforce learning.

Using the language of position and movement

Using appropriate language for position and movement should be part of the everyday language used in the early years setting and should incorporate both indoor and outdoor activities. Maths trails encourage the use of positional vocabulary, for example 'behind', 'over', 'under', 'beside', 'on top of', etc. As children become involved with dance, movement and drama, the language will have more meaning and can be reinforced by developing games involving instructions using position and direction. 'Simon says' is an activity that might be adapted in different ways to include direction, position and movement.

Measuring length and area, weight, volume and capacity

Length can be measured using a variety of bases, for example hand spans, fixed length blocks, spoonfuls, cups, foot length and stride length. It is important to make activities interesting, purposeful and practical. Children need to know the reason for measures and that they can be applied to a number of different situations, for example plant growth, floor space, and quantities of liquid and solid materials. As children mature they will be able to solve problems posed by using the skills gained.

Mathematical language is essential to the further development of skills. Initially, terms such as 'heavier than', 'lighter than', may be the only language associated with weighing materials and people, but you need to use the language effectively and introduce new vocabulary at appropriate times.

Resources will include balances, kitchen scales and bathroom scales, and children should have opportunity to estimate weight and consider weight in relation to other items. Sand, water play and other activities help develop the concepts of volume and capacity. Early years workers involved with these activities can assist by asking appropriate questions or posing problems that the child can solve. Working out how many times a child needs to pour water from one smaller container to fill the larger one, or how many cups of juice can be poured from the jug are everyday activities that the child will feel comfortable with.

Time

Time is often a difficult concept for children to grasp, but as they are involved in routines during the day they will realise that the day has a structure to it. Adults and early years workers should reinforce this understanding whenever possible, for example 'We will do that after lunch, this afternoon.'

You can develop games and activities that will help with understanding daily structure, for example sequence cards:

- card 1 – picture of child getting out of bed on a morning, sun shining
- card 2 – child in early years setting, playing with toys
- card 3 – child being collected from setting, waving goodbye
- card 4 – child going to bed, moon showing through window.

The cards will then be mixed up and the child encouraged to place them in the correct order. More cards can be added in order to extend the game or different themes can be used.

Other activities encourage the awareness of time, for example cooking activities and timing how long something takes to bake, growing plants and observing them each day. Some of the most difficult concepts are 'yesterday', 'today' and 'tomorrow', and it is useful to reinforce this language whenever possible and in appropriate contexts. Children will then move on to telling the time on a clock face and they will need to be aware of different ways of telling the time and different types of clocks.

Extension activity

Devise an activity for children in the 4–5 age range which might help them develop the concept of time. It may be a sequence game or something else that will help with an understanding of the structure of the day or some part of it.

Appropriate language

Adults and early years workers must always be aware of using the correct language so that children do not become confused in any way. When speaking about shape, it is common for the words 'rectangle' and 'oblong' to be interchangeable, whereas in reality a rectangle is a four-sided figure with four right angles; therefore a square is a particular type of rectangle. An oblong is a rectangle where each opposite pair of sides is the same length. We should be using the words 'square' and 'oblong' to differentiate between the two shapes.

Materials, settings and environment

Enabling children to choose and use different media for sorting

Children should be provided with different types of media when carrying out sorting activities and they

should be encouraged to sort using different criteria. Some examples of sorting are:

- shapes of leaves
- natural and man-made items
- texture
- colours of collage materials
- category, e.g. flying
- shapes of objects
- colours of beads
- sizes of dolls, etc.

Experimenting with shape, space and pattern

The setting should be conducive for children to explore and experiment in a safe and secure environment. The role of the adult is to ensure that the resources and activities are appropriate and that there is a child-centred approach to learning. Recognising patterns in nature enables children to develop a sense of wonder and involvement in a much wider range of resources. Children can experiment with various shapes and when considering the patterns in different types of flooring it is possible to introduce tessellation and then the extension could be to design flooring patterns using different shapes. Children are quite often fascinated with camouflage and this could be introduced in the use of pattern and shape in nature, for example how shape can be broken up by pattern, such as the giraffe and zebra.

Children's opportunity to use and apply mathematics in practical tasks

A further aspect of the role of the adult is to make mathematics as practical as possible and to relate it to everyday activities, so that children can see a purpose, application and meaning for their activities. Cooking is one of the most obvious areas where there is a practical relationship to mathematical concepts and the day-to-day activities in a kitchen. Often a child might have difficulty with a purely mechanical activity, for example 5 + 3, but if this is translated into everyday objects, such as pieces of fruit, and it is explained that the whole problem relates to someone having enough pieces of fruit for the children, then the problem can be worked out on a practical level.

Encouraging children to explain their thinking to support the development of their reasoning

It is important to encourage children to talk through and explain their thought processes in a logical and structured way. It is part of the role of the adult to listen carefully as children do this, as it may be possible to identify a simple error in calculation rather than in the process of dealing with the problem. If the child has not talked through and enunciated the process and only given the answer, which is incorrect, they may well believe that the process by which they arrived at that answer is also incorrect. This will, in turn, have a detrimental effect on the child's self-confidence. Conversely, if the child has talked through the process in a logical way, it is often possible to identify where the error has occurred and the child will be praised and encouraged in the process and corrected accordingly.

How to maintain interest, motivation and focus

Maintaining interest and motivation has much to do with the practical level of activities and their level of fun. If a child enjoys carrying out activities, then they will wish to be further involved. There must be capacity to develop skills to a more detailed level and if you consider interests that you have, and how you gain enjoyment from them, you will understand why it is vital to provide an interesting, stimulating environment for children so that the learning process will be self-perpetuating and enjoyable.

How to use praise and constructive feedback to promote further learning

In general, children love mathematics especially when they are young. They choose to play and become involved in activities that contain a great deal of mathematical thinking and will choose rhymes and songs with numbers. Adults and early years workers must use praise to reinforce these ideals and positive reinforcement is powerful. Children like to please and we have a responsibility to make maths fun and to use encouragement and praise as appropriate. In praising and encouraging a child, you are telling them that

whatever they are doing is pleasing, good and gives pleasure to others and they will wish to repeat it. Some settings use additional methods of providing positive reinforcement such as using stickers or star charts. These methods should ensure that reward is achievable by every child in the setting and that they do not just rely on academic achievement.

Theory into practice

Listen to adults speaking to children.
- How often do they praise the child?
- Is the body language positive?
- How often do they smile at the child?
- Do they criticise?
- Comment on other relevant points.

Assessment activity 17.4

You have been asked by your supervisor to plan and implement some activities with children that will help develop skills and understanding of shape space and measure.

1 Plan one activity for children 3–5 years of age, and one activity for children 5–8 years of age. **P6**

2 State the aims and learning outcomes for the activities.

3 Implement and evaluate one of your chosen activities. **M4** **D2**

End of unit assessment

1 You are working in the early years sector and have been asked to produce a display, on 'The development of mathematical skills in the early years', which will be useful for trainee early years workers and parents of the children in the setting.

a) In your display you should provide details of two different theories of mathematical development. **P1**

b) Look critically at the differences between them, giving examples from your experiences to support the theories or challenge them. **M1**

c) You will need to add a chart (or a number of different charts) in which you describe mathematical development in children under 8 years of age. In addition, you should describe the role of the adult in the development of numeracy skills in young children. **P2 P3**

d) Describe how one piece of current legislation has an influence and impact on children's numeracy development. **P4**

e) Explain how it is implemented in the early years setting and evaluate its effectiveness. You should provide some examples, if you can, to give support to your work. **M2**

f) As a follow-up activity, write a handout to give to trainee early years workers evaluating the effectiveness of national initiatives in promoting children's numeracy skills. **D1**

2 As an early years worker you will be involved in planning, preparing, implementing and evaluating a variety of activities for young children.

a) Plan:
- two activities to promote children's number skills **P5**
- two activities to promote children's understanding of shape, space and measure. **P6**

b) Implement:
- one of the number skills activities **M3**
- one of the shape, space and measures activities. **M4**

When planning and carrying out these activities, consider the age and number of children, the resources required, the aim of the activity, the identified outcomes for the child, and the description of the activity.

c) Once the children have carried out the activities, write an evaluation for each one. **D2** You should include what went well and not so well, what you would change, whether the children achieved the desired outcomes, and if not, why not?

References and further reading

Blinko, J. (2000) *Shape, Space and Measure*, A&C Black

Clemson, D. and Clemson, W. (1994) *Mathematics in the Early Years*, Routledge

Edgar, V. (2001) *Christmas Activities for the Early Years*, Brilliant

Headington, R. (1997) *Supporting Numeracy*, Fulton

Macleod-Brudenell, I. (2004) *Advanced Early Years Care and Education*, Heinemann

Miller, L., Cable, C. and Devereux, J. (2005) *Developing Early Years Practice*, Fulton

Mortimer, H. (2003) *100 Number Games for Ages 0–3*, Scholastic

Wright, J. (2006) *Talking Maths*, Everything Early Years

Useful websites

Department for Education and Skills – www.dfes.gov.uk

DfES Standards Unit – www.dfesstandards.gov.uk

Grading criteria	Assessment activity	Page number
To achieve a pass grade the evidence must show that the learner is able to:		
P1 describe two different theories of how understanding of mathematical concepts develops in children	End of unit assessment	478
P2 describe the stages in the development of children's mathematical understanding	17.1 End of unit assessment	461 478
P3 describe the role of the adult in developing children's numeracy skills	17.2 End of unit assessment	467 478
P4 describe the influence of one piece of legislation/curriculum guidance on supporting the development of children's numeracy skills	17.2 End of unit assessment	467 478
P5 develop two activities to promote children's number skills	17.3 End of unit assessment	473 478
P6 develop two activities to promote children's understanding of shape, space and measure	17.4 End of unit assessment	477 478
To achieve a merit grade the evidence must show that, in addition to the pass criteria, the learner is able to:		
M1 compare and contrast the two theories using practical examples	End of unit assessment	478
M2 explain how the identified legislation/curriculum guidance is used in an early years setting to promote children's numeracy skills	End of unit assessment	478
M3 implement one of the activities to promote children's number skills	17.3 End of unit assessment	473 478
M4 implement one of the activities to support understanding of space, shape and measure	17.4 End of unit assessment	477 478
To achieve a distinction grade the evidence must show that, in addition to the pass and merit criteria, the learner is able to:		
D1 evaluate the effectiveness of national initiatives in promoting children's numeracy skills	End of unit assessment	478
D2 evaluate the effectiveness of the two implemented activities	17.3 17.4 End of unit assessment	473 477 478

Supporting children's literacy skills

Introduction

Using language effectively is one of the most important skills that anyone will learn in their life. The ability to communicate with other people is one of the basics of a society working together towards a common goal. Children need the opportunity to develop these skills in a supportive and secure environment and all individuals who come into contact with young children will have some influence on this.

In this unit you will have the opportunity to consider some of the theories of language development, which will also link with the stages of the development of literacy skills. The role of the adult is particularly important in this area as you need to be aware of the scope of their responsibility in planning, observing and assessing the language and literacy skills of children in their care.

As in all areas of childcare, it is important to be aware of the individual needs of the child and you will need to consider specific or special issues that may affect the child's ability to learn. In order to provide effectively for the child in the home or early years setting, you should be aware of current legislation and guidelines and how this has an impact on the early years curriculum. You will need to build up a range of activities designed to promote the development of, initially, speaking and listening skills and, later, the skills used in reading, writing and comprehension. Involvement across the age range will provide you with the knowledge and skills required to support all children with literacy and language development.

There will inevitably be some overlap with Unit 17, Supporting Numeracy Skills and it is recommended that these two units are studied together.

What you need to learn

- The development of literacy skills
- Current national initiatives and curriculum guidance relating to the development of children's literacy skills
- How to implement a range of speaking and listening activities that can be used to support the development of children's skills
- How to implement a range of reading and writing that can be used to support the development of children's skills

Thinking points

Children see the written word all around them, in books, magazines, notice-boards and on the television screen. Gradually their own literacy skills will emerge and the early years worker will have opportunity to plan to promote the development of those skills.

Within the early years care and education setting there are many opportunities for children to enlarge their vocabulary and to link the written to the spoken word.

How do you think literacy and language development could be incorporated into the following activities?

- Drama
- Stories and rhymes
- Music
- Sand play
- Water play
- Cooking activities
- Role play, for example, a shop, clinic, opticians, café
- Creative activities.

Why do you think it is important to focus on the development of these skills?

Literacy skills involve:

- speaking
- listening
- reading
- writing
- fine motor skills.

Each child moves through the stages of developing literacy skills at their own pace but this can be helped with support and input by the adults that the child comes into contact with on a daily basis.

Key term

Literacy skills are the skills required in order to be able to read and write effectively.

Theories of language development

Over the years, various people have put forward theories as to how children might develop language and there have been diverse views on this topic. We will look at five such theorists in more detail and consider their main points in the acquisition of language in young children.

Each of the theorists mentioned in the table below have very positive and distinct views as to how language develops. You will be able to compare their views and form your own opinion about the process.

▼ Theories on the development of language

Theorist	Main points of theory
Noam Chomsky	Noam Chomsky believed that a child is born with an innate capacity to understand and develop language. He acknowledged that vocabulary has to be learned and that certain parts of grammar are influenced by interaction. He felt that each person is innately able to acquire language – unlike other animals – through a Language Acquisition Device (LAD), which is activated by language input. This equips the individual with the ability to acquire language and, in a similar way that a child learns to walk, the LAD provides the wherewithal to acquire language. He later acknowledged that the environment has some influence on building language skills.
Burrhus Frederic Skinner	Skinner believed that learning language was a matter of conditioning and reinforcement. Children play with sounds in the 'babbling' stage and when an adult feels that a sound is almost recognisable as a word, for example 'dadadada', they will reinforce it with praise and smiles and modify the word to 'dada'. This will in turn encourage the child to repeat it and it will gradually become 'daddy'. As children become older, they try to copy adults and when you listen to children engaged in role play they might use phrases that they would not normally use. Skinner's views on positive and negative reinforcement as responsible for shaping children's language is accepted by many as the main way that language is learned.
Jean Piaget	Piaget felt that language development was part of general cognitive development (see Unit 17, page 450). As children move into symbolic play, he envisaged that language would develop alongside this. Language development and cognitive development are intertwined and symbolic representation is a crucial stage in a child's ability to develop literacy skills.
Lev Vygotsky	Vygotsky felt that thinking skills and language skills were totally separate, initially, and it was only as a child grew and matured that these became linked together. After that children can use language to express their thoughts and feelings. This inter-relationship between thought and language is essential for the understanding of cognitive development. The level of development for an individual child became known as 'the zone of actual development' but Vygotsky felt that children were capable of higher levels with support and assistance from adults. The difference between these two levels was known as the 'zone of proximal development' and this has huge implications for the adult who would help extend the child's vocabulary and reinforce sentence structure and grammar.
Jerome Bruner	Bruner leans towards social interaction as a major influence in language development but does not claim that it is totally responsible. He claimed that this is a support mechanism, which builds on the child's innate ability to acquire language. However, it is in the social context that the child experiences language on a regular and familiar basis and this enables children to understand the 'codes' of language and grammar. He was a constructivist who felt that children move through specific stages in their intellectual development (see Unit 17, page 450).

Theory into practice

Vygotsky's theory in practice

John is almost 4 years old and attends his local nursery school. He has been trying to copy his name when the teacher writes it on his work. His ability to form the letters is improving on a daily basis, but he has a tendency to write his name with the letters following each other but to the left, i.e. he starts with J but then puts the o to the left of it so that his name appears as nhoJ. (This is his stage of actual development.)

The zone of proximal development will be what can be achieved with adult support. His teacher does not want to dishearten his attempts and so she begins to write his name in the top left-hand corner of the paper instead of the right-hand side as she had been doing. When he tries to copy his name it is now difficult for him to write to the left as there is no paper and with her support and direction he eventually begins to copy his name with the letters in the correct order and reading from left to right. John will eventually write his name unaided and this will become the new stage of actual development.

Sequences and stages

Children develop their literacy skills from very early on in their life with speaking and listening skills being developed before those used in reading and writing. The development of language skills begins very much immediately after birth with the first sounds that a child makes being related to crying which also enables that child to fully use its lungs.

The development of listening and speaking skills

The table below shows the development of listening and speaking in the young child.

▼ Development of listening and speaking skills

Approximate age	Listening	Speaking
Birth–3 months	Has a startle reflex to sudden sounds Will quieten down when talked to Can recognise some voices	Many theorists now believe that the recognition of speech patterns begins prior to birth as the child would be able to hear its mother's voice and respond to it After the birth the child cries and can make different sounds for different needs, for example hunger Makes cooing sounds
4–6 months	Responds to direction of sound Responds to tone, for example friendly; angry Enjoys toys that make sounds Enjoys music	Babbling Can practise sounds using tongue and lips to change tone Vowels are used initially as with cooing Later consonants are introduced
7 months–1 year	Enjoys rhymes such as 'Round and round the garden' and can anticipate the ending Enjoys 'hiding' games, for example peek-a-boo Turns head in direction of sound Has an understanding of some words Can respond to directions, for example 'come here'	Babbling continues and runs of sounds are used, for example 'mamama'. 'babbaba' Uses sounds to gain attention Starts to copy some speech sounds Motherese (or parentese) is the speech patterns used by adults when talking to the very young. The pronunciation is very clear and the speech is slower and this helps the child. This distinct method of speech helps the child recognise and understand words as this precedes the vocalisation of the sounds Has a few words but usually with repetitive syllables, for example 'mama', 'dada', 'bye-bye'

Approximate age	Listening	Speaking
1–2 years	Can follow simple instructions Listens to rhymes Enjoys short stories	Initially one word is used perhaps with a pointing gesture, for example 'toy'. This is known as holophrase, i.e. one word conveying meaning Building up a vocabulary Can later string two words together, for example 'doggy gone' Understands more words Can become frustrated due to inability to vocalise effectively
2–3 years	Follows more complicated directions, for example 'get the ball and bring it over here'	Continues to build vocabulary Uses two- and three-word sentences Speech can be understood especially by those closely linked to the child Adult reinforcement confirms correct pronunciation
3–4 years	Understands simple questions Responds to sound even when source is out of sight Enjoys stories and action rhymes	Begins to use connecting words such as 'is', 'in' Uses longer sentences Sentences become more grammatically correct
4–5 years	Listens to adult conversations and has a good understanding of the content Enjoys more complex stories and can answer questions about them	Uses more complex sentences Tells stories in a logical sequence Grammar is improving
5–6 years	Can follow instructions of three parts Can re-tell stories or events	Language is complex Repeats events accurately Vocabulary increasing
6–7 years	Can understand complex stories Can relay messages with few errors	Understands opposites Carries out meaningful conversations with peers and adults
7–8 years	Can follow complicated directions Listening skills are finely tuned	Converses at adult level Follows complex instructions Uses complex sentences

As children get older, they enjoy more complex stories ▶

BTEC National | Children's Care, Learning and Development

Key terms

Motherese is the type of language used by adults when speaking to babies. It is very precise and often repetitive. The pronunciation is clear and the adult will speak more slowly than usual.

A **holophrase** is when a child uses a single word to convey information, for example when the child points to a cup and says 'drink'.

Theory into practice

Children need to listen carefully in order to repeat the words they hear. The adult can help children build up their listening skills by using games that encourage active listening, such as sound lotto, using musical instruments, games, for example one child tiptoes up behind another and the first child listens carefully for them, playing games where words rhyme.

- Visit an early years setting and note the activities which encourage the use of listening skills.

language skills and vocabulary will probably find reading an easy progression of literacy skills.

Story telling helps the development of language in a number of ways and the time spent with children in a homely environment sharing a book is invaluable. It conveys the message that stories and books are enjoyable, that the written word conveys important messages and eventually that they can impart information in a similar way by writing.

The illustrations in children's books are extremely important as they reinforce the text and provide important cues to enable understanding.

Most children love to hear stories. There is a gradual process by which children see that there is a definite relationship between the telling of a story and the written word. It is helpful to record whether or not a child:

- likes to hear stories
- enjoys looking at books
- realises that there is a connection between the written word and the story.

Eventually the child will start to behave like a reader and will:

- know how to use a book, that there is a front and back, and can turn pages effectively

Developing reading skills

Learning to read and write is not something that happens suddenly when a child starts to attend school. The foundations of the skills start to be laid as soon as the child is shown its first book.

Children need to become familiar with written words and then they will eventually reach an understanding that these symbols have meanings. They will need to be able to master activities which include visual discrimination and communication skills. A child with a wide range of

I wonder what this is about?

- know that there is a sequence to a story
- know that the illustrations contain relevant information
- understand that there is a relationship between the letters and sounds
- enjoy and use a range of picture and story books
- record own experiences and ideas through drawing, painting and writing.

Extension activity

Arrange to visit your local library when there is a story-telling session for young children.

- Note how the story teller starts the session and how she or he relates to the children.
- Watch the children as the story progresses and listen to the changes in voice and tone as the tale unfolds.
- Evaluate the session and consider ways it might have been improved.

Developing fine motor skills

Before children can develop the specific and precise skills used for writing, they must develop their general fine motor skills and strengthen the small muscles in the hand. This can be helped by activities such as modelling with clay or play dough, spending time at sand and water play or by developing their manipulative skills in the art area or with small construction toys and drawing activities.

Developing writing skills

Children should have the opportunity to become familiar with the written word in many different ways and, when they indulge in role-play activities, there should be opportunity for the child to write and make marks and to see written words. For example, in a hospital setting there would be magazines and the nurse, receptionist and doctors would be making notes or taking messages via the telephone.

Children develop the ability to write by using mark-making implements and following or copying patterns. The development of drawing skills and the development of writing skills are closely linked. Once the child has mastered the use of crayons or pencils, they may well try to copy letters, especially their own name, when this has been written on the paper. Initially the letters will be indistinct and may just form a similar pattern, but they will gradually take on more shape and will become more recognisable as the letters of the child's name.

When a child realises that there is a link between information and marks on paper, then they will also wish to 'write'. Again there are certain stages to be noted. The child will:

- 'write' shopping lists, notes, messages from telephone calls, etc.
- make letter-like marks

▲ Developing writing skills

- form some letters
- make up stories which adults write down or scribe
- write own stories.

It is worth noting any developments and information about the child's literacy development from home.

The table below gives some indication of approximate ages and stages of the development of writing skills. The development of drawing skills and writing skills are very closely linked.

▼ The development of writing skills

Age	Stage of development
1–2 years	Can hold crayon with whole hand and scribbles Enjoys books with pictures
2 years	Can hold pencil near the point and is developing a preferred hand Draws using scribbles and dots Turns the pages of books
2½ years	Preferred hand is more dominant Will attempt to copy some shapes, for example circle, line, V and T
3 years	Can draw a recognisable shape of a person with facial features, arms and legs
4 years	Is developing good control of pencil Can draw detailed person, house, etc. May attempt to copy name Scribble can resemble writing, for example in lines Starts to make shapes which resemble letters
5 years	Good control of writing/drawing implements Copies letters Can write own name spontaneously
6 years	Simple writing skills Some invented spelling, for example 'wen' – when; 'pla' – play
7 years	Writes in short sentences, often disjointed Sentences do not always relate to each other
8 years	Writing with meaning Text relates to topic Letter formation is clear and precise with good pencil/pen control

Assessing literacy skills and development

You will need to be able to assess children in order to monitor their progress and to find out if there are any areas of concern. Most assessments in the early years are carried out through interaction with the children and through regular observations. Assessments should not be based solely on one observation as children react differently on different days and there may be other circumstances to take into consideration. These observations will gradually build up to give an overall picture of the child in each area of development. Observations will include a range linked to language use and speech development, early writing and reading skills, and in the very young child this will include interests in books and the written word, the use of writing and drawing implements alongside pictures and examples of emergent writing.

Children learn at a faster rate in their early years than they do at any other time. If you have contact with young children, you will realise that they vary greatly in the skills that they possess. Some children may be able to communicate with only a few words, whereas others will be able to hold fairly complex conversations. There will also be great differences in all other areas of the child's development.

Good practice checklist

All assessments and records must be factual and based on hard evidence. When you are recording your findings from observations or interactions, check that:

- you have recorded the child's age
- you have dated your records
- they are based on fact
- there is evidence to substantiate your findings
- you report any concerns
- you maintain confidentiality.

Types of records used

Within an early years setting, it is beneficial to keep records of the child's progression in their literacy development record.

Record-keeping takes many forms, but it is important that, as the child moves from one area to another or one setting up to another, a record of their abilities goes with them. If a child goes through a period of regression, it is important to try to find the root cause.

Record-keeping should begin with the full co-operation of the parents as they have a great deal of knowledge, which can help build up the complete picture of the child. It is important to consider the child's background as there are many factors which need to be taken into account when planning learning experiences. Religious and cultural differences will need to be acknowledged and provided for. Record-keeping is vital for the informed structured planning that is expected from a sensitive early years worker. If we do not know the scope of children's experiences, skills and knowledge, how can we effectively plan for the next stage in their development?

There are a number of different methods of keeping records. Often a simple tick list is used, but as each new skill is ticked it should also be dated so that timescales can be recorded alongside skills achieved. Other assessments may take the form of observation records, charts and diagrams. Many settings devise their own.

In language development, it is important that a child uses language with confidence. When assessing language development, you need to be aware that movement from one stage to another may be very gradual.

It is useful to note when a child:

- speaks in one word answers
- uses phrases
- uses complete sentences
- converses freely with confidence
- discusses points of view
- recalls past experiences
- speculates about the future
- describes places
- describes feelings.

Each of the above can be broken down into more detailed components and it is important that the recording of stages suits the purpose for which it is intended.

It is also essential to recognise that records should be accurate and factual as they may be used for more formal assessment purposes, for example the statementing process. This is the process whereby children with special or specific needs are formally assessed – a statement records their needs and states how those needs will be supported.

Name of child:			Date of birth:		
Activity	Achieved	Date	Activity	Achieved	Date
Enjoys stories			Can hold a crayon		
Can turn pages correctly			Makes marks with crayon		
Talks about pictures			Can copy shape		

▲ Examples of other types of record keeping

The role of the adult

Observation and assessment

One of the main methods of assessing the development in young children is to observe them closely. This will enable you to assess the stage of development for that child and to plan effectively for future activities, which will aid consolidation and progression. It is mainly through observation, assessment and record-keeping that you can evaluate the setting's provision and ensure that you are meeting the individual needs of the children. It is also necessary to check that the setting provides quality experiences, which extend learning.

As you have more contact with young children, you will become more aware of the importance of observation. This is covered in more detail in Unit 3, Promoting Children's Development.

Observing children and accurately recording your findings is essential. The conclusions you draw will be extremely valuable in your assessment of any individual child. Observing children effectively takes practice, but it is important to remember that a relaxed atmosphere will produce a more realistic observation than one where the children feel under scrutiny and may change their behaviour accordingly.

Extension activity

- Observe a child in an early years setting for 10 minutes.
- Make a list of the activities the child was engaged in that helped develop language and literacy skills.

Reinforcement, praise and encouragement

B.F. Skinner was probably the best-known exponent for positive reinforcement and you need to recognise that praise and encouragement are very powerful, as children like to please others. In praising and encouraging a child, you are telling them that whatever they are doing is pleasing, good and gives pleasure to others, and they will wish to repeat it. Verbal praise and encouragement is a powerful tool for you and it is essential when children are trying to master language and literacy skills. Verbal correction of poor grammar should be carried out in a sensitive manner and it is usually enough to give the correct version in your feedback, for example:

Child: I have some pet mouses at home.

You: Well that's wonderful, how many mice do you have?

Similarly, positive feedback with attempts at reading, writing and letter formation will promote learning and foster good relationships. Some settings will use additional methods of providing positive reinforcement, such as using stickers or star charts. However, always remember that these rewards should be attainable by every member of the class or group, as it would be demotivating if a child did not receive a reward at all.

Theory into practice

Think about times when you have been praised for something well done.
- How did you feel?
- Did it encourage you to try to do other things well?
- Did you feel that you had a standard to be maintained?

Working with parents

Parents are the child's first teachers and have much valuable information about the development of the individual child. It is important for you to build up a positive relationship with the child's parents so that each will be able to reinforce the work of the other.

Parents have a right to know about the structure of the setting and the curriculum planning and should be involved at all stages. Progress should be reported to them on a daily and regular basis and the child should be praised and encouraged when their parents are present so that they can develop their self-confidence and self-esteem.

Theory into practice

Arrange to visit an early years setting and observe how the members of staff relate to the parents/carers when they come to collect the children. Take note of:

- body language
- facial expressions
- tone of voice.

Are children's achievements reported to their parents? Are the children praised and encouraged?

يولد جميع الناس أحراراً متساوين في الكرامة والحقوق. وقد وهبوا عقلاً وضميراً وعليهم ان يعامل بعضهم بعضاً بروح الإخاء.

简体中文字
人人生而自由，在尊严和权利上一律平等。他们赋有理性和良心，并应以兄弟关系的精神互相对待。

כׇּל בְּנֵי הָאָדָם נוֹלְדוּ בְּנֵי חוֹרִין וְשָׁוִים בְּעֶרְכָּם וּבִזְכֻיּוֹתֵיהֶם. כֻּלָּם חוֹנְנוּ בַּתְּבוּנָה וּבַמַּצְפּוּן, לְפִיכָךְ חוֹבָה עֲלֵיהֶם לִנְהֹוג אִישׁ בְּרֵעֵהוּ בְּרוּחַ שֶׁל אַחֲוָה.

▲ **Examples of different writing systems**

Planning activities

When planning activities for children, it is important to build upon their previous experience. Providing activities that are too difficult or too remote will undermine the child's confidence and affect self-esteem. Child-centred activities, where the child plays an integral part and has had involvement in choosing and implementing the activity, will be more valuable and beneficial to the development of the child. If a child chooses a book, they will pay more attention and gain more from the activity than if the book is chosen by someone else. The number of children involved will determine the level of individual attention that any child has. A one-to-one session reading a story will have a different outcome from a session with 15 children.

You need to be aware of the range of needs to be addressed and developed by the activities, and plan accordingly. This will, additionally, include the size of the group taking part at any given time and the resources required.

Awareness of diversity and cultural needs

You should be aware of the background of the children in your care and cater for cultural and religious specifics. In some cultures, reading and writing does not follow the established pattern of reading in the UK. Remember, that letters are not always used and in some countries it is usual to use characters to convey messages rather than letters building up into words, for example Arabic, Chinese/Mandarin characters will read vertically, and in some cultures the writing reads from right to left.

Types of planning

Early years workers must be able to plan effectively for the needs of all children in their care, as shown in the following table.

Establishing an effective, confident and caring relationship with children

Helping children develop literacy skills is a very personal course of action and developing a good relationship with children is vital in this process. It is through the building up of these relationships that the child's self-confidence and self-esteem will increase and so will their willingness to engage in conversation and interact with others. Corrections in grammar and other linguistic errors should be corrected in a sensitive way so that the child's skills are increased and the individual does not feel belittled in any way.

▼ Planning activities

Planning	Detail
Individual	It is important that you know about the individual needs of each child, including their actual stage of development. A child may be displaying signs of delayed development against the norms and it is essential that their needs be planned for, rather than a whole-class or group approach. For example, a child may be experiencing difficulty in gripping writing implements and may need activities which will strengthen the small muscles in the hand.
Long-term	Long-term planning may be over a number of months and future targets set for the child. Details of the planning will include topics and strategies for each area of learning. The long-term planning might be in broad strokes with the detail more defined in the medium- to short-term planning, for example, on a topic basis within which there will be activities to develop reading and writing skills which will be related to the chosen theme.
Medium-term	Medium-term planning might be on a weekly or monthly basis but will include detailed goals within the long-term planning. It is important that resources are available for all the activities planned and that they are set in a logical and structured way and cover all areas of learning. Similar to long-term planning in relation to literacy activities but they will be more detailed in content.
Short-term	Short-term planning may be on a daily basis and will have smaller goals to be achieved. You will have planned the small details and have decided on the resources, staffing and materials required. Achievements and progress will be recorded so that future planning can be based on realistic targets. Planning on a daily or weekly basis will have more detail and be less prone to changes, for example planning stories for the day and related reading and writing activities.

Theory into practice

A child holds out a toy that they have and says, 'I've bringed you this.' Your response could be, 'Well that's a silly thing to say, it's brought not bringed – I don't know – we'll have to get this right won't we?'

- Is this an appropriate response? Give reasons for your answer.
- What response might you give? Give reasons for your answer.

When and how to intervene

Knowing when to intervene in a children's activity takes sensitivity and experience. The child should be able to develop skills independently but occasionally adult assistance might be beneficial.

It is important not to take over the task but to ask if the child requires any assistance. You will need to observe the child and make a judgement as to whether your intervention is going to help the situation or hinder it.

Theory into practice

Intervention and providing assistance may help the child move on to the next stage of development. A child may be having difficulty fitting the pieces into a jigsaw puzzle. You may spend time with the child and suggest where the piece might go. It is important that you do not take over.

Case study: Will it fit together?

Jason is 3 years old and is engaged in an activity that is quite complicated for him. In the process of carrying out the activity, he wants to link three pieces of Lego together in a particular way. The early years worker sees that he is struggling with the physical fine motor skills and decides to intervene.

1 **Which of the two phrases do you think the early years worker should use?**
   - 'I'll do that for you.'
   - 'Would you like me to help?'

2 **What might be the negative effects of each phrase?**

3 **What might be the positive effects of each phrase?**

4 **Suggest two other activities that will promote fine motor development.**

5 **How else might you support the child?**

Confidentiality

Confidentiality is one of the most important underlying basics for the early years worker. It is fundamental to the trust and respect that must be developed when building a positive relationship with parents and carers. Once confidentiality is broken it is impossible to fully re-establish the relationship. Not only can a breach of confidentiality destroy carefully established relationships, it can have far-reaching effects, which may even have legal implications for the setting and the staff involved. Confidentiality is covered in more detail in Unit 6, Promoting Children's Rights.

Inclusion

It is vital that all children feel valued and are able to access the curriculum. Children will arrive at a setting with individual needs and abilities and you must cater for all. Activities must be presented in a way that they

Case study: Gossip hurts!

Sarah and Shema are both early years workers at a family centre in Blankington. They had finished work for the day and were waiting at the bus stop to go home. Both of them had been concerned about a child in their care who was displaying unusual and disturbing behaviour and they began discussing the situation as no one else was around. However, they became so involved that they did not notice that other people had joined them and a small queue had formed.

The following day they were both asked to go to the manager's office. One of the other people at the bus stop was a neighbour of the child's family and they had returned home and told the child's parents that personal details about their family were being openly discussed in public.

1 **Why was this poor practice by the two early years workers?**

2 **What might the consequences be for them?**

3 **What might the consequences be for the setting?**

4 **What might be the consequences for the child and family?**

can be adapted to suit the needs of the individual child. It is part of your role to ensure that the needs of all children are met. When considering language and literacy development, it is particularly important that any specific needs are addressed and that the child has the appropriate support, especially if they are visually impaired. There is a range of measures that might be put in place, such as large print books and clear, brightly coloured illustrations. If the child has speech impairments, speech and language therapists may be available to provide specialist provision and assistance within the mainstream setting.

Good practice checklist

- Consider the setting and ensure that all barriers are removed, if at all possible.
- Provide additional resources if they can benefit the child in any way.
- Observe children to ascertain their level of expertise.
- Make informed judgements to plan for their future needs on an individual basis.

Addressing specific needs

Each child must be considered on an individual basis and their needs addressed as and when they occur. Some children will have long-term needs which will require specialist help, whilst others will have temporary needs which might need support on a short-term basis. Occasionally children are ill and need to be away from the early years setting for a while, recovering or recuperating, and as a result they may fall behind. They may require additional help for a while and might quickly catch up. On the other hand, children may have more severe needs that may require support over a much longer period of time and specific equipment and resources may also be required; for example children with fine muscle difficulties may need special pencil grips to enable them to grasp writing implements. It is important that their needs are assessed and appropriate strategies put in place.

Reducing barriers to learning

Children present a variety of needs and resources must be made available to ensure that those needs are met. There are many resources that any setting should have readily available, for example scissors for left-handed children, easy grip handles, pencil grips for children who find holding a conventional pencil difficult, handles on jigsaw pieces. However, there are other resources that may need to be introduced to meet the needs of a specific child, for example standing frames, tables at correct heights for wheelchair users, larger print books for partially-sighted children.

Each child should have enough space for their own comfort. Children who use walking aids or wheelchairs should have enough space to move comfortably in order to maintain their independence. Buildings may need to be altered or adapted to meet the legal requirements for accessibility.

There should be areas of the setting where children can relax in comfort and an area where noise and other distractions are at a minimum level. Children who have some degree of hearing impairment will find background noise very distracting if they are trying to listen to stories or hold a conversation. The whole layout of the setting should be planned to take into consideration the activities that are likely to generate a greater amount of noise and these should not be close to the areas for quieter activities. This will also help the child who finds it difficult to concentrate and activities should be structured to be of shorter duration. Interesting, stimulating activities are needed that will increase motivation levels and this will also assist the child with low self-esteem who will need praise and encouragement throughout the day. A child with low self-esteem will need activities that engender success and so build self-confidence. This is yet another example of the importance of early years workers knowing the stage of development of the children in their care and planning activities accordingly.

▲ Supporting the child on a one-to-one basis

Specific needs

Meeting children's individual learning needs

It is essential that early years workers meet the needs of all children and it must be recognised that certain conditions require additional resources including a higher adult–child ratio. There are a number of reasons why children will need an individual learning programme and some are shown in the diagram below.

It is important that the child receives the help and assistance required, but it is equally important that they do not feel undermined or that their confidence or self-esteem is affected in a negative way. Adults must have the resources to provide the best for children and may require specialist input to meet the needs of children with specific needs.

Key terms

Dysphasia is a condition which is often caused by damage to the brain and results in speech and comprehension impairment.

Dyspraxia is difficulty in thinking out and executing movements or tasks, including those requiring fine motor skills, such as drawing or writing; also known as 'clumsy child syndrome', developmental co-ordination disorder (DCD).

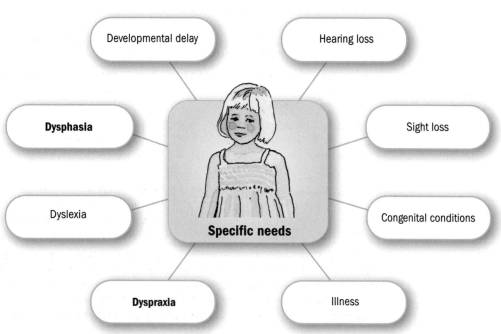

Developmental delay

Hearing loss

Dysphasia

Sight loss

Dyslexia

Congenital conditions

Specific needs

Dyspraxia

Illness

Case study: Assessing learning needs

Joan is an early years worker in a day nursery and she has moved into a new area of the setting where a little boy named Sayed has just started attending. He is a very friendly child but Joan begins to notice that he is not able to do many of the activities that the other children his age are doing. He does not attempt the jigsaws but bangs the pieces on the table, happily making different sounds, and he has difficulty holding crayons and paint brushes.

1 How could Joan find out if Sayed has any developmental delay?

2 If he appears to have delay in some areas, what should Joan then do?

3 Who should she speak with?

4 How else might she gather more information?

▼ Meeting individual learning needs

Condition	Detail
Hearing loss	This might be a permanent or temporary condition and you may be the first to realise that there is a degree of hearing loss. Children might only hear correctly if sitting close to the adult. They may be disruptive because they do not fully understand the situation. This must be diagnosed correctly and parents involved at all times. It may be that the child needs corrective treatment or to use an aid to help hearing. Adults should be aware of the situation and speak clearly when talking to the children. It is good practice to face children when talking to them but adults need to be careful to ensure they do not cover their mouth when speaking.
Sight loss	Sight loss or impairment can be in varying degrees and care should be taken to ensure the child has the best opportunity to see what is happening. Spectacles may be able to correct the situation to a certain degree but there are screens for computers, which can enlarge the print and large print books. Bright, clear illustrations and posters can be used to make the area more homely. Often one-to-one work is required to help develop reading and writing skills.
Illness	If a child has had a severe or lengthy illness then there may be delay in a number of areas of learning and this must be taken into consideration when preparing a programme of study. Many children 'catch up' quite quickly but may need more individual help for a while.
Congenital conditions	There are a vast number of congenital conditions, which might result in learning difficulties and require specific help. Each condition will be individual to the child involved and require a personal or individual learning plan with short-, medium- and long-term goals to be achieved. In many instances this will also involve guidance from other professionals, for example speech therapists, curriculum advisers and health visitors.
Developmental delay	Developmental delay might have a variety of different causes, for example illness, premature birth, separation, as well as congenital conditions. The situation may be permanent or temporary and will need to be addressed accordingly and on an individual basis.
Dysphasia	Dysphasia is a condition which is often caused by damage to the brain and it will result in speech and comprehension impairment. There may be difficulty with talking, listening, writing and understanding. Speech therapy can be very helpful in improving communication. Speaking slowly and clearly and using other methods of communication, for example gestures and drawing, can also help.
Dyslexia	This is a difficulty with reading and writing despite the individual having normal development of cognitive skills and intelligence. Many children with dyslexia are capable, intelligent and articulate yet they are unable to read, write or spell at a developmental level appropriate for their age. As children with this condition have literacy problems in general they will also have some difficulty with handwriting. Again, children benefit from one-to-one help by specialist staff.
Dyspraxia	Dyspraxia is also known by other names such as 'clumsy child syndrome' or developmental co-ordination disorder (DCD). There are a number of signs for this conditions which also include some difficulty with reading and writing, and speech problems – may have been slow to learn to talk and speech may be indistinct; understanding of positional vocabulary ('in', 'on', 'behind', 'under', etc.) is often very limited. Many children benefit from one-to-one therapy by qualified professionals and they will require help whilst at school.

When and how to access help

Help is available to support children with any condition and you will be able to access specialist professionals in this area. Many early years settings have a key worker system where one member of staff is allocated to a child as their particular contact and link within the setting. This enables the individual child to develop a sense of security and belonging. It is possible to refer the child to other specialists, such as speech therapists, and in some areas of the UK they visit early years settings, on a regular basis. The health visitor is often the first point of contact for many families when there is some indication that the child has difficulties with vision, hearing or speech problems. Within an education setting, there is opportunity to contact curriculum advisers who can help staff provide a detailed learning plan for a specific child.

When English is not the child's main language

When English is not a child's first language, there are support mechanisms which can be put in place, and most early years settings have literature and welcome packs in a variety of languages. Books within the setting should celebrate the diversity of race and culture within the country and there should be books with stories in other languages. Multi-cultural images should be portrayed in posters and photographs. Labels should reflect different writing styles and languages. There are also interpreters who can provide support for the child and the family for as long as they require it.

There are a number of support mechanisms that can be put in place for children and a few are mentioned in the table in Unit 17, page 461, Sources of support.

Assessment activity 18.1

You are working in the early years sector and have been asked to be involved in producing information sheets for some in-service training on language and literacy skills in the early years sector.

1 Explain how theories of language development have affected practice in the early years setting. **P1** **M1**

2 Produce some information sheets for parents about different activities, for example role play, creative play, with details about how those activities promote language and literacy development in young children. **P2**

3 In your information sheets, explain how adults can help young children develop these skills. **P4**

Legislation and curriculum guidance are discussed in detail in Unit 17, pages 462–67. The information in this section highlights the aspects relating to literacy skills.

Legislation

Over the years, legislation has been put in place to ensure the education of children covers all the relevant and important aspects required for the individual to take an active role in society. Care of the child and their emotional security plays a large part in providing safe and secure environments for the individual. Part of this whole-child development includes the right to education and the opportunity to develop literacy and numeracy skills. The development of numeracy skills is looked at in detail in Unit 17, Supporting Numeracy Skills.

Some of the main aspects of legislation are listed in the table in Unit 17, page 462, Legislation relating to numeracy skills and literacy skills.

Curriculum guidance

You will find more detail below about the curriculum guidance specifically in the areas of learning for communication, language and literacy. The early years curriculum is generally considered in three broad age groups: under 3 years of age, 3–5 years of age and over 5 years of age.

Birth to Three Matters framework

This framework for children under 3 years of age is discussed in Unit 17, page 463. The area 'A skilful communicator' relates directly to the development of language and literacy skills. Infants need to hear language on a regular basis and the positive body language that is associated with fun and learning.

Good practice checklist

Current issues

Ensure that you are up to date in your knowledge of the early years curriculum, especially in areas of communication, language and literacy, and that you are using the current documentation.

Check that you have:

- read and understand the current documentation
- attended any relevant training (if applicable)
- discussed issues with appropriate members of staff
- been involved in planning meetings
- understand observation and assessment procedures.

Theory into practice

Arrange to visit an early years setting where children under the age of 3 attend. Talk to the staff and observe how the Birth to Three Matters framework is structured and implemented, particularly in relation to the Skilful Communicator.

Curriculum guidance for the Foundation Stage, specifically the area of learning for communication, language and literacy

This curriculum for children aged 3–5 years of age is described in detail in Unit 17, page 464.

The second Early Learning Goal, 'Communication, language and literacy' is divided into 'competences' linked to: using language as a means to communicate; using language as a tool in thinking; developing the ability to link sounds and letters; developing reading skills and developing writing skills.

Extension activity

Find the Early Learning Goals for communication, language and literacy and see how the Stepping Stones relate for that specific area.

A good place to start your research might be www.dfes.gov.uk.

▲ The National Literacy Strategy aims to improve literacy

National Curriculum/Cwricwlwm Cymreig/ Northern Ireland Curriculum

This curriculum for children over 5 years of age is discussed in detail in Unit 17, page 464.

English is sub-divided into areas covering the spoken language, reading skills and writing skills and this has further been extended into, originally, the National Literacy strategy and, more recently, the Primary National Strategy.

Theory into practice

Arrange to visit an early years department in a primary school and talk to staff about how language and literacy skills are promoted in the classroom. Take note of sessions specifically designed to meet the National Strategy.

Theory into practice

Think of a general theme or topic, for example 'Myself' or 'Toys'. List some activities around that subject that could promote language and literacy skills in the 5–6-year-old child (Year 1).

■ Primary National Strategy (PNS)

This is described in detail in Unit 17, page 465.

Under the PNS, children will continue to receive discrete teaching relating to language and literacy and greater emphasis is placed on the use of phonics (recognising the sounds of parts of the words). Greater emphasis is also placed on group or whole class work. It is anticipated that materials will be available from the Primary National Strategy to support this area of work. In the PNS for literacy, there are 12 strands, the first four of which relate to the spoken word and the remainder link with reading and writing skills. They are:

National Literacy Strategy

The National Literacy Strategy was first introduced in 1998 to raise the levels of literacy in schools. Teachers and support staff were trained so that literacy standards might be improved on a national level. The Literacy Hour was split into four sections, each considering different aspects of literacy. Some of the time was spent on whole-class activities such as comprehension, spelling, grammar, punctuation and vocabulary. The remainder would be spent on individual and/or group work linked to reading and writing.

- Speaking
- Listening and responding
- Group discussion and interaction
- Drama
- Word reading skills and strategies
- Understanding and interpreting texts
- Engaging with and responding to texts

- Write a wide range of texts on paper and on screen
- Text structure and organisation
- Sentence structure and punctuality
- Word structure and spelling
- Presentation.

Extension activity

Carry out some research into the introduction of the Primary National Strategy and consider how it will positively affect early years education, and in particular literacy. A useful website is www.dfesstandards.gov.uk.

Case study: Preparation for practice

Jessica has just qualified as an early years worker and is employed at the Orange Grove Day Nursery. She is currently working with the children aged 3–4 years. Part of her role is to be involved with the planning of activities, which are specifically designed to promote certain skills and she has been asked to prepare two which will promote communication skills.

1 **Suggest two activities that she might consider.**

2 **Describe the activities.**

3 **List the learning outcomes for the child for each activity.**

4 **How might the activities be extended?**

Learning through play

Play is the vehicle by which all young children find out and develop the skills and knowledge to extend experiences and move on to the next levels in learning. There are five main areas of development and early years workers, parents and carers need to ensure that all areas are catered for. Play specifically allows the children to extend and increase their vocabulary and provide them with numerous examples of the written word. Stories are greatly loved by young children and they will try to write their own stories given the right encouragement. Literacy and language skills can be promoted through all aspects of play and it is the responsibility of the adults to provide the appropriate resources so that every opportunity is used to encourage enjoyment of the written and spoken word.

You will become skilled at providing for these areas of learning but all areas of play will provide for communication skills. Play and associated learning activities are covered in more detail in Unit 7, Learning Activities and Play. It is important to ensure that children have ample opportunity to talk, read and, at whatever level, by having access to reading and writing materials at all times. Children will take advantage of all the materials presented to them and will develop vital skills for the ongoing refinement of reading and writing skills. The use of language for different purposes and the introduction of new vocabulary is best developed through the natural play situations children engage in every day.

Impact of legislation/guidance on practice

Legislation and curriculum guidance ensures that good practice is available for children at all times. The introduction of the Early Years Curriculum (incorporating Birth to Three Matters framework, the Foundation Stage and the National Curriculum) means that early years workers follow a flexible yet structured curriculum that will help raise standards in all areas of development, particularly language and literacy. The detail of the curricula mean that adults have a set of standards that the majority of children can achieve by the end of the curriculum stage. Training events are often arranged to provide for the development of staff and to ensure that standards are being maintained.

Teaching methods might include the whole-word approach, where children are taught to recognise key words usually printed on card and linked to a reading scheme. This is often useful for learning difficult words but does not enable children to build up words by themselves. Using phonics means that the children learn the sound that the letter makes and this helps children develop a method of working out new words for themselves. The Rose Review indicated that there should be more emphasis on teaching in this way.

Theory into practice

Arrange to interview a teacher in a school and find out how current legislation impacts on their classroom practice, particularly for language and literacy development.

Assessment activity 18.2

Write a short report about one piece of current legislation that has an influence and impact on children's literacy development. Explain how it is implemented in the early years setting and evaluate its effectiveness. Try to provide some examples if you can to support your work. **P3** **M2** **D1**

18.3 How to implement a range of speaking and listening activities that can be used to support the development of children's skills

Activities

There are many activities to encourage the development of literacy skills including:

- story sacks
- story telling
- music
- dance
- story tapes
- small world
- circle time
- drama
- role play.

Role play

From a very early age, children will embark on role-play activities which fulfil many aspects of overall development. There are a number of mathematical activities involved in role play and these have been discussed more fully in Unit 17, Supporting Numeracy Skills. However, all aspects of language and literacy development will be addressed in some way during role-play activities. Children will have the opportunity to take on the role or character of someone else and will often use words and phrases that they might otherwise have no opportunity to use. Within the whole role-play area, there should be paper and pencils so that notes might be made or messages taken down. There should be magazines or posters to show the written word in context. Much of what is presented for the child to use will depend on the type of role-play area selected. The choice is only limited by the imagination and could include:

- the home
- hospital
- shop, for example baker's
- garden centre
- optician
- baby clinic
- post office.

Children will have the opportunity to live out their fantasies and fears but, in addition, they will be able to extend their language and literacy skills in a number of different ways.

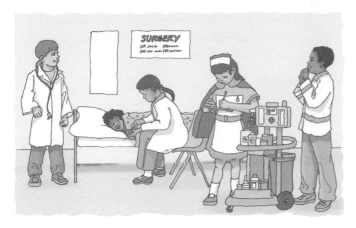

▲ How are you feeling today?

Story telling

This is one of the world's oldest ways of passing down information through generations. It has been revered over time even before the majority of people mastered the written word and it is still an art form in its own right.

Story telling in childhood has further benefits as it provides the comfort and security a child needs. It is learning in the best way. Story telling can often be under-estimated, but it allows the children to expand their vocabulary by providing new sentence patterns. Additionally, it provides an opportunity to listen and widen the child's experiences in a new and interesting form. Stories also help with the emotional development of the child as they stimulate the senses. Story telling should never be hurried and the story teller should use plenty of expression when reading. Many children have never experienced the joy of listening to stories and so initially the story teller should be prepared for interruptions and questions. If you are going to read stories to children, always allow time for preparation beforehand as you may have to read from a book that is not directly in front of you so the children can see the pictures. It should be an enjoyable experience for the teller and the listener.

Story sacks

These are used to encourage adults to share stories with children and usually consist of a bag or sack containing a book plus other materials which will be related to the story and might consist of soft toys or puppets of the main characters, pieces of scenery or anything that might help bring the story to life for the child. There might be an audiotape of the story so that it can be heard in a different way.

Initially story sacks were a Basic Skills Agency National Support Project and they are now used by a wide range of groups including libraries, schools, Sure Start, speech therapists and family centres. They were designed to encourage a love of books and to have a positive effect on reading success in schools. It is important to encourage parents to have books in the home so that children are surrounded by the written word in a meaningful way.

Theory into practice

- Have you come across the use of story sacks in your involvement with children in the early years? How are they used? If you have not been involved with them, consider if other learning aids, for example puppets, might be useful in reinforcing a story.
- Choose two stories and make a list of resources which might help reinforce the text or language.

Music

Children should be encouraged to listen to a variety of types of music so that they can become familiar with a wide range. Some of the first musical items that a child is introduced to consist of rhymes and songs or a lullaby that a parent might sing to help a child sleep. These encourage the child and make them aware of the different tones and pitch that the human voice is capable of. Music can also evoke a whole range of emotions in the individual and is beneficial for the child expressing their feelings.

Dance

Free expression in dance is beneficial for the overall development of the child. Freedom of movement helps a child acknowledge that they are a unique and individual person. Careful listening to the music will allow children to interpret sounds into personal meaning and children will often talk about their experiences enthusiastically.

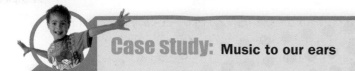
Drama

Drama with young children is excellent for the development of literacy skills as the child has an ideal opportunity to express a familiar story in their own words. Drama sessions may begin with a traditional story, with the early years worker telling the background and the children taking the parts of the characters. If an adult is relating the story then the child is not under any pressure to say the words but will be encouraged to do so as the story moves along. Occasionally, very shy and timid children will come 'out of their shell' and be very vocal if playing the role of someone else. As children become older, they often gain great enjoyment from dramatising stories and will display an increase in self-confidence and self-esteem.

Story tapes

Story tapes are useful as they present a different way for the child to hear stories. They should never replace the face-to-face contact that adults have with children, but they will allow children to listen to favourite stories repeatedly at a time suitable to them. Listening centres should have a stock of audio tapes suitable for the age group using them. This will empower children to choose their story and to listen to it when they wish to. The listening centre needs to be situated in a place away from the more lively and noisy activities so that the child can concentrate on the matter in hand.

Circle time

Many early years settings have incorporated circle time into their daily routine. This enables each individual child to speak about their choices of the day and to tell others what they have done and why. News items and other features can be linked into circle time, but it is important that each child has the opportunity to speak without interruption. Some settings have a hat that the child must wear in order to have the attention of everyone else and speak. Other establishments have a toy, for example a teddy, that the child can hold whilst speaking. However it is organised, circle time provides an opportunity to give each child, regardless of ability, a unique opportunity to be the centre of positive attention each day.

Small world

Small world play includes many aspects of role play, but on a much smaller scale. It might include a doll's house, farmyard, garage, etc. and the children can take on a number of roles and responsibilities whilst playing on a carpet or at the table with other children. The relaxed atmosphere and the artefacts enable them to use their language skills in a slightly different way and use role-related vocabulary fluently.

Theory into practice

- Arrange to visit an early years setting and ask permission to listen to an early years worker tell a story to a group of children. Take notes on the skills involved and different tones of voice used.
- Make arrangements for you to tell a story to a small group of children. Remember to practise first so that you are familiar with the structure.
- Evaluate your story telling session, for example what went right, what went wrong, what you would change, etc. Be fairly critical as it will help you to improve your skills.

Materials and resources

Stories

Children should have many opportunities to listen to stories. They may be from books which can be shared in a caring and secure environment, but stories can also be made up or told from memory – young children often like to hear stories about when their parents or grandparents were younger. There should be a variety of books of different types for children to look at.

Children need to be taught to care for books and the best way is by example. Story books should be repaired as soon as they are damaged and children will often bring books with a torn page to be repaired before it becomes much worse. Children very soon learn that anything can happen in a story book and that they are places of fantasy and enjoyment.

When children are very young, they may not have developed the level of listening skills required and the story teller must be prepared for a number of interruptions. Gradually the child will listen for longer periods of time and stories are the best way of encouraging children to develop good listening skills.

It is useful to check understanding of the story by asking questions afterwards. This should take the form of a discussion rather than a series of questions, which

How do you think they will cross the river?

▲ **Sharing a story**

might sound like interrogation. Children can later be encouraged to solve problems which might be posed, for example in the story of 'The Three Billy Goats Gruff' there might be some discussion as to how the three goats could cross the river if the bridge did not exist.

Rhymes

Children enjoy rhymes from a very early age and will quickly learn to anticipate the end. This will encourage them to listen carefully, especially when rhymes for the older child include sections with the words missing, for example 'Head, shoulders, knees and toes' where a word is omitted but the actions are still used.

Rhymes and songs teach children about the complexity of language and encourage children to think of rhyming words. They find that they can play with language and that it serves many different purposes.

Group size

The size of the group will affect the way in which the rhymes, songs or stories are delivered.

- When working with children on a one-to-one basis, the atmosphere tends to be less formal with adult and child usually sitting together on a settee or chair. There is usually a closeness that creates a good learning experience.
- Small group work tends to be slightly more formal as all the children in the group need to be catered for and must be able to see the pictures in the book. It depends on the size of the group as to how close they can get to the reader and the book.
- Larger groups need to be managed in such a way that all children can see and it is usual for the children to be sitting on the floor in a semi-circle so that they can. This type of session is still friendly even though it tends to be more formal.

Spoken language

It is important to talk to and converse with children regularly throughout the day, to reinforce good practice, introduce new words and help build self-confidence and increase self-esteem. Children deserve our attention and we should face them when we are speaking to them and let them know that we value their efforts and actions. It is also essential that early years workers and other adults speak with and talk to the children who do not speak in return. We must not fall into the trap of only talking to people where we receive a response. We should not make the reluctant speaker feel under pressure, as they will respond more readily if the atmosphere is relaxed and conducive to conversation.

Poetry

Poetry is a form of language that readily develops from rhymes and songs of early childhood, but it is often neglected as children grow older. As children develop literacy and language skills, they enjoy playing with words and finding rhyming pairs. As with all language, poetry can be amusing, striking and emotive, and children should be given the opportunity to hear poetry and compose poems.

Theory into practice

- Arrange to visit a school setting for children under the age of 8 years. Find out if poetry is used on a regular basis in the development of language and literacy skills.
- Make a list of five poems suitable for the age group you have chosen to visit.

Tape recorder

Providing children with the opportunities to record their own voices allows them to enjoy sounds in a different way. They enjoy saying rhymes, singing songs and telling stories. In general, they take great joy in this type of activity as long as they do not feel that their privacy has been invaded.

Theory into practice

In pairs or small groups, consider different activities in which a tape recorder might be used in the promotion of language and literacy skills.

Write down your suggestions and make a list of other resources you might need to support your ideas.

Listening centre

Many early years settings provide listening centres or areas where children can experiment with sound and can also listen to music, rhymes and stories in a quiet area. The area should be situated in a quieter part of the setting but it enables children to listen to music, rhymes, stories, etc. when they wish to and they can listen to the same recording as many times as they want.

English as an additional language

Children for whom English is an additional language often feel vulnerable in an environment that is different in many ways. It is beneficial if the child feels more at home and relaxed and the setting should include books, posters, labels, etc. in the child's home language. Other children in the setting may wish to learn new words in another language and there might be a mutual learning of new words. Audio tapes can be useful and many authorities have specialist classes and groups so that children can learn with their peers.

Extension activity

Make a poster which might be used in the entry area of an early years setting. Design it so that children and families who do not have English as their first language will be made welcome.

Remember, it should be bright and eye-catching. You might like to use pictures or graphics in your design.

Assessment activity 18.3

You have been asked to plan and carry out some activities that will promote language development. Plan one activity to promote children's speaking skills and one activity to promote children's listening skills. Try to be detailed in your planning. Implement and evaluate one of the activities. **P5 M3 D2**

Contexts for reading and comprehension skills

Children have many opportunities on a daily basis to read and develop the skills related to reading and writing. It is important that the child becomes fluent in reading and comprehension skills and not just looking at one word at a time out of context.

Situations

Fluent reading means that the child has to be able to recognise groups of symbols and transfer them into meaningful words. In addition they need to be able to decipher these symbols in a left to right manner and from the top of the page to the bottom. Other cultures deal with reading in different ways, for example characters rather than letters and from the top of the page to the bottom, starting at the right.

These are complex skills for the child to master. Children quickly learn that words present information in various forms and in differing situations, for example directions, labels, street names, recipes, letters, ICT, story books, shopping list, etc. Children will reproduce the same forms of writing in their everyday activities whether through play or structured activities.

Shared reading

Shared reading is an integral part of the Primary National Strategy, with all the children reading together. The reading is usually from a large book and the early years professional will introduce the book by talking about the title and author before encouraging the children to read aloud. The children will join in as they feel more confident and even the shy child will participate eventually as they gain in confidence. Children also enjoy reading in pairs as it reinforces the enjoyment and communal spirit.

Reading aloud alone

Children will often read aloud when alone. In this way the spoken word and the written word are very closely linked and this is reinforced as the child can hear the sounds the words make. It also provides neuro-linguistic links and helps with comprehension and memory. You may notice adults reading aloud when they are trying to make sense of a sentence or paragraph.

Reading for pleasure

If children enjoy stories and rhymes, they will wish to learn to read for themselves. If this process is handled carefully and sensitively then reading independently will also be an enjoyable and pleasurable experience. Children will eventually reach a stage when they wish to read for its own sake and a love of reading for pleasure will be encouraged. If children do not enjoy reading, they might well continue to read but it may just serve a purpose, for example finding information, rather than being a pleasurable activity in its own right.

Reading linked to other activities

Reading is a skill that is integral to so many other activities, especially as the child grows older, that it is essential that the child has good literacy skills that are embedded in other experiences. As a child matures, other curriculum subjects rely on positive literacy skills. For example, in mathematics, problems are often presented in written form and the child must decode the writing before solving the mathematical problem. Instructions for using equipment or taking part in activities often require a certain level of language and literacy skills.

Listening to stories and rhymes

Ensuring that children have the opportunity to listen to stories and rhymes is vitally important for the overall development of the child. A caring and relaxed atmosphere is essential for children to enjoy stories and rhymes, which form the foundations for language development which then leads to reading and writing skills. In addition, this helps develop the listening skills, which help with the reinforcement of correct pronunciation. Listening to stories and rhymes can be on a one-to-one basis, in a small group and as a whole-class.

Theory into practice

It is useful for children to hear stories from a variety of sources. Write a short story for a child of 2–3 years of age. It might be a real story from your family or from when you were younger. Remember the age group so don't make it too complicated – keep it simple. It needs to have a definite beginning, middle and end.

You might then like to tell it to a young child and even draw some pictures to accompany it.

Cues and conventions

When children begin reading, they need to know certain conventions such as reading from left to right and from the top of the page to the bottom. If this has been reinforced from early on in the development of literacy skills, the child will very quickly manage this skill. Cues as to the content of the text can be gleaned from the illustrations accompanying the text. As children gain in maturity and the development of complex literacy skills, then the graphics and illustrations do not need to be as large or important and the child will be able to internally visualise the context.

Learning to write involves learning other conventions such as those related to letter shapes, sequence of letters in a word and the sequence of words in a sentence. Many of the activities used in developing reading skills are very useful in the development of writing skills.

Organisation/structure of text

Children learn very quickly that there are a number of ways that text is organised and structured. There are times, as in story books, when the written words are organised into sentences and then the sentences are structured into a logical order so that sense can be made of the story. There are other times when the order of the text is less important, such as in shopping lists. The more children are exposed to different forms of writing, the more they will realise that writing is used for a variety of purposes, for example: message taking (as from a telephone call); lists; stories; taking orders (as in a café); completing forms and charts. The structure of the text is different in each case and children need opportunities to become familiar with as many types as possible.

Phonic cues

Phonics relates to the sound that a letter makes and the written form it takes. The Rose Review suggested that phonics be taught earlier than before in order to raise the standard of literacy in schools. Phonics is a very important part of reading and children will learn that the sounds of the letters go to make up the words. Visual cues from the text are also used to make sense of the written words, but knowing the sounds and building up words provides important cues for the child. Research has been carried out which indicates that children who are taught phonics from an early age become fluent readers. However, it is difficult to remove the influences that access to books and listening to stories has on the overall reading ability of the individual child.

Extension activity

1 Carry out some research into the Primary National Strategy, looking particularly at the suggested outcomes for literacy in Year 1 of the National Curriculum.

2 Design an activity to promote either reading or writing skills in children who are 5–6 years of age.

Writing forms

Writing is used for many purposes and takes different forms. As children develop writing skills, they will need to structure their writing to meet its purpose. Letters are structured in a different way from an item of news or from a shopping list. An order taken in a restaurant varies greatly from a report written in a surgery. Children will gradually accept that there are a multitude of forms of writing and with encouragement will develop the skills to differentiate between them. Children should be given the opportunity to write and send cards for various occasions: thank you letters; shopping lists; stories and poems.

Theory into practice

1 Make a list of all the different uses for the written word that you can think of. You may like to work with another person for this activity.
2 How many of these ways do you or your friends use on a regular basis?

Awareness of writing process

Children usually learn to read and write together, as the processes are closely related and it helps the children make the connections between the letters and the sounds they make when read aloud.

Often children of approximately 3–4 years old will start making meaningful marks on paper and may even begin trying to copy their name or other words. They realise that the symbols have meaning that can be translated into sounds and words. Once a child has shown this readiness, they should be given other opportunities to develop the skills used for writing, for example the correct hold for a pencil and correct formation of letters. This should not be rushed and children will need the physical co-ordination and dexterity to perform fine movements whilst holding a pencil or crayon. Activities which will help develop these skills, include:

- painting
- drawing
- tracing
- modelling using clay, play dough, etc.
- threading activities
- cutting and sticking activities.

Initially children may not have a preferred hand for holding pencils and other writing or mark-making implements, but try to avoid the temptation of placing the pencil in the child's hand. It is good practice to place the implement in front of the child and allow them to pick it up with their preferred hand. They may change hands regularly but eventually they will use one hand more than the other. Once the child has picked it up, it may be possible to adjust the grip if necessary.

Composition

The composition of the written work will vary according to its purpose and children need to be aware of the range of uses of the written word. Gradually, as children listen to stories and have opportunity to read, they will become more aware of the structure of a written article, for example beginning, middle and end. However, it must be recognised that this is not always the case but that all work should be structured in a logical way. When children first start to record their thoughts in writing, the adult may find that the process of writing stops the creative flow as the child has not developed the fluency required. At times like this, it is helpful for the child to 'dictate' their thoughts and ideas to the adult who will then act as a scribe to put the words on paper more quickly.

Characteristics of a variety of forms/genres

Children need to understand that writing is used in a variety of ways and takes different forms. It is beneficial if children can have experience of these different forms. If they have a variety of examples to fit the context, they will gain an understanding of the characteristics, for example lists, message pads, report forms, prescription pads, memos, letters. If children are exposed to these different forms, they will gradually accept this into their day-to-day routines.

Bilingual children may have developed literacy skills in languages that are totally different from each other. There may be different writing systems within a household or a child may speak a language but not be able to write it. Children may be familiar with writing which moves from right to left, as in Arabic and Hebrew, or they may be more familiar with vertical writing, as in Japanese and Mandarin Chinese. This is in total contrast to English, which is written in a horizontal plane and from left to right. Developing literacy skills can be very difficult for some children and they need every encouragement from sensitive and positive adults.

Using displays

Displays may be free-standing, on a table or a wall but should always provide a focal point for a stimulating topic or idea. They fulfil a variety of needs and many of these link to the development of literacy skills. A lively, stimulating display will encourage children to talk and use a variety of language. If the display has a title or other written notes, labels or perhaps a poem or rhyme displayed alongside it, this will reinforce the relationship between the display and the written word.

Children should be encouraged to think of the display as theirs and it should, wherever possible, be their work that is shown. Labels might be added to enhance the display but should never detract from it. Often table displays are active and might be added to on a daily basis by the children, for example a colour display or natural science. The children might bring items of interest to add to the display and these could be labelled accordingly. It might be useful to have displays which include families of words or words which relate to a specific topic the setting may be involved in. Whatever the initial purpose of the display, it must help fulfil the needs of the children in the setting.

Theory into practice

When you are on placement or visiting an early years setting, you might be involved in setting up a display. Choose one of the following and consider how you would carry out your task:

- interest table
- natural science display
- wall frieze (you can choose the topic)
- display of children's work.

You will need to consider colour, background, lettering and composition of the display area. Be innovative and remember to make it interesting and attractive.

Activities

There are numerous activities in the early years setting which will provide opportunity for children to develop reading and writing skills. Some are mentioned below but the list is not exhaustive.

Role play

It is good practice to have various shaped pieces of paper and different writing implements in role-play areas so that children can make marks and notes as and when required. Types of writing will depend on the type of role-play activity, for example a telephone and pad for taking orders in a shop, shopping lists, order pad in a restaurant, mock prescription pads in hospital, record cards in a clinic – the list is endless.

▲ Displaying children's work

Sand play

Making tracks in sand and following them with a finger or cars, etc. will help develop writing skills. Children can practise making shapes and patterns in the sand and eventually they may practise letters.

Painting

Children love to paint. It is an opportunity to produce a very personal piece of work. They will often practise other skills whilst painting and this helps develop the specific skills used for reading and writing. Holding a brush, making meaningful marks on paper and talking about their creations are all skills relating to the development of literacy. Children often move on to painting their name and become more refined in depicting images on paper.

Story sacks

Story sacks contain a variety of items related to the story book and these provide opportunities to reinforce the spoken and written word as being closely related. Many libraries and early years settings use story sacks to encourage parents and children to read together and use story aids to bring the text to life. Children will then develop a love of stories and enjoy reading for themselves as they develop the skills.

Print making

Children enjoy making prints and they have the opportunity to see the relationship between the material used for the print and the mark left behind on the card or paper. Hand prints, finger prints, bobbin prints and potato prints are all examples of ways in which permanent marks might be made.

Patterns

The formation of patterns is important in the development of literacy skills. Children need to be able to see word patterns and be able to visually discriminate between words. Patterns can be made using the print making activities above or by threading coloured beads in specific order and fitting together similar shapes, for example hexagons of different colours. The ability to relate to patterns in art work helps children to relate to patterns in the written word. When letters form a specific pattern, they will always have the same sound and meaning and as children become familiar with the patterns of letters they will grow in confidence as they develop reading and writing skills.

Story telling

Story telling is so enjoyable for children and begins at a very early age. It is through story telling that the foundations of language and literacy are laid down. For many adults the ability to tell stories is very natural, but for others they need to develop these skills in order for the children to fully benefit. It is usually through stories that children begin to realise that the marks on paper have meaning and that the words flow from left to right. The astute early years worker will use story sessions to talk about the book in general and when telling the children the book title may run their finger under the words so that the children will link the spoken and the written word.

Poetry

Poetry is first introduced to children in the rhymes we use when they are very young. Children very quickly learn to anticipate the ending and will eventually complete the lines in a familiar rhyme. As they grow older, they enjoy playing and experimenting with words and gain pleasure from rhyming words. Poetry is a natural progression, but sadly it is often a neglected aspect of literacy development.

Music

Music helps children express themselves in so many ways and provides for the holistic development of the child. Enjoying different types of music in their own right is important, but the development of listening skills and the conversations arising from listening to music are invaluable. Children must learn that they can express their feelings in many different ways and that they can record their emotions in writing. Making up rhymes and songs will also engender a love of words and show how they can be used in different contexts.

Drama

Drama helps bring stories to life for the child and enables them to portray characters in their own way. As well as having a strong connection with the development of literacy skills, it also provides outlets for the emotional development. As well as being invaluable for the development of language, drama can be used in various ways. Children can be encouraged to write short plays of their own and then act them out with others in the setting.

Adult as a scribe

There are times when a child wishes to 'write' a story but does not have the skills at that time. It is quite acceptable for the adult to act as a scribe for the child and write down what they say. A variety of pictures on a writing table may trigger the imagination and the child's 'scribed' work might be displayed alongside the picture. The adult must display a sensitive approach so that they do not take over but merely offer assistance for the child.

Use of technology

Many early years settings and homes have computers and other technological items that will be of benefit to the development of literacy skills in the early years. There is a wide variety of computer programmes that can be used for this purpose. Television programmes have been designed and commissioned specifically for children and meet educational needs in ways that the average setting could not achieve. There are other electronic games and devices which might have appropriate programmes.

Writing for different audiences

Children very quickly come to realise that writing fulfils numerous purposes, for example letters, postcards, menus, notes, newspaper articles and poetry. They will try to copy some of these styles but may need encouragement with others.

Group/individual books

Within an early years setting, it is common to see the use of 'big books' for story telling or for use in the PNS. This enables all the children in a group to see clearly the text and illustrations. However, smaller books are more usual when used on an individual basis but must always be age- and stage-appropriate.

Cutting and sticking

Cutting and sticking activities provide for the creative nature of the child but additionally help strengthen the small muscles in the hands, which will be needed for writing skills. The positioning of the individual pieces also relates to the patterns and overall nature of the activity.

And then Billy Goat saw the bridge.....

▲ Adult as a scribe

Theory into practice

Arrange to visit an early years setting and take note of the use of technology in the centre. Pay particular attention as to how it is used for promoting language and literacy skills. If you have the opportunity, visit a setting with a different age range and note how the use of technology differs.

Good practice checklist

You must ensure the safety of the child at all times and it is your responsibility to maintain standards and check resources prior to use. You will need to ensure:

- a risk assessment is carried out for activities
- the area is safe
- resources are safe to use
- there are enough resources for the number of children involved
- materials and equipment are age- and stage-appropriate
- activities or equipment can be adapted to meet the individual needs of the child.

Materials, settings and environments

The importance of providing a wide variety of materials and resources for reading and stimuli for writing

It is the responsibility of the parents, carers and early years workers to provide the materials and resources which will encourage children to develop the appropriate skills. Children need to be exposed to the written word in a variety of forms and should have enough materials to be able to practise skills as they develop. Resources will also include the people who will be with the children, to tell stories, to reinforce correct use of grammar, increase vocabulary and provide the praise and positive reward to provide the stimuli and make the experience enjoyable.

Enabling children to choose own reading materials and appropriate writing forms for particular contexts

In order for children to have opportunity to choose reading materials and writing forms, it is necessary to provide a wide range of resources and activities.

There should be a range of books covering as wide a scope as possible, for example books for information, dictionaries, simple story books, action stories, topic/theme books, books with rhymes and poetry books. For the very young child, there will be picture books in various materials. There ought to be a variety of writing materials and activities to promote letter formation and writing skills. Appropriate cards and paper should be placed in role-play areas so that the children can record messages and writing forms in context.

How the setting/environment may affect children's reading performance and comprehension

The setting and the environment can have a strong influence on the child's reading performance and understanding. If the setting and environment is sparse and without books or opportunities to develop writing skills, or adults who will tell stories and encourage children, the children will have greater difficulty in developing the appropriate skills for fluency in reading and writing. The setting and environment should have the necessary materials and resources to allow the child the opportunities to see and use the written word. The atmosphere should be pleasant, relaxed and conducive to learning. Children should have access to a wide range of books and activities, which will promote reading and writing skills. Adult involvement and sensitive intervention of the right type, which will help build self-confidence and self-esteem, is also required. It is the overall environment which will lead to a positive response to developing language and literacy skills.

Assessment activity 18.4

You have been asked to plan and carry out some activities that will promote reading and writing development. Plan one activity to promote children's reading skills and one activity to promote children's writing skills. Try to be detailed in your planning. You might then implement and evaluate one of the activities. **P6 M4 D2**

End of unit assessment

1 You are working in the early years sector and have been asked to produce a display, on 'The development of language and literacy skills in the early years', which will be useful for trainee early years workers and parents of the children in the setting.

a) In your display you should provide details of two different theories of language development. **P1**

b) Look critically at the differences between them, giving examples from your experiences to support the theories or challenge them. **M1**

c) Add a chart (or a number of different charts) in which you describe listening, speaking, reading and writing development in children under 8 years of age. Describe the role of the adult in the development of literacy skills and how they might meet the differing needs of individual children. **P2** **P4**

d) Describe how one piece of current legislation has an influence and impact on children's literacy development. **P3**

e) Explain how it is implemented in the early years setting and evaluate its effectiveness. You should provide some examples if you can to support your work. **M2**

f) As a follow-up activity, write a handout to give to trainee early years workers evaluating the effectiveness of national initiatives in promoting children's literacy skills. **D1**

2 As an early years worker you will be involved in planning, preparing, implementing and evaluating a variety of activities for young children.

a) Plan:
   • two activities to promote children's speaking and listening skills **P5**
   • two activities to promote children's reading and writing skills. **P6**

b) Implement:
   • one of the speaking and listening skills activities **M3**
   • one of the reading and writing activities. **M4**

c) When planning and carrying out these activities, consider the age and number of children, the resources required, the aim of the activity, the identified outcomes for the child, and the description of the activity.

d) Once the children have carried out the activities, write an evaluation for each one. **D2** You should include what went well and not so well, what you would change, whether the children achieved the desired outcomes, and if not, why not?

References and further reading

Macleod-Brudenell, I. (2004) *Advanced Early Years Care and Education*, Heinemann

Miller, L., Cable, C. and Devereux, J. (2005) *Developing Early Years Practice*, Fulton

Nutbrown, C. (1997) *Recognising Early Literacy Development*, Paul Chapman

Palmer, S. and Bayley, R. (2004) *Foundations to Literacy*, Network Education Press

Smith, D. (2001) *Supporting the Literacy Needs of Children in the Early Years*, Tarquin Pub

Whitehead, M.R. and Makin, L. (2003) *How to Develop Children's Early Literacy*, Paul Chapman

Useful websites

Department for Education and Skills – www.dfes.gov.uk

DfES Standards Unit – www.dfesstandards.gov.uk

Grading criteria	Assessment activity	Page number
To achieve a pass grade the evidence must show that the learner is able to:		
P1 identify two different theories of language development	18.1 End of unit assessment	496 512
P2 describe the sequences and stages in the development of children's reading, writing, speaking and listening skills	18.1 End of unit assessment	496 512
P3 identify one piece of legislation/curriculum document and its influence on supporting children's literacy skills	18.2 End of unit assessment	500 512
P4 describe the role of the adult in developing literacy skills and meeting specific needs	18.1 End of unit assessment	496 512
P5 develop two activities to promote children's speaking and listening skills	18.3 End of unit assessment	504 512
P6 develop two activities to promote reading and writing skills	18.4 End of unit assessment	511 512
To achieve a merit grade the evidence must show that, in addition to the pass criteria, the learner is able to:		
M1 compare and contrast the two theories of language development using practical examples to support or contradict the theories	18.1 End of unit assessment	496 512
M2 explain how the identified legislation/curriculum guidance is used in a children's setting to support the development of literacy skills	18.2 End of unit assessment	500 512
M3 implement at least one of the planned activities to support the development of children's speaking and listening skills	18.3 End of unit assessment	504 512
M4 implement at least one of the planned activities to support the development of children's reading and writing skills	18.4 End of unit assessment	511 512
To achieve a distinction grade the evidence must show that, in addition to the pass and merit criteria, the learner is able to:		
D1 evaluate the effectiveness of the identified legislation/curriculum guidance in promoting children's literacy skills	18.2 End of unit assessment	500 512
D2 evaluate the effectiveness of the implemented activities	18.3 18.4 End of unit assessment	504 511 512

The development and care of babies and children under 3 years

Introduction

The care of young children in their early months is probably one of the most important periods of care. Babies need consistency in their carers as they are starting to form those all so important bonds with others. By the age of 3 years, a child has developed from a totally helpless baby to having the foundations of all the major skills and abilities they need to progress through life. The rate of growth and development in these first three years is very rapid and changes occur over a very short period of time.

This unit reflects the importance of these early years as recognised in the principles of the Birth to Three Matters framework and helps you to apply the principles and practice of the framework in your work with the under-3s. By the time you qualify in the early years sector, it is likely that you will be working with the new Early Years Foundation Stage (EYFS). This is due to start being used in September 2008 and will provide a single framework for care, learning and development for children in all early years settings from birth to 5 years. The EYFS builds on the existing Foundation Stage, Birth to Three Matters and the National Standards for Under-8s Day Care and Childminding. It will provide a flexible approach to care and learning and raise quality throughout the early years sector to help to improve the life chances of all children, by setting a clear expectation of the care, learning and development they will receive, whatever the setting they attend.

What you need to learn

- The expected sequence and development of babies and children in the first three years of life
- How to help provide physical care requirements for babies and children under 3
- How to provide play activities to encourage learning and development
- How to communicate with babies and children under 3, interpret their needs and respond to them

Thinking points

Birth to Three really does Matter!
Most parents are very keen to help their child grow into the most intelligent, best looking, caring and happy person possible. Yet we know that this does not happen for some children. The most important years of a child's life are the first three – the foundations of future development are very much set at this time.

You are a qualified and experienced childcare worker working in a nursery. You have been asked by friends who are expecting their first child how they can help to make sure they will be able to provide the right sort of physical care and play activities for their child and to respond to their needs. They also want to know how to promote good communication with them.

- What would you tell them?

Development

The basic principles of development apply to all children:
- Development starts from the head and works down the body (**cephalocaudal**), and from the mid line to the extremities.
- All development happens in the same order, but can occur at different rates.
- All areas of development are linked together.

Key term

Cephalocaudal refers to the maturation of gross and fine motor skills from the head down the spine.

Although development happens at different rates, there are certain stages that most children will reach by a certain age. These are known as the milestones of development, for example, walking alone by 18 months, smiling at 6 weeks.

The four key areas of development are:
- *physical development* – this refers to the body increasing in skill and performance and includes:
  - gross motor development (using large muscles), for example legs and arms
  - fine motor development (precise use of muscles), for example hands and fingers
- *social and emotional development* – the development of a child's identity and self-image and the development of relationships and feelings about him or herself, learning the skills to live in society with other people
- *intellectual development* – learning the skills of understanding, memory and concentration
- *communication and speech development* – learning to communicate with friends, family and all others.

The Birth to Three Matters framework (see page 524) looks at a child's learning, growth, development and environment in four areas:
- a strong child
- a skilful communicator

- a competent learner
- a healthy child.

Each aspect links in with four broad developmental age groupings, which will be used in this unit:
- heads up, lookers and communicators (0–8 months)
- sitters, standers and explorers (8–18 months)
- movers, shakers and players (18–24 months)
- walkers, talkers and pretenders (24–36 months).

Theory into practice

How has Birth to Three Matters been implemented in your placement? Have all the staff had the training? Try to find out how it has changed their practice.

Heads up, lookers and communicators (0–8 months)

■ At birth

Movement

Newborn babies have very little if any control over their bodies. They are scrunched up and will curl into the foetal position. Movements are **automatic reflexes** rather than deliberate. These reflexes are amazing to watch. They include:
- grasp reflex – grasping an object that has touched the palm of their hand or sole of foot
- rooting – turning their head to look for a nipple or teat if their cheek is touched
- sucking and swallowing and eliminating reflexes
- placing – trying to make stepping movements if they are held upright with their feet on a firm surface
- startle in response to a sudden sound or bright light
- Moro reflex – stretching their arms suddenly and then bringing them in if they feel they are falling

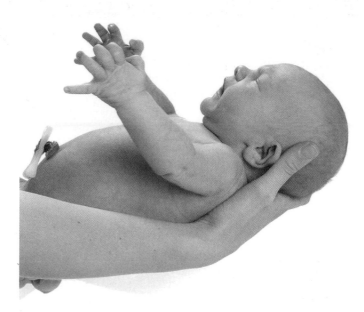

▲ Babies are born with a number of automatic reflexes. What reflex is this an example of?

■ By 1 month

Babies of this age need:

- firm but gentle handling
- constant holding when awake
- lots of cuddles and touch
- talking and singing
- music to listen to
- feeding, bathing, changing
- bright colours and mobiles within 20–25 cm of their faces.

Physical

The typical physical movements of a 1-month old baby are:

- lies on back with head to one side – arms and legs on face side outstretched
- head lags when pulled up to sitting position
- when held sitting, back is a full curve
- primitive reflexes, such as rooting, sucking, stepping, grasping are still present.

Social and emotional

The baby:

- responds positively to main carer
- imitates facial expressions
- stares at bright shiny objects
- gazes intently at carers
- social smile at carers (by 6 weeks).

Intellectual

The baby:

- blinks in reaction to bright light
- turns to soft light
- stares at carer
- cries when basic needs require attention.

Communication

The baby:

- cries when basic needs require attention such as hunger, tiredness and distress
- 'freezes' when a bell is rung gently close to the ear and moves head towards the sound
- stops crying at sound of human voice (unless very upset)
- coos in response to carer's talk.

- recognising their mother's voice and smell
- crying when they are hungry, in pain, need feeding, changing or just cuddling. Cries usually cease in response to continuous quiet adult voices.

Senses

Babies use their senses from birth, for example:

- smell and taste – responding to sour or sweet tastes
- hearing and communication – crying is a baby's only means of communication. Different cries for different meanings develop very quickly. Loud sounds make babies jump but they enjoy listening to voices
- sight can focus at 20–25 cm which is close facial contact distance. Otherwise vision is fuzzy.

Key term

Automatic reflexes 'Survival' reflexes that mostly disappear by about 3–4 months of age – babies can locate the source of food and suck, react to loud noises and even appear to walk at a very young age.

3 months

Physical

At 3 months, the baby:

- kicks legs and waves arms
- brings hands together over chest or chin
- watches movements of own hands, plays with own hands
- holds rattle for a few seconds if placed in hand
- can lift head and upper chest and turn when on front.

Social and emotional

The baby:

- fixes gaze on carer's face when feeding
- smiles, starting to engage and vocalise with carers
- recognises preparation for routine e.g. bath, feeding.

Intellectual

The baby follows movements of large and smaller objects.

Communication

The baby:

- becomes quiet and turns head towards sound of rattle near head
- can be upset by sudden loud noises
- cries when uncomfortable or annoyed
- vocalises when spoken to and when alone
- sucks lips in response to food preparation
- shows excitement at sound of voices, footsteps.

■ 6 months

Physical

At 6 months, the baby:

- sits with support
- rolls over
- pushes head, neck and chest off floor with arms when on front
- holds arms out to be lifted up
- when held standing, bears weight on feet and bounces
- uses whole hand in palmar grasp, passes toy from one hand to another.

Social and emotional

The baby:

- starts to show interest in other babies, smiling
- becomes more interested in social interaction, depending on amount of time spent with other children and their personality
- shows fear of strangers and distress at separation from carer
- interacts differently with various family members
- uses comfort object, such as a blanket
- puts hand to bottle or cup and pats it when feeding
- seeks attention.

Intellectual

The baby:

- is very curious, easily distracted by movements
- immediately fixes sight on small objects close by and reaches out to grasp them
- puts everything in mouth
- finds feet interesting objects
- watches toys fall from hand within range of vision
- immediately reaches for rattle when offered and shakes it to make sound.

Communication

The baby:

- makes sing-song vowel sounds
- laughs and chuckles and squeals aloud in play
- screams with annoyance
- responds differently to different tones of voice
- turns immediately to main carer's voice
- is starting to respond to noises out of sight with correct visual response.

■ 8 months

Physical

At 8 months, the baby:

- sits alone for 10–15 minutes without support
- reaches out for toys when sitting
- may crawl or shuffle
- pulls body to stand but cannot lift lower body so falls backwards
- pokes at small items with index finger

- uses index and middle fingers with thumb in pincer grip to pick up small items
- will take and hold a small brick in each hand
- lifts block but can only release by dropping.

Social and emotional

The baby:

- is very interested in all around
- recognises familiar and unfamiliar faces
- shows stranger anxiety
- takes everything to mouth ('mouthing', from 6 months)
- holds, bites and chews firm object, for example a biscuit.

Intellectual

The baby:

- looks in correct direction for falling toys
- might find toy hidden under a cushion or cup if he watches it being hidden
- holds toy out but cannot release it.

Communication

The baby:

- vocalises for communication, shouts for attention
- **babbles** loudly and tunefully – dual syllables in long strings, for example 'dad-dad', 'baba', 'mam-mam'
- imitates adult vocal sounds, for example coughs, smacking lips
- understands 'no' and 'bye-bye'
- shows an instant response to hearing test conducted 1 m behind child, out of sight.

Key term

Babbling is a repetitive type of vocalisation, such as 'dada', 'mamma', which has no special meaning, but is applied to having social meaning by the reactions of adults, i.e. dad or mum. Reinforcement helps the sounds to develop into meaning. Deaf babies babble, but it soon ends as there is no feedback for them.

At 12 months, babies are starting to move to a standing position ▶

Sitters, standers and explorers (8–18 months)

■ 12 months

Physical

At 12 months, the baby:

- pulls to stand then can stand alone and starts to walk holding on – 'cruising'
- becomes mobile through crawling or shuffling
- enjoys self-feeding and holds cup with help
- has a neat pincer grip – picks up anything tiny from the floor
- starts to show hand preference
- clicks two cubes together
- puts cubes in box when shown.

Social and emotional

The baby:

- shows a strong attachments to carers
- shows definite emotions and is aware of emotions of others
- will play alone
- is starting to develop **object permanence**.

Intellectual

The baby:

- will hold two cubes, one in each hand, and click together in imitation
- drops toys deliberately and watches them fall – this is called 'casting'
- looks in correct place for toys that have rolled out of sight
- will crawl to retrieve rolling ball
- recognises familiar people at 6 metres
- watches movements of people, animals, cars, etc. with great interest.

Communication

The baby:

- knows and turns to own name
- **jargons** loudly in 'conversations', includes most vowels sounds
- understands about 20 words in context, for example 'cup', 'dog', 'dinner', and understands simple messages, for example 'clap hands', 'where are your shoes?'
- may hand adult common objects on request.

Key terms

Object permanence The understanding that objects that have disappeared from view still exist, even though a child cannot see them.

Jargons The last stage of babbling, from 10 months and older, when it seems as though children are speaking in whole sentences using their 'own' language.

■ 18 months

Physical

By 18 months, the child:

- can walk alone – with legs far apart
- drops from standing to sitting
- pushes and pulls toys when walking
- can walk downstairs with hand held.

- tries to kick a ball, rolls and throws ball
- squats to pick objects from floor
- assists with dressing and undressing
- can use spoon with increasing skill
- uses delicate pincer grasp for tiny objects
- can build tower of two cubes
- holds crayon in primitive tripod grasp and scribbles
- turns handles
- pulls off shoes.

Social and emotional

The child:

- is becoming more independent
- is joyful and full of fun
- starts toilet training
- is beginning to have tantrums when upset
- has a separate sense of self (egocentric), only concerned with his or her own view of the world
- has little idea of sharing and strong sense of 'mine'
- is more demanding and assertive, emotionally volatile
- expresses rage at being told 'no'
- may have a comforter, such as soft doll or teddy.

Intellectual

The child:

- turns pages of books, several at a time, enjoys picture books and can point to a named object
- points to interesting objects outside
- points to parts of the body
- understands use of everyday objects, for example vacuum cleaner
- helps to undress
- enjoys pretend play, for example talking on the phone.

Communication

The child:

- starts to use first words – six or more recognisable words, understands many more
- echoes prominent or last word in sentences
- tries to join in with nursery rhymes
- responds to simple instructions – 'fetch your shoes', 'shut the door'.

■ 2 years

Physical

By 2 years, the child:

- walks up and down stairs with both feet on one step
- climbs on furniture
- runs and changes direction
- opens, shuts doors and turns handles
- kicks ball without falling
- builds tower of six bricks
- uses spoon for self-feeding
- puts shoes on
- draws circles and dots
- starts to use preferred hand.

Social and emotional

The child:

- enjoys other children's company but reluctant to share toys
- needs clear boundaries and routines
- is able to choose from limited range of options
- may show concern when another child is upset
- engages in parallel play (alongside others)
- remains egocentric
- is becoming emotionally stable, but still prone to mood swings
- is learning to separate from carer for short periods, for example while at nursery
- knows own identity.

Intellectual

The child:

- names and points to parts of the body
- recognises self in mirror
- draws and makes marks
- imitates household tasks
- is extremely curious
- enjoys simple puzzles and building towers.

▲ At 18 months, physical skills are developing rapidly

Communication

The child:

- can link two words together
- uses more than 200 words by 2 years
- makes simple two-word sentences refers to own name, talks to self during play
- uses **telegraphic speech** – using key essential words and missing out connecting words
- has a rapidly expanding vocabulary, including plurals
- holds simple conversations
- enjoys repetition of favourite stories
- counts to ten.

Key term

Telegraphic speech comprises shortened sentences without words such as 'and' and 'the' spoken by children from about 18–24 months, for example 'go walk park'.

■ 3 years

Physical

By 3 years, the child:

- stands and walks on tiptoe
- can kick a ball confidently and throw overhead and catch with arms out
- jumps from low steps
- pedals tricycle
- turns single pages in book
- can copy a circle
- builds bridges with blocks when shown and tall towers
- undoes buttons
- threads large beads.

Social and emotional

The child:

- shows greater social awareness
- will play in twos or threes, sharing ideas
- may have close friends
- engages in a lot of mixed play of the sexes
- is stable and emotionally secure
- is friendly to other children, increasing independence, but still needs support from adults
- fears loss of carers
- has a sense of gender, ethnic and cultural identity
- is less anxious about separation but easily upset.

Intellectual

The child:

- copies circle and cross, draws man with head
- matches two or three primary colours
- can sort into simple categories
- paints with large brush, cuts with scissors
- will talk about paintings
- constantly asks 'why'
- confuses fact and fiction
- is developing role and fantasy play
- remembers songs, rhymes and stories.

▲ At 3 years, a child's fine motor skills are increasingly developed

Communication

The child:

- imitates adult speech
- has an increasing vocabulary
- can listen well if interested
- has a developing use of grammar
- can describe feelings at simple level e.g. happy, sad
- talks to self in play
- can be understood by strangers
- uses short, grammatically correct sentences
- knows parts of body, animals
- is still making errors of tenses.

Patterns of development are also covered in detail in Unit 3, pages 88–115.

Theories of development

Over the years, psychologists have suggested a number of different theories about how and why babies and children develop. Some of these theories have influenced advice and guidance given to parents and carers. It is interesting to look at old childcare books and see the differences in advice on leaving babies to cry, how often they should be played with and whether mothers should go back to work. All these points have been hotly debated in the past.

The general themes of developmental theory that you explored in Unit 3 obviously apply to babies and the under-3s. However, some of them are especially relevant.

■ Bonding, attachment and communication

All babies need to develop close links with at least one important adult within the first year of their life. This is the start of a person's emotional security. John Bowlby (1907–90) became well known for his research findings that if a baby has long separations from their mother in their early years, there would be serious problems for the child in later life. Bowlby's research was critical in the late 1940s in persuading mothers who had been working during the Second World War that they should not go out to work but stay at home to care for their children.

Many researchers followed Bowlby's findings, notably Michael Rutter, and refined Bowlby's theory that close emotional attachments are essential, but not necessarily with the mother, and that babies can make attachments to more than one person.

The first close emotional bond is, however, usually with the baby's mother. Before birth, the baby has been listening to the mother's voice, hearing her heart beat, and generally becoming familiar with the rhythms of the mother. In a normal delivery, the mother often holds the baby while the placenta is being delivered and a breast-feeding mother may start to feed at this point. If there are complications in the birth, every effort is made to ensure that the mother can hold or touch the baby as much as possible, even if the baby has to be in an incubator.

All this helps with the process of bonding, which is strengthened by:

- skin-to-skin contact
- eye-to-eye contact
- familiar sounds of voices
- familiar smells.

It is important for a baby to develop relationships with significant others. This not only allows more flexible caring, but is part of the process of primary socialisation. We cannot learn to develop relationships and mix with people in society generally until we have developed a range of relationships in our early months with different family members and other close carers. Ideally, a baby needs one or more constant caring figures, usually mother and father or grandparents. A good bonding relationship can and does develop with non-family members; you will see this yourself as you progress in your work with babies. If a baby is cared for outside the home, then the carer should not be constantly changing. It is unusual for this to happen, as all child care professionals are aware of the need to encourage the development of close bonds with consistent carers. Many settings now use a key worker system, where one person has the prime responsibility for a child.

Bonding and attachment are also discussed in Unit 1, page 5, and Unit 14, pages 424–30.

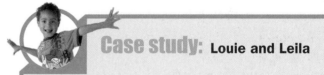

Case study: Louie and Leila

Louie, aged 9 months, attends a day nursery every day from 8.00 a.m. to 6.00 p.m. The baby room is staffed by whoever is available from the main nursery. Louie's mother is concerned because she never seems to see the same person when she drops Louie off or picks him up. Louie seems to be losing interest in nursery and cries or is miserable most of the time.

Leila is also aged 9 months and attends a different nursery from 8 a.m. to 6 p.m. The baby room has its own team of staff, with two key workers responsible for each baby. They are never on duty together, but have a good communication system to inform each other of how the babies are progressing. There is also a meeting once a week for the key workers to discuss 'their' babies. Leila's mother feels confident that she is leaving Leila with the same people all the time and Leila greets her carers with a big smile every morning.

Why do you think Leila and Louie react so differently to their day care?

■ The nature–nurture debate

Many experiments and studies have been carried out, including studies on identical twins who have been separated since birth. After many years of debate, a fairly balanced view is that we do inherit some aspects of development, whilst others are more influenced by our upbringing and environment.

Even our height can be influenced by the quality of our diet and may be affected by illness. Parental involvement and access to learning materials will influence the intellectual achievement of a child.

The nature–nurture debate is also discussed in Unit 3, page 90, and Unit 14, page 404.

Current frameworks for effective practice: Birth to Three Matters

In 2003, the UK government launched Birth to Three Matters to provide a framework to most effectively support children from birth to 3 years. Research has shown that even babies have highly developed learning skills and that the first three years are extremely critical in giving a child the best start in life. The importance of the first three years has been increasingly recognised in the changes to the expectations of childcare provision. It is no longer enough to just provide care for babies and young children; the importance of supporting and enhancing a child's development and learning is firmly embedded now in all provisions from childminders to nurseries. Birth to Three Matters provides information on child development, effective practice, examples of play activities to promote play and learning, guidance on planning and resourcing and meeting diverse needs.

The framework reflects the diversity of types of organised provision for children in this age group and recognises the importance of wider issues including equal opportunities and relationships with parents. All of your work with the under-3s should be shaped by the principles which underpin the Birth to Three Matters framework.

These principles have evolved from the combined experience and wisdom of representative children's organisations, leading childcare writers, experts and practitioners and are as follows:

- Parents and families are central to the well-being of the child.
- Relationships with other people (both adults and children) are of crucial importance in a child's life.
- A relationship with a key person at home and in the setting is essential to young children's well-being.
- Babies and young children are social beings; they are competent learners from birth.
- Learning is a shared process and children learn most effectively when, with the support of a knowledgeable and trusted adult, they are actively involved and interested.
- Caring adults count more than resources and equipment.
- Schedules and routines must flow with the child's needs.
- Children learn when they are given appropriate responsibility, allowed to make errors, decisions and choices, and respected as autonomous and competent learners.
- Children learn by doing rather than by being told.
- Young children are vulnerable. They learn to be independent by having someone they can depend upon.

Theory into practice

As you work through this unit and in your practical experiences, keep referring back to these principles. Tasks in the unit will ask you to apply them in practice. In the meantime, go though the list and try to imagine a child not growing up within the support of these vital principles. What effect might this have?

Observations

Observing the progress in the development of a baby or young child is a fascinating activity and an excellent way to learn about the development of children and their needs. Observation is discussed in detail in Unit 3, pages 127–36.

Observations are also a requirement of the Foundation Stage guidance for children aged 3 to school age and are included in the Birth to Three Matters framework. However, there are a few ground rules that are vitally important to follow to protect the child and yourself:

- Make sure you have a clear understanding of the normal range of development for the child you are observing.
- Remember the wide normal variations that can occur in any child's development.
- Always report any concerns you may think there are about any child's development to your supervisor, never directly to the child's parents.
- Never pass information about a child's development to anyone who does not need it; always go through your supervisor.
- Be sure to keep to the policies and procedures of your placement relating to observations.
- Remember that personal information on children and their parents is subject to the **Data Protection Act** and so is restricted in its distribution.

Key term

The **Data Protection Act** is legislation that protects individuals from material that may be recorded about them or their children. Everyone has the right to see what is recorded – in all written and electronic formats.

Theory into practice

Find out what the Data Protection Act means to your placement. Look it up on the internet and ask your supervisor about the setting's policy.

The term 'observation' can be used in a number of ways. An effective, skilled childcare worker is constantly observing the children they work with. In being observant, you can often identify things that need further investigation or simply note points of development. Observations can be formal or informal.

Informal observation

Case study: Informal observation

Jake is supervising a small group of toddlers. He notices that Ruby, who is 1½ and usually very happy when playing, is very unsettled and keeps crying. He then notices that she seems very flushed. After the session, Jake discusses Ruby with his supervisor. She has noticed that Ruby is not as settled as usual and ate very little lunch. That evening the supervisor has a word with Ruby's dad when he picks her up. He thanks the supervisor for noticing and says they will keep an eye on her at home. The next morning Ruby's parents ring the nursery to say that she is not well and they are taking her to the doctor.

This is an example of Jake and the supervisor making good use of informal observation. Identify the number of points they both noticed through informal observation.

The key points of a formal observation are:

- Observing is spending time watching and recording certain things about a child and then drawing conclusions from that record.
- Observations should be objective.
- Observations should be confidential.

Theory into practice

Explain the following observation techniques, giving examples from your placement where possible:

- checklists, tick charts
  written records/snapshot observations
- time samples
- event samples.

You may need to refer to Unit 3.

Good practice checklist

How to carry out observations

- Always ask your supervisor before carrying out any observation on a child.
- Make sure that parents have consented to observations being carried out on their child.
- Carry out observations and assessments in line with your placement's policy.
- Make sure that you have everything you need to hand.
- Observe children sensitively and without them noticing.
- Write up your observations in a sensitive and non-judgemental way.
- Avoid making any negative judgements about children.
- Make sure that any conclusions are based directly on the observations.
- Share your findings with your supervisor so that they can be passed on to parents.

Assessment activity 35.1

1 Describe the development, including communication, of babies and young children in the first three years of life, building on what you already know from Unit 3.

Think about:

- the different aspects of development
- the sequence and expected pattern of development
- the acceptable range
- current theories, for example the nature–nurture debate
- current frameworks of effective practice, for example Birth to Three Matters. **P1**

2 Outline what needs to be considered when observing babies and children under 3 years. **P2**

3 Now describe in detail how to undertake observations of babies and young children under 3 years. **M1**

4 Identify what can be learned about babies and young children in the first three years of life through observing them. **P3**

5 Justify (give the reasons for) the use of observation of babies and young children in the first three years of life. **D1**

Feeding

Infant feeding

National guidelines relating to the feeding of babies clearly state that breast-feeding is best for babies until they are 6 months old. At 3–4 months, solids may be gradually introduced, avoiding cow's milk, wheat, nuts, eggs, salt and sugar. The debate between breast- and bottle-feeding has raged on for many years. Until modern baby milks were produced, babies who could not be breast-fed had to be fed on cow's milk which is totally unsuitable for babies under 1 year. It was often contaminated and many babies died if they were not breast-fed. It was not until the early 1900s that milk started to be treated to make it free of bacteria and viruses. Modern infant formula milks are now scientifically modified to make them as near to human milk as possible.

■ Advantages of breast-feeding

The main advantages of breast-feeding are that it:

- contains the right amounts of nutrients, at the right temperature, and is always available without risk of contamination
- contains antibodies to boost the immunity gained in the uterus
- is less likely to result in an overweight baby
- helps delay or avoids eczema
- has little additional cost
- helps in the bonding process
- helps the uterus shrink more quickly
- delays the return of the mother's periods.

■ Advantages of bottle-feeding

Although breast-feeding is the ideal way of infant feeding, not all mothers wish to use this method, or they may not be able to breast-feed, for example if they are taking certain prescription medication. There are claims that bottle-feeding has some advantages in comparison to breast-feeding:

- It is obvious how much milk the baby is taking.
- There is no risk of embarrassment with public feeding.
- Other people can feed the baby, such as the father.
- It can be helpful for mothers returning to work.

■ Parental choice

A childcare professional's role in the choice between breast- and bottle-feeding is only to give impartial information if asked, and then support the parents in their choice. The choice about feeding is a personal one for the parents of the baby, with support from midwives, health visitors and doctors.

Breast-feeding is one of the most natural functions of motherhood and when established is an immensely satisfying experience. It can take some time to establish a good feeding pattern and milk supply. Mothers who are breast-feeding need support to ensure they have enough rest and a good diet to promote good milk production.

Mothers who are breast-feeding may need help to find some privacy when feeding their baby. Discreet public feeding is possible, as mothers can usually find a quiet corner away from the public gaze and if some thought is given to clothing it is quite possible to feed a baby without anyone really being aware.

Never suggest or support a suggestion that a mother could use a public toilet to feed. Would you like to have your lunch in such a place? Being informed about breast-feeding and offering support is a role of childcare workers.

Returning to work may need some thought if a baby is being breast-fed. Some enlightened employers are supportive of mothers taking feeding breaks if the baby is near to the place of work. Working mothers can express milk and may use a breast pump. The milk should be kept in a sterilised bottle in the fridge until needed and then warmed and bottle-fed to the baby. Some babies find it very difficult to adapt to taking milk from a rubber teat as it is a very different prospect to a human nipple. You also need to make sure that all the usual hygiene rules related to bottle-feeding are followed to avoid the risk of contamination and infection.

Formula feeds

Current formula infant feeds are almost a replica of breast milk as they are manufactured to match the protein and salts in breast milk. In one important respect, however, formula feeds cannot match breast milk: the antibodies that are passed on from mother to baby in breast milk cannot be replaced in formula milk. However, a well-prepared formula bottle given in a caring environment with close interaction between baby and feeder can be a satisfying experience for both parties.

Poor practice in bottle-feeding can, however, be dangerous and unsatisfying for a baby. Poor hygiene and preparation of bottle feeds can lead to potentially fatal gastro-enteritis. 'Prop' feeding can result in choking, and not stimulating the bond between carer and baby can lead to emotional problems.

Equipment for feeding

Large chemists and baby shops have a wide range of bottles, sterilisers and associated equipment that, if added together, would be very expensive. There are some essentials for formula feeding:

- feeding bottles – up to 12 to allow rotation and advance preparation
- teats with holes of a suitable size to allow milk to flow without choking the baby
- covers for the teats, usually a top for the bottle that allows the teat to be put upside down in the bottle during storage in the fridge

▲ Sterilising equipment

- bottle brush and teat cleaner
- sterilising equipment
- clean surface to prepare feeds
- a clean and safe water supply (especially important in developing countries).

Sterilising the bottles and equipment used in bottle-feeding is essential to kill the bacteria that thrive in warm milk. There is no substitute for sterilising and it must be done after each use of a bottle and teat. The first stage in sterilising is a thorough wash in hot soapy water, paying particular attention to the inside of the teat and the curves and edges of the bottle using a bottle brush. After rinsing, the equipment then needs sterilising.

The methods of sterilising are explained in Unit 2, pages 77–78

Microwaving
Takes about 10 minutes; equipment is sterile for 2–3 hours

Steaming
Takes about 10 minutes; equipment is sterile for up to 3 hours

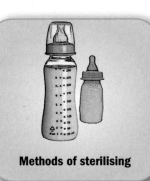

Methods of sterilising

Boiling
Takes at least 5 minutes; tends to damage plastic bottles if used regularly; equipment is sterile for 3 hours

Cold water sterilising
Takes about 30 minutes; equipment is sterile for up to 24 hours

▼ **Principles of safe feeding**

	Action needed	Comments
Environment (kitchen)	Clean, dry worktops No other foodstuffs around Keep pets, etc. from surfaces	Contamination can easily occur due to carelessness
Operator (person preparing feed)	Always wash hands before starting work Do not touch any surface or equipment that will come into contact with milk Avoid touching the head, face, etc. during preparation Carefully read and follow the exact instructions on formula and sterilising solution packets Exact quantities of milk powder and water should be used	Risk of contamination and bacteria Very easy to make a feed that is too strong or too weak as proportions are carefully calculated by the manufacturer
Equipment (bottles, teats, etc.)	All should be assembled before the start of preparation. All bottles, teats, jugs, spoons must be thoroughly cleaned in hot soapy water, rinsed and left fully immersed in sterilising solution for minimum recommended time Formula should be checked as fresh and within date of use on packet Check that the water supply is a safe supply and water is boiled before use	Milk and milk residue is an ideal medium for bacteria to breed Even a tiny amount of residue under a bottle rim can be enough to cause illness in a baby if bacteria multiply Any food stuff deteriorates with age and may cause harm if not within the use-by date Water supplies can carry bacteria that can cause gastro-enteritis. This can kill small babies due to the dehydration caused by vomiting and diarrhoea
Storage	Packets of formula should be kept in a dry cupboard, tops safely and securely closed Bottles should be kept in refrigerator when made, teats covered Bottles should never be left out at room temperature Contents of part-used bottles should be disposed of	All important to prevent contamination and potential gastro-enteritis

Following the common-sense rules of hygiene is the first step on the road to safe feeding. The table above examines the principles of good practice.

Giving a baby a stronger feed is dangerous because the feed will contain too much protein and too many salts; a baby's body cannot cope with this and convulsions and brain damage could occur as the body dehydrates. Too high a concentration of salts can lead to kidney damage. To avoid accidentally making the feed too strong:

- always check the number of scoops of powder that are needed
- only use the scoop provided in the packet
- do not be tempted to use heaped scoops; level off the powder with a plastic knife
- always read and follow the directions on the packet.

Giving the feed

There is no nutritional benefit in warming a bottle feed, but if it is heated to a suitable temperature it will be more enjoyable for the baby.

- Heat the bottle in a commercial bottle warmer or in a jug of water. Never use a microwave oven as there is a serious risk of hot spots in the milk in the bottle that will scald the baby's mouth and digestive tract.
- Check the temperature is correct and not too hot. A test of the temperature should always be carried out (not by having a sample yourself). Your inner wrist is a sensitive area of skin and this should be used for testing purposes. The feed is at the correct temperature if a few drops sprinkled on the inside of your wrist feel comfortable.

- Sit in a comfortable position with the baby. Be sure he or she can see your face and is in close contact. Talk to the baby while you are feeding,
- Make sure the bottle is tilted to ensure the teat is filled with milk – this will prevent air being swallowed with the milk. If the baby swallows a lot of air, the resulting wind and pain will disrupt the feed. However, some air is needed in the bottle as the feed is taken because, as the milk is taken in by the baby, a vacuum (no air) results in the bottle and it can be very difficult for the baby to take the milk in.
- After a few minutes remove the teat from the baby's mouth and allow air into the bottle to prevent a vacuum forming.
- Whenever possible, the baby should be fed by the main carers, so that bonding will take place. Whoever feeds the baby must ensure it is done in a comfortable position that allows for eye-contact and close bodily contact. Talking and smiling to the baby is an important part of the feeding experience.
- Remember that a baby should never be left alone to feed from a bottle that has been propped up, because:
  - there is a high risk of choking
  - the baby is being deprived of important contact with the carer
  - too much air will be taken in.

Extension activity

Work out the cost of bottle-feeding a baby for the first year of life. Think about the cost of formula milk, sterilising equipment and bottles. How do you think this compares to breast-feeding?

Infant feeding is also discussed in Unit 2, pages 68, and 77–79.

Weaning

Weaning is the term used to describe the process of changing a child's feeding from being dependent on milk to eating family foods. A newborn baby does not have the digestive system to cope with solid foods. A baby of 1 year has a more mature system able to cope with different foods. The process of learning to enjoy a wide range of foods can be an easy one or it can be difficult for carers and the baby alike.

Case study: Running late

Jamie has slept in this morning. She is supposed to be meeting her friend in town for a day's shopping and is very late. Her baby is crying, so she rushes down to the kitchen and takes the last bottle of milk out of the fridge. She pops it in the microwave to heat and then props the bottle up with a pillow so that her baby can reach the teat and take her feed while Jamie makes another bottle to take out with her. She puts the kettle on, grabs a bottle from the pile of dirty dishes beside the sink and gives it a quick rinse under the hot tap. She finds the formula but cannot find a measuring spoon so she scoops a few teaspoons of powder into the bottle before adding the boiling water. She quickly packs a couple of nappies and the newly made bottle into a bag before putting the baby into her pram and setting off to meet her friend and have a day out at the shops.

1 **Make a list of all the mistakes that Jamie has made.**

2 **What might happen as a result of these mistakes?**

Theory into practice

There are many fashions related to weaning. Ask your parents and grandparents when they weaned their children and what foods they used, and you will probably receive several different answers. Parents in the UK may say they started their child on baby rice, while parents in Israel may have used avocado pear as a first weaning food.

The important thing to remember about weaning is the purpose of it, which is to safely introduce children into the normal eating patterns of their family by familiarising them with a wide range of new tastes. Trying to rush the process can at best overwhelm a child's taste buds and at worst cause health problems through the use of inappropriate foods.

It is very easy for carers of children to transfer their own food dislikes to them. How difficult is it to feed a baby with something you dislike? Think about your body language and facial expressions if you are in that situation.

■ Starting the weaning process

There are national guidelines relating to the start of weaning and it is a good idea to try to collect some government leaflets from baby clinics to check on the latest guidelines. The UK and Irish Department of Health guidelines of August 2005 recommend that a baby should have nothing but infant milk for the first six months of life. The guidelines recognise that all babies develop at a different rate but advise that it is not a good idea to introduce solid food before they are 20 weeks old because the digestive system and kidneys are too immature to cope.

A baby could thrive very well on milk alone until the age of 12 months but, at this age, the iron stores from birth will be diminishing and the baby will be at risk of becoming anaemic. Leaving the start as late as 12 months could make it difficult for a baby to make the change from a breast or bottle to eating from a spoon.

Within the guidelines, the best judge of when to wean a baby is actually the baby. Babies are ready to start weaning when they:

● are still hungry after feeds
● can sit up
● shows interest in solid food
● pick up food and put it in their mouth
● want to chew.

Sucking the fists is not a sign of being ready for weaning; this is a normal part of development as the baby has found how interesting their hands are. (Neither is it a sign of teething!)

■ Commercial and home-produced weaning food

Nutritionally there is little difference between commercial baby foods in jars or packets and home-produced weaning food. Commercial foods can be expensive, however, and the consistency is often unlike ordinary food. As a result, some parents will only feed a baby home-produced food which is fine, but can be difficult if the family is out for the day or the rest of the family are having a meal that is spicy or otherwise unsuitable. A sensible mix of commercial and home foods is a good compromise. Home-produced weaning foods are nearer in texture and taste to the child's eventual diet, but can take time and effort to prepare.

Theory into practice

Investigate all the different commercial weaning foods available in the shops. How easy do you think it would be to provide similar foods at home?

■ How to start weaning

● Offer the first spoonfuls of a bland, very liquid mix, part way through a milk feed or near the end, when the first pangs of hunger have been satisfied.
● Introduce new tastes gradually. Offer only one new taste a day in the first months of weaning and if a new food is rejected one day, try it again later; it may then be accepted with pleasure.

- Gradually thicken food, eventually mashing it with a fork.
- As the amounts of solid food increases, the amount of milk feed offered should be reduced. By the time a baby is eating three substantial meals of solids a day, milk feeds should be reduced to night-time, with water or fresh juice between meals and at mealtimes.
- As soon as the baby starts trying, let him or her join in feeding, even though everything will fall off the spoon and it will go anywhere but in the mouth.
- Offer finger foods as much as possible, for example lumps of cheese, apple pieces, small sandwiches. (It is no coincidence that a baby is ready to start self-feeding when his or her gross and fine motor skills have reached the stage of sitting up and a pincer grip.)
- A vital piece of equipment at this stage is a sheet of plastic to protect the floor if it is not washable.

A suggested day's menu as a baby progresses towards a normal family diet could be like the one shown below.

Nutritional requirements

The general guidelines of a healthy diet that you looked at in Unit 9 apply to children and babies who are being weaned. However, there are one or two differences until their digestive system is fully mature.

▲ Give babies the opportunity to feed themselves

From 9 months, each day a baby needs:
- 3–4 servings of starchy food
- 3–4 helpings of fruit and vegetables
- 2 servings a day of protein
- vitamin drops until they are 5 years old.

Babies have small tummies and need energy for growth.
- They should have full fat dairy products but no cow's milk as a drink until 1 year old.

▼ Suggested day's menu for 6–12 months+

Time of day	Daily diet 6–9 months	Daily diet 9–12 months	Daily diet 12+ months
On waking	Breast-or bottle-feed	Breast-or bottle-feed	Drink of milk
Breakfast	Baby breakfast cereal with pureed fruit	Porridge made with 90 ml infant/follow-on milk	1 slice of toast, weetabix with milk, well-diluted orange juice
Mid-morning	4 satsuma segments	2 breadsticks and cheese cubes	Carrot sticks and chickpea puree (hummus)
Lunch	3 tbsp broccoli and potato with cheesy sauce, 90 ml infant/follow-on milk, chopped melon pieces	1 hard boiled egg with soldiers, 1 fromage frais, 90 ml water or well-diluted orange juice	Scrambled egg on toast, banana and custard, 90 ml water or well-diluted orange juice
Mid-afternoon	Half a small mashed banana or mango, water as a drink	Toast fingers, water as a drink	90 ml fruit smoothie, 1 pitta bread or bread with cheese or ham
Tea	Tomato sauce with mince and pasta shapes, 90 ml follow-on milk, 1 small yogurt	Shepherd's pie with meat or lentils, broccoli, carrots, 1 banana, water or juice	Fish pie and vegetables, seedless grapes or stewed fruit, water or juice
Evening	Breast-or bottle-feed	Breast-or bottle-feed	Breast-feed or milk

- Never give a child nuts until the age of 5 years as there is a strong risk of allergy and also of choking.
- Avoid products containing wheat until at least 6 months of age. Some babies are allergic to the gluten in wheat, resulting in coeliac disease.
- Eggs should be well cooked and only offered after 6 months.
- Citrus food and shell fish should not be given before 6 months.
- Never add any salt at all and avoid salty products until 12 months.
- Avoid honey, soft and blue cheese until 12 months.

Feeding problems

It is rare for a child to make the transition to everyday family meals without a few tears and tantrums on the way. Many children are seen to have a food problem at some time. The approach that carers take is an important part of dealing with this.

Refusing food at a designated mealtime is not a problem. Any child who has food offered in a relaxed, thoughtful manner will eat as much as he or she needs if opportunities are provided. This continues throughout childhood; eating and not eating only become a problem if the child's carers see them as a problem. Babies have every right not to eat if they do not feel hungry, in the same way as you have. Why would a toddler want to sit down and eat when he or she is in the middle of an exciting play activity or investigating what is in the cupboard in the hallway? Sometimes a child is simply too busy, too tired or still full from the last meal to want to eat. Simply removing the plate and letting the child go back to play is the best approach.

Extension activity

Many people who are overweight or suffer from eating problems, such as anorexia or bulimia, remember mealtimes as a battle zone in childhood. Research some of the literature on eating disorders for examples.

Supporting parents' wishes

Feeding a baby can be a difficult and emotional topic for parents. Many people see a thriving child as the sign of 'good' parenting. A child who does not eat well could be regarded as not being cared for properly.

We develop our attitudes to food from a very early age, from our parents and our own experiences. Parents can become upset about what their child is or is not eating and many parents come under pressure from grandparents. Despite being aware of the latest healthy diet issues, they may find it hard not to follow their own parents' suggestions. You may need to offer support to parents in encouraging healthy eating in their babies. However, it is important to remember that parents are responsible for their child's diet.

Theory into practice

Survey the menus of all the babies at your placement. Do they all eat the standard menu of the nursery? If they do, find out what provision there is for following parents' wishes where they have different requirements for their child's diet. How would the nursery support those parents?

- Cultural variations should always be respected when you are designing menus for young children.
- Always avoid offering 'forbidden' foods, such as pork to Muslims or meat to vegetarians.
- Always follow instructions about children's allergies to certain foods as failing to do so could cause a child to die. Remember that the allergen could be hidden in a seemingly innocent food so you must always read food labels!

For more information on special diets, food preferences and food intolerances, see Unit 11, pages 381–83 and 388–91.

Routine care

Babies and children under 3 years need help with their personal hygiene including:

- washing and dressing
- care of the skin
- care of hair
- care of teeth
- changing nappies
- help with toilet training.

At birth a baby may not like being disturbed and changed, but by the age of 3 a young child will be doing much of the task involved for themselves with minimal support from adults. It is important to respond to the individual child in the way you handle them, bearing in mind the important points of good practice.

Good practice checklist

- Always be gentle when changing a baby, think about the way their limbs move and always lift them firmly under the arms using both hands.
- Always support the head according to the baby's stage of development.
- Keep undressing and handling for very young babies to a minimum.
- Encourage older babies to 'help' with dressing by pushing arms through sleeves.
- Remember that even young babies require attention to their dignity and privacy during changing.
- Make sure you are respecting parental wishes at all times with regard to lotions, clothes, etc.
- Always be sure you have everything you need before starting any task.
- Never leave a baby alone on a changing surface; ask someone else to fetch something you need.

It is unlikely that you would be in a situation of bathing a baby in your placement as bathing is usually done at home. However, babies and young children need frequent washing as it can be very dirty work being a baby.

A baby's skin can very easily become sore as they have very sensitive skin. Even with the highest standard of care, babies can get rashes or sore spots.

Good practice checklist

Care of skin

The key principles for caring for baby's skin are as follows:

- Hands and faces must be cleaned after feeds.
- Never share cleaning cloths between children.
- Always carefully dry the skin.
- Nappy areas must be cleaned regularly, especially when changing a dirty nappy.
- Skin creases, for example armpits, neck, groin, need care to keep dry.
- Avoid the use of perfumed products that can irritate sensitive skins.
- Use creams, etc. as advised by parents.
- Never poke around in a child's ears with cotton buds; just clean around the outside with cotton wool if necessary.
- Baby boys' foreskins should be left alone and they should not be pulled back at this age.

Washing and changing a baby is a good opportunity to notice any skin problems. Some of the common ones are shown in the following table.

▼ Common skin problems

Problem	Description	Cause	Treatment
Sweat rash (milaria)	Rash of small red spots on face and chest	Overheating Immature sweat glands	Cool child down by removing clothes Use cotton next to skin and avoid synthetic fibres Avoid overheating with clothes and room heating
Cradle cap	Yellow/brown crusting on the scalp, particularly on anterior fontanelle (soft spot)	Build-up of sebum	Soften with olive oil or baby shampoo and rinse well. Special shampoos are also available
Chafing	Soreness in body creases, for example neck, groin and armpits	Insufficient washing and drying of skin Excessive sweating	Prevent by good skin care, especially in the neck area due to baby dribbling. Apply mild cream, for example zinc and castor oil
Eczema	Sore red rash, may affect face or any part of the body, particularly skin folds. Can be very severe, with bleeding and weeping due to scratching	Usually an allergic response, possibly to cows' milk or detergents	Requires medical treatment Avoid soap and using bio detergents for washing clothes Keep nails short to stop scratching Use emulsifiers in the bath Breast-feeding helps to lessen severity and delay onset

Dressing

Parents will have provided the clothes for babies in your care but there a few basic points about baby clothes that are important to remember:

- Natural fibres are more comfortable to wear as they absorb perspiration.
- Two or three thin layers of clothing are better than one very thick layer. Clothing can then be adjusted to suit the temperature.
- Overheating can be dangerous for a baby.
- Clothes that are machine washable are easier to care for.
- Clothes should be loose and easy to put on and take off.
- Avoid ribbons and cords that could easily cut off the circulation around a finger or neck.
- All materials should be flame resistant.
- Care should be taken with clothes that have feet in them, for example stretch 'babygro' suits. It is important to check frequently that there is enough room for the baby's feet to move as wearing too tight a suit will damage the soft, growing bones of the feet.

Hair care

Babies have very fine hair and if it is fairly long it can tangle easily and need careful brushing. As they grow and start to eat solids, food can easily get mixed up in

their hair in which case it needs careful sponging out.

If you need to brush a baby's hair, ensure you use a soft brush which must be only used for that baby.

Some cultural groups have specific requirements for hair care. For example, many African-Caribbean babies have their hair braided into plaits that stay intact during washing.

Theory into practice

Find out about any particular hair styles and care that apply to children in your placement.

Care of teeth

Teething is a big event in the development of a baby. The arrival of a baby's first tooth is often a cause for celebration but also of discomfort for some babies.

The usual pattern of the arrival of teeth is:

- bottom front teeth at around 4–7 months
- two middle top teeth
- teeth along the sides from front to back
- second molars at the back at around age 12 months.

By the age of 3, most children have a full set of 20 baby teeth which remain until the second teeth start to appear at around the age of 6 years.

Teeth need careful care even before they start to appear. Good care of the teeth includes:

- avoiding sweet drinks in bottles and soothers
- limiting the amount of fruit juices as they contain acid that can damage the teeth
- encouraging children to drink plain water
- avoiding foods with sugar

Case study: Dental health

Despite significant improvement since 1983, dental decay is one of the most widespread diseases amongst children in the UK – occurring five times more frequently than asthma.

In the 2003 Children's Dental Health Survey (a ten-yearly report commissioned by the four UK Health Departments) results showed:

- a decrease in the average number of filled primary teeth in both 5- and 8-year-olds from 0.5 teeth in 1983, to 0.3 teeth in 1993 and 0.2 teeth in 2003 in 5 year-olds and from 1.2 teeth in 1983 to 0.7 teeth in 1993 and 0.5 teeth in 2003 in 8-year-olds
- at age 5, 79 per cent of children had visited the dentist but had not an extraction or filling, 16 per cent had received an extraction or filling, and 6 per cent had never visited the dentist
- 31 per cent of 5-year-olds in 2003 had first visited the dentist before the age of 2 years compared with 7 per cent in 1983.
- among children from social classes IV and V (see Unit 6, page 224), 13 per cent of 5-year-olds had never visited the dentist compared with 2 per cent of children from social classes I, II and III non-manual.

1 If you can, find out how many children in your placement have been to the dentist.

2 Of these how many have had a filling or a tooth out?

3 Why do you think that dental health appears to be improving in young children?

- wiping gums before teeth appear with a piece of gauze after feeding
- brushing teeth as soon as they appear with a soft brush twice a day
- only using a very small pea-size amount of toothpaste under supervision to avoid swallowing.

▲ Teeth should be brushed with a soft brush twice a day

Nappy changing

When William Cadogen was writing about childcare in 1748, he suggested babies should be changed just once a day!

Disposable nappies have taken over from terry nappies in the past 20 years, with the result that millions of dirty paper and plastic nappies must be destroyed daily. Disposable nappies are convenient as they do not require washing or carrying around if you are out, but they are very expensive and present society with the big problem of disposal. A move back to using terry nappies is slowly gaining ground. You may find yourself caring for a baby who uses them, so being able to change one is a useful skill.

The best way to learn the mechanics of changing a nappy is to watch a competent person. The folding of terry nappies is almost an art form and there are many ways to do it depending on the size and sex of the baby. This is one of their advantages as the nappy can be folded to be thickest at the position of urination. The same sized terry serves a tiny 3 kg baby and a bouncing 2-year-old. They need to be covered with some form of plastic outer to prevent wetness coming through and are often used with a thin paper lining to make the disposal of faeces easier. There are also tailored varieties of terry nappies available. Disposable nappies come in many different sizes and shapes with a range of special compounds to absorb wetness, built-in cream to prevent soreness, etc.

Theory into practice

- Have a look at the range of nappies used by babies in your placement. Are they all disposable or are some parents using terry nappies of some sort?
- Research the pros and cons of parents using terry or disposable nappies for their child. Consider the cost, convenience and environmental impact.

Nappy rash

Nappy rash appears as a red, sore area over the buttocks. In severe cases it can look like chafing. Sometimes a baby can develop thrush on the buttocks; this can be seen as small outbreaks of spot-type lesions away from the main red area. Medical advice is needed to deal with a nappy rash caused by thrush.

A barrier cream applied to the napkin area is useful to prevent nappy rash and petroleum jelly is a good standby. There are many different creams on the market, all claiming efficiency, but few babies will reach the age of 2 without having a nappy rash.

The first defence to prevent nappy rash is to ensure a baby does not spend too long in a wet nappy and certainly never to leave a baby in a wet and dirty nappy. Applying a barrier cream is a second defence. All babies will benefit from spending some time each day without a nappy on. A warm room and a covered mat on the floor are a suitable place to let the child have time without a nappy.

Good practice checklist

Changing a nappy

The following procedure for changing a nappy is recommended.

1. Wash your hands.
2. Collect all your equipment: nappy, water, soap, cotton wool or baby wipes, cream, changing mat, bucket or bag for the dirty nappy.
3. After removing the nappy, clean the baby's bottom. If the nappy is a dirty one this will need greater care than if the nappy is wet. Using clean water is fine, but baby wipes contain a solution to neutralise ammonia and so help to prevent nappy rash.
4. When cleaning female babies, always clean from front to back to avoid introducing infection into the vagina. With boys, try to avoid soiling the foreskin area.
5. Apply a protective barrier cream if used. Be careful not to get cream on the adhesive fixings of a disposable nappy; if you do they will not stick.
6. Put the nappy on, being very careful with nappy pins if used, and dress the baby.
7. Dispose of the soiled nappy. Roll it up and put it into a nappy sack if disposable. If it is a terry nappy, dispose of the paper liner and put the nappy into a bucket of sterilising solution.
8. Wash your hands.

Always wear gloves and follow the policy of the setting. Terry nappies should be washed – after soaking in solution – at a temperature of at least 60°C and in non-biological powder. They should be rinsed thoroughly.

Toilet training

Children are not in nappies forever. As a child's body develops, they start (around 18–24 months) to become aware when their bowels and bladder are full and need emptying. This is the ideal time to start toilet training.

Theory into practice

Read about the physiology of bladder control. Why isn't it possible to potty train a child under the age of 18–24 months? You could start by looking at Unit 2, page 76.

There is often great pressure on parents to toilet train children as soon as possible, but trying to get a child to use the toilet too early can lead to many problems. Sometimes there almost seems to be a 'race' between parents to see whose child is 'dry' earliest. Early years settings too can often inadvertently put pressure on parents by admission policies, which only allow children over 3 who are toilet trained to come to the setting.

Theory into practice

Does your placement allow children over a certain age who are not toilet trained to attend? How do they support children and parents with toilet training?

Remember these points when helping children with their toilet training:

- Only start when the child is ready – this varies with every child.
- Toilet training takes time, for example it can take three months for the child to get the idea and then this will still only be daytime success.
- Girls appear to be easier to toilet train than boys, but no one really knows why.

A child is ready to start toilet training when:

- the child begins to have bowel movements more regularly and often at predictable times, for example in the morning after breakfast
- the child can try to pull pants up and down and shows an interest in wearing pants rather than nappies
- there are signs of awareness that a bowel movement is happening such as grunting, squatting, telling you, etc. The child has words for stool and urine such as 'poo' and 'wee' or 'wee wee,' etc. (It is helpful to find out what words the family uses for these bodily functions so that a child with minimal language can be readily understood.)
- toddlers begin to show that they understand the feelings they have in their bodies which mean they need to 'go'. Over time they will be able to signal or tell you that they need the potty or the toilet. In the early stages, signals such as the child holding him or herself in the groin area, wriggling, looking uncomfortable or pulling at clothing may all be letting you know that the child is aware of different sensations
- the child may dislike the feeling of being in a dirty nappy and nappies can be dry for a few hours at a time.

It is important that a child is starting to want to be independent and do things for him or herself. Being able to manage bodily functions is a huge step towards becoming independent. The child must also be able to physically walk and sit down safely and comfortably. This may seem obvious but these are all skills that have to be learned.

Extension activity

At one time parents were encouraged to put babies as young as two weeks old on a potty to try to turn the reflex post-feed bowel emptying into a habit! Why do you think this was not a good idea?

There are some times in a toddler's life when it is not a good idea to try toilet training:

- if the family is moving house
- at the time of arrival of a new baby
- changes in parental relationships
- illness
- changes in care settings or even carers.

Toilet training requires a lot of learning and effort on the part of the child, so it is better not to ask them to cope with too many new things at once.

Good practice checklist

Toilet training

- Parents' wishes should be followed to make sure there is consistency between home and setting.
- Take things slowly. Some children become dry during the day very quickly and others take much longer, so be patient.
- Do praise the child when successful but do not make such a fuss that the child begins to become anxious and fretful.
- Do not make a fuss if a child has an 'accident'. Toilet training like any other skill needs lots of practice so 'accidents' are bound to happen. Never make a child feel stupid or 'bad' if they wet or mess their pants.
- Don't put pressure on the child – slow and steady is the rule, and be guided by the child's pace. If the child starts to appear anxious or worried, don't persist.
- Gentle encouragement, stories, songs and fun potties or using the toilet with specially adapted seats and steps are all good ideas, so long as the child does not see going to the toilet as a 'performance' which must be achieved at all costs.

Care routines are also discussed in Unit 2, page 74.

Hygiene, health and safety

Babies and young children are vulnerable and need protection. There are some basic, essential rules which should always be followed when working with any child, but are particularly important with babies.

Good practice checklist

Working with babies and young children

- Always wash your hands:
  - before picking up a baby
  - before preparing or giving feeds
  - after changing a baby
  - after taking older children or yourself to the toilet
  - after playing with pets.
- Poor attention to hygiene and safety can be serious:
  - Never reuse a partly finished bottle of feed.
  - Never leave a bottle of feed out at room temperature.
  - Always keep bottle teats covered when not in use.
  - Always test the temperature of a bottle feed – check it on the back of your hand.
  - Do not allow other children or pets to touch spoons or dishes that are for a baby's food.
  - Never prop feed a baby, that is, leave a baby in a pram or seat with the bottle propped up on a pillow, etc.
  - Never thicken a baby's bottle with rice or rusk otherwise babies may choke.
  - Always supervise an older baby when eating, particularly hard foods such as rusks or apple.
  - Never give a child anything containing a food product they are allergic to.
- Always remember that young children, and babies in particular, have no sense of danger. They need protecting from:
  - animals, even family pets
  - dangers from heat, household objects, etc.
  - falls as they become more mobile; a baby should never be left alone on a surface above ground level
  - other children who may injure them through exuberance or jealousy.
- Avoid exposing babies to known infections, although this is not always easy, as many conditions are infectious before symptoms appear.
- Always put a baby to sleep on his or her back, with the feet at the bottom of the cot, and use blankets that can be tucked in and will not billow over the face. This will help to prevent sudden infant death syndrome (cot death).
- Never smoke in a room where a baby may be cared for or anywhere near to a baby or child. Apart from the risks associated with passive smoking, the effect of smoking by a baby's carers is a high risk factor involved in sudden infant death syndrome.

Theory into practice

What policies and procedures are in your placement to protect babies and young children?

Physical signs of illness

Babies can become ill very quickly. Minor symptoms that an adult would not worry about can rapidly cause serious illness or death in a baby. If you are ever worried about a baby's health, speak to your supervisor as a matter of urgency.

Appropriate response

Some conditions need urgent medical help by dialling 999 for an ambulance:

- stopping breathing or going blue
- not responding, floppy or glazed expression
- cannot be woken
- having a fit or convulsion
- vomiting with a fever and/or diarrhoea
- any injury
- unusual or high pitched crying
- difficulty in breathing.

Babies are prone to many other types of health problems that can cause concern to parents and carers. If a carer is concerned, medical help or advice should be sought from the family doctor or through phoning NHS Direct

or taking the child to an NHS Walk in Centre. This applies to the following:

- fever with a headache or stiff neck
- fever that does not settle
- earache or discharge from ears
- pain in the head
- vomiting for more than 12 hours
- refusing several feeds
- any blood in the faeces
- painful urinating or blood
- any bad smelling discharge
- abdominal pain
- cuts or scrapes that ooze pus or are red and inflamed
- sudden rashes or large areas of blisters
- sore throat causing difficulty swallowing.

Always seek help if you are worried by letting your supervisor know in the first instance. Medical staff would far rather see a baby unnecessarily than risk a tragedy.

For signs and symptoms of some common childhood illnesses, see Unit 2, page 57.

Assessment activity 35.2

1 Describe all aspects of the feeding and routine care of babies and young children under 3 years. **P4**

2 Explain how babies and young children under 3 years should be fed and cared for safely. **M2**

Play activities

It is never too early to learn. Babies and young children benefit from new experiences and learn through a variety of activities, interaction with people and by exploring the world around them.

Activities for different aspects of learning and development

If you think about the four areas for a child's learning, growth and development as defined by Birth to Three Matters, you have a good guide to the type of activities you can use to encourage learning and development in babies and young children:

- a strong child
- a skilful communicator
- a competent learner
- a healthy child.

■ A strong child

Between the ages of birth and 3, a child finds out who they are, what they like and what they can do. They experiment with different ways of relating to those around them and need to be recognised and valued.

Play and practical activities include:

- providing a variety of mirrors in different places to help babies explore what they look like and who they are
- letting children make decisions about how and where to display their paintings or allow them to select which toys to play with
- using different voices to tell stories and getting children to join in wherever possible, using puppets or soft toys
- providing dressing-up clothes and materials that help children find out what it feels like to be someone else
- providing experiences that involve using all the senses, such as relaxing music, soft lighting and pleasant smells.

Encouragement and support help children develop emotionally and respond to successes and challenges.

■ A skilful communicator

As a child grows, they become increasingly sociable, learn to communicate effectively, understand others and make choices.

Play and practical activities include:

- role playing and dressing up, visits to parks, shops, libraries, encouraging children to take on roles, meet others and express feelings and thoughts
- listening to tapes of rhymes and stories, spoken words; some that require children to respond, others that engage them to listen
- responding to what children show they're interested in and want to do by providing activities, stories and games
- providing opportunities for babies to make choices, for example which spoon to choose, which bib to wear, the size of paintbrush to use, whether to go outdoors or stay in.

■ A competent learner

Drawings, words and imaginative play encourage a child to explore and develop their creativity. Play and practical activities include:

- resources for babies to play with, for example pots and pans, wooden blocks, soft toys
- diaries of photographs with children to record an important occasion such as visiting a special place
- opportunities to play with sand, water and play dough
- collections of everyday objects such as wooden pegs, spoons, pans, corks, cones and boxes that can be safely explored alone, shared with adults or other children.

■ A healthy child

As a child grows they learn to express feelings and cope with new situations. A child develops physical skills and learns about their body. They also learn about boundaries, rules and asking for help.

Play and practical activities include:

- stories, pictures and puppets which allow children to experience and talk about feelings

- a consistent approach when responding to challenging behaviour such as scratching and biting
- non-specific play materials such as boxes and blankets so that play can move in different directions.

Activities for different age groupings

The four age groupings in Birth to Three Matters are also useful to think about:

- heads up, lookers and communicators (0–8 months)
- sitters, standers and explorers (8–18 months)
- movers, shakers and players (18–24 months)
- walkers, talkers and pretenders (24–36 months).

Some activities are difficult to classify as supporting only one aspect of development but many will have a key focus and it is worth trying to balance the activities throughout a period of time. Look at the tables below.

▲ Early play

▼ Activities for heads up, lookers and communicators (0–8 months)

Aspect of development	Suggested activities
Motor development	Time to enjoy freedom for kicking in the bath or on a changing mat without a nappy Playing with hands and feet whilst changing or washing Noisy paper to kick against Finger games, for example 'This little piggy'
Hand–eye co-ordination	Mobiles hung over cot, chair, changing mat Objects to hold and look at with a range of textures
Social and emotional	Cuddles
Intellectual including creative skills	Brightly coloured pictures and objects Watching trees in the wind
Language and communication	Singing and talking to baby Imitating a baby's noises and expressions Sound-making toys such as rattles Songs and movement

▼ Activities for sitters, standers and explorers (8–18 months)

Aspect of development	Suggested activities
Motor development	Stacking and nesting toys Playing ball New experiences using the body, for example swimming Encouraging mobility by putting toys slightly out of reach Push and pull toys, toys that make sounds or pop up when a button is pressed, etc.
Hand–eye co-ordination	Mirrors Building stacks and knocking them down using toy bricks, boxes
Social and emotional	Household opportunities, for example pots and pans, boxes, cans Games cleaning teeth, brushing hair Outdoor trips to the park, shops, to see the horses
Intellectual including creative skills	Great enjoyment of water play, for example in the bath with toys, in small washing-up bowl A treasure box made from a strong cardboard box with changing items aimed at different senses Large, easy-to-hold crayons with big sheets of card to scribble on Books with bright pictures to look at Simple hide and seek with increasing difficulty
Language and communication	Action songs, for example 'The wheels on the bus' Constant communication

▼ **Activities for movers, shakers and players (18–24 months)**

Aspect of development	Suggested activities
Motor development	Blowing bubbles and blowing out candles, riding toys
Hand–eye co-ordination	Music and rhythm toys including 'home made' as well as bought instruments, music boxes and music tapes Peg boards and work benches
Social and emotional	'Grown-up' items such as keys, pens, bags and hats of all kinds Games that include getting, hiding and retrieving objects Make-believe games and resources to support fantasy play, such as materials from different cultures, dressing-up clothes, props such as puppets, etc.
Intellectual including creative skills	Show and label pictures – put the pictures in context Art supplies for mark-making, painting, play dough or clay
Language and communication	Talking about what is happening now and what happened this morning, yesterday, what you might do together tomorrow Talking about the child's day-to-day experience such as 'what did you have for lunch today?' Reading and talking about books or picture-books with repeated words, rhymes and phrases that a toddler can remember and will want time after time Pretend play such as having a conversation on a toy phone Talk to the child about the marks they make and the colours they may have used Point to familiar written words that occur naturally such as signs on doors, or when outside or on an outing Reading, singing, rhymes, clapping hands, etc.

▼ **Activities for walkers, talkers and pretenders (24–36 months)**

Aspect of development	Suggested activities
Social and emotional	Fantasy or imaginative play, for example pretending to be someone else either in the child's family or someone from a TV series or film
Intellectual, including creative skills	Dressing up with a supply of materials such as hats, pieces of material and bags

Even a young baby will have preferences for some activities rather than others. It is important to observe the response to an activity and adapt or change it if necessary.

Observations of carers with young babies shows that boys are often handled much more firmly than girls and have the opportunity for more 'rough and tumble' play than their sisters! The setting of ideas and views is also rapidly developing at this age. Think carefully about avoiding stereotyping activities, even for young babies. Do not think in terms of boys' or girls' activities.

Giving praise, support and encouragement

All the basic principles of encouragement and supporting the building of self-esteem apply to young babies as well as older children. Always remember during play to praise, support and encourage.

▲ Remember to give praise and encouragement

Babies and young children, unless actively discouraged by adults or not given appropriate opportunities to explore their surroundings, are curious about everything. Motivation is not a problem. However, the role of adults is to provide safe opportunities for babies and young children and to give praise and encouragement so that their positive attitude remains. They will then continue to grow and develop in the best way they can.

Theory into practice

Listen to most adults with a baby or young child. When any degree of a new skill is shown, the adult will usually exclaim something on the lines of, 'Well done, aren't you clever!' to which the baby laughs and does it again. This is an excellent example of learning through reinforcement!

In your placement, notice what forms of encouragement are given to children.

Links with development

During any developmental phase, you will want to encourage children while they are 'practising' a new skill and also help them to move on when they seem to have mastered the skill. For example, when they learn to walk they will have to practise a great deal before they can confidently walk away on their own. Children need practice and support in order to progress.

New and challenging activities

Everyone needs some challenge, and babies and young children are no different. A challenging activity is one that is just a little bit more difficult than what the child is able to do at any one time. Activities that are challenging help to extend a child's knowledge or skills, in other words to fulfil more of the child's possible potential. The key factors that help babies and young children achieve more of their developmental potential are:

- to be given activities, which 'stretch' their current knowledge or skills a little further
- to be motivated to try something new

- to be encouraged by adults
- to receive praise and encouragement
- to be successful through their own efforts.

Placing an attractive toy just out of reach can encourage the newly crawling baby to make an extra effort, as can simply getting to the child's 'floor level' and encouraging the child to come to you. The important thing is to observe, to find out what interests the child and to find out what development stage the child may be reaching so that you can support the child in the best way possible.

Procedures and practice

Babies and young children need to be kept safe while they are learning all their new skills of rolling, crawling, pulling to stand, etc. There will be a health and safety policy in your placement and you must be aware of this. You must also make sure that you understand the potential risks in your environment.

For information on how to carry out a risk assessment, see Unit 2, page 45.

Special care is needed when babies start to crawl or shuffle. Just imagine, for around eight months or so they have been limited to looking at things in sight or reliant on others to bring things to them. All of a sudden they can move and reach all those interesting looking objects. A baby does not know that many of them may injure and hurt.

Theory into practice

- Do you know where to find your setting's health and safety policy? Are there any special requirements for the care of young babies?
- Look around the rooms in your placement. Can you spot any potential danger areas? For example, are doors kept free from any obstacles? Are there any safety issues concerning plugs, wires, where art materials are stored, etc?

You should, as always, make sure that any activities you are involved with follow your placements plans and that you check them with your supervisor.

For more about play, see Unit 7, Children's Learning Activities and Play.

Assessment activity 35.3

1 Identify and choose five play activities to support different aspects of learning and development. These areas of development and learning need to include the following:
   - gross and fine motor development
   - hand–eye co-ordination
   - language development through listening and responding

   - emotional expression and social competence
   - intellectual skills and understanding
   - imagination and creative skills.

2 Explain (describe in detail) what is meant by challenge in play activities.

35.4 How to communicate with babies and children under 3, interpret their needs and respond to them

Development of language and responding to children

Babies need their carers to help them survive – without carers to feed them, change them, keep them warm and safe and provide them with bodily contact, babies would not survive very long. To make sure their carers know they need something, babies need to communicate. Babies' first vocal communication is crying. The pitch seems to be particularly useful for attracting the attention of adults who (usually) quickly go to find out what is wrong, soothe and comfort. As a result of this, babies begin to make relationships with their carers. Babies learn about the world through what their carers do and the opportunities they give to babies to look at and feel objects.

Children all over the world develop most of their communication skills by the time they are 3 or 4 years old. When they start school, children can vary speech to suit the social occasion, know the meaning and pronunciation of thousands of words and use correct grammatical formats. So how does this amazing process take place?

At birth, a baby's brain and senses are programmed for the task of acquiring language. Babies can hear before birth – they respond to noises whilst in the uterus.

Early language

A child's first words usually start around the time they take their first steps. This is the same all over the world in all societies. The period before a baby starts to use words is called the preverbal stage – they are finding out how to communicate long before they say their first words. This is through:

- gazing into the eyes of carers
- being sensitive to the emotional tones around them
- 'turn taking' in conversation by gurgles and other sounds
- making their needs known by crying, responding, etc.
- babbling which later blends into early speech.

Talking and interacting with babies and young children helps them to socialise, to get to know other people and to learn about themselves. Babies learn from the way other people behave. Some researchers have shown that babies as young as 42 minutes can imitate someone sticking out their tongue. These babies watch and then, with a bit of effort, stick out their tongues too!

It is very upsetting for babies if the adult they are with does not talk to them, turns away from them, pays attention to someone else and so on. They do not know the reasons and work very hard to try to get the adult's attention.

Language development

Language development requires children to master four sub-systems of language which are

- *phonology* – the ability to understand and produce speech sounds
- *semantics* – the ability to understand words and the different combinations of words
- *grammar* – the ability to understand the rules by which words are arranged into sentences and the rules by which words can indicate tense and gender
- *pragmatics* – the ability to understand the rules of effective communication such as turn-taking, initiating and ending conversations.

There are two key theories of language development which have parallels with theories for other forms of social development:

- *Behaviourist theories* These stress that the conditioning and imitation a child is exposed to is important in language development.
- *Nativist or inherent theories* Noam Chomsky's theory of language is that it is a human-specific skill that develops as a result of an inbuilt language acquisition device.

For more about this, see Unit 18, page 482.

Case study: Language – nature or nurture?

Staff at Jason's (age 4) nursery were puzzled by the amount of bad language that he used. Almost every other word was an obscenity. His grandmother who brought him to nursery seemed such a mild person. One day when she finished work early Jason's mum collected him. Every other word was an obscenity, and staff could not help but suppress a smile when she commented that she could not understand why Jason used such bad language

Children whose first language is not English usually learn to speak English and adopt the regional accent where they learn the language. Liesel, age 3, belongs to a dual-nationality family. Her mother is from Germany, her father from England. Leisel is fluent in both German and English and happily chatters to her German grandparents on the phone. Her mother has always spoken to her in German and her father speaks to her in English.

1 How do you think these children have learned their language skills?

2 Why do you think that children without hearing have difficulty learning to talk and yet babble and vocalise the same as other babies in their early months?

Theory into practice

Look at the table opposite outlining the sequence (order of) of language development from birth. What do you think the most important thing is that you can do to support communication at each of the stages?

▼ The sequence of language development

Age	Language and communication skills
Pre-linguistic or pre-verbal stage	**Birth to 12 months**
Birth–4 weeks	Cries when basic needs require attention – hunger, tiredness, distress
1 month	'Freezes' when a bell is rung gently close to the ear, moves head towards the sound Stops crying at sound of human voice (unless very upset) Coos in response to carer's talk
3 months	Becomes quiet and turns head towards sound of rattle near head Vocalises when spoken to and when alone
6 months	Makes sing-song vowel sounds, for example 'aah-aah', 'goo'. Laughs and chuckles and squeals aloud in play Responds differently to different tones of voice. Starting to respond to noises out of sight with correct visual response
9 months	Vocalises for communication, shouts for attention Babbles loudly and tunefully – dual syllables in long strings, for example 'dad-dad', 'baba', 'mam-mam' Imitates adult vocal sounds, for example coughs, smacking lips. Understands 'no' and 'bye-bye' Instant response to hearing test conducted 1 m behind child, out of sight
1 year	Knows own name Jargons loudly in 'conversations', includes most vowels sounds Understands about 20 words in context, for example 'cup', 'dog', 'dinner', and understands simple messages, for example 'clap hands', 'where are your shoes?'
Linguistic stage	**12 months onwards**
12–18 months	First words appear – uses 6–20 recognisable words, understands many more Echoes prominent or last word in sentences Tries to join in with nursery rhymes Responds to simple instructions – 'fetch your shoes', 'shut the door'
18–24 months	Two words linked together Uses more than 200 words by 2 years Makes simple 2-word sentences. Refers to own name, talks to self during play Telegraphic speech – using key essential words – missing out connecting words
2–3 years	Rapidly expanding vocabulary, including plurals Holds simple conversations Enjoys repetition of favourite stories Counts to 10

Theory into practice

Watch a parent or a colleague talking to a young baby. Notice how the adult gives the baby time to 'reply' and so keep up a conversation.

Early communication ▶

Good practice checklist

Supporting the development of communication

- Always give a baby your full attention or include them in conversations. Conversations with colleagues can wait until later.
- Watch, listen and respond to the baby.
- Talk aloud to the baby as you are doing something.
- Use simple gestures to support what you are saying.
- Make sure that the tone of your voice, the rhythm (how 'up and down' your voice goes), the pitch (how high or low) and the tempo (how quickly or slowly you speak) change as you speak to make you interesting and help the baby work out sounds.
- Talk and sing to and with the baby.
- Make sure that your facial expression matches your mood. Babies will look at your face and see a smile or a frown or a blank expression and they will sense your mood and respond to it. (Research has shown that babies show distress or worry when their normally responsive carer suddenly shows a very still or blank face.)
- Pay attention to what a baby is 'saying' to you by their responses.
- Take time to let the baby respond to you – they learn about turn-taking in the two-way 'talking' and listening that they will do with a partner.
- Copying what a baby does helps to establish a 'dialogue' so that they can imitate and be imitated.
- Help an older baby or child to learn about the names of objects, colours, etc. by naming them in a natural way, for example, 'Oh, look at the black dog/the red bus', and so on.
- Repeat an older child's phrases without correcting to both check that you understand and to help the child hear the usual way of sentence construction, tenses.
- If English is not the first language, find out some phrases in the child's home language to encourage continuity between home and the setting. This will illustrate that the home language is valued and will support bilingual learning.
- Parents' views must also be taken into account.

Use a range of different communication methods

Some children may be visually or hearing impaired. They require special attention to ensure they do not miss out on communication and learning. It is vital that all staff respond to the child's cues which signal a need for interaction or to explore. Think about:

- opportunities to involve touch in communication for blind children
- visual cues for deaf children; careful positioning of the head and body so that the baby or child can clearly see mouth movements and eye direction will be very important
- making sure that lighting is good to maximise the child's vision
- using exaggerated facial expressions to support meaning
- making sure noise levels in the room are not disruptive
- using games, such as peek-a-boo, or rhymes such as 'Round and round the garden' where the same actions are repeated, which are suitable for all children but especially for a deaf child.

■ Sign language

Young children who are deaf may well be learning an alternative form of communication. The earlier sign language is taught, the more 'natural' and fluent the signing.

There are different sign languages such as:

- British Sign Language (BSL) – a language with its own grammar used fluently by deaf people in the UK
- American Sign Language (ASL).

Different countries have their own sign language but some movements are common to many, such as a headshake meaning 'no'. Men and women may use different signs and there are regional variations in signing for the same objects.

A signing method known as Makaton is often used instead of BSL with people with learning difficulties. Makaton also uses speech alongside signing. This method helps children to link a word to an action or object and is an aid to communication. Makaton signing is based on BSL signs. As with spoken languages, where there are regional variations of dialect and accent, so there are also variations in the signs that are used throughout the UK. The Makaton signs have been standardised to dialect/accents variations used in the south-east/London region. This standardisation avoids confusion for Makaton users if they move around the UK.

Look back at work you have done on communication. What do you remember about non-verbal communication? Babies and young children are very good at picking up non-verbal communication. You do not have to say anything for a baby or young child to recognise that you are feeling sad, angry or happy.

Talking to parents

Parents are consulted regarding any intervention programmes and specialist help via speech and language therapists. If parents would like their child to use sign language, carers will also need to learn basic signs to support the child. As with all other matters involving parents, you should pass on information about a child's communication skills or otherwise to your supervisor. It is perfectly acceptable to pass on to parents that their child has said a new word today but, as a student, never to tell them of any concerns.

For more about language development, see Unit 18, Supporting Literacy Skills.

Assessment activity 35.4

1 Describe the different methods used to communicate with babies and young children under 3 years.

Think about:

- the sequence in which communication develops from birth to 3 years, as well as how and why babies communicate from birth and the pre-verbal stage
- the importance of using recognised language formats and non-verbal forms, such as Makaton when this is appropriate
- why it is important to recognise and reward communication efforts in babies and young children to encourage language development
- a range of different communication methods
- responding to pre-verbal speech
- identifying needs from the communication of babies and young children
- other methods of communication when meaning is not clear
- recognising and responding to behavioural reactions to communication failures. **P6**

2 Explain how to interpret needs and respond to children and young babies. **M4**

3 Evaluate the range of methods used in communication with babies and children under 3 to ensure that understanding is taking place. **D2**

End of unit assessment

You have been shortlisted for the job of nanny/family support to a family who have had twins. The babies are still in hospital as they were very premature. One twin has had serious problems with his breathing, and the doctors think there may be some developmental delay. The parents want to employ someone who will really know the issues and help the twins to make the best start in life.

You have already shown that you understand the basics about development and care of children, using some of the assessment activities you have carried out for this unit.

As part of the final selection procedure for the job, you have been asked to make a presentation outlining the following:

1 The important features of a good observation. **M1**
2 The role and importance of observations of babies and young children. **D1**
3 The key features of good quality care of young babies and how you know what they need. **M2 M4**
4 The range and benefits of different communication styles with babies and young children. **D2**

References and further reading

Books

Gleason, J.B. (1997) *Development of Language*, 4th edition, Allyn and Bacon

Horton, C. (ed.) (2005) *Working with Children 2005–06: facts, figures and information* (Guardian Books), Sage

Leach, P. (2003) *From Birth to Age Five*, Dorling Kindersley

Sheridan, M. (1997) *From Birth to Five Years*, Routledge

St Andrews Association, British Red Cross and St Johns Ambulance (2006) *First Aid Manual*, Dorling Kindersley

Sylva, K. and Lunt, A. (1998) *Child Development: A First Course*, Blackwell

Useful websites

Department of Health – www.dh.gov.uk

NCH (children's charity) – www.nch.org.uk

Sure Start – www.surestart.gov.uk

Grading criteria	Assessment activity	Page number
To achieve a pass grade the evidence must show that the learner is able to:		
P1 describe the development, including communication, of babies and young children in the first three years of life	35.1	526
P2 outline what needs to be considered when observing babies and children in the first three years of life	35.1	526
P3 identify what can be learned through observation about babies and children in the first three years of life	35.1	526
P4 describe the feeding and routine care of babies and young children under three years	35.2	540
P5 identify five different play activities that help to support different aspects of learning and development	35.3	545
P6 describe the different methods used to communicate with babies and children under three years	35.4	549
To achieve a merit grade the evidence must show that, in addition to the pass criteria, the learner is able to:		
M1 explain how to undertake observations of babies and young children under three years	35.1 End of unit assessment	526 550
M2 explain how babies and young children under three years should be fed and cared for safely	35.2 End of unit assessment	540 550
M3 explain what is meant by challenge in play activities	35.3	545
M4 explain how to interpret needs and respond to babies and young children	35.4 End of unit assessment	549 550
To achieve a distinction grade the evidence must show that, in addition to the pass and merit criteria, the learner is able to:		
D1 justify the use of observation of babies and young children in the first three years of life	35.1 End of unit assessment	526 550
D2 evaluate the range of methods used in communication with babies and children under three to ensure that understanding is taking place	35.4 End of unit assessment	549 550

Glossary

Absolute poverty A lack of income to provide all the basic requirements of living: food, housing, clothing, etc.

Accommodation Information is modified and adapted to account for new experiences and knowledge. (Piaget)

Adaptation Adapting thoughts and concepts through the process of assimilation and accommodation. (Piaget)

Adequate control Ensuring that risks are sufficiently managed and organised to prevent injury.

Advocate To be an advocate for a child or young person is to speak or act on their behalf to maintain their best interests if they are unable to do so themselves.

Amino acids The building blocks of protein.

Anaemia A lack of iron in the diet or poor iron absorption.

Anaphylactic reaction An allergic reaction caused by the sudden release of chemical substances in the body in response to an allergen.

Anti-discriminatory practice Taking positive action to counter discrimination.

Assimilation New information is taken in which fits with the child's existing understanding. (Piaget)

Attachment See **bonding**.

Attention deficit hyperactivity disorder (ADHD) A disorder linked to low arousal levels in which a child shows significant problems in focusing attention and hyperactivity.

Automatic reflexes 'Survival' reflexes that mostly disappear by about 3–4 months of age – babies can locate the source of food and suck, react to loud noises and even appear to walk at a very young age.

Babbling Repetitive type of vocalisation, such as 'dada', 'mamma', which has no special meaning, but is applied to having social meaning by the reactions of adults, i.e. dad or mum. Reinforcement helps the sounds to develop into meaning. Deaf babies babble, but it soon ends as there is no feedback for them.

Basal metabolic rate (BMR) The number of calories needed by the body when resting in order to breathe, for the heart to beat, for body temperature to be maintained and for other involuntary activities, including brain function to occur.

Body language How you communicate non-verbally, including tone of voice, facial expressions, stance, gestures, touch.

Bonding The process through which young children form close relationships with a small number of well-known adults – their parents, their grandparents, their key worker in a nursery, their childminder or nanny. Also known as attachment.

Boundaries The limits to acceptable behaviour.

Care value base Sets the standards and provides guidelines for professional practice in health and social care in order to improve clients' quality of life.

Case conference A multi-disciplinary meeting to discuss a child or young person and their family.

Cause for concern When there is need for support for the child and their family to ensure the needs of the child or young person are being met.

Cephalocaudal Refers to the maturation of gross and fine motor skills from the head down the spine.

Child abuse Ill-treatment or harm inflicted on a child or young person, either deliberately or through neglect, which impairs or damages the child or young person's health, welfare or development.

Child protection procedure Part of the child protection service and starts at the point of referral; the child is the central focus.

Childminder Home-based childcare provision covering all age ranges (from a few months onwards) in the childminder's own home for a small number of children.

Children's centre Centre-based provision for various age group.

Classical conditioning A method of learning where a response can be triggered by a recognised cue.

Code of conduct The rules of your setting and practice you should demonstrate when working with the children in your care.

Coeliac disease A condition where the body reacts to gluten, the protein which is found in wheat and some other cereals.

Cognitive behaviour therapies A mix of psychotherapy and behavioural therapy, which works by challenging and changing attitudes and behaviour.

Cognitive development A process by which thought processes develop so children are able to increase their knowledge and understanding of the world around them; sometimes called intellectual development.

Confidentiality Not sharing with other people, or passing on, personal information about the children and families you are working with, unless you have been given permission to do so or it is in the interests of the child to do so.

Conformity Complying with social standards, attitudes and practices.

Congenital conditions Conditions that a child is born with; can include genetic conditions and those which occur during the pre-birth development of the child.

Conservation The understanding that the number of objects (or the weight or volume) remains the same even when they are rearranged spatially. (Piaget)

Co-operative play By 3 and 4 years, children begin to play with other children.

Critical period A set period of time within which some theorist have speculated that an attachment must occur

Cross-sectional study Information gathered about a group of people at one point in time.

Culture A set of attitudes, behaviour patterns and beliefs belonging to a group of people.

Curriculum A programme of study, courses or syllabus.

Cycle of abuse When a parent who has suffered abuse as a child themselves then abuses their own child.

Data Protection Act Legislation that protects individuals from material that may be recorded about them or their children. Everyone has the right to see what is recorded – in all written and electronic formats.

Deprivation The term used when babies and toddlers are separated on a long-term basis from their main attachment.

Developmental delay When a child or young person's development (physical, emotional, intellectual, language or social) is delayed or regressing due to other factors, such as an abusive situation.

Disability A physical or mental impairment which has a substantial and long-term adverse effect on the child's ability to carry out normal day-to-activities.

Disclosure When a child tells you that they are being, or have been, abused.

Discrimination Treating someone less favourably than other people, because they or their family are seen as belonging to a particular group in society.

Diversity Recognises people's different characteristics, making sure they are considered so that they can get maximum benefit from their uniqueness. Treating people fairly means that their differences are recognised and are respected and acted upon as needed.

Dyscalculia A learning condition that affects the individual's ability to carry out calculations. This will also affect their general mathematical reasoning.

Dyslexia Difficulty with reading and writing despite the individual having normal development of cognitive skills and intelligence.

Dysphasia A condition which is often caused by damage to the brain and results in speech and comprehension impairment.

Dyspraxia Difficulty in thinking out and executing movements or tasks, including those requiring fine motor skills, such as drawing or writing; also known as 'clumsy child syndrome', developmental co-ordination disorder (DCD).

Emotional abuse The persistent emotional ill-treatment of a child or young person which causes adverse effects on the child or young person's emotional well-being.

Emotional development The process of a child developing an understanding of and controlling their own emotions and learning how to express and control emotions that they show to others.

Empathy Understanding what it is like to be someone else.

Equality of opportunity Ensuring that everyone, irrespective of their diversity (for example, age, gender, disability or race) has equal access to opportunities at work, through education and other services.

Equilibrium The balance of existing and new concepts as the child makes sense of its environment.(Piaget)

Equity Fairness, impartiality.

Essential fatty acids Linoleic acid and alpha-linolenic acid, which are essential for our immune systems and for proper brain development and cannot be synthesised in the body and must be supplied in the diet.

Evaluate To assess the quality of your practice by asking yourself questions such as, 'Is what I do good enough? Does it lead to the best possible outcomes for children and families?'

Expectations Indicate to children how adults expect them to behave.

Feedback Commenting on the work of other people by saying what they are doing well (so that they know it is good and can carry on doing it – positive feedback) or could do better (so they can work more effectively – constructive feedback).

Food intolerance May be an adverse reaction, an allergy or an aversion to a particular food.

Formative assessment A continual review by both you and the assessor during the draft process of producing your study.

Framework for Assessment of Need A common framework used by all professionals in an initial assessment to establish whether or not there are child protection issues; it provides a common approach that all professionals and agencies involved must use.

Gender concept The understanding that gender is constant and permanent.

Glue ear A condition in which the middle ear fills up with a sticky fluid which muffles sound.

Good health Positive social and mental health and the absence of disease.

Health promotion A process, activity or event carried out with the aim of improving, protecting or maintaining people's health.

Heuristic play Play in which children are allowed to discover for themselves. The adult provides a range of objects to explore but sits nearby and observes.

Hidden curriculum The things that children learn at school that are not part of the formal curriculum.

Holistic development 'Seeing a child in the round, as a whole person, emotionally, socially, intellectually, physically, healthily, culturally and spiritually.' (Birth to Three Matters)

Holophrase When a child uses a single word to convey information, for example when the child points to cup and says 'drink.'

Homeostasis The process of maintaining constant physical and chemical conditions within the body despite outside influences.

Idiographic approach to assessment Studying the child's own individual progress.

Inclusion The process of identifying, understanding and breaking down barriers to participation and belonging, to make sure that everyone in an activity or setting is included.

Innate sociability The theory that humans are designed to make attachments and form relationships.

Inter-agency working Information sharing and shared decision-making between agencies to jointly and collaboratively meet the needs of families, children and young people.

Jargon The last stage of babbling, from 10 months and older, when it seems as though children are speaking in whole sentences using their 'own' language.

Key worker A member of staff allocated to a child so that a strong relationship might develop. They will work alongside the child to get to know their likes, dislikes, interests and strengths.

Labelling Using spoken words to give the names of objects and people; supplying the vocabulary to enable the child to talk about the object or person.

Literacy skills The skills required in order to be able to read and write effectively.

Local authority The local representation of government and law, which provides services to everyone in the local community.

Local Safeguarding Children's Boards (LSCBs) This system oversees inter-agency working in child protection in England, Wales and Northern Ireland; they replace Area Child Protection Committees (ACPS).

Longitudinal study The study of an individual or group of people over a period of time.

Macro-nutrients Nutrients which occur in large quantities in the body: carbohydrates, proteins and fats.

Makaton A language system which uses signs and symbols to enable people who cannot speak or write to communicate.

Malnutrition Too much (over-nutrition) or too little food (under-nutrition).

Marginalisation The exclusion of a particular group of people on the fringe of mainstream society (for example, travellers, asylum seekers, older people).

Micro-nutrients Nutrients which occur in small quantities: vitamins and minerals.

Milestones The ages at which the majority of children will reach certain significant stages of development, for example sitting up unsupported, walking.

Monitor To take a long hard look at the way you work, how you do it, what the results are, and why you work as you do.

Monotropy In early theories of attachment, it was proposed that babies made only one key attachment.

Motherese The type of language used by adults when speaking to babies, including a higher pitch of voice and slower speech. It is very precise and often repetitive. The pronunciation is clear and the adult will speak more slowly than usual. Also known as infant-directed speech.

Multi-disciplinary team A team of people from different professional backgrounds, training and qualifications who work together to provide services for children and families.

Multiple attachment Later theories of attachment proposed that babies were able to simultaneously to make several strong attachments.

Nature–nurture debate Whether children's development is influenced by nature (the effect of inherited factors) or nurture (environmental factors).

Neglect is the persistent failure to meet the child or young person's basic needs.

Nomothetic approach to assessment Comparing children's progress according to identified levels of development according to age and other factors such as racial origin.

Non-verbal communication Occurs without words, for example, through **body language** or by signing.

Numeracy skills The skills required in order to be able to use numbers, shape, measures, time and space effectively.

Nursery school State-maintained provision for children aged 3 up to starting primary school.

Nutrients Components in food which produce energy, provide material for growth, repair of the body or reproduction, or undertake chemical reactions to regulate these activities.

Object permanence The understanding that objects that have disappeared from view still exist, even when a child cannot see them.

Objective Looking at the facts, being free from bias or your own point of view.

Open questions Cannot be answered by 'Yes', 'No' or any other single word (such questions are 'closed' questions). Don't say 'Did you enjoy the party yesterday?' but do say 'What did you do at the party yesterday?'

Operant conditioning A method of learning which is based on the type of consequence or reinforcement that follows our initial behaviour.

Parallel play By the age of 2 years, children may play side by side but do not interact very much.

Parental responsibility In law, parents have both rights and responsibilities towards their children.

Participant observation When the observer becomes involved with the children, either by working alongside a child or by becoming part of the group of the children being observed.

Perception The process by which each of us gains direct awareness through our senses of the world around us.

Personal care routines Individual daily practices to care for personal hygiene, for example washing, cleaning teeth.

Physical abuse May involve hitting, shaking, throwing, poisoning, scalding or burning, drowning, suffocating, biting, or otherwise causing physical harm to a child or young person; also referred to as non-accidental injury.

Physical development A gradual process by which children develop the use and control of muscles.

Planned approach The processes of: collecting information (through observation and discussion) about the child; assessment of current stage of development; planning experiences to meet current needs and help them progress; implementation of the plan; monitoring and evaluating the plan.

Policies Documents to demonstrate how you should carry out your duties in certain situations, such as during an evacuation.

Population A group of people or objects that share particular characteristics, for example a year group in a school or group of schools that have similar characteristics.

Poverty line The amount of money below which, after adjusting for size and composition of household and after housing costs, a family is categorised as being poor.

Pre-disposing factors Factors in the child's background or make-up which might make them more vulnerable or susceptible to abuse, for example if a child has parents who have themselves been abused.

Prejudice An unfavourable opinion of a person or group, usually arising from inaccurate information or lack of information, and which leads to **discrimination**.

Pre-school Community-based provision for (usually) up to 25 children aged 2½–4 years

Pre-value judgement When a person makes a judgement about another person based on something they feel is the truth, for example that all poor people do noteat well.

Primary research Original research; the collection of information by the person or persons carrying out the research.

Private nursery Centre-based provision for any number of children, from a few months up to 4 years.

Privation The term used when no attachment is made.

Provision Can be a physical setting or a peripatetic service based in the community, or other service.

Qualitative information Information gathered in narrative (non-numeric) form, for example an interview.

Quantitative information Information gathered in the form of numbers.

Random sample A subgroup of a **population** selected to represent the entire population in which the people in the population have an equal chance of being chosen to be in the subgroup.

Reciprocal behaviour Attachments and relationships are often mutual. A mother has strong feelings for her baby, whilst the baby has strong feelings for her.

Referral When someone contacts social services or the authorities with concerns about a child or young person.

Reflective practitioner Someone who takes a questioning approach to their work, thinking critically about what they do, analysing how and why they do it that way, and assessing the effectiveness of what they are doing and how they can become more effective.

Relative poverty Enough income for basics but not for those items considered usual in the society you live in, for example not being able to afford a TV set.

Reliability The method used to obtain any information can be repeated and is consistent. '

Rules Describe what people may or may not do.

Sample A subgroup of a population selected to represent the entire **population**, for example a selection of pupils from a year group within a school or group of schools.

Schema A mental structure or concept which relates to a pattern of behaviour and can be used in a variety of situations. (Piaget)

Secondary research The use of information collected by others.

Section 47 enquiry An investigation (legally supported by the Children Act 1989) where a child has been suffering significant harm.

Self-concept Our vision of our whole selves, including our self-esteem, our self-image and our ideal self.

Self-esteem How we judge ourselves: how close are we to being the person we want to be? This judgement either gives us high or low self-esteem, also referred to as self-confidence.

Self-fulfilling prophecy A prediction that, in being made, actually causes itself to become true.

Sensory integration therapy Provides controlled sensory stimulation to increase adaptive behaviours/responses.

Separation The term used when a parent or main attachment leaves the baby or toddler.

Separation anxiety Difficulty, in many children aged 2 and under, in being apart from people and places they know and feel secure with.

Sex-role concept The understanding how, as a boy or girl, children are expected to act.

Sexual abuse Forcing or coercing a child or young person to take part in sexual activities, whether or not the child is aware of what is happening.

Sign Anything that you perceive using your senses, for example something you smell, hear, see or feel.

Significant harm The criteria which helps professionals decide if there is need for intervention and or support because there has been ill-treatment or impairment of health to the child or young person.

Social development Children learning how to develop relationships and interactions with other people.

Social learning theory Suggests we learn by imitating others.

Social services The services provided by the government to support those members of the community that are in need and often the most vulnerable.

Socialisation The process that happens during a child's early life – they are influenced by the people in the environment around them.

Sociogram Shows the relationships between different members of a group or the relationship of one member within a group.

Solitary play Babies and under-2s mostly play alone.

Special educational needs Children with special educational needs learn differently from most children of the same age. They may need extra or different help.

Stereotypes Generalisations about people, assumptions that because a person is part of a particular group, they will be the same as others in that group. Such assumptions are usually inaccurate.

Stranger anxiety An aversion to people whom babies do not know; occurs towards the end of the first year. They cling to the familiar adults they trust and feel safe with.

Subjective Looking at things from your own point of view, being influenced by pre-conceived ideas, not looking at the facts and being impartial.

Summative assessment Carried out at the end of your study in order to make final judgements.

Symptom What the casualty tells you, for example 'I went a bit dizzy.'

Target child The child being observed.

Telegraphic speech Shortened sentences without words such as 'and' and 'the' spoken by children from about 18–24 months, for example 'go walk park'.

Therapeutic communication Non-directive communication to encourage a child to communicate their feelings, such as 'Is there something you would like to talk about?', 'Where would you like to start?'

Tolerance An underlying part of **equity**. Tolerance means respecting difference and not expecting that everyone should be, act or behave as you think they should.

Unconditional regard Letting children know that they are valued just for being them, not always for what they can achieve.

Validity The information gathered and the method used are relevant to the study being undertaken.

Variable A factor that changes or can be changed.

Verbal communication Communication using the spoken word.

Weaning The process of introducing solid foods.

Index

economic diversity 219–23
economic factors and development 113
educare 62
Education Act (1996) 233–4
embryo 91
embryonic development 92–3
  factors affecting 93–4
emergency situations 52–61
  accident procedures 56
  fire emergency 58–60
  flood/bomb scare 59
  gas leak emergency 59
  rehearsing procedures 59
  types of 58
  see also first aid; injury
Emerson, P. E. 104, 427
emotional abuse 172, 173–5
emotional development 88, 103–6, 335, 516
  birth to 3 years 517–23, 542–3
  and play 207, 270
empathy 21
empowering children
  for self-protection 198
  to protect rights 199–200
encouragement 117, 120, 121
environment 259
  anti-discriminatory 116, 119, 121
  cleaning 48–50
  and development 116–17, 119, 121,
    122–3, 339
  indoor 42
  outdoor 42–3
  physical 46
  risk assessment 41–7
equal concern 10–11
equal opportunities 223
  National Standards 233
equality 238
  formal policies 232–5
  of opportunity 225
equipment 74, 82
  defective 46
  storage of 82
equity 224–6
Erikson, Erik 115, 406, 411
ethical issues in research 324–7
ethnic groups 212–13, 339
  access to services 228–9
  defined 212
  life chances 222
evacuation 59
  evidence of rehearsals 36
evaluating your practice 159–60
event sampling 131, 133, 444
Every Child Matters 41, 114, 365, 442–3
  outcomes 62, 184, 363
expectations of children 114
  and behaviour 22, 437
experimental method 306–7
exploratory play 115, 269
extended family 181, 214, 431

extended schools 119, 122
eye contact 13, 14, 80, 121
  cultural differences 17

F

family 180–2
  and abuse 179
  and behaviour 436
  behavioural therapy 432
  breakdown 435
  changing structures 181
  role of 431–2
  social disadvantage 181
  types 180–1, 214–15, 431
fantasy play 115, 268
Fantz, R.L. 110
fast foods 378
fathers, role of 429
fats 344, 350–2
feedback
  from supervisor 161
  receiving 148, 149
  to children 472, 477
  to parents 202
feeding 68–70, 527–33
  appropriate foods 342
  and attachment 429
  bottle-feeding 69, 78–9, 527–30
  breast-feeding 68–9, 527
  cleaning equipment 82
  inadvisable foods 70, 342
  parents' wishes 533
  problems 533
  sterilising equipment 77–8
  water 358–9
  weaning 69–70, 79, 530–2
  see also bottle-feeding;
    healthy eating
fine motor skills 98, 522
  development 0–3 years 101
  development 4–7 years 102
  and play 270
  for writing 486
finger brush 75
Finkelhor, D. 208
fire emergency checklist 58–60
  reviewing and monitoring 60
first aid 52
  3 Bs 52
  emergency action 53–4, 55
  prioritising treatment 52–3
  recovery position 54
  unconscious casualty 53–4
first aid box 58
Flynn, B. 186
Flynn, H. 176
foetal development 92–3
  factors affecting 93–4
food
  developing preferences 375–6, 381
  encouraging independence 347

hygienic preparation 347
  personal preferences 380-3
  presentation 379
  social aspects 380
  storage and equipment 49
  and tooth decay 385–6
  see also feeding; healthy eating
food additives 376
food allergies 388, 390–1
food handling 49
Food Hygiene Certificate 41, 49
food intolerance 346, 388, 389–90
food poisoning 394–8
  good practice checklist 397
  reasons for 394
  types of bacteria 395–6
  vulnerable groups 394
food safety 392–8
  Critical Control Points 393
  legislation 392–3
  temperature control 393
Food Safety Act (1990) 41, 392–3
footwear 73
Ford, Gina 431
formative assessment 135, 284
formula feeding 69, 78, 527–30
fostering 205–6
Foundation Stage 155, 462
  mathematical development 464
  see also Early Years
Framework for Assessment of
  Children in Need 186–7
Freedom of Information Act 246
frequency distributions 318
Freud, Anna 271
Freud, Sigmund 108, 404, 406
  moral development 414
  personality development 410
  psychosexual stages 410–11
frustration–aggression
  hypothesis 413
furniture positioning 46

G

Garvey, Catherine 261
gas leak emergency checklist 59
gender
  concept 411, 412
  constancy 412
  and development 113
  health needs 339
  nutritional needs 343
  and sex 215
gender identity 412
  development of 543
gender schema theory 412–13
genetic inheritance 94, 114
  disorders 94
  health conditions 337, 338
Gibson, E.J. 110
globalisation 223

glue ear 17
government initiatives 114, 116
government provision 228
grammar 546
graphs and charts 130, 133, 444
gross motor development 98
   in first year 99–100
   1–3 years 100
   4–8 years 102
groups, observation of 132
growth charts 98

H

hair care 63, 64–5, 75, 535
Halverson, C.F. 109
hand washing 48
hand–eye co-ordination 542, 543
Hazard Analysis Critical Control Points
   393
hazardous substances 40, 43
head lice 63
Head Start programme 231
health
   definition 336
   and physical activity 342, 344
   regional differences 339–40
Health Divide 221–2
health education 366–7
health promotion campaigns 367–8
   different approaches 368
health and safety
   activities 272, 277, 288
   in care of babies 539
   good practice 260
   legislation 40, 45, 58, 117
   policy 544
Health and Safety at Work Act (1974) 40, 58
Health and Safety Executive 40
health status 114
   diversity of 214
health visitor 460–1, 496
healthy child 541–2
healthy development 332–71
   in adults 338
   factors affecting 336–42
   groups at risk 336–7
   life expectancy 335–6
   meeting potential 334
   needs by age 336–9
   skills and competencies 335
healthy eating
   6–9 months 532
   balanced diet 359–61
   from 9 months 532–3
   national guidelines 341–2, 347
   special diets 346–7
healthy lifestyles 119–20, 123, 334–5
   effects of choices on 365–6
   government programmes 362–4
   influencing factors 365
   involving children 364

involving families 364–5
   making changes 366–7
   opportunities to promote 362–5
Healthy Living Centres 363
healthy, safe and secure environment
   36–51
   indoor areas 42
   outdoor areas 42–3
   risk assessment 41–7
hearing 110
   at birth 517
   impairment 17, 548
   loss 459, 460, 494, 495
heating 45
heuristic play 71
hidden curriculum 287, 436
hierarchy of needs 406, 422
historical child rearing
   theories 430–1
HIV infection 49, 337
holding and lifting babies 80
holistic development 88–9
holophrase 485
homosexuality 215
hormones and birth 94
Horton, C. 231
hospitalisation 337, 434
   deprivation 428
Howard, G. 336
human rights 210, 228
   legislation 235–7
   overriding 237
   UN Declaration 324
   see also rights
Human Rights Act (1998) 183, 235, 237
Human Rights, UN Declaration of 125
humanist perspectives 405, 406
Hutt, C. 115
hygiene control procedures 48–51
   confidentiality 51
   good practice 48, 539
   reporting information 50, 51
hyperactivity 376, 391, 418
hypothesis 306

I

ICT use in activities 286
ideal self 421
idiographic approach 97
illness 459, 460
   difficulties caused by 494, 495
   physical signs 540
   when to get help 540
imaginative play 266
imitation 107
immigration 223
immunisation 337
Incident Form 59
inclusion 9–10, 233, 459
   in activities 274, 286, 492–3
   and healthy living 365

inclusive practice 242–5
   personal awareness 241–2
   promoting 241–7
income differentials 219, 223
independence 120
   in adolescence 123
   and physical development 98
   and risk 121
   routines promoting 67–8, 77
individual learning programmes 275–6
indoor play 289
inequality 220–1, 226–7
   vulnerable groups 227
infant feeding 68–9
infection 337
   and foetal development 93
infection control 45, 49–50, 57
infectious diseases, signs and
   symptoms of 57
information 36
   and confidentiality 245–6
   and data protection 36–7
information processing theory 418–19
information sharing 36, 198
   observation findings 135
   supporting transitions 117
injury 540
   complications 56
   emergency action 55
   major 55–6
   minor 55
   procedures to follow 52–4
   signs and symptoms 52
   treatment of 55–6
   when to call ambulance 56
   see also first aid
instructions, giving 15
intellectual development 516
   0–36 months 517–23, 542–3
inter-agency working 185
Internet for research 298
interpersonal skills 146–9, 287
interviews 303–6
   good practice 304–5
   types of 303

J

Jacobson, L. 437
James, William 418
jargon, childcare 28–9
jargons 520

K

Kempe, C. 178
Kempe, R. 178
key worker system 460, 461, 523
   and child protection 190
King, Truby 430
Kitzinger, Sheila 431
knowledge of world 286
Kohlberg, Lawrence 412, 415–17